Nursing Management: Principles and Practice

Edited by
Mary Magee Gullatte, RN, MN, ANP, AOCN®, FAAMA

Oncology Nursing Society
Pittsburgh, Pennsylvania

Nursing Management: Principles and Practice

ONS Publishing Division
Publisher: Leonard Mafrica, MBA, CAE
Director, Commercial Publishing: Barbara Sigler, RN, MNEd
Production Manager: Lisa M. George, BA
Technical Editor: Angela Klimaszewski, RN, MSN
Staff Editor: Lori Wilson, BA
Copy Editor: Amy Nicoletti, BA
Graphic Designer: Dany Sjoen

Nursing Management: Principles and Practice

First printing, March 2005
Second printing, October 2006

Library of Congress Control Number: 2005923610

ISBN 1-890504-52-1

Publisher's Note

Printed in the United States of America

Oncology Nursing Society
Integrity • Innovation • Stewardship • Advocacy • Excellence • Inclusiveness

DEDICATION

This book is dedicated in loving honor and memory of my parents:
Bilbo Magee 1915–2002 WWII Veteran
and Hazel Magee

For the many blessings I have received, including a loving and supportive
husband and children: Rodney Gullatte, Sr., Rodney Gullatte, Jr., and
Ronda Gullatte. You are my strength and my joy. To all my brothers and
sisters: Selma, Billy, Lester, Amanda, Winnie, Willace, Hope, Donna,
and Sue Ann, thank you for your love and support.

*"I shall pass through this world but once.
If therefore, there be any kindness I can show
or any good thing I can do, let me do it now . . .
For I shall not pass this way again."*

—Etienne de Grellet

CONTRIBUTORS

Editor/Author

Mary Magee Gullatte, RN, MN, ANP, AOCN®, FAAMA
Director of Nursing
Inpatient Oncology and Transplant Services
Emory University and Crawford Long Hospitals
Director, Oncology Data Center
Winship Cancer Institute
Emory University
Adjunct Clinical Faculty
Nell Hodgson Woodruff School of Nursing
Emory University
Atlanta, Georgia

Chapter 8. Flexible Budgets and Staffing Matrix, Chapter 11. Workforce Diversity: Valuing and Embracing Differences, Chapter 12. Retention and Recruitment: Reversing the Order, Chapter 14. Interviewing and Selecting the Right Candidate, Chapter 18. Lifelong Learning and Continuing Competency

Authors

Delorese Ambrose, EdD
President, Ambrose Consulting & Training
Atlanta, Georgia
Chapter 1. Managing Self to Lead Others

Margaret L. Anthony, RN, MHS, CNOR
Nurse Manager
Hollings Cancer Center
Medical University of South Carolina
Charleston, South Carolina
Chapter 24. Quality and Process Improvement

Susan M. Bauer-Wu, DNSc, RN
Director, Phyllis F. Cantor Center
Dana-Farber Cancer Institute
Boston, Massachusetts
Instructor of Medicine, Harvard Medical School
Boston, Massachusetts
Chapter 33. Nursing Research: Current Perspectives and Future Trends

Marilyn K. Bedell, MS, RN, OCN®
Nursing Director—Oncology
Norris Cotton Cancer Center
Dartmouth-Hitchcock Medical Center
Lebanon, New Hampshire
Chapter 19. Mentoring: Promoting the Development of Nurses

Margaret A. Bloomquist, SPHR
Associate Administrator, Human Resources
Emory Healthcare
Atlanta, Georgia
Chapter 14. Interviewing and Selecting the Right Candidate

Cynthia Braswell, RN, MS
Director of Business Development
Portsbridge Hospice
Atlanta, Georgia
Chapter 30. Management of Hospice Services

Patricia A. Calico, DNS, RN
Branch Chief, Advanced Education Nursing
Division of Nursing, Bureau of Health Professions
Health Resources and Services Administration
Department of Health and Human Services
Rockville, Maryland
Chairperson, Baccalaureate Nursing Program
Midway College
Midway, Kentucky
Assistant Professor
College of Nursing and Health
University of Cincinnati
Cincinnati, Ohio
Clinical Nurse Educator
Cincinnati VA Medical Center
Cincinnati, Ohio
Chapter 9. Nursing Workforce: Challenges and Opportunities

Connie J. Carson, PhD
Principal
Carson Consulting
Littleton, Colorado
Chapter 2. Transforming Theory Into Practice

Frances Cartwright-Alcarese, RN, MS, AOCN®
Clinical Director, Neuroscience, Oncology, Surgical Specialties, and Transplant Institute
Mount Sinai Hospital of New York
New York, New York
Chapter 27. Radiation Oncology Management

Mary E. Cooley, PhD, CRNP, CS
Nurse Scientist
Phyllis F. Cantor Center
Dana-Farber Cancer Institute
Boston, Massachusetts
Instructor of Psychiatry, Harvard Medical School
Boston, Massachusetts
Chapter 33. Nursing Research: Current Perspectives and Future Trends

Colleen L. Corish, RN, MN, OCN®
Clinical Director
Oncology and Medical/Surgical Services
Medical University of South Carolina and The Hollings Cancer Center
Charleston, South Carolina
Chapter 24. Quality and Process Improvement

Gregory L. Crow, RN, BSN, MSN, EdD
Graduate Director
Sonoma State University
School of Science and Technology
Department of Nursing
Rohnert Park, California
Senior Consultant
Tim Porter-O'Grady Associates
San Rafael, California
Professor Emeritus
Sonoma State University
Rohnert Park, California
Chapter 11. Workforce Diversity: Valuing and Embracing Differences

Annette Tyree Debisette, DNSc, ANP, RN
Senior Advisor to the Associate Administrator for Health Professions
Health Resources and Services Administration
Department of Health and Human Services
Rockville, Maryland
Interim Director, Medical-Surgical Services
Northern Virginia Community Hospital
Arlington, Virginia
Assistant Professor
School of Health Professions, Department of Nursing
Marymount University
Arlington, Virginia
Director, Medical-Surgical Nursing
Pentagon City Hospital (formerly National Hospital for Orthopedics and Rehabilitation)
Arlington, Virginia
Chapter 9. Nursing Workforce: Challenges and Opportunities

Kathleen A. Ducey, RN, MS, AOCN®
Director of Clinical Operations, Cancer
  Center
University of Kansas Hospital
Kansas City, Kansas
Chapter 6. Healthcare Economics

Patricia Stanfill Edens, RN, MS, MBA,
  FACHE
Assistant Vice President, Quality
Hospital Corporation of America
Nashville, Tennessee
Chapter 20. Workplace Reengineering, Reorganization, and Redesign

Marilyn B. Farrand, BSIE, MSHS
Senior Management Engineer
Emory Hospitals Patient Services
Atlanta, Georgia
Chapter 8. Flexible Budgets and Staffing Matrix

Patricia E. Frank, RN, BSN, OCN®
Former Oncology Nurse Coordinator
Penn Home Infusion
University of Pennsylvania Health System
King of Prussia, Pennsylvania
Chapter 29. Homecare Issues

Catherine Glennon, RN, BC, CNA, MHS,
  OCN®
Health Center Administrator, Oncology
  Services
Private Diagnostic Clinics, PLLC
Duke University Medical Center
Durham, North Carolina
Chapter 17. Performance Appraisals

Ilisa M. Halpern, MPP
Managing Government Relations Director
Gardner, Carton, & Douglas, LLC
Washington, DC
Chapter 36. Advocacy and Health Policy

Joanne M. Hambleton, RN, MSN, CNA
Vice President, Nursing and Patient
  Services
Fox Chase Cancer Center
Philadelphia, Pennsylvania
Chapter 31. In Search of Nursing Excellence

Connie Hampton, MSN, RN, FNP
Nurse Manager, Medical/Oncology Unit
Atlanta Veterans Administration Medical
  Center
Decatur, Georgia
Chapter 26. Program Development in a Veterans Healthcare System

Janet Y. Harris, RN, MSN, CNAA
National Director, Professional Services
Cardinal Health, Pyxis Products
San Diego, California
Chapter 5. Organizational Design and Structure

Corinne Haviley, RN, MS
Director, Radiology
Northwestern Memorial Hospital
Chicago, Illinois
Chapter 6. Healthcare Economics

Martha W. Healey, RN, MS, FNP
Project Director
Phyllis F. Cantor Center
Dana-Farber Cancer Institute
Boston, Massachusetts
Chapter 33. Nursing Research: Current Perspectives and Future Trends

Susan Lasker Hertz, RN, MSN, AOCN®
Vice President, Medical Services
Namaste Comfort Care
Denver, Colorado
Chapter 2. Transforming Theory Into Practice

Deborah A. Houston, MS, RN, CPHIMS
Director, Enterprise Applications
The University of Texas M.D. Anderson
  Cancer Center
Houston, Texas
Chapter 32. Nursing Information Systems

Anne M. Ireland, RN, MSN, AOCN®
Oncology Consultant
Fletcher Allen Health Care
Burlington, Vermont
Chapter 28. Ambulatory Care Management

Evelyn Q. Jirasakhiran, RN, MSN
Department Director
Transplant Services & Rollins Pavilion
Emory University Hospital
Atlanta, Georgia
Chapter 12. Retention and Recruitment:
Reversing the Order

Marilyn Jones-Bradshaw, MBA, MN, RN,
  CCS
Legal Nurse Consultant
Atlanta, Georgia
Chapter 25. Legal and Risk Management Issues

Marjorie Kagawa-Singer, PhD, MN, RN
Associate Professor
UCLA School of Public Health and Asian
  American Studies
Los Angeles, California
Chapter 10. Culturally Competent Organiza-
tions

Shaheen Kassim-Lakha, MPH, DrPH
Department of Health Services
UCLA School of Public Health
Los Angeles, California
Chapter 10. Culturally Competent Organiza-
tions

Sharon Krumm, PhD, RN
Administrator and Director of Nursing
Sidney Kimmel Comprehensive Cancer
  Center
The Johns Hopkins Hospital
Baltimore, Maryland
Chapter 35. Cancer Centers of Excellence

Luana R. Lamkin, RN, MPH
Administrator
Mountain States Tumor Institute
Boise, Idaho
Chapter 7. Financial Management for the
Nurse Manager

Casey T. Liddy, MHA
Business Manager
Oncology and Medical/Surgical Services
Medical University of South Carolina
Charleston, South Carolina
Chapter 24. Quality and Process Improvement

Joan Such Lockhart, PhD, RN, CORLN,
  AOCN®, FAAN
Professor, and Associate Dean for Aca-
  demic Affairs
Duquesne University School of Nursing
Pittsburgh, Pennsylvania
Chapter 18. Lifelong Learning and Continu-
ing Competency

Adair D. Maller, MA, SPHR
Director, Human Resources
Emory Healthcare
Atlanta, Georgia
Chapter 15. Employment Laws and Regulations

Virginia R. Martin, RN, MSN, AOCN®
Clinical Director, Ambulatory Care
Fox Chase Cancer Center
Philadelphia, Pennsylvania
Chapter 28. Ambulatory Care Management

Mary Dee McEvoy, PhD, RN, AOCN®
Director
Joseph F. Cullman Jr. Institute for Patient
  Care
Mount Sinai Hospital
New York, New York
Chapter 16. Labor Relations and Collective
Bargaining

Brenda M. Nevidjon, RN, MSN
Associate Clinical Professor and Chief
Division of Health Care Leadership,
  Education, and Management
Duke University School of Nursing
Durham, North Carolina
Chapter 37. Managerial Rejuvenation

Diane M. Otte, RN, MS, OCN®
Director, Cancer Center
Franciscan Skemp Healthcare
La Crosse, Wisconsin
Chapter 13. Assistive Personnel

Patti L. Owen, MN, RN
Director, Oncology Services
Northside Hospital
Atlanta, Georgia
Chapter 23. Accreditation: A Method for
Measuring Compliance

Guadalupe Palos, RN, LMSW, DrPH
Instructor
Department of Symptom Research
The University of Texas M.D. Anderson
  Cancer Center
Houston, Texas
*Chapter 11. Workforce Diversity: Valuing and
Embracing Differences*

Janice Mitchell Phillips, PhD, RN, FAAN
Senior Research Specialist
American Institutes for Research
Silver Spring, Maryland
Former Program Director
National Institutes of Health
National Institute of Nursing Research
Bethesda, Maryland
*Chapter 34. Securing Funding for Nursing
Research*

Tim Porter-O'Grady, EdD, RN, FAAN
Senior Partner, Tim Porter-O'Grady As-
  sociates
Associate Professor, School of Nursing
Emory University
Atlanta, Georgia
Adjunct Professor
School of Public Health
Lakehead University
Chapter 3. Leadership Development

Mary L. Scott, RN, MS, OCN®
Director, Oncology Nursing
Huntsman Cancer Hospital
University of Utah Hospitals and Clinics
Salt Lake City, Utah
*Chapter 5. Organizational Design and
Structure*

Linda J. Shinn, MBA, RN, CAE
Principal
Consensus Management Group
Indianapolis, Indiana
Chapter 21. Writing a Business Plan

Joseph Spallina, FAAMA, FACHE
Director
Arvina Group, LLC
Ann Arbor, Michigan
*Chapter 22. Cancer Program Strategic Plan-
ning and Marketing*

Veronica Stone, RN, OCN®, NMCC
Catastrophic Case Manager
Intracorp—A CIGNA Healthcare Com-
  pany
Chattanooga, Tennessee
Chapter 29. Homecare Issues

James N. Thomas, PhD
Vice President, Consulting Services
Development Dimensions International
Atlanta, Georgia
*Chapter 14. Interviewing and Selecting the
Right Candidate*

Carol Thompson, RN, MSN, AOCN®, CS
Manager, Bone Marrow Transplant Unit
Oncology Supervisor
South Texas Veterans Health Care System
San Antonio, Texas
*Chapter 26. Program Development in a Veter-
ans Healthcare System*

Madeline Turkeltaub, RN, PhD, CRNP,
  FAAN
Nurse Consultant, Diversity and Basic
  Nurse Education Branch
Division of Nursing, Bureau of Health
  Professions
Health Resources and Services Adminis-
  tration
Department of Health and Human
  Services
Rockville, Maryland
Assistant Professor
University of Maryland School of Nurs-
  ing
Baltimore, Maryland
Senior Vice President for Patient Services
Collingswood Nursing Center
Rockville, Maryland
Director, Clinical Nursing Research and
  Development, and Acting Vice Presi-
  dent for Patient Services
Suburban Hospital
Bethesda, Maryland
Director, Nursing Program
Montgomery College
Takoma Park, Maryland
*Chapter 9. Nursing Workforce: Challenges
and Opportunities*

Alice Forsha Vautier, RN, EdD
Associate Administrator, Patient Services,
    and Chief Nursing Officer
Emory University Hospital
Crawford Long Hospital
Wesley Woods Geriatric Hospital
Atlanta, Georgia
*Chapter 8. Flexible Budgets and Staffing
Matrix*

Mary E. Warner, BSN, RN, OCN®
Patient Care Manager/Oncology Coor-
    dinator
Mercy Fitzgerald Hospital
Darby, Pennsylvania
Chapter 29. Homecare Issues

Barbara L. Young Summers, PhD, RN,
    MSN
Vice President and Chief Nursing Officer
Head, Division of Nursing
The University of Texas M.D. Anderson
    Cancer Center
Houston, Texas
Chapter 4. Clinical Leadership Challenge

Chapter Reviewers

Karen Marl Banoff, BSN, RN, MPA
Internal Consultant
Mount Sinai Medical Center
Principal
KMB Consulting, LLC
Trumbull, Connecticut

Andrea Barsevick, DNSc, RN, AOCN®
Director, Nursing Research
Fox Chase Cancer Center
Philadelphia, Pennsylvania

Melissa Bennett, BSN, RN, OCN®
Unit Leader of the Hematology/Oncol-
    ogy Special Care Unit
Dartmouth-Hitchcock Medical Center
Lebanon, New Hampshire

Brenda F. Berrian, PhD
Professor, Department of Africana Studies
University of Pittsburgh
Pittsburgh, Pennsylvania

Jamie Cesaretti, MD
Department of Radiation Oncology
Mount Sinai Medical Center of New York
New York, New York

Joseph Cirrone, MD
Department of Radiation Oncology
Mount Sinai Medical Center of New York
New York, New York

Elizabeth Clark-Morrison
Attorney
Associate General Council
Emory University
Atlanta, Georgia

Ruth Collins, MSN, RN, CRNP
Research Coordinator
Department of Radiology
University of Pennsylvania
Philadelphia, Pennsylvania

Arthur Duron, RN
Office of the Director, Administrative
    Resident
South Texas Veterans Health Care System
San Antonio, Texas

Rosemary Ellis, MSN, RN
Director of Quality
Medical University of South Carolina
Charleston, South Carolina

Marilyn Frank-Stromborg, EdD, JD, RN, ANP, FAAN
Chair and Distinguished Research Professor
Northern Illinois University
School of Nursing
DeKalb, Illinois

Richard Friend, PhD
Founder, Friend & Associates, Inc.
Chicago, Illinois

Laura A. Hanen, MPP
Master of Public Health Policy
Director, Government Relations
National Alliance of State & Territorial AIDS Directors
Washington, DC

Jose M. Hernandez, MSN, RN
Data Support System Clinical Coordinator
South Texas Veterans Health Care System
San Antonio, Texas

Anne Jadwin, MSN, RN, AOCN®, CNA
Director, Nursing Services
Fox Chase Cancer Center
Philadelphia, Pennsylvania

Eula Keen-Woods, MHSM, RN
Department Director
Oncology Services
Emory Crawford Long Hospital
Atlanta, Georgia

Gloria Kersey-Matusiak, PhD, RN
Associate Professor
Holy Family University
Philadelphia, Pennsylvania

Willace D. Magee, JD
Attorney at Law
Decatur, Georgia

Nancy McDaniel, MA, RN
Team Supervisor
American Red Cross
Marietta, Georgia

Marthe J. Moseley, PhD, RN, CCRN, CCNS
Clinical Nurse Specialist for Critical Care
South Texas Veterans Health Care System
San Antonio, Texas

Belinda S. Puetz, PhD, RN
President and CEO
Puetz and Associates
Pensacola, Florida

Margaret Riley, MN, RN, CNAA
Director, Center for Cancer Care & Research
Saint Joseph's Hospital of Atlanta
Atlanta, Georgia

Barbara Barnes Rogers, MN, RN, CRNP, AOCN®
Adult Hematology-Oncology Nurse Practitioner
Fox Chase Cancer Center
Philadelphia, Pennsylvania

Marcia A. Satryan, MSN, RN, AOCN®
Adjunct Clinical Faculty
Penn State Altoona
Independent Oncology Consultant
Satryan Consulting Services
Hollidaysburg, Pennsylvania

Margaret Vettese, PhD, RN
Nurse Scientist
Dana-Farber Cancer Institute
Boston, Massachusetts

Donna G. Weber, MS, CTR, FAAMA
Director, Accreditation and Data Management
Hospital Corporation of America
Nashville, Tennessee

TABLE OF CONTENTS

FOREWORD

A chain of events that threatens the quality of health care nationwide has led professional nursing to its greatest challenge in more than a century. All nurses share the goal of providing top quality care to patients in an efficient and comprehensive manner. The burden of quality lies, in large part, with nursing leaders. Today's nurse leader wears many hats and has the awesome responsibility of managing at a time when we face the most serious global nursing shortage in our history. Aging of the workforce—for nurses in education, research, and practice—coupled with fewer people choosing nursing threatens the very fabric of patient care and the supply of RNs to meet the needs of the future.

Before my election to Congress in 1998, I was a registered nurse for more than 30 years. That is why one of my first legislative priorities was to use public policy to stem the nursing shortage before it truly cripples our healthcare system.

In 2001, Congress passed my bill, the Nurse Reinvestment Act. The Nurse Reinvestment Act focuses federal resources on recruitment of new nurses and retention of current nurses already in the workforce. The bill establishes scholarships for nursing education as well as Career Ladder grants to encourage promotion and advancement for those in the nursing profession.

Passage of the Nurse Reinvestment Act was a key first step in bringing awareness to the critical nature of the nurse shortage, but it is just the beginning. Now we also must focus on the working conditions that lead so many nurses to leave the profession, as well as more funding for nursing education programs that are essential to ensuring nurses have the continuing education they need in this changing world.

Nurse managers are key members of the healthcare team. These managers have the responsibility for nurse recruitment and retention, staff development, coaching and counseling, and leadership and mentorship of the nursing team. In times of high demand, nurse managers may be promoted from the ranks due to their expertise, leadership, and professionalism as a bedside nurse. However, too often the nurse may not have access to the professional development opportunities that can provide guidance for the many new challenges that will be present in new positions. This is why it is vital that nurses have the management training they need to succeed in these roles. Strong nurse leaders and managers are correlated with a stable and experienced nurse workforce.

We face great economic challenges in the healthcare industry. We must turn challenge into opportunity as it relates to mentoring staff and developing leaders. This textbook will serve as a comprehensive resource for nurse managers, clinicians, and new nurses who aspire to leadership roles in their profession. Together, we can build and improve upon the already fundamental role of the nurse in our healthcare system and ensure the highest quality care for our patients.

Lois Capps, RN
United States Congresswoman
23rd Congressional District of California

PREFACE

The task of managing, organizing, delivering, and improving safe and effective nursing care has likely never been more challenging than today. When one considers the extraordinary challenges of delivering care within multiple settings and, along with that, ensuring that patients have access to the enormous array of new, experimental therapies, it is no surprise that the management role demands tremendous more expertise, skill, and commitment than ever before. Nurse managers and administrators are being asked to meet the needs of patients, families, institutions, corporations, and society at large; they face competing demands and constrained resources.

Help is on its way! *Nursing Management: Principles and Practice* goes a long way toward providing key knowledge to guide the practice and development of nurse managers. This book provides an important resource for managers in virtually every aspect of nursing practice. It also gives important insights for nursing administration and management students whose sights are set on making a real difference in the care context. In short, this book is a real gem!

There are many special features to this book; however, most important among them is its editor and author, Mary Gullatte. Mary is an expert in oncology nursing and management who is well known in the field for her leadership in the improvement of care for patients with cancer. Her previous edited book, *Clinical Guide to Antineoplastic Therapy: A Chemotherapy Handbook*, is highly acclaimed as a clinical resource to oncology nurses and clinicians. Because Mary brings her own expertise, wisdom, vision, and experience to this publication, it is crafted to meet the needs of real nurses who are working in very challenging conditions. In addition, Mary brings her vast network of expert colleagues from around the country to contribute to this volume. Together, these authors create a recipe for interesting, thought provoking, and instructional reading.

On a personal note, I have known Mary Gullatte for a number of years. She is, indeed, a true clinician and scholar whose life is dedicated to the improvement of care of patients, families, and communities. The gift of her unflagging commitment is evident in this book, as it is in all of her life's work. Although it is most unusual for someone writing a preface to dedicate it to another individual, in this instance, it is most fitting. I dedicate this preface to Mary Magee Gullatte—the nurse that I wish for all who need care; the manager that I wish for all who provide care; and the teacher I wish for all who aspire to make a true difference. Thank you, Mary, for the important gifts that you have given in this book and in all of the work that you do.

Marla E. Salmon, ScD, RN, FAAN
Dean and Professor
Director, Lillian Carter Center for International Nursing
The Nell Hodgson Woodruff School of Nursing
Emory University
Atlanta, Georgia

ACKNOWLEDGMENTS

The editor wishes to express special thanks to individuals and mentors who have had a positive impact on helping to shape her professional growth and practice and for encouraging her to pursue personal and professional goals with persistence and determination:

Nurses: Mary Beth McDowell, Mary F. Woody, Mary Huch, Charlotte McHenry, Laura Porter-Kimble, Marla Salmon, Brenda Brown, Robbin Moore, Pat Stanfil-Edens, Carrie Gullatte, Edith Folsom Honeycutt, Nelza Levine, Sandra Herring, Rose McGee, Linda Nauright, Sandra Millon-Underwood, Janice Phillips, Pearl Moore, Clara Jenkins, Jessie Anderson, Cynthia Crank, Ryan Iwamoto, Kevin Sowers, Sharon Krumm, Melba Hill-Paschel, Marjorie Kagawa-Singer, Roberta Strohl, Deborah McGuire, Catherine Futch, Ann Belcher, Brenda Nevidjon, Kathi Mooney, Susan Beck, Mary Scott, Laura Hurt, and all of the nurses with whom I have worked and who have coached and mentored me over the decades.

Physicians: James Bennett, James Fisher, Imani Vannoy, Douglas Murray, Daniel Nixon, David Lawson, Harold Freeman, Michael Fanucchi, Leonard Heffner, Elliott Winton, Toncred Styblo, Kamal Mansour, William Wood, Louis Sullivan, Tina Jones, Robert Hermann, Edmund Waller, Rein Saral, Fadlo Khuri, Douglas Collins, and Lloyd Geddes.

I also wish to express sincere appreciation to the administrative leadership at Emory Healthcare: Alice Vautier, Chief Nursing Officer, Emory Hospitals; John Fox, President and CEO of Emory Healthcare; Jonathan Simons, Director, and Sandra Murdock, DrPH, COO, Winship Cancer Institute; for their support of my professional growth. To the Directors of Nursing colleagues: June Connor, Jane Vosloh, Cathy Wood, Barbara Sverdlik, Sherry Tiller, Becky Provine, Mary Hart, Marilyn Margolis, James Mullen, and administrators: Robert Bachman, Margaret Bloomquist, David Pugh, Jimmy Hatcher, Mark Aycock, Albert Blackwelder, and other coworkers, managers, staff, and friends, past and present, across all departments of these institutions who have contributed in some measure to my professional growth, love of people, and passion for nursing.

Community leaders: Andrew Young, Rev. (s) Kenneth and Cassandra Marcus, John D. Henry, Sr., and Coach Kenneth Carter.

Special thanks to Leonard Mafrica, Barbara Sigler, and the staff of the Oncology Nursing Society for their work on this publication. Thank you, Sherrill Ross, for making sure I am in the right place at the right time. Special thanks to Rhonda Everett, medical librarian, Emory University Hospital Branch.

Special Thanks to the Chapter Reviewers

My sincere appreciation to all of the contributing authors, consultants, and reviewers of this book and to a wonderful and caring team of healthcare professionals and leaders.

CHAPTER 1

Managing Self to Lead Others

Delorese Ambrose, EdD

"Leadership is putting character into action." (Hunter, 1998)

Nursing management is simultaneously more exciting and more difficult than ever. In addition to the intrinsic rewards of healing lives, the healthcare environment offers endless opportunities to innovate, to grow personally, and to inspire medical excellence. At the same time, health care is a system in transition. With each change come new stressors and complexities to manage. Changing expectations, staffing shortages, and the challenges of managing care, costs, access, and quality require leadership that is increasingly adept as the healthcare industry redefines itself for the future.

In every practice setting, leadership responsibilities are compounded by the need to juggle multiple priorities, log long hours, balance work and home life, maintain personal and staff morale, mediate conflicts, influence policies, and keep abreast of the latest information and technology. Indeed, the primary leadership challenge in health care today is how to provide access to safe, reliable, low-cost, high-quality patient care in a climate of turbulence and complex new precedents.

If you have chosen to lead and manage others in this environment, you will need to be highly skilled, motivated, and committed to your field. You must develop a sophisticated understanding of the business aspects of medicine, expertise in human relations, and an ability to create a motivating environment for self and others. You must be dedicated to lifelong learning and clinical competence, because skills and technology become rapidly obsolete, and in your role as manager, you do best if you model the excellence you seek from others. You also must cultivate personal values such as integrity, courage, and a caring human spirit. But this is not the end. To be most effective, you will need to develop a keen awareness of yourself as an instrument of leadership.

With this in mind, this chapter discusses what nurse leaders (e.g., managers, administrators, clinical directors, other healthcare executives) can do to better manage themselves to lead others. Throughout the text you will gain practical tips for self-mastery, managerial and moral courage, and interpersonal relations as we explore what it means to manage and lead from the inside out. The chapter is organized under two sections.

The first section, "Managing Self: The Journey Inward," will

- Review the relationship between managing, leading, and the use of self to influence people and organizational outcomes.
- Define what values are and examine how personal values shape the manager's character, perceived trustworthiness, behavioral choices, and impact as a leader.

The second section, "Leading Others: Putting Character Into Action," will

- Explore three dimensions of character development (personal mastery, managerial courage, and interpersonal relations) as pathways to exemplary leadership.
- Offer guidelines for managing yourself in each of these areas in order to lead others more effectively.

Managing Self: The Journey Inward

Managing, Leading, and the Use of Self

Management is the art and science of getting things done through people. Successful managers are skilled at planning, organizing, monitoring, supervising, and coordinating people and activities. They also are skilled at leadership—thinking strategically, challenging the status quo, envisioning future direction, and inspiring, coaching, and empowering people so they *want to* go in that direction.

Take a nurse manager or a nurse director for example. In their respective roles, each has different organizational responsibilities. Yet both must plan, organize, handle staffing and staff assignments, set performance goals, oversee the activities of others, monitor the quality of patient care, and allocate financial and technologic resources appropriately. They must create a stable, efficient, well-run organization. This requires *managerial* expertise.

The nurse manager and the nurse director also must be agents of change. They must demonstrate the courage needed to innovate and transform the organization in ways that will ensure clinical or professional excellence. They must develop a work culture and climate that support high-performing teams and cultivate in people a willingness to change, innovate, and embrace core organizational values that support quality service. This requires *leadership* abilities.

Discussions about management and leadership tend to focus on the wise and efficient use of resources, such as people, time, money, and technology, to reach organizational goals. What is often overlooked is the *use of self* to achieve this.

Take a closer look at the role of leadership and you will discover that it is impossible to talk about leading others without considering how you manage and deploy yourself in that role. Leadership is a process of persuasion and example by which you inspire and engage others in achieving a shared vision (Kouzes & Posner, 1999). The workplace offers countless opportunities for everyone to exercise leadership. Professionals pioneer new medical advances. Supervisors coach and inspire workers to go the extra mile or hone new skills. Managers establish new goals and priorities and engage people in change aimed at excellence. In each of these instances, you are, in effect, using yourself to influence people and outcomes.

Use of self is a term used by organization development specialists to describe the ways in which we bring *all* that we are and all we have experienced to our work: our bodies, minds, personality, creativity, and talents, as well as our values and biases, strengths and shortcomings, positive self-regard or self-loathing.

Personal Values

In managing yourself and leading others, your personal values become the most important consideration. Every choice and every communication exchange is guided by values—*your conscious or unconscious beliefs about how the world works or how it ought to.* Where do these values come from? The first set of values is formed in childhood. These are usually the same as your parents' or primary caregivers', including teachers and even television, in some cases. Later, as you grow into adulthood, you may challenge and change some of these values, but many remain with you for life, serving as organizing principles as you make decisions and form relationships. These beliefs shape your perceptions of what is important and serve as perceptual filters from one situation and one interaction to the next.

As individuals (and by extension, as organizations), we perceive, experience, and live out our values in multifaceted ways. Figure 1-1 summarizes ways our values come into play as we interact with others and make behavioral choices.

Figure 1-1. Manifestations of Personal Values

1. As *beliefs* or a core "world view": We would never give up, no matter what.
2. As *thought patterns* or filters: We use them to interpret events and people's behaviors.
3. As our *priorities* that show up in the day-to-day choices we make
4. As our *self-concept*: how we see ourselves and how we ideally would like to be seen by others
5. As our *self-esteem*: how we positively regard ourselves
6. As the *state of being* we strive for (e.g., love, happiness, freedom, peace, security)
7. As the *motives* that drive our choices (e.g., control, power, creativity, fame, wealth, service to humanity)
8. As the things we *fear* (e.g., loss, being bored, criticism, abandonment, loneliness)

Some values are said to be "terminal." Others are described as "instrumental." Terminal values determine how you want to be seen or remembered by others—the type of person you would like to become. Do you want to be seen, for example, as a manager who cares deeply about people? Do you want to be remembered as engaging and likeable, or do you think it is enough that people respect you and do as you ask?

Instrumental values govern your daily behavioral choices from situation to situation. Do you go the extra mile regardless of the level of your compensation? Do you treat people as though they are basically trustworthy, or do you act as though most are untrustworthy? Are you extremely frugal, or do you believe in spending whatever it takes to get the results you want?

Of course, the two types of values always intersect. For example, if one of your terminal values is to be someone who has a great deal of *integrity*, instrumentally, you would choose behaviors such as keeping your word or "walking your talk." Several years ago, I took on a consulting assignment with a new CEO who was the hospital's fifth CEO in 11 years. With each CEO that had come and gone, employees had to deal with a new senior administrative team and new strategic initiatives. Needless to say, they were jaded by the lack of leadership continuity, and their morale, performance, and productivity were negatively impacted. The new CEO, anxious to break the cycle of aborted leadership, conducted a series of focus groups to gather feedback. Repeatedly, employees across all levels and units made comments such as, "We feel the CEO position here is a pass-through assignment," or "No one cares enough to stick with us until the espoused values and programs become a reality."

The CEO gave his word that he would stay for the long haul; he would continue his dialogue with employees and would make every effort to seek and apply their input wherever practical. He used terms like "shared leadership" and commitment to "excellence in service" and set about living these principles by holding employee town meetings, rewarding excellence, and engaging people as what he called "partners in change." After several months of skepticism, employees began to make note of the consistency with which the CEO followed through on his promise. They reported a noticeable difference in the behavior of senior leadership and commitment levels. They expressed appreciation for minor behavioral changes, such as the CEO often walked the halls and would greet employees who had attended his town meetings by name. As of this writing, four years later, the CEO is reported to be one of the most admired executives the hospital has known. The hospital has survived a difficult merger with another institution, led by this man and his team. Throughout the trying period, the integrity with which he lives his values has earned him the continued trust and support of managers, staff, and professionals systemwide.

Values and Character

Values are an important focus of leadership development because of their impact on shaping character. A body of leadership scholars, labeled "trait theorists," concern themselves primarily with the study of how values undergird the character of the leader. They pay special attention to the ways in which the leader's stated values and the behaviors of the leader are linked to those values and shape subordinate perceptions of the leader's credibility or trustworthiness. This body of work has given useful insights into leader values and character traits that followers seek. The following are among the ones most often cited:

1. *Honesty and integrity*—your word is good and your behaviors are consistent with stated values.
2. *Self-knowledge and self-mastery*—you are clear about your strengths and shortcomings, willing to learn from others, and generally exhibit positive self-regard.
3. *Courage*—you are willing to put yourself on the line, based on conviction and a willingness to take risks; you possess inner strength and demonstrate confidence.

4. *Vision*—you are forward-thinking and future-oriented and believe in possibilities.
5. *Passion*—you are both inspired and inspiring to others and approach life with gusto.
6. *Concern for others*—you demonstrate caring and goodwill toward others and tend to be respectful, supportive, and fair-minded in your dealings with people.
7. *Competence*—you are a strategic thinker who is effective at goal attainment. You are consistent and reliable.
8. *Cooperativeness*—you are community-minded, team-oriented, willing to collaborate with others, and skilled at resolving conflicts or creating harmonious relationships.
9. *Inclusivity*—you create an environment that enables all employees to contribute to their fullest potential, and that allows you to make quality decisions in the midst of diversity, similarities, and polarities.

Values and Behaviors

As you work with and manage employees, you will notice that there is an elaborate interplay of personal, social, and organizational values that govern behaviors. Consider, for example, how values related to power, authority, inclusion, security, competition, well-being, safety, teamwork, and autonomy coincide and/or collide in your workplace, dictating behaviors and creating harmony or conflict. Consider, too, how the values held by those in leadership roles ultimately shape the organization's culture and climate. Clearly, if you are in a leadership role, you must be grounded on a solid platform of values that will steer your actions in the right direction for yourself and for your organization.

In preparing to lead others, you must work on value alignment. This means your espoused values (what you *say* you believe in and want) must consistently match your lived values (how you *act* in each situation). Unfortunately, value alignment often is difficult to achieve. Life obligations, fears, habits, poverty, and the challenges of working in a stressful healthcare environment can compromise your ability to act in ways that are in alignment. A classic example is the parent who believes in ample quality time with the children and who, at the same time, must put in long hours at work, arriving home too exhausted for quality parenting. Over time, these inconsistencies can erode our self-concept (how we see ourselves) and our self-esteem (the degree of positive regard we hold for ourselves). If self-esteem is low, we gravitate toward values that defend or protect our fragile psyches. Conversely, if self-esteem is high, we are more likely to be aligned with values and practices that support personal mastery and the highest human good.

Hultman and Gellermann (2001) suggested that people who exhibit traits such as a lack of concern for others, dishonesty, and slovenliness are more likely to be low in self-esteem. In contrast, people who are caring, honest, and committed to excellence tend to have higher self-esteem. The implications of this for managing self and for leading others are endless. For starters, such findings suggest that a core competency for leadership is the development of positive self-regard, both in the leader and in those he or she seeks to influence and support.

Values and Trust

The nurse leader or manager who is so task-oriented that there is no time to get feedback from or develop others is likely to create a work climate that is ultimately demoralizing and ineffective. This is a sobering observation. It means that eventually each organization becomes an extension of the values of those whose leadership, management, and professional choices shape the day-to-day experiences of its employees and customers. If you are a manager charged with decision-making clout, your personal impact is even more profound. Every employee expects the supervisor to lead and manage with integrity, fairness, and sound judgment. Employees look to the leader for guidance and support. Staff want to know that their leader is guided by the right set of values that will assure them that the leadership is consistent and in the best interests of all. At times, the staff will defer to the wishes of the leader, assuming or hoping that the leader is trustworthy.

Trustworthiness is closely related to three core values (Ambrose, 1996), *competence, integrity*, and *goodwill*, which are summarized in Table 1-1.

Table 1-1. Three Dimensions of Trust		
Dimension	**Examples**	**How It Works**
Competence	Personal: creativity, excellence, curiosity, a learning stance Social: concern for people, emotional intelligence, customer service skills, community mindedness, inclusivity Technical: business acumen, professional know-how, technologic skills	People trust you if they sense that you know what you are doing.
Integrity	Honesty, dependability, alignment of words and deeds and of inner and outer worlds, fair-mindedness	People trust you if they believe your word is good and they see you "walking your talk."
Goodwill	Open communication, caring, open-mindedness, cooperation, positive outlook, and visionary stance	People trust you if they sense you care about them.
Note. Based on information from Ambrose, 1996.		

Your willingness to seek and incorporate feedback from those you supervise, those you serve, your peers, and your supervisors is an important mindset for managerial excellence. As you solicit feedback, a focus on the dimensions of competence, integrity, and goodwill will go a long way toward building your "trustworthiness" as a leader.

Leading Others: Putting Character Into Action

In managing self to lead others, three dimensions of character development become important (Ambrose, 2002): personal mastery, interpersonal skills, and managerial courage. These are summarized in Table 1-2.

Table 1-2. Dimensions of Character Development and Leadership	
Dimension	**Examples**
Personal mastery: *The ability to reflect on yourself, take steps necessary for personal and professional growth, and make choices that are congruent with your vision and values.*	• Live your values and play to your strengths. • Solicit and use feedback to build character and skills. • Make self-care, lifelong learning, and support networks a priority in your life and work.
Managerial courage: *Deployment of personal and interpersonal mastery in service of the organization's strategic goals marked by an ability to demonstrate wisdom, exercise leadership, and take risks necessary to foster innovation.*	• Be willing to challenge the status quo and take risks. • Engage head and heart, warrior and healer. • Articulate and model a compelling vision for your organization. • Communicate with integrity. • Be comfortable with being uncomfortable.
Interpersonal skills: *The ability to build relationships, manage differences, and create a motivating environment that inspires self and others to achieve high performance.*	• Develop cultural competence in working with diverse customers and employees. • Focus on relationship building, common interests, and mutual gain as you resolve conflicts. • Develop a healthy awareness of personal and organizational power.

Here are some specific steps you can take under each of these dimensions as you manage yourself to better carry out your leadership responsibilities.

Personal Mastery

Personal mastery begins with self-awareness, self-acceptance, and self-confidence, coupled with a readiness to change and develop in the areas you choose. Managers who fail often do so because they lack these traits. Rather than figuring out who they are and relying on their own values, competencies, and personal style, ineffective managers ignore their instincts and talents as they try to emulate others. They lack the courage to stand up for what they believe or to take decisive action. Instead they may adopt one management fad after another, looking for the right model or magical formula for leadership effectiveness.

In contrast, effective managers tend to be people who build their competence and confidence by playing to their values and strengths. At the same time, these managers know their personal shortcomings and take steps to manage these shortcomings. They are adept at getting support from others and at hiring, developing, and delegating to people with complementary characteristics and skill sets.

Live Your Values and Play to Your Strengths

Rather than trying to emulate others, clarify your values and value your own style, strengths, and life experiences. What works for another manager might be different from what works for you. Once you are clear about your values, share them with the people who report to you and others, and invite them to give you honest feedback when you are not living your values. This is important because to model integrity in your life and as a leader, your walk (how you act) must match your talk (what you say you believe in).

In a recent culture audit for a major hospital where employee morale was at an all-time low, the number one issue cited by frontline employees was failure of management to keep their word and to do what they said they believed in. One impact of this was that employees tended to drag their feet on important change initiatives, cynically assuming that things would not pan out. When checking with the supervisors and middle managers, they blamed senior management for lacking the "moral courage" to establish clear values, priorities, and direction in the face of difficult politics and mandates.

What was most interesting about this study was the fact that one unit in the hospital was able to maintain high morale and to outperform the other units. A closer look revealed a most important difference. The unit manager ran her floor as though she had created an oasis in the midst of chaos. In her words, *"As a manager, I focus my leadership attention on the things over which I have control: my commitment, my ability to develop and support people, and the goals I have set for my unit. I simply drill it into my staff that we must never lose sight of our number one priority, which is a commitment to our patients' well-being. Then I do everything in my power to inspire and enable them to do their best work"* (personal communication). This manager demonstrated many characteristics of personal mastery: self-knowledge, clarity, willingness to stand up for what she believes in, and congruence between her beliefs and actions.

Be aware, too, that there will be situations where your values differ from those of your coworkers or the organization itself. Learn to discuss these differences openly and honestly without judging self or others. The goal here is to foster mutual respect and understanding.

If you discover that you embrace values that create disharmony for self or others, you may set a personal growth goal of modifying those values or developing new ones. If, for example, your perfectionism leaves no room for flexibility or is taking a toll on your family or coworkers, you may want to develop the ability to be a perfectionist in some areas and not others. As you make these shifts in your personal development, talk with others about the changes you are trying to make. One manager took the time to explain to her staff which areas she was working on being more flexible about. She then, very explicitly, listed several areas that because of safety implications were non-negotiable.

Solicit and Use Feedback to Build Character and Skills

This may sound like overstating the case, but, in fact, the effectiveness of a leader is entirely dependent on people's *perception* of that leader's trustworthiness—competence, wisdom, and credibility. Because good leadership is in the eye of the beholder, you must regularly ask, *"How am I doing?"* to improve your performance as a manager. Ask this question of those you serve, those you supervise, and those who supervise you. This represents 360-degree feedback.

In addition to informal dialogue, patient satisfaction surveys and 360-degree feedback from your direct reports, peers, and supervisors will be very useful in this respect. Patients are whom you ultimately serve. As a healthcare leader, the most important gift you can give to patients is a well-managed, well-led environment that supports their healing. As you manage the human, financial, and technologic resources at your disposal to provide the best clinical service, the voice of your patients provides a critical barometer for measuring your success. Likewise, the employees you supervise and work with have a lot to say (perhaps behind your back) that can benefit you and your organization. Ask for feedback from your direct supervisor. You do not have to wait for the formal year-end performance management feedback session. Check with your supervisor or director regularly to discuss not only your own performance but also larger strategic goals for clinical and leadership excellence.

As you solicit feedback, do not shoot the messenger! Thank the person or group giving you feedback, even if you disagree. Later you can decide whether, or how, to use their contribution. This way you leave the door open to get continual input for your personal leadership development.

Make Self-Care and Support Networks a Priority in Your Life and Work

There is a useful adage that says, "Fill your own cup first, then you can feed others from the overflow." This sage advice reminds us that to lead others with integrity, we must nurture and develop ourselves so that we can become credible models of the behaviors we seek in others. Unfortunately, in the field of medicine where practitioners and executives at all levels routinely log long hours and endure great stress, there is little time for self-reflection and self-renewal. To be successful in your personal and professional life, you must take proactive steps to nurture and manage yourself. The 21st century healthcare environment, like workplaces in every sector, creates many barriers to work/life balance. The majority of U.S. families with small children now have both parents in the workforce. To compound this picture, a growing percentage of managers and senior healthcare administrators are baby boomers, many of whom (especially women) are charged with primary care responsibilities for elderly parents as well as for high school- or college-aged children still at home.

When thinking about self-care, we think about the obvious: proper diet, sufficient exercise and rest, and regular check-ups. But it is the less tangible interventions that often trip us up: how to manage the boundaries and interfaces between our relationships, our workplace, and the demands placed on us by self and others in order to find the time and resources necessary for self-care. For starters, you must learn to negotiate these boundaries. For example, learn to say "no." Challenge unnecessary meetings. Establish with your significant others special time alone that is yours and only yours for rejuvenation and down time. Try to take one or two retreats each year with or without family and colleagues. These do not have to be lengthy but should afford quality time, allow deep reflection, include leisure activities, be spiritually uplifting or mentally stimulating, and above all, restful.

Self-care also means taking time out for learning. By staying abreast of the latest thinking and technology in your field, you give yourself the gifts of knowledge and credibility needed to be self-assured and to make meaningful contributions to your field and your institution. Make attendance at internal training programs and external conferences a routine part of your work life. Take control of your career by embracing lifelong learning and initiating these opportunities rather than waiting for recommendations from your supervisor. Join professional organizations such as your state nurses association and/or specialty organizations, such as the Oncology Nursing Society, American Association of Critical Care Nurses, Association of Operating Room Nurses, or American Academy of Ambulatory Care Nursing, that place member education and leadership development as top priorities.

As you do so for yourself, cultivate the value of learning in your work team. Wherever possible, hire employees whose talents and backgrounds complement your own. Coach, develop, and expose staff members to the best training and education available. Groom them to function as co-leaders and highly skilled professionals who support you in achieving organizational goals.

You cannot care for self and build your expertise in a vacuum. *Who* you know goes hand in hand with *what* you know. You will need wise guides and caregivers who support you in supporting others. Throughout your career, consciously develop a support network of people who serve as your personal or spiritual anchors, service providers, professional contacts, and staff team members.

Managerial Courage

Because leadership is aimed at change, you must be willing to challenge the status quo and try new things. At times, you will have to embark on paths that have not yet been proven. Your efforts will often be met with resistance. There will be situations where you are expected to stand tall and "be the boss," making unpopular command decisions, enforcing safety mandates, cutting costs, or even cutting jobs. Naturally you will experience trepidation in many of these situations. But as Mark Twain once put it, "Courage is not the absence of fear, it is the mastery of fear." This is the nature of management and leadership. Being in charge takes both moral and managerial courage. The following are several ways to develop and exhibit managerial courage.

Be Willing to Challenge the Status Quo and Take Risks

Managerial courage relies on an ability to deploy your knowledge, instincts, and interpersonal skills in the service of the strategic goals of the organization. It means being willing to stand on principle and to risk failing as you speak your truth or make bold choices to achieve the outcomes envisioned for the team.

But courage is not the same as recklessness. To the extent that you spend time gathering data, learning from others, and developing your moral compass and problem-solving skills, you can be more calculated in your approach, thereby minimizing failure. However, be prepared to manage the occasional fallout from your risk-taking. This is where self-mastery kicks in. When mistakes happen, ask, "What did we learn?" instead of focusing on "Who is to blame?" Smart leaders view change as involving incremental steps in which learning occurs along the way. If you learn from mistakes, you are not only showing courage, you are gathering wisdom.

Engage Both Head and Heart, Warrior and Healer

Courage does not mean being ruthless or heartless. Regardless of your preferred leadership style, you must develop a wide repertoire of decision-making approaches that allow you to be directive when you seek compliance and collaborative when you seek commitment.

As the leader, learn to use your head to make difficult decisions and your heart to implement them in ways that speak to the needs of those impacted by the decision. If you take a tough, directive stance all the time, ultimately you will lose the trust and support of people as they begin to feel like victims and who may attempt to sabotage your efforts. Conversely, if you are always conciliatory and "touchy feely," you will lose the very respect you seek, as they perceive you as spineless or unable to handle tough decisions well. The challenge lies in knowing when to be tough-minded or autocratic and when to be a follower, seeking guidance and input from others. It is very easy to fall back on your personality or preferred leadership style. It takes courage to modify the approach in different situations and with different people to achieve the desired managerial outcomes.

Tap the expertise of those around you, and engage others in a process of shared leadership, where appropriate. This allows an opportunity to get commitment or buy-in for the changes you are leading. Multiple contributions also generate better ideas for implementation than a single leader can.

Articulate and Model a Clear, Compelling Vision for Your Organization

Perhaps the most important practice successful leaders engage in is the practice of creating a shared vision. This practice is key because it ultimately shapes the culture of the organization—the set of values, priorities, and practices that hold the organization together. It is important to do this first for yourself as a manager or executive, then for the team you are charged with leading. In crafting your vision, be sure to seek input and to take your needs and values, as well as the needs and values of your direct reports and those you serve, into account. Then communicate your vision honestly, excessively, and redundantly.

With your vision in mind, develop a sound strategy and set clear expectations and priorities for self and others. If people do not have a clear sense of direction and expected final outcomes, the confusion causes them to move away from change, even if they believe change is necessary.

Communicate With Integrity

While I was conducting a management seminar, a trainee handed me a quote that I now post in my meeting rooms. It reads, *"Don't talk big in the back room; talk back in the big room."* This is a timely reminder. Employees at every level lack the courage to speak their truth. Instead, they retreat to the safety of the "parking lot meeting" after the meeting. There they say all the important things that could have served the organization well if shared openly and honestly in the context of the staff meeting. This practice is not acceptable for nurse managers or leaders who want to encourage effectiveness and integrity at work. It is also the fastest way to erode trust and morale. Be sure to impress upon people that you are trying to create a culture and work climate in which it is safe for people to differ and to bring their unique perspectives to the table.

Communicating with integrity means that one has the courage to bring inner thoughts and spoken words into alignment. When you talk *with* people rather than *about* them, you will be a truth caller in your organization. Even if you hold a minority position, be willing to share your views and equally willing to hear what others have to say in response. This kind of communication is an important component of character development. Behaving this way will eventually distinguish you from others as a trustworthy person who takes the moral higher ground.

Figure 1-2 identifies guidelines to use as you interact with people and inculcate the value of honest communication in the workplace. Consider posting these in your meeting areas as a way of teaching these principles and skill sets to others.

Figure 1-2. Guidelines for Communicating With Integrity

- Take the risk to say what you really think.
- Speak for yourself. Do not hide behind the "we" of your group.
- Encourage others to speak their truth also.
- Listen nondefensively; probe to make sure you understand the other before responding.
- Be clear, direct, and unambiguous about your expectations of others and your position on important issues.
- If you change your mind, let others know.
- Seek and offer feedback as a pathway to personal effectiveness.
- Ensure that opinions are fact-based.

The ability of the leader to set performance goals and offer performance feedback is the foundation of good managerial practice, yet it is the area in which many supervisors and managers are most timid. This is understandable. Egos tend to be easily bruised, and feedback (especially negative or corrective) can be easily met with resentment or embarrassment by both parties. I often have coached supervisors who are ineffective because they lack the gumption to give explicit, honest feedback to their direct reports. The cost to productivity, safety, morale, and general organizational effectiveness is high.

To be an effective manager, strive to create a work culture in which feedback is the norm. To maintain goodwill, work hard to protect the self-esteem of the person receiving feedback from you. Choose the right time, place, and tone. Give both positive and negative feedback (not necessarily at the same time). When giving both positive and negative feedback in one discussion, avoid using "but" to connect the two. The word "but" in that context has the psychological impact of diminishing the positive feedback. For example, instead of saying, "You are good with our patients, *but* you do not always follow through on details," say *"You are good with our patients. Now I need you to work on following through on details."*

If the feedback is corrective or negative, observe the following guidelines:

- Address only behaviors that can be changed.

- Attack the problem, not the person.
- Be descriptive, not judgmental.
- Be clear about the impact of the person's behaviors.
- Speak for yourself. "You" tends to be accusatory. "I" tends to be more effective as you describe the situation and its impact on you.
- State future expectations clearly.
- Have the facts supported with examples whenever possible.
- Be clear that intentions are in the best interest of the people and the organization.
- Develop your character such that you act with heart and integrity, and you will gain the courage it takes to give and receive honest feedback and reap its many rewards.

Be Comfortable With Being Uncomfortable

Leadership can be a messy process as differences and competing needs collide. Because leaders are agents of change, they also create discomfort for people. It is human nature to resist change because it moves us out of our comfort zone. Change also leaves people feeling less competent than before as they are forced to learn new skills, embrace new technology, and take on more or different responsibilities. Sabotage, resistance, and disagreements are all part of the tension that ensues as we lead, implement, and manage change. Effective leaders are aware of this inevitability. They address and mediate conflict head-on in ways that facilitate win-win outcomes.

Interpersonal Relations

Develop Cultural Competence in Working With Diverse Customers and Employees

In 2002, the American Hospital Association (AHA) Commission on Workforce for Hospital and Health Systems published a report aimed at helping hospital leaders to build a more effective workforce (AHA, 2002). Among their recommendations was the need to improve workplace partnerships by "creating a culture in which hospital staff—including clinical, support, and managerial—are valued, [and] have a sustained voice in shaping the institutional policies . . ." (p. 5). This recommendation and the findings that support it are not surprising. Healthcare systems are beginning to come to terms with a history of classism and exclusionary practices that have challenged managers and leaders for decades. Today, the escalation of cultural competence and diversity management programs are visible acknowledgments that things are changing for the better. But much work remains to be done in this area. As a manager, you have a key role to play.

One of the most interesting challenges for a manager is how to create inclusive workplaces where patients and workers feel valued, respected, and are able to get their needs met regardless of their ethnicity, race, sexual orientation, and socio-economic status. Chapters 3, 4, 12, and 13 offer insights into how to develop effective leadership skills in cultural competence and diversity.

Focus on Relationship Building, Common Interests, and Mutual Gain in Resolving Differences

Conflict is inevitable whenever people interact. In the workplace, competing needs, styles, values, and expectations are bound to clash. As a manager, you are challenged to manage differences, resolve conflicts, and reach agreements that last and that leave relationships intact or enhanced.

Fisher, Ury, and Patton (1991) wrote an all-time best-selling negotiation primer-based book on research they conducted at the Harvard Negotiation Project. The book, *Getting To Yes*, teaches how to negotiate in ways that build relationships and create mutually satisfying outcomes. It is built around four negotiation concepts labeled "principled negotiation." The goal of this approach is to reach agreement rather than "win." Using a collaborative, rather than adversarial, mindset allows you to listen to people across your differences, generate multiple options for resolving the conflict, and, thereby, reach wise, mutually satisfying and lasting agreements. Drawing on popular negotiation theory, the differences between "principled" and adversarial approaches are summarized in Figure 1-3.

Figure 1-3. Reaching Agreements That Last	
Principled Goal: Agreement (win-win)	**Adversarial Goal: Victory (win-lose)**
Emphasize common interests ("needs") and mutual gain.	Emphasize positions ("wants"), differences, and unilateral gains.
Seek to preserve and enhance relationships.	Disregard relationships.
Attack the problem, not the person. Rely on objective criteria and joint problem solving.	Attack the problem and the person. Use pressure and threats.

Build Trusting Relationships

Trustworthiness is based on competence (being knowledgeable about people, processes, and resources), integrity (being honest and consistent), and goodwill (demonstrating you care). To build competence, learn as much as you can from all available sources. Be a good communicator and listener who is willing to learn from anyone and from various perspectives. To develop integrity, act in ways that model what you say you believe. Speak the truth as you see it and invite/make it safe for others to do the same. Never shoot the messenger. Rather, create a climate where people are rewarded for sharing their best insights and information. To create goodwill, show appreciation for the contributions of others. Value people for who they are and what they have to offer. Show you care by practicing acts of kindness and thoughtfulness toward others.

Develop a Healthy Awareness of Personal and Organizational Power

The most effective leaders cultivate humility and never lose touch with their humanness. At the same time, they have a healthy relationship with power—neither hoarding it nor fearing it, but using it wisely in achieving personal and organizational goals. Ambrose (2003) defined power as the capacity to ensure the outcomes we want. As such, power becomes the fuel of leadership that enables you to drive organizational change and effectiveness.

Hagberg (2002) made an important distinction between internal and external power. She has contributed much to our understanding of personal and organizational leadership by suggesting that we experience power differently at different stages of personal growth, in different situations, and with different people. She taught that while outer power is linked to our status, credentials, connections, or achievements, inner power derives from our capacity for reflection and wisdom. The key, according to Hagberg, lies in combining both sources of power in order to be personally more effective, ultimately becoming a "true" leader, someone who is willing to be other than who the world wants him or her to be and who is guided by such values as self-knowledge, purpose, humility, wisdom, and dedication to community.

In the early stages of your journey of managing self and leading others, it will be natural to find yourself concerned with basic external needs: "How can I survive?" "How can I grow?" "How can I succeed?" But as you move closer to self-mastery, you become more introspective and clearer about who you are and how you can best serve your clients. If you are willing to take the necessary risks, you can create an exciting career in which you transcend the ordinary in your responsibilities as a nurse leader or manager. In doing so, you will find yourself integrating work and life in a holistic way. You will be guided by a more powerful set of questions: "How can I bring my inner world and my outer world into better alignment?" "How can I find meaning in my work and my life?" "What risks am I willing to take to become a more effective human being, leader, and parent?" "How can I transcend the ordinary to approach my career from a stance of purpose and enlightenment?" As you manage yourself to lead others, this awareness will translate into excellence in interpersonal relations and service to humanity.

Conclusion

The key message of this chapter is that to transform and successfully affect organizations, communities, or the lives of self and or others, we must first transform ourselves. Personal leadership development is a process of self-reflection and self-renewal that requires feedback from others and a willingness to pay attention to lessons of life experiences. What is your own life teaching you about leadership? What are the core values that guide and serve you? What obstacles have you overcome that gave you insights into people and the nature of organizational or community life? Instead of focusing inordinately on eradicating weaknesses, you are better served by building on existing strengths. What strengths can you draw on to do your best work? If you are not sure what your strengths are, ask for feedback about what you do well. Learn to listen to your gut. For example, at the end of the day, what energizes you? What depletes your energy? Your answers to these questions can reveal much about where your commitment and passions reside and how you can quickly draw on them.

References

Ambrose, D. (1996). *Healing the downsized organization.* New York: Three Rivers Press.

Ambrose, D. (2002). *Fifty ways to heal your work life.* Retrieved February 2003 from http://www. ambroseconsulting.com/keynoteSpeeches.html

Ambrose, D. (2003). *Leadership: The journey inward* (3rd ed.). Dubuque, IA: Kendall/Hunt.

American Hospital Association Commission on Workforce for Hospital and Health Systems. (2002). *In our hands: How hospital leaders can build a thriving workforce.* Washington, DC: Author.

Fisher, R., Ury, W., & Patton, B. (1991). *Getting to yes* (2nd ed.). New York: Penguin.

Hagberg, J. (2002). *Stages of personal power in organizations* (3rd ed.). Salem, WI: Sheffield Publishing Company.

Hultman, K., & Gellermann, B. (2001). *Balancing individual and organizational values: Walking the tightrope to success.* New York: Jossey-Bass/Pfeiffer.

Hunter, J.C. (1998). *The servant: A simple story about the true essence of leadership.* New York: Random House.

Kouzes, J.M., & Posner, B.Z. (1999). *Encouraging the heart: A leader's guide to rewarding and recognizing others.* San Francisco: Jossey-Bass.

CHAPTER 2

Transforming Theory Into Practice

Susan Lasker Hertz, RN, MSN, AOCN®
Connie J. Carson, PhD

Change is rampant in health care today, placing increased demands on all health-care providers. Managers must possess and master a subset of skills, employ novel approaches to change, and use emerging technologies to make their jobs easier and more efficient in a fast-paced workplace. This chapter provides a foundation for acquiring some of the necessary concepts and skills that oncology managers require to establish and enhance their expertise.

The manager is pressured by a combination of factors, many of which are present in the workforce for the first time. Multigenerational workforces include both men and women from various countries of origin. Managers face an increasing demand for accountability by an all-inclusive customer base, as well as by their employees. Rapid and constant technologic advances require mastery of both oncology-specific advances and "time-saving" technologies. Healthcare delivery demands a service orientation by all employees. Hospitals are downsizing in both size and amount of services offered. Available healthcare dollars are shrinking for all patient care delivery organizations.

Fundamental to successfully navigating these challenges is the knowledge of general management concepts and theories that are covered in this chapter. The theoretical background for both managerial change theory and systems theory is presented in the following pages. An overall paradigm is developed by which an oncology manager at any level can assess his or her environment and begin to develop a working vision or direction. These fundamental concepts concern the interrelatedness of three different perspectives of the organization or workplace: structural design, flow of information and work processes, and human factors that must be effectively assessed and managed (Robbins & DeCenzo, 2003). A discussion of management and leadership assessment inventories that are crucial tools to enhance the oncology manager's understanding of his or her own behavior and the behavior of people with whom he or she works is included. Personality profiles, leadership profiles, and work-behavior profiles are presented here, as all are relevant in the workplace. Finally, specific communication and time-management skills are discussed to establish a working toolbox for today's oncology manager.

Foundations for Understanding

Scientific Management Theories

Management theory was first developed and applied in the early 20th century to present a systematic and objective approach to expose and correct inefficient manufacturing operations. These theories form the basis of the Scientific School of Management Theory in which "the one best way" for work to be done is discovered and implemented. Frederick Taylor first presented early scientific systems theories in his 1911 book *Principles of Scientific Management*. Taylor's theories and those of other early management consultants or engineers are thought to be old-fashioned; however, many of their methods and structures are still applicable. For example, Taylor founded the movement to improve organizational performance by employing objective observations, such as the use of time and motion studies. In addition, Taylor's principles of management included (a) the development of a science for each element of an individual's work, (b) each worker should be specifically selected and trained for each job, (c) managers and workers should cooperate so that work can be completed, and (d) managers had specific work for which they were uniquely suited (Taylor, 1911). These early organizational principles contributed to the perception of management as distinct from work production.

Max Weber was a German sociologist who wrote early in the 20th century about the ideal work organization. In his writings, Weber identified the best organization as one in which there is a distinct division of labor and a clearly defined hierarchy. Detailed rules and regulations direct the work structure and should be applied impartially. Weber also suggested that managers functioned most ideally when they were professional officials who worked for specific salaries and pursued their careers within the organization (Weber, 1957).

Henri Fayol's contribution to the scientific theories of management was to describe a set of activities that was specific to managers. He documented the specialized relationships of line versus functional staff positions, still used in organizations today. Line positions, as Fayol defined them, are direct chain of command positions in a top to bottom hierarchy, whereas functional staff positions involve more specialized positions outside of the chain of command in support of specific tasks or duties (Koehler, Anatol, & Applebaum, 1976).

Fayol's management structure included the classic hierarchical pyramid structure in which decisions move from top down. Manager tasks, according to Fayol, included planning, organizing, commanding, coordinating, and controlling. The purpose of organizations was to bring together equipment, workers, and materials required to achieve specific organizational objectives. Managers were responsible for planning and assessing these factors to devise a strategy to achieve organizational goals. Managers used tools to organize and coordinate a unifying effort and to control the workforce, supplies, and other forces so that work objectives could be achieved.

Today's managers apply some of these scientific management theories when they match people to specific jobs and teach them to be more effective in these positions

(Robbins & DeCenzo, 2003). Using videotape or other tools of time-motion study to suggest improvements in work processes or creating an organizational chart that illustrates the relationships for both line and staff positions are applications derived from scientific management theories.

Humanistic Management Theories

While advocates of the scientific management theories sought to look at the structure of work and organizations and increase production and work performance through that application, other early theorists focused on more people-centered concepts to improve organizational performance or describe management responsibilities. These theories are known as the humanistic approach to management. The Hawthorne Studies conducted at the Western Electric Company's Hawthorne Works in Illinois in the 1920s and 1930s did much to provide new insights into group norms and behaviors and the effects of these on productivity (Robbins & DeCenzo, 2003). Initial studies attempted to determine whether increased illumination in the factory would correlate with increased productivity by factory workers. In fact, what was found was that the illumination had little or no impact on productivity at all. Instead, it was through a variety of consultant-based studies at this factory over the next several years that it was discovered that group standards, group sentiment, and general security (known as the Hawthorne Effect) more significantly affected worker output and production. Up until these studies were conducted, management viewed workers as no different than machines. It was the study of the Hawthorne Effect that drove home the importance of people and human relations in making management more humane.

Most familiar to nurses is the work of Abraham Maslow, a humanistic psychologist and author of the well-known Hierarchy of Needs (1954). He postulated that the five basic needs (physiologic, safety, social, self-esteem, and self-actualization) when not satisfied will motivate behavior. Maslow (1954) suggested that each need is arranged in hierarchical importance, and each step in the hierarchy must be met before the next level of achievement can be reached. Research, unfortunately, does not always support Maslow's theory.

Douglas McFregor's Theory X and Theory Y assumptions about human nature have contributed greatly to the humanistic approach to management. McFregor in *The Human Side of Enterprise* (1985) indicated that the scientific approach to management, as expounded by Theory X, looked at the worker as having an aversion to work, being unmotivated to perform well unless threatened or forced to do so, being indolent and unambitious, and valuing security about all (Koehler et al., 1976). Theory Y looks at work as being as natural to humans as play or rest. Work makes life rewarding and full; all humans welcome responsibility under the right circumstances; and organizations waste the potential of most employees. McFregor suggested that it is Theory Y's view of the positive nature of humans and work that should guide management practices. However, these theories have not been explored fully as a comprehensive organizational theory but are widely accepted for empowering employees and managers to be more participative in work behaviors.

The last humanistic management theory for discussion is the Motivator-Hygiene Theory or two-factor theory by Frederick Herzberg. Herzberg's theory assumes that there are two sets of factors that contribute to motivation and job satisfaction that are not direct opposites of each other. Factors that influence satisfaction are called motivational factors, whereas another set of hygiene factors influence dissatisfaction (Herzberg, Mausner, & Snyderman, 1959). Motivational factors include achievement, recognition, advancement, growth, and responsibility. Hygiene factors include supervision, pay, status, job security, and administrative policies. There is still wide debate as to whether there are two distinct dimensions that contribute to work satisfaction and dissatisfaction, but positing this idea brings into focus the variety of factors that may influence work satisfaction. In fact, the National Study of Changing Workforce indicated that although employers for the most part identify "good wages" as the most important factor for employees at work, the employees themselves cite a "full appreciation for work done" as most important (Nelson, 1996, p. 4).

The differences between the scientific and humanistic theories are vast. The conceptual models of both approaches were historically presented at about the same time. In the previous century, many organizations had either a scientific or humanistic approach toward management and employees. Today, organizations are able to draw from the strengths of both concepts. The oncology nursing manager must be able to conduct time-motion studies and gain input from employee forums synonymously. Corporate mandates require specific employee performance with designated role expectations. It is the challenge of the nursing manager to fulfill these obligations with both scientific rigor and humanistic style.

The presentation of both scientific and humanistic management theories is a useful foundation for approaching management problems and devising solutions. Brief summaries of the two schools of management theory are presented in Table 2-1. Both schools of management theory assist managers in systematically approaching management challenges they may face in today's healthcare arena. However, without the framework for dealing with change, the next constant construct to be presented, managers may find themselves without a complete understanding of how to better manage their environments, employees, and corporate structures.

Table 2-1. Relevance of Scientific and Humanistic Management Theories for Today's Nurse Managers

	Scientific Theory	Humanistic Theory
General concepts	Development of rational principles to make organizations more efficient and effective	Tolerance of individual work methods; relies on the employee's sense of responsibility for quality and quantity of work produced
Best known theorists	Frederick Taylor, Max Weber, and Henri Fayol	Abraham Maslow, Douglas McFregor, and Frederick Herzberg

(Continued on next page)

Table 2-1. Relevance of Scientific and Humanistic Management Theories for Today's Nurse Managers *(Continued)*

	Scientific Theory	Humanistic Theory
Strengths	Hires, trains, educates, and matches workers to specific jobs. Carves out specifics of a manager's role	Values the ideas of individual employees and encourages general participation at work in planning and decision making
Weaknesses	Emphasizes material incentives and disregards human factors	Theories are well known but not borne by research. Sometimes flowery compliments are given as "lip-service" instead of real monetary or work environmental "fixes."
Management tools in current use	Organizational chart Time-motion studies	Suggestions box Open employee forums

Note. Based on information from Robbins & DeCenzo, 2003.

Managing and Embracing Continuous Change

Handling change, knowing what it is, embracing it, learning to modulate its effects on everyday operations, and strategic challenges are vital aspects of management. This discussion of change includes several well-known paradigms for understanding the change process, including Lewin's (1935) three-step change process and Bridges' (1980) model for understanding and managing transitions. Also described are suggestions for managing the change process successfully and overcoming the natural inclination to resist change.

Organizational change is defined as "an alteration of an organization's environment, structure, technology, or people brought about by either external or internal forces" (Robbins & DeCenzo, 2003, p. 203). In cancer care, for example, improvements in the effectiveness of antiemetic therapy were key external forces in changing the point of service for the delivery of cancer chemotherapy from an inpatient hospital stay to outpatient cancer centers. Internal forces for change may include a change in available personnel, such as a shortage of RNs or a new chief nursing officer. In either case, the fact of change must be recognized and embraced, and a new strategy must be employed to counter these forces. Understanding the stages of change can assist in this process.

Classically, Karl Lewin (1935) has described the change process. In his model, successful change first requires that the status quo be *unfrozen* so that stakeholders are readied to consider change. In the early 1980s, for example, the implementation of diagnosis-related groups as a payment vehicle for Medicare provided an external force that changed the status quo and unfroze hospital stakeholders, allowing them to adopt changes in healthcare delivery. Once the "business as usual" approach has been disrupted, the second phase, *change,* can be implemented. To use the example cited above, changes such as disease management or best-practice care maps could be implemented once the environment was softened up to require and embrace this change in healthcare delivery. The last step in Lewin's three-step process, called *refreezing*, ensures that this change will be sustained and adopted as the new standard or new status quo.

William Bridges' (1980) work on transitions builds on Lewin's three-step model. It is somewhat more explicit in describing the effects of change and therefore offers more insight for managers wishing to understand and manage staff resistance to changes that are constant in today's healthcare environment. Bridges described environments of change as chaotic "whirlwinds" in which the process of change includes the stages of *endings, exploration,* and *new beginnings* (Bridges).

For Bridges (1980), every transition or change begins with an ending or a letting go of the old. Successfully managing the end before beginning change goes against the grain of our culture. Bridges recommended not focusing solely on the results or the end-point of change but rather offered methods to manage the transitions of the change process. The process of embracing change requires that managers live with the discomfort of the change process. Feelings of denial, anxiety, and anger give rise to many intense and difficult to manage behaviors in staff, patients, or managers themselves when change is occurring. Bridges advised that these normal responses to change initially give rise to the exploration phase from which comes creative, novel solutions and opportunities to "think outside of the box." After this time of exploration comes the unveiling of new beginnings, which first may be met with skepticism but gradually will move people toward acceptance and bring renewed energy and enthusiasm to the environment. Figure 2-1 is a schematic depiction of this three-step evolutionary process.

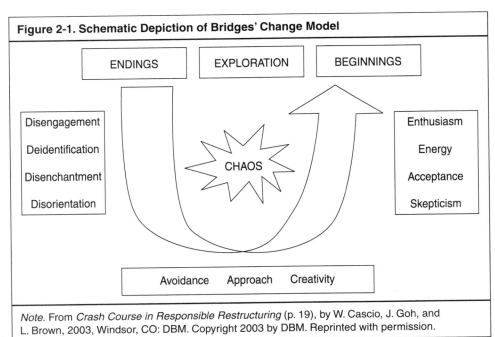

Figure 2-1. Schematic Depiction of Bridges' Change Model

| ENDINGS | EXPLORATION | BEGINNINGS |

Disengagement
Deidentification
Disenchantment
Disorientation

CHAOS

Enthusiasm
Energy
Acceptance
Skepticism

Avoidance   Approach   Creativity

Note. From *Crash Course in Responsible Restructuring* (p. 19), by W. Cascio, J. Goh, and L. Brown, 2003, Windsor, CO: DBM. Copyright 2003 by DBM. Reprinted with permission.

Although Lewin's and Bridges' models assist managers in better understanding how the change process occurs, it is helpful to know specific hints to manage the various phases of the change as it is occurring. In *The Tipping Point*, Gladwell (2000) explored why some ideas, behaviors, or products produce a greater change than others. It is at the "tipping point" or the moment of critical mass when some type of threshold or boiling point is reached that sets into motion the process of change. He boils down the act of change into three rules or constructs. First, some people matter more than others. This is the *law of the few*. Find those people, sell them on your ideas for changes, and the change may be more easily accepted. Second, ideas or changes need to be memorable and move us to action (Gladwell). This is the *importance of stickiness* for those ideas that are easily remembered. An example of this is the assassination of President John F. Kennedy, which had a very big impact on the baby boom generation. The *power of context* recognizes that humans are more sensitive to their environments than they may seem (Gladwell). Consideration of individuals' responses to change or new ideas is often a result of the situation in which one finds him or herself. It may not be a response driven by their inherent personality or genetic predisposition. The responses to change then are not absolute nor are they always the same. By understanding Gladwell's three constructs, it is possible to begin to manage change and achieve stronger outcomes.

Jennings, Miller, and Materna (1997) offered concrete steps in managing change as helpful tools for managers. First, foster some sense of dissatisfaction with the status quo to begin to position the need for change. Retrieve information from the marketplace or competitors. Demonstrate a personal commitment to the change, whether it is a change in personal behavior or new work operation. Plan for the communication of the change, identify the key audience, build trust, and ensure that the change is communicated from top down and bottom up. Develop methods to make the change happen in everyday work situations. Set goals and targets that are consistent with the change vision. Give people structure as to how to perform the new task to make the change happen. Finally, sustain the change by removing barriers that stand in the way of the change being embraced. To assist in describing how to bring about change in the workplace, these 10 dangers of the change process are presented (Nickols, 2004).

1. Be unclear about why there is a need for change.
2. Begin the process of change with a victim's mentality.
3. Assume everything will fall into place.
4. Under-resource the change effort.
5. Send folks in for the change ill-prepared.
6. Initiate the change process without a communication plan.
7. Do not anticipate chaos.
8. Forget to "hand-hold" during the process.
9. Fight the whole war all at once.
10. Expect the new way to win first and all the time.

In conclusion, change is a constant in health care today. Hospitals merge and acquire other care delivery systems; staff and bosses come and go at both planned and unexpected times. Sometimes you as a manager are required to lead the change effort, other times you may find yourself an unwilling participant in implementing change. In all cases, a good understanding of the change process is an advantage in whichever circumstances managers may find themselves. Implementing some of the techniques to assist in managing change through education, communication, participation, facilitation, or negotiation make this process more manageable.

Personality Profiles

One device that often is used at management training workshops or team-building seminars is the process of inventorying those characteristics or traits that make each person unique. Validating these specific characteristics that you bring to the workplace helps define your personality strengths and weaknesses and provides those same insights into your coworkers, managers, leaders, and subordinates. Many types of these inventory tools have been researched and developed. Presented here are common examples of a *personality trait inventory*, the Myers-Briggs Type Indicator® (MBTI), a *behavioral styles* inventory, the Dominance, Influence, Steadiness, Conscientiousness (DiSC®) Inventory, and a *measurement of leadership behavior* developed by Kouzes and Posner (1997). Any of these may have application in the workplace because all of these tools are currently being used in healthcare organizations. Also presented is a discussion of whether understanding variations in personality or behavior can help managers to be more effective.

Personality inventories are designed to assess the relatively stable and enduring personal characteristics that may have an effect on job performance and workplace behavior. MBTI inventory initially was developed in 1943 based on the work of Carl Jung. Although not originally developed to be applicable to work situations, it has a very broad research base, is used most appropriately with people of high school age through adulthood, and is a measure of normal personality traits. The test is widely available, is copyrighted and trademarked, and can be scored by computer or by a stencil. It consists of 100+ forced choice pairs that measure the personality dimensions of introversion/extroversion, sensing/intuition, judging/perceiving, and thinking/feeling.

MBTI differentiates and measures perceptions, judgments, and attitudes used by different types of people to make decisions. As a managerial tool, MBTI helps managers become aware of themselves and how they interact with people. It often is used in team-building exercises to improve interpersonal relationships (Costello, 1993). Another study looked at the relationship between nursing orientees and their staff nurse preceptors. Anderson (1998) found that those orientees who matched their primary preceptors on the personality trait of introversion/extroversion reported higher levels of satisfaction with their overall orientation than those who did not have a match. Although widely used in many industries—approximately two million people have taken the MBTI in the United States alone—it is not the only useful tool available (Robbins & DeCenzo, 2003).

The Big 5 model of personality seeks to provide a more direct relationship between personality and job performance. Its five major factors include extroversion, agreeableness, conscientiousness, openness to experiences, and emotional stability or the degree to which someone is calm and secure or tense, nervous, or depressed. In a study conducted by Gambles, Wilkinson, and Dissanayake (2003), a personality profile based on the Big 5 model was used to explore the existence of a personality profile for nurses working in palliative and critical care in the United Kingdom. A specific personality inventory was completed by 178 nurses, half of whom were staff nurses. The nurses scored highest in extroversion, empathy, trust, openness, and group orientation. The nurses studied were cautious when faced with new ideas and were somewhat lacking in objectivity. Another study using MBTI as the personality inventory found that healthcare clinicians tended to be more introverted and scored higher in feeling and perceiving dimensions than did healthcare administrators, who scored higher in extroversion, thinking, and judging scales (O'Connor & Shewchuk, 1993). Understanding these personality differences may help to bridge the communication differences felt by healthcare clinicians and their administrative counterparts.

One of the concerns that is sometimes expressed about MBTI and other personality inventories is that evaluating personalities of people at work may not be appropriate; this may be more personal than is proper in the work environment. To address these concerns, behavioral styles inventories may be better suited to the workplace. Behavioral styles inventories evaluate and suggest how a person prefers to behave in a certain situation. These inventories are concerned with the behaviors exhibited on the job, which may be more appropriate workplace activities. Inventories of this type include the Dimensions of Behavior—DiSC Inventory. This inventory is given very quickly in the workplace, is well validated, and has been used for approximately 30 years. The DiSC inventory provides information about how a person will behave in the workplace with the understanding that behavior is changeable or adaptable and may be different under different situations. From the results of the inventory, an extensive profile is chosen that describes the strengths and weaknesses of the individual who takes the inventory. The results also include how to work with and communicate with coworkers who score differently on the inventory.

The last type of inventory features a measurement of specific leadership behaviors developed and researched in the 1980s by Kouzes and Posner (1997). Thirty behavioral statements are described on a 10-point Likert scale as to how often a manager or person uses these behaviors. Challenging the process, inspiring shared vision, enabling others to act, modeling the way, and encouraging were identified most frequently as the characteristics that leaders display. This leadership inventory is used to point out one's own strengths and weaknesses with respect to leadership behaviors. Further work by this team identified that leaders most frequently combine the traits of trustworthiness, expertise, and dynamism. Can these traits be honed or taught as part of successful management training? Kouzes and Posner offer a mechanism with this inventory to measure leadership development. Over time, that would indicate these behaviors can be modeled, described, and therefore embedded in managers.

Personality inventories and other types of inventories have an important role in personal management development and in growth and development of effective work teams. Used judiciously, they can be useful as personal growth tools and enhance the manager's feeling of confidence and goodwill in the workplace. In addition, they can be fun exercises to use with staff for team-building purposes to assist in embracing personality and behavioral diversity at work.

Communication and the Relevance of Listening

"In organizations, as in the rest of life, many of the greatest joys and most intense sorrows, the highest peaks and the deepest valleys, occur in relationships with others" (Bolman & Deal, 1999, p. 134). At least three recurrent questions haunt managers in their relationships in the healthcare environment (Bolman & Deal, pp. 134–135).

- What is really happening in this hospital/unit?
- Why do other people behave as they do?
- What can I do about it?

Communication Principles

The genesis of the theoretical base of managerial concepts coincided with the advent of research into communication principles. As research formed the foundation for managerial perspectives, an awareness of the relevance of communication in the organizational setting also was being established. Everything a manager does involves communicating. Not just some things but everything. Without communication, a manager cannot develop a strategic plan, staff the floor for nursing coverage, plan a budget, or ensure excellent care. Although good communication alone does not make a good manager, a good manager must possess effective communication skills.

In 1976, Dance and Larson cited more than 126 definitions of the term "communication" and summarized that a comprehensive definition did not exist. In the past three decades, many more attempts have been unsuccessfully made. Some of these attempts include the following.

> Communication is the process by which we understand others and in turn endeavor to be understood by them. It is dynamic, constantly changing, and shifting in response to the total situation. (Anderson, 1959, p. 5)
>
> Communication cannot be understood except as a dynamic process in which listener and speaker, reader and writer act reciprocally, the speaker acting to provide direct and indirect sensory stimulation to the listener; the listener acting on the stimulation by taking it in, investing it with meaning by calling up images in the mind, testing those images against present information and feelings, and sooner or later acting upon those images. (Martin & Anderson, 1968, p. 53)
>
> Communication is a process that makes common to two or several what was the monopoly of one or some. (Gode, 1959, p. 5)

Communication travels in many different channels. Interpersonal communication involves a few individuals, whereas mass communication can reach multitudes of people. Communication can be confidential or quickly spread through the grapevine, where it is random and often inaccurate. In the organizational setting, communication travels upward, downward, laterally, or in networks.

Bookstores abound with current best sellers on communication. Although they may contain numerous tenets or principles of communication, the following five have stood the test of time.

Tenet Number One

Communication requires a two-way flow of information. It cannot be done in a vacuum. Baker (1971) stated that when one writes, there is an assumption that someone (known or unknown) may read, and when one speaks, there is the intention that someone may hear, even if one speaks to oneself. Whereas one person in isolation can dispense language, communication requires reciprocity. The term "communication" is derived from the Latin word for "to share." Effective communication involves listening as much as speaking. The act of conveying extensive information to staff will fall on silent ears if a means of response is not established. If your staff cannot respond, you do not have a communication system, but rather an information channel (Jay, 1999). An effective manager establishes the environment where both positive and negative situations are heard. Staff members must be able to respond, to know that their replies are being openly received, and to see that their contributions are making a difference in the decision-making process of their department.

Tenet Number Two

Communication is not retrievable. Dance and Larson (1972) compared communication to an extended Slinky® toy when held upright: "When viewed as helical, one's speech communication at one and the same time moves toward and yet gracefully curves back on itself in progressive motion. The intertwining of two or more helices, as in interpersonal or person-to-persons speech communication . . . testifies to the fantastic and fascinating complexity of human speech communication" (p. 184). Our conversations continue to be shaped by the actions of others, ongoing events, and conversational dynamics. Once a sentence is said, it cannot be taken back. Even with apologies, the content has been launched.

Tenet Number Three

Rules and expectations exist. Weaver and Strausbaugh (1964) stated that these patterns make it possible for us to put words together in ways that meet the expectations of the listener and heighten the degree of communication. Some rules are specific to individual relationships. Others are influenced by cultural differences or mandates of the employment setting. These rules change due to fluctuations in the dynamics of the people involved, their employment position, and the institution itself. Eisenberg and Goodall (2001) stated that the definition of effective communication does not remain constant; rather it varies by company or industry, the people involved, and the culture. Communication styles that work well in a small clinic may be inappropriate for an inner city teaching hospital. Patterns of interaction that were effective last year may be outdated today because of changes in technology, patient preferences, or the nature of health care.

Tenet Number Four

Interpersonal communication is constantly changing. "Speech communication is a process by which meanings are exchanged, information is sent and received" (Brooks, 1971, p. 5). In the employment setting, at home, or with friends, communication is constantly moving—coming apart, expanding, deepening, or distancing. People working together may become friends; that relationship may deepen or tensions may occur. Colleagues may be promoted or demoted, and the change in positions can alter the communication dynamics between the two. The workload may intensify and time previously available for more personal interactions may be limited. Changes in the corporate structure may expand or constrict opportunities for more personal interactions. Regardless of these changes, communication still occurs. It might take a different form, it may be fragmented, and it may become more meaningful, but it does change.

Tenet Number Five

One cannot function effectively in a managerial position without an awareness of the importance of communication. As Zelko and Dance (1978) noted, the management of today's business organization relies on and makes more use of speech communication than any other commodity or ingredient" (p. 20). This holds true even today. Unfortunately, becoming an effective communicator takes time. Conferences, seminars, and expensive consultants can help but are not sufficient in helping professionals master the art of communication. The best teachers are role models and practice. Principles of communication need to be taught and practiced. Examples of excellence must be evidenced in the oncology manager if he or she is to nurture the communication skills of his or her staff.

Benefits of Effective Communication in the Healthcare Arena

Managers today are challenged to be effective communicators. Table 2-2 outlines some of the significant advantages of good communication. What does it mean to be an effective or good communicator? The following list includes elements of effective communication (Jennings et al., 1997).

Table 2-2. Benefits of Effective Communication in the Healthcare Arena	
	Benefits
Patients	When patients are involved in the development of their treatment plan, compliance improves. Patients who are able to communicate their concerns to listening ears experience greater satisfaction with the care given, regardless of the extent of their disease.
	(Continued on next page)

Table 2-2. Benefits of Effective Communication in the Healthcare Arena *(Continued)*	
	Benefits
Family members	Good communication increases confidence in the healthcare team and institutions, which decreases potential friction over care decisions, present and future.
Hospital or clinical care setting	Good communication produces well-motivated staff, resulting in higher patient satisfaction, fewer complaints, and a better community image.
Oncology managers	When information is flowing freely, oncology managers are able to prioritize issues, obtain appropriate input, make specific recommendations, and see action plans enacted.
Physicians	Treatment planning is communicated more effectively. Patients respond better, relationships improve with all stakeholders, and medical care improves.
Nursing staff	Staff works more efficiently and effectively. Job satisfaction and productivity increase.
Allied healthcare providers	Job expectations are clearer, roles are better defined, and job performance and satisfaction improve.
Administration	Ideally, effective communication should begin at the top administrative levels and filter down through the hospital infrastructure.
Community	The institution is perceived as a positive neighbor that enhances any community in which it is a part.
Financial bottom line	Satisfied patients return to their healthcare setting for future care, change physicians less often, and file fewer complaints.

1. Engage in active listening of what is said and what is not said.
2. Pose open-ended questions.
3. Establish rapport.
4. Clarify.
5. Stimulate.
6. Give support and encouragement.
7. Intervene when necessary to clarify issues.
8. Observe; note the whole person, including his or her voice, phraseology, and body language.
9. Offer genuine praise to build self-esteem and high performance.
10. Comfortably compliment staff in public.
11. Build rapport by concentrating on common ground.
12. Build trust by demonstrating reliability, openness, and sensitivity.

An organization staffed by effective communicators benefits the patient, the patient's family members, the hospital or clinical care setting, oncology managers, the physicians, nursing staff, allied healthcare providers, the human resource department, administration, the community, and the financial bottom line.

Four forms of communication are used in the healthcare setting: the spoken word, the perceived word, the written word, and nonverbal communication.

The Spoken Word—Verbal Communication

The relevance of the spoken word cannot be overemphasized. Satir (1972) saw communication as "a huge umbrella that covers and affects all that goes on between human beings. Once a human being has arrived on this earth, communication is the largest single factor determining what kinds of relationships s/he makes with others and what happens to him in the world about him. How he manages his survival, how he develops intimacy, how productive he is, how he makes sense . . . are largely dependent on his communication skills" (p. 30).

Most of us have remarked, "It wasn't what he said, but how he said it that made me angry." The tone of one's voice, the emphasis or inflections given to certain words, and the pauses inserted in a sentence contribute special meaning to the spoken word. Increasing loudness expresses anger or alarm. Depending on the tone and emphasis, a simple "yes" can convey anger, resentment, acknowledgment, happiness, or fated resolution. Vocal inflections and pitch can communicate alarm, annoyance, and fear. An extremely fast tempo conveys hyperactivity or anxiety; a slow tempo often signals uncertainty.

A simple sentence, "I gave Jane *the* paper" can have a different meaning if the emphasis is placed on one word rather than another. When *I* is emphasized, it means that I completed the action, not someone else. When *gave* is stressed, it means that I personally handed it to her, I did not phone her, mail it, or e-mail it. Emphasizing *Jane* implies that it was delivered to her, not anyone else. *The* paper implores that a specific sheet of paper was delivered, and placing the accent on paper infers that it was a paper, not another object. The same sentence can have five different meanings based on where the accent is placed.

Verbal Communication Styles—Traditional Definitions

Figure 2-2 depicts four types of communication styles (Sutch, 1994). When dealing with each of these four different kinds of people, it is ideal to tailor your message so they all will be able to listen. For example, if you feel the person to whom you are speaking has an *Explorer* communication style, provide additional technical information; whereas the technical information will not be as effective if you are speaking to a person with more of a *Free Thinker* type of communicative style. Figure 2-3 depicts these styles in more detail.

Le Boeuf (1985) identified the five most important words in our language: "You did a good job"; the four most important words: "What is your opinion?"; the three most important words: "Let's work together"; the two most important words: "thank you"; and the single most important word: "we" (pp. 88–89).

The Perceived Word—Listening

The earliest and possibly the most thorough study on listening was cited by Baker (1971) but executed by Rankin in 1929. Rankin's subjects reported that

42% of one's communicative interaction was spent listening. Although it might be difficult to believe, most people speak less than they listen, as 32% of the average communicative interaction is spent in talking. Replications of his study have confirmed Rankin's findings (Canary & Cody, 1993). Male and female discrepancies were not reported.

Figure 2-2. Description of Communication Styles	
Mr./Ms. Fix-it **Concrete sequential (CS)** Prefers learning from hands-on experience, logically organized, uses the five senses to absorb information. These individuals like to focus on ideas and tasks. They think methodically and predictably and do not adjust easily to change.	**Utilitarian** **Abstract sequential (AS)** This type of individual prefers learning from a logical presentation of ideas. They rely on impersonal analysis and systematic planning to solve their problems. They create theoretical models from a wide range of information, are slow to decide, and are less concerned with people than with ideas.
Explorer **Concrete random (CR)** These people prefer learning from trial and error. They rely heavily on experience-based intuition. They do best when they can find a practical use for ideas and theories. They base their decisions on finding solutions, are quick to make decisions, and are risk takers. They rely more on people than technical analysis for information. They thrive on change.	**Free Thinker** **Abstract random (AR)** Prefers learning from lots of free-form ideas. These people form opinions from feelings. They view experiences from different perspectives. They think intuitively and do not usually rely on logic. They balk at structure and are great brainstormers because they like to generate new ideas.

Note. From *Interpersonal Communication Skills: Training to Minimize Conflict and Build Collaboration in Today's Team-Oriented Workplace*, by D. Sutch, 1994, Boulder, CO: Career Track. Copyright 1994 by Career Track. Reprinted with permission.

People engage in active and passive listening. Active listening requires attention; passive listening does not. You might have heard someone say, "I know you are hearing me, but are you really listening?" Active listening takes many forms, and a given interaction rarely requires only one form of listening. Listening is a process; by its very nature it is constantly in a state of fluctuation.

Appreciative listening involves recognizing the tone and mood, visualizing images from the message, and gleaning satisfaction or gratification from being involved in the activity. *Conversational* listening requires the receiver to switch roles from being the listener, to the speaker, and then back again to listener. *Courteous* listening is practiced in conversational settings where the listener is expected to accept the responsibility of listening with an open mind and allowing the speaker to dominate most of the conversation. People also listen to indicate love and respect. The mere showing of attention to the speaker is a reward in itself. We often use *selective* listening when hearing only segments of a message, whereas concentrated listening involves hearing the entire message and attempting to comprehend all of its components. *Critical* listening requires that the receiver analyze the evidence or ideas presented and make judgments about the validity and quality of the message presented. This requires one to distinguish fact from opinion, differentiate between the emotional and the logical, and identify bias and prejudice. Usually this occurs in an open forum. *Discriminative* listening is listening for the purpose of understanding and retaining information. This requires skills in comprehending the relationship of details to main points, following a sequence of thought, retaining information, and recognizing the purpose of the presentation (Baker, 1971).

Figure 2-3. How to Tailor Your Message so People Listen

Mr./Ms. Fix-it **Concrete sequential (CS)** With *Mr./Ms. Fix-it*, it is ideal to focus on experiences because they are more concrete/sequential. Use a logical organization and present details before the big picture. Use practical and realistic applications. All five senses can be used in your presentation to these people.	***Utilitarian*** **Abstract sequential (AS)** When dealing with these people, focus on ideas. Have a logical organization to your presentation. Present goals and objectives first, and list the pros and cons of each alternative. Be brief and concise.
Explorer **Concrete random (CR)** Remember that these people are comfortable with trial and error. Focus on experience. Present points of agreement first and support your ideas with practical suggestions. Multimedia presentations might be effective.	***Free Thinker*** **Abstract random (AR)** Focus on ideas and options. Trust your instincts. Present broad issues first, and remember they like novel and unusual suggestions. Use entire body to communicate.

Note. From *Interpersonal Communication Skills: Training to Minimize Conflict and Build Collaboration in Today's Team-Oriented Workplace*, by D. Sutch, 1994, Boulder, CO: Career Track. Copyright 1994 by Career Track. Reprinted with permission.

It takes more effort to be an active listener than to be an effective speaker. Active listeners are cautious of interruptions, wait for responses, and are comfortable with periods of silence. They use "um-hum" appropriately. When they listen well, they use empathy, suspend judgment, and ask questions. Active listeners may even take notes. They try to listen long enough to hear what the person is intending to say. Lewis (1956) wrote that to be truly heard "is the whole art and joy of words" (pp. 293–294).

Obstacles to communication are shown by gaps in the ratio between the amount of time we speak and the amount of time spent listening. We show we are not listening by nonverbal clues that convey a lack of concern. These clues lead to breakdowns in communication, disinterest, and eventually distrust (Sutch, 1994). Jay (1999) stated that good managers tell their staff as much as they can, as soon as they can, and never lie. The excellent manager then listens to their responses.

The Written Word

There are times when the only means of communicating to staff is in writing. This especially happens with shift changes, job sharing, and flex time. Memos, notice boards, staff letters, e-mail messages, faxes, and internal newsletters all have their place in the toolbox of an effective manager. Written communication is ideal when wanting to impart a perception of formality and authority, when a permanent record is desired, or when you want to ensure that a large number of people will have exactly the same information. For legal reasons, it might be important to put information to staff in writing. In some instances, information may have been presented verbally and written follow-up is necessary. When complimenting staff, it provides a record of your thanks and appreciation. In some instances, the information is quite detailed, and staff members will benefit from having all of the information in one document. E-mail messages might be a quicker way of communicating. In situations requiring diplomacy, you can choose your words more carefully.

There are definite disadvantages to the written word. It limits immediate feedback when staff members need to ask questions or seek clarification. It takes more time to put information into writing than it does to leave a voicemail message or contact an individual personally. In 1657, the French philosopher Blaise Pascal wrote, "I have only made this [letter] longer because I have not had the time to make it shorter."

Sutch (1994) identified six guidelines for making a written messages easier to read: "Use 25 or fewer words per sentence; 12 or fewer words per punctuated pause; 75 or fewer words per paragraph; and 150 or fewer syllables per hundred words. Use short words, highlight the most important information, and utilize white space so the document is easier to read—at least one inch on all sides" (p. 39).

Nonverbal

Nonverbal communication includes, but is not limited to, body language and physical movements. What we wear and how we sound also are considered nonverbal communication. When a conflict occurs between the verbal and nonverbal message, almost always the nonverbal is more accurate (Nelson & Golant, 2004). We have become subtle in our verbal relationships with others, but we still rarely know how to lie nonverbally. Our true intent is conveyed by the tone of our voice, eye contact, facial expressions, gestures, and posture. When a manager says "I'm really interested in your opinion" but says this with crossed arms, a downward gaze, and a tapping foot, a different message is conveyed nonverbally. The nonverbal trumps the verbal in accuracy.

Clues help us to discern a person's response when it is thought to be inaccurate. There may be a greater lag time in response to a question. People who are avoiding the truth may make less eye contact than normal. Body posture might shift. They smile less often and speak more slowly. Occasionally they use a higher pitch in their voice and pronounce words more deliberately. Be cautious; if a person is showing these nonverbal behaviors, he or she may not necessarily be avoiding the truth.

Sutch (1994) stated that nonverbal behaviors may be used to build rapport. Some of the most influential responses are the smile, touch, affirmative head nods, and eye contact. It is advisable to maintain a comfortable amount of distance between you and the person to whom you are speaking, usually an arm's length apart. When possible, try to avoid height differences between you and the person to whom you are speaking, as this can produce an uncomfortable barrier. Be natural about your nonverbal communication style.

Vehicles for Organizational Communication

Communications is not merely the plural of communication. The distinction we make between these two is the same as that between medicine and medicines. We speak of medicines when referring to separate and distinct pharmaceutical preparations and of medicine when referring to the total field of treatment of disease and preservation of health. Likewise, communications includes various types—e-mails, letters, phone calls, conversations—as well as the technical means of transmitting messages, such as the Internet, radio, television, and the cinema (Zelko & Dance, 1978).

The following suggestions are provided to facilitate communication in staff meetings, telephone conversations, counseling sessions, and internal written messages, such as memos, notice boards, staff letters, technologic or electronic communications, and newsletters.

- Staff meetings are the most effective way that a group of people can communicate directly, but they are expensive. Doyle and Straus (1976) stated that most organizations spend between 7% and 15% of their personnel budgets directly on meetings. When an interactive discussion is required, a meeting is the ideal way to obtain the input from several different people. Three basic functions of a meeting are to inform, discuss, and decide (Jay, 1999). Prior to scheduling a meeting, identify the information you want to convey to your staff, the discussion you wish to facilitate, and the decisions that need to be made.

- Telephone conversations convey more information than just the spoken word. First impressions happen in the first 10–15 seconds. Over the phone, that is the first 25–30 words. Ninety percent of an emotional message is nonverbal. One could assume, incorrectly, that emotional content is not conveyed through the telephone. Anxiety is conveyed in one's tone and the quickness of speech. When one is preoccupied or simply tacitly listening to the phone conversation, that message is easily conveyed to the listener. A smile, surprisingly, is transmitted through the telephone wires, as is lack of concern or disinterest.

- Counseling sessions are a means of giving feedback to an employee. Schedule uninterrupted time and meet privately. Be direct but not brutal. Listen with understanding. Focus on issues by distinguishing between perceptions and fact. State specific, observable behaviors and list probable outcomes or possible improvements. It might be better to have the employee generate those options. Avoid loaded terms, and try to deal with emotions first. When possible, focus on the value to the person. Share information and ideas. Link behaviors to be changed to the expected behavior identified in the employee's job description.

Remember employees might respond in one of several ways. Be prepared for all of these responses. They may accept the criticism. If they do, you might want to schedule a meeting at a later date to check on progress and encourage their behaviors. They may deny the problem. If so, try to listen to their side of the story. Some people will plead ignorance. They may be honestly unaware of the situation. Unfortunately, some will get angry and defensive. Even in these situations, try to listen to their viewpoint. If possible, try to get the angry individual to explore options and problem solve. Others may become quiet, imply that it is not a significant issue, or even minimize the complaint. Remember, just when you think you are prepared for the situation, the employee may throw a curve ball that will surprise you. Try to be prepared for all options.

- Memos often are read and discarded. Memos are seen as a more public form of communication and should not be used to convey confidential information. Even if the news is only moderately disappointing, they should not be used to convey bad news. That always should be given face-to-face.

- Notice boards are ideally run by staff members for themselves. It is not an appropriate vehicle for managers to transmit operational information. Either there is so much on them that nothing can be read, or they are read so rarely that they are ineffective.

- Staff letters usually are meant as a private means of communicating between a person and a small group of people. They are used most effectively when you have something confidential to say to an employee and want a permanent record. You might be responding to a request for budget increase, formally complimenting a staff member, replying to a complaint, or giving a disciplinary written warning. A letter can confirm a decision and shows that you have taken the request seriously and provided a written response.

- Technologic communications rely on telephones, faxes, e-mails, and electronic chat rooms to communicate. Although many argue these advances have broadened our ability to communicate, for many, it is less satisfying than face-to-face interactions. Interpersonal communication via e-mail can be as effective or even more effective as face-to-face interactions, but it does require an awareness of simple rules of "Netiquette" (Grimes, 1998). Be considerate of others; keep your message short and to the point. Remember that TYPING IN ALL CAPITAL LETTERS is the equivalent of shouting. Writing in sentence or lower case presents a less urgent message. Some prefer to simplify their message by eliminating punctuation. Sentences that are run-on imply a prompt response is expected. Consider the message you are implying before changing from standard sentence case. Breakdowns in communication sent electronically can be just as devastating as breakdowns in face-to-face interactions. Clarify uncertain implications to maintain accurate and effective communication. Verbally describing one's emotions assists in clarifying the written message. For example, "I laughed when I received your e-mail." Others use "emoticons" or keyboard symbols that are easily read when the head is tilted slightly to the left. In the most basic emoticon (the smiley face), a colon, hyphen, and a right parenthesis become the eyes, nose, and mouth of the smile, which is easily changed to a frown by simply using the left parenthesis. Emoticons convey a more casual message, so use them sparingly (Grimes).

- An internal newsletter is rarely used as effectively as it might be. It is an ideal means of imparting small but necessary pieces of information, for conveying good news, and for keeping people posted on daily operational activities. They can enable people and departments to talk to each other, create a feeling of unity, increase departmental loyalty, and improve staff morale. Staff will perceive management's attitude toward them by the esteem given to their newsletter. When effort is placed on the importance of communicating with employees, the attitude is conveyed that they are important to you. Do not feel that this is "your" newsletter. Encourage staff participation and make it a prestigious job. Commit and stick to deadlines. Internal newsletters are not the place to impart important company information, announce bad news, or present financial data. Their tone should be upbeat, personal, and informal.

When Communication Fails

The ability to manage conflict is one of the most important skills for the healthcare manager to possess, whether it be conflict between staff members, the manager and staff, or manager and other employees of the hospital. Whenever any conversation occurs, there are at least six people present: (a) who you think you are, (b) who you think the other person is, (c) who you think the other person thinks you are, (d) who the other person thinks he or she is, (e) who the other person thinks you are, and (f) who the other person thinks you think he or she is. That is only when two people are involved in the conversation. When others are added, it becomes even more complicated (Barnlund, 1968). Each "person" does not have an equal voice at the same time. When conflict occurs, who you think the other person is and who the other person thinks you are often interfere with who you think you are and who the other person thinks he or she is. Voices get muddled, perceptions are confused, and tension increases.

Whether the differences are real is irrelevant. If people perceive differences, a conflict state exists. Over the years, three differing views have emerged in the understanding of organizational conflict. The *traditional* view assumed that conflict was bad and management had the responsibility of ridding the organization of conflict. This perspective dominated the management literature during the late 19th century and continued until the mid-1940s. The *human relations* view argued that conflict was natural and inevitable. Because it could not be eliminated, it was accepted as part of the human condition. This position was held from the late 1940s through the mid-1970s. The *current view* of conflict supports an interactionist view where conflict is encouraged because a harmonious, tranquil organization is prone to become apathetic and unresponsive to the needs for change and innovation. It is the challenge of the healthcare manager to foster an optimal level of conflict, enough to keep units viable, self-critical, and creative (Robbins & DeCenzo, 2003).

Unfortunately, it is difficult for the manager to determine whether conflict is valuable or dysfunctional. Neither too much nor too little conflict is desirable. One conflict resolution method is not appropriate for all situations. Not every conflict justifies your involvement. Some need to be resolved solely between the involved parties; other conflicts will never be resolved. Choose your battles wisely, saving your energy for those that really affect your department. Do not be lured into the naïve belief that a good manager always has a cohesive department. Crucial questions surface: To what degree does an individual attempt to rectify the conflict by satisfying the other person's concerns? By satisfying their own concerns? What happens if no action is taken to resolve the conflict?

Research has indicated that although conflict occurs for a multitude of reasons, it can be separated into three categories: communicational differences, structural differences, and personal differences (Robbins & DeCenzo, 2003). Communication differences arise from conversational misunderstandings and semantic differences. Structural differences occur over disagreement over goals, decision alternatives, performance criteria, and resource allegations. These conflicts are not caused by poor communication but are rooted in one's position in the organization. Personal differences arise out of individual preferences, idiosyncrasies, and values. One person may perceive an individual to be abrasive and untrustworthy; another may find the same individual to be a valuable team member.

In addressing conflict, it is the challenge of the manager to convey the message that conflict has its legitimate place and that offering divergent opinions and demonstrating original thinking are welcome. Techniques for conflict resolution should be presented before conflict occurs. Managers should set the model of excellence by acknowledging mistakes and encouraging staff to do likewise. When mistakes are made, first and foremost, be honest. Give the facts. Tell who was involved without finger pointing. Admit responsibility. Tell everyone who needs to know. Explain your actions to remedy the situation. Solicit suggestions. Have a plan to prevent the mistake from occurring again.

Trenholm and Jensen (1992) defined five basic conflict styles in terms of their ability to meet two kinds of goals: personal and relationship. Individuals with an *aggressive* communication style have a primary concern to achieve personal goals, even at the expense of a relationship. Conflicts are competitive games; they may even enjoy the fights, as long as they win. The *withdrawing* style typifies individuals who try to avoid conflict. For them, nothing is worth the hassle of a fight. People with an *accommodating* style have a high concern for the relationship, while the need to achieve personal goals is low. They try to smooth over disagreements. Those with a moderate concern for personal and relational goals often try to cut a deal by using a *compromising* style. Individuals who are committed both to personal and relational goals seek solutions through which everyone will benefit. These people have a *problem-solving style* and are open to rational cooperation.

Which style of conflict resolution is best? It all depends. There are times when each style is effective. When a hospital is downsizing and eliminating staff, a problem-solving or compromising style may not be as effective as an aggressive style. When hospital expansion is occurring, this same aggressive style can stymie creativity and team building. The ideal manager is able to develop the abilities to enact all of these styles in the appropriate situation.

Managers who are able to use effective communication, address conflict, and build an effective team are exhibiting leadership. The next section defines leadership, differentiates between a leader and a manager, addresses the characteristics of a good leader, presents transgenerational differences, provides examples of magnet hospitals where innovative leadership policies are practiced, and discusses ways to handle less than ideal leadership situations.

Leadership

Leadership is offered as the solution for most of the world's problems. Although thousands of pages have been written about it, leadership remains an elusive concept. The English word "leader" is more than a thousand years old and little changed from its Anglo-Saxon root *laedare*, which meant to lead people on a journey (Bolman & Deal, 1999). It is a commonly held axiom that leadership is a good thing; yet, there is discrepancy about what leadership really means.

We do know that it is not a thing. Like communication, it happens only in a relationship and only in the imagination and perception of the parties to a relationship. Ultimately, it means different things to different people. In defining leadership, it is appropriate to establish what it is not. It is not merely the ability to get others to do what you want, as this can be self-effacing. It is not judged only by what it accomplishes but also by the integrity and values it instills in the process. It is not solely visionary, as that neglects to ask if others support the leader's vision. It is elitist to imagine that leadership is provided only by people in positions of authority. Although it is responsive to organizational needs, it is not like a weathervane that responds to whichever way the wind is blowing. Having existed for centuries, it is relevant to distinguish leadership from management, as the two are commonly confused (Bolman & Deal, 1999).

Just because you are an effective manager does not mean that you are a leader. A good leader is not necessarily a good manager. The fact that you might not be a leader does not mean that you are not a good manager. A manager is a position on an organizational chart, defined by specific expectations and roles. Focus on being a good manager and you will most likely succeed at accomplishing yearly goals, meeting your quotas, obtaining appropriate pay increases, and building a successful department. A good manager recognizes the leaders, change agents, and how those individuals work in the managerial scheme. Good managers hire individuals to complement their strengths and weaknesses and are not intimidated by people who possess leadership strengths different from their own.

The last two decades have spawned doctoral dissertations, a plethora of magazine articles, and endless books by successful corporate executives on the attributes of effective leadership. Vision is the only universal characteristic in all of these reports. Effective leaders identify possibilities, help focus the vision, and create direction for organizational efforts. Other leadership characteristics also surface, including the ability to communicate that vision effectively to others, commitment and passion, and the ability to inspire trust and build relationships (Bolman & Deal, 1999).

All organizations need vision, but that vision can take many different forms. Some need vision with blinders; others enjoy the luxury of limitless possibilities; and others require vision, but it is not their only need. When budgetary constraints limit development, a vision of expansion is inappropriate. Cost-cutting measures might dictate the deferring of new programs and development. A visionary leader might struggle with the imposed necessity to eliminate programs and make necessary cuts but can do so in creative and visionary ways.

McNeese-Smith (1993) applied the five leadership practices identified by the research of Kouzes and Posner (1997) to the hospital setting. She noted

1. Leaders challenge the process by taking risks, questioning routine, exploring innovative possibilities, and looking for newer and better ways to complete a task. Willing to learn from their mistakes, they are not afraid to admit when they are wrong.

2. Not only are they visionaries, but they also enlist others in the vision. They know how to build momentum, picture the possible, and take pride in team accomplishments. They are expressive, energetic, and charismatic.

3. They foster collaboration, cooperation, trust, and trustworthiness. They involve everyone, including those employees outside their unit. An empowering nurse manager involves all staff in policy formation, procedures, standards, and the evaluation process that results in responsibility, ownership, and unit pride.

4. These leaders earn employee respect because they lead by doing. They handle difficult times with absolute honesty. Their conversations show thoughtfulness and sensitivity.

5. Effective leaders recognize that patient care is difficult and personally exhausting. They understand the emotional demands and drains placed upon their staff and acknowledge the value of this work. They set high expectations and enable staff to achieve these goals. They empower their staff and are not hesitant to give important jobs to others, along with the authority to accomplish these tasks. Leaders are not threatened by individuals with differing values and aspirations.

At a 2003 presentation to the chief nursing officers of a major hospital corporation, Marston (2003) addressed the challenge of managing and retaining the best of today's workforce. He defined four generations according to birth years, their attitudes toward work, and how these four generations face the challenges in the workforce. "Maturers" were born prior to 1945, "baby boomers" between 1946 and 1964, generation Xers between 1965 and 1977, and millennials (also known as generation Y) between 1977 and the current date. An interesting parallel exists in that most healthcare organizations were controlled by physicians prior to 1945, by administrators during the era of the boomers, by insurance providers during the time of the Xers, and now by cash flow considerations regardless of who is captaining the ship.

Individuals cannot be placed in a given category solely by chronologic age, as some people fall in between groups. This might be because they are on the cusp related to age or because they have a different life perspective. Just because an individual has a specific chronologic age does not necessarily mean that he or she will automatically fit a specific category.

Maturers entered their career during the time that research on the scientific and humanistic perspectives of management and communication theories was emerging. If they are women, they feel pride in being the first generation of females who joined the workforce. Throughout their careers, they have averaged 5–10 years at each position. They respect honor, dedication, sacrifice, and duty. Their commitment is to the company and the field of nursing. Their bosses in the past have been primarily male, and they have had a hierarchical respect for physicians. Advancement in the company was primal. Awed by technology, they initially were reticent computer users. Although they are computer literate, it may have been difficult for them to become so. They are not going quietly into old age, as they are intolerant of their aches and pains. They may appear to be angry that their investments did not materialize as anticipated, thus they are working more years than they previously had planned and hoped. Their heroes are teams, not individuals. They responded best to clearly defined, measurable work goals with established deadlines.

Baby boomers used to think they were incredible risk takers; they marched in Selma and avoided the draft. They grew up with stay-at-home moms but worked full time while raising their families. Their loyalty is to the people they work with and the hands-on experience they gain from their patients. Passion is a driving force. They want to feel that they make a significant contribution to the world. They are motivated by money, have a strong work ethic, and know what good medical care is. Many boomers are working today because they want to, because they enjoy the challenge and seek a position that is personally fulfilling. They are motivated by mentoring, flexible schedules, and rewarding work. They see technology as an important vehicle but do not have the computer savvy of generation Xers. For many years, they have been workaholics, competitive and successful. They are defined by their jobs and take personal satisfaction in their accomplishments. They do well in a mentor role.

Generation Xers are the victims of dot.com companies. They have seen huge opportunities for personal advancement shatter by corporate infrastructure. As a result, they are skeptical of the company and more trusting of their individual boss. They are highly motivated by the now, see a satisfying position as one that makes them happy, and place their personal needs over the needs of the organization. Nursing is not necessarily a lifelong calling; it is something they are doing for the present. Generation Xers have few heroes. They grew up as latchkey kids, have been independent at an early age, and are loyal to themselves and their personal needs. When placed on a team, they are interested in knowing how they will benefit from the experience. They want to be formulators of the plan and involved in decision-making strategies. Maturer or boomer managers will be most effective in directing the energy and focus of Xers by allowing these employees to have a much broader course of possibilities than previous generations ever would have considered or anticipated as necessary. A team for the Xers will look different from anything previously seen. They are directing their own course; expect innovative solutions. "You should . . ." is not an effective managerial strategy. They show a reluctance to accept an authority figure merely because of the position held in the company. They have an ease and comfort with technology that boomers and maturers envy. They are suspicious of the work ethics of baby boomers because they want more individual freedom than they see in the lives of the boomers or maturers. They are excellent negotiators. Although they might appear to be bored, they want to develop their skills. Remember, a good job for them is one in which they are happy. Working weekends and Christmas does not make them happy. You might need to do creative problem solving (alternative scheduling) to keep them motivated.

The jury is still out on the needs and motivational factors for employees born from 1977 to the current date, as the newest group of people enters the workforce. It is natural to hope that they will be the "brightest and best," able to learn from the mistakes and accomplishments of the maturers, boomers, and generation Xers. As new entrants to the workforce, they are optimistic but do not have an employment history to substantiate their dreams. They are interested in their future, their goals, and their personal options. Their heroes are themselves. It is anticipated that they will stay in a position for 1.1–2.2 years. Many millennials were computer literate in grade school. The have a comfort with technological advancements that many maturers and boomers will never be able to experience. Teams for them will take different forms, including virtual teams—team members they may never personally meet. They have high expectations but lack the blue print of getting from where they are today to where they would like to go in the future. Millennial employees comprise a workforce of more than 80 million people. Someday they will want your job, whether you are a boomer, a maturer, or a generation Xer. They are ambitious but need direction and the ability to make their own mistakes and choose their own course.

Effective managers recognize generational and individual differences, challenge their staff appropriately, and establish a work environment that tolerates and welcomes the needs of transgenerational employees.

Numerous issues face the hospital striving to staff its facility with seasoned professionals and qualified nurse managers. The serious shortage of nurses stems from the expanding numbers of professionals reaching retirement years, fewer individuals entering the profession, and decreased job satisfaction with those remaining in the workforce. Suggestions for dealing with downsizing, increased workloads, poor working conditions, governmental regulations, patient safety issues, and higher acuity rates have led some institutions to promote autonomy and encourage empowerment. Magnet hospitals, so named for their ability to attract and retain nurses, have been operating since the early 1980s (Upenieks, 2003). Magnet hospitals strive to provide opportunities for their nursing staff where they are able to make decisions based on their own professional judgment, be involved in decisions that affect their working conditions, and perceive managers as collaborative and supportive (Laschinger, Almost, & Tuer-Hodes, 2003). They have a supportive organizational climate, collaborative nurse–physician relationships, an autonomous climate, opportunities for nursing advancement, participatory management, and adequate staffing (Upenieks).

Obviously, not only magnet hospitals have these perspectives; however, magnet hospitals have set the foundation for other hospitals to follow. Institutions with this perspective have improved patient care while increasing job satisfaction, organizational commitment, and trust in management, lowered levels of job stress, and improved nurse–physician working relationships (Aiken & Slone, 2000). Magnet nurse leaders are identified as supportive, visionary, knowledgeable, visible to clinical nurses, responsive, and able to preserve power and status within the hospital system. Hospitals choosing to implement the strategies of magnet hospitals must reduce barriers to empowerment and build bridges to access relevant information, resources, and support.

Although there is an abundance of literature that considers the characteristics of successful leaders in general and nursing leaders in specific, little has been published on leadership development (Allen, 1998). Nurse managers interested in empowering their staff to become effective managers in the future must recognize that every day they are role models in leadership techniques, either positive or negative. Their staff is learning from them. Managers groom the leaders of the future by taking pride in their accomplishments, nurturing the growth of self-confidence, encouraging curiosity and critical thinking, communicating clear expectations, providing a progression of experiences for self-improvement and advancement, and supporting the leadership potential in others. Mentoring begins with the hiring process. Empowered leaders recruit employees who seek new challenges and show an interest in growth. In some organizations, you might have to fight for educational opportunities, as these are seen as nonproductive hours. Your battles in developing problem-solving groups, journal clubs, in-service programs, and mentoring programs for your staff are worth your efforts, as they can provide a competitive edge over departments or facilities without them.

Not all leadership theories are applicable to the demands of a given institution (McDaniel & Wolf, 1992). Although leadership quality is key to the culture of magnet hospitals, many facilities lack the infrastructure to nurture these concepts. Because of the financial constraints or the perspectives of top management, some facilities support a more traditional style that focuses on "just getting the job done." In this environment, one can choose to go with the flow, paddle upstream, or become a true visionary.

Unfortunately, some employment settings are not ideal. Hochheiser (1987) described the "Tooth Fairy Theory of Business Management." He defined several flawed premises.

- All employees have a genuine interest in the success of the organization.
- Conflicts are nothing more than honest differences of opinion as to how to meet the needs of the organization.
- Better communication will improve employee–management relationships and productivity.

Some employees (or employers) do not care whether the bottom line is met, that the company has a good image in the community, or that patients get excellent care. Some want the organization to be successful enough to let them get what they want out of it. You may have differences with this employee (or employer) and try every trick there is to communicate. Your dedication, hard work, loyalty, accomplishments, and all the advice in the management books on earth are no match. Some people are incompetent, but in many other instances, they are jerks only if you fail to look at what they have done for themselves. If he or she is your boss, be especially cautious. They have advanced in the organization because some other person respected their values.

When faced with this type of situation, if you are the manager, you can fire the employee, change the person to whom he or she reports, or ask the employee/employer for assistance in handling the situation. If the jerk is your boss, you can change jobs, compromise, get into therapy, change your tactics, change your own goals, change your profession, or even become your own boss. Always remember that you have options in dealing with disgruntled employees or employers. The way you handle these situations makes you the manager you will want to be.

Organization, Time Management, and Delegation

Accomplishing goals is impossible without effective time-management skills. In today's work frenzy, it is common to assume that obstacles can be overcome by working longer and that "you're the only one who can do the job." Saying "no" means that you are a less effective employee. Davidson and Losure (1999) encapsulated volumes of books on the concept of time management: "Ultimately, you'll be treated by your boss in the way you teach your boss to treat you" (p. 94). Those who continually take on more than they can feasibly accomplish will be given more by their boss. When faced with new opportunities, Davidson and Losure posed the following questions to help determine whether you can safely take on another commitment.

- Is it in alignment with my priorities and goals?
- Am I likely to be prone to say yes to such a request tomorrow or next week?
- What else could I do with the same amount of time that might be more appropriate and/or rewarding?
- What other pressing tasks and responsibilities am I likely to face around that time?
- Does the other party have other options besides you?

If you decide to decline the task, Davidson and Losure suggested you do so by phone, mail, or fax. "It's much easier to decline when you don't have to do so in person" (p. 96).

Eight Basic Pointers in Becoming More Time Efficient

1. Distinguish between what is "urgent" and what is "vital." An urgent task is something that demands immediate attention; a vital task is one that encompasses the highest priorities in one's life. Urgent demands often pressure vital priorities. Take the time to identify your governing issues by identifying the issues of greatest importance. As these issues emerge on paper, you will experience a sense of clarity and purpose. Remember, the vital issues identified are yours alone, and there are no "incorrect answers"; they do not need to be defended to anyone (Smith, 1994).

2. Strengthen your managerial voice. Avoid jargon; own the message. Identify what you are willing to do and what you are not. Create a powerful voice by empowering your staff. Set a model of excellence. Recognize that you cannot accomplish all tasks alone. Remove obstacles that prevent employees from helping you accomplish goals and perform their jobs effectively. Coach your staff on their options and negotiate with them the latitude within which they can act. Encourage staff to use their own judgment, to take initiative to make their jobs more effective, and to solve their own problems. Leebov and Scott (1990) suggested the following as strategies to change, from directing your staff to empowering your staff.

   - Solicit input from your employees by providing regular "input opportunities." Routinely encourage employees to consider opportunities and problems that extend beyond the scope of their specific job, to make constructive contributions, and to know that their ideas and concerns are treated credibly.
   - Help employees exercise sound judgment in choice situations. Assist them in examining alternatives and appropriate responses to a variety of situations.
   - Replace obstacles with backup systems. To empower your employees, you must identify the obstacles that prevent them from taking initiative and making decisions. You might want to identify certain "quick action" tasks that employees can handle without approval, or set an expenditure level at which employees can make decisions on their own.
   - Coach; do not supply answers.

3. Effective time managers know the difference between control and power. "Power enables employees to be more effective; control can limit the potential that

power enables. To increase your power in the organization, you need to loosen the reins and give employees the freedom to act creatively to accomplish their tasks and satisfy customers. Employees with great potential will be energized and increase their contributions to the organization. You are responsible for the results achieved in your area. If you let go and enable your employees to act, your status will be enhanced by their accomplishments" (Leebov & Scott, 1990, p. 76).

4. Differentiate between those issues that are imposed by the demands of the work environment and those that are self-imposed. Have you noticed that the things that matter the most often are tabled by less important issues? Smith (1994) referred to the following as "time robbers" in the workforce: interruptions, unanswered questions, unnecessary meetings, poor communication, unclear job descriptions, shifting priorities, equipment failures, ineffective organizational hierarchy, red tape, and conflicting priorities. Failure to delegate, a poor attitude, personal disorganization, absentmindedness, failure to listen, indecision, fatigue, lack of self-discipline, procrastination, paper shuffling, and an inability to prioritize are self-imposed factors.

5. In organizing your time, know that your desk is among the most important areas of your life. Take charge of your desk to help take charge of your time. Peruse all of your papers to determine what is relevant and what can be discarded. Continually discard what is not needed and acquire what is. Revisit the relevant pile and divide it into mini-piles; use date stamping if that is beneficial. Organize your files so that you can find what is necessary. Be creative in labeling files. You might want to include files labeled: "Where to file this?" "Fun Stuff," "Check in one Month," "To Read," or "Things to Think About." Develop a system for grouping your files so that you will be able to find necessary information when needed. The time you spend synthesizing your office space will lead to effective time management.

6. Establish time management perimeters in your daily routine. For example, voice mail can be a simple dumping ground for others to deposit requests. In many instances, once a voicemail message is left, the ownership of action is placed on the person receiving the call. You can change this by clarifying your expectations of the people who choose to contact you by phone. Your recorded message might state, "Please leave me a message regarding the situation, what you feel might be an appropriate solution, and how you would like my assistance." This message places ownership of action on others and specifies needed outcomes.

7. Implement an effective means of communication with your staff to update situations, explore possible solutions, identify actions, and acknowledge issues that they can handle independently and those that require managerial input. The 5-15 Report is a simple tool that by definition takes 5 minutes for the recipient to read and take appropriate action and takes no more than 15 minutes for the sender to write. It might be handwritten, sent by e-mail, or written on a word processor. This technique forces the sender to identify priorities and multiple solutions. It might include true-false options and multiple-choice possibilities. A sample 5-15 Report might state, "Today, Dr. Smith asked me to report the status

of our complementary therapy program at Tumor Boards. I don't know whether or not I'm the person to do that. Should I:

- Schedule it; I am excited about it, and we can work out the details later.
- Tell him that I would like to do it in three months when there is more information to report.
- Tell him that I would like to handle this and he should speak directly with me.
- Make no decision; let's talk about this together and develop a plan. We could meet on _____ at _____ o'clock."

8. Establish a means of organizing your day and stick with it. For some this is accomplished using a Palm Pilot®, Day-Timers®, or simple calendars. Extensive seminars have been held on organizational techniques to manage your day. Identify what works for you, acknowledge your own work habits, and be willing to learn from others while setting your own course.

Conclusion

The concepts (e.g., assessment inventories, leadership styles, communication skills) presented provide an overview of important ideas in nursing management. The historical perspectives of systems theory and change theory are important constructs in assessing managerial problems and opportunities that are faced today. Personality and behavioral inventories are in use to provide managers with a way to view themselves as they adapt to new roles and find themselves in leadership situations. Leadership style is a key component to personal managerial success and the overall success of nursing organizations. The skills of communication, listening, delegating, and time management, when added to the understanding of leadership, provide a significant toolbox with which managers can succeed.

References

Aiken, L.H., & Slone, D.M. (2000). The magnet nursing services recognition program: A comparison of two groups of magnet hospitals. *American Journal of Nursing, 100*(3), 26–36.

Allen, D.W. (1998). How nurses become leaders: Perceptions and beliefs about leadership development. *Journal of Nursing Administration, 28*(9), 15–20.

Anderson, J.K. (1998). Orientation with style. *Journal of Nursing Staff Development, 14,* 192–197.

Anderson, M.P. (1959). What is communication? *Journal of Communication, 9*(1), 5.

Baker, L.L. (1971). *Listening behavior.* Englewood Cliffs, NJ: Prentice Hall.

Barnlund, D. (1968). *Interpersonal communication: Survey and studies.* Boston: Houghton Mifflin.

Bolman, L.F., & Deal, T.E. (1999). *Reframing organizations: Artistry, choice and leadership.* San Francisco: Jossey-Bass.

Bridges, W. (1980). *Transitions: Making sense of life's changes.* Reading, MA: Addison-Wesley.

Brooks, W.D. (1971). *Speech communication.* Dubuque, IA: William C. Brown Co.

Canary, D.J., & Cody, M.J. (1993). *Interpersonal communication: A goals-based approach.* New York: St. Martin's Press.

Costello, K. (1993). The Myers-Briggs Type Indicator: A management tool. *Nursing Management, 24*(5), 46–47, 50–51.

Dance, F.E.X., & Larson, C.E. (1972). *Speech communication: Concepts and behavior.* New York: Holt, Rinehart, and Winston.

Dance, F.E.X., & Larson, C.E. (1976). *Functions of human communication: A theoretical approach.* New York: Holt, Rinehart, and Winston.

Davidson, J., & Losure, B. (1999). *Complete idiot's guide to managing your time.* London: MacMillan.

Doyle, M., & Straus, D. (1976). *How to make meetings work: The new interaction method.* New York: Wyden Books.

Eisenberg, E.M., & Goodall, H.L. (2001). *Organizational communication: Balancing creativity and constraint.* New York: Bedford/St. Martin's Press.

Gambles, M., Wilkinson, S.M., & Dissanayake, C. (2003). What are you like?: A personality profile of cancer and palliative care nurses in the United Kingdom. *Cancer Nursing, 26*(2), 97–104.

Gladwell, M. (2000). *The tipping point.* New York: Little, Brown and Co.

Gode, A. (1959). What is communication? *Journal of Communication, 9*(1), 5.

Grimes, G. (1998). *The internet: Quick steps for fast results.* Indianapolis, IN: MacMillan.

Herzberg, F., Mausner, B., & Snyderman, B. (1959). *The motivation to work* (2nd ed.). New York: Wiley.

Hochheiser, R.M. (1987). *How to work for a jerk—Your success is the best revenge.* New York: Vintage Books.

Jay, R. (1999). *The seven deadly skills of communicating.* Belmont, CA: International Thompson Business Press.

Jennings, K., Miller, K., & Materna, S. (1997). *Changing health care.* Lanham, MD: National Book Network.

Koehler, J.W., Anatol, K.W.E., & Applebaum, R.L. (1976). *Organizational communication.* New York: Holt, Rinehart, and Winston.

Kouzes, J.M., & Posner, B.Z. (1997). *The leadership challenge: How to keep getting extraordinary things done in organizations.* San Francisco: Jossey-Bass.

Laschinger, H.K.S., Almost, J., & Tuer-Hodes, D. (2003). Workplace empowerment and magnet hospital characteristics: Making the link. *Journal of Nursing Administration, 33,* 410–421.

Le Boeuf, M. (1985). *The greatest management principle in the world.* New York: Berkley Books.

Leebov, W., & Scott, G. (1990). *Healthcare managers in transition: Shifting roles and changing organizations.* San Francisco: Jossey-Bass.

Lewin, K. (1935). *A dynamic theory of personality.* New York: McGraw-Hill.

Lewis, C.S. (1956). *Till we have faces: A myth retold.* Grand Rapids, MI: William B. Eerdman.

Marston, C. (2003, November). *Managing and retaining the best of today's workforce.* Paper presented to Chief Nursing Officers at the HCA/CNO Summit, New Orleans, LA.

Martin, H.H., & Anderson, K.E. (1968). *Speech communication.* New York: Allyn and Bacon.

Maslow, A. (1954). *Motivation and personality.* New York: Harper and Row.

McDaniel, C., & Wolf, G.A. (1992). A test of theory. *Journal of Nursing Administration, 22*(2), 60–65.

McFregor, D. (1985). *The human side of enterprise.* New York: McGraw-Hill/Irwin.

McNeese-Smith, D. (1993). Leadership behavior and employee effectiveness. *Nursing Management 24*(5), 38–39.

Nelson, A., & Golant, S. (2004). *You don't say: Navigating nonverbal communication between the sexes.* Upper Saddle River, NJ: Prentice Hall.

Nelson, B. (1996). *Motivating today's employees.* San Diego, CA: Nelson Motivation.

Nickols, F. (2004). *Change management 101: A primer.* Retrieved July 1, 2004, from http://home.att.net/~nickols/change.htm

O'Connor, S.J., & Shewchuk, R.M. (1993). Enhancing administrator–clinician relationships: The role of psychological type. *Health Care Management Review, 18*(2), 57–65.

Robbins, S.P., & DeCenzo, D.A. (2003). *Fundamentals of management: Essential concepts and applications* (4th ed.). Upper Saddle River, NJ: Prentice Hall.

Satir, V. (1972). *Peoplemaking.* Palo Alto, CA: Science and Behavior Books.

Smith, H.W. (1994). *The ten natural laws of successful time and life management: Proven strategies for increased productivity and inner peace.* New York: Warner Books.

Sutch, D. (1994). *Interpersonal communication skills: Training to minimize conflict and build collaboration in today's team-oriented workplace.* Boulder, CO: Career Track.

Taylor, F. (1911). *The principles of scientific management.* New York: Harper.

Trenholm, S., & Jensen, A. (1992). *Interpersonal communication.* New York: Wadsworth.

Upenieks, V.V. (2003). What constitutes effective leadership? *Journal of Nursing Administration, 33,* 456–467.

Weaver, C.H., & Strausbaugh, W.L. (1964). *Fundamentals of speech communication.* New York: American Book Co.

Weber, M. (1957). *The theory of social and economic organizations.* New York: Free Press.

Zelko, H.P., & Dance, F.E.X. (1978). *Business and professional speech communication* (2nd ed.). Chicago: Holt, Rinehart, and Winston.

Leadership Development

3

Tim Porter-O'Grady, EdD, RN, FAAN

Recognizing Leadership

Defining leadership is an elusive pursuit at best. Over the years, great leaders have been identified (Kets de Vries, 1993). We have had less success, however, in enumerating specific characteristics of leadership that can be universally replicated and form a firm foundation for identifying the full range of leadership characteristics (Kotter, 2001). It appears that we know leadership when we see it, yet we are less able to define exactly what it is we see (see Figure 3-1).

Figure 3-1. Leadership Characteristics

- Vision
- Determination
- Personality

- Vulnerability
- Identification

- Energy
- Communication

Over the past 40–50 years, much effort in the academic and business communities has been dedicated to assessing characteristics of leadership (Heifetz & Laurie, 2001). Great leaders have been studied in detail, and traits of leadership have been defined, researched, and explicated as a way of getting at some fundamental numerators of leadership that conform with the foundations of our understanding and become the content of formalized programs directed toward teaching leadership (Drucker & Stone, 1998). Leadership is known to be a valid and meaningful part of the human experience. Leaders have surfaced under all kinds of circumstances, from war to great political and social change, from religious and moral foundations, and from cultural and social transformations (Ferris, 1889).

Each age of human experience has produced a leader who represents the characteristics of the times. As we review the course of human experience, it becomes clear to anyone who understands history that leadership changes and adjusts depending on demand, social circumstances, and the particular needs of the time. Indeed, each generation of human interaction created the conditions from which leadership would emerge. These conditions are fundamental circumstances within which any model of leadership responds to the demands of the time. Leadership operates through the expression of vision, determination, and force of personality and will, converging to create a significant change in the order of things (Sorcher & Brant, 2002).

Leadership is about more than generalized characteristics. Leadership is about people. Leaders are both born and made. Leaders are born insofar as they are influenced by the genetic characteristics of their heredity. Leaders are made insofar as social development, circumstances, and personal experience converge to create the conditions and context within which specific leaders could emerge. This happens at the point of convergence where there is a good fit among the times, the demand, and the personal characteristics of the individual who would be leader (Pearman, 1998).

Some generic and identifiable characteristics of leadership can be learned and replicated. Although these characteristics can be taught, the circumstances and knowledge in which leadership characteristics can be expressed are important considerations for the success of specific leadership traits. A good leader recognizes this convergence of forces and conditions and responds to them with such clarity and appropriateness that the actions undertaken are congruent with the demand for them, and a meaningful transformation occurs or valued outcomes are achieved.

Developing Leaders for the Time

Pursuing the characteristics of leadership and enumerating the basic elements and traits of leadership that lead to good leaders are the foci of other chapters in this book. This chapter looks at developing leaders. What is critical in the process of leadership development is that the elements of development are congruent with the demands of the time. Although leadership was studied during the entire 20th century, many of the characteristics that enabled successful leadership in a 20th-century "Newtonian" model of social organization and work (vertical, structural, institutional, fixed, and finite) will not transfer into the 21st century, which is driven by "Quantum" models of work and workplace and exemplified by complexity, chaos, mobility, and the need for fast-paced responses (Wheatley, 1999).

The emerging 21st-century workplace demands a different kind of leader with a different set of skills than those that were successful in the past. Developing this leader calls for a novel mix of strategies. This new landscape for work creates conditions within which the leader must incorporate the technologic revolution. This reality creates the foundation for a unique and dynamic role for the leader. Furthermore, increased globalization and the communication competencies that drive it are influenced by the elements of interaction, communication, and relationships (Anderson, 2001). The leader must be able to thrive and engage both the role and people in a way that best fits these challenging and changing circumstances.

Understanding the Quantum context changes the foundational understanding of leadership. In the 21st century, recognizing the signposts of change and the forces of integration and connectedness creates a context for leadership that demands an updated expression of leadership skills. The leader in the workplace must be fast, fluid, and flexible in personal style, orientation, and role expression. The leader of the 21st century must be able to engage a diverse workforce within a wide variety of work circumstances (see Figure 3-2).

Figure 3-2. Age Characteristics		
• Quantum models • Complexity • Highly mobile	• Fast change • Outsourced work	• Portable services • Technologic

As outsourcing in short-term work arrangements becomes increasingly popular, the leader must enforce a different set of leadership skills than those used when a workforce is directly employed (Drucker, 2002). The leader must be able to deal with an ever-widening range of role and personality characteristics in the employees. Because of the span of generations employed in the workplace, blending and managing these multifocal, multigenerational workers in a highly transforming work environment is a critical requirement for good and effective leadership (Lancaster & Stillman, 2002). Different from the 20th-century focus on stability and process, the leader of the 21st century must focus on agility, adaptability, relevance, and value.

In a technologically advanced world, outcome and value become increasingly important. As the 20th century focused on "give" service technologies, the 21st century emphasizes "get" service technologies. However, the differences extend beyond that focus (Porter-O'Grady, 2002). Technology makes it possible for outcomes to be more clearly delineated now than in the past. We can identify outcomes and then determine the most appropriate processes directed at obtaining them. In past processes, orientation and work were the primary emphases of effort, often at the expense, certainly in the service environment, of having identified unachievable service deliverables. Through the use of technology and service algorithms, we can identify desirable outcomes and "back into" specific processes that can directly advance these outcomes (Evans & Wurster, 1999). The use of models of information technology in health care provides the "user" (called the "patient" in the 20th century) with a choice of processes based on desired skills and specifically customized outcomes. This user-driven, mass-customized approach to service delivery emphasizes customer ownership rather than unilateral provider-controlled changes. These new rules alter the foundations of healthcare service (McKenna, 2002). This dramatic move away from provider-driven orientation in clinical work toward more customer-driven and value-based clinical activities changes the conditions and circumstances of health care with which leaders must now contend at every level of service activity.

To develop effective managers for this transforming work is a creative process. While a new workplace unfolds, management and leadership must be continuous and dynamic. The challenge in this situation is recognizing that both leadership and the circumstances within which it is applied are changing together at precisely the same rate. The difficulty in developing leaders in this context is that much of what one would develop a leader for is shifting before the leader has an opportunity to act. This dynamic means, more specifically, that leadership development must occur within the context of a changing and transforming view that will shift and adjust the leadership skills and expectations at the same time the leader plays out the role. In short, leaders must learn on the run.

The Knowledge Worker

As the leader must adjust to the constant state of change in the workplace, the worker also is challenged to adapt to these changes. The interplay between worker and workplace changes because of the complexity of the workplace and the demand for high-level skills. As the workplace comes to depend more on the knowledge and skills of the worker, the locus of control shifts from workplace to worker (McKenna, 2002). In 21st-century organizational circumstances, the workplace is more dependent on the skills and talents of the worker than the worker is dependent on the resources and rewards of the workplace. This shift in locus of control creates more dependence on knowledge workers and creates more mobility and value for knowledge work (see Figure 3-3). As a result, the traditional worker value expressed in commitment to the

Figure 3-3. Knowledge Workers		
• Owns work	• Seeks life balance	• Independent
• Self-directed	• Technological	• Value focused
• Noncompliant		

workplace has shifted to commitment to the work. The emerging reality now is that nursing work can be done anywhere. Nurses are recognizing the inherent value of their knowledge and the application of it. The worker no longer has to be committed to a specific workplace for a long period of time to claim the kinds of rewards or remunerations that this knowledge worker has now come to expect (Jensen, 2002).

Leading Professionals Is Different

Professionals do not owe their allegiance to institutions or organizations. They are instead aligned with those they serve. Professionals are not committed to the workplace; they are, instead, committed to the work of the profession. To the professional, it is the obligation of leadership to see to it that the professional can do his or her work well, with the requisite resources and the level of quality both the professional and those they serve expect. If this "balance" of variables affecting professional work is not achieved and maintained, the relationship between the leader and the professional and the organization and profession break down. When that happens, it is very difficult to reconstruct.

Leading the knowledge worker requires that leaders recognize that they are leading a worker over whom they have no ownership or long-term control. This mobility in the worker and a fluid relationship of the worker to the workplace creates a change in the dynamic between leader and worker. It changes the conditions and circumstances of leadership itself. Vertical and controlling models of leadership and decision making are no longer effective methods of leadership. Leadership is moving from exerting mechanisms of control over work and the worker to processes of partnership and co-ownership in relationship to performance, expectations, and work outcomes. Managing and leading a partnership is considerably different from controlling and directing employees (Amar, 2002).

As the nursing profession assumes more accountability for the outcome of its members, organizational leaders must change their relationship to the profession and the professional. Professions are composed of knowledge workers with specific skills and expectations for performance. In any mature profession, the expectation of the professional will be that he or she fulfills the obligations for the activities of the profession and will meet the standards of performance and practice exemplified through the profession's values (Porter-O'Grady, 2001). Here again, the professional model of work parallels the work conditions of the knowledge worker. The need for interdependence, accountability, clarity of expectations, and the commitment to defined outcomes for all practices are common values between the profession and its members. In this professional frame of reference, knowledge workers have a right to expect that they will have ownership over their work but that ownership will be disciplined by clear expectations, well-delineated accountability, and enumeration and clarity around work outcomes.

In a professional work environment, the leader carries out different approaches to the exercise of the role. The professional leader plays a predominantly facilitating (gathering) role. The expectations of this leader are exemplified in her or his ability to focus the professional worker on the work and its value to the patient, as well as to fulfilling the purposes of the profession. The leader, in this circumstance, does not own the work; rather, he or she facilitates the integration, coordination, and implementation of the profession's work in a consistent, integrated format that ultimately has an impact on those served with acceptable clinical outcomes.

Clearly, to exercise the role of leader in this context requires the structure of empowerment and partnership that has hitherto not existed in organizations over most of the span of the 20th century. Newer models of shared leadership and decision making, which engage the profession in a partnership model, create a different set of expectations for organizational leaders (Pearce & Conger, 2003). This professional partnership calls into play more adult-to-adult relationships and intersections between the organization and the professional (knowledge worker). Now the leader must exhibit both content and context skills. The content of leadership is disciplined by the context of partnership, accountability, equity, and ownership, all characteristics of a professional organization (Porter-O'Grady, 1992). These contextual characteristics create the format through which the nurse leader must operate. These characteristics help to form the framework within which the leader must develop the role and skills necessary to provide meaningful and viable leadership within the professional organization.

Creating a Context for Leadership

It is difficult to develop leadership in others if the context for the expression of leadership and learning is not appropriate. Too often leaders focus on skill development in others without recognizing that the contextual framework for leadership is as important as the skill content. Creating a "safe place" for potential leaders to learn and develop is an important corollary to building excellent leadership skills (Fetterman, 2001) (see Figure 3-4).

Figure 3-4. Current Work Context		
• Uncertain	• High patient turnover	• Short-term
• Ever-changing	• Nonresidential	• User-driven
• High-technology based		

The changing context for work does not lend itself well to creating a stable and calm environment within which to develop leadership skills. The challenge for the leader, mentor, and teacher is to be able to evidence good leadership skills in a context of high mobility and constantly shifting change in the workplace. A part of the dynamic that this represents creates a mosaic of opportunities and experiences that the emerging leader must recognize and be able to unfold potential leadership skills within it. This real-world orientation to the expression and experience of leadership is a critical value in the developing and maturing of leadership skills (Murphy & National Society for the Study of Education, 2002).

In a contemporary professional workplace, it is important for leaders to recognize that they are managing and leading a practice environment. The expectations emerging in the practice environment are requiring higher levels of interdependent judgments, better skills in relationship building, greater interaction goal proficiency, and greater individual maturity and self-management. It is within this frame of reference that the emerging leader confronts the development of personal leadership skills.

Empowerment

The leader does not give empowerment to anyone. Empowerment is the recognition of the power already present in a role and allowing it to be legitimately expressed. For true empowerment to exist, both leader and staff must know what the expectation of the practice role is and give it all it needs to ensure that the outcomes expected from it are achieved. The best expression of empowerment in any role is the successful and satisfying achievement of the expectations of the role.

Empowerment means recognizing the power already present in a situation or a person and allowing this power to be legitimately expressed (Spears, Lawrence, & NetLibrary, 2002). The emerging leaders, therefore, must have a clear commitment to individual empowerment and the capacity to build a context for empowerment that supports the growing interdependence and independence of individual practitioners in the expression of their nursing practice. Those responsible for educating the new leader must recognize that creating an appropriate and valid context for the expression of leadership gives a frame of reference for the empowered skills that will be necessary within the emerging complex work environment. Development of appropriate leadership skills helps to focus the emerging leader on those abilities that best fit the emerging conditions and circumstances influencing nursing practice. If this context or framework for leadership expression is established and a better fit is created between the leadership learned and that expressed, the greater the potential for ensuring the appropriate, meaningful, and valid expression of nursing practice.

This situation calls for a high level of maturity within the expression of leadership (Warner, 2002). Today we are watching the nursing profession move out of its historical adolescence into an adulthood requiring a different level of behavior and intersection with others in the healthcare system. As nurses begin to coordinate, facilitate, and integrate care across the broader spectrum of service environments, the interface with other disciplines and persons in the delivery of healthcare services will grow in volume and in intensity. This situation now calls the individual nurse to a higher level of skill with regard to communication, interaction, and goal achievement. Leaders must represent in their own practice a commitment to this understanding and a willingness to advance it in the role of all those they lead. In developing this next generation of leaders, the educator and/or mentor will need to be alert to the following circumstances.

- The ability of the emerging leader to conceptualize complexity
- The leader's potential for handling future conflict
- The ability of the new leader to engage others' issues without owning them
- The leader's skill with group process management
- The emerging leader's sense of self and personal confidence in the face of conflict, aggression, and negativity
- The ability of the leader to envision the direction of the changing journey within the cultural, social, and economic realities of a given organization

Mentoring Leaders

To "create" this effective new leader, current leaders must recognize that the development of leadership in others is an outflow of the leadership present in themselves. The mentoring process involves setting an example from personal lived experience that others can emulate, build upon, and incorporate into their own practice (Spouse & Redfern, 2000). The mentor provides both framework and format within which the emerging leader can safely develop skills and make sure opportunities exist for the individual's own leadership expression. Mentors, through their own behavior, set patterns of process and skill that, when emulated, produce meaningful outcomes and advance the value of the expression of leadership in those being mentored (Zachary, 2000).

The mentor must be aware of the significant value that role has in the life of others. Mentors are not free of flaws; instead, they honestly recognize the content of their character and use this knowledge for their personal growth and development, as well as their own accommodation to the realities inherent in their personal and professional journey. The journey is not perfect for the mentor, but the mentor actualizes the adjustment to personal imperfection, accommodates for it, and practices moving beyond its limitations. The mentor exemplifies the imperfections of human expression and acknowledges these imperfections and adjusts leadership style and skill to compensate for the negative potential that personal human frailty may have on the expression of competent leadership. By exemplifying the conflicts inherent in this personal and professional journey of leadership, the mentor creates a safe and meaningful opportunity for the recognition of deficits in the emerging leader, allows for the celebration of human frailties, and exemplifies the challenge and excitement in the human effort to triumph over adversity and limitation. The mentor sees leadership as a journey of growth, a sign of commitment to one's personal advancement. Finally, this commitment to movement within the role of leader serves as a signpost to others of the willingness and ability to engage and embrace the challenges of clinical practice in the face of the vagaries and contradictions of the human work environment (see Figure 3-5).

Figure 3-5. Traits of the Mentor

• Vulnerable	• Firm	• Strategic
• Open	• Insightful	• Empathetic
• Flawed	• Experienced	• Patient
• Clear	• Practical	• Available

Most mature leaders have suggested in their developmental process the specific contribution of their mentors during the personal leadership journey. Mentoring for the learner provides an opportunity to identify with solid leadership skills and to be able to access another individual, who is mature in the experience of leadership, with the frank and open discourse related to any developmental issue associated with growing and maturing as a leader. The mentor serves as a demarcation between one level of behavior and another in the developing role of leader. Furthermore, the mentor serves as an evaluator of the growing level of skill in the emerging leader (Brown, 2001). The mentor sometimes is the parental replacement in an "adult-to-adult" relationship, creating a much stronger and equitable foundation for interaction and communication as an adult. Still present is the safety and support necessary for effective growth and development embedded in the mentoring relationship, creating an interchange of value, meaning, and support for the emerging leader experimenting with new facets of the leadership experience. From the mentor, the new leader gets a better understanding of the circumstances and the conditions of effective leadership provided, a political and contextual frame for the ever-present challenges inherent in the pathway from emergent to mature leader (Murray, 2001).

Leading Change

Perhaps the most significant activity of the leader is the process of leading change (Beer & Nohria, 2000). Without a doubt, change is the most significant element of organizational life. Regardless of the activities the leader will be engaged in, change processes will be the most definitive and capture most of the leader's energy. Understanding change within a long-term context is critical to the success of the individual leader.

> ### Change in the 21st Century
> Today's change is different. We are living in a world of high techno-logic innovations in work and life. The opportunity to learn a practice or ritual and keep it has disappeared—a practice or procedure lasts only as long as it takes to obtain the next level of technologic innova-tion. Practitioners cannot be attached to ritual and routine or expect to see an environment where skill sets can be maintained for lengthy periods of time. The successful clinician is the one who is committed to making a difference in the lives of others, not to any particular way or method of meeting that goal.

Leaders recognize that change exists. Change is constant, cyclical, and never ending (Gilbert & Bower, 2002). This is critical to understanding the basic concepts influencing all leadership expression. Helping individuals engage and embrace their own roles in change will be a major element of the expression of the role of leader. Because change is the most constant element of work, the leader is challenged with the workers' frequent negative disposition to personal change. Bringing a level of concert between the constant demand for change and individual's reluctance to undertake personal change will pose a significant leadership challenge. Much of the development of the leader will relate to his or her ability to identify specific change and to lead others into identifying and addressing that change in their personal roles.

Leaders must be able to identify with the changes that are emerging to know how critical these changes are and the ability of the organization to drive them. Through their personal passion for movement, leaders must inspire responses from others to incorporate change into their own lives. The point of change, such as it is experienced today, allows no time for complacency. All change has an impact on individual performance. In assessing individual performance outcomes, the leader must be able to comfortably confront change directly, translating it into a language that has meaning for those whom the individual leads. At this time, the leader must persuade individuals how the change makes a substantial and meaningful difference in their lives and work. The leader should identify the best way to communicate effectively with a knowledge worker from each generation's workforce and lead the individuals accordingly (Marston, 2003).

The leader best exemplifies commitment to change through personal actions. If leaders do not demonstrate a willingness to embrace and adapt to the demands of change in their behavior, attempting to encourage others to do so will have minimal success. Therefore, leadership skill development around the process of change has more to do with how the leader incorporates the drama and cycle of change within the role. The leader evidences for others the application of this rule and, subsequently, journeys with the team in a way that establishes new behaviors, performance, and expectations (Davis & Meyer, 1998). In this way, for the leader, change becomes a lived experience. In the process of action learning and lived experience, the leader models for others the positive action of change and the advancement of clinical practice in response to the demand for change.

Loss Management

In the development of the leader, it is important to be able to assist others in the management of loss. Inherent in all change is not only the aggregation of new and exciting opportunities for growth but also the embedded old practices and performances to which people have become accustomed. Change always brings both loss and gain (Newman, 2000). They are necessary parts of the continuous and dynamic cycle of change. However, moving into new practice patterns and behaviors cannot be sustained nor can success be ensured over the long term unless the opportunity for mourning the loss of past practices is embedded in the change journey. The emerging leader must develop skills in helping others acknowledge what will be left behind in their personal change process. The meaning and value associated with past practices and traditional activities must be enumerated and celebrated before they can be safely put away and people can move on to new challenges and opportunities. The skill of loss management is perhaps one of the least practiced skills in dealing with change and one that impacts the ability to create sustainable and successful change over the long term (Black & NetLibrary, 2002).

Communicating Direction

All leaders must have a vision of the direction of change and the change journey for the organization. Leaders are consistently managing mobility and movement; however, they are not inherently valuable. The value of movement is disciplined by the direction to which one is moving and the meaning that movement has in achieving specified and clear outcomes for all participants. The leader, in this role, is essentially a "signpost reader." This means that the leader constantly lives in the "potential" of the journey as it moves toward goals and outcomes that have value for the organization and the people in it (Coffman & Gonzales-Molina, 2002). The leader must be able to see the direction of the journey and then translate that direction into a language followers can understand. The leader can break down the direction of change into increments and elements, allowing staff members to slowly incorporate the changes into their work.

The leader is a translator of organizational goals and priorities, economic and financial realities that must be accommodated, and the ultimate work requisites of driving a competitive and complex healthcare environment. Although nurses recognize the reality associated with these issues, they often have a difficult time incorporating these realities into the practices and processes associated with nursing care. Through the substance of translation, the leader assists the staff in accommodating and incorporating changes into their own practice experience (see Figure 3-6).

Figure 3-6. Translation Skills

- Clear vision
- Broad view of the issues
- In the language of staff

- What does it mean to me?
- What do I do?

- Impact of the act
- Ensuring competence

Translation of Change

Contemporary research shows that individuals do not embrace change unless it has meaning within the context of their own experience (Briggs & Peat, 1999). The emerging leader must recognize that the fundamental requirement of translation of change is making that change clear, meaningful, and amenable to the role of the practitioner in a way that can be understood and applicable as perceived by the individual. People do not change because the change is good for the organization. The new leader must recognize that the change needs to be identified as good by the individual before it will be incorporated into the individual's set of values (Hultman & Gellermann, 2002). The translation role of the leader brings change within the content of the practitioner's role, embedding the understanding of the change in a framework of applied practice. In this way, the reality of the change is both meaningful and invaluable for the individual and incorporated within the framework of work. It is in this way that the vision and strategy, as well as goals and objectives of the organization, become real for those working at the organization's point of service (Albrecht, 2003). Furthermore, in this way, the goals and values of the organization become those of the individual. Through this process, the role of the leader finds its value in how successful the translation from vision and strategy into action and performance has been incorporated into the practitioner's role.

This core level of understanding about the role of translating vision is critical to the sustainability and the success of the leader and that of the staff members who will be charged with fully exercising in their own roles the actions and elements of practice and patient care, which serve as the culmination of the purposes and goals of the organization. There is, perhaps, no greater skill in the tool chest of a leader than good visioning and translation abilities. Creating a good fit between the purposes of the organization and work of the staff is one of the more important applied skills for any good leader.

Developing Leaders for a New Era

The new leader must recognize that the age into which the profession is moving requires a different set of skills from the nursing professional. With this understanding, the emerging leader begins to see his or her role as a pioneer developing a road map that will help to guide the practitioner into a new era of practice. The challenge for the leader is ensuring a personal willingness to change practice and performance.

Willingness

Mentors and educators committed to developing the new leader must recognize in the leader the presence of willingness. The willingness of the leader to confront the challenges of change creates a context for hope within which others also can exemplify their own willingness to change. Important for leaders is to engage others in their efforts to participate in creating a better future. For health care, this willingness means openness to what needs to be done to meet the needs of patient care, establish new standards of practice, and address the challenges of the changing payment environment. In this effort, the leader will need to exhibit the courage, passion, energy, discipline, and trust that will be necessary to thrive in the presence of the chaos of change (Channer & Hope, 2000).

A leader willing to live in this set of circumstances, of course, must be considerably adaptable. The "metal" essential to this kind of leadership must be found within. The leader must recognize that the exemplars of good leadership in this set of circumstances represent more about who the leader is than what the leader does. The manager should be aware that the culture of the organization and the nature of mentorship must be such that it enables, indeed influences, the growing leader to trust and express a personal willingness to risk. Often leaders will need to exhibit in their own practice changes others might not yet be willing to make. This places the leader outside the norm and in a position to challenge others to alter rituals and routines and shift expectations. This often puts the leader on the cutting edge of the change process, at the greatest point of risk, and raises the stakes with regard to the role and the relationship of the leader with others in the work environment. The good leader recognizes the normative resistance to change that exists in all people. Therefore, this leader expects, even anticipates, that there will be some level of opposition to any change process (Hambrick, Nadler, & Tushman, 1998). To this leader, the understanding that all change begins with an individual act informs others of his or her willingness to undertake a change action. The leader develops coalitions (even conspiracies) with others to expand the cycle of change person by person until it becomes a normative way of doing things.

Emotional Competence

In the past decade, the importance of maturity and the emotional stability of leaders in the expression of their role have been more clearly identified. Under the rubric of emotional competence or intelligence, this set of skills has become of equal value to all other expressions of the leader's role (Goleman, 2000). Emotional competence represents a leader's regard for the needs of colleagues and subordinates, a strong understanding of basic human motivators, a willingness to be responsible, an ability to identify core problems, and an ability to act decisively. Quantum organizations are viewed in the context of "wholes" rather than in the traditionally compartmentalized structures of the past (Zimmerman, Lindberg, & Plsek, 1998). This creates for the leader a deeper understanding of the goodness-of-fit between all the elements of the organization and the components of the human dynamics of work. In this set of circumstances, the leader needs skills that synthesize all the elements of both the work and the workplace in a mosaic of intersections that resonate in a "dance" that moves the organization to fulfilling its mission and advancing its purpose. The leader has the capacity to intuitively understand these system[s] interfaces and to synthesize the efforts necessary to keep all the elements of the workplace operating in a synergistic manner. The good leader recognizes that providing leadership is only a small component of the life of the organization; all efforts must converge to move the whole organization to fulfill its purpose.

Emotional Competence

The old model of a strong, independent, and "cool-headed" leader appears to be more myth than ideal. Great leaders exemplify great passion with all the strength and weakness that circumstance implies. Exceptional leaders are in touch with how they feel and how they can engage the feelings and sentiments of others. Leadership is mostly relationship and engagement. Being able to identify and resonate with the experiences and lives of others and harnessing that to the challenges of work is the great attribute of good leaders.

The emotionally competent leader expresses a high degree of self-knowledge (Goleman, Boyatzis, & McKee, 2002). This means that both strengths and weaknesses in the expression of the leader's role are understood in light of their impact. The leader develops an appreciation for imperfection. It is recognized that everybody exemplifies a different mix of characteristics. The emotionally competent leader sees that it is only when patterns of behavior are aggregated that the balance in the team or work group is identified and maintained. This leader can use all the skills present in an infinite variety in the work group to move the team into advancing goals. However, it is inherent in this leader that the emotional maturity that recognizes the variety of skills in others is also able to express the full appreciation of the variabilities in others' performances as part of the exercise of the role of the leader. Emotionally competent leaders exemplify an openness to new ideas, the value of others' knowledge, compassion for others' situations, a true and complete presence to others, and the mindfulness of the needs of others.

The leader exemplifying the traits of emotional competence is aware of his or her own emotional needs. This individual is an exceptionally resilient person with the capacity to cope with the unanticipated, the uncertain, and the chaos of change. Through this resilience, the leader is able to gain insight and maturity and learn to translate it into the expression of the role. The emotionally intelligent leader seeks to find balance in life between the personal and professional, between the emotional and intellectual, and between learning and doing. This individual exemplifies characteristics of maturity and self-control. The emotionally competent leader is capable of self-regulation, personal motivation, and empathy and can develop and exercise a high level of social skill without sacrificing character and personal integrity. Increasingly, these characteristics of emotional competence are becoming essential corollaries to the appropriate and meaningful expression of the role of the leader (Kotter & Cohen, 2002).

Confronting Conflict

In the last two decades, much progress has been made in understanding the nature of conflict in human organizations. We know that all conflict is normative (Costantino & Merchant, 1998). It is not true that conflict is inappropriate and unnecessary, representing relational inadequacy. All human conflict has meaning and can be addressed if there is understanding and a process for resolving it. The leader looks at conflict through the eyes of opportunity (Levine, 1998). Developing this frame of reference for the leader is an important skill for both mentor and educator. The concept of conflict as a fundamental part of all of human interaction must be a cornerstone of all leadership as individuals respond to conflict situations.

Conflict is always a means for growth and transformation (Kottler, 1996). Conflict management takes into account that people differ in any number of ways. Factors related to culture, race, gender, social status, and income as well as personal beliefs, family position, mental and physical health, intelligence, and emotional maturity all influence the nature and interaction of human relationships. Leaders understand this complex mosaic of factors influencing the expression of behaviors. Nursing leaders have an additional set of concerns regarding conflict, including the historical subordination and powerlessness experienced by women and nurses throughout most of the 20th century (Ashley, 1976). This confluence of both personal and professional circumstances creates a framework for conflict that is often unique to the nursing profession. The clinical leader, aware of this confluence, develops special awareness of the potential for conflict arising from each of these loci.

The emerging leader is taught that good conflict resolution begins with an environment that makes open and free communication possible (Wenger & Mockli, 2003). The leader creates a safe place within which to deal with conflicts as a normative part of doing the business of service. The leader addresses conflict between the organization and the profession, creating an environment that rewards and supports the professional work of the nurse (Kritek, 2002). Always aware of the normative conflict between profession and organization, the leader seeks to reduce the intensity of that conflict and to create a place where good relationships can be continuously addressed and renegotiated (Levine, 1998).

Working together to provide healthcare services creates a level of intensity and difficulty unparalleled in any other work field. In nursing, the potential for a group-based conflict is always present. These conflicts are not to be avoided; instead, they are to be identified early. The earlier the leader identifies a conflict, the easier the process for its resolution. This calls for a level of awareness and clarity at two levels:

one, with regard to the potential for conflict, and two, the careful engagement of conflict at critical moments with an eye for dealing with the conflict at a time most potent to its resolution (Moore, 2003). The growing and developing leader refines skills in conflict assessment, identification, and timely resolution. The continuing development and refinement of conflict process skills, interactional capacity, relational management, and moving people to resolution of conflict are requisites of the leader. As the leader develops and matures, he or she comes to understand that the role operates forever in the presence of conflict. This leader is continuously involved in managing differences and actualizing those differences as a mechanism for honoring human diversity, advancing relationships, and improving practice (Blackard & Gibson, 2002).

Living Leadership: The Vulnerable and Growing Leader

Historically, vulnerability has been seen as weakness. Yet, when examined critically, all great leaders used their vulnerability as a tool to advance their leadership and relationships with others. Vulnerability is not weakness; it is the recognition of the need for growth and the capacity to identify with that need in others. Vulnerable leaders have a willingness to exhibit their limits and to extend the capacities of others to compensate for those limits. The growing and maturing leader recognizes that by embracing the strengths in others not present in the leader, the influence and power of leadership is extended and enhanced. With this understanding, the role of leader is to effectively create the conditions and circumstances that allow those who are led to maximize their own contribution to work initiatives and to the goals to which each is connected (Sample, 2001).

Good leaders incorporate in their management of power expression of their personal identification with those whom they lead. The leader recognizes in others a need to be recognized for individual contribution to an initiative or the enterprise. The leader identifies with the desires, needs, and values of those he or she leads so that these things can be touched and expressed within the context of the leader's own role. It is said that Julius Caesar was so loved by his army that he could lead them into any situation and they would go not only willingly but with great enthusiasm, regardless of the horrendous circumstances. When his military exploits were studied in great detail, it was evidenced that Julius Caesar could so identify with the needs, desires, and wishes of his soldiers, and they with him, that his army was able to act as an extension of his own will. He expressed this resonance with them in his willingness to fight side by side, to visit the sick, to take meals with the soldiers, and to identify with their personal and family concerns. This expression of human solidarity, this vulnerability before those he led created a strong identification between the army and its leader. This powerful image indicates how living vulnerably and the willingness to understand it and to use it as a part of the leadership dynamic is a critical element in the expression of good leadership.

Vulnerability means openness. This openness is expressed in the willingness of the leader to engage others in confronting risks by being willing to confront themselves, stretching one's capacity beyond current skill levels. Willingness is expressed in raising the risk of failure in one's performance and in living with the ambiguity of emerging challenges and opportunities not yet fully incorporated into the competence and skills of the person (leader). The vulnerable leader cherishes the journey and enjoins people with it. This recognition of the value of the journey, rather than the moment of arrival or the achievement of the outcome, is the critical variable in the viable and continuing expression of good leadership. The vulnerable leader does not back away from a challenge simply because the personal capacity to address it may be uncertain. Leaders cultivate opportunity for challenge and change and exemplify in their behavior the excitement and energy necessary to positively respond to impending opportunity. They give these challenges the correct form and bring the team through them with energy and commitment, obtaining good outcomes. For the leader, the expression of the role is as chief learner with all the vulnerability and vagaries that experience implies. It ensures for the follower that the leader is a fellow traveler on the journey of growth, maturity, and advancement for both person and profession.

The Leadership Journey

The leader is forever learning. All good leaders live within a developmental context. The work of learning and leadership never ends. All leaders must be as committed to their own development as they are to their role. Leadership is a living journey that represents a personal commitment to individual growth and development. The good leader joins in the effort to develop the roles of the professional staff, other workers, and the organization. The maturity and growth of the leader serves as an exemplar to those who are on an earlier stage of their leadership journey. The obligations of mentorship and the development of other leaders are both inherent in the role. Growing in leadership competence is a shared experience, the expectation of which is communicated from one leader to another. Those who are leaders have an opportunity and an obligation to extend to each other what has been learned through experience and the development of the role. All leaders must realize that they are on a life journey that will never end as long as they are in the role. The most viable and successful leaders always will know that they are not fully competent in the expression of leadership. They know that competence is not completely obtainable and understand that leadership is a journey, not an event. The significance and joy of leadership is in its continuing dynamic and ever-challenging call to personal mastery and entry into the never ending mystery of human growth and relationship.

References

Albrecht, K. (2003). *The power of minds at work: Organizational intelligence in action.* New York: AMACOM.

Amar, A.D. (2002). *Managing knowledge workers: Unleashing innovation and productivity.* Westport, CT: Quorum Books.

Anderson, W.T. (2001). *All connected now: Life in the first global civilization.* Los Angeles: Westview Press.

Ashley, J.A. (1976). *Hospitals, paternalism, and the role of the nurse.* New York: Teachers College Press.

Beer, M., & Nohria, N. (2000). *Breaking the code of change.* Boston: Harvard Business School.

Black, C., & NetLibrary. (2002). *Changing course: Healing from loss, abandonment, and fear* (2nd ed.). Center City, MN: Hazelden.

Blackard, K., & Gibson, J.W. (2002). *Capitalizing on conflict: Strategies and practices for turning conflict into synergy in organizations: A manager's handbook.* Palo Alto, CA: Davies-Black.

Briggs, J., & Peat, D. (1999). *Seven life lessons of chaos.* New York: HarperPerennial.

Brown, B.L. (2001). *Mentoring and work-based learning.* Columbus, OH: ERIC Clearinghouse.

Channer, P., & Hope, T. (2000). *Emotional impact: Passionate leaders and corporate transformation.* New York: Palgrave.

Coffman, C., & Gonzales-Molina, G. (2002). *Follow this path: How the world's greatest organizations unleash human potential.* New York: Warner Books.

Costantino, C., & Merchant, C. (1998). *Designing conflict management systems.* San Francisco: Jossey-Bass.

Davis, S., & Meyer, C. (1998). *Blur: The speed of change in the connected economy.* New York: Addison-Wesley.

Drucker, P. (2002). They're not employees, they're people. *Harvard Business Review, 80*(2), 70–77.

Drucker, P., & Stone, N. (1998). *On the profession of management.* Boston: Harvard Business School.

Evans, P., & Wurster, T. (1999). *Blown to bits: How the new economics of information transforms strategy.* Boston: Harvard Business School.

Ferris, G.T. (1889). *Great leaders: Historic portraits from the great historians.* New York: Appleton.

Fetterman, D.M. (2001). *Foundations of empowerment evaluation.* Thousand Oaks, CA: Sage.

Gilbert, C., & Bower, J. (2002). Disruptive change. *Harvard Business Review, 80*(5), 95–101.

Goleman, D. (2000). *Working with emotional intelligence.* New York: Bantam Books.

Goleman, D., Boyatzis, R., & McKee, A. (2002). *Primal leadership.* Boston: Harvard Business School.

Hambrick, D., Nadler, D., & Tushman, M. (1998). *Navigating change.* Boston: Harvard Business School.

Heifetz, R., & Laurie, D. (2001). The work of leadership. *Harvard Business Review, 79*(11), 131–140.

Hultman, K., & Gellermann, W. (2002). *Balancing individual and organizational values: Walking the tightrope to success.* San Francisco: Jossey-Bass/Pfeiffer.

Jensen, B. (2002). *Work 2.0: Rewriting the contract.* New York: Perseus.

Kets de Vries, M. (1993). *Leaders, fools, and imposters.* San Francisco: Jossey-Bass.

Kotter, J.P. (2001). What leaders really do. *Harvard Business Review, 79*(11), 85–96.

Kotter, J.P., & Cohen, D. (2002). *The heart of change: Real-life stories of how people change their organizations.* Boston: Harvard Business School.

Kottler, J.A. (1996). *Beyond blame: A new way of resolving conflicts in relationships.* San Francisco: Jossey-Bass.

Kritek, P.B. (2002). *Negotiating at an uneven table: Developing moral courage in resolving our conflicts* (2nd ed.). San Francisco: Jossey-Bass.

Lancaster, L., & Stillman, D. (2002). *When generations collide.* New York: Harper Business School.

Levine, S. (1998). *Getting to resolution.* San Francisco: Berrett-Koehler.

Marston, C. (2003, November). *Managing and retaining the best of today's workforce.* Paper presented at the HCA/CNO Summit, New Orleans, LA.

McKenna, R. (2002). *Total access: Giving customers what they want in an anytime, anywhere world.* Boston: Harvard Business School.

Moore, C.W. (2003). *The mediation process: Practical strategies for resolving conflict* (3rd ed.). San Francisco: Jossey-Bass.

Murphy, J., & National Society for the Study of Education. (2002). *The educational leadership challenge: Redefining leadership for the 21st century.* Chicago: NSSE—distributed by University of Chicago Press.

Murray, M. (2001). *Beyond the myths and magic of mentoring: How to facilitate an effective mentoring process.* San Francisco: Jossey-Bass.

Newman, J.H. (2000). *Loss and gain.* Cambridge, England: Chadwyck-Healey.

Pearce, C.L., & Conger, J.A. (2003). *Shared leadership: Reframing the hows and whys of leadership*. Thousand Oaks, CA: Sage.

Pearman, R. (1998). *Hard wired leadership*. New York: Davies-Black.

Porter-O'Grady, T. (1992). *Implementing shared governance*. Baltimore: Mosby.

Porter-O'Grady, T. (2001). Profound change: 21st century nursing. *Nursing Outlook, 49*(1), 182–186.

Porter-O'Grady, T. (2002, January/February). Reforming the healthcare structure. *Health Progress,* pp. 17–20.

Sample, S. (2001). *The contrarian's guide to leadership*. San Francisco: Jossey-Bass.

Sorcher, M., & Brant, J. (2002). Are you picking the right leaders? *Harvard Business Review, 80*(2), 78–87.

Spears, L.C., Lawrence, M., & NetLibrary. (2002). *Focus on leadership servant-leadership for the twenty-first century*. New York: Wiley.

Spouse, J., & Redfern, L. (2000). *Successful supervision in health care practice: Promoting professional development*. Malden, MA: Blackwell Science.

Warner, J. (2002). *Aspirations of greatness: Mapping the midlife leader's reconnection to self and soul*. New York: Wiley.

Wenger, A., & Mockli, D. (2003). *Conflict prevention: The untapped potential of the business sector*. Boulder, CO: Lynne Rienner.

Wheatley, M.J. (1999). *Leadership and the new science: Discovering order in a chaotic world* (2nd ed.). San Francisco: Berrett-Koehler.

Zachary, L.J. (2000). *The mentor's guide: Facilitating effective learning relationships*. San Francisco: Jossey-Bass.

Zimmerman, B., Lindberg, C., & Plsek, P. (1998). *Edgeware*. Irving, TX: VHA.

Clinical Leadership Challenge

Barbara L. Young Summers, PhD, RN, MSN

"Nurse leaders can have their heads in the clouds, but they must have their feet on the ground and their hands on the patient." Dame Kathleen Raven (Royal College of Nursing, 2003)

Nursing is a clinical practice discipline, grounded in the professional relationship between the patient and nurse. Within this relationship, the nurse applies the nursing process to assess, diagnose, and identify outcomes and plan, implement, and evaluate a plan of care for the patient/client. This foundation of nursing in clinical decision making and action requires those in management and administration roles to engage in the provision of clinical leadership in addition to financial and human resources management.

A challenge of clinical leadership is that it is a concept that has not benefited from a commonly accepted definition or set of roles and responsibilities. The absence of clinical leadership role descriptions and implementation strategies is confirmed by a review of the literature that produced few documents on the subject. Countries in the United Kingdom have published the most in-depth studies of clinical leadership in nursing; however, even these are few in number (Cook, 2001; Ham, 2003; Royal College of Nursing, 2003). This lack of specificity regarding clinical leadership roles and functions provides nurse managers, administrators, and clinical nurses with opportunities to develop the concept in ways that are most likely to be successful within their organization's culture.

Despite the limited availability of published research and thought regarding clinical leadership, the available definitions deserve review and consideration. These definitions include "a nurse directly involved in providing care that continuously improves care through influencing others" (Cook, 2001, p. 39). This perspective is expanded in the following: "A clinical nursing leader is someone with specialist clinical expertise combined with effective leadership skills in areas such as negotiation, communication, and influencing others" (Royal College of Nursing, 2003, p. 31). The American Association of Colleges of Nursing (AACN) described clinical leadership through the clinical nurse leader (CNL) roles (AACN, 2003). These roles are proposed to include clinician, outcomes manager, patient advocate, educator, information manager, team manager, systems analyst and risk anticipator, and member of a profession.

Clinical leadership for the new realities of nursing means engaging clinicians in adapting to the new circumstances of health care—letting go of the old and familiar and reaching for the uncharted future. The nurse manager, administrator, and clinician must partner in this process of adaptation, and the development of a program or framework for clinical leadership must occur within the context of the changing culture of each organization. Clinical leadership is not confined to one particular role, although some organizations may opt to create positions for designated clinical leaders. Clinical leadership must become an integral component of the practice of not only managers and administrators but also clinical nurses.

This chapter presents a variety of perspectives and paths that may be pursued in an effort to develop a clinical leadership program. Contemporary leadership thought is shown not only from nursing but also from medicine, healthcare administration, and business. The imperative for building clinical leadership will be presented, followed by a review of clinical performance management and improvement activities. Finally, clinical leadership competence will be discussed from several perspectives, concluding with thoughts about leadership coaching.

Creating a Practice Culture

Creating a practice culture is imperative for clinical leadership. Health care is provided by clinical practitioners, and clinical leaders can shape the culture within which this practice occurs. The development of a practice culture is largely dependent upon the clinical leadership within an organization. According to Porter-O'Grady and Malloch (2003), the convergence of three culture constituent groups results in the drive of a system to succeed. These cultures include the patients, the community, and the members or workers who give focus to the culture. The most numerous workers in health care are clinicians, and within this group, nurses are the largest subgroup. Therefore, the culture of a healthcare organization is shaped, in part, by the nurses who are concerned about clinical practice. Review Chapter 3 for more information on leadership development.

Others have addressed the key roles of clinical leaders in developing a practice culture. "Clinicians ought to be playing a central role in making the changes in the health care system that will allow the system to offer better outcomes, greater ease of use, lower cost, and more social justice in health status" (Berwick, 1994, p. 797). Clinical leaders build the capacity for change and innovation in their colleagues. They engage clinicians to bring about change in providing leadership development and the time, information, and resources needed to achieve the desired change (Ham, 2003).

In the late 1990s, professional organizations and individual researchers began describing phenomena occurring within health care that highlighted the importance of clinical leadership (Institute of Medicine [IOM], 1999). In 1999, IOM published a landmark report that focused on the impact of medical errors on patient safety and identified fragmentation in health services delivery as a primary contributing factor to these errors. This IOM report was followed by a study conducted by Buerhaus, Staiger, and Auerbach (2000) that described the impact of an aging nursing workforce on the future delivery of health care. Additional reports on the nursing workforce shortage and its impacts were published in rapid succession by organizations including the Joint Commission on Accreditation of Healthcare Organizations (2002), the American Hospital Association (2002), and the Robert Wood Johnson Foundation (Kimball & O'Neil, 2002). Although each of these reports took slightly differing approaches to the workforce issues, all addressed the critical clinical leadership role of the nurse.

IOM (2001) published a report that further explored the frailties of the healthcare delivery system. Among the many findings and recommendations from this report, IOM clearly identified the requirement for healthcare organizations and professional groups to partner in developing systems of care that are safe, effective, timely, client-centered, efficient, and equitable. In 2003, IOM released another report that identified key areas of focus for the education of healthcare professionals. These foci are consistent with clinical leadership practices and include interdisciplinary collaboration, quality management, and evidence-based practice.

AACN (2003) published a draft of a paper describing the CNL role as a response to the challenges and calls for change in the healthcare system. AACN proposed the CNL as a leader "in the health care delivery system across all settings in which health care is delivered . . .", assuming "accountability for client care outcomes through the assimilation and application of research-based information to design, implement, and evaluate client plans of care. . . . The CNL is a provider and manager of care at the point of care," designing, implementing, and evaluating client care (p. 3). The CNL provides direction to the care delivery team, coordinating individual efforts toward goal achievement. Although the role of the CNL is conceptualized by AACN as an entry into practice level, the competencies, core knowledge areas, and roles described have potential application to a broader context of clinical leadership in nursing practice.

Clinical Performance Management and Improvement

Clinical leaders are required to recognize their role as both members and leaders of interdisciplinary teams. The clinical leader directs the team focus toward desired outcomes and opportunities for improvement while attending to individual member focus on specific performance. The clinical leader serves as a mirror for team progress as well as a stimulus for continued improvement and advocate for change. Berwick (1994) stated, "Clinician-led reform, however, would require that we establish clear improvement aims, monitor our progress, and above all willingly make changes in the way we do our work in an effort to better meet the aims" (p. 797). Clinical leaders engage in key practices to promote attainment of desired clinical outcomes. These include leading through influence, application of standards of practice and performance, and evaluation of factors contributing to outcomes.

Leadership Through Influence

Many clinical professionals view their practice as being highly autonomous and may resist efforts to focus on team-based outcomes. Work with professional nurses and other healthcare professionals necessitates that the clinical leader manage relationships with others as colleagues and partners. The leader strikes a balance between respect for the autonomy of the individual practitioner and the requirement for attainment of specific outcomes. This includes the balance of standardization of clinical practices and the individualization of patients' needs and practitioners' preference. The clinical leader manages the relationships among the team members; leadership through influence is a key practice. Influence is a derivative of the power of personal relationships and of persuasion, and the clinical leader uses influence to set and maintain a direction for the team, encouraging each member along. Through the use of influence, the clinical leader provides a sense of direction for the future, inspiring others to act and influencing change.

Application of Standards

Clinical leadership includes the establishment of standards of nursing practice and the application, supervision, and guidance in the use of the standards for patient care delivery. Practice standards must be consistent with national and professional benchmarks and regulatory agency requirements. Practice standards include both standards of care and standards of performance. Standards of care serve as the framework for measuring clinician performance in use of the nursing process, whereas standards of performance describe performance in professional nursing roles (Brant & Wickham, 2004). Clinical leadership requires that such standards be identified as providing the basis for clinician practice. Both generic and specialty practice standards have applicability in the delivery of healthcare services.

Elevating the Quality of Patient Care Outcomes

For clinical leaders, the focus of quality is evolving from processes of care to the outcomes of care, from performing the right clinical processes to attaining the desired clinical outcomes (Porter-O'Grady & Malloch, 2003). Clinical leadership involves assessment of both nurse-sensitive outcomes and multidisciplinary outcomes. These outcomes may be obtained from multiple national organizations as well as from internally derived organizational data sets. Regardless of the source of outcome measures, clinical leaders communicate the expected standards of performance to achieve the desired outcomes. The results of clinical practice when measured in relationship to the selected outcomes provide clinical leaders with information to engage staff in evaluating performance, devising staff education programs, and developing individual staff coaching plans. In addition, clinical outcomes should be reviewed in relationship to acuity systems and staffing patterns as well as patient care assignments to determine any relationships that may be contributing to the outcomes.

Clinical Leadership Competency

How does the manager, administrator, or clinician develop competence in clinical leadership? What are the key role functions of the clinical leader? The absence of a commonly accepted standard of performance or definition of role provides an opportunity to craft the role functions and competencies in a way that best fits the needs of an organization or profession. With that flexibility in mind, the following section will provide some information for consideration in developing clinical leadership roles. Managers and administrators may use this information to develop a list of desired role functions and competencies. The list can be further refined with a rating of importance of each role function and competency to the overall role and another rating of the skill competence of individuals relative to each role function and competency. A comparison of the two ratings will provide insight into areas for potential skill and knowledge development for the CNL.

Authoritative Clinical Knowledge, Skills, and Wisdom

Clinical leadership is the application of authoritative clinical knowledge in combination with clinical skills and the wisdom obtained from practice experience. The caduceus was initially used by the Greeks to depict Hermes, the god of medicine and science. The caduceus is a staff with two serpents coiled around it: one to represent knowledge and the other to represent wisdom. Knowledge is the acquaintance with a body of facts and principles, whereas wisdom is acquired from a base of practice knowledge, experiences, and understanding (*Webster's II New College Dictionary*, 2001). Both are essential to the balance of clinical practice and the work of clinical leadership. The effective clinical leader possesses and seeks out both knowledge and wisdom.

Clinical Leader Mind-Sets

Although the term "clinical leadership" has been used throughout this chapter, the role of the clinical leader also includes management functions. Gosling and Mintzberg (2003) described the interdependencies of leadership and management, with both being necessary but neither sufficient alone. The authors proposed that managers adopt various "mind-sets" that assist the manager to bridge action and reflection. Although the authors addressed the general field of management, the concepts can be applied to clinical leadership. The challenge for the clinical leader, in this case, is to bridge the duality in order to "function at the point where reflective thinking meets practical doing" (Gosling & Mintzberg, p. 56).

Gosling and Mintzberg (2003) described five mind-sets, including managing self, managing organizations, managing context, managing relationships, and managing change. The application of these to clinical leadership would take the following form.

Managing self—The active engagement in reflection on the meaning of experiences. Clinicians typically find themselves in a state of nonstop action during the course of a day. Rarely do they make the time to stop and reflect upon experiences. However, it is through reflection that clinical leaders begin to discern patterns and create explanations based upon thoughtful review of experiences.

Managing organizations—The process of analysis of data from multiple sources. Clinicians routinely find themselves engaged in deep analysis of clinical patient problems, taking into account complex sets of data obtained from many sources, including their own practice experience. The challenge for clinical leadership is to apply that same depth of analysis to organizational issues and problems, developing competence in seeking data from multiple sources and in calling upon their leadership practice experiences.

Managing context—The action of intentionally looking for alternative perspectives of one's world view. In the case of the clinical leader, this involves
- Moving out of the office into the practice arena to observe the actions and interactions of clinicians
- Spending time with the client or patient to better appreciate the view of the recipient of clinical care
- Talking with professionals from disciplines other than nursing to gain an appreciation of the challenges and perspectives they bring to care delivery and clinical outcomes.

The result of these and similar activities is a more wholly informed view of the arena of clinical practice and thus an improved leadership capacity to elevate practice and enhance outcomes.

Managing relationships—The recognition that a leader cannot manage the actions of others, especially not other autonomous professionals. However, relationships can be negotiated, and it is in the space of these relationships between and among people that shared commitment and understanding emerge. Managing relationships requires the clinical leader to recognize the limited reach of her or his individual action as the source of achieving goals. The clinical leader instead must create systems and structures and an environment that supports others in goal attainment.

Managing change—Involves a bias toward action that is both collaborative and reflective. The clinical leader is knowledgeable about the capacity of the team, the capabilities of its members, and the context of the organization; and change is managed with these insights. Clinical leaders recognize that change rarely occurs in a linear manner or according to a predetermined plan involving specific activities that occur in a particular order. Leaders also know that it is undesirable to change everything all of the time. Instead, change is viewed as a state-of-being, a constant that is occurring in some portion of our existence. The clinical leader manages change by creating a focus on the relationship between change and continuity. Action focuses on the specific area that needs to be changed, while it reflects on the change within the context of continuity (all the areas that are not changing at once). Effective clinical leaders will manage the dynamic tension between that which changes and that which remains constant, using both to support the effective functioning of the team.

Clinical Leadership Core Knowledge and Competencies

AACN (2003) included areas of core knowledge and four key competencies. While recognizing the intent of this document to describe expectations for clinical nurses at point of entry into practice, the content has applicability to the larger context of clinical leadership. Many of the areas of core knowledge can be used to build a curriculum for clinical leadership, including

- Health promotion, disease prevention, and maintenance of the client or patient function to achieve and maintain an optimal level of wellness
- Illness and disease management as well as management of treatment interventions that are geared to support the client or patient in optimizing functioning and quality of life throughout the care continuum
- Proficiency in the application of information technology for the documentation, retrieval, and use of data in clinical practice as well as knowledge of healthcare technology to support and monitor patient functioning
- Ethics in the form of values and principles that provide guidance in decision making.
- Human diversity is used to gain an understanding of the contribution of cultural, racial, ethnic, gender, socioeconomic, and religious factors to the delivery of clinical care.
- Knowledge of systems within health care, including the organization within which care is delivered and the external environment that influences the larger professional practice context.

The competencies AACN identified include *critical thinking,* which provides the foundation for decision making; *communication,* which is the basis for creating and sustaining relationships; *assessment* of individuals, groups, and systems, including skills at data gathering, analysis and synthesis of the data, making good judgments, and evaluating outcomes; and *management of technology and resources* to achieve desired outcomes.

Berwick (1994) described clinical leadership skills that are required to create healing systems.

- Viewing and understanding the whole healthcare system, not simply the specific nursing world view
- Gathering and interpretating care outcome data
- Working collaboratively across disciplines
- Developing interdependent, trusting relationships with others in which the motives and intelligence of diverse groups of others are valued and respected
- Being skilled in the application of new approaches to work instead of sticking to the safety of the status quo
- Interpreting the needs of patients in a manner that respectfully places care improvement efforts in the hands of the recipients of the care (p. 801).

Coaching to Leadership Strengths

Some thoughts about how managers and administrators can coach others to build their leadership strengths are in order. Mintzberg (1999) described the practices of inspiring others, caring, infusing, and initiating, each of which seems particularly well-suited to a clinical practice discipline.

Inspiring others is not the same as empowering; rather, it assumes others have the power to act and do not need permission to do so. The creation of a climate that fosters openness and the release of creative energy allows the interaction that permits the strengthening of bonds, treating each member as an essential part of a social community. These actions support the need of each person to see the link between self and the something larger than self—the organization.

Caring in the case of the CNL involves caring for staff that they may care for the patient, providing for the caring of the patient and the attainment of desired outcomes through the actions of clinical leadership.

Infusing change is not management by intrusion where a "fix" is imposed upon a problem. Infusion allows change to slowly, quietly seep in, in a steady yet deep and durable manner.

Initiating provides an alternative to the leader performing the role of delivering the message from "on high"—a practice that encourages dependence on the heroic leader figure. Rather, initiating is about connecting with the base to assess the current circumstance and never losing that connection. This allows the leader to serve as a champion for the initiatives of the clinical team.

Conclusion

There is bad news and good news, danger and opportunity, in the absence of clearly defined competencies for clinical leadership. The bad news is a consequence of the lack of specific attention dedicated to this critical set of nursing role functions, and the danger comes from the potential lost opportunities to nursing. The good news is that the significant role of clinical leaders is gaining recognition and there are no existing preconceptions about the role to constrain our ability to craft the role in a way that will meet the challenges of health care. This good news provides the greatest of opportunities. It often is more difficult to forget a reality we have known than it is to create one from the unknown. Nursing has the opportunity to leverage the gap of knowledge and, in doing so, to firmly embed clinical leadership within the profession.

References

American Association of Colleges of Nursing. (2003). *The role of the clinical nurse leader.* Retrieved December 16, 2003, from http://www.aacn.nche.edu/publications/whitepapers/clinicalnurse-leader.html

American Hospital Association. (2002). *In our hands. How hospital leaders can build a thriving workforce.* Washington, DC: Author.

Berwick, D.M. (1994). Eleven worthy aims for clinical leadership of health system reform. *JAMA, 272,* 797–802.

Brant, J.M., & Wickham, R.S. (2004). *Statement on the scope and standards of oncology nursing practice.* Pittsburgh, PA: Oncology Nursing Society.

Buerhaus, P., Staiger, D.O., & Auerbach, D.I. (2000). Implications of an aging registered nurse workforce. *JAMA, 283,* 2948–2954.

Cook, M.J. (2001). The renaissance of clinical leadership. *International Nursing Review, 48,* 34–36.

Gosling, J., & Mintzberg, H. (2003). The five minds of a manager. *Harvard Business Review, 81*(11), 54–63.

Ham, C. (2003). Improving the performance of health services: The role of clinical leadership. *Lancet, 361,* 1978–1980.

Institute of Medicine. (1999). *To err is human: Building a safer health system.* Washington, DC: National Academy Press.

Institute of Medicine. (2001). *Crossing the quality chasm.* Washington, DC: National Academy Press.

Institute of Medicine. (2003). *Health professions education: A bridge to quality.* Washington, DC: National Academy Press.

Joint Commission on Accreditation of Healthcare Organizations. (2002). *Health care at the crossroads: Strategies for addressing the evolving nursing crisis.* Oakbrook Terrace, IL: Author.

Kimball, B., & O'Neil, E. (2002). *Health care's human crisis: The American nursing shortage.* Princeton, NJ: Robert Wood Johnson Foundation.

Mintzberg, H. (1999, Spring). Managing quietly. *Leader to Leader, 12,* 24–30. Retrieved December 2, 2003, from http://l2li.org/leaderbooks/L2L/spring99/mintzberg.html

Porter-O'Grady, T., & Malloch, K. (2003). *Quantum leadership: A textbook of new leadership.* Sudbury, MA: Jones and Bartlett.

Royal College of Nursing. (2003). *A framework for adult cancer nursing.* Retrieved December 30, 2003, from http://www.rcn.org.uk/members/downloads/RCNCancerFrameworkAug2003.pdf

Webster's II new college dictionary. (2001). Boston: Houghton Mifflin.

Organizational Design and Structure

Mary L. Scott, RN, MS, OCN®
Janet Y. Harris, RN, MSN, CNAA

A well-designed and carefully executed planning process is the foundation for an overall strategy that can be used within a healthcare organization. This design format outlines a systematic process resulting in the development of all parts of the plan. The process includes the development of a mission statement, identification of goals and objectives, realistic policies and procedures, and the implementation of an effective plan (see Figure 5-1).

Figure 5-1. The Planning Process

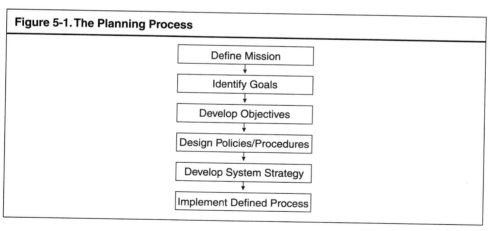

Mission and Philosophy

The mission of an organization articulates the overall role and purpose. The statement identifies the reason why the organization exists as well as the constituents it serves. It addresses the organizational position regarding ethics, principles, and relevant standards of practice. The statement itself should be broad enough to allow creativity but limited enough to provide guidance related to the specific activities required for implementation. Rowland and Rowland (1984) stated that prior to the development of the statement, four basic questions need to be answered: What is the business being planned?; What do customers (i.e., patients) need?; What will the organization be allowed to do?; and What financial and human resources are needed to do what needs to be done?

The mission statement is the highest priority in the planning process because it directs the philosophy, objectives, policies, procedures, and rules of the organization. The philosophy flows directly from the mission statement and outlines the ethics and values that guide the organization's values. The organizational philosophy provides the framework for development of the overall nursing and patient care unit philosophies. Although written in concert with the overall organizational philosophy, the nursing philosophy outlines the basic beliefs about nursing and patient care, the quality and scope of services, and methods for accomplishing organizational goals. At this point in the planning process, specific nursing models may be evaluated and included (Marquis & Huston, 2003). The philosophy can incorporate the leadership and practitioner vision of how nursing management and practice should be viewed in the organization. The philosophy for each patient care area then can be adapted from the general nursing philosophy. The unit or area philosophy should specify the way it relates to nursing and the overall organizational goals.

According to Brooks (2003), philosophy development can be an activity used for reengineering a nursing care delivery system. In this process, the group states a valued ideal and proposes methods that could make the ideal a reality.

Goals and Objectives

Following the development of the mission statement outlining the overall purpose, the goals and objectives detail the strategies needed to accomplish the mission. Goals outline the strategy, whereas objectives operationalize the strategy. A goal may be defined as the desired result toward which work activity is directed. Goals should change as the organization changes, and although global in nature, goals clearly delineate the end product. Healthcare organizations often set short-term and long-term goals that include new and ongoing services offered, customer (and patient) satisfaction, and resources required.

Objectives are similar to goals and direct individuals toward a specific outcome. Objectives are meant to be more specific than goals because they identify how and when specific actions will be accomplished. According to Pegels and Rogers (1998), if ". . . goal setting is a policy-making, agenda-building process, then objective setting is a management response of what will be achieved toward those goals in a specific time frame" (p. 32).

Objectives often are written in a one-year time frame, but some organizations use multi-year plans to achieve strategic goals. The more specifically an objective is defined, the easier it is for individuals to get involved and to clearly communicate the expected outcome. According to Rowland and Rowland (1984), well-written objectives should be measurable and have structured time lines and people responsible for completion identified.

Objective development generally is accomplished at the staff level but is a response to the corporate or hospital mission, philosophy, and goals. Objectives are the basis for measuring management success during the year and should be written in a way that evaluates progress at regular, consistent intervals. Clearly written goals and objectives must be effectively communicated throughout the organization. This is a vital role for the unit manager or leader. Well-developed and refined communication skills are required to involve staff at all levels, as well as to modify objectives, as needed, in relation to environmental changes.

Policies and Procedures

Policies provide an operational framework for organizational goals and objectives. Although some policies are required by regulatory and/or accrediting agencies, many are specific to an institution to promote internal control. Policies are written and available through an organization to encourage consistency of behavior and standardization of practice. Although executive level staff members are ultimately accountable for organizational policy, unit managers or leaders often are responsible for determining the process for implementation at the unit level. Feedback from staff during the development process is critical because their support and involvement is crucial. After policy has been developed, the manager or leader is again responsible to communicate the policy to the staff that will be affected.

Once policies are implemented in an institution, consistent administration of the policies is imperative. Fiesta (1993) stated that the healthcare worker can be held liable for failure to follow policies if a patient is harmed as the result of the failure. The courts have rejected the argument that policies are general goals; rather, the courts state that policies are required for consistency in care delivery. It is better for an institution to have no policy at all than to have those that are not consistently followed (Fiesta).

Procedures provide a guideline and outline of acceptable ways to accomplish a specific task. Procedures typically define the task in a step-by-step fashion, and manuals of current procedures can be found on each patient care unit. Involvement of direct caregivers in procedure development yields a better product and outcome. The unit manager is responsible for making sure that policy manuals are current and that care providers are informed of new or revised procedures. The manager or director also may be responsible for referring new procedures to a practice committee or seek counsel from the appropriate licensing organization if there are questions or concerns about what might be necessary.

Many hospitals and healthcare facilities are developing online/Intranet accessibility to policies and procedures. This can assist in information dissemination and provide quick access to the most current information needed.

Rules

Rules and regulations usually are included in organizational policy statements. They allow only one option or alternative. Few rules should exist within an organization; however, they should be consistently enforced, and appropriate discipline should be applied for violations.

Organizational Structure

Once the mission, goals, objectives, and policies and procedures have been developed, selection of an appropriate structure is necessary to facilitate and accomplish the mission. Definitions of how work is organized, how decisions are made, and the authority and responsibility of workers are defined by the organizational structure. The organizational structure depends on the services that need to be provided and a careful evaluation of the complexity of these services. Although the organizational structure may change, the key factor is that the structure must support the mission and philosophy of the organization.

Organizational structure and design most often are characterized by their formality, complexity, and centralization. Formality is the degree to which an organization has stated policies that define staff functions. Complexity addresses the division of labor, specialization of that labor, the number of levels, and the geography of the organizational units (Brooks, 2003; Steven, 2003). Centralization refers to the point at which decisions are made. In a centralized organization, decisions are made at the top and communicated downward. In a more decentralized structure, decision making occurs at staff levels and is communicated laterally and upward.

Variance in structure may exist, but three basic types are outlined in the literature: bureaucratic, matrix, and flat. These three basic types may be modified or combined into a hybrid model (Brooks, 2003; Steven, 2003).

Bureaucratic structures are formal, centralized, and hierarchical. Communication flows from the top of the organization to the bottom with little staff level involvement in either planning or decision making. Policies and rules dictate actions and limit individuality. This type of structure has been considered efficient in controlling workers and met specific needs when services were minimal and workers had a limited knowledge base. This structure is used in varying degrees, and staff may be given decision-making authority in some areas but not in others. These structures often are called "line" structures, and a vertical line on the organizational chart designates reporting and decision-making responsibility. Lines on the organizational chart connect to the central authority.

In this model, people in "line" positions are responsible for accomplishing the goals and objectives of the institution. In hospitals and other healthcare organizations, this includes RNs, licensed practical or vocational nurses, and assistive personnel. Staff positions provide support and advice but have no responsibility for the goals and objectives. The effectiveness of this structure is influenced by the clarity of the job descriptions. Line positions are indicated with solid lines, whereas staff positions are connected with dotted lines. Figure 5-2 demonstrates an example of a bureaucratic model.

Matrix structures have been effective in the current healthcare environment. Matrix structures combine bureaucratic and flat structures and enable rapid response to changes in the external environment. These structures have been demonstrated effectively in service line or product line models. Matrix structures use horizontal program management that is overlaid on a traditional hierarchical structure (see Figure 5-3). In this organization, a manager of a patient care area reports both to a functional manager and a product manager. The line manager and the product manager operate in a collaborative mode. Personnel from different functional departments report to two different bosses—the traditional department head and a program or product manager—creating an interdisciplinary team.

Within the matrix model, patient care is delivered collaboratively. A nurse reports to the nurse manager for patient care and to the product or project manager when working on projects or product line processes. Because of the complex relationships in this model, good communication and team-based skills are imperative.

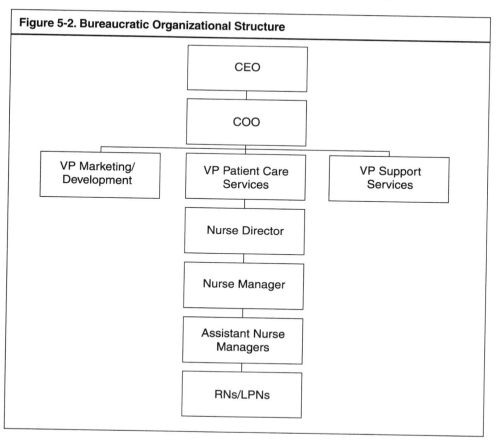

Figure 5-2. Bureaucratic Organizational Structure

In a *flat* organization, authority to act is at the action level. Decision making is delegated to the professional doing the work. This often is referred to as participatory management. It is "flat" because the hierarchical layers are removed. A decentralized structure provides staff with the ability to make decisions about care in a timely manner. There is no longer a need to pass requests up the formal chain of command to the centralized authority. Flat structures are less formal and have fewer policies and rules to dictate behavior. Individual decisions can be made to meet the needs of the particular patient and situation.

Figure 5-3. Matrix Organizational Structure

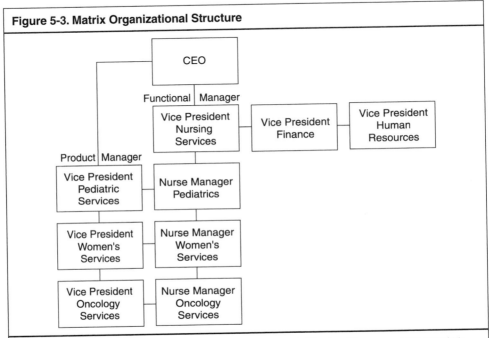

Note. From *Leadership Roles and Management Functions in Nursing: Theory and Practice* (4th ed.) (p. 171), by B.L. Marquis and C.J. Huston, 2003, Philadelphia: Lippincott Williams & Wilkins. Copyright 2003 by Lippincott Williams & Wilkins. Reprinted with permission.

In addition to the three basic models, a fourth alternative, *self-governance*, has gained considerable popularity in healthcare organizations in recent years. Self-governance is the result of defined structures that allow professionals to govern themselves. Professional accountability is the foundation of the model, and authority is given to each professional, allowing individuals to make decisions regarding all aspects of practice and patient care. Self-governance, also called a professional practice model (see Figure 5-4), goes beyond decentralization. Authority and autonomy are placed in appropriately defined areas. Staff nurses, for example, make decisions regarding nursing practice, and management staff function as facilitators. As might be expected, this model demands a different or higher level skill set. Relationship management and conflict resolution must be added to the traditional need for good interpersonal skills.

Although four different structures have been identified, it is important to note that certain situations may cause staff to respond in an alternative way. For example, an organization that operates in a self-governance structure may convert to a bureaucratic mode when an emergency arises. In an emergency situation, someone must be "in charge" and designated to make decisions quickly. In this instance, there is no time for a committee meeting to discuss possible alternatives for action. When the emergency situation is resolved, the staff can return to the normal processes that promote operating within the self-governance structure.

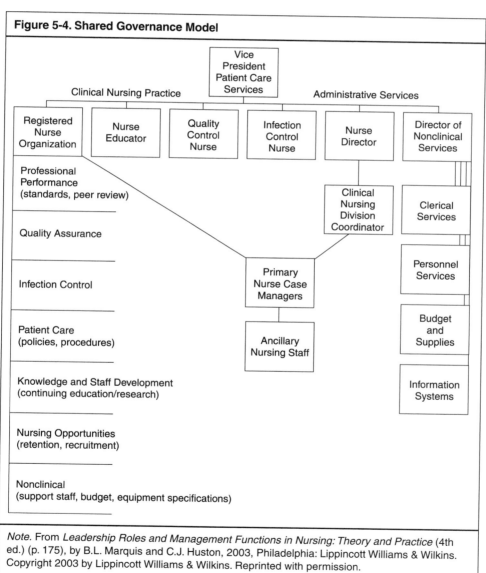

Figure 5-4. Shared Governance Model

Note. From *Leadership Roles and Management Functions in Nursing: Theory and Practice* (4th ed.) (p. 175), by B.L. Marquis and C.J. Huston, 2003, Philadelphia: Lippincott Williams & Wilkins. Copyright 2003 by Lippincott Williams & Wilkins. Reprinted with permission.

Delivery Systems and Models of Nursing Care

Several models and systems of nursing care have been developed that support improved quality patient care, effective use of resources, and staff growth and development. The development of these systems has been based on organizing and managing care in varying organizational settings and has combined concern for quality of care and the appropriate use of resources (Grohar-Murray & DiCroce, 2003).

The *case* method and *functional* method were early models of care, each with its own characteristics and design. In the early days of nursing, the nurse provided care to patients. Medication administration and treatments were done, and the patient's status was reported to the head nurse. The functional method of nursing care was used to provide care by many caregivers at different levels. Care was assigned by tasks, and nursing assistants and professional nurses had these task assignments based on education and experience. Care was fragmented, and staff was frequently dissatisfied. Team nursing developed after World War II, with teams of professional nurses, licensed practical nurses, nursing assistants, and orderlies organized into work groups to provide care to patients. Team leaders made assignments, delegated work, made rounds, and held end-of-shift conferences to evaluate care and update nursing care plans. Team nursing resulted in changes made to the nursing units. The team leader became responsible for the care of the patients, and the head nurse functioned in a decentralized manner, depending on the team leader to manage the team effectively. Team nursing represented a philosophy of nursing and a new method for patient care organization. The concern was that the nurse was not constantly present at the bedside, and the knowledge and attention of the nurse was directed toward other team members and away from the patient (Grohar-Murray & DiCroce, 2003).

Other models of nursing care evolved and have been based on the nature of the work to be performed and the evolution of healthcare systems. The development of primary nursing by Marie Manthey in the 1970s returned the nurse to being accountable for planning, providing, administering, communicating, and evaluating the care being provided to a group of patients. The principles of decentralization and empowerment and the involvement of the patient in decision making are hallmarks of this model (Manthey, 2001). In Manthey's view, ". . . primary nursing was a path to humanizing patient care by empowering staff nurses, who, in turn, could empower patients" (Manthey, p. 56). Based on providing total care, the establishment of therapeutic relationships, and 24-hour continuity through written care plans and communication with other care team members, primary nursing and the role of the RN in direct care have contributed the essential ingredients of the RN as a major participant in patient care delivery, regardless of the model or system being used (Manthey).

Case management is another method of nursing care delivery. It is a system of health assessment, planning, obtaining services, and delivery of those services, coordination of care, and ongoing monitoring that will meet the needs of patients and families. The system is designed to provide care that decreases fragmentation, maximizes the individualization of care, and can be provided in hospitals, ambulatory settings, and through home healthcare agencies. The case manager, often a nurse, follows a caseload of patients with specialized plans for each patient based on disease entity, resources available, and defined outcomes desired. This model improves the efficiency of the primary nursing model, continuing to create accountability and responsibility but also noting the response of the patient to specific therapies. A multidisciplinary comprehensive care plan is the source of the evaluation process and provides direction and communication to all participants providing care (Grohar-Murray & DiCroce, 2003).

Clinical and professional practice models currently are being explored and used. The clinical practice model and its use of guidelines support patient care delivery in a consistent manner by defining nursing services and practice and assisting in documenting the steps in the nursing process (Wesorick, 2002; Westmoreland, Wesorick, Hanson, & Wyngarden, 2000). The focus of the clinical practice model is an ". . . integrated interdisciplinary professional practice at the point of care" (Westmoreland et al., p. 17). The model seeks to define a practice infrastructure within a strong, healthy work culture that is positive for healthcare providers and the recipients of the care (Westmoreland et al.). Clinical practice guidelines are evidence-based and are quickly available where care is provided. These guidelines assist the nurse in critical thinking and the development of individualized patient care. Institutional and organizational procedures are used in conjunction with clinical practice guidelines to support nursing practice.

Accountability is a hallmark of the nursing models currently being developed and implemented. This characteristic places the professional nurse in the role of decision maker in providing patient care and allows the nurse to evaluate and monitor the patient's progress or condition in collaboration with the physician and other members of the healthcare team (O'Rourke, 2003). The accountability factor promotes the ethics of the providers and the responsibility of developing a knowledge base that is applicable to practice. It becomes the task of the accountable individual to request the training needed and master the skills necessary to be able to use the knowledge appropriately in rigorous decision-making process(es) (O'Rourke, p. 101). Organizational performance standards and performance and clinical practice standards are the components of the patient care model based on interdisciplinary professional practice (O'Rourke).

Healthcare Networks

During the past decade, changes in the social, political, and economic environments in the United States have led to major transformations in healthcare organizations. Upheaval in the insurance and financial environments has driven organizations to focus on improving patient outcomes by defining quality care and working to ensure patient satisfaction with every encounter (Clifford, 1998; Grohar-Murray & DiCroce, 2003). In addition, the increased use and expense of new technologies have created additional strains on healthcare systems.

In efforts to respond to these changes, many organizations have restructured relationships and made changes in how services are delivered. Integrated healthcare networks are being developed with the goals of decreasing costs and becoming more competitive in response to the growth in the managed care market, the decreases in reimbursement, and the imminence of capitation. Many observers believe that integrated healthcare networks provide solutions to the issues of delivering health care to meet consumer needs. In these networks, the primary objectives are to keep people healthy and treat them in the primary care setting, where costs will be the lowest (Grohar-Murray & DiCroce, 2003).

Consolidation has created networks composed of acute care hospitals partnering with primary care providers, same-day surgery centers, skilled nursing facilities, home health and hospice, and other types of outpatient and diagnostic organizations. In some geographic areas, this consolidation has resulted in formerly competing facilities now working together to provide incentives to patients and insurance providers, share in the financial risks, and continuously evaluate care provided through the organization based on standardized measures of patient satisfaction, cost, and quality. Reengineering and retraining, reduction in managers and some levels of management, and the use of data in decision making are characteristics that have marked the development of integrated healthcare systems (Grohar-Murray & DiCroce, 2003). An increase in market competition for healthcare dollars also has emerged.

The restructuring processes and the development of integrated networks have had an impact on nursing services in hospitals and other defined settings within the organization. Clifford (1998) believed that nurses have been less visible than physicians during these reorganizations, even though nurses are the largest group of healthcare professionals and critically important to the successful delivery of quality patient care. Clifford further elaborated on the "invisibility" of nursing in these processes by attributing this phenomenon to four factors: (a) the identity of nurses with hospitals and the idea that nurses are integrated into the general discussions of the restructuring process; (b) nurses are not independently financed; (c) the discipline of nursing is not recognized and independent from physicians; and (d) the female-dominated roles in nursing account for the lack of professional autonomy in relation to the predominately male physician group. The role of the chief nursing officer is critical to the emergence of nursing services as a dynamic and important part of the reorganization process. In this time of change, nursing clearly has the opportunity to make significant contributions to the success of these new and emerging care delivery systems. The use of the mass media can assist in this process and help focus attention on the role of the nurse in providing necessary high-quality care.

Governing Boards: Roles and Responsibilities

The role of the governing board of a healthcare institution is especially challenging in today's healthcare environment. This dynamic environment, coupled with the diverse and complex needs and expectations of those being served, and shared responsibilities are some of the challenges facing hospital leadership (Longest, Beaufort, & Darr, 1993).

Complex organizational structures and the relationships between the chief executive officer (CEO), governing body, and professional staff organizations (medical staff) have created interesting and diverse positions on critical issues. Governance, hospital administration, and medical staff have developed roles based on the type of organization and community services offered by a particular facility (Genovich-Richards, Gorenberg, & Deremo, 2000). The literature suggests that it is the role of management and the CEO to lead, and it is the role of the governing body ". . . to be supportive, to establish a current mission and the policies by which management will implement plans and programs to carry out the organizational mission" (Longest et al., 1993, p. 13). Boards have become involved in strategic planning; clinicians have been appointed as voting and nonvoting members; and the regulatory and accrediting agencies have pursued governance's responsibilities for quality and improved outcomes.

The need for healthcare administrators and governing boards to measure and improve clinical, financial, and patient satisfaction outcomes presents new possibilities for nurses to participate with governance. Genovich-Richards et al. (2000) believed that governance will regularly need to provide performance measurement outcomes for consumer use, conduct specific studies on interventions in care, and identify specific healthcare and social needs that will require provider resources.

Currently, the nurse executive frequently interacts with the board as part of the senior leadership staff. Nursing can provide board members with a structured orientation that includes information about nursing practices, performance improvement efforts, and the preparation and use of specific reports. In addition, quality improvement initiatives, the use of specific patient care examples when making a point, and the incorporation of data are a few ideas that can assist nurses when serving on a governing board, either in a hospital or for another healthcare organization (Genovich-Richards et al., 2000).

There is also a role for nurses to participate in community or patient advocacy organization boards. The specialized knowledge base regarding the continuum of care and how hospitals and healthcare organizations function can bring a rich experience to a community board. Shared values, an understanding of the healthcare environment in a community, and strong problem solving and communication skills make nurses ideal members for these boards. It is important to note that listening to different points of view from other community members, relationship building, and participating in cause-related fund-raising can be rewarding and satisfying experiences for a nurse with a desire to participate in a community activity.

Program Development and Market-Driven Strategies

One of the functions of health organizations and health professions is to provide services to meet the needs of specific groups and/or populations. Strategic planning processes are used to assist organizations and professions to evaluate and respond to changes in the healthcare environment. Outcomes that improve the health status of the populations designated are the measures of effectiveness that can be used to determine if a program has been successful. Careful strategic planning that develops an idea into a program is the preferred method that determines the overall purpose and direction of an organization. Strategic planning for a specific program is systematic and continuous and consists of a sequence of steps that begin by identifying and defining a problem, formulating strategies, and implementing solutions that lead to successful outcomes for a program (Glick & Thompson, 1999; Wheeler-Harbaugh, 2003; Zuckerman, 1998).

Drenkard (2001) suggested that before beginning the planning process, consideration should be given to the level of commitment from the organizational leadership that the project be a match with the organizational culture and that there is an ability to integrate the plan into action. Following the completion of this process, an initial step can be an evaluation of the originating organization's strengths and weaknesses. The skill of the medical staff, number of specialists that might be needed, the current reputation of the hospital and its existing programs, nursing expertise, available and planned technology, support services, and funding are all areas that need scrutiny. The support of hospital administration and its willingness to provide the necessary human and financial resources aimed toward a common goal can assist the program planners in presenting the plans initially to the hospital board and then to the community. A similar evaluation of any competitors also can be performed. External factors can include the existing market, area demographics, patient population trends, and current referral patterns for the population being evaluated (Konski, 1996). A needs assessment is a parallel process and consists of data collection, data analysis, and conclusions. The components of a needs assessment include

- An examination of previous programs that might be similar to the program under consideration
- Morbidity and mortality data that can provide information about the health problems of the groups in question
- Demographic data that reveal population size, age, race, sex, ethnicity, family structures, education, occupation, income, and health insurance status
- An examination of existing programs and resources so that duplication or gaps in services might be avoided
- An evaluation of community perceptions to evaluate support for the planned program and identify those who might be affected by the program
- An identification of legal constraints (e.g., professional practice, federal regulations, reimbursement issues, local ordinances)
- An evaluation of the political climate and identification of any environmental issues or trends that might have an impact on the project.

Following the data collection and analysis, the strategic planning process can proceed. The identification of the planning group is critical. It is important to involve key stakeholders who are able to commit time and energy to the process; however, care must be taken that the group be able to meet deadlines and carry out the necessary functions needed to design and implement the plan. The plan elaborates on the strengths and weaknesses of each hospital department as it might relate to the new enterprise. The process flows from the development of vision and mission statements to determining strategic objectives. Formulation, implementation, and evaluation of strategies then can be planned. The time frame should be three to five years, with an evaluation process that supports regular "revisits" of the plan and its original objectives.

If a community development approach is used, community members are encouraged to participate in the initial assessment, planning, and delivery of the services. This construct promotes support of the program by the target population and assists in the achievement of objectives (Glick & Thompson, 1999).

As strategies are developed, defined tactics, action plans, and measurements are needed (Drenkard, 2001). An accompanying business plan may be necessary to support the strategic planning process. A financial analysis can assist in determining the financial feasibility of the strategic plan by determining necessary projections, time lines for financial milestones, and additional evaluation criteria. It is important to determine if reimbursement might cover new services and what the long-term projections might be.

Service Line Leadership

The success of an organization depends on the ability of the leadership to instill in its members a common vision and the determination of the members to support and internalize the vision. The environment created by a nursing leader and the way the leader relates to the workforce are keys to success. It is important for leaders to establish goals, instill values into the organization, build the necessary coalitions, and respond to challenges and opportunities presented.

Several leadership models have been developed and discussed in the literature. Wolf's (2000) Transformational Model for Professional Practice in Healthcare Organizations has been developed as a framework to support an organizational approach to learning and development, with a focus on innovation and creativity. This model has significant implications for service line management, and its four components can promote and support the development of a specific program. The *professional practice component* encompasses transformational leadership, the care delivery system, professional growth, and collaborative practice. The *process component* emphasizes the need for "purposeful and deliberate critical thinking" (Wolf, p. 46) along with negotiation and decision making. These factors consider the needs of the patient, the use of professional recommendations, and the management of resources. The results of the process component bring about the *primary outcome component*. These outcomes support quality patient care, patient satisfaction, and caregiver satisfaction. The fourth or *strategic outcomes component* results in the willingness of the consumer to ". . . promote or engage in future relationships with the organization" (Wolf, p. 48). The implementation of this model requires an organized process that consists of determining the overall organizational vision, assessing the current reality, planning action, developing priorities, and carrying them through. With careful attention to the model, outcomes can be measured within the structure of the components described and progress attained.

Perra's (2000) Integrated Leadership Practice Model also lends itself to service line leadership. Based on defining fundamental leadership qualities, Perra proposed that the qualities will produce positive outcomes in staff nurses and promote job satisfaction, improvement in practice, and staff participation in enhancing the quality of patient care. The leadership qualities are self-knowledge, respect, trust, integrity, shared vision, learning, participation, communication, and the ability to be a change facilitator. Support from top-level management as well as the ability of frontline managers to develop efficient teams provide the foundations for this model. The implications for service line leadership can be seen in the achievement of improved efficiency and organization and, ultimately, patient satisfaction.

Another approach to service line leadership can be found in the principles developed by Studer (2003). Although developed for hospitals and large healthcare organizations, the changes proposed by this process can be easily applied to service line development. The process of taking an organization through a major change is based on "five pillars": service, quality, people, finance, and growth. Nine principles are explained: a commitment to excellence, measuring the important things, building a culture around service, creating and developing leaders, a focus on employee satisfaction, building individual accountability, aligning behaviors with goals and values, communicating at all levels, and recognizing and rewarding success (Studer). The culture changes also focus on the "must haves" of effective leader rounding, such as thank-you notes to staff, discharge phone calls to patients, key words at key times, aligning leader evaluations with desired behaviors, and employee selection and early retention (Studer). The implementation of these ideas and principles require major changes in behavior and frequent self-evaluations by the leadership. This approach, however, has been quite successful in many organizations and has been shown to be effective in promoting positive behaviors in hospital leaders, resulting in improvements in staff morale and, ultimately, direct patient care.

Summary

The role of nursing leadership in designing organizations and structures is well documented in the nursing literature. The current climate provides endless challenges and opportunities and will certainly require our creativity and commitment to sound and evidence-based nursing practice. Strong leadership, vision, organization, and communication can assist in building structures in which care can be provided. Strategies support innovation, and plans support how nurses work together, use resources, and obtain the outcomes desired. These concepts will help us define our future and its endless possibilities.

References

Brooks, C.A. (2003). Understanding and designing organizational structures. In P. Yoder-Wise (Ed.), *Leading and managing nursing* (pp. 139–149). St. Louis, MO: Mosby.

Clifford, J. (1998). *Restructuring: The impact of hospital organization on nursing leadership.* Chicago: American Hospital Publishing.

Drenkard, K. (2001). Creating a future worth experiencing: Nursing strategic planning in an integrated health care delivery system. *Journal of Nursing Administration, 31,* 364–376.

Fiesta, J. (1993). Legal aspects—standards of care: Part 1. *Nursing Management, 24*(7), 30–32.

Genovich-Richards, J., Gorenberg, B., & Deremo, D. (2000). The role of governance in improving clinical outcomes: Opportunities for nursing. *Nursing Administration Quarterly, 42*(2), 62–71.

Glick, D., & Thompson, K. (1999). Program and project management. In J. Lancaster (Ed.), *Nursing issues in leading and managing change* (pp. 483–504). St. Louis, MO: Mosby.

Grohar-Murray, M.E., & DiCroce, H. (2003). *Leadership and management in nursing.* Upper Saddle River, NJ: Prentice Hall.

Konski, A. (1996). Physician involvement and assessment in the development of hospital oncology programs. *American Journal of Clinical Oncology, 19,* 311–316.

Longest, J., Beaufort, B., & Darr, K. (1993). Organizational leadership in hospitals. *Hospital Topics, 71*(3), 11–15.

Manthey, M. (2001). Two miracles in one career. *Nursing Administration Quarterly, 25*(2), 55–60.

Marquis, B.L., & Huston, C.J. (2003). *Leadership roles and management functions in nursing: Theory and application* (4th ed.). Philadelphia: Lippincott Williams & Wilkins.

O'Rourke, M. (2003). Rebuilding a professional practice model: The return of role-based practice accountability. *Nursing Administration Quarterly, 27*(2), 95–105.

Pegels, C.S., & Rogers, K. (1998). *Strategic management of hospitals and healthcare facilities.* Rockville, MD: Aspen.

Perra, B. (2000). Leadership: The key to quality outcomes. *Nursing Administration Quarterly, 24*(2), 56–61.

Rowland, H.S., & Rowland, B.L. (1984). *Hospital administration handbook.* Rockville, MD: Aspen.

Steven, D. (2003). Strategic planning, goal setting, and marketing. In P. Yoder-Wise (Ed.), *Leading and managing nursing* (pp. 107–120). St. Louis, MO: Mosby.

Studer, Q. (2003). *Taking you and your organization to the next level.* Pensacola, FL: Studer Group Training Institutes.

Wesorick, B. (2002). 21st century leadership challenge: Creating and sustaining healthy, healing work cultures and integrated service at the point of care. *Nursing Administration Quarterly, 26*(5), 18–32.

Westmoreland, D., Wesorick, B., Hanson, D., & Wyngarden, K. (2000). Consensual validation of clinical model practice guidelines. *Journal of Nursing Quality, 14*(4), 16–27.

Wheeler-Harbaugh, J. (2003). Guest editorial: Strategic planning: Drafting your roadmap to success. *Gastroenterology Nursing, 26,* 93–95.

Wolf, G. (2000). Vision 2000: The transformation of professional practice. *Nursing Administration Quarterly, 24*(2), 45–51.

Zuckerman, A.M. (1998). *Healthcare strategic planning: Approaches for the 21st century.* Chicago: Health Administration Press.

Healthcare Economics

Corinne Haviley, MS, RN
Kathleen A. Ducey, MS, RN, AOCN®

The economics of our healthcare environment are dependent upon multiple factors, which include the production and consumption of income. The distribution of healthcare expenses has been studied globally and within communities and organizations to track, monitor, plan for, and control spent dollars. On a national level, the following is a description of key indicators that reflect how resources are reportedly being used and how dollars are being allocated.

U.S. healthcare expenditures represent 17% of the gross domestic product and have increased 69% between the years 1990 and 2000 (Ferman, 2003; Wilson, 2002). Fifty-four percent of the $1.3 trillion spent in 2000 was attributed to hospitals and physicians (Ferman; Wilson). See Figure 6-1 for the distribution of healthcare expenditures in 2000. Healthcare spending and growth rates have increased higher than the inflation rate and the consumer price index (Ferman; Wilson).

According to the National Institutes of Health, the overall cost of cancer in the United States in 2002 was estimated at $171.6 billion; $60.9 billion was allocated to direct medical costs, $15.5 billion was because of indirect morbidity (loss of productivity because of illness), and $95.2 billion was related to indirect mortality (loss of productivity because of premature death) (American Cancer Society, 2003). The four most common tumor types associated with total treatment expenditures are breast (13.1%), colorectal (13.1%), lung (12.1%), and prostate (11.3%) (National Cancer Institute, 2003).

Hospital and prescription drug spending has grown very rapidly, especially when compared to other components in health care. This escalation has stimulated the increased purchase of prescription drugs outside the United States. When the distribution of expenses is compared to the increased cost, as shown in Figure 6-1, prescription drugs appear to be disproportionately growing. This is especially concerning because prescription drugs (e.g., chemotherapy, antibiotics, growth factors, antiemetics) are a critical component in the care of patients with cancer and can be a significant financial burden. According to an outpatient cancer drug cost study analyzing pharmacy and outpatient professional claims, chemotherapy costs represented 76% of the increase in insurance claims from health maintenance organizations and commercial carriers in 1995 and 1998 (Halbert et al., 2002). The majority of patients with cancer receive some portion of care in hospitals, where expenses continue to rise.

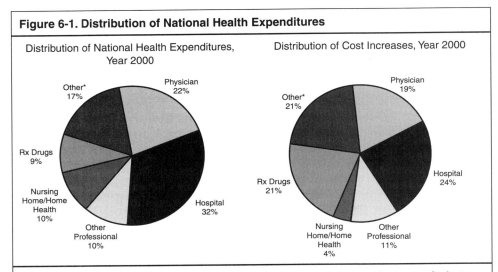

Figure 6-1. Distribution of National Health Expenditures

Distribution of National Health Expenditures, Year 2000

- Physician 22%
- Hospital 32%
- Other Professional 10%
- Nursing Home/Home Health 10%
- Rx Drugs 9%
- Other* 17%

Distribution of Cost Increases, Year 2000

- Physician 19%
- Hospital 24%
- Other Professional 11%
- Nursing Home/Home Health 4%
- Rx Drugs 21%
- Other* 21%

*"Other" is a collective category comprised of government administration and net cost of private health insurance, government public health activities, and non-prescription drug components of the retail outlet sales category (e.g., durable medical equipment, other nondurable medical products). Some 37% of the "other" category is comprised of administration (government administration and net cost of private insurance); this translates to administrative costs equal to 6% of total national health expenditures.

Note. Based on information from Department of Health and Human Services, 2002.

Medicare and Medicaid generally reimburse at a lower rate as compared to commercial insurance and self-paying policies. What is important to healthcare organizations is the proportion of commercial and self-paying patients versus those with Medicare/Medicaid because of the reimbursement rate differences. Therefore, it is important for healthcare organizations to know the proportion, as it affects income.

Commercial insurance pays for approximately 35.6% of hospital expenses. Public funds account for 60.5%, including Medicare (31.8%), Medicaid (16.3%), and others (12.4%). From a national perspective, in the United States, out-of-pocket and private funds account for the smallest proportion, equaling 3.9% (Department of Health and Human Services, 2002) (see Figure 6-2). The variability of payors can challenge organizations' overall financial strength.

The ever-changing business environment affects healthcare economics. The economic unpredictability because of the war in Iraq and national disasters such as September 11th has affected the United States. There has been a direct correlation with these incidents and the cost of transportation, oil prices, a diminishing return on investments, corporate bankruptcy, layoffs, and declining consumer confidence. Other major challenges such as severe workforce shortages, pharmaceutical costs, regulatory compliance requirements, error reduction and risk assessment initiatives, liability insurance, technology costs, disaster preparedness, and general healthcare reimbursement issues have had a considerable impact. Figure 6-3 represents a summary of the many current economic pressures experienced by healthcare organizations.

Figure 6-2. Distribution of National Health Expenditures by Source of Funds

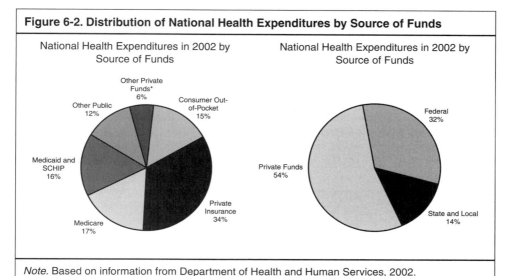

National Health Expenditures in 2002 by Source of Funds

National Health Expenditures in 2002 by Source of Funds

Note. Based on information from Department of Health and Human Services, 2002.

Figure 6-3. Economic Pressures

Severe workforce shortages—Salaries have risen as a result of shortages, especially for nurses, pharmacists, and technologists. Agency or traveling staff often cover vacant staff positions, further driving up the cost of care.

Increased cost of pharmaceuticals and blood products—Prescription drugs rose 17.3% in 2000. Blood transfusions increased by an average of 31% during that same year.

New Health Insurance Portability and Accountability Acts (HIPAA) regulations—Compliance with new federal regulations are imposing administrative and financial burdens (e.g., HIPPA privacy regulation due to the increased amount of paperwork and policy development).

New Accreditation Council for Graduate Medical Education regulations—Effective July 2003, resident work hours and resident training mandates will affect physician support within hospitals because of significant changes in practice.

Increased liability insurance—Professional liability insurance has had a 30% increase, which covers both hospitals and physicians during the past year.

Technologic improvements—Technology improvements have increased the purchase price and maintenance of equipment because of the complexity of new equipment (e.g., the cost of a general x-ray unit [$175,000] versus a CT scanner [$1,300,000] versus a PET imaging machine [$2,000,000]). The cost of a maintenance agreement on a standard mammography unit is $10,000 per year, whereas it costs $40,000 to cover a digital mammogram unit per year.

Disaster preparedness—Disaster readiness has required healthcare facilities to upgrade their preparedness to respond to and protect from biologic, nuclear, and chemical emergencies. These expenditures cost $11 billion in 2003.

Government reimbursement has not been adequate to cover cost—Government reimbursement is not keeping up with cost, especially for academic facilities. Medicare reimbursed hospitals 1% less than the cost of services in the year 2000. The Medicare payments are projected to be $18 billion less than cost in the year 2005. It is estimated that 65% of all hospitals will lose money on Medicare patients.

(Continued on next page)

Figure 6-3. Economic Pressures *(Continued)*

Uncompensated care has increased—Uncompensated care for the underinsured and/or uninsured population has added to the decrease in hospital revenue. In 2000, $21.6 billion of uncompensated care was reportedly delivered in the United Sates.

Priority investments are changing for many healthcare organizations—Historically, hospitals and agencies committed significant dollars to new construction, renovating, and purchasing diagnostic and therapeutic equipment (e.g., radiology equipment, surgical instruments). Organizations bill for services delivered in a new or renovated building or through the use of medical devices or equipment, which contribute to the profit. The information technology era has caused a shift in fund allocation as communication, imaging, medical records, and tele-medicine have become electronic. Revenue generated from information technology has limitations or may be nonexistent. Financial pressure has resulted because it is difficult to justify a return on these investments.

Note. Based on information from Cap Gemini Ernst & Young, 2003.

The following key factors support a stable outlook for the healthcare industry.

- Hospital use rate, advances in technology, and an increase in patient volume have led to a 3% annual growth rate as measured by not-for-profit hospital admissions in 2001 (Moody's Investor Service, 2002).
- A 9% revenue growth rate in 2001 was attributed to commercial reimbursement as the result of rising provisions and overall market performance (Moody's Investor Service).
- In spite of the cuts in reimbursement under the Balanced Budget Act of 1997, Medicare reimbursement is anticipated to improve (Department of Health and Human Services, 2002).
- Unprofitable services such as small clinics, underutilized services, and screening programs are being restructured, which has contributed to a positive hospital operation performance.

A Historical Look at Healthcare Reimbursement

To fully understand the current complexities of healthcare billing and reimbursement, it is helpful to take a step back and review the chronology and trajectory that make up this complex structure. Figure 6-4 is a timeline of events of the development and implementation of Medicare and Medicaid, the first national healthcare coverage for the elderly and the poor.

Out of this quagmire grew other national reimbursement strategies aimed at reducing the mounting cost of health care, including diagnosis-related groups (DRGs) and ambulatory patient classifications (APCs).

Diagnosis-Related Groups

DRGs were instituted in 1983 with the implementation of the Prospective Payment System for inpatients. The Health Care Finance Administration (HCFA) developed a classification system consisting of groups of services so that the services within each group would be comparable both clinically and with respect to the use of resources. HCFA established a "weighted payment" for each group based on median hospital costs and estimated frequencies of use of services. These groups are known as DRGs. Payments from Medicare to the hospital are determined based upon the patients' diagnosis and group of services in which this diagnosis falls.

Figure 6-4. Timeline of Events

Medicare

1935: National health insurance was discussed when the first government health insurance bill was introduced in Congress (s. 3253).

1965: The Social Security Act established Medicare and Medicaid for healthcare coverage for the elderly (Medicare) and the poor (Medicaid). Lyndon Johnson signed the Medicare Program into law.

1967: Nixon expanded Medicare to include the disabled receiving Social Security benefits and those with end-stage renal disease.

1965–1977: The Social Security Administration was responsible for administering Medicare.

1972: Public Law 92-603: Medicare required hospitals to establish a plan for utilization review to ensure that services provided were medically necessary. This act required a concurrent review of Medicare and Medicaid patients.

1973: The Health Maintenance Organization (HMO) Act provides start-up funds for HMOs by requiring employers to offer at least one HMO to employees.

1977: Medicare administration is now the responsibility of the Health Care Financing Administration (HCFA). President Johnson's original proposal does not cover outpatient or physician services. Congressman Wilbur Mills combines Johnson's proposal to cover institutional care, joining Medicare "Part A" with a voluntary program called Medicare "Part B" for outpatient and physician services.

1982: Peer Review Improvement Act redesigned the PRSO program to Peer Review Organization. At this time, hospitals began to review the appropriateness of admissions prior to hospital admission.

1983: Public Law 98-21: The prospective payment system for inpatient hospital care was implemented in October. Under this prospective payment system (PPS), reimbursement for hospital care to Medicare inpatients is based on a diagnosis-related group (DRG). Hospitals are reimbursed at a predetermined level of reimbursement, no matter how long the patient stays or how many services are provided.

1989: OBRA Omnibus Budget Reconciliation Act. Federal legislation was passed that mandated inpatient changes in the payment rules for Medicare physicians. This act established the Agency for Health Care Policy and Research. This agency was renamed in 1999 to Agency for Healthcare Research and Quality (AHRQ). AHRQ looks at issues related to healthcare quality, disease protocols, outcomes, and care delivery systems. Data gathered by this agency through its major initiative, the Healthcare Cost and Utilization Project, help develop quality indicators.

1997: The Balanced Budget Act required HCFA to implement a Medicare prospective payment system for certain healthcare services. This act was designed to assist in the development of a standardization of payment for comparable services. Section 4523 of the Balance Budget Act of 1997 provided authority for the Centers for Medicare and Medicaid Services (CMS) (formerly known as HCFA) to implement a PPS under Medicare for hospital outpatient services.

2000: HCFA's final rule for the new system is published in the Federal Register on April 7, 2000 (65RF18434). New system went into effect on August 1, 2000.

2001: HCFA was renamed CMS as a part of the initiative to create a new culture of responsiveness in the agency.

2003: Medicare Prescription Drug Improvement and Moderinzation Act of 2003: Implementation of a new Medicare fee schedule for drug reimbursement in the ambulatory setting.

Note. Based on information from LaTour & Eichenwald, 2002.

The positive effects of the DRG system are that hospitals know in advance the predetermined amount of payment that they will receive for each Medicare patient who has an inpatient stay. The implementation of the DRG system served as a catalyst in healthcare organizations to develop and improve outpatient services, including outpatient oncology services. Now, most patient care that was once delivered as an inpatient can be effectively and efficiently delivered as an outpatient.

After its implementation, DRGs had a significant effect upon Medicare expenditures for post-acute care benefits. Decreased reimbursement as a result of the DRG system has put a burden upon healthcare budgets. Because DRGs authorize payment for a pre-specified number of inpatient days based upon the diagnosis, inpatient patient lengths of stay have shortened dramatically, in some cases precipitating early discharges of patients who still may benefit from inpatient services.

Ambulatory Payment Classifications

As a direct result of the implementation of DRGs, ambulatory care services have developed rapidly and have grown exponentially in most healthcare organizations. Not unexpectedly, a prospective payment system for ambulatory services, similar to the inpatient prospective payment system of DRGs, was developed for hospital outpatient services in 2000.

All services paid under the new outpatient prospective payment system are classified into groups called APCs. Services in each APC are similar clinically and in terms of the resources they require. A payment rate is established for each APC. Depending on the services provided, hospitals may be paid for more than one APC for an encounter. The key to appropriate payment to hospitals for the services that they render is in careful billing and documentation of all of the outpatient services that they provide.

APCs were developed for the Medicare population by the government to encompass the full range of ambulatory settings, including same-day surgery units, hospital emergency rooms, and outpatient clinics. They represent ambulatory care across the entire potential patient population, not just Medicare patients. The APC system is designed to explain the amount and type of resources used in the ambulatory visit. Patients in each APC have similar clinical characteristics and similar resource use and cost. APCs do not address the physician's cost of care, phone contacts, home visits, nursing home services, or inpatient services.

Medicare Changes—Consumer Impact

Section 4523 of the Balanced Budget Act of 1997 changed the way beneficiary coinsurance is determined for the services included under the prospective payment service. As a result of these changes, the amount of co-insurance that patients must pay is calculated for each APC based upon 20% of the national median charge for services in that APC. The APC payment and the portion that patients must pay as co-insurance amounts are adjusted to reflect geographic wage variations. This represents a huge change in co-insurance payment potentials for patients and may significantly burden patients already on fixed incomes.

Medicare Effect on Outpatient Oncology Services

The prospective payment systems developed for inpatient (DRGs) and outpatient (APCs) services have dramatically impacted the resources available to healthcare organizations and have challenged organizations to develop greater efficiencies in the delivery of care.

Changes in the reimbursement rates of APCs continue to occur on a regular basis. For example, in 2003, Medicare issued changes that resulted in a 20%–30% decrease in reimbursement for hospital-based infusion centers (Oncology Roundtable, 2002).

The Overall Financial Impact: Attention to Detail in Outpatient Coding

A decrease in drug reimbursement along with an increase in expenses has greatly raised the scrutiny of oncology finances. This scrutiny translates into an increased importance upon correct billing, coding, and documentation during all points of patient contact to maximize the potential that all billable charges are being captured. The reimbursement system is dynamic and complex. Hospitals are challenged with keeping up with rapidly changing regulations as well as constantly changing coding and billing procedures.

Even when institutions develop sophisticated internal systems to capture charges, some services offered are "non-covered services." Medicare coding is known to change throughout the calendar year and requires constant attention by knowledgeable reimbursement professionals.

Examples of Drug Reimbursement Changes

An example of drug reimbursement changes is Medicare's regular change in coding and reimbursement and can be found in Table 6-1. On January 1, 2004, Medicare changed coding for chemotherapy administration. For example, Medicare no longer pays for Healthcare Common Procedure Coding System (HCPCS) Q0085, which included chemotherapy infusion the first hour and IV push. Medicare will accept Q0084 for IV infusion chemotherapy. If additional chemotherapy is administered (i.e., subcutaneous, intramuscular, or push), a charge code of Q0083 is used (Gledhill, 2004). The key for nursing management is to have an acute awareness of coding and charges and be alert to changes.

Administration Payments

In the final rule of 2003, the Centers for Medicare and Medicaid Services (CMS) lowered reimbursement rates for all administration of APCs (see Table 6-2). APC 120, infusion therapy except chemotherapy, decreased 27.9% in 2002. APC 352, level I injections, decreased 44.3%, and APC 359, level II injections, decreased 35.5% (Abbey & Abbey Consultants, Inc., 2002).

Table 6-1. Reimbursement Rates for Chemotherapy-Related Anemia Drugs (Example Only [Kansas City, KS])

Healthcare Common Procedure Coding System	Description	Ambulatory Payment Classification	2002 Payment	2003 Payment	Percent Change
Q0136	(Epoetin alfa) 1,000 units	733	$12.26	$9.10	25.8%
C1774	(Darbepoetin alfa), 1 mcg	734	$4.74	$2.37[a]	50.0%

[a] Derived from CMS conversion ratio (for billing purposes only) of 260 units: 1 mcg.

Note. Based on information from Federal Register, 2002.

Table 6-2. Chemotherapy Drug Administration Ambulatory Payment Classification Payment Rates (Example Only [Kansas City, KS])

APC	Description	2001 Payment Rate	2002 Payment Rate	2003 Final Payment Rate	Percent Change
116	Chemotherapy administration by other technique	$117.57	$46.32	$40.43	12.7%
117	Chemotherapy administration by infusion only	$92.45	$205.14	$187.98	8.4%

Note. Based on information from Oncology Roundtable, 2003.

Health Insurance Plans Other Than Medicare

Changes in national healthcare reimbursements often are followed by changes in private payor/third party reimbursement. Healthcare providers and consumers are faced with a multitude of health insurance plans, each with their own specific requirements. The popular health insurance plans (health maintenance organizations [HMOs] and preferred provider organizations [PPOs]) and associated provider challenges will be reviewed in the next segment.

Health Maintenance Organizations

In this healthcare plan, a fixed monthly fee is paid for healthcare services to covered enrollees, and a primary care physician (PCP) is chosen from a network of providers.

Enrollees are required to pre-select a PCP at the time of annual enrollment. The PCP is the first-line provider and will determine referrals (within a pre-approved network of healthcare providers) for specialized care when necessary.

Specialty Provider Challenges

The nurse manager must have a working understanding of requirements and limitations of various medical plans. Patients may need to be scheduled at different places for specific testing (e.g., MRI, CT) at freestanding imaging centers and laboratories in order to receive adequate/maximum entitled payment. PCP referral may need to be obtained for each test. Acquiring referrals, scheduling, testing, and obtaining results for a varied group of ancillary providers can be a challenge during the timely care of patients with cancer.

Preferred Provider Organizations

A group of physicians and hospitals work under one service umbrella to provide healthcare services to PPO participants at a discounted rate. The percentage of reimbursement depends on the healthcare policy and the previously established rate agreement with the provider. Participants are not required to choose a PCP and may choose any provider they wish. PPO enrollees are encouraged to select doctors within the PPO system; if they choose to seek care "out of network," they will incur higher co-payments.

Challenges to Providers

Providers are faced with the challenge of trying to keep all of the different plan requirements in mind from patient to patient, which can change annually and usually is tied to the patient's employment. In addition, providers are faced with understanding how changes in carrier requirements will affect their ability to provide and or coordinate care. Most oncology care providers will work with patients so care and diagnostic support will remain within network. If patients seek care outside of their insurance network, co-pays and co-insurance payments will be higher on the enrollees' part.

Nurses in independent practice are providers of health care. In ambulatory care centers, the nurse manager or administrator is involved in daily operations of the outpatient cancer care center, which must be supported by enough revenue or income to cover expenses associated with providing healthcare services. Revenue is money earned through the delivery of billable services, such as chemotherapy, injections, infusions, and patient teaching. Expenses are the costs associated with providing these services, such as drugs, supplies, and staff. Several chapters in this book provide in-depth information on financial healthcare management.

Historically, nurses have been known to "not charge" patients for supplies and services. With the decrease in reimbursement over the past two decades from Medicare and other providers, it is essential that nurses charge for all services and supplies. The nurse manager is responsible for monitoring the expenses of clinical operations.

The manager must educate the staff on the importance of maintaining a balanced budget and teach the healthcare team to

- Report all services provided to the patient.
- Document all services performed. If it was not documented, it was not done.

Services provided are assigned current procedural terminology (CPT) codes (American Medical Association, 2003). Each CPT code has an attached amount that is billable to the patient. For example, 96408 is the CPT code for administration of chemotherapy by IV push (HCPC-Q0083). In 2003, the charge associated with this service was $80. First hour of IV chemotherapy was $175.

It is essential for the documentation be present to support the code so the bill may be processed. Nurse managers and oncology coders must monitor billing and charge code practices carefully to maximize timely reimbursement, minimize claim denials, and, above all, prevent the appearance of healthcare billing fraud. The Medicare Prescription Drug Improvement and Modernization Act of 2003 is bringing additional changes to the Cancer Care Delivery System. Until January 2004, physician office practices were reimbursed at 95% of the AWP. Since January 2004, payments for chemotherapy drugs have been reduced by 10%–15%, while payments for administration of chemotherapy drugs have increased. Additional reductions for chemotherapy drugs are scheduled for 2005 and 2006. Payments for chemotherapy administered in the hospital setting differs from the physician practice and is based on cost of acquisition pricing. Beginning in 2006, payments to hospitals will be based on a survey for hospital drug acquisition prices. The Government Accountability Office, a government agency, will conduct the survey (Bailes & Coleman, 2004).

Implications for Nursing Practice

Nurse managers must assist their staff to charge correctly and to understand the implications of a missed or incorrect charge. Staff meetings may be used to update everyone on the latest external (Medicare) or internal (finance) charge changes. Additionally, an annually updated policy and procedure or guideline on correct charging and billing practices is essential. Remember

- Many supplies are no longer paid separately.
- Ancillary staff are able to bill for services rendered using E and M codes in the hospital outpatient setting.
- Documentation must support services rendered.
- Charges can be denied if the CPT on the claim is incorrect or missing. All charges, including chemotherapy drugs provided, pumps, IV fluids, and needles, must be included or Medicare may not pay for the services.
- Services such as infusions and procedures must be attached to a correct code.

Case Study

Linda S., a 52-year-old patient, has arrived in the outpatient oncology clinic for her first visit following lumpectomy and lymph node dissection. Linda had an implanted port placed for chemotherapy in the special procedures department last week. Linda then was scheduled for chemotherapy administration the following week. At her first visit, the nurse practitioner completed chemotherapy teaching, and Linda was sent to the treatment area for her chemotherapy infusion. On arrival, her port is accessed, fluids started, and treatment given. Documentation was completed using the treatment nursing flow sheet. Charges for nursing care were entered in the charge entry system.

Documentation

Documentation is key to appropriate and maximized reimbursement. The nurse manager may use a number of sources to monitor compliance and determine strategies for improvement. This includes performing chart reviews and monitoring billing forms.

Documentation using a patient flow sheet (see Figure 6-5) can be helpful in triggering thoughts regarding what was used during that visit. Additional narrative to support extended patient care is essential. In the case of Linda S., the expanded chemotherapy teaching can be written in the notes section, or a teaching plan can be used.

Charge Forms

Charge forms must be linked to the institution's current chargemaster (see Figure 6-6). Correct ICD-9 and CPT coding are essential for complete and timely payment of services provided to patients. Each service or procedure provided is linked to a code and a pre-determined payment amount. If the incorrect code is entered, the result may be a decreased reimbursement amount or denial of payment.

Documentation to Support Billing Services

Documentation in the patient record has become increasingly important to support the billing process in addition to the clinical requirements relative to optimum patient care. Radiation therapy departments and facilities can charge for nursing care when it includes educating and treating patients. For example, when patients initially present to determine if radiation therapy is a treatment option, charges may be issued. Further, throughout the course of treatment, when nurses administer select injections such as amifostine or provide wound care, charges may be appropriate. The key, however, is to ensure that there is a physician order and clear nursing documentation to support the care delivered.

In radiation therapy, typically nurses see the patient upon initial consult to conduct a nursing assessment and educate the patient and family regarding the overall treatment experience and potential effects from therapy. This process can take anywhere from 30 minutes to one hour, depending upon the depth of information delivered and the patient's ability to learn. Nurses generally conduct a weekly assessment separate from physician clinic visits to determine patient needs, observe for side effects, and determine the effectiveness of interventions throughout the course of treatment. A separate E and M code may be used to charge for the nurse's care. Two points to remember are (a) facility charges for an E and M code (i.e., 99211–99215) must be billed on the UB92 form. If they are billed on the 1500 form, they will cross as a physician charge, not the facility's charge for nursing care; and (b) weekly nursing visits using the E and M facility fee may not, in 2004, be charged on the same day a patient receives a radiation treatment. Skin changes frequently require nursing care, which depends upon the treatment site and patient condition. Check with your local fiscal intermediary for Medicare to be certain your charges are reimbursable.

Figure 6-5. Cancer Center Nursing Documentation Sheet

Cancer Center
Nursing Documentation Sheet

Linda S
DOB 02/05/52

ADMISSION Ht 6'3" Wt 140	**Date:** 03-06-04 0930 Reason For Visit: Chemotherapy AC [X] Ambulatory [ ] W/C Time/RN: 10:46

ASSESSMENT	**WNL**	**See Notes**
Neuro - Alert, Orient x 4, Appropriate		
Neuro - Sensation intact, Gait Steady		
CV - Heart, R/R, pulses		
Pulmonary - Lungs Clear, No Cough, SOB		
GI - Oral - Appetite/Taste Alterations/wt		
GI - Nausea/Vomiting/Diarrhea/Constipation		
GU - Dysuria/Frequency		
Integumentary - Skin Warm, Dry, Intact		
Fatigue	0 - (1) - 2 - 3 - 4 - 5 - 6 - 7 - 8 - 9 - 10	
Pain Rating (0 = No pain) Location	(0) - 1 - 2 - 3 - 4 - 5 - 6 - 7 - 8 - 9 - 10	
Psychosocial: alterations in coping, learning	[x] Coping WNL [x] See Notes	
Environmental Factors		
Self Care Factors		
Standard of Care Initial Chemo RX	[x] Chemotherapy [ ] Pain Management [ ] Blood Product Tx [ ] Other ____	

Allergies	O2 Sat	**Vital Signs**		
PCN		Time: 11AM		
		T= 97.8		
		P= 80		
		R= 20		
		BP= 120/76		

RN/CA Signature	Initials/Print Name KD *Kathy Ducey*

NOTES:

* Chemotherapy teaching completed by Susan Allen, ARNP (see Teaching Record)
* CBC - Hgb 13.0, ANC 2500
* Patient did well during initial treatment - expressing fear over inpending Alopecia.

Information on head coverings and wigs given to patient.

* Appointment with LCMSW Jan set up for next Tuesday following her CBC.

(KD)

Continued on Back

CVC
- [ ] Hickman
- [ ] Infusaport
- [x] Pas-Port
- [ ] PICC
- [ ] Groshong
- [ ] Vas-cath
- [ ] Hepatic Artery Cath
- [ ] Other

- [ ] Dressing Dry & Intact
- [ ] Dressing Changed:
  Alcohol/Betadine
  Hibiclens/Neosporin
  Other:
  Site Clear [x] Yes [ ] No
  Sutures Intact [ ] Yes [ ] No
- [ ] Sutures Removed
- [ ] Cap Change
- [x] Port Access
- [x] Blood Return
- [ ] Huber Needle Change

Peripheral IV
- [ ] Skin Prep for IV Start
Site:
____g Cath ____g Butterfly
By: ____ R.N

Vesicant Administration
- [x] Vesicant Precautions
- [x] Blood return before, during & after admin.

Infusion Pump [x] Yes [ ] No

PATIENT EDUCATION

I = Initial
R = Review
W = Written

___ Disease:
_X_ Chemotherapy:
___ Radiation
___ Radiation Site:
___ Diagnostic Tests:
CBC & Chem 7
_X_ Medications:
See MAR
_I_ Nutrition
_I_ Mouth Care
_I_ Neutropenia
_I_ Thrombocytopenia
___ CVC
___ Sm Infusion Pump
___ Pain Management
___ Procedure/Surgery
___ Transfusions
___ Sexual Dysfunction
___ Other:

Patient Responses:
- [x] Patient verbalized understanding
- [x] See Note
- [ ] Pt/Fm have name/phone # of contact person

DISCHARGE PLANNING

Plan for Next Visit:
CBC Weekly
RTC for next Chemo in 2 weeks

DISCHARGE

Time/RN: KD 1130
- [x] Ambulatory [ ] W/C
- [ ] Home [ ] Home Infusion
- [ ] Phone # for assistance
- [ ] Return appointment confirmed
- [ ] Hospital, Report called
- [ ] Summary note written

Figure 6-6. Cancer Center Charge Sheet

Cancer Center
Examination/Treatment
Charge Sheet

Date: 3/6/200X

Time In: 0930   Time Out: 1130

		VACCINE/TRANSFUSION	
	60301843	Admin of influenza vaccine	90471
	60302064	Admin of Hepatitis B Vaccine	90471
	60302056	Admin of Pneumococcal vaccine	90471
	60301819	Transfusion of Blood/Platelets	36430
		CHEMOTHERAPY	
	60301900	Chemo Admin, Sub-Q or IM (1 per visit)	Q0083
X	60301918	Chemo Admin, IV Push (1 per visit)	Q0083
X	60301926	Chemo Infusion, 1st Hour	Q0084
	60301934	Chemo Infusion, Ea Add'l Hour	Q0084
	60302098	Chemo Via Ommaya Reservoir	95990
		NON-CHEMOTHERAPY	
	60301835	Non-Chemo Injection, Sub-Q or IM	90782
	60301884	Infusion Non-Chemo, 1st Hour	Q0081
	60301892	Infusion Non-Chemo, Ea Add'l Hour	Q0081
		LAB	
	60301470	Blood Draw	G0001
X	60301223	CVC blood draw	36540
		HEPARIN FLUSHES	
	60420502	Heparin Inj 500UN(PED)	J1644
	60420478	Heparin Inj 2,500UN(ADULT)	J1644
		VISITS	
	60301330	New/Old Patient (Statistic)	Stat
	60301249	Second Opinion Consult (Statistic)	Stat
	60301561	E&M New Pt - Level I (Minimal)	9920125
	60301579	E&M New Pt - Level II (Limited)	9920225
X	60301587	E&M New Pt - Level III (Expanded)	9920325
	60301595	E&M New Pt - Level IV (Detailed)	9920425
	60301603	E&M New Pt - Level V (Comprehensive)	9920525
	60301611	E&M Established Pt - Level I (Minimal)	9921125
	60301629	E&M Established Pt - Level II (Limited)	9921225
	60301637	E&M Established Pt - Level III (Expanded)	9921325
	60301645	E&M Established Pt - Level IV (Detailed)	9921425
	60301652	E&M Est. Pt - Level V (Comprehensive)	9921525
	60301660	Interdisciplinary Meeting	G0175
		PROCEDURES FOR EXAM/TREATMENT	
	60301983	Bx Breast, with Guidance	19102
	60301975	Ultrasound Guidance	76942
	60301991	Bx Breast, w/o Guidance	19100
	60301389	Colposcopy	57452
	60301876	Colposcopy Cervix w/ Biopsy	57455
	60301868	Colp Cervix w/Biopsy & Curret	57454
	60302015	FNA with Guidance	10022
	60301975	Ultrasound Guidance	76942
	60302007	FNA without Guidance	10021

		PROCEDURES FOR EXAM/TREATMENT (CONT.)	
	60301272	Lumbar Puncture, Diagnostic	62270
	60302031	Debridmnt, Non-Sel/Dressing Ch	97602
	60302049	Debridement Sharp Selective	97601
	60302080	Port Maint ONLY inc Hep Flush	90784
	60301421	Paracentesis, Initial	49080
	60301967	Paracentesis, Subsequent	49081
	60302023	Puncture Asp Seroma/Hematoma	10160
	60301439	Thoracentesis	32000
		PROCEDURE ROOM	
	60800034	Bladder washing	51700
	60800356	Bone Marrow Biopsy	38221
	60800364	Bone Marrow, Aspiration Only	38220
	60800497	Bx Breast, with Guidance	19102
	60800471	Ultrasound Guidance	76942
	60800505	Bx Breast, w/o Guidance	19100
	60800430	Bx, Prostate Needle Punch	55700
	60800471	Ultrasound Guidance	76942
	60800257	Central Line Removal	36535
	60800042	Chest tube placement	32002
	60800489	Conscious Sedation	99141
	60800059	Cystoscopy Flex w/ Visual Aid	52000
	60800562	Cystoscopy, Rigid	52000
	60800570	Cystoscopy, Flexible	52000
	60800463	Cystourethroscopy,Remov Stent	52310
	60800547	Debridment, Non-Sel/Dressing Ch	97602
	60800554	Debridement, Sharp Selective	97601
	60800448	Dilat Urethra, Female, Init'l	53660
	60800455	Dilat Urethra, Female, Subseq	53661
	60800240	Dilation Urethra, Male, Initial	53600
	60800422	Dilation Urethra, Male, Subseq	53601
	60800091	Exc Biopsy, Single Lesion	11100
	60800588	Exc Biopsy, 1st Lesion w/Cautery	11100
	60800406	Exc Biopsy, Ea Add'l Lesion	11101
	60800521	FNA with Guidance	10022
	60800471	Ultrasound Guidance	76942
	60800513	FNA without Guidance	10021
	60800026	Bladder Instillation	51720
	60800315	LEEP	57522
	60800372	Lumbar Puncture, Diagnostic	62270
	60800117	Paracentesis, Initial	49080
	60800414	Paracentesis, Subseq	49081
	60800539	Puncture Asp Seroma/Hematoma	10160
	60800216	Thoracentesis	32000

Consider the case studies depicting a patient undergoing radiation therapy. Consider the two different documentation scenarios to support billing practices.

Case Study

Jeannine L. is a 52-year-old female diagnosed with stage II breast cancer. Her pathologic staging is T2N1M0 adenocarcinoma, estrogen receptor and progesterone receptor negative. She underwent a lumpectomy with sentinel node biopsy, which was positive. Subsequently, she had an axillary node dissection with one node positive. Postoperatively, she received four courses of chemotherapy and reportedly did well throughout the treatment.

Jeannine L. has no other significant health problems. She is postmenopausal and taking Fosamax® (Merck, Whitehouse Station, NJ) 70 mg per week for osteopenia and oral calcium supplements weekly. She is married with two daughters, one a freshman in college and the other a sophomore in high school. Her support system is reportedly good; however, she has demonstrated increased anxiety related to initiating radiation treatments.

Initial Consult—Part I

Decision Tree

Choose favorable documentation that supports an initial consult with the intent to start radiation therapy. Please choose the optimal documentation.

Scenario A

PATIENT Jeannine L	MR#/RT# 555555	DATE 06/23/200X

RADIATION THERAPY PATIENT CARE RECORD—BREAST

Site	Right Upper Quad 12pnt	Surgical Procedure		Lumpectomy
Histology	Adeno	Recurrence (Y / N) Location	N	
Grade/Stage	II/II	Genetic Counseling (Y / N)	N	
ER/PR Status	Neg	Protocol		None
HER-2 Status	Neg	Other		
Menopausal Status	Post			

Dates		06/23/200X								
(cGy or Gy) / Fx										
Comfort Alteration KPS		100%								
Fatigue		1								
Pain Location										
Pain Intensity										
Pain Intervention		0								
Effectiveness of Pain Intervention										
Hot Flashes/Flushes										
Nutrition Alteration Anorexia		0								
Weight		0								
Skin Alteration Skin Sensation		0								
Radiation Dermatitis										
Mucous Membrane Alteration Drainage		0								
Drainage Odor										
Lymphedema Upper Arm	RT									
(____ cm above elbow)	LT									
Lymphedema Lower Arm	RT									
(____ cm below elbow)	LT									
Emotional Alteration Coping		0								
Sexuality Alteration		0								
Injury, Potential	Date	0								
Bleeding/Infection										
WBC										
Hemoglobin/Hematocrit										
Platelets										
Vital Signs TPR		96.9-80-20								
BP		120/80								
Other										
INITIALS										

Copyright © 2002, Oncology Nursing Society. Used with permission.

Assessment Parameters and Common Toxicity Criteria
Radiation Therapy Patient Care Record—Breast

COMFORT ALTERATION

Karnofsky Performance Score (KPS)
100% Normal, no complaints
90% Can perform normal activity, minor signs of disease
80% Can perform normal activity with effort, some signs of disease
70% Cannot do active work, but can care for self
60% Requires assistance, but can meet most needs with assistance
50% Requires considerable assistance and frequent medical care
40% Disabled, requires special care
30% Severely disabled, hospitalization indicated
20% Very sick, supportive hospitalization needed
10% Moribund, fatal processes progressing rapidly

Fatigue (ONS scale)
1 No fatigue
2 Mild fatigue
3 Moderate fatigue
4 Extreme fatigue
5 Worst fatigue

Pain Location
Write, in the box, the location of pain.

Pain Intensity
Record the patient's subjective rating of degree of pain, with ratings ranging from 0 (no pain) to 10 (severe pain).

Pain Intervention[c]
0 None
1 Over-the-counter medications
2 Nonsteroidal anti-inflammatory agents or non-opioids
3 Opioids
4 Adjuvant medication (e.g., neuroleptics [amitriptyline, carbamazepine])
5 Complementary and/or alternative methods

MUCOUS MEMBRANE ALTERATION

Drainage[c]
0 Absent
1 Present

Drainage Odor[c]
0 Absent
1 Present

EMOTIONAL ALTERATION

Coping[c]
0 Effective
1 Ineffective

Effectiveness of Pain Intervention[c]
0 No relief
1 Pain relieved 25%
2 Pain relieved 50%
3 Pain relieved 75%
4 Pain relieved 100%

Hot Flashes and/or Flushes[a]
0 None
1 Mild or no more than 1 per day
2 Moderate and greater than 1 per day
3 —
4 —

NUTRITION ALTERATION

Anorexia[a]
0 None
1 Loss of appetite
2 Oral intake significantly decreased
3 Requiring IV fluids
4 Requiring feeding tube or parenteral nutrition

SKIN ALTERATION

Skin Sensation[b]
0 No problem
1 Pruritus
2 Burning
3 Painful

Radiation Dermatitis[a]
0 None
1 Faint erythema or dry desquamation
2 Moderate to brisk erythema or patchy moist desquamation, mostly confined to skin folds and creases; or moderate edema
3 Confluent moist desquamation ≥ 1.5 cm diameter and not confined to skin folds; pitting edema
4 Skin necrosis or ulceration of full-thickness dermis; may include bleeding not induced by minor trauma or abrasion

SEXUALITY ALTERATION

0 Absent
1 Present

The cited parameters were established by
[a]National Cancer Institute (NCI) Common Toxicity Criteria, Version 2.0
[b]Radiation Therapy Oncology Group (RTOG), Version 2.0 or the RTOG SOMA Scales
[c]Oncology Nursing Society Radiation Documentation Tool Workgroup

Patient Education Documentation

Patient _Jeannine L_

MR#/RT#_ 555555 _

CODES

Barriers	Response	Follow-Up
A. Physical Limitations	S States essential concepts	1. Teaching complete
B. Language Barrier	PV States or performs c verbal cues	2. Reinforce teaching
C. Cognitive Limitation	PI Performs independently	3. Reteach
D. Religious/Cultural Practices	PA Performs c physical assistance	4. Teaching post-discharge
E. Emotional Barriers	O Offered and refused teaching	5. Case Management
F. Desire/Motivation	N No evidence of learning	
G. Pain/Discomfort	PN See progress note	
H. None		

Active Patient Problem/Need requiring Intervention during treatment	Contact/ MD Order	Expected Outcome/ Goal with time frame	Approaches/ Interventions	EDUCATION Date/Initials	Barriers	Response/ Follow-up	Date/Initials	Barriers	Response/ Follow-up
General Radiation Education Discuss purposes and effects of Radiation Therapy				06/23/xx CH	H	S/2			
Explain the importance of discussing with physician any new medications				06/23/xx CH	H	S/2			
Describe why aspirin and aspirin containing products should be avoided				06/23/xx CH	H	S/2			
Discuss when to call Radiation Oncologist e.g. temp>100°, chills, diarrhea, pain, flu symptoms, etc.				06/23/xx CH	H	S/2			
Explain radiation treatment schedule e.g., number of treatments				06/23/xx CH	H	S/2			
Provide resource information. Bill of Rights, radiation brochure, ACS, etc.				06/23/xx CH	H	S/2			
Identification, prevention and treatment of side effects discussed: Nausea/Vomiting				06/23/xx CH	H	S/2			
Anorexia				06/23/xx CH	H	S/2			
Dehydration				06/23/xx CH	H	S/2			
Constipation				06/23/xx CH	H	S/2			
Diarrhea				06/23/xx CH	H	S/2			
Infection				06/23/xx CH	H	S/2			
Bleeding				06/23/xx CH	H	S/2			
Anemia				06/23/xx CH	H	S/2			
Fatigue				06/23/xx CH	H	S/2			
Alopecia				06/23/xx CH	H	S/2			
Stomatitis				06/23/xx CH	H	S/2			
Esophagitis				06/23/xx CH	H	S/2			
Flu Symptoms				06/23/xx CH	H	S/2			
Skin change				06/23/xx CH	H	S/2			
Pain (0-10 scale)				06/23/xx CH	H	S/2			
Neurological changes									
Bladder irritability									
Allergic reactions									
Other									
Medications Administration, dose, purpose, side effects, potential Food/Drug interactions. Expected response. Signs and symptoms to be reported to MD	Start Date	DC Date							
Fosomax 70mg POq week									

Scenario B

Progress note:
Patient seen for initial consult for treatment. Reviewed treatment plan and set patient up for simulation.

Corinne Haviley, RN

Note. From *Radiation Therapy Patient Care Record: A Tool for Documenting Nursing Care*, by C. Catlin-Huth, M. Haas, and V. Pollock (Eds.), 2002, Pittsburgh, PA: Oncology Nursing Society. Copyright 2002 by the Oncology Nursing Society. Reprinted with permission.

Discussion

A comprehensive overview of patient education and assessment is preferred to support an initial consult. The amount of detailed information also supports the time required to deliver the care. History is important; however, preparation for treatment is very important from an educational perspective.

During Treatment—Part II

Decision Tree

Six weeks into therapy, Jeannine develops an axillary skin reaction requiring intervention. The nurse conducts an assessment and teaches the patient how to apply Vigilon® (Bard, Inc., Murray Hill, NJ). Please choose the optimal documentation.

Scenario A

PATIENT Jeannine L   **MR#/RT#** 555555   **DATE** 06/23/200X

RADIATION THERAPY PATIENT CARE RECORD—BREAST

Site	Right Upper Quad 12pnt	Surgical Procedure		Lumpectomy
Histology	Adeno	Recurrence (Y / N) Location	N	
Grade/Stage	II/II	Genetic Counseling (Y / N)	N	
ER/PR Status	Neg	Protocol		None
HER-2 Status	Neg	Other		
Menopausal Status	Post			

Dates		06/23/200X				08/10/200X				
(cGy or Gy) / Fx										
Comfort Alteration										
KPS		100%				100%				
Fatigue		1				1				
Pain Location										
Pain Intensity		0				4				
Pain Intervention						Vigilon				
Effectiveness of Pain Intervention										
Hot Flashes/Flushes						2				
Nutrition Alteration										
Anorexia		0				0				
Weight		0				0				
Skin Alteration										
Skin Sensation		0				0				
Radiation Dermatitis						3				
Mucous Membrane Alteration										
Drainage		0				1				
Drainage Odor						0				
Lymphedema Upper Arm	RT									
(____ cm above elbow)	LT									
Lymphedema Lower Arm	RT									
(____ cm below elbow)	LT									
Emotional Alteration										
Coping		0				0				
Sexuality Alteration		0				0				
Injury, Potential	Date	0				0				
Bleeding/Infection										
WBC										
Hemoglobin/Hematocrit										
Platelets										
Vital Signs										
TPR		96.9-80-20				98.6-82-16				
BP		120/80				118-72				
Other										
INITIALS										

Assessment Parameters and Common Toxicity Criteria
Radiation Therapy Patient Care Record—Breast

COMFORT ALTERATION

Karnofsky Performance Score (KPS)
100% Normal, no complaints
90% Can perform normal activity, minor signs of disease
80% Can perform normal activity with effort, some signs of disease
70% Cannot do active work, but can care for self
60% Requires assistance, but can meet most needs with assistance
50% Requires considerable assistance and frequent medical care
40% Disabled, requires special care
30% Severely disabled, hospitalization indicated
20% Very sick, supportive hospitalization needed
10% Moribund, fatal processes progressing rapidly

Fatigue (ONS scale)
1 No fatigue
2 Mild fatigue
3 Moderate fatigue
4 Extreme fatigue
5 Worst fatigue

Pain Location
Write, in the box, the location of pain.

Pain Intensity
Record the patient's subjective rating of degree of pain, with ratings ranging from 0 (no pain) to 10 (severe pain).

Pain Intervention[c]
0 None
1 Over-the-counter medications
2 Nonsteroidal anti-inflammatory agents or non-opioids
3 Opioids
4 Adjuvant medication (e.g., neuroleptics [amitriptyline, carbamazepine])
5 Complementary and/or alternative methods

MUCOUS MEMBRANE ALTERATION

Drainage[c]
0 Absent
1 Present

Drainage Odor[c]
0 Absent
1 Present

EMOTIONAL ALTERATION

Coping[c]
0 Effective
1 Ineffective

Effectiveness of Pain Intervention[c]
0 No relief
1 Pain relieved 25%
2 Pain relieved 50%
3 Pain relieved 75%
4 Pain relieved 100%

Hot Flashes and/or Flushes[a]
0 None
1 Mild or no more than 1 per day
2 Moderate and greater than 1 per day
3 —
4 —

NUTRITION ALTERATION

Anorexia[a]
0 None
1 Loss of appetite
2 Oral intake significantly decreased
3 Requiring IV fluids
4 Requiring feeding tube or parenteral nutrition

SKIN ALTERATION

Skin Sensation[b]
0 No problem
1 Pruritus
2 Burning
3 Painful

Radiation Dermatitis[a]
0 None
1 Faint erythema or dry desquamation
2 Moderate to brisk erythema or patchy moist desquamation, mostly confined to skin folds and creases; or moderate edema
3 Confluent moist desquamation $\geq$ 1.5 cm diameter and not confined to skin folds; pitting edema
4 Skin necrosis or ulceration of full-thickness dermis; may include bleeding not induced by minor trauma or abrasion

SEXUALITY ALTERATION

0 Absent
1 Present

The cited parameters were established by
[a]National Cancer Institute (NCI) Common Toxicity Criteria, Version 2.0
[b]Radiation Therapy Oncology Group (RTOG), Version 2.0 or the RTOG SOMA Scales
[c]Oncology Nursing Society Radiation Documentation Tool Workgroup

Note. From Radiation Therapy Patient Care Record: A Tool for Documenting Nursing Care, by C. Catlin-Huth, M. Haas, and V. Pollock (Eds.), 2002, Pittsburgh, PA: Oncology Nursing Society. Copyright 2002 by the Oncology Nursing Society. Reprinted with permission.

Scenario B

08/10/200x

Ms. Lawrence presents with wet desquamation changes in her right axilla measuring 6cm x 4 cm. She complains of dryness and aching pain (pain rating of 4 on scale of 0–10) in area. The patient reports applying Aquaphor® ointment (Beiersdorf Inc., Wilton, CT) three times daily without relief. The skin change does not have signs of infection; however, a clear exudate has been noted in moderate amount.

Vital signs: Temperature 98.6°; pulse 82; respiration 16; blood pressure 118/72. No change in weight or appetite. No lymphedema.

Vigilon dressing was applied with immediate relief (pain rating decreased to 2). Patient and husband instructed on Vigilon use that is to be applied two times daily, with first application after morning radiation treatment. Reviewed standard protocol for care of axilla and treatment side. Patient and husband are able to return and demonstrate dressing change appropriately without any barriers.

Plan: Reassess in three days.

Corinne Haviley, RN

Discussion

Although in scenario A an assessment is documented, details of the intervention were missing. The assessment form is helpful to quickly facilitate documentation of signs and symptoms of problems; however, it does not allow for the capture of treatment. The assessment form should have an accompanying nursing note to clarify the intervention delivered and patient response. Details such as these help support the amount of time involved with and the quality of the intervention, including physical assessment and treatment. An example of consult times is as follows.

Level 1:	0–10 minutes
Level 2:	11–20 minutes
Level 3:	21–30 minutes
Level 4:	31–45 minutes
Level 5:	46+ minutes

Without sufficient documentation that validates the time, reimbursement may not occur because of insufficient evidence. E and M coding must be established for each medical and radiation oncology outpatient visit. A score card may be developed to assist with weighting and acuity to determine the correct code to be charged. Weighting includes the number of nursing interventions, depth of assessment, topics discussed and reinforced, and the number of resources used.

For example, your patient visit included vital signs, skin assessment dressing change and review of skin care with patient and husband. Time spent with this patient was 209 minutes.

The E and M charge code would be

99212–Established patient

APC 0600; Payment rate $43.96 (Oncology Roundtable, 2003).

Summary

No margin. No mission. Healthcare organizations generate revenue or income from many different sources. The majority of income is due to inpatient and outpatient billable services. Revenue also may be generated through other services or contracts, such as home health and hospice care, selling of equipment (dated or not useful to the organization), ambulatory care, office and clinic space rental, gift and coffee shops, and parking facilities. Donations from philanthropy and foundation organizations may contribute to support organizations and are most commonly directed toward new construction, purchase of new equipment, program development, and/or research. Organizations often invest dollars into stocks and bonds, which bring additional income from the interest gained or when the bonds are due, "cashed in," or sold. The economic recession and market downturn during the past three years have had a significant impact on return on investment of healthcare industry.

Revenue comes from different payor sources most often categorized as private or public. These sources reimburse services at varying rates. Private sources include self-payment from patients, commercial healthcare insurance, and managed care companies. Public funds include Medicare, Medicaid, S-CHIP funds, and multiple federal, state, and locally funded programs. Both private and public sources dictate or negotiate reimbursement rates often on a yearly or monthly calendar. Once the rates have been established, they generally cannot be changed. In some cases there may be exceptions, however, generally not without a penalty. Reimbursable services are specified that are included in the rates.

It is imperative that the nurse manager has an understanding of the healthcare economics that have been covered in this chapter. The next two chapters provide some basics of financial management for the nurse manager. Fiduciary responsibility for managing unit, department, or organizational budgets is an integral part of the nurse managers' daily activities.

References

Abbey & Abbey Consultants, Inc. (2002). *CY2001 Versus CY2002 APC Payments.* Retrieved November 16, 2004, from http://www.apcnow.com/CompareAPCs2003.xls

American Cancer Society. (2003). *Cancer facts and figures 2003.* Atlanta, GA: Author.

American Medical Association. (2003). *Current procedural terminology, standard edition.* Chicago: Author.

Bailes, J., & Coleman, T. (2004). The new Medicare bill: Far-reaching effects on cancer treatment. *Clinical Advances in Hematology and Oncology, 2*(5), 292–294.

Cap Gemini Ernst & Young. (2003). *Forecast: Health care's top 10 business issues and impacts for 2003.* Retrieved March 26, 2003, from http://www.us.cgey.com/health

Department of Health and Human Services, Centers for Medicare and Medicaid Services. (2002). *National health accounts.* Washington, DC: Author. Retrieved March 26, 2003, from http://www.cms.hhs.gov/statistics/nhe/default.asp

Federal Register. (2002, November 1). *Medicare program: Changes to the hospital outpatient prospective payment system and calendar year 2003 payment rates.* Retrieved September 3, 2004, from http://frwebgate3.access.gpo.gov/cgi-bin/waisgate.cgi?WAISdocID=23285313237+7+0+0&WAISaction=retrieve

Ferman, J. (2003). The rising cost of healthcare. *Healthcare Executive, 18*(2), 70–71.

Gledhill, L. (2004). Coding for hospital outpatient infusion services in 2004. *Oncology Issues, Oncology Economics, and Program Management, 19*(1), 14.

Halbert, R., Zaher, C., Wade, S., Malin, J., Lawless, G., & Dubois, R. (2002). Outpatient cancer drug costs: Changes, drivers, and the future. *Cancer, 94,* 1142–1150.

LaTour, K., & Eichenwald, S. (Eds.). (2002). *Health information management: Concepts, principles and practice.* Chicago: American Health Information Management Association.

Moody's Investor Service. (2002). *Not-for-profit healthcare: 2002 outlook and medians.* New York: Author.

National Cancer Institute. (2003). *Cancer progress report—2003 update. Costs of cancer care.* Retrieved September 3, 2004, from http://progressreport.cancer.gov/doc.asp?pid=1&did=21&mid=vcol &chid=13

Oncology Roundtable. (2002). *Outpatient oncology revenues: Early lessons on managing under APCs.* Washington, DC: Advisory Board Company.

Oncology Roundtable. (2003). *Maximizing oncology reimbursement: Next generation strategies for optimizing revenue capture.* Washington, DC: Advisory Board Company.

Wilson, K. (2002). *Healthcare costs 101.* Oakland, CA: California Healthcare Foundation.

Financial Management for the Nurse Manager

Luana R. Lamkin, RN, MPH

> *"Every man has a right to his opinion, but no man has a right to be wrong with his facts."* Bernard Baruch (Field, 1944)

Financial management requires that its practitioners know the facts and be equipped to articulate their opinions based on evidence. Nursing leaders are challenged to use this knowledge to enhance patient care through the management of fiscal and human resources.

The experts in financial management in nursing always seem to find a way to get the new project off the ground, provide new services, maintain optimal staffing levels, and excel personally and professionally. In her summary of chief nursing officers' (CNOs') assessment of nurse manager skills, Schmidt (1999) reported that although 55% of nurse managers are viewed as successful in implementing operational standards, only 40% are viewed as successful in managing financial standards. This chapter is intended to help the other 60% reach their potential in this leadership skill. A glossary of frequently used budget terms can be found in Figure 7-1.

Figure 7-1. Glossary of Terms

Average Daily Census (ADC)—The average number of inpatients on a given day; number of patients divided by the number of days in a certain time frame.

Average Length of Stay (ALOS)—The average number of days a group of inpatients stays in the hospital.

Benchmark—The best practice that can be found.

Budget—A formal documentation of management's plans and expectations, usually financial in nature.

(Continued on next page)

Figure 7-1. Glossary of Terms *(Continued)*

Business Plan—A formal documentation of a proposed program, project, or service, including the manner of judging its success.

Capital Budget—A formal documentation of management's plan to acquire buildings and equipment that will be used by the organization for more than one year. Generally, a capital budget item also is defined by a minimum cost.

Census—The number of patients occupying a bed at a certain time, usually midnight.

Chart of Accounts—A document created by an organization to define cost centers and assign numbers to each line item in a budget or financial report.

Direct Expenses—The expenses that can be directly related to the work to be accomplished in a given work area, such as personnel and supplies.

Expenses—The total cost to provide a good or service, including both direct and indirect expenses.

Fixed Costs—Costs to provide a good or service that is not dependent on volume.

Full-Time Equivalent (FTE)—The equivalent of one full-time employee working for one year. Usually calculated as 40 hours per week and 2,080 hours per year, including both productive and nonproductive time.

Hours Per Patient Day (HPPD)—Paid hours divided by patient days; the number of productive and non-productive hours of care devoted to one patient in one 24-hour period.

Indirect Expenses—Costs that relate to housekeeping, building maintenance, and administration. Indirect expenses are shared by a number of cost centers.

Nonproductive Time—Sick, holiday, vacation, and other paid, non-worked hours. May include work time not devoted to patient care, such as required education.

Operating Budget—The formal documentation of the management's plan for day-to-day expenses and revenue; does not include capital budget items.

Patient Day—One patient in one bed for 24 hours.

Productive Time—Straight time, overtime, and premium time worked and paid for.

Responsibility Center—Cost center used to emphasize the manager's responsibility for both expenses and revenue.

Strategic Plan—A formal documentation of the long-range plan for an area, including the resources needed to meet the goals.

Unit of Service—A measurement of output, such as patient days, visits, and surgeries.

Variance—The difference between the budgeted and actual amount; usually expressed in dollars and/or percentages.

Variable Expense—Cost for providing goods or services that vary with volume.

Workload—The volume of work in a department or organization.

Year to Date (YTD)—The cumulative total of the budget, actual expenses, or revenue for the months from the beginning of the fiscal year to the present.

Zero-Based Budget—A formal document of expenses and revenues that were built from a zero dollar starting point, as opposed to building a budget based on incremental changes.

Budgeting is not the only activity involved in financial management, but it does seem to be the most forbidding to many. Financial management also includes planning programs, monitoring revenue and expenses, revising actions based on current conditions, keeping up to date in the changes that impact practice from the institutional level to the bedside, and always looking for new ways to provide better patient care at reasonable costs. Financial management is providing value to the patients and the organization and is the support for the delivery of care.

For many nurse managers, there is nothing quite as intimidating as the budgeting process. It can be an arduous process that causes the finest of clinicians and human resource managers to throw up their arms in frustration. The questions ring in their heads: Why do I have to budget? Why do I have to budget? Why do I have to budget? We do it to confirm for ourselves, our staff, and management our financial and clinical goals. The manager does budgeting because he or she is the one voice championing the care needs of the patients and staff on that unit. The manager will be held accountable for the financial success of the areas managed, and the manager certainly wants to design the plan for that success. It is budgeting that backs up the blueprint for the functioning of the clinical area for the year.

In a simplistic form, the budgeting process is just like the nursing process or the research process. Assess the situation, just like a patient assessment, plan for the interventions that are necessary, put the numbers on paper, implement the budget, monitor the spending, and then reassess and revise the plan or budget. As in patient care, communicating the plan and enlisting the help of the experts and staff in the process is critical.

The forms, the series of events leading to the budget, and the ability to negotiate the budget vary widely depending on the setting. In this chapter, generalities about the process, formats for the budget itself, and the documents that surround it will be presented, but it is up to the individual to translate these formats to the specific situation.

Financial Management Philosophy

Understanding the budget philosophy in a specific setting is a crucial first step. Organizations vary in the amount of accountability placed upon the manager. It is critical to understand what is expected and how the patient care philosophy of the manager corresponds with that of the organization. Ask peers the following questions to get an idea of the philosophy.

- Does the organization most highly prize and monitor the number of staff or the cost of staff members? That is, do they measure full-time equivalent (FTE) staff or FTEs per adjusted occupied bed?
- Is the emphasis on monthly adherence to the budget or the year-end totals? How much flexibility is acceptable throughout the year?
- Is the budget flexible enough to take into account the number of patients cared for on a day-to-day basis, or is the budget fixed based on the estimate of the number of patients cared for throughout the year?
- Is the CNO accountable for the nursing budgets, or is it the chief financial officer (CFO) that truly oversees the budgets closely?
- Are special projects—initiating a palliative care program—budgeted separately, or is that part of the ongoing annual budget?
- Is the budget prepared based on last year's budget or last year's spending, or is the budget zero-based, meaning starting from scratch every year?
- Does the culture allow negotiation with peers for sharing or trading resources?
- What is the definition of capital budget, and is capital budgeting for major items such as beds done by individual departments or by a larger entity?

If a manager is uncomfortable with the answers to any of these questions, there is a responsibility to become the impetus to change the culture. It is important to know the answers to these questions in a specific setting. A manager new to the organization or new to a manager role is advised not to assume to know all the answers. Ask peers, supervisors, or the business office manager for their analysis of these questions. Asking questions like this does not make one appear ill prepared. In fact, seeking answers to thoughtful questions confirms that the manager wants to do the work correctly and takes this part of the role seriously. Be sure to get a thorough orientation to the process, the timetable, and the forms to be used early in the process. Nearly everyone starts out with an inherited budget (meaning that the unit or service is already established); understand what thinking went behind the numbers and how much flexibility exists to negotiate alternative plans and spending.

Revenue and Expense

In its purest form, there are only two parts to financial management and the plan or budget: how much money is forecasted to be brought in as revenue, and how much is forecasted to be spent to do the work of caring for patients. If confined to the spending part of the budget, one has only cost containment as a weapon against a budget out of control. If, however, one has accountability for the revenue portion of the budget, there exist two methods of control: bringing in new revenue and reducing expenses. Frequently, nurse managers voice helplessness in the revenue side of budgeting: "How can I control how many patients are admitted?" Look at it from the physician point of view. No one has more impact on the physician interest in admitting patients to the unit than the manager. Every day while dealing with physicians and their patients, the manager confirms the physicians' belief that this is a good place to admit patients. When a patient asks, "Who can I tell that you give wonderful care here?" answer with a written list of names that includes both the administrator or supervisor and the physician who admitted the patient. The supervisor may have an immediate impact on the performance evaluation of the manager, but the satisfied physician who admits more patients will have a much longer positive effect on the success of the hospital, the unit, and the manager.

Think of the budgeting process as an opportunity to think big, to set goals that will improve the care, the skill mix, and the new programs that make the unit shine. Even if the manager is not successful in every proposal, the seeds have been planted that there are ideas for growth, ideas for higher quality, and ideas for involving staff in designing the work to be accomplished.

Terminology

Terminology will vary by organization, and getting the language right is imperative to articulating the plan for care and financial management. Finkler and Kovner (2000) created a good glossary. Make sure the terms are the same in the current place of employment. Nothing is more frustrating than filling out the wrong form to get what is needed. Completing a CER at one organization might mean a capital expenditure request but be a corporate exception report at another.

Assessment

If the budget is truly the support to the delivery of patient care, one cannot budget until the plan for that care is established. This is an excellent time to do a strategic plan for the unit or area of responsibility. This can be a formal retreat from the hospital with selected staff and physicians to determine the future in a written document. An alternative is a less formal method of staff meetings and suggestions from staff about what they see changing and what they would like to be able to offer patients. The unit plan must be in concert with the mission, vision, and goals of the organization. Be attuned to the organization's emphasis upon process improvement, patient satisfaction, and recruitment and retention goals, and then build the unit plan based on these tenets that resonate with the organization and the unit philosophy of care.

Take time to read everything available about the budget process. Timelines are nearly always included that can guide personal planning. Review all the forms that are included in the budgeting process and the monitoring process (see Table 7-1). Understanding that the personnel budgeting is done separately from supply budgeting can save inordinate time.

Revenue

Generally, revenue budgets are completed first. The finance department usually does a good deal of this work. They assess a variety of internal and external factors. Is the population growing or shrinking in the market? The organization's success in negotiating reimbursement rates for the coming year and goals for profit or revenue in excess of expense to be reinvested in the organization also play a big role in determining the revenue budget. The finance department should consult the manager and perhaps key physicians to determine changes specific to the area. Figure 7-2 lists some specific items the manager is encouraged to consider in determining the revenue budget or in advising the finance department. Changes in practice patterns and reimbursement will help determine the revenue budget. For example, when chemotherapy administration for primary medical oncology treatment shifted to the outpatient arena, fewer inpatient admissions were evident.

Do not hesitate to point out and share knowledge about what is impacting cancer care in the nation, predictions for the specific unit, or ideas for service expansion. This conversation with the finance department and senior administrator offers an opportunity to suggest that untapped revenue may come from the introduction of a palliative care unit, or that the length of stay may increase because of a new drug that requires inpatient stays for longer than the average. The people in the finance department and perhaps the CNO know little about oncology as a specialty. The oncology manager is the expert and needs to articulate the trends.

Table 7-1. Sample Unit Budget

JFK Hospital Final Approved Budget													
Oncology Unit	Jul	Aug	Sep	Oct	Nov	Dec	Jan	Feb	Mar	Apr	May	Jun	Total
ROOM CARE REVENUE	435,104	474,988	442,960	490,700	444,773	444,168	570,348	494,568	521,822	525,811	506,533	477,949	5,829,724
IP ANCILLARY REVENUE	87	95	88	98	89	89	114	99	104	105	101	95	1,164
TOTAL INPATIENT INCOME	435,191	475,083	443,048	490,798	444,862	444,257	570,462	494,667	521,926	525,916	506,634	478,044	5,830,888
TOTAL OUTPATIENT ANCILLARY	19,732	21,816	20,427	22,511	20,427	20,427	26,290	22,470	23,998	23,998	23,234	21,706	267,036
TOTAL OTHER PATIENT SERVICES	0	0	0	0	0	0	0	0	0	0	0	0	0
TOTAL OTHER OPERATING REVENUE	0	0	0	0	0	0	0	0	0	0	0	0	0
TOTAL INCOME	454,923	496,899	463,475	513,309	465,289	464,684	596,752	517,137	545,924	549,914	529,868	499,750	6,097,924
530200 SUPERVISORY	16,429	14,120	13,665	17,632	13,665	14,120	14,120	13,209	14,120	13,665	14,120	15,931	174,796
530300 PROFESSIONAL	141,896	136,341	131,968	136,384	132,459	136,552	136,614	127,800	137,491	135,315	136,956	132,974	1,622,750
530500 NON-REG/NON-CERT TECH	2,231	2,231	2,159	2,231	2,159	2,231	2,231	2,087	2,247	2,174	2,247	2,174	26,402
530600 NON-PROFESSIONAL ASST.	22,109	21,442	20,759	21,451	20,778	21,494	21,494	20,107	22,012	20,854	21,549	20,854	254,903
530700 SUPPORT/ADMIN ASSISTANTS	15,808	14,996	14,436	14,955	14,495	14,988	14,988	14,021	14,988	14,504	14,988	14,524	177,691
531200 STRETCH OBJECTIVE WAGE	(1,344)	(1,344)	(1,301)	(1,344)	(1,301)	(1,344)	(1,344)	(1,257)	(1,344)	(1,301)	(1,344)	(1,301)	(15,869)
533005 TEMPORARY HELP	24,197	24,197	23,416	24,197	23,416	24,197	24,197	22,636	24,197	23,416	24,197	23,416	285,679
TOTAL SALARIES & WAGES	221,326	211,983	205,102	215,506	205,671	212,238	212,300	198,603	213,711	208,627	212,713	208,572	2,526,352
533500 FICA EMPLOYER EXPENSE	12,305	11,726	11,345	11,944	11,380	11,742	11,746	10,988	11,833	11,564	11,771	11,560	139,904
533510 MEDICARE EMPLOYER EXPENSE	2,878	2,742	2,653	2,793	2,662	2,746	2,747	2,570	2,767	2,704	2,753	2,704	32,719
536700 RECOGNITION DEPT EMPLOYEE	42	42	42	42	42	42	42	42	41	41	41	41	500
538000 FLEX CREDIT EXPENSE	121	121	117	121	117	121	121	114	121	117	121	117	1,429
TOTAL EMPLOYEE BENEFITS	15,346	14,631	14,157	14,900	14,201	14,651	14,656	13,714	14,762	14,426	14,686	14,422	174,552

(Continued on next page)

Table 7-1. Sample Unit Budget (Continued)

Oncology Unit		Jul	Aug	Sep	Oct	Nov	Dec	Jan	Feb	Mar	Apr	May	Jun	Total
545100	COST OF DRUGS SOLD	468	453	387	474	414	413	455	416	466	468	449	421	5,284
546100	MEDSURG SUPPLIES GENERAL	10,062	9,740	8,317	10,198	8,898	8,873	9,789	8,935	10,012	10,062	9,653	9,059	113,598
546110	MEDSURG SUPPLIES IV SOLUTIONS	1	1	1	1	1	1	1	1	1	1	1	1	12
546140	MEDSURG SUPPLIES CATHETERS	1,151	1,115	952	1,167	1,018	1,015	1,120	1,023	1,146	1,151	1,105	1,037	13,000
546150	MEDSURG SUPPLIES ELECTRODES	7	7	6	7	6	6	7	6	7	7	7	6	79
546160	MEDSURG SUPPLIES CUSTOM PACKS	464	449	384	470	410	409	451	412	462	464	445	418	5,238
546180	MEDSURG SUPPLIES SUTURES	18	17	15	18	16	16	17	16	18	18	17	16	202
546190	MEDSURG SUPPLIES WIRES	3	3	2	3	2	2	3	2	3	3	3	2	31
546500	MEDSURG IMPLANTS PROSTHETICS	1	1	1	1	1	1	1	1	1	1	1	1	12
548700	INBOUND FREIGHT CHARGES	6	6	5	6	5	5	6	5	6	6	6	5	67
550900	MINOR EQUIPMENT	531	514	439	539	470	469	517	472	529	531	510	478	5,999
550910	SURGICAL INSTRUMENTS	5	5	4	5	5	5	5	5	5	5	5	5	59
551000	OFFICE AND ADMIN SUPPLIES	466	451	385	473	412	411	454	414	464	466	447	420	5,263
551020	FORMS	887	859	733	899	785	782	863	788	883	887	851	799	10,016
551100	FOOD	603	584	499	611	533	532	587	536	600	603	579	543	6,810
551150	NOURISHMENTS	204	197	168	206	180	180	198	181	203	204	195	183	2,299
551800	MAINTENANCE SUPPLIES	3	3	3	3	3	3	3	3	3	3	3	3	36
551830	LIGHT TUBES AND BULBS	3	3	2	3	2	2	3	2	3	3	3	2	31
552200	SERVICES RELATED SUPPLIES	521	504	431	528	461	459	507	463	518	521	500	469	5,882
552500	MEDICAL CHEMICALS	14	13	11	14	12	12	13	12	14	14	13	12	154
552600	GLASSWARE	2	2	1	2	2	2	2	2	2	2	2	2	23
552700	BIOLOGICS	2	2	1	2	2	2	2	2	2	2	2	2	23
552800	QUALITY CONTROL MATERIALS	363	352	300	368	321	320	353	323	361	363	348	327	4,099
552900	BACTERIA MEDIA	6	6	5	6	5	5	6	5	6	6	6	5	67
	TOTAL DRUGS & SUPPLIES	15,791	15,287	13,052	16,004	13,964	13,925	15,363	14,025	15,715	15,791	15,151	14,216	178,284

(Continued on next page)

Table 7-1. Sample Unit Budget (Continued)

Oncology Unit		Jul	Aug	Sep	Oct	Nov	Dec	Jan	Feb	Mar	Apr	May	Jun	Total
553140	PURCHASED SERVICES OTHER	186	186	186	186	186	186	186	186	186	186	186	186	2,232
553141	AUDIOLOGY FEES	17	17	17	17	17	17	17	17	17	17	17	17	204
566600	CATERED MEALS	50	50	50	50	50	50	50	50	50	50	50	50	600
	TOTAL PURCHASED SERVICES	253	253	253	253	253	253	253	253	253	253	253	253	3,036
560700	REPAIR AND MAINT-PURCHASED	53	53	53	53	53	53	53	53	53	53	53	53	636
561910	ELECTRONIC SUPPLIES	14	14	14	14	14	14	14	14	14	14	14	14	168
	TOTAL REPAIRS AND MAINT	67	67	67	67	67	67	67	67	67	67	67	67	804
	TOTAL RENT	0	0	0	0	0	0	0	0	0	0	0	0	0
	TOTAL INSURANCE EXPENSE	0	0	0	0	0	0	0	0	0	0	0	0	0
	TOTAL UTILITIES	0	0	0	0	0	0	0	0	0	0	0	0	0
	TOTAL INTEREST	0	0	0	0	0	0	0	0	0	0	0	0	0
564700	TRAVEL AND MEETINGS	300	300	300	300	300	300	300	300	300	300	300	300	3,600
	TOTAL OTHER	300	300	300	300	300	300	300	300	300	300	300	300	3,600
	TOTAL BAD DEBT	0	0	0	0	0	0	0	0	0	0	0	0	0
	TOTAL DEPRECIATION & AMORT	0	0	0	0	0	0	0	0	0	0	0	0	0
	TOTAL OPERATING EXPENSES	253,083	242,521	232,931	247,030	234,456	241,434	242,939	226,962	244,808	239,464	243,170	237,830	2,886,628
901106	PATIENT DAYS	709	773	722	799	724	724	845	732	772	778	750	708	9,036
901202	ADMISSIONS	120	130	122	135	122	122	143	124	130	131	127	119	1,525
901306	PROCEDURES IP	35	38	36	40	36	36	42	36	38	39	37	35	448
916400	OBSERVATION HOURS	35	34	29	36	31	31	34	31	35	35	34	32	397
916405	OP IN A BED HOURS	2	2	1	2	1	1	2	1	2	2	2	1	19
916410	OBSERVATION PTS	31	34	32	35	32	32	37	32	34	34	33	31	397

(Continued on next page)

Table 7-1. Sample Unit Budget (Continued)

Oncology Unit	Jul	Aug	Sep	Oct	Nov	Dec	Jan	Feb	Mar	Apr	May	Jun	Total
916415 OP IN A BED	1	2	1	2	1	1	2	1	2	2	1	1	17
TOTAL STATISTICS	933	1,013	943	1,049	947	947	1,105	957	1,013	1,021	984	927	11,839
VOLUME DRIVEN STATISTIC	738	806	752	833	754	754	881	762	805	811	781	737	9,414
FTES	43.69	43.69	43.69	43.69	43.69	43.69	43.69	43.69	43.69	43.69	43.69	43.69	43.69

Legend: IP = inpatient, OP = outpatient, non-reg/non-cert tech = non-registered and non-certified technicians, FICA = Federal Insurance Compensation Act, or Social Security Tax, IV = intravenous

Generally, the revenue budget is determined and translated into a volume or workload statistic for use by the manager. For instance, an inpatient unit may be given the information that the average daily census on a unit will be 22, and the average length of stay is budgeted at four days. These are fairly straightforward data that the manager must translate into the number of staff necessary. A determination that an outpatient infusion or chemotherapy unit will have an average daily number of 36 patients does not detail those having eight-hour infusions versus those who have single-dose injections. Contact the financial representative to make sure you are both in agreement about the kind of patients expected during the next year, and apply the comparable workload and volume statistic. The kind of patients cared for will have a major impact on the revenue as well as staffing and supply budgeting. The recent bundling of outpatient procedures by Medicare has had enormous impact on outpatient chemotherapy infusion reimbursement. Do not assume the financial liaison is up to date on the nuances for every specialty. Recent bundling of services by Medicare for radiation therapy has caused the volume of procedures to appear to have declined, although the number of patients treated remained the same and reimbursement generally increased.

Expenses

The finance department will generally create documents that detail the financial experience from last year. If the budget has been well monitored during the last year, any possible errors will be obvious. If the manager is new to the process, these documents provide help to see where changes need to be made. The people that do financial work are, in general, very detail oriented, but they are people, and people make errors. Be sure to check the work and confirm the accuracy. If the figures from last fiscal year show 18 staff members and 6 full-time temporary agency personnel were used to care for patients but are not reflected in the finance department's spending history, the manager is likely the only one who has that detailed information to correct this figure, which could mean a big difference in future budget projections.

Figure 7-2. Considerations in Forecasting Revenue and Volume

- Addition of new physicians to existing practices that admit to the work unit
- Retirement or relocation of physicians
- Addition of new services on the unit, such as hospice respite beds and palliative care beds
- Addition of new services in the facility, such as prostate seed implants, that will reduce inpatient admissions
- Addition of new drugs that might cause new admissions or shift to outpatient admissions
- Closure of surrounding facilities or services
- Addition of new services by competitors
- Addition of new technology, such as endoscopic procedures or ports
- Change in the number or type of clinical trial patients
- Shift to oral chemotherapy drugs

Table 7-2 is a sample nonwage budget worksheet for a 28-bed oncology unit. This organization's budget year is July 1 to June 30. The budgeting process begins in March, when Table 7-2, the budgeting worksheet, and other documents are distributed to managers. Because the year is not complete, only actual expenditures for the current year through February (Column X) appear. The year-to-date (YTD) expenditures are Column Y. Frequently, forms such as these include an estimate on the part of the finance team of the expenses for the coming year based on current spending (Column Z). The manager uses Column AA to submit the budget proposal for the coming year. Figure 7-3 details some items to consider when making forecasts for expenses.

Only managers who care for patients on a daily basis have a thorough idea of the changes at the bedside. Frequently, nurse managers' roles do not allow them to have up-to-the-minute experience with the day-to-day changes, nor is it necessary. Be sure to tap the experience of staff. Long-term staff members are especially good at noting subtle changes that are impacting work routines. Newer staff members bring the experience from a previous workplace. Asking the opinions of staff will ensure their observations are considered and make them feel more a part of any changes that will take place as a result of the budget.

Another good source for data is key physicians. Select the ones who are especially well read or will be the first to introduce new treatments, put patients on clinical trials, or are instrumental in making changes in their practices and in the hospital. If a new clinical trial is being processed through the institutional review board that calls for 1:1 nurse-to-patient care for hours after the injection, planning for additional staff to accommodate this research protocol is easier to justify. In cases like this, the manager should review the protocols for workload impact and be ready to justify staffing adjustments and equipment needs.

Putting the Budget on Paper

At least three pieces of information are necessary prior to putting a budget on paper: the volume of patients projected, changes in technology and oncology practice, and changes in nursing care and personnel. When these data have been analyzed for

Table 7-2. Sample Budget Worksheet

Budget Worksheet

Oncology Account Number and Description	FY2005 Sep	FY2005 Oct	FY2005 Nov	FY2005 Dec	FY2005 Jan	Column X FY2005 Feb	FY2005 Mar	FY2005 Apr	FY2005 May	FY2005 Jun	Column Y FY2005 Total	FY2004 Total	Column Z FY06 Projection	Column AA FY2006 Total	2006 FY	2005	2004
551150 NOURISHMENTS	76	305	312	281	227	27	0	0	0	0	1,655	1,343	1,685	0			
551800 MAINTENANCE SUPPLIES	0	5	0	2	2	0	0	0	0	0	9	7	8	0			
551830 LIGHT TUBES AND BULBS	0	0	0	0	0	0	0	0	0	0	0	4	0	0			
552200 SERVICES RELATED SUPPLIES	482	501	469	466	521	487	0	0	0	0	4,051	946	4,200	0			
552500 MEDICAL CHEMICALS	19	13	13	3	19	14	0	0	0	0	102	97	100	0			
552600 GLASSWARE	0	0	0	0	0	(18)	0	0	0	0	(18)	0	0	0			
552700 BIOLOGICS	0	0	0	0	0	0	0	0	0	0	0	(17)	0	0			
552800 QUALITY CONTROL MATERIALS	264	289	295	361	471	292	0	0	0	0	2,739	4,618	3,200	0			
552900 BACTERIA MEDIA	6	9	9	0	9	6	0	0	0	0	50	2	25	0			
TOTAL DRUGS & SUPPLIES	13,921	17,314	17,290	14,520	15,704	12,946	0	0	0	0	123,111	177,457		0			
553140 PURCHASED SERVICES OTHER	0	0	0	0	1,671	0	0	0	0	0	1,671	0	1,000	0			
553141 AUDIOLOGY FEES	0	0	0	0	0	0	0	0	0	0	0	115	0	0			
557000 HOUSEKEEPING	0	0	0	0	0	0	0	0	0	0	0	261	0	0			
566600 CATERED MEALS	0	0	0	0	0	26	0	0	0	0	26	92	0	0			
568100 WASTE MANAGEMENT	0	0	0	0	0	0	0	0	0	0	0	1,466	0	0			
TOTAL PURCHASED SERVICES	0	0	0	0	1,671	26	0	0	0	0	1,696	1,934	0	0			

(Continued on next page)

Table 7-2. Sample Budget Worksheet (Continued)

Oncology Account Number and Description	FY2005 Sep	FY2005 Oct	FY2005 Nov	FY2005 Dec	FY2005 Jan	Column X FY2005 Feb	FY2005 Mar	FY2005 Apr	FY2005 May	FY2005 Jun	Column Y FY2005 Total	FY2004 Total	Column Z FY06 Projection	Column AA FY2006 Total	2006 FY	2005	2004
560700 REPAIR AND MAINT-PURCHASED	110	90	45	0	0	45	0	0	0	0	483	1,889	855	0			
561910 ELECTRONIC SUPPLIES	9	20	12	21	13	8	0	0	0	0	125	129	145	0			
562000 REPAIRS AND MAINT-EQUIP	0	0	0	0	0	0	0	0	0	0	0	1,633	0	0			
TOTAL REPAIRS AND MAINT	120	110	57	21	13	53	0	0	0	0	608	3,651	0	0			
TOTAL RENT	0	0	0	0	0	0	0	0	0	0	0	0	0	0			
TOTAL INSURANCE EXPENSE	0	0	0	0	0	0	0	0	0	0	0	0	0	0			
TOTAL UTILITIES	0	0	0	0	0	0	0	0	0	0	0	0	0	0			
TOTAL INTEREST	0	0	0	0	0	0	0	0	0	0	0	0	0	0			
564700 TRAVEL AND MEETINGS	0	0	0	0	377	0	0	0	0	0	377	40	200	200			
564750 MILEAGE	0	0	0	0	0	0	0	0	0	0	0	104	0	0			
598999 HBOC CASH RECEIPTS-OTHER	0	0	0	0	0	0	0	0	0	0	0	(40)	0	0			
TOTAL OTHER	0	0	0	0	377	0	0	0	0	0	377	104	0	0			
TOTAL BAD DEBT	0	0	0	0	0	0	0	0	0	0	0	0	0	0			
TOTAL DEPRECIATION & AMORT	0	0	0	0	0	0	0	0	0	0	0	0	0	0			
TOTAL OPERATING EXPENSES (EXCLUDING SAL & BENEFITS)	14,041	17,424	17,348	14,541	17,765	13,025	0	0	0	0	125,792	183,145	0	0			

(Continued on next page)

Table 7-2. Sample Budget Worksheet (Continued)

Oncology Account Number and Description	FY2005 Sep	FY2005 Oct	FY2005 Nov	FY2005 Dec	FY2005 Jan	Column X FY2005 Feb	FY2005 Mar	FY2005 Apr	FY2005 May	FY2005 Jun	Column Y FY2005 Total	FY2004 Total	Column Z FY06 Projection	Column AA FY2006 Total	2006 FY	2005	2004
901106 PATIENT DAYS	652	804	705	703	772	710	0	0	0	0	5,912	9,206		9,179			
901202 ADMISSIONS	134	164	122	135	137	81	0	0	0	0	1,056	1,569		0			
901306 PROCEDURES IP	0	37	72	27	35	17	0	0	0	0	188	0		449			
916400 OBSERVATION HOURS	22	41	31	25	31	22	0	0	0	0	228	295		396			
916405 OP IN A BED HOURS	2	2	4	1	2	2	0	0	0	0	14	21		18			
916410 OBSERVATION PTS	22	41	31	25	31	22	0	0	0	0	228	295		396			
TOTAL STATISTICS	832	1,089	965	916	1,008	854	0	0	0	0	7,626	11,386		10,438			
VOLUME DRIVEN STATISTIC	0	0	0	0	0	0	0	0	0	0	9,501	9,501		0			

Legend: PT = patients, IP = inpatients, OP = outpatients

their impact, it is time to record the money that will support these changes and plans. Generally, think of three areas of spending: staff, supplies, and capital expenses.

Capital Budgets

Capital expense is for larger items usually defined by their useful life (such as greater than five years) and cost (greater than $1,000 for one item). Scales, lifts, beds, refrigerators, monitors, and furniture usually fit into this category. Managers will be asked to delineate these items and attach exact or estimated cost and justification for their purchase. See Figures 7-4 and 7-5 for a capital request form example that additionally asks for the justification based on regulatory needs, patient safety, efficiency, revenue production, and the priority order of the list. Organizations must make decisions on which capital items to purchase from lists of requests that may exceed funds available. The new bed scale for one unit may be in competition with colonoscopes and computer technology needs in another clinical area. Take time to write a justification that answers the questions and speaks to the organizational priorities and patient care needs.

Staffing Budget

The staffing budget is perhaps the most complicated work to be accomplished. The basic number of staff needed to care for the patients is called the *staff productive time*. Everyone has days off, vacation, and sick time; in addition, there is in-service education time on and off the work unit, required meetings, and time for project development. All these extras are unfortunately called *nonproductive time*. Exactly what constitutes nonproductive time varies by institution. The manager should have this clearly defined prior to budget planning.

Figure 7-3. Considerations in Forecasting Expenses

- Changes to the nursing role, such as drawing blood samples, or the addition of lift teams
- Changes in nursing staff mix because of an inability to attract RNs or a desire to reduce expenses
- Change in the number or type of clinical trials requiring additional nursing time
- Additions in technology, such as cell phones and electronic record keeping
- Change in practice or chemotherapy regimens requiring additional monitoring by nurses
- New chemotherapy that requires additional supplies

How much staff does it take to care for the budgeted number of patients? Most organizations use benchmarks from pooled data to determine the number of *hours of care per patient day* (HPPD) by nursing unit. Benchmarking firms may be hired by large organizations to study specific nursing areas and determine the HPPD. Other organizations rely upon data published by national organizations; those data vary in specificity. In general, the number of hours per patient day is highest in intensive care units and lowest in general medical-surgical areas. Oncology units generally are judged to need more hours than general medical-surgical areas and fewer hours than intensive care areas. Some organizations rely upon their experience or their acuity systems to determine HPPD internally. Regardless of the source of the data, the nurse manager must understand if the HPPD figure is productive or a combination of productive and nonproductive time, usually called total HPPD. Lamkin, Rosiak, Buerhaus, Mallory, and Williams (2002) recently published data on the state-of-the-art of staffing. Because the data are survey- and opinion-based, not evidence-based, the Oncology Nursing Society chose not to publish staffing standards. The article provides a good sampling of staffing ranges throughout the country.

Table 7-4 is a staffing matrix for an oncology unit based upon 8.43 productive HPPD. This unit of 28 beds is budgeted to have an average daily census of 26, or 9,484 patient days in the year (26 patients per day x 365 days per year). Multiplying the number of patient days (9,484) times the HPPD (8.43) equals the productive staff hours, 79,945. Every FTE works 36–40 hours a week as defined by the organization. Dividing the productive hours needed by 40 hours per person results in 38.4 FTEs to care for patients. This unit schedules all eight-hour shifts.

Now the manager determines the skill mix and then the number of staff to schedule on each shift throughout the week. On this unit, three skill levels are identified: skill level 1 is staff RNs, skill level 2 is unit management and the educator, and skill 3 is assistive personnel (AP), such as patient care assistants, patient care technicians, and unit clerks or secretaries. Table 7-5 shows that the nurse manager determines the skill mix goal to be primarily RNs (56%), AP (38%), and management (6%). Skill mix usually is negotiable and often determined by the manager based on patient care requirements. Changes in the type of patients,

Figure 7-4. 2005 Capital Requests Routine and Replacement Capital

Prioritization Criteria:

1. Equipment is broken and requires replacement.

2. Equipment is no longer supported by the vendor and must be replaced.

3. Equipment replacement or acquisition is required for patient or employee safety.

4. Maintenance costs of equipment are prohibitive, and replacement/upgrade would be more cost effective.

5. Capital item is critical to achieving the 2004 operating budget.

6. Profitable business is at risk of being lost if equipment is not replaced.

7. The project has a cash payback of less than 2 years.

8. Capital equipment purchase is required by JCAHO or other regulatory body, or by a legal contractual commitment.

Department	Dept#	Capital Item Requested	Estimated Cost	Justification#	Rank Order	Facilities Rank Order	Prioritization Criteria (Chack all that apply)								Needed during the		Outside/ Foundation Funding
							1	2	3	4	5	6	7	8	First 6 Months	Last 6 Months	

nursing care philosophy and model, and the organization's structure all cause a need for reevaluation of the skill mix. If patients on ventilators are introduced to the unit, the need for a higher RN mix is required. If licensed practical nurses are introduced or eliminated from the model of care, a change is warranted. If the laboratory no longer performs venipunctures, some new mix will be required.

RN staff members are more expensive than AP. In organizations where the dollars spent on human resources are more highly managed than the raw number of staff members, efforts continue to revise the skill mix to lower-level, less-expensive staff.

Figure 7-5. Capital Budget Request Form

1. Detailed description of the equipment and its purpose: _____
   _____

2. Describe briefly the benefits of this expenditure: _____
   _____

3. Will the acquisition of this item require any construction or remodeling? If yes, have you included those costs in the price of the item? _____
   _____

4. How will this equipment purchase affect annual revenue for this accounting unit?

   a.) Will it increase procedures? Yes or No (circle one) If yes, how many procedures and what
       is the charge associated with the procedures? _____
       _____

   b.) Will the purchase have any effect on full-time equivalent (FTE) numbers, requiring either
       more FTEs or a reduction in FTEs because of gained efficiencies from the purchase?
       Please indicate here the increase or decrease in FTEs and the amount of salary related to
       it. _____
       _____

   5. What is the cost to lease the equipment versus to purchase the equipment?
      _____

6. Will the purchase have any effect on expenses? _____
   _____

   a.) What are the maintenance agreements and annual costs associated with them? _____
       _____

   b.) Will the new equipment require any additional supply items? If so, what is the cost of
       these items? _____
       _____

7. What are the consequences of postponing the purchase? _____
   _____

   _____

   Manager Signature   Date

However, recent studies by Aiken, Clarke, Sloan, Sochalski, and Silber (2002) and Needleman, Buerhaus, Mattke, Stewart, and Zelevinsky (2002) have shown the advantage to having RNs in higher ratio.

Table 7-4. Budgeted Staffing Matrix Plan for the ABC Medical Center Oncology Unit									
Sample Staffing Skill Level		**Sun.**	**Mon.**	**Tues.**	**Wed.**	**Thur.**	**Fri.**	**Sat.**	**Totals**
Days	1	5	5.2	6	6	6	6	6	40.2
	2	0	2.23	2.23	2.23	2.23	2.23	0	11.15
	3	3	5	5	5	5	5	4.3	32.3
Evenings	1	5	6	6	6	6	6	5	40
	2	0	0	0	0	0	0	0	0
	3	3	4	4	4	4	4	3	26
Nights	1	4	4	4	4	4	4	4	28
	2	0	0	0	0	0	0	0	0
	3	2	2	2	2	2	2	2	14
Budgeted staffing matrix for 26 patients ADC (average daily census) providing 8.43 productive hours of care per patient day, by shift, and by day of the week.									

A general staffing plan is completed based upon the total number of staff and the anticipated acuity of patients around the clock and the average daily census by day of the week. Figure 7-6 shows the general staffing plan for three 8-hour shifts, 7 days a week, on a 13-bed medical oncology unit. This nurse manager knows that chemotherapy infusions and trips to imaging varies little between days and evenings and between weekdays and Saturdays. There is less activity on nights, therefore less work for the less-skilled staff to perform. The staffing pattern calls for six RNs Monday through Saturday on days and Monday through Friday on evenings and a lower number on other shifts. New managers and staff are easily confused by percentages of staff members, such as the 2.23 management staff planned for Monday through Friday on the day schedule in Table 7-4. This is a full-time nurse manager, a full-time assistant nurse manager, and a half-time educator. Both the manager and assistant are "productive" staff 90% of the time (10% of the time they are attending education activities or other nonproductive time), and the educator is productive 86% of the time (or .43 FTE), adding up to 2.23 on average Monday through Friday during day shift.

Nonproductive time is critical to the functioning of a nursing area. In the example in Figure 7-7, nonproductive vacation, holiday, and sick time equals 4.4 additional

FTEs, the mandatory education is 0.9 FTE, and the coverage for new hire orientation is 1.0 FTE, for a total of 6.3 additional FTEs. This is equivalent to an additional 14% staff. At this facility, a fairly rigorous process is in place to identify how many new orientees there will be and the number of hours of education that will be required. In some facilities, an agreed upon addition of 12%–15% is added on to the productive FTE figure to arrive at the total paid FTE number.

Table 7-5. Staffing Skill Mix Worksheet		
Item		**Number**
Patient days		9,484
O/P Obs patients		0
Budget average daily census		26.0
Budget hours per patient day (HPPD)		8.43
Variable staff hours required (9,484 x 8.43)		79,945
Variable full-time equivalents required (79,945: 40 hours per week)		38.4
Hours per shift		8
Patient days/week (9,484: 52 weeks a year)		181.9
Total shifts/week		191.65
Variable hours/week		1,533
Calculated HPPD		8.4
Skill mix	1 RN	56.46%
	2 management	5.82%
	3 assistive personnel	37.73%

Flexibility in staffing is perhaps the most critical financial task of the nurse manager. Because the census of patients varies, the number of staff necessary to care for the patients must be flexible. The census in most facilities is the number of bedded patients at the midnight count. That number fluctuates based on admissions, discharges, and transfers throughout the day. The shortened length of stay can mean that an RN assigned to five beds during her shift may see seven, eight, or nine different patients in those five beds. That is why inpatient staffing is called "variable," allowing the nurse manager to "flex up" the number of staff when the census or acuity is higher and "flex down" when it is lower. Most managers are skilled at *knowing* when to flex their staff up and down for patient care, but *implementing* the flexing and especially flexing down is difficult. Most hospitals have an in-house pool of nurses that go to the unit most in need of their help to cover high acuity or sick calls for their shift, making flexing up possible. Sending people home or calling them prior to their shift to stay home, or flexing down, is a more difficult decision to make, not only for the variable patient care reasons but also for the human reasons of impacting the ability of the staff to meet their personal financial needs. Most units create a matrix, such as that shown in Figure 7-5, to show the average number of staff needed to care for a certain number of patients. This figure reflects the number and mix for a 13-bed oncology unit with a budgeted 9.62 total HPPD. This is an invaluable tool for charge nurses in determining the need to flex staff when the nurse manager is not present.

Unfortunately, the nursing shortage has caused all of us to frequently work with fewer than budgeted staff because nursing staff is not available to care for patients. The caution here is to determine if budgets are based upon the experience of last

---

Figure 7-6. Hospital Variable Staffing Plan

Fiscal Year 2006, June 2004–May 2005

Unit = oncology 13-bed unit plus outpatients
Budgeted average daily census = 14.3 patients
Budgeted hours of care = 9.62 hours/patient day

Daily fixed staff
- Assistant nurse manager (ANM) for unit: Monday–Friday, 0700–1530 (in charge/daily operations) included only in unit budget
- Patient care coordinator (PCC): Monday–Friday, 0700–1530
- Health unit secretary: Monday–Friday, 0700–1930; Saturday–Sunday, 0700–1530
- Nurse tech: Monday–Sunday, 0700–1900; three nights/week; Monday–Sunday, 1900–0700 (alternating with night tech)

Daily variable staff	Monday–Friday	Saturday–Sunday
12–13 patients • 0700–1900, 3 RNs + 1 LPN	• ANM in charge • Staff RN as charge (with patients) after 1500	• Staff RN as charge with fewer patients
• 1900–0700, 2 RNs + 1 LPN	• Staff RN as charge with patients • Tech only as specifically needed	• Staff RN as charge with patients • Tech only as specifically needed
10–11 patients • 0700–1900, 2 RNs + 1 LPN	• ANM in charge • Staff RN as charge (with patients) after 1530 • Tech only as specifically needed after 1530	• Staff RN as charge with fewer patients • Tech only as specifically needed after 1530
• 1900–0700, 2 RNs + 1 LPN	• Staff RN as charge with patients • Tech only if specifically needed	• Staff RN as charge with patients • Tech only if specifically needed

(Continued on next page)

Figure 7-6. Hospital Variable Staffing Plan *(Continued)*

9 patients		
• 0700–1900, 2 RNs + 1 LPN	• ANM in charge • Staff RN as charge (with patients) after 1530	• Staff RN as charge with patients
• 1900–0700, 2 RNs	• Staff RN as charge with patients • 7p–11p tech	• Staff RN as charge with patients • 7p–11p tech
7–8 patients		
• 0700–1900, 2 RNs	• ANM in charge; PCC with patients • Staff RN as charge (with patients) after 1530 • No techs/HUS for (7) patients • 7a–3p tech/HUS with (8) patients	• Staff RN as charge with patients • No tech for (7) patients • Tech for (8) patients, if needed
• 1900–0700, 2 RNs	• Staff RN as charge with patients • 7p–11p tech at (8) patients	• Staff RN as charge with patients • 7p–11p tech at (8) patients
< 7 patients		
• 0700–1900, 2 RNs	• ANM in charge; PCC with patients • Staff RN as charge (with patients) after 1530; no tech/HUS	• Staff RN as charge with patients • No tech • No health unit secretary
• 1900–0700, 2 RNs	• Staff nurse as charge with patients • No tech	• Staff RN as charge with patients • No tech

Illness coverage plan
- Staffing adjustments will be made within the cluster, if possible.
- Any available hospital float staff will be identified with administrative supervisor.
- ANM/PCC will be used to cover patient care needs.
- Unit/cluster call lists will be initiated.

year's expenses and not on last year's budget. If vacancies in the staffing pattern are unfilled over a year, and the budget is based on last year's experience, the nurse manager must justify maintaining the budgeted expense for staff and couple the justification with a plan to recruit new staff into existing vacant positions. It often is risky going into budget session with long-term unfilled vacancies, as these vacant FTEs could be viewed as not needed and end up on the cutting room floor.

In general, nurse managers are responsible for determining their productive and nonproductive budgets and staffing plans but are not responsible for determining the additional benefits of employees. The finance department determines benefits and payroll taxes based upon their past experiences and predictions for the future. The same is generally true of budgeting salary increases.

Figure 7-7. Nonproductive Time Budget Worksheet: ABC Medical Center, Oncology Unit

Orientation staff:
Replacement:

Skill level	Number of staff	Hours/ staff	Total hours
1	3.0	400	1,200
2	0.0	160	0
3	6.0	160	960
			2,160
FTEs:			1.0
Calculated % to variable hours:			2.70%

Mandatory education:

Skill level	Number of staff	Hours/ staff	Total hours
1	35.0	39	1,365
2	0.0	0	0
3	24.0	24	576
			1,941
FTEs:			.09
Calculated % to variable hours:			2.43%

Earned time off (ETO)/sick hours:

	Total
Estimated ETO/sick hours:	9,194
FTEs:	4.4
Calculated % to variable hours:	11.50%

Nonproductive budget worksheet allows the manager to determine how many hours are necessary to budget for staff orientation, mandatory education, earned time off, and sickness. In total, this unit will add 6.3 full-time equivalents (FTEs) for nonproductive time (1.0 for orientation + 0.9 for education + 4.4 for earned time off and sick time). Staffing levels refer to 1 = RNs, 2 = management, and 3 = assistive personnel. Calculated % to variable hours means that 1.0 FTE to cover for orientation is equal to 2.7% of the productive variable budgeted for this unit.

Nonwage Budgets

Usually, human resources are by far the greatest expenses on a nursing unit and can be as much as 70%–95% of the budgeted expenses. The additional expenses that are attributed to the nursing area vary widely among facilities. For some, the linen use is carefully monitored and attributed to individual units or cost centers, for others it is treated as an overall expense of the organization. The same holds true for stock drugs, non-chargeable medical-surgical supplies, specialty beds, forms, and copying. Regardless of where the expense for these items falls, it is the responsibility of the nurse manager to monitor the use of supplies and drugs. In general, if the manager budgets the supplies, there are data to monitor ongoing use of the supplies. The manager should ask questions prior to developing the nonwage expense budget; for instance, will any new charges be attributed to the area in the coming year? Usually, this part of the budget is based considerably on the previous year's actual expenses or the previous year's budget and varies much less than personnel cost. Table 7-6 is the nonwage expense budget for a 28-bed oncology unit and the monthly report created by the finance department to help the nurse manager monitor variations.

Negotiating the Budget

If the manager has been innovative and is recommending the addition of new services or expansion of staffing, the manager will have the opportunity to persuade someone to approve the changes. The challenge to trim the budget or persuade someone against trimming it is almost an annual event in many organizations. This is the opportunity for the real nursing leader to excel with budget acquisition and management.

The first step is to identify exactly where one might reduce expenses. Think of every possible way, and then determine what can be eliminated or reduced without compromising patient care. Make sure the audience understands the impact of the proposals on the hospital as a whole, not just the specific area. Get affirmation from the finance department that it concurs with the numbers submitted. Make sure the plans for expanding a program or for trimming services to reduce a budget are supported by staff and physicians. A powerful argument can be made when speaking for many. The most powerful argument is supported with data to justify any budget increases. Seek the assistance of successful peers in determining how they have added programs or cut expenses without endangering patients. Elicit the support of peers in trading or sharing staff or expenses. Do not make suggestions that reduce cost on one unit by shifting the cost to another department. Offer cross-departmental suggestions, such as reducing one RN at $50,000 and hiring one AP at $25,000 or one phlebotomist in the lab at $25,000. Always provide the rationale from an organizational perspective, not a specific cost center. If all else fails and approval is not granted to expand a program or major cuts must be made, make sure to identify and document the impact expected from the changes on the organization and potential patient outcomes.

Budget Surveillance and Monitoring

All organizations provide some kind of data about monthly revenue and expenses for the manager to use to judge the success of the plan or budget. Monthly reports are too late to impact the expense of that month. Many organizations provide daily productivity staffing figures to the manager so that quick corrections can be made. If daily reports are not available, creating them is a good possibility. Table 7-7 is an example of a form that one nurse manager created with the help of a financial analyst. It is a simple electronic spreadsheet that keeps a running picture of how well the manager is doing on staffing. The manager or designee enters the midnight census and the number of staff working for the 24-hour period. The spreadsheet calculates the daily variance in FTEs from the budgeted staffing for that census and keeps a comprehensive total for the month.

Table 7-6. Nonwage Expense ABC Medical Center Responsibility Center Report, Cost Center: Oncology

Account	Description	Current Month Actual	Current Month Budget	Variance	Prior Year Actual	Year-To-Date Actual	Year-To-Date Budget	Variance	Prior Year Actual
816015-0000	Recognition expense	0	30	(30)	0	0	60	(60)	0
840012-0000	Commercial printing	66	44	22	0	66	88	(22)	151
840020-0000	Office supplies	113	317	(204)	340	443	634	(191)	458
840022-0000	Subscriptions	0	14	(14)	0	0	28	(28)	0
840024-0000	Books	0	38	(38)	0	0	76	(76)	0
840056-0000	Membership dues	0	13	(13)	0	0	26	(26)	0
840059-0000	Education/training	0	83	(83)	0	0	166	(166)	0
840060-0000	Travel	0	147	(147)	0	0	294	(294)	(400)
840068-0000	Minor equipment	0	322	(322)	0	176	644	(468)	0
840099-0000	Other expenses	0	7	(7)	0	0	14	(14)	0
852040-0000	Other housekeeping supplies	28	14	14	16	63	28	35	30
855012-0000	Catheters and tubing	208	279	(71)	252	410	549	(139)	511
855020-0000	Prep and protective	581	697	(116)	676	1,084	1,371	(287)	1,377
855031-0000	Packs trays and kits	42	3	39	2	46	6	40	2
855099-0000	Misc. medical supplies	2,327	2,117	210	1,740	4,200	4,166	34	3,301
856020-0000	Irrigating solutions	1	4	(3)	5	6	8	(2)	6

(Continued on next page)

Table 7-6. Nonwage Expense ABC Medical Center Responsibility Center Report, Cost Center: Oncology (Continued)									
Account	Description	Current Month		Variance	Prior Year Actual	Year-To-Date		Variance	Prior Year Actual
		Actual	Budget			Actual	Budget		
856030-0000	Drugs	4	33	(29)	13	7	65	(58)	14
860012-0000	Equipment repairs	0	69	(69)	0	0	138	(138)	0
870030-0000	Service agreements	0	250	(250)	0	0	500	(500)	0
Total non-payroll expense		**4,398**	**5,721**	**(1,323)**	**4,041**	**8,538**	**11,341**	**(2,803)**	**7,443**

This Responsibility Center Report is of the financial transactions and activities for this oncology unit for August 31, 2005, the second month of this organization's fiscal year. Read the chart left to right, and look at the description commercial printing. This unit spent $66 on printing and was budgeted to spend $44 this month. The monthly variance is $22 more than budgeted. Last year, in August 2004, this unit spent no money on printing. Year-to-date, meaning the two months of the year thus far, $66 has been spent and $88 was budgeted to have been spent after two months, for a variance of positive $22. At this time last year, $151 had been spent on printing.

For total non-wage or non-payroll expense, $4,398 has been spent this month on a budget of $5,721, so the unit has under spent in the month of August by a total of $1,323. At this time last year, the unit had spent $4,041. For the two months of this year (year-to-date), the unit has spent $8,538 and was budgeted to spend $11,341, for a positive year-to-date variance of $2,803. At this time last year, the unit had spent $7,443. In summary, the unit is under budget by $1,323 for the month and under budget $2,803 for the year but has spent $1,095 more than it spent at this time last year ($8,538 − $7,443 = $1,095).

Table 7-7. MNO Medical Center Daily Staff Monitoring Tool						
Unit: Oncology						
Month: February						
Date	Census	Number of RNs	Number of Management	Number of Assistive Personnel	Variance	Cumulative Variance
1	24	13	0	9	−3.29	−3.29
2	31	16	2	10	−4.67	−7.96
3	30	16	2	10	−4.06	−12.02
4	23	14	2	9	+2.4	−9.62
5	20	12	2	8	+3.6	−6.02
6						

This computerized staffing monitoring sheet allows the nurse manager to insert the number of staff who worked each day of the month. The program keeps track of the daily variance of shifts worked and the cumulative variance for the month. The unit was overstaffed by three or four (−3.29 and −4.67 above) people on the first, second, and third of the month and understaffed on the fourth and fifth days by two or three people (+2.4 and 3.6 above). The cumulative for the month is understaffed by 6.02 shifts.

This unit does not staff any licensed practical nurses.

Many organizations ask for an understanding of variances on a daily, weekly, or monthly basis. Most create guidelines for writing variance explanations, such as a variance greater than 3% a month or a variance of greater than a certain dollar figure. These forms usually do not list an explanation of positive variances, but add those, too. If quality, patient satisfaction, or outcome changes have resulted from negative variances, add that as well.

In trying to determine the cause of your variances, consider the following. Overstaffing may be a result of

- Inexperienced staff or manager
- Poor delegation
- Poor ancillary support
- Inability of charge nurses or of the manager to flex down
- Use of expensive agency personnel
- Orientation of new staff
- Supply expenses over budget
- Too many supplies ordered
- Too many supplies used
- Patient acuity or census causing more supplies to be used
- Staff not charging for supplies
- Staff providing free take-home supplies to patients.

If expenses are considerably over budget, then look at revenue and the census to see if the expense was justified. A justification that reads staff expense is over by 7% or $14,000 for the month accompanied by census over budget by 10% and revenue over budget by $36,000 is sure to be better received than a justification that just notes the overspending. Be a data-driven manager.

Table 7-8 is an abbreviated monthly department responsibility report for an inpatient oncology unit. The full monthly report is three and one-half pages in length and details actual revenue and budgeted revenue and expense for the month and YTD. Upon receiving this monthly report, the manager sits down for some solitary review time. This manager would note the following in analyzing this report.

- Total income for the month is $484,277 and budgeted for $524,688 or under by 7.7% for the month. YTD total income is also under budget but only by 3.7%. The manager then will notice that total patient days are over budget by 4.7% for the month, but admissions are under budget by 31%. One could surmise from this that although admissions are down, the length of stay is up. This could be related to patient acuity, poor discharge planning, or poor case management. One immediate action would be to check with the utilization review or case manager to see how many patients' insurance plans denied days or stays during the month and what actions can be taken to reduce the number. A part of the organization's budget may be to set target length of stay (LOS) goals for certain procedures, treatments, or diagnosis, in which case the nurse manager is responsible for taking the necessary action to maintain targeted LOS or below.

- In the salary and wage category, the manager sees that the salaries for the month are over in total by $2,177, but the overage occurs in two areas: temporary help and support/administrative assistants. The manager is not surprised by the temporary help category because there are two full-time travel RNs working on the unit, but she is surprised by the support staff figure of $11,489 spent this month and the $122,003 spent YTD. It takes only a quick check of the staffing for the month to realize there is a problem with "sitters" or aides who are hired to sit with combative patients or patients at risk for falls. The action plan is to institute a new fall prevention plan that, over time, will eliminate the need for sitters, without increasing the use of patient restraints, a patient safety goal initiative.

- Scanning the drugs and supplies expenses, the manager sees that, overall, the unit is under budget by 13% this month, but the largest overage this month and for the year is in catheters. A check with the staff determines that no more catheters have been used, but one particular physician always orders a special kind of catheter. The central supply department confirms that the special catheter is approximately $50 more per unit. The manager resolves to have a conversation with the physician and present a comparison of the two catheters to convince the physician to select the standard, less expensive catheter when possible.

This process of reviewing revenue and expenses on a monthly basis is only worthwhile if the manager is willing to evaluate the data, find the answers, and change clinical or administrative practices. The process of budget monitoring is similar to research: evaluate the situation, determine possible solutions, take action, and reevaluate again next month.

Table 7-8. Department Responsibility Report

Oncology Inpatient Unit As of May 31

	May ACTUAL	May BUDGET	DOLLAR VARIANCE FAV/(UNFAV)	PERCENT VARIANCE FAV/(UNFAV)	PRIOR YEAR ACTUAL	YTD ACTUAL	YTD BUDGET	DOLLAR VARIANCE FAV/(UNFAV)	PERCENT VARIANCE FAV/(UNFAV)	PRIOR YEAR ACTUAL
REVENUE										
ROOM CARE REVENUE	471,195	514,656	(43,461)	(8.44)	426,147	4,922,453	5,199,991	(277,538)	(5.34)	4,380,271
IP ANCILLARY REVENUE	356	344	12	3.49	178	1,958	3,479	(1,521)	(43.72)	3,300
TOTAL INPATIENT INCOME	471,551	515,000	(43,449)	(8.44)	426,325	4,924,411	5,203,470	(279,059)	(5.36)	4,383,571
TOTAL OUTPATIENT ANCILLARY	12,726	9,688	3,038	31.36	14,942	187,601	107,110	80,491	75.15	96,698
TOTAL OTHER PATIENT SERVICES	0	0	0	0.00	0	0	0	0	0.00	0
TOTAL OTHER OPERATING REVENUE	0	0	0	0.00	0	0	0	0	0.00	0
TOTAL INCOME	484,277	524,688	(40,411)	(7.70)	441,267	5,112,012	5,310,580	(198,568)	(3.74)	4,480,269
SALARY and WAGES										
SUPERVISORY	13,329	13,225	(104)	(0.79)	12,219	145,192	142,953	(2,239)	(1.57)	134,872
PROFESSIONAL	104,372	116,761	12,389	10.61	113,177	1,298,652	1,284,298	(14,354)	(1.12)	1,330,307
REGISTERED CERTIFIED TECH	(46)	0	46	0.00	90	736	0	(736)	0.00	422
NON-REG/NON-CERT TECH	1,463	12,874	11,411	88.63	3,033	17,961	139,341	121,380	87.11	20,517
NON-PROFESSIONAL ASST.	20,917	23,249	2,332	10.03	21,245	223,607	256,587	32,980	12.85	258,315
SUPPORT/ADMIN ASSISTANTS	11,489	77	(11,412)	(14,820.51)	11,668	122,003	3,300	(118,703)	(3,597.07)	120,047
TEMPORARY HELP	35,786	19,790	(15,996)	(80.83)	8,446	262,840	213,817	(49,023)	(22.93)	225,068
SALARY TRANSFER OUT	0	0	0	0.00	390	0	0	0	0.00	3,408
SALARY TRANSFER IN	843	0	(843)	0.00	3,014	10,085	0	(10,085)	0.00	14,083
TOTAL SALARIES AND WAGES	188,153	185,976	(2,177)	(1.17)	173,282	2,081,075	2,040,296	(40,779)	(2.00)	2,107,039

(Continued on next page)

Table 7-8. Department Responsibility Report (Continued)

May ACTUAL	May BUDGET	DOLLAR VARIANCE FAV/(UNFAV)	PERCENT VARIANCE FAV/(UNFAV)	PRIOR YEAR ACTUAL	DRUGS AND SUPPLIES	YTD ACTUAL	YTD BUDGET	DOLLAR VARIANCE FAV/(UNFAV)	PERCENT VARIANCE FAV/(UNFAV)	PRIOR YEAR ACTUAL
469	291	(178)	(61.23)	207	COST OF DRUGS SOLD	4,913	2,950	(1,963)	(66.55)	2,899
8,720	11,414	2,694	23.60	10,959	MEDSURG SUPPLIES GENERAL	105,231	115,550	10,319	8.93	116,276
2	1	(1)	(66.00)	23	MEDSURG SUPPLIES IV SOLUTIONS	13	11	(2)	(17.45)	27
1,582	964	(618)	(64.10)	840	MEDSURG SUPPLIES CATHETERS	13,731	9,758	(3,973)	(40.72)	9,727
59	2	(57)	(2,874.00)	0	MEDSURG SUPPLIES ELECTRODES	127	13	(114)	(880.08)	(147)
465	238	(227)	(95.37)	298	MEDSURG SUPPLIES CUSTOM PACKS	5,124	2,413	(2,711)	(112.35)	2,498
0	195	195	100.00	0	MEDSURG SUPPLIES SUTURES	269	1,975	1,706	86.39	179
0	0	0	0.00	0	MEDSURG SUPPLIES WIRES	16	0	(16)	0.00	0
0	0	0	0.00	0	MEDSURG IMPLANTS PROSTHETICS	3	0	(3)	0.00	0
6	0	(6)	0.00	0	INBOUND FREIGHT CHARGES	56	0	(56)	0.00	0
0	0	0	0.00	0	VENDOR REBATES	32	0	(32)	0.00	0
0	1	1	100.00	0	LINEN AND BEDDING	0	11	11	100.00	5
0	26	26	100.00	0	EMPLOYEE WEARING APPAREL	0	264	264	100.00	242
0	268	268	100.00	0	MINOR EQUIPMENT	4,506	2,710	(1,796)	(66.29)	229
3	1	(2)	(222.00)	12	SURGICAL INSTRUMENTS	51	11	(40)	(365.64)	24
269	361	92	25.48	232	OFFICE AND ADMIN SUPPLIES	4,354	3,653	(701)	(19.19)	8,543
977	831	(146)	(17.61)	1,679	FORMS	9,123	8,411	(712)	(8.46)	9,354

(Continued on next page)

Table 7-8. Department Responsibility Report (Continued)

	May ACTUAL	May BUDGET	DOLLAR VARIANCE FAV/(UNFAV)	PERCENT VARIANCE FAV/(UNFAV)	PRIOR YEAR ACTUAL	YTD ACTUAL	YTD BUDGET	DOLLAR VARIANCE FAV/(UNFAV)	PERCENT VARIANCE FAV/(UNFAV)	PRIOR YEAR ACTUAL
FOOD	305	733	428	58.34	458	5,985	7,424	1,439	19.38	6,928
NOURISHMENTS	52	125	73	58.58	70	2,093	1,263	(830)	(65.75)	1,219
MAINTENANCE SUPPLIES	0	1	1	100.00	0	9	2	(7)	(356.00)	7
LIGHT TUBES AND BULBS	0	0	0	0.00	0	0	0	0	0.00	4
SERVICES-RELATED SUPPLIES	549	40	(509)	(1,273.43)	100	5,660	406	(5,254)	(1,294.09)	471
MEDICAL CHEMICALS	16	9	(7)	(74.67)	14	128	89	(39)	(43.31)	95
GLASSWARE	0	0	0	0.00	0	(5)	0	5	0.00	0
BIOLOGICS	0	182	182	100.00	0	0	1,840	1,840	100.00	(17)
QUALITY CONTROL MATERIALS	415	433	18	4.22	225	4,023	4,387	364	8.30	4,225
BACTERIA MEDIA	4	0	(4)	0.00	(4)	65	0	(65)	0.00	(4)
TOTAL DRUGS AND SUPPLIES	13,895	16,116	2,221	13.78	15,113	165,509	163,141	(2,368)	(1.45)	162,784
STATISTICS										
PATIENT DAYS	776	741	35	4.72	764	8,135	8,555	(420)	(4.91)	8,485
ADMISSIONS	93	135	(42)	(31.11)	121	1,327	1,397	(70)	(5.01)	1,425
PROCEDURES IP	5	0	5	0.00	0	217	0	217	0.00	0
OBSERVATION HOURS	0	0	0	0.00	34	228	0	228	0.00	258
OP IN-A-BED HOURS	0	0	0	0.00	0	14	0	14	0.00	19
OBSERVATION PTS	21	18	3	16.67	34	301	199	102	51.26	258
OP IN A BED	1	0	1	0.00	0	3	0	3	0.00	0
TOTAL STATISTICS	896	894	2	0.22	953	10,225	10,151	74	0.73	10,445

This is the monitoring tool used by the oncology unit on a monthly basis to follow revenue and supplies. This is a month-to-date and year-to-date report as of May 31 for a facility that budgets July to June, so the 11th month of the year is displayed.

FAV = favorable, IP = inpatient, OP = outpatient, PT = patient, UNFAV = unfavorable, YDT = year to date

Special Considerations

Many organizations ask nurse managers to develop business plans for new programs. Business plan formats vary widely by facility, as does the degree of autonomy the manager has in developing the financial section of the business plan. Figure 7-8 includes some of the basic requirements for the manager to consider when thinking about proposing a new service, whether the actual forms require all these data or not. Chapter 36 details the specifics of business planning.

Figure 7-8. Business Plan Considerations

1. Introduction
   a. Title
   b. Purpose
   c. Fit with mission, vision, and values of the organization
   d. Fit with the organization's strategic plan
   e. Fit with the cancer program's strategic plan
2. Community assessment
   a. Community need
   b. Competition's present programs or plans
3. Risk assessment
   a. Degree of financial risk
   b. Degree of liability risk
   c. Degree of lost opportunity risk
4. Implementation plan
   a. Resources required; human, operation, and capital expense; and space
   b. Structure and organizational relationships
5. Evaluation plan
   a. Evaluation measures: financial, quality, patient satisfaction, physician satisfaction
   b. Evaluation timeline
6. Financial analysis
   a. Demand, volume, revenue, market share, payor mix, rate setting
   b. Expense: full-time equivalents, nonwage expense, capital expense, space, renovations, overhead
   c. Review of best-practices experience
7. Three- to five-year proforma income statement
8. Three- to five-year net present value analysis
9. Recommendation

Another possible area of financial management for the nurse manager is the development of payor contracts. When the organization is negotiating with payors for the most favorable contracts, the finance department does this work. A wise contract negotiator will seek the advice of the manager to determine what it will cost to provide care prior to developing the contract specifics. This is especially important when a particular service such as bone marrow transplantation is being negotiated as a stand alone or "carved-out" benefit or when capitation contracts are being negotiated.

Summary

Financial management is one of the core competencies of the nurse manager. The manager who is ill prepared for the task is encouraged to seek all the mentoring that is available, either via peers, supervisors, or financial analysts in the organization or by taking classes at a local university or college. The purpose of managing one's finances is to have a firm plan of how to best care for patients given the resources available. It takes careful planning on the front end and close scrutiny to determine how one can improve performance. Not every manager will enjoy this particular part of the role of manager, but every manager realizes that only via skilled financial management can we best care for our patients. Deeps and Sussman (1993) quoted Dag Hammerskjold as saying, "Never, for the sake of peace and quiet, deny your own experience or convictions." Managers are empowered to commit to their patient care convictions by excelling in financial management.

References

Aiken, L.H., Clarke, S.P., Sloan, D.M., Sochalski, J., & Silber, J.H. (2002). Hospital nurse staffing and patient mortality, nurse burnout, and job dissatisfaction. *JAMA, 288,* 1987–1993.

Deeps, S., & Sussman, L. (1993). *Smart moves.* Upper Saddle River, NJ: Addison-Wesley.

Field, C. (1944). *Bernard Baruch, park bench statesman.* Columbus, OH: McGraw-Hill.

Finkler, S.A., & Kovner, C.T. (2000). *Financial management for nurse managers and executives* (2nd ed.). Philadelphia: Saunders.

Lamkin, L., Rosiak, J., Buerhaus, P., Mallory, G., & Williams, M. (2002). Oncology Nursing Society workforce survey part II: Perception of the nursing workforce environment and adequacy of nurse staffing in outpatient and inpatient oncology settings. *Oncology Nursing Forum, 29,* 93–100.

Needleman, J., Buerhaus, P., Mattke, S., Stewart, M., & Zelevinsky, K. (2002). Nurse-staffing levels and the quality of care in hospitals. *New England Journal of Medicine, 346,* 1715–1722.

Schmidt, D.Y. (1999). Financial and operational skills for the nurse manager. *Nursing Administration Quarterly, 23*(4), 16–28.

Flexible Budgets and Staffing Matrix

Alice Forsha Vautier, RN, EdD
Marilyn B. Farrand, BSIE, MSHS
Mary Gullatte, RN, MN, ANP, AOCN®, FAAMA

One of the most important and difficult tasks of nursing leadership is to manage the full-time equivalent (FTE) staffing budget. The title does not matter: nurse manager, department director, director of nursing, or chief nursing officer, the number of staff budgeted is critical. Without enough staff to care for patients, the manager is stopped from making change in care delivery systems, improving quality, and improving patient, physician, and staff satisfaction. One of the first steps is to ensure that the budgeted dollars are appropriate; the second step is the recruitment and retention of staff. This chapter is devoted to the concept of a flexible budget, based on hours of nursing care per patient day. It addresses the change in census on a daily basis and outlines the impact on staff and retention. Because the budget is a constantly moving target, how to monitor it on a shift-by-shift and month-by-month basis also will be discussed. During times of staffing shortages, the manager must ensure that systems exist for nurses to access resources should care requirements change beyond the capability of involved practitioners (White, 2003).

In the midst of budget planning, the manager must come with a sound strategy to secure the appropriate number of staff to meet fluctuating patient care demands. During budget negotiations, the first step is to reach agreement on the number of hours per patient day. The key is to build enough core staffing to cover patient care needs around the average patient census. The average patient census should be the *budgeted census per patient unit*. Multiple databases are used to see if there is consistency in the recommended hours per patient type. As an example, the cardiac surgery intensive care units all close within the recommended hours per patient day, compared by multiple databases. If inconsistencies are found, then additional time is spent finding an agreed upon number of hours of care per patient type. For the most part, the hours per patient day are consistent.

The second step is to get administrative approval for a flexible budget. Nursing leadership has struggled with how to get the staff members needed when the census is high and how to decrease staff when the census is lower than budget. If the census is higher than budget, it needs to be addressed quickly, which shows support of staff and aide retention. The solution is built into the system during the budget process. One multiplies the approved hours per patient day by the census. One does not have to look for a trend in census or seek approval for additional FTEs. A flexible budget is an immediate response to a change from budgeted census.

In many ways, flexible budgets produce a similar end result to patient care needs on a nursing unit. The advantages of a flexible budget are

- The hours of care are approved in the budget process.
- The system is easy to administer.
- It does not depend on the opinions of a large number of nurses.
- It is not easy to have false projections of staffing needs.
- It requires very little time to determine staffing needs shift by shift.
- The change in staffing needs does not have to wait until the classification forms are filled out and a report run.

The disadvantage is a shift-by-shift fine-tuning of staffing based on patient acuity.

Both budgeting and patient classification systems should be used as a management tool, and individual judgment by the person responsible for the daily operation of the unit needs to be in place. Both systems give the average care needed for patients, and sometimes the manager may increase or decrease the staffing required based on expert knowledge of the unit. There are numerous examples throughout this chapter to assist the nurse manager in determining unit-flexible staffing standards and matrices based on average daily census and worked hours per unit of service or hours per patient day. Over the course of a month, actual staffing will be within the flexible budget or patient classification requirements. If the actual is consistently above or below the staffing requirements, the systems need to be evaluated for having the correct allocation of time for patient care.

For the flexible budget, the hours per patient day are evaluated during the budget process, and any changes required should be made at this time. The databases from which the hours per patient day are derived need to be part of the annual review. The acuity of patients across the nation continues to increase, and that impacts the hours recommended for each patient type.

Recruitment and retention of staff are critical for the delivery of safe and effective patient care. A system that allows the budget to change based on the number of patients also allows the addition of staff at the time of increased patient hours of care. It is not very helpful if the nurse manager has to go through a long involved process to add or decrease staff. Staff is needed on the same day the facility has increased patient hours of care. Staff need to feel supported by nursing and hospital leadership, so an effort must be made to keep the nurse-to-patient ratio manageable. If staff members feel that no one cares about the ratio, it is nearly impossible to retain staff.

Staffing and budgeting are two of the most important functions of nursing leadership. Chapters 6 and 7 have provided in-depth information on healthcare economics and financial management, respectively, as base preparation for this chapter, which is meant to give insight into the process of flexible budgeting. Tools on how to successfully implement flexible budgeting are included. A glossary of terms used throughout this chapter can be found in Figure 8-1. The content of this chapter primarily focuses on inpatient acute care units.

Figure 8-1. Terms and Definitions

Average Daily Census (ADC)—equivalent patient days for a specified period of time (e.g., month, year) divided by number of days in the period. (For example, a 38-bed medical nursing unit had 912 patient days for the month of September. ADC 912/30 = 30.4.)

Direct Care Providers—staff who care for patients at the bedside; typically includes RNs, LPNs, nurse technicians, nurse aides, and patient care assistants. The number of these positions should fluctuate with number of patients.

Full-Time Equivalent (FTE)—a measurement used to determine the percent of time worked based on a 40-hour workweek. For example, an employee who works 20 hours/week is equivalent to 0.5 FTE and 40 hours/week is equivalent to 1.0 FTE.

Hours/UOS (Target)—total worked hours per UOS. Monitors how well a department staffs to budget; also may be referred to as hours per patient day in inpatient nursing units.

Indirect Care Providers—staff who do not directly care for the patient at bedside and do not generally fluctuate with number of patients. These positions typically include unit clerks, monitor technicians, and department managers who do not take patient assignments.

Nonproductive Hours (Paid time off)—amount of hours paid for vacation, holiday, or sick time for benefited hospital employees.

Paid Hours—worked hours + nonproductive hours.

Patient Mix—the breakdown of patients in a group by hospital service, such as BMT or general medicine.

Patient:RN Ratio—the number of patients to RNs.

Percentage of Nonproductive Hours—nonproductive hours/paid hours.

Skill Mix—the breakdown of staff by skill, such as percent of RNs or technicians.

Unit of Service (UOS)—the workload measurement used to quantify service of a unit or a department. Examples include equivalent patient days, nursery days, visits, and procedures. Most inpatient nursing units use equivalent patient day = number inpatients residing on unit at midnight plus observation days (patients admitted–23 hours).

Variance Hours/UOS—budgeted hours/UOS–actual hours/UOS.

Worked (Productive) Hours—the amount of hours worked in a department; this should include all internal hospital employees as well as any outside agency staff. It is important to understand what is included in the hospital's productive hours. Sometimes hours for orientation, professional time, and meetings are included, which should not be counted in staffing.

Workload Volume—the numerical value of the UOS provided during a specified period of time.

Static Versus Flexible Budget
(With Biweekly Example)

Most hospitals will develop an annual budget for each department at a particular volume, resulting in a fixed number of FTEs. However, it may not be feasible to operate at this level if the budgeted volume is unrealistically lower than the actual volume. Thus, most patient care departments tend to operate with a flexible budget to achieve the level of service necessary for a department. The difference between static and flexible budgets is illustrated in Tables 8-1 and 8-2.

In a static budget, the number of budgeted paid FTEs does not change with volume. In Table 8-1, the two periods have different budgeted volumes at 490 and 525, respectively. The number of budgeted paid FTEs is fixed at 56.2 regardless of fluctuations in volume; this results in the hours/UOS (unit of service) (target) to differ at 8.19 and 7.64, respectively. To manage effectively, a department should not have a moving target as an objective to reach.

Table 8-1. Static Budget

| Period | Volume | | Paid FTEs | | Hours/UOS | | Variance Hours/Unit of Service |
	Budgeted	Actual	Budgeted*	Actual	Budgeted**	Actual	
1	490	510	56.2	58.0	8.19	8.12	.07
2	525	475	56.2	56.1	7.64	8.43	(.79)

* Budgeted paid full-time equivalents remain fixed.
** Budgeted hours per unit of service adjusted by census.

In Table 8-2, the two periods have different budgeted volumes at 490 and 525, respectively. The number of Budgeted Paid FTEs changes so that the Hours/UOS (target) is static at 8.31. Flexible budgeting is when staffing fluctuates at different volumes to maintain a fixed hours/UOS target.

Table 8-2. Flexible Budget

| Period | Volume | | Paid FTEs | | Hours/UOS | | Variance Hours/Unit of Service |
	Budgeted	Actual	Budgeted***	Actual	Budgeted****	Actual	
1	490	510	57.0	58.0	8.31	8.12	.19
2	525	475	61.0	56.1	8.31	8.43	(.12)

*** Budgeted paid full-time equivalents adjusted by census.
**** Budgeted hours per each unit of service remains fixed.

Annual FTE Budget

Many hospitals develop an annual FTE budget to plan salary expenses for the next year. The FTEs would represent a static budget because a set projected volume number is applied. Typically, during the budget process, the budgeted worked hours/UOS is reviewed. Many times comparative databases or benchmarks are used to validate if the budgeted worked hours are appropriate. These are some of the most important numbers set during the budget process because they will be used throughout in a flexible budget. In Figure 8-2, Unit T4 has budgeted worked hours/UOS = 9.50, which is equal to the benchmark hospital group.

Patient Classification Systems

Historically, healthcare settings, particularly in acute care, relied on formal or institutionally developed patient classification systems (PCSs) to determine staffing needs. In the 1980s, most hospitals embraced an industrial PCS in an effort to quantify

Figure 8-2. Nursing Services Annual Full-Time Equivalent Budget Spreadsheet Sample

Cost Center	Department Name	No. Beds	UOS	A Volume Statistics			B Wk/Hr UOS Statistics			C Paid FTE Statistics	
				FY Bud Annual Volume	FY Bud Budget ADC	FY-1 Actual ADC	FY Budget Wk Hr/UOS	FY-1 Actual Wk Hr/UOS	Bench Target Wk Hr/UOS	FY Budget FTEs	FY Actual FTEs
20280	Unit G1 (Cardiac)	39	Pt Days	11,734	32.1	35.6	9.00	8.05	9.50	56.7	56.2
20330	Unit T4 (Oncology)	40	Pt Days	11,680	32.0	30.1	9.50	10.34	9.50	59.6	61.0
20430	IMC Nursery	16	Nsy Days	4,700	12.9	13.7	12.00	13.03	11.50	30.3	35.0
20470	Emergency		Visits	32,000	87.7	81.2	2.14	2.57	2.50	36.7	40.9
20500	Labor and Delivery		RVUs	52,000	142.5	147.9	1.55	1.59	1.60	43.3	46.0

Formula to Calculate FY Bud Wk Hr/UOS
FYBud WkHr/UOS = (FYBudFTEs x 2080 x .895) (FYBud Annual Volume)
B = ((C x 2080 x .895))/A

For Example (T4):
(59.6 x 2080 x .895)/11,680 = 9.46 WkHr/UOS

Formula to Calculate FY Bud FTEs
FY Bud FTEs = (FY Bud Wk Hr/UOS x FY Bud Annual Volume)/2080/.895
C = (A x B)/2080/.895

For example (G1):
(9.00 x 11,734)/2080/.895 = 56.7 Pd FTEs

Notes on formulas:
Annual FTE conversion factor = 2,080 hrs
Budget paid time off % = 10.5%
1 – PTO% = 1 – .105 = .895

Average Daily Census–ADC; Full-Time Equivalent–FTE; Fiscal Year–FY; Relative Value Unit–RVU; Unit of Service–UOS and assign individualized patient acuity attributes per patient, per shift. This process was arduous for the nursing staff that had little confidence in the validity of the system to accurately reflect what the nurse perceived as the true patient acuity and resultant workload assignment.

As changes in healthcare reimbursement in the 1990s brought declining inpatient census and major restructuring and reorganizing of healthcare processes, including care delivery, many of the formal acuity systems fell out of favor. In 2000, de Vries, Vissers, and de Vries looked at PCS for production control in hospitals. They compared PCSs relative to three measures: (a) general purpose criteria: stability, simplicity, validity, and reliability; (b) application-dependent criteria: financial control, quality control, and logistics; and (c) decision level criteria: operations, institutional, and macro, and found that existing PCSs did not fulfill all those requirements. The classification systems used for comparison included international classification of diseases (ICD-9), diagnosis-related groups, disease staging, diagnosis treatment combinations, and various hospital-specific systems.

Some organizations continue to rely on patient classification and acuity models for determining staffing and workload. The dawn of the millennium has seen improvement in the quality, validity, and reliability of some classification systems products such as EVALISYS PCS®. This product reportedly takes into consideration the "step-mixed" reality of staffing requirements in which staff members continuously adjust care priorities throughout the work shift. The goals of this tool are to provide for staffing flexibility, balance patient assignments, provide for effective staff utilization, and provide an objective and sound method for the manager to prepare for budget and defense (Catalyst Systems, 2003).

A second commercial tool is the Expert Nurse Estimation Patient Classification System (ENEPCS™). This contemporary model incorporates all activities and care needs of the patient using eight categories of care: cognitive status, self-care status, emotional psychosocial support, comfort/pain management, family information and support, treatment, interdisciplinary coordination, patient teaching and documentation, and transition planning (Malloch, 2002).

A third product is the RES-Q® Healthcare Systems (2004). This product is Windows®-based and provides for assigning of individualized acuity attributes to each patient or patient bed location. Each attribute has a relative workload value assigned to it, which then determines the patient acuity level. This, in turn, becomes the basis for determining the correct mix of staff and skills to provide the required patient care need.

Some current PCSs offer computer-based models, eliminating the old paper and pencil tools of the past. Regardless of the process or product used to determine staffing level and skill mix, it is imperative that the nurse manager be actively engaged in ensuring appropriate staffing for each shift, seven days a week.

Benchmarking

Benchmarking is another method managers use to determine the appropriate level and skill of staffing to provide safe and effective patient care. Benchmarking is a process by which comparative hospital groups often are used to obtain information and indicators when reviewing worked hours/UOS levels. Several databases exist in the healthcare industry to use for this purpose. Generally, global hospital criteria, such as type of hospital—teaching or nonteaching, locale—community or urban, bed size, and case mix index, are used to identify and compare hospital groups. To further streamline appropriate benchmark hospitals from a departmental or operational angle, departmental questionnaires, which are completed by participating hospitals in the database, can be used as additional criteria.

For hospitals that do not participate in a comparative database, the *Hospital Blue Book* (Metzer, 2001) or calling/surveying hospitals can be used to identify potential "compare" hospitals. Then, a departmental questionnaire or survey can be administered via phone or e-mail. Many books and professional organizations have listings of hospitals and contacts that can be used in this endeavor. Some examples of recommended departmental data include

1. Monthly volume
2. Patient to RN ratio
3. Service mix breakdown
4. Staffed beds (if appropriate) or number of rooms (if appropriate)
5. Target/budgeted worked hours/UOS
6. Number of indirect care FTEs by job class and FTE amount (i.e., educator = 1.0, unit clerk = 4.5)
7. Core coverage of master staffing plan by skill
8. Number of procedures with volume (in nursing areas, this is not always looked at)

Once comparative data are obtained for worked hours/UOS, this information should be used to determine whether existing hospital-targeted worked hours/UOS are appropriate on a departmental level.

Management of Staffing Resources

There are two stages to effectively use labor resources: core staffing and adjusted daily staffing. Core staffing includes reviewing workload trends, managing position control, and maintaining appropriate core coverage to build staff schedules for future periods. Adjusted daily staffing involves the daily management of staffing levels required with actual workload levels.

Core Staffing

Workload (Census/Volume) Trends

It is important to understand the workload trend of each department to schedule staff most effectively. If possible, workload data should be gathered and summarized by day of week and shift. In most nursing inpatient units, the shifts reviewed should include 7 am, 3 pm, and 11 pm; it also is helpful to quantify census at 7 pm if it is not too labor intensive to collect. Census statistics that can be reviewed for this purpose include actual average daily census, most frequent census level, and the census level, which represents 80% of the days in a specific period of time.

Position Control

It is recommended to track employees by skill to know how many FTEs are in filled positions. A spreadsheet, such as the one shown in Figure 8-3 can be used to monitor unfilled (vacant) positions. It is recommended to have employees available to work on a per diem or as needed basis, as these positions can be added to staffing as census warrants. It is not advisable to hire too many permanent positions, which can result in staffing numbers to be over budget.

Figure 8-3. Bone Marrow Transplantation Position Control

Skill	Name	FTE
RN	XXXXXXXXX	1.0
RN	XXXXXXXXX	0.6
RN	XXXXXXXXX	1.0
RN	XXXXXXXXX	0.9
RN	XXXXXXXXX	1.0
RN	XXXXXXXXX	1.0
RN	Vacant	1.0
RN	Vacant	1.0
RN subtotal		7.5

Skill	Name	FTE
NT	XXXXXXXXX	1.0
NT	XXXXXXXXX	1.0
NT	XXXXXXXXX	1.0
NT	XXXXXXXXX	0.8
NT	Vacant	1.0
NT subtotal		4.8

(Continued on next page)

Figure 8-3. Bone Marrow Transplantation Position Control *(Continued)*		
Skill	**Name**	**FTE**
UC	XXXXXXXXX	1.0
UC	XXXXXXXXX	0.6
UC	XXXXXXXXX	1.0
UC	XXXXXXXXX	1.0
UC subtotal		3.6
RN Mgr	XXXXXXXXX	1.0
Total paid FTEs		16.9
Full-Time Equivalent–FTE; Manager–Mgr; Nurse Technician–NT; Unit Clerk–UC		

Core Coverage

Each unit should have a staffing plan that is used to build future schedule periods. Figure 8-4 shows the staffing plan for a bone marrow transplant (BMT) nursing unit. It is helpful to quantify the FTE numbers associated with the staffing plan to see how well the position control will supply these positions on a regular basis. In general, the core coverage should be set at a level where staff is not always called off or short.

Figure 8-4. BMT Nursing Unit Core Coverage									
Day Shift									
Skill Name	**Su**	**M**	**T**	**W**	**Th**	**F**	**S**	**Wk FTEs**	**Pd FTEs**
RN	7	9	9	9	9	9	7	11.8	13.2
Nurse technician	2	2	2	2	2	2	2	2.8	3.1
Unit clerk	1	2	2	2	2	2	1	2.4	2.7
RN Mgr	0	1	1	1	1	1	0	1.0	1.0
Total	10	14	14	14	14	14	10	18.0	20.0
Evening Shift									
Skill Name	**Su**	**M**	**T**	**W**	**Th**	**F**	**S**	**Wk FTEs**	**Pd FTEs**
RN	6	7	7	7	7	7	6	9.4	10.5
								(Continued on next page)	

Figure 8-4. BMT Nursing Unit Core Coverage *(Continued)*									
Nurse technician	1	1	1	1	1	1	1	1.4	1.6
Unit clerk	1	1	1	1	1	1	1	1.4	1.6
RN Mgr	0	0	0	0	0	0	0	0.0	0.0
Total	8	9	9	9	9	9	8	12.2	13.7
Night Shift									
Skill Name	**Su**	**M**	**T**	**W**	**Th**	**F**	**S**	**Wk FTEs**	**Pd FTEs**
RN	5	6	6	6	6	6	5	8.0	8.9
Nurse technician	1	1	1	1	1	1	1	1.4	1.6
Unit clerk	0	1	1	1	1	1	0	1.0	1.1
RN Mgr	0	0	0	0	0	0	0	0.0	0.0
Total	6	8	8	8	8	8	6	10.4	11.6

Budget Variance				
Skill Name	**Total/Week**	**Total Paid**	**Budget**	**Variance**
RN	29.2	32.6	30.0	-2.6
Nurse technician	5.6	6.3	7.0	0.7
Unit clerk	4.8	5.4	5.4	0.0
RN Mgr	1.0	1.0	1.0	0.0
Total	40.6	45.3	43.4	-1.9

Adjusted Daily Staffing

Staffing Guidelines

There are primarily two types of staffing guideline tables used in inpatient nursing units: the lookup table and the staffing matrix. Typically, lookup tables are used in a homogeneous patient mix, whereas staffing matrices are used on a heterogeneous patient mix. The purpose of these tables is to quantify staffing levels at each census level that will be within the approved budgeted hours/UOS target. It should be noted that these tables are "guidelines," and, thus, some variation may be needed if patient acuity warrants it. These staffing guidelines represent only direct care (DC) providers that would be fluctuated to staff within budget at different census levels.

Lookup Table Example (for homogeneous patient mix)

Lookup tables are developed by manually inputting the number of positions by skill, such as RN or nurse technician (NT), into a spreadsheet for each census level to reach an hours/UOS of equal to or less than the budgeted hours/UOS for direct care providers.

The number of positions represents the actual number of people working and is generally in terms of .5 FTE increments; direct care providers generally start at 7 am, 11 am, 3 pm, 7 pm, or 11 pm. Finally, the FTE variance column is used to measure whether the FTE numbers at each census level is within budget. The objective of the lookup table is to have positive FTE variances. In general, a lookup table can have an infrequent FTE variance of –0.1 or –0.2 if there are a large number of positive variances. This way, the positive variances will cause the negative variances to average out to a positive number because of the fluctuating census.

To develop a lookup table, the worked hours/UOS for only direct care providers must first be calculated. This is illustrated in Figure 8-5. The indirect care provider core coverage was validated, and the amount of patient FTEs quantified was 4.0

Figure 8-5. Oncology Department		
Available beds: 23		
Budget Information	Year XX	
Patient days	7,150	
ADC	19.5	
PTO %	10.5%	
Total paid FTEs	42.5	
HPPD (wk hr/UOS)	11.12	
Direct Care Providers		
Skill Level	**Paid**	**Worked**
RN	33.2	29.7
Nurse technician	4.3	3.8
Subtotal DC	37.5	33.5
% Direct Care (DC) 88.3% DC Hours/UOS 9.82** ** (for staffing guideline tables)		
Indirect Care Providers		
Skill Level	**Paid**	**Worked**
RN5 manager	1.0	1.0
Unit clerk	4.0	3.6
Subtotal indirect	5.0	4.6

unit clerks and 1.0 RN manager. The percent of DC then is determined by factoring out these indirect providers. In Figure 8-5, $(42.5-5)/42.5 = 88.3\%$. The worked hours/UOS for DC providers only (DC hours/UOS) = 11.12 x .883 = 9.82. Then, the DC hours/UOS is used in the lookup table shown in Figure 8-6. Formulas for the lookup table are shown in Figure 8-7.

Figure 8-6. Oncology Department Lookup Table

Budget Hours/UOS 9.82	Day Shift			Evening Shift			Night Shift		
	Care	RN	NT	Care	RN	NT	Care	RN	NT
	40.9%	84.6%	15.4%	32.6%	87.8%	12.2%	26.6%	83.8%	16.3%

ADC	FTEs for 24 Hours	Day Shift			Evening Shift			Night Shift			Hours/ UOS	FTE Variance
		Tot DC	RN	NT	Tot DC	RN	NT	Tot DC	RN	NT		
5.0	2.0	2.0	2.0	0.0	2.0	2.0	0.0	2.0	2.0	0.0	9.60	0.1
6.0	3.0	3.0	3.0	0.0	2.0	2.0	0.0	2.0	2.0	0.0	9.33	0.4
7.0	3.0	3.0	3.0	0.0	3.0	3.0	0.0	2.0	2.0	0.0	9.14	0.6
8.0	4.0	4.0	4.0	0.0	3.0	3.0	0.0	3.0	3.0	0.0	10.00	-0.2
9.0	4.0	4.0	4.0	0.0	4.0	4.0	0.0	3.0	3.0	0.0	9.78	0.1
10.0	5.0	5.0	5.0	0.0	4.0	4.0	0.0	3.0	3.0	0.0	9.60	0.3
11.0	5.0	5.0	5.0	0.0	4.0	4.0	0.0	4.0	3.0	1.0	9.45	0.5
12.0	5.0	5.0	5.0	0.0	5.0	4.0	1.0	4.0	3.0	1.0	9.33	0.7
13.0	7.0	7.0	6.0	1.0	5.0	4.0	1.0	4.0	3.0	1.0	9.85	0.0
14.0	7.0	7.0	6.0	1.0	5.0	4.0	1.0	5.0	4.0	1.0	9.71	0.2
15.0	7.0	7.0	6.0	1.0	6.0	5.0	1.0	5.0	4.0	1.0	9.60	0.4
16.0	8.0	8.0	6.0	2.0	6.0	5.0	1.0	5.0	4.0	1.0	9.50	0.6
17.0	9.0	9.0	7.0	2.0	7.0	6.0	1.0	5.0	4.0	1.0	9.88	-0.1
18.0	9.0	9.0	7.0	2.0	7.0	6.0	1.0	6.0	5.0	1.0	9.78	0.1
19.0	9.0	9.0	7.0	2.0	8.0	7.0	1.0	6.0	5.0	1.0	9.68	0.3
20.0	10.0	10.0	8.0	2.0	8.0	7.0	1.0	6.0	5.0	1.0	9.60	0.6
21.0	11.0	11.0	9.0	2.0	8.0	7.0	1.0	7.0	6.0	1.0	9.90	-0.2
22.0	11.0	11.0	9.0	2.0	9.0	8.0	1.0	7.0	6.0	1.0	9.82	0.0
23.0	12.0	12.0	10.0	2.0	9.0	8.0	1.0	7.0	6.0	1.0	9.74	0.2

Average Daily Census–ADC; Full-Time Equivalent–FTE; Nurse Technician–NT; Total Direct Care–Tot DC; Unit of Service–UOS

Figure 8-7. Formulas for Lookup Table
FTEs for 24 hours = total FTEs for all shifts Tot DC = total FTEs for each specific shift Hours/UOS = ((FTEs for 24 hours) x 8)/ADC FTE variance = ((budget hours/UOS – hours/UOS) x ADC)/8
Average Daily Census–ADC; Full-Time Equivalent–FTE; Tot DC–Total Direct Care; Unit of Service–UOS

In Figure 8-6, at census = 23, a total of 28 positions can be scheduled over a 24-hour period, which results in 9.74 hours/UOS. This would result in an FTE variance under budget of 0.2. Day shift has a total of 12 positions (10 RNs/2 NTs), evening shift has a total of 9 positions (8 RNs/1 NT), and night shift has a total of 7 positions (6 RNs/1 NT). The breakdown by shift is generally done by looking at the ratio of patients to RNs and patients to NTs. Admissions, discharges, and transfers are considered when distributing FTEs by shift of skill.

Staffing Matrix Example for Homogeneous Patient Mix

Staffing matrices are developed by using formulas to calculate the number of positions by skill, such as RN or NT, for each census level to equal budgeted hours/UOS for DC providers. Judgment must then be used to round the number of RNs or NTs to a number that will be staffed.

The percent of FTEs for each shift and the skill mix percent breakdown for a department should be estimated in order to perform the calculations; both can be calculated from the core coverage. For example, subtotal the DC FTEs across each shift, and then use the following formulas:

% shift FTEs = (shift DC FTEs)/(total DC across all shifts)

% skill = (FTEs per skill)/(total DC FTEs)

The formulas for the staffing matrix are shown in Figure 8-8.

Figure 8-8. Formulas for Staffing Matrix
Hours/UOS = ((FTE for 24 hours) x 8)/census FTE for 24 hours = ((budgeted hours/UOS) x census)/8 Tot DC FTEs for shift = (FTE for 24 hours) x (% FTE on shift) RN for shift = (Tot DC FTEs for shift) x (% RNs) NT for shift = (Tot DC FTEs for shift) x (% NTs)
Full-Time Equivalent–FTE; Nurse Technician–NT; Tot DC–Total Direct Care; Unit of Service–UOS

FTE for 24 hours = (10.50 x 21)/8 = 27.6
Tot DC FTEs for day shift = 27.6 x .381 = 10.5 FTEs
RN for day shift = 10.5 x .80 = 8.4 RN FTEs
NT for day shift = 10.5 x .2 = 2.1 NT FTEs

Figure 8-9 shows an example of a staffing matrix. Using Figure 8-9, how many RNs would be staffed for day shift at 21 patients?

Figure 8-9. Bone Marrow Transplantation Staffing Matrix

FTE% by Shift:
Day 38.1% | Evening 38.1% | Night 7.6%

Skill Mix %: RN 80.0% | NT 20.0%

Budget Hours/UOS 10.53		Day Shift			Evening Shift			Night Shift			
		Care	RN	NT	Care	RN	NT	Care	RN	NT	Hours/UOS
	38.1%	38.1%	30.5%	7.6%	38.1%	30.5%	7.6%	23.8%	19.0%	4.8%	10.53

Number of Patients	FTEs for 24 Hours	Day Shift			Evening Shift			Night Shift			Hours/UOS
		Tot DC	RN	NT	Tot DC	RN	NT	Tot DC	RN	NT	
5.0	6.6	2.5	2.0	0.5	2.5	2.0	0.5	1.6	1.3	0.3	10.53
6.0	7.9	3.0	2.4	0.6	3.0	2.4	0.6	1.9	1.5	0.4	10.53
7.0	9.2	3.5	2.8	0.7	3.5	2.8	0.7	2.2	1.8	0.4	10.53
8.0	10.5	4.0	3.2	0.8	4.0	3.2	0.8	2.5	2.0	0.5	10.53
9.0	11.8	4.5	3.6	0.9	4.5	3.6	0.9	2.8	2.3	0.6	10.53
10.0	13.2	5.0	4.0	1.0	5.0	4.0	1.0	3.1	2.5	0.6	10.53
11.0	14.5	5.5	4.4	1.1	5.5	4.4	1.1	3.4	2.8	0.7	10.53
12.0	15.8	6.0	4.8	1.2	6.0	4.8	1.2	3.8	3.0	0.8	10.53
13.0	17.1	6.5	5.2	1.3	6.5	5.2	1.3	4.1	3.3	0.8	10.53
14.0	18.4	7.0	5.6	1.4	7.0	5.6	1.4	4.4	3.5	0.9	10.53
15.0	19.7	7.5	6.0	1.5	7.5	6.0	1.5	4.7	3.8	0.9	10.53
16.0	21.1	8.0	6.4	1.6	8.0	6.4	1.6	5.0	4.0	1.0	10.53
17.0	22.4	8.5	6.8	1.7	8.5	6.8	1.7	5.3	4.3	1.1	10.53
18.0	23.7	9.0	7.2	1.8	9.0	7.2	1.8	5.6	4.5	1.1	10.53
19.0	25.0	9.5	7.6	1.9	9.5	7.6	1.9	6.0	4.8	1.2	10.53
20.0	26.3	10.0	8.0	2.0	10.0	8.0	2.0	6.3	5.0	1.3	10.53
21.0	27.6	10.5	8.4	2.1	10.5	8.4	2.1	6.6	5.3	1.3	10.53
22.0	29.0	11.0	8.8	2.2	11.0	8.8	2.2	6.9	5.5	1.4	10.53
23.0	30.3	11.5	9.2	2.3	11.5	9.2	2.3	7.2	5.8	1.4	10.53

Full-Time Equivalent–FTE; Nurse Technician–NT; Tot DC–Total Direct Care; Unit of Service–UOS

Staffing Matrix for Heterogeneous Patient Mix

Staffing matrices can be used for departments that have two very distinct patient types that have significantly different hours/UOS. The same formulas (Figure 8-8) are used from the staffing matrix for a homogeneous patient mix to calculate the amount of FTEs for one patient of each patient type. These "per patient" values are multiplied by the number within each patient type and added together.

Using Figure 8-10, what would be the number of RNs on evening shift for a unit that has 8 BMT patients and 10 general medicine patients? BMT patients have a budgeted hours/UOS of 10.53, whereas general medicine patients have a budgeted hours/UOS of 7.12.

Figure 8-10. Staffing Matrix for Nursing Unit With Blood and Marrow Transplant and General Medicine Patients

FTE% by Shift:

Day	Evening	Night
38.1%	38.1%	7.6%

Skill Mix %:

RN	NT
80.0%	20.0%

Patient Type	Hours/UOS	Number of Patients
BMT	10.53	8
General medicine	7.12	10

BMT — Budget Hours/UOS 10.53

	Day Shift			Day Shift			Evening Shift			Evening Shift			Night Shift			Night Shift			Hours/UOS
	% Care	% RN	% NT	Tot DC	RN	NT	% Care	% RN	% NT	Tot DC	RN	NT	% Care	% RN	% NT	Tot DC	RN	NT	
BMT	38.1%	30.5%	7.6%				38.1%	30.5%	7.6%				23.8%	19.0%	4.8%				10.53
Per patient (FTEs for 24 Hrs 1.3)				0.5	0.4	0.1				0.5	0.4	0.1				0.3	0.3	0.1	

General Medicine — Budget Hours/UOS 7.12

	Day Shift			Evening Shift			Night Shift			Hours/UOS
	Tot DC	RN	NT	Tot DC	RN	NT	Tot DC	RN	NT	
Per patient (FTEs for 24 Hrs 0.9)	0.3	0.3	0.1	0.3	0.3	0.1	0.2	0.2	0.0	7.12

Staffing Needs for Combined Patient Mix of BMT and General Medicine

	Day Shift			Evening Shift			Night Shift			Hours/UOS
	Tot DC	RN	NT	Tot DC	RN	NT	Tot DC	RN	NT	
Combined Number of Patients 18 (FTEs for 24 Hrs 19.4)	7.4	5.9	1.5	7.4	5.9	1.5	4.6	3.7	0.9	8.64

BMT (per patient)
FTE for 24 hours = (10.53 x 1 pt)/8 = 1.3
Tot DC FTEs for shift = 1.3 x .381 = .5
RN for shift = .5 x .80 = .4
NT for shift = .5 x .20 = .1

General Medicine (per patient)
FTE for 24 hours = (7.12 x 1 pt)/8 = .9
Tot DC FTEs for shift = .9 x .381 = .34
RN for shift = .34 x .80 = .27
NT for shift = .34 x .20 = .13

(8 pts x .4) + (10 x .27) = 5.9 RNs on evening shift

Monitoring Budget Variance

It is essential to monitor how actual staffing levels compare to budget and document reasons of overages in objective terms. Figure 8-11 is a report that displays the worked FTE variance by month. Total worked hours should include all worked hours, including outside agency.

Monthly FTE Conversion Factors
28 days: 160.0
29 days: 165.7
30 days: 174.4
31 days: 177.1

Using Figure 8-11, Dept. A was four FTEs over budget in August
[(9.5 − 10.93) x 535]/177.1 = 4.0

Formulas on Report
Actual work hours/UOS = actual work hours/actual volume trend
Flex work FTEs = (budget work hours/UOS − actual work
$$\frac{\text{hours/UOS}) \times (\text{actual volume trend})}{\text{FTE conversion factor}}$$

It is very important to look at trend data as well as year-to-date (YTD) information. Sometimes only one month may be negative (over budget), with most other months and YTD data positive. In this case, management should not react to only the one month, as the "trend" is still positive. At the end of a month, it is hard to remember what may have caused a department to run over budget. Thus, it is strongly recommended to department managers to quantify reasons as they occur.

Figure 8-11. Flex Work Full-Time Equivalent Trend Report

Fiscal Year Flex Work FTEs Trend

Department	UOS	Sept	Oct	Nov	Dec	Jan	Feb	Mar	Apr	May	Jun	Jul	Aug	YTD
Dept. A	Pt days	(1.0)	(0.2)	(2.3)	(2.8)	1.7	0.8	(1.5)	(1.2)	(5.7)	(3.3)	(4.6)	(4.0)	(2.0)
Dept. B	Visits	3.5	(4.5)	(9.6)	0.0	(0.7)	(17.3)	4.0	(5.6)	3.7	2.6	(4.3)	0.2	(1.9)
Subtotal		2.5	(4.8)	(11.9)	(2.8)	1.0	(16.6)	2.5	(6.8)	(2.0)	(0.7)	(9.0)	(3.8)	(3.9)

Fiscal Year Flex Actual Volume

Department	UOS	Sept	Oct	Nov	Dec	Jan	Feb	Mar	Apr	May	Jun	Jul	Aug	YTD
Dept. A	Pt days	547	592	501	563	616	529	616	585	473	535	514	535	6,606
Dept. B	Visits	1,500	1,600	1,650	2,000	1,200	1,850	1,000	1,200	1,320	1,460	1,100	1,500	17,380

Fiscal Year Flex Actual Work Hr/UOS

Department	UOS	Sept	Oct	Nov	Dec	Jan	Feb	Mar	Apr	May	Jun	Jul	Aug	YTD
Dept. A	Pt days	9.92	9.67	10.39	10.48	9.10	9.37	10.02	9.96	11.73	10.65	11.20	10.93	10.24
Dept. B	Visits	6.10	7.00	7.0	6.50	6.60	8.00	5.80	7.30	6.00	6.20	7.20	6.48	6.72

Note. The parentheses above indicate a negative number.

The concepts of managing a department of nursing using a flexible budget have been presented to help you be successful in a nurse executive role. While managing tight budgets for health care, it is very helpful to be able to flex your budget both upward for higher census and lower for a drop in census to maintain balance to support safe patient care and staff satisfaction. The nature of our business provides us broad fluctuations in patient care demands. This concept of flexible budgeting is meant to be one of several management tools for the nurse executive to help make sound staffing decisions. It should not be used as a sole staffing decision tool but used with assessment of staff experience and any crisis that may require additional adjustments to staffing requirements. Experience and crisis only add minor adjustments to the flexible budget. Using this model across two major university teaching hospitals for more than 10 years, the nursing department has been on budget with less than a 1% variance of required hours.

References

Catalyst Systems. (2003). *EVALISYS patient classification system (PCS)*. Retrieved February 29, 2004, from http://www.catsys.com

de Vries, G., Vissers, J., & de Vries, G. (2000). The use of patient classification systems for production control of hospitals. *Casemix Quarterly, 2*(2), 65–70.

Malloch, K. (2002). *Expert Nurse Estimation Patient Classification System*. Retrieved February 29, 2004, from http://www.kathymalloch.com

Metzer, J. (2001). *Hospital blue book*. Atlanta, GA: Billian.

RES-Q® Healthcare Systems. (2004). *Patient attribute module*. Retrieved February 29, 2004, from http://www.res-q.com

White, K. (2003). Effective staffing as a guardian of care. *Nursing Management, 34*(7), 20–24.

CHAPTER 9

Nursing Workforce: Challenges and Opportunities

Patricia A. Calico, DNS, RN
Annette Tyree Debisette, DNSc, ANP, RN
Madeline Turkeltaub, PhD, RN, CRNP, FAAN

The challenges of a dwindling RN workforce in the 21st century mark a new era of professional-corporate-private partnerships aimed at identifying and launching old and new strategies to combat the global shortage of RNs. The healthcare system is in transition, and it is essential that leaders from all the stakeholders who cherish excellence in healthcare for all citizens of the United States make excellent decisions. To contribute toward that end, we have before us an "opportunity to reformulate and recreate postmodern nursing as the most caring, respected, and unified of the health care professions" (Clark, 2002, p. 19).

This chapter provides an overview of the history of the nursing shortage, nursing image, trends in the nursing workforce, and recommendations for the future.

History of Nursing Shortages

In 2003, the RN workforce received mass media coverage regarding the distinctive nursing shortage in the United States. Numerous reports of current RN staffing and projections of continued staffing shortages through the year 2020 reveal the integral connection between staffing shortages and patient outcomes. National attention focused on an adequate supply of clinically competent RNs as essential to the provision of quality health care in the United States (Aiken et al., 2001b; Blendon et al.,

The views expressed in this chapter do not necessarily represent the views of the Department of Health and Human Services, Health Resources and Services Administration, or the United States Government.

2002; Joint Commission on Accreditation of Healthcare Organizations [JCAHO], 2002; Page, 2003; Steinbrook, 2002).

A historic look of nursing workforce shortages in the United States and actions taken to relieve shortages provide perspective to the current nursing shortage and the community involvement required to address the need for RNs.

RN shortages have been reported in the United States beginning during World War I, when an increased demand for nurses occurred and resolution was achieved by increasing enrollments in schools of nursing. World War II brought another nursing shortage. The army and navy military services signed up more than 65,000 RNs. The defense industry also had great need for nurses and employed more than twice the number of RNs during this time of national need. As hospitals experienced an acute shortage of RNs, enrollments in schools of nursing were increased again, and schools of nursing were encouraged to accelerate programs of study. The federal government intervened to resolve the shortage by passing the Bolton Act of 1943 (also called the Nurse Training Act) and establishing the U.S. Cadet Nurse Corps. The Corps provided an entirely subsidized nursing education for students who agreed to serve as essential military or civilian nurses throughout the time of war. From 1943 to 1948, 124,065 nurses were subsidized by the Nurse Cadet Corps and graduated from schools of nursing (American Nurses Association, 1994). The Corps set a precedent for federal involvement in basic nursing education and made significant improvements in nursing education.

Also as a result of the Bolton Act, a Division of Nurse Education was created within the Public Health Service. The Division's major responsibilities included monitoring the final phase of the Cadet Nurse Corps program, assessing nursing needs within the Public Health Service, conducting nursing research studies, ensuring quality of nursing education and practice, and representing nursing on the national level (Division of Nursing, 1997).

In 1945, following enactment of the Bolton Act, nursing school enrollments were at a high of 130,900 students, but enrollments decreased to a low of 94,133 following the war. Despite the low enrollments and the struggle to fill nursing classes, few men or individuals from minority backgrounds were enrolled in or graduated from nursing programs (Kalisch & Kalisch, 1995).

The need for personnel to provide care during these times of shortage encouraged the growth of practical nurse programs and the use of assistive personnel who provided essential services during the war. Licensed practical nurses and assistive personnel remain as part of the landscape of providers and are vital to care provision, particularly in long-term care settings.

The RN shortage persisted, and, in 1950, there were reports of "critical" and "acute" nursing shortages in cities and rural hospitals throughout the United States. Hospital units were closed, moratoriums were placed on new programs, 12- and 16-hour shifts were instituted in hospitals, and more licensed practical nurses were employed. The need for more RNs during this shortage was attributed to market demands, including the growth in healthcare services, and an increase in the population and the availability of health insurance plans that made healthcare available to more people. Opportunities became available for nurses to work outside of hospitals, which further decreased the supply of nurses available to work in the hospital setting (Berliner & Ginzberg, 2002; Kalisch & Kalisch, 1995).

Major changes in nursing education were being considered as a result of the Brown Report (Brown, 1948). Reminiscent of the Goldmark Report of 1923 that advocated the university setting for nursing education and higher standards for nursing education and practice, the Brown Report committee recommended that nursing education be moved to universities and colleges and that hospital schools of nursing be phased out of existence. The committee also addressed a recruitment process that would enhance nursing care and create a more open profession:

> We recommend that nurses everywhere seek to recruit students and personnel without regard to sex, marital status, economic background, or ethnic, racial, and religious origins. We recommend particularly that positive steps be taken by the profession to create an atmosphere conducive to attracting carefully selected representatives of a true cross-section of the population to nursing. (Brown, p. 197)

The enhanced standards for nursing education published in the Brown Report were actualized in the development of the State Board Test Pool. The test pool was expected to produce valid and reliable examinations that could be used by all states. The examination established minimum standards and facilitated the licensure of nurses from one state to another but may have placed more restrictions on the enrollment of students to ensure the success of graduates on the examination. Although more emphasis was placed on the quality of nursing graduates and baccalaureate nursing programs began to replace diploma programs, little progress was made in ensuring a more diverse workforce.

The introduction of a new type of RN education program at the associate degree level established another player to prepare nursing graduates. Associate degree programs proliferated at community colleges and over the years began to graduate more nurses than diploma or baccalaureate programs (Spratley, Johnson, Sochalski, Fritz, & Spencer, 2002).

The availability of RN personnel to provide quality nursing care in a growing healthcare industry received national attention when the Report of the Surgeon General's Consultant Group on Nursing was published in 1963. The report authors indicated that an adequate supply of nurses could not be ensured without federal support. Their recommendation for federal intervention inspired the Nurse Training Act of 1964, which provided for student loan and scholarship programs and monies for nursing school infrastructure development. In the 1970s, following the Nurse Training Act, "graduations from basic nursing education programs grew more rapidly ... than at any time since 1873" (Kalisch & Kalisch, 1995, p. 450). The Medicare and Medicaid programs were accompanied by a large growth in healthcare services. As healthcare costs began to rise and reimbursements changed in the late 1970s, the nation's hospitals downsized, and hospital staffing was eased, but shortages began to surface again in the 1980s.

The introduction of diagnostic-related groups (DRGs) as a mechanism for cost reimbursements resulted in shorter hospital stays and the discharge of sick patients. Nurses experienced decreased autonomy in care management and were stifled in their ability to provide safe, quality nursing care based on professional standards. Healthcare organizations cut costs by abolishing nurse executive positions and reducing the numbers of nurse managers. Staff nurses were without close management support at the same time that they assumed new management responsibilities and provided patient care. Few staff nurses were educationally or experientially prepared with leadership and management skills or had developed the political savvy to affect changes in the practice environment, thus burnout occurred (Aiken, Clarke, Sloane, & Sochalski, 2001a; Summer & Townsend-Rocchicioli, 2003). Administrators often did not engage nurses in solutions to the problem and reintroduced previous solutions to reduce shortages, such as offering sign-on bonuses and the recruitment of foreign nurses, which in some instances proved to be adversary to the nursing community and did not ameliorate the nursing shortage.

The introduction of technology for computerized records and communication often increased burden on the nurse, as its use was accompanied with a steep learning curve. The work environment grew increasingly difficult for nurses, and the shortages continued and grew exponentially to the present time. An Institute of Medicine committee investigated nurse staffing in hospitals and nursing homes and recommended an evaluation of the workforce related to the educational level and the number of nurses to better understand the workforce issues (Wunderlich, Sloan, & Davis, 1996).

A pattern of RN shortages occurred in the 1950s, late 1970s, late 1980s, and again in the 21st century. The shortage emerging is the most complex of any shortage to this time related to its length, fewer new nurses, the large cohort of retiring nurses, and changes in the reimbursement structure and healthcare delivery systems (Berliner & Ginzberg, 2002; Kalisch & Kalisch, 1995; Trofino, 2003).

The U.S. Department of Health and Human Services (DHHS, 2002) reported that 30 states had nursing shortages in the year 2000 and predicted that 44 states would experience shortages by 2020. The Bureau of Labor Statistics projected the need for another one million nurses by 2010 (Hecker, 2001). Numerous healthcare organizations report unfilled RN positions and significant turnover in the RN workforce. School of nursing enrollments declined 15% between 1995 and 2000 (American Association of Colleges of Nursing [AACN], 2001), and potential students were turned away because there were insufficient numbers of faculty or clinical sites and classrooms to support learning (AACN, 2004). A major reason for the shortage of nurses is that the RN workforce is aging, and retiring nurses are not being replaced at an adequate rate. Fewer young people are entering nursing, and the representation of individuals from minority backgrounds in nursing remains disproportionate with the U.S. population. The numbers of graduates are not keeping pace with the increasing demand for care generated by an aging population (Buerhaus, Staiger, & Auerbach, 2003; Heller & Lichtenberg, 2003; Smart & Kotzer, 2003).

Physicians and members of the public view nurse understaffing as a major threat to the safe care of patients in hospitals within the United States (Blendon et al., 2002; Kimball & O'Neil, 2002). Families are concerned for the health of their hospitalized relatives (Berwick, 2002), and 50% of RNs surveyed would not recommend nursing as a profession to their family and friends (General Accounting Office, 2001). The solutions to this unique and severe nursing shortage do not lie solely on the shoulders of the nursing profession. Education, healthcare organizations, the federal government, and the public at large have a stake in protecting the health of the nation by ensuring a competent RN workforce to provide the best possible care for health promotion and for healing of those in need.

Actions to address the nursing shortage today include the old standards of hiring bonuses, recruiting foreign trained nurses, closing hospital units, decreasing services, and establishing state nursing commissions to study the problem, in addition to some new initiatives. Congress passed the Nurse Reinvestment Act (NRA), Public Law 107-205, which was signed by President George W. Bush in August 2002. The NRA provided more funds for nursing education program development, nursing workforce development programs, nurse scholarships, and nursing education loan repayment. It also addressed the faculty shortage by establishing a nurse faculty loan cancellation program to support nurses studying to become nurse educators. Healthcare organizations and nursing education programs are collaborating to increase the number of enrollments in schools of nursing by providing tuition support, developing accelerated programs, and enrolling second degree students who progress more quickly through entry level programs than traditional students. AACN (2004) recently reported that enrollments in baccalaureate schools of nursing had increased by 16.6% in 2003. Johnson & Johnson (2002) initiated a massive national media campaign to recruit new nurses into the profession. Efforts also are under way to prepare a pipeline of future nursing students through Kids Into Health Careers programs that are far reaching into K-12 schools to introduce young people and their families to careers in health care. Programs inform students that opportunities as healthcare professionals are attainable with support, even though they may face educational or economical disadvantages (Bureau of Health Professions, Health Resources and Services Administration, 2004).

Healthcare organizations are improving the work environments to retain nurses and enhance the quality of patient care. The Magnet Hospital Program is one model to develop excellence in nursing service (American Nurses Credentialing Center, 2004).

The primary mission of the Federal Division of Nursing is to ensure an adequate nursing workforce. "Through the division's leadership, federal resources . . . are proactively deployed in ways that greatly benefit society. The vision of the DN's directors and staff continues to guide their judicious use of federal resources to advanced nursing education and practice" (Division of Nursing, 1997, p. 32).

The nursing profession has experienced cycles of nursing shortages, each one perceived as worse than the others. Unprecedented media coverage, new alliances, more visibility of nursing studies in medical journals, a greater understanding of the profession by forces outside of nursing, and well-prepared professional nursing leadership are all forces converging to guide the trajectory of the nursing profession for successful transformation in the 21st century.

Current RN Statistics

The 2.2 million strong RN workforce in the United States is the largest in the history of the profession and has more nurses prepared at the baccalaureate and higher degree levels than ever before. Of the estimated 2.6 million nurses in the United States who hold licenses (81.7% are in the workforce) as of March 2000, approximately 5.4% are male, 31.7% are younger than 40 years of age, and 12% are from racial and ethnic minority backgrounds. RNs who obtained their basic nursing education within the past five years were most likely to graduate from an associate degree nursing program (55.4%). Although 38% graduated from baccalaureate programs, the number graduating from diploma programs was only 6% (Spratley et al., 2002).

Advanced practice RNs (7.3% of the RN population) were most likely to be prepared as nurse practitioners (44.9%), followed by clinical nurse specialists (27.7%), and nurse anesthetists (15.2%). Nurses prepared as both nurse practitioners and clinical nurse specialists (7.5%) and those prepared as nurse midwives (4.7%) are among those expanding care provision and increasing access to care. Approximately 10% of advanced practice nurses indicated they were from racial and ethnic minority backgrounds (Spratley et al., 2002). Figure 9-1 shows a breakdown of practice roles.

Figure 9-1. Registered Nurses Prepared for Advanced Practice, March 2000

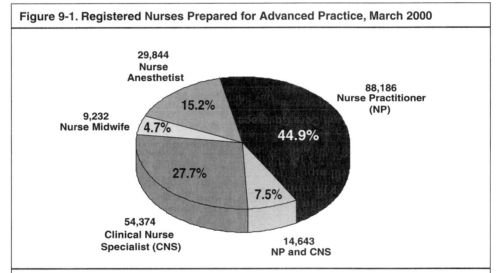

Note. From *The Registered Nurse Population March 2000: Findings From the National Sample Survey of Registered Nurses,* by E. Spratley, A. Johnson, J. Sochalski, M. Fritz, & W. Spencer, 2002, U.S. Department of Health and Human Services, Health Resources and Services Administration, Bureau of Health Professions, Division of Nursing. Retrieved July 22, 2004, from http://bhpr.hrsa.gov/healthworkforce/reports/rnsurvey/rnss1.htm

Nurses responding to the National Sample Survey of RNs were most likely to work in hospital settings. Of the 59.1% of nurses who reported working in hospitals, 74% worked more than 50% of their time in direct patient care. Others worked in administration, consultation, research, teaching, supervision, and other roles. Outside of hospitals, nurses were most likely to work in public/community health settings (18.2%), ambulatory care settings (9.5%), and long-term care settings (6.9%) (Spratley et al., 2002).

RNs function autonomously and interdependently as healthcare team members in basic and advanced practice roles to coordinate the care of 290,809,777 Americans (U.S. Census Bureau, 2004). Their collective knowledge and skill, judgment, expert care provision, and compassion are essential to the provision of quality health care. Nurses are the primary source of care and support of hospitalized patients at a time in their lives when they are most vulnerable (JCAHO, 2002), and nurses are the most trusted of healthcare professionals (Gallup Organization, 2003). Nurses are said to like the work they do but are leaving their positions in fear of causing harm to patients when there are not enough nurses to provide safe care. According to a report by the JCAHO, in 2002, inadequate nurse staffing levels were associated with 24% of the sentinel events reported to the organization. It has been documented that significantly better patient outcomes occur in hospitals where more RNs provide care (Aiken, Clarke, Cheung, Sloane, & Silber, 2003; Needleman, Buerhaus, Mattke, Stewart, & Zelevinsky, 2002) and more highly educated RNs are at the bedside (Aiken et al., 2003). Hospitals with "magnet like" qualities, such as shared governance, sufficient staffing levels, educationally and experientially prepared staff, excellent leadership at the executive and middle management levels, adequate salaries, and a supportive learning environment for practice, are the best models for quality patient care and retention of nurses (AACN, 2004). The presence of an influential nurse executive and strong middle managers also encourage retention of nurses at the bedside.

Nursing Image

The demand for RNs is significantly greater than the supply (U.S. DHHS, 2002), and the necessity to establish a pipeline to ensure an adequate supply of nurses in the future offers an opportunity to showcase the nursing profession in a positive light to young people who are forming their attitudes about careers (Feldman, 2003) and adults who are considering second careers. Consumers of nursing care may be the best recruiters of nurses, based on their perceptions of and interactions with nurses who caringly deliver sophisticated and competent care. Nurses are challenged to maintain the respect reflected in public surveys in which they receive high ratings for honesty and ethics (Murray, 2002). Kelly and Joel (1999) reported that in 1997, the American public depicted the nurse as the key measure of quality in hospitals and voiced their displeasure when nurses were replaced by less skilled providers when organizations sought to cut healthcare costs. As advocates for patient health and safety, nurses are viewed by consumers as "an untapped resource for the nation's health" (Kelly & Joel, p. 249).

The media have not always been so kind to nurses on a host of issues. Negative comments related to employment, salary, role function, position, age, education, clinical competency, appearance, and the quality of patient care given have been highlighted in the public arena. Public perceptions of nurses have varied over the years from the Sairy Gamp image (from the Charles Dickens novel *Martin Chuzzlewitt*) of an unprofessional, unkempt, and uncaring nurse and midwife to nursing heroes like Florence Nightingale, Lillian Wald, and Mary Eliza Mahoney. Major media campaigns to bolster the image of nursing, when it needed help, were implemented in 1989 by the National Commission on Nursing Implementation Project and the Ad Council and in 2002 by the Johnson & Johnson Company.

Fagin (1992) noted the necessity to promote high levels of education, professionalism, and leadership in nursing. Lehna et al. (1999) studied the effect that nursing attire has on the image of nursing and found that identifying attire, such as a name badge, was important to patients in knowing their nurse caregiver. Efforts must be continued to portray nurses positively in print and visual media, particularly those media that are attractive to elementary and older students, males, and people of color, if we wish to attract them to the nursing profession.

The 21st-Century Nurse

Today's RN, as surveyed in the 2000 National Sample Survey of nurses, was found to be white (non-Hispanic), female, married, and a graduate from an associate degree nursing program (Spratley et al., 2002).

The average age of the RN in 2000 was 45.2 years, quite a bit older than those in previous national surveys conducted in 1992 and 1996. The majority or 59.1% of the nursing workforce self-reported working in hospitals, and 18.2 % reported working in public/community health settings, community health centers, student health services, and occupational health services. Of the 59% working in hospitals, the majority of RNs were providing direct care. Seven percent of RNs practice at advanced practice levels as clinical nurse specialists, nurse practitioners, nurse midwives, and nurse anesthetists (Spratley et al., 2002). Advanced practice nurses have a tremendous impact on access to care and improved health of the underserved, but it is often invisible to the public (Gordon, 1997). Gordon depicted the care provided by three nurses in practice as so intimate that the nurse was almost invisible in the context of the patient condition.

Nurses must wholeheartedly embrace the opportunity for crafting new care opportunities with older adults and individuals living with chronic illness. As the U.S. population is reportedly aging in large numbers and living longer, nurses are faced with concerns of how best to respond to an increased emphasis on chronic health needs, like cancer (U.S. DHHS, 2000).

The description of the RN population is emerging into a more diverse and culturally appropriate workforce that will best represent the population and character of the people of America. Through Title VIII legislation, more specialized nurses are being prepared to care for the various cultures and needs of the population. Oncology nurses provide a specialized form of nursing to patients with cancer and their families. In the National Sample Survey of RNs, nurses reported studying oncology nursing in their clinical nurse specialist and nurse practitioner programs (Spratley et al., 2002). Research supports the need for nursing to focus on addressing priority areas related to cancer treatment and therapies and being sensitive to the illness and consumer enhancement of improvements in the quality of life (Rankin, Newell, Sanson-Fisher, & Girgis, 2000).

Media Image and Credibility

Credentialing brings credibility to practice and implies a high standard of attainment of specialty knowledge and skills. Certification options and opportunities are available for all levels of practicing oncology RNs. Additional credentials specific to oncology nursing are available and enhance the image of the specialty. Certifications for the Oncology Certified Nurse (OCN®), Advanced Oncology Certified Nurse Practitioner (AOCNP™), Advanced Oncology Certified Clinical Nurse Specialist (AOCNS™), and Certified Pediatric Oncology Nurse (CPON®) are available through the Oncology Nursing Certification Corporation (ONCC), and the American Nurses Credentialing Center offers certification for an advanced role designated as a palliative care clinical nurse specialist. Other professional specialty nursing organizations, such as Critical Care Nurses and Operating Room Nurses, also offer specialty certification. The public and the profession value the positive image of the nurse and the nursing workforce. It is the responsibility of each nurse to continue to enhance the positive image and to work collaboratively to care for all members of the public.

Trends in the Nursing Workforce

The Health Resources and Service Administration, Bureau of Health Professions, is the primary federal agency responsible for providing information and analysis relating to the supply and demand for healthcare professionals, including RNs (U.S. DHHS, 2002, p. 2). The National Sample Survey for RNs provides a summary of the data on the number and characteristics of the RN population. This survey was developed as a result of the need for more comprehensive data on the nursing workforce, concerns about the limitations of the nursing inventories, and the enactment of public law (Public Law 94-63). In July 1975, the Bureau of Health Professions, Division of Nursing began to investigate methodologic approaches that could best obtain data on the RN population (Moses, 1990). In response to legislation passed by Congress that called for the surveying and gathering of data on a continuous basis on the number of nurses, activity status, location and area of practice, compensation, and those with advanced training or graduate degrees in nursing, the study design, using sampling techniques, was developed in 1976 (Moses, 1990). That design has formed the basis for each of the studies in the National Sample Survey series.

The National Sample Survey of RNs is the nation's most extensive and comprehensive source of statistics on the RN workforce. The first study was carried out in September 1977. Subsequent studies were done in November 1980 and 1984 and March 1988, 1992, 1996, and 2000. The population studied for these surveys is anyone with a current RN license to practice in the United States. Because there is no centralized national listing of all licensees in the United States, sample selections are carried out on a state-by-state basis. The personal characteristics covered in the survey include gender, age, marital status, presence of children, family income, and geographic location of residence. The professional characteristics covered include educational background, employment status, employment setting, position type, hours of work, salary, and geographic location of employment. In addition, there is a series of questions related to the previous year's geographic location and employment status (Moses, 1990, 1994). Workforce issues usually are centered around supply and demand. The following passages will explore the supply and demand phenomena and the impact it has on the current shortage.

Trends in the RN Supply

In March 1988, there were an estimated 2,033,032 individuals in the United States with current licenses to practice as RNs. An estimated 1,627,035 were employed in nursing (80%), the majority on a full-time basis. The RN population was 45% greater in the 1988 survey than in the first study (September 1977) and approximately 8% greater than in the November 1984 study. The number of employed nurses increased at an even greater rate than the overall RN population (U.S. DHHS, 1990). The years between 1996 and 2000 marked the slowest growth in the RN population over the 20-year period between 1980 and 2000. On average, the RN population grew only about 1.3% each year between 1996 and 2000 compared with average annual increases of 2%–3% in earlier years. During this time, the total number of RNs employed in nursing increased by 85,998, and the number of full-time nurses increased slightly from 1996. This slow down in growth reflects fewer new entrants to the nurse population coupled with greater attrition from the nurse population than in earlier years. A loss of nurses from the workplace can be related to a variety of factors, including aging of the nursing workforce and inadequate compensation for the work being done (Spratley et al., 2002). Factors affecting trends include education, age, gender, and salary.

Education

Recent concerns about a shortage of RNs have centered, in part, on the availability of applicants for nursing programs. Because there is no unduplicated list of applicants to nursing programs, the focus has been placed on the number of admissions or first-time enrollments. The number of admissions had declined from its peak of 123,824 in the 1983–1984 academic year to 90,693 in the 1986–1987 academic year. However, in the 1987–1988 academic year, admissions to nursing education programs rose 4.3%, to 94,594. Although all three types of programs showed some increase, associate degree programs had the largest increase, with 5.7% more admissions than in 1986–1987 (U.S. DHHS, 1990).

The projected number of new graduates until 2020 falls far short of the numbers needed to replace those retiring between 2000 and 2020. During the last decade, major changes have taken place in the educational background of the U.S. RN population. The 1988 sample survey estimated that less than half the nurses had received basic nursing education in a diploma program compared to 75% in 1977 (Moses, 1990). Conversely, only 11% of nurses in 1977 were prepared in associate degree programs compared to 28% in 1988 (U.S. DHHS, 1990). Diploma program graduates have become an increasingly smaller proportion of the total RN population and associate degree graduates an increasingly higher proportion. Among the RN population in March 1988 who had graduated from initial nursing education programs within the last five years, 15% were from diploma programs and 53% from associate degree programs. Among those who had graduated 5–10 years earlier, 21% were from diploma programs and 46% from associate degree programs. Approximately 32% of the newer RNs and 34% of those graduating 5–10 years ago were graduates of basic baccalaureate programs (U.S. DHHS, 1990).

Between 1996 and 2000, the number of RNs who received their basic education in baccalaureate programs increased at a higher rate than those who received their basic education in associate degree programs (increases of 17% and 13%, respectively). This was a reversal of the trend for the past two decades in which the number of nurses educated at the associate degree level increased at a faster rate than those receiving their basic education in a BSN program. AACN reported a 3.7% increase in baccalaureate enrollment between 2000 and 2001 (AACN, 2001; U.S. DHHS, 2002) (see Figure 9-2).

Figure 9-2. Total Number of RN Graduates by Degree Program, 1995–2000

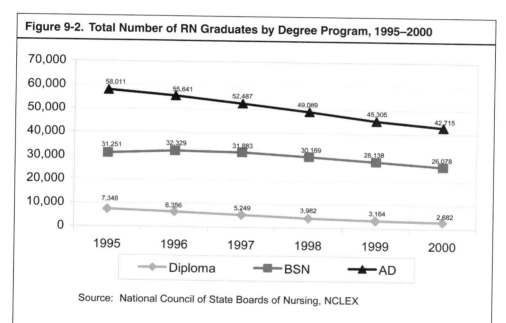

Source: National Council of State Boards of Nursing, NCLEX

Associate degree graduates are declining at a somewhat faster rate than baccalaureate graduates, with the net results that baccalaureate graduates now comprise an increasingly greater share of total graduates (see Figure 9-3).

Note. From *Projected Supply, Demand and Shortages of Registered Nurses,* by U.S. Department of Health and Human Services, Health Resources and Services Administration, Bureau of Health Professions, National Center for Health Workforce Analysis, 2002, Washington, DC: U.S. Department of Health and Human Services. Retrieved July 22, 2004, from ftp://ftp.hrsa.gov/bhpr/national-center/rnproject.pdf

Graduate programs provide nurses the important preparation for leadership positions. As researchers, administrators, teachers, and expert clinicians, these nurses provide the management structure and guidance to ensure the sound practice of nursing in the healthcare system. In addition to advanced nursing education programs, individuals already licensed as an RN also may seek baccalaureate nursing education if their initial education was in an associate degree or diploma program (U.S. DHHS, 1990).

The trend toward completion of advanced degrees in nursing specialties for those with advanced education at the master's or doctoral levels continues to increase. Clinical practice is now the predominant area, with 50.7% (65,400) of nurses with master's or doctoral degrees estimated to have this specialty. A little less than one-third specialized in some part of the clinical practice area in 1977, as compared with approximately 46% in 1984 (U.S. DHHS, 1990) and 49.2% in 2000 (U.S. DHHS, 2002). The predominant area of concentration within clinical practice has remained medical-surgical nursing. The clinical specialty of oncology nursing has not been specifically identified in the National Sample Surveys conducted to this point.

Clinical nurse specialists and nurse clinicians, experts in a specific area of clinical nursing practice, are a relatively small percentage of the RN supply. In March 1988, there were an estimated 28,975 (1.8%) clinical nurse specialists and 17,628 nurse clinicians (1.1%). The major employment setting was the hospital (68%), although about 15% were employed in ambulatory care settings, 11% in public health/community health, and 3% were self-employed. Although it is generally expected that these nurses would have master's degrees, the majority reporting did not. Thirty-four percent of clinical nursing specialists and 11.5% of nurse clinicians had master's degree preparation in 1988 (U.S. DHHS, 1990).

In 2000, 33.2% of clinical specialists and 9.4% of nurse clinicians reported having master's degree preparation, showing little change from 1988. However, the number of RNs whose highest level of preparation was either a master's or doctorate degree tripled over the last 20 years. Nurses with advanced education now make up 10% of the RN population, versus 5% in 1980 (Spratley et al., 2002).

Although oncology was not specified as an area of clinical practice in 2000, one person self-reported as an oncology nurse practitioner and 38 reported that they were employed as clinical specialists in oncology (M. Fritz, personal communication, December 29, 2003). Because of the sampling methodology used, projections to the larger nurse population cannot be made (see Figure 9-3).

Age and Gender

There is a continuing trend related to the aging RN population. In 1980, the majority of the RN population was under the age of 40, whereas in 2000, less than one-third were under 40 (Spratley et al., 2002). The average age of the RN population in 2000 was 45.2, compared to 44.3 in 1996 (Spratley et al.). It is estimated that males made up approximately 5.4% of the nursing workforce in 2000. In 1988, 3.5% were less than 25 years old. In 1988, nurses between 40 and 50 years old made up 23.7% of the workforce, whereas in 2000, they were 34.4%. The average age of male nurses is lower than females with 38% under 40 (Spratley et al.) (see Figure 9-4).

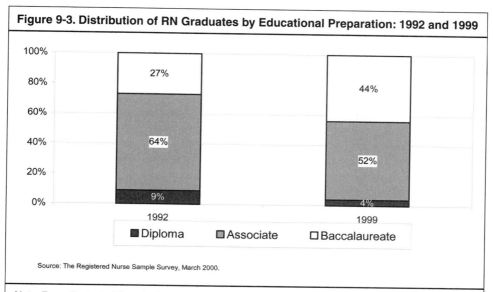

Figure 9-3. Distribution of RN Graduates by Educational Preparation: 1992 and 1999

Source: The Registered Nurse Sample Survey, March 2000.

Note. From *Projected Supply, Demand and Shortages of Registered Nurses,* by U.S. Department of Health and Human Services, Health Resources and Services Administration, Bureau of Health Professions, National Center for Health Workforce Analysis, 2002, Washington, DC: U.S. Department of Health and Human Services. Retrieved July 22, 2004, from ftp://ftp.hrsa.gov/bhpr/national-center/rnproject.pdf

Salary

It is likely that salary compression is playing a role in the declining supply of RNs. Although actual earning for RNs increased steadily from 1983–2000, "real" earnings—the amount available after adjusting for inflation—have remained relatively flat during this period. A good portion of the wage growth for nurses reported over the years generally occurs early in their careers, then tapers off with time. The average annual income of nurses in 2000 was $46,782, whereas the average annual income of nurses working in hospital settings was approximately $43,000 (Spratley et al., 2002). It is hypothesized that "as their potential for increased earnings diminishes over time, staff nurses may be motivated to leave patient care for additional education and/or other careers in nursing or outside the profession" (U.S. DHHS, 2002).

Trends in the RN Demand

In 2000, the national supply of full-time equivalent RNs was estimated at 1.89 million, while the demand was estimated at 2 million, a shortage of 110,000 or 6%. Based on what is known about trends in the supply of RNs and their anticipated demand, the shortage is expected to grow relatively slowly until 2010, at which time it will have reached a deficit of 275,215 RNs. However, in 2020, that number is anticipated to escalate to 808,416 (U.S. DHHS, 2002).

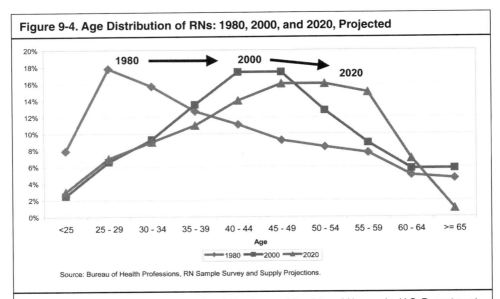

Figure 9-4. Age Distribution of RNs: 1980, 2000, and 2020, Projected

Source: Bureau of Health Professions, RN Sample Survey and Supply Projections.

Note. From *Projected Supply, Demand and Shortages of Registered Nurses,* by U.S. Department of Health and Human Services, Health Resources and Services Administration, Bureau of Health Professions, National Center for Health Workforce Analysis, 2002, Washington, DC: U.S. Department of Health and Human Services. Retrieved July 22, 2004, from ftp://ftp.hrsa.gov/bhpr/national-center/rnproject.pdf

Although the actual number of nurses has increased consistently over time, so has the demand for the number of nurses needed. The increase in demand is anticipated to be greater than the increase in supply. The projected shortage in 2020 results from a projected 40% increase in demand between 2000 and 2020 compared to a projected 6% growth in supply. It is expected that by 2011, the number of nurses leaving the profession will exceed the number that enter (U.S. DHHS, 2002).

The demand for nurses is accelerated by population growth, aging of the population, increased per capita demand for health care, and trends in healthcare financing, as well as retirements and resignations of nurses. After balancing projected losses against projected new entrants, the RN supply is projected to grow 1.3% between 2008 and 2012, and by the end of the projection period, to decline by 1.9% between 2016 and 2020 (U.S. DHHS, 2002) (see Figure 9-5).

If the projected path continues, there is good indication that at least five states (Alaska, Connecticut, Delaware, Idaho, and Wisconsin) will have a greater than 50% discrepancy between the supply of nurses available and the demand in those states (U.S. DHHS, 2002). Although it is the general belief that a larger proportion of nurses is now working in settings other than hospitals, analysis of nurse survey results indicate that approximately the same percentage of nurses worked in hospitals in

1962 (60%–64%) as in 2000 (59%) (Marshall & Moses, 1965; Spratley et al., 2002; U.S. Department of Health, Education, and Welfare, 1974).

Figure 9-5. New Entrants and Losses From the Licensed Pool of RNs for Selected Periods

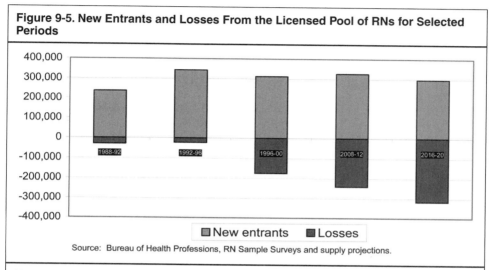

Source: Bureau of Health Professions, RN Sample Surveys and supply projections.

Note. From *Projected Supply, Demand and Shortages of Registered Nurses,* by U.S. Department of Health and Human Services, Health Resources and Services Administration, Bureau of Health Professions, National Center for Health Workforce Analysis, 2002, Washington, DC: U.S. Department of Health and Human Services. Retrieved July 22, 2004, from ftp://ftp.hrsa.gov/bhpr/national-center/rnproject.pdf

---

Opportunities

Recent reports (2003) indicated that students are being turned away from schools of nursing because of inadequate numbers of faculty, clinical sites, and classrooms (AACN, 2003). The projections of supply and demand are based on the projection rates of nursing school graduations from existing programs. The nursing community responded to the demand for nurses by developing creative strategies to attract individuals into nursing. As reported by AACN (2003), the number of accelerated second degree nursing programs has increased from 105 in 2002 to 129 in 2003. Eighty percent of the fiscal year (FY) 2003 HRSA/BHPR funded grants developed to increase baccalaureate nursing program enrollment focus on accelerated nursing programs for individuals with baccalaureate degrees in other areas (Division of Nursing, 2003). Although these programs are not entirely new, the focus on a population that has prior education has increased. These programs range from 11 to 18 months and have the potential to increase the number of projected baccalaureate nurse graduates within the next year or two. At this time, the anticipated increase in the accelerated nursing programs by themselves is not adequate to forestall the expected shortage.

The Nurse Reinvestment Act, passed in 2003, includes several strategies to address nurse education, practice, and retention, as well as faculty development. A variety of scholarship, loan repayment programs for individuals with outstanding loan balances from nursing education loans, faculty loan programs, and projects that increase access to education at all levels of nursing education through the use of distance learning methodologies are being offered through grants funded by the appropriations for this legislation. The ability to expand nursing programs through grants that support faculty salaries during the grant period are helpful in developing an infrastructure to support increased access to nursing education; however, decreases in many state budgets make it difficult to project if faculty lines will be funded once the grant period is completed.

The National Advisory Council on Nurse Education and Practice (NACNEP) (2002) noted that the faculty shortage can be mitigated by maintaining current faculty and attracting new faculty members from a currently inactive but appropriately educated nursing workforce. In addition, NACNEP recommended such strategies as funding demonstration projects that support mentoring programs for new faculty; developing roles for teaching assistants in nursing education and developing doctoral programs that prepare individuals who are expert in both clinical nursing and nursing education; and providing faculty development with a focus on the use of distance learning methodologies to increase access to all levels of nursing education.

To be effective, strategies must be both short term and long term. Once individuals become nurses, it is imperative that they are retained in the workforce. The Nurse Reinvestment Act, enacted in FY 2003, includes strategies to provide internship/residency programs to give nurses in new professional roles a good start; career ladder strategies to maintain individuals in the nursing workforce through providing well-articulated educational programs and additional opportunities for cross-training and specialty training; and strategies that provide a strong focus on organizational changes in the workplace through interventions such as increased opportunity for shared governance, improved communication in the workplace, and the ability to have an impact on improving patient outcomes. Outcomes from the projects supported in the first year of the Nurse Reinvestment Act are not yet available; however, the projects funded in FY 2003 will be carefully evaluated with regard to improvement of retention of nurses in the workplace and in nursing as a profession.

Common themes in the literature for long-term solutions to the nursing shortage include a better prepared workforce for bedside nurses and nurse managers, competitive compensation, and collaboration between nursing education and healthcare organizations to develop creative and innovative approaches to changing the work design of nurses and their work environments. Interdisciplinary healthcare professional education is thought to be essential to changing the healthcare environment and enhancing patient safety (Aiken et al., 2001a; Berliner & Ginzberg, 2002; Berwick, 2002; Greiner & Knebel, 2003; Heller & Lichtenberg, 2003; Institute of Medicine, 2001; Peterson, 2001; Spetz & Given, 2003; Steinbrook, 2002).

The great challenges we see at this point in the history of nursing shortages provide the opportunity to inspire new and creative solutions to change the course of the projected shortage. Data and trends should inform decisions that are made to prevent the dire predictions related to the nursing population of 2020. Professional organizations, federal agencies and departments, educational institutions, and private entities working together to maintain the storehouse of information, data, and trends will allow close monitoring of strategic outcomes targeted toward decreasing the current shortage and proactively meeting demands for nurses in the future.

References

Aiken, L.H., Clarke, S.P., Cheung, R.B., Sloane, D.M., & Silber, J.H. (2003). Educational levels of hospital nurses and surgical patient mortality. *JAMA, 290,* 1617–1623.

Aiken, L.H., Clarke, S.P., Sloane, D.M., & Sochalski, J.A. (2001a). An international perspective on hospital nurse's work environments: The case for reform. *Policy, Politics, & Nursing Practice, 2,* 255–263.

Aiken, L.H., Clarke, S.P., Sloane, D.M., Sochalski, J.A., Busse, R., Clarke, H., et al. (2001b). Nurses' reports on hospital care in five countries. *Health Affairs, 20*(3), 43–53.

American Association of Colleges of Nursing. (2001, December). Enrollments rise at U.S. nursing colleges and universities ending a six-year period of decline. *Media Relations.* Retrieved July 22, 2004, from http://www.aacb.nche.edu/Media/NewsReleases/enrl01.htm

American Association of Colleges of Nursing. (2003, December). Thousands of students turned away from the nation's nursing schools despite sharp increase in enrollment. *Media relations.* Retrieved December 22, 2003, from http://www.aacn.nche.edu/Media/NewsReleases/enrl03.htm

American Association of Colleges of Nursing. (2004, January). Schools turn away more than 11,000 qualified applicants last year. *AACN news watch.* Retrieved January 24, 2004, from http://www.aacn.nche.edu/Media/NewsWatch/list.htm

American Nurses Association. (1994). *Historical perspective of the U.S. Cadet Nurse Corp.* Washington, DC: American Nurses Association, Inc./Foundation.

American Nurses Credentialing Center. (2004). *ANCC Magnet Program: Recognizing excellence in nursing services.* Retrieved July 1, 2004, from http://www.nursingworld.org/ancc.cert.html

Berliner, H.S., & Ginzberg, E. (2002). Why this hospital nursing shortage is different. *JAMA, 288,* 2742–2744.

Berwick, D.M. (2002). *Escape fire.* New York: The Commonwealth Fund.

Blendon, R.J., DesRoches, C.M., Brodie, M., Benson, J.M., Rosen, A.B., Schneider, E., et al. (2002). Views of practicing physicians and the public on medical errors. *New England Journal of Medicine, 347,* 1933–1940.

Brown, E.L. (1948). *Nursing for the future: A report prepared for the National Nursing Council.* New York: Russell Sage Foundation.

Buerhaus, P.I., Staiger, D.O., & Auerback, D.I. (2003). Is the current shortage of hospital nurses ending? *Health Affairs, 22*(6), 191–198.

Bureau of Health Professions, Health Resources and Services Administration. (2004). *Kids into health careers.* Retrieved January 30, 2004, from http://bhpr,hrsa.gov/kidscareers/

Clark, C.S. (2002). The nursing shortage as a community transformational opportunity. *Advances in Nursing Science, 25*(1), 18–31.

Division of Nursing. (1997, April). *Fifty years at the division of Nursing.* Washington, DC: Author.

Division of Nursing. (2003). *Basic nurse education FY 2003 grantee abstracts (Purpose 5).* Retrieved July 22, 2004, from http://bhpr.hrsa.gov/nursing/03abstracts/bne.htm

Fagin, C. (1992). Revisiting nursing's media image. *Nursing and Health Care, 13,* 494–495.

Feldman, H. (Ed.). (2003). *The nursing shortage: Strategies for recruitment and retention in clinical practice and education.* New York: Springer.

Gallup Organization. (2003). *Public rates nursing as most honest and ethical profession.* Retrieved January 24, 2004, from http://www.gallup.com/subscription/?m=f&c_id=14141

General Accounting Office. (2001, July). Nursing workforce: Emerging nurse shortages due to multiple factors. *GAO report to health subcommittee on health: GAO-01-944.* Washington, DC: United States General Accounting Office.

Gordon, S. (1997). *Life support: Three nurses on the front lines.* Boston: Little, Brown.

Greiner, A.C., & Knebel, E. (Eds.). (2003). *Health professions education: A bridge to quality*. Washington, DC: National Academy Press.

Hecker, D.E. (2001). Occupational employment projections to 2010. *Monthly Labor Review, 124*(11), 57–84.

Heller, B.R., & Lichtenberg, L.P. (2003). The role of nursing schools in addressing the shortage. In H. Feldman (Ed.), *The nursing shortage: Strategies for recruitment and retention in clinical practice and education* (pp. 57–69). New York: Springer.

Institute of Medicine, Committee on Quality of Health Care in America. (2001). *Crossing the quality chasm: A new health system for the 21st century*. Washington, DC: National Academy Press.

Johnson & Johnson. (2002, February 11). *Johnson & Johnson launches ad, recruiting campaign to reduce nursing shortage*. Retrieved January 30, 2004, from http://www.jnj.com/news/jnj_news/20020418_1558.htm

Joint Commission on Accreditation of Healthcare Organizations. (2002). *Health care at the crossroads: Strategies for addressing the evolving nursing crisis*. Chicago: Author.

Kalisch, P.A., & Kalisch, B.J. (1995). *The advance of American nursing* (3rd ed.). Philadelphia: Lippincott Williams and Wilkins.

Kelly, L.Y., & Joel, L.A. (1999). *Dimensions of professional nursing* (8th ed.). New York: McGraw Hill.

Kimball, B., & O'Neil, E. (2002). *The American nursing shortage*. Princeton, NJ: Robert Wood Johnson Foundation.

Lehna, C., Proutz, S., Peterson, T.G., Degner, K., Grubaugh, K., Lorenz, L., et al. (1999). Nursing attire: Indicators of professionalism? *Journal of Professional Nursing, 15*, 192–199.

Marshall, E.D., & Moses, E.B. (1965). *The nation's nurses: The 1962 inventory of professional registered nurses*. New York: American Nurses Association.

Moses, E. (1990). *The RN population—1988*. U.S. Department of Health and Human Services, Health Resources and Services Administration, Bureau of Health Professions, Division of Nursing. Washington, DC: U.S. Department of Health and Human Services.

Moses, E. (1994). *The RN population—1992*. U.S. Department of Health and Human Services, Health Resources and Services Administration, Bureau of Health Professions, Division of Nursing. Washington, DC: U.S. Department of Health and Human Services.

Murray, M.K. (2002). The nursing shortage. *Journal of Nursing Administration, 32*, 79–84.

National Advisory Council on Nurse Education and Practice. (2002). *Second report to the secretary of Health and Human Services and Congress*. Rockville, MD: U.S. Department of Health and Human Services, Health Resources and Services Administration, Bureau of Health Professions, Division of Nursing.

Needleman, J., Buerhaus, P., Mattke, S., Stewart, M., & Zelevinsky, K. (2002). Nurse-staffing levels and the quality of care in hospitals. *New England Journal of Medicine, 346*, 1715–1722.

Page, A. (Ed.). (2003). *Keeping patients safe: Transforming the work environment of nurses*. Washington, DC: National Academies Press.

Peterson, C.A. (2001, January 31). Nursing shortage: Not a simple problem—No easy answers. *Online Journal of Issues in Nursing, 6*(1). Retrieved October 1, 2003, from http://www.nursingworld.org/ojin/topic14/tpc14_1.htm

Rankin, N., Newell, S., Sanson-Fisher, R., & Girgis, A. (2000). Consumer participation in the development of psychosocial clinical practice guidelines: Opinions of women with breast cancer. *European Journal of Cancer Care, 9*, 97–104.

Smart, G., & Kotzer, A.M. (2003). STAT! A four-step approach to nursing recruitment and retention in a tertiary pediatric setting. In H. Feldman (Ed.), *The nursing shortage: Strategies for recruitment and retention in clinical practice and education* (pp. 136–148). New York: Springer.

Spetz, J., & Given, R. (2003). The future of the nurse shortage: Will wage increases close the gap? *Health Affairs, 22*(6), 199–206.

Spratley, E., Johnson, A., Sochalski, J., Fritz, M., & Spencer, W. (2002). *The registered nurse population March 2000: Findings from the National Sample Survey of Registered Nurses*. Washington, DC: U.S. Department of Health and Human Services, Health Resources and Services Administration, Bureau of Health Professions, Division of Nursing.

Steinbrook, R. (2002). Nursing in the crossfire. *New England Journal of Medicine, 346*, 1757–1766.

Summer, J., & Townsend-Rocchicioli, J. (2003). Why are nurses leaving nursing? *Nursing Administration Quarterly, 27,* 164–171.

Trofino, J. (2003). Power sharing: A strategy for nurse retention. In H. Feldman (Ed.), *The nursing shortage: Strategies for recruitment and retention in clinical practice and education* (pp. 120–133). New York: Springer.

U.S. Census Bureau. (2004). *Annual estimates of the population for the United States and for Puerto Rico: April 1, 2000 to July 1, 2003.* Retrieved January 26, 2004, from http://eire.census.gov/pepest/data/states/tables/NST-EST2004-01.php

U.S. Department of Health, Education, and Welfare. (1974). *Source book: Nursing personnel.* Washington, DC: Author.

U.S. Department of Health and Human Services. (2000, November). *Healthy people 2010* (2nd ed.). Washington, DC: U.S. Government Printing Office.

U.S. Department of Health and Human Services, Health Resources and Services Administration, Bureau of Health Professions. (1990). *Seventh report to the president and Congress on the status of health personnel in the United States.* Washington, DC: U.S. Department of Health and Human Services.

U.S. Department of Health and Human Services, Health Resources and Services Administration, Bureau of Health Professions, National Center for Health Workforce Analysis. (2002). *Projected supply, demand, and shortages of RNs.* Washington, DC: U.S. Department of Health and Human Services.

Wunderlich, G.S., Sloan, F.A., & Davis, C.K. (Eds.). (1996). *Nursing staff in hospitals and nursing homes: Is it adequate?* Washington, DC: National Academy Press.

Culturally Competent Organizations

Shaheen Kassim-Lakha, MPH, DrPH
Marjorie Kagawa-Singer, PhD, MN, RN

Healthcare providers and organizations are being held increasingly accountable for the quality of care, safety, and clinical outcomes of the patients entrusted in their care. At the same time, there has been a significant change in the demographic profile of these patients who now include individuals from numerous minority groups of diverse geographic and cultural backgrounds. In order to achieve the organizational mission to provide high quality care for all patients regardless of background, healthcare institutions and agencies need to ensure that nurses, medical staff, and other healthcare professionals deliver effective and respectful quality health care. This chapter will focus on theoretical constructs, definitions, and approaches to promote the level of cultural competence in the management of healthcare organizations. Included in this chapter are an examination of the fundamental relationship between culture and health, a paradigm designed to reduce the risk of cross-cultural miscommunication, and suggestions for successful multicultural management strategies that organizations may implement to potentially improve health outcomes for diverse populations.

Why Does Culture Matter?

Health and the means to maintain, regain, or attain well-being are culturally defined (Angel & Thoits, 1987; Foster, 1978); cultures function to maintain the well-being of their members and provide meaning to life. Notably, cultures are dynamic, responsive, and coherent systems of belief, values, and lifestyles. They evolved within particular geographic locations using available technology and economic resources as integrated systems of language, thoughts, actions, customs, beliefs, and institutions of racial, ethnic, social, or religious groups (Cross, Bazron, Dennis, & Isaacs, 1989; Hammond, 1978). The lifestyle patterns characteristic of each cultural group (e.g., diet, means of livelihood) influence the physical well-being of its members in gene expression, health status, and disease prevalence (Bronfenbrenner & Ceci, 1994) and provide the meaning of life events. Through beliefs, values, and rituals that define responses to communicate caring, ensure safety, and provide social support for its members, culture makes predictable and controllable what might otherwise be unpredictable and uncontrollable, such as sickness and death (Kagawa-Singer, 1996). Thus, culture is fundamental to medical care.

The literature documents that ethnic minority populations lag behind European-Americans (whites) on almost every health indicator, including healthcare coverage, access to care, and life expectancy, and they surpass whites in almost all acute and chronic disease rates (Bradley, Given, & Roberts, 2001; Institute of Medicine [IOM], 2002; President's Initiative on Race, 1999; Satcher, 1999). For example, infant mortality rates among African Americans and Native Americans are twice as high compared to whites; the mortality rate for pregnant African Americans is four times higher than for whites; and Vietnamese and Hispanic women are at significantly greater risk for cervical cancer (Kirschstein, 1999). Although not completely understood or well explained, these disparities are variously attributed to barriers to routine access to preventive care, low levels of cultural competence among healthcare professionals, and lack of proportional representation of minorities in the health profession (Bhopal, 1998; Smith, 1999). Moreover, as the organization and delivery of health services are increasingly based on the distinct values associated with the business model of managed care that views health as a commodity, these health disparities may be further exacerbated by clashes with the belief systems and expectations of particular sub-populations (Lavizzo-Mourey & Mackenzie, 1996).

Why Should Cultural Competence Matter to an Organization?

Ethnic minorities now comprise approximately 25% of the U.S. population and will form the majority by 2050 (U.S. Census Bureau, 2001). It is unlikely that the statistics on health disparities will improve without concerted efforts on the part of healthcare organizations to transform the structure and delivery of services and train practitioners to reduce the dissonance that occurs across cultural differences. Hospitals continue to be associated with problems of racism and health disparities in the medical establishment in terms of the intensity and quality of care as well as length of stay (IOM, 2002; Klessig, 1992; Yergan, Glood, LoGerfo, & Diehr, 1987). A study using Medical Expenditure Panel Survey data found that minority patients had more trouble getting appointments, had to wait longer to see the physician, and were less satisfied with their interaction with healthcare staff (Shi, 1999). Existing literature on cultural competence in clinical practice underscores the need for change in practitioners' self-awareness and attitudes toward diverse patients in order to eliminate differential care based on race (Levy, 1985; Schulman et al., 1999; Tervalon & Murray-Garcia, 1997; Todd, Samaroo, & Hoffman, 1993).

Professional groups and government agencies are now using "cultural competency" as a means to address the miscommunication that occurs in culturally discordant clinical encounters and eliminating the probable resultant racial/ethnic disparities in health outcomes (Jackson, 1993). Although definitions abound, empirical evidence is lacking. More problematic than the lack of clarity in the definition, however, is the lack of discussion on the goal or the "why" of these skills and empirical evidence of its effect.

The past 25 years have seen successive waves of immigrants from diverse cultures arrive in the United States. Every culture has interwoven into its basic world view certain beliefs and practices about health, disease, treatment, and healthcare providers. As these immigrants, sometimes with limited use of the English language and literacy skills, interact with the healthcare environment, their beliefs and practices may present a challenge to healthcare professionals trained in the philosophy, concepts, and practices of Western medicine (Gilbert, 2002). For example, a belief in the primary place of mankind in the cosmic order is fundamental in Western thought and permeates the Western healthcare system. This view frames how professionals are educated to provide care and how recipients of care are expected to respond within the system. Similarly, individuality and the values of autonomy form the basis of Western bioethics (Airhihenbuwa, 1995). This belief system, however, is not universal, and failure to understand the nature of culture and the integrity of differing belief systems leads to the risk of conflict and its negative impact on health outcomes (Blackhall et al., 1999). Thus, to provide optimal care in a more equitable manner to all segments of society, mainstream healthcare organizations based on the Euro-American cultural model need to transform themselves into multicultural agencies by making both the structure of the organizations and the process of delivering services culturally competent.

Culture is vaguely conceptualized and inaccurately used in health care. Most often, it is glossed erroneously as synonymous with race or as a monolithic term to describe people that are phenotypically similar and assumed to have the same beliefs, values, and behaviors. Such use results in stereotypical, not scientific, thinking. Genetic variation by population groups is not the cause of health disparities. Less than 5% of diseases are genetically caused; 95% are due to lifestyle or environmental factors (Kagawa-Singer & Kassim-Lakha, 2003). Culture informs lifestyle. Notably, culture usually is not the cause of poor health outcomes; rather, being identified as a member of a cultural group more often underlies the variations in health status. Differential treatment in medical care occurs when external identifiers of group membership, such as skin color, language, or religion, are used to judge the relative value of individuals, and resources are allocated based upon those criteria in a prejudicial manner (Kagawa-Singer, 2001; LaVeist, 2000; Williams, Yan, Jackson, & Anderson, 1997). The effects of discrimination and racism are much more difficult to overcome as barriers to optimal care than appreciating cultural differences, because, most often, these reactions occur unconsciously (Levy, 1985; Schneider, Cleary, Zaslavsky, & Epstein, 2001; Schulman et al., 1999; Tervalon & Murray-Garcia, 1997; Todd, Deaton, D'Adamo, & Goe, 2000; Todd et al., 1993). However, if acknowledged, these prejudices might be better addressed through systematic efforts to promote cultural competence. The role of a healthcare/nurse manager in supporting the concept of a culturally competent organization is to eliminate disparities within the organization.

The U.S. Census uses five racial categories (White, African American or Black, Asian, American Indian or Alaska Native, and Native Hawaiian or Other Pacific

Islander) and two ethnic categories (Hispanic and non-Hispanic). The Office of Management and Budget (OMB) developed these primarily to monitor political allocation of resources, not as scientific evidence of genetic differences, as is implicitly assumed in most medical and health studies when reporting ethnic/racial differences in health outcomes (OMB, 1997). These categories create significant problems for clinical care. First is the lack of scientific evidence for any biologic basis for these categories or assumptions that underlie differential care for physiologic reasons. Second is the lack of attention to diversity within groups. Each of the OMB categories contains several distinct national groups and multiple ethnic groups within each national group, with their own culture or subculture. Genetic studies indicate greater within-group variation among these categories than between groups, thus rendering the categories as social/political constructs based on the color of one's skin and not on biologic differences (LaVeist, 2000; Schneider et al., 2001; Williams et al., 1997). Finally, race does not equal culture.

Cultures respond to environmental challenges. They are not homogeneous, monolithic, or static. Varying levels of acculturation, assimilation, age, education, income, family structure, gender, wealth, foreign versus U.S.-born status, and immigrant status all modify the degree to which the cultural group membership of an individual will influence health practices and health status. In a multicultural society such as the U.S., each cultural group is contemporaneously undergoing modifications and mixtures that render it uniquely different than the native culture. Individual expressions of cultural beliefs and practices differ, further underscoring the need for assessment of individual variation both within and between cultural groups (Kagawa-Singer, 2000). Failure to recognize these differences perpetuates stereotypical evaluations of behavior by individuals different than oneself and can divert the nurse from accurately assessing the strengths of and potential conflicts among staff, patients, and their families (Ying, Lee, Tsai, Yeh, & Huang, 2000). Such misinterpretation can, in turn, lead to mismanagement of staff or impact patient outcomes through biased and differential care.

Communication is fundamental for effective cross-cultural relationships. When we understand that every culture defines good character and acceptable, respectful behavior as well as the communication styles required for these standards, the stage is set to respectfully negotiate with patients, their families, and staff among a wider set of options for the goals of care and the means to achieve them. Many of the "vulnerabilities" attributed to cultures other than European-American cultures are due to misinterpretations of these cultural values, beliefs, and practices (Kagawa-Singer & Chung, 1994). Variations that exist in leadership styles of cultural groups other than the dominant population are rarely addressed in management training. Instead, most training assumes the universality and primacy of Euro-American communication and leadership styles. This bias clouds the ability to see equal validity among different cultural communication strategies for interpersonal communication and work relationships. Management of institutions in which discordant encounters occur must be culturally competent to foster and support optimal behavior among its constituents. Such circumstances require an organization that is sophisticated, aware, and prepared to support discussions to resolve these issues personally, interpersonally, and legally.

Organizational Commitment to Cultural Competence

Cultural competence is a term used frequently today in management and clinical care to refer to a process that requires individuals and systems to respond to cultural diversity. In this chapter, culturally competent practice is defined as a skill set. Culturally competent managers are able to respectfully elicit and identify culturally framed values, views, and beliefs from all stakeholders in the organization. Identification of variations in cultural values, communication styles, and acceptable interpersonal practices is essential for organizations seeking to promote culturally competent practices. A culturally competent management style is one that develops organizational goals and standards of care that are responsive to such differences and nurtures programs and policies that enhance and reward such practices.

Three elements must be present to achieve organizational cultural competence: competence in the individual caregiver, culturally appropriate delivery of health care to multicultural populations in an institution, and the organizational will and skill to promote such care (Cross et al., 1989; Isaacs & Benjamin, 1991; Dana, Behn, & Gonwa, 1992). Before providing cultural competence training to healthcare professionals, managers need to assess the willingness and ability of the organization to support such training (Gilbert, 2002). They must also have a clear idea of what concepts, attitudes, knowledge, and skills need to be taught. A first step might be a comparison of their own service delivery policies and practices with the 14 National Standards for Culturally and Linguistically Appropriate Services (CLAS) for Healthcare Organizations, developed by the Office of Minority Health in the U.S. Department of Health and Human Services to serve as a guide to quality healthcare for diverse populations (www.omhrc.gov/clas).

Increasingly, accreditation organizations, such as the Joint Commission on Accreditation of Healthcare Organizations (JCAHO), state Medicaid agencies, and the federal Centers for Medicare and Medicaid Services (CMS) are recommending or requiring organizations to provide culturally and linguistically appropriate care. Numerous healthcare professional associations, including the American Nurses Association, have urged professional schools to pay attention to cross-cultural medicine and health disparities in their basic educational programs. The task of adhering to the accreditation requirement and CLAS standards for training healthcare professionals already in practice, however, has fallen to managers in healthcare organizations (Gilbert, 2002). The concern for managers is twofold. They must consider the difference between *workforce* diversity training and *cultural competence* training for healthcare professionals. The former focuses on improving relationships and interactions among members of a diverse workforce and is discussed in another chapter. The latter focuses on improving the quality of care and enhancing service delivery to diverse patient populations. Both require an examination of the institutional commitment and infrastructure to promote patient and employee diversity as well as management support of and sensitivity to pluralism in the clinical setting.

Organizational Gains

Clearly healthcare institutions and providers need to address the disparities that exist in the health outcomes of patients of different ethnic and cultural backgrounds and the medically underserved. Failure to address the issues of effective cross-cultural communication and variations in health-related belief systems and cultural norms between patients and nurses and other healthcare personnel potentially threaten patient satisfaction, clinical outcomes, and population health outcomes (Lavizzo-Mourey & Mackenzie, 1996). The nursing community, specifically, needs to better determine measures of quality of care, particularly for multi-ethnic populations. Management is challenged to define and measure training outcomes and choose instructional strategies that relate cultural competent practice to measures of quality. Such acknowledgment requires recognition of the structural and organizational issues that contribute to the cultural competence of their employees. For example, the extent to which the demographic profile of the faculty and hospital staff reflects the diversity of the population served and the extent to which an institution supports and rewards behavior that is more inclusive or respectful of all individuals from all cultures are tangible measures of success in culturally based care.

Effective cross-cultural interaction requires attention to and integration of three areas of culture in the clinical encounter: the patient/family, the nurse, and the healthcare institution. Successful integration of these areas constitutes cultural competence or *ethnorelative practice*, that is, the ability to evaluate behavior relative to its cultural context so that the clinicians and patient/family are able to promote, maintain, and/or regain mutually desired and obtainable levels of health within the realities of their life circumstances (Kagawa-Singer & Kassim-Lakha, 2003).

Successful Strategies

Culturally competent organizations require institutional commitment to and the creation of infrastructure to promote patient and employee diversity as well as management support of and sensitivity to cross-culture issues in the healthcare setting. Specific interventions include

- Delineation of the strategic direction of culturally competent practice provided by the governing board and senior management
- A formal communication plan outlining the initiative
- The alignment of management incentive goals and performance appraisal criteria to conform with the strategic direction in terms of promoting cultural competence and effectively managing workplace diversity
- Hiring of bicultural personnel at all levels of staffing and management from populations that are more reflective of the patients served
- Recruitment of hospital faculty and nursing consultants
- Development of policies and procedures that integrate the principles of cultural competence into the ongoing work of the organization

- A formal means of consultation with the community to be served for the verification of need for the program and appropriateness of the intervention, including patient educational materials to be used (U.S. Department of Health and Human Services, 1998).

The last should be particularly emphasized in the program planning and implementation phases to ensure availability, accessibility, and acceptability of appropriate, culturally responsive services (Mokuau, 1994).

The quality improvement model familiar to healthcare organizations also may be used to overcome these difficulties. An internal project team comprised of multidisciplinary staff from all levels of the organization and reflecting the diversity of the populations served would be most effective in achieving this institutional transformation if it were charged with guiding and leading the initiative. Existing accreditation guidelines and standards, such as those described earlier, may be used to promote, maintain, and measure nursing interest and leadership (JCAHO, 2004; U.S. Department of Health and Human Services, 2000).

The cross-cultural education curricula should be based on the values and principles outlined in numerous theoretical models for nurses, including the Oncology Nursing Society's (ONS's) multicultural guidelines, as well as for other health practitioners (Betancourt & King, 2000; Bobo, Womeodu, & Knox, 1991; Campinha-Bacote, 1999; Kagawa-Singer, 1996; Kagawa-Singer & Kassim-Lakha, 2003; ONS, 1999; Scott, 1997; Tervalon & Murray-Garcia, 1997). Educational interventions require that all healthcare agency personnel (e.g., nurses, social workers, allied health personnel, management, administrative staff) as well as physicians be included and trained together and in their respective professional groups for more specific job-related skills, because the care practices of each profession differ, as do the issues of multicultural medicine that confront them (Gilbert, 2002). Attendance at trainings by institutional leaders, such as nursing and medical directors, and hospital administrators communicates an endorsement of its importance.

Educational activities may include a variety of communication mechanisms, ranging from audiovisual to grand rounds, and workshops. In addition to such traditional instruction methods, self-directed and computer-assisted learning activities may be developed to facilitate self-learning with minimal interruption to patient care responsibilities (Marrone, 1999). Healthcare team experiential modules are essential in facilitating communication and coordination of care across diverse care settings, disciplinary perspectives, and multiple ethnic backgrounds. Every effort should be made to organize trainings so that continuing education credits can be given to participants. Workshops and courses offering these credits are likely to have much better attendance than those that do not (Gilbert, 2002). The ONS multicultural toolkit provides important materials for cultural competence in oncology nursing practice (ONS, 2001).

Donabedian's (1985) model of structure, process, and outcome that is used widely in the health services field provides a useful theoretical framework for assessing the infrastructure needed to support the culturally competent practice. This model examines outcomes in terms of how well the care provided meets or exceeds clinical/administrative standards given the characteristics of the environment and use of resources. The evaluation question has two parts:

(i) Does the adoption of a multifaceted, strategic cultural competence initiative by executive management improve the level of culturally competent care provided by the institution?

(ii) Does the implementation of a cultural competence training program for healthcare professionals result in (a) improved patient satisfaction and (b) better health outcomes across all ethnic groups being served by the healthcare organization?

Other proposed but untested measures of structure and process include

- Level of representation of cultural diversity among nursing staff, physicians, and management
- Administrative support and accountability for cultural competence training of staff
- Staff motivation to participate in training
- Multidisciplinary participation in training
- Employee awareness of cultural competence strategic initiative
- Achievement of related management goals
- Integration of cultural competence principles into ongoing work of the department
- Degree of institutionalization of cultural competence values (e.g., language capacity, communication etiquette by cultural groups, behaviors that engender trust, appropriate foods on menus, patient entertainment, patient education, hospital rules and regulations consonant with various cultural beliefs).

Such changes should be reflected in measures of patient satisfaction. Current patient satisfaction questionnaires need to be validated for cross-cultural assessment purposes. Indicators such as better adherence to medical care, follow-up appointments, healthcare utilization patterns, modification of high-risk health behaviors, promotion of culturally based health protective behaviors, and reductions in disparities of health outcomes across cultural diverse groups could serve as outcome measures.

Conclusion/Opportunities

Culture is fundamental to the development and management of disease in every population, for its purpose is to teach its members what to do to survive, how to do it, and why they should persist in the face of adversity (Kagawa-Singer & Kassim-Lakha, 2003). The metaphor of weaving is useful to understand cultural variations. The technique of weaving is universal, but the patterns in the fabric that emerge from each group are culturally identifiable (Kagawa-Singer, 1996). Specific discrete beliefs and behaviors are like the threads in the tapestry. Taken out of context, a single thread, like a belief or behavior, may be misinterpreted or even disregarded as unnecessary or maladaptive, especially if evaluated against a standard appropriate for another culture. As such, healthcare organizations, nursing directors, and managers would benefit both themselves as well as their patients to learn how to be cross-culturally effective in the delivery of medical care. If organizations attend to cultural differences and build the skills necessary for cross-cultural expertise, they will improve health outcomes and increase quality of life for patients from a wider array of cultural backgrounds. If they ignore them, they will perpetuate and exacerbate the differential outcomes and unequal distribution of disease burden present today.

References

Airhihenbuwa, C. (1995). *Health and culture: Beyond the Western paradigm.* Thousand Oaks, CA: Sage Publications.

Angel, R., & Thoits, P. (1987). The impact of culture on the cognitive structure of illness. *Culture, Medicine, and Psychiatry, 11,* 465–494.

Betancourt, J.R., & King, R.K. (2000). Diversity in health care: Expanding our perspectives. *Archives of Pediatrics and Adolescent Medicine, 154,* 871–872.

Bhopal, R. (1998). Specter of racism in health and health care: Lessons from history and the United States. *BMJ, 316,* 1970–1973.

Blackhall, L.J., Frank, G., Murphy, S.T., Michel, V., Palmer, J.M., & Azen, S.P. (1999). Ethnicity and attitudes towards life sustaining technology. *Social Science and Medicine, 48,* 1779–1789.

Bobo, L., Womeodu, R.J., & Knox, A.L., Jr. (1991). Principles of intercultural medicine in an internal medicine program. *American Journal of the Medical Sciences, 302,* 244–248.

Bradley, C.J., Given, C.W., & Roberts, C. (2001). Disparities in cancer diagnosis and survival. *Cancer, 91,* 178–188.

Bronfenbrenner, U., & Ceci, S. (1994). Nature-nurture reconceptualized in developmental perspective: A bioecologic model. *Psychological Review, 101,* 568–586.

Campinha-Bacote, J. (1999). A model and instrument for addressing cultural competence in health care. *Journal of Nursing Education, 38*(5), 203–207.

Cross, T., Bazron, B., Dennis, K., & Isaacs, M. (1989). *Towards a culturally competent system of care* (Vol. 1). Washington, DC: Child and Adolescent Service System Program Technical Assistance Center, Center for Child Health and Mental Health Policy, Georgetown University Child Development Center.

Dana, R.H., Behn, J.D., & Gonwa, T. (1992). A checklist for the examination of cultural competence in social service agencies. *Research on Social Work Practice, 2*(2), 220–233.

Donabedian, A. (1985). *The methods and findings of quality assessment and monitoring: An illustrated analysis* (Vol. 3). Ann Arbor, MI: Health Administration Press.

Foster, G. (1978). *Medical anthropology.* New York: John Wiley & Sons.

Gilbert, M.J. (2002). *A manager's guide to cultural competence training for healthcare professionals.* Woodland Hills, CA: The California Endowment.

Hammond, P. (1978). *An introduction to cultural and social anthropology.* New York: McMillan.

Institute of Medicine. (2002). *Examining unequal treatment in American health care.* Washington, DC: National Academy of Sciences.

Isaacs, M.R., & Benjamin, M.P. (1991). *Towards a culturally competent system of care Vol. II: Programs which utilize culturally competent principles.* Washington, DC: Child and Adolescent Service System Program Technical Assistance Center, Center for Child Health and Mental Health Policy, Georgetown University Child Development Center.

Jackson, L.E. (1993). Understanding, eliciting, and negotiating clients' multicultural health beliefs. *The Nurse Practitioner, 18*(4), 30–43.

Joint Commission on Accreditation of Healthcare Organizations. (2004). *Where can I find the standards?* Retrieved August 13, 2004, from http://www.jcaho.org/accredited+organizations/hospitals/standards/index.htm

Kagawa-Singer, M. (1996). Cultural systems related to cancer. In R. McCorkle, M. Grant, M. Frank-Stromberg, & S. Baird (Eds.), *Cancer nursing: A comprehensive textbook* (pp. 38–52). Philadelphia: Saunders.

Kagawa-Singer, M. (2000). Improving the validity and generalizability of studies with underserved U.S. populations: Expanding the research paradigm. *Annals of Epidemiology, 10*(8 Suppl. 1), S92–S103.

Kagawa-Singer, M. (2001). From genes to social science: Color coding cancer. *Cancer, 91*(Suppl. 1), 226–232.

Kagawa-Singer, M., & Chung, R. (1994). A paradigm for culturally based care for minority populations. *Journal of Community Psychology, 22*(2), 192–208.

Kagawa-Singer, M., & Kassim-Lakha, S. (2003). A strategy to reduce cross-cultural miscommunication and increase the likelihood of improving health outcomes. *Academic Medicine, 78*, 577–587.

Kirschstein, R. (1999). *Wide use leads to push to test safety of four herbs* [Press release]. Bethesda, MD: National Institutes of Health.

Klessig, J. (1992). Cross-cultural medicine, a decade later: The effect of values and culture on life-support decisions. *Western Journal of Medicine, 157*, 316–322.

LaVeist, T.A. (2000). On the study of race, racism, and health: A shift from description to explanation. *International Journal of Health Services, 30*, 217–219.

Lavizzo-Mourey, R., & Mackenzie, E.R. (1996). Cultural competence: Essential measurements of quality for managed care organizations. *Annals of Internal Medicine, 124*, 919–921.

Levy, D. (1985). White doctors and black patients: Influence of race on the doctor-physician relationship. *Pediatrics, 75*, 639–643.

Marrone, S. (1999). Designing a competency-based nursing practice model in a multicultural setting. *Journal of Nurses in Staff Development, 15*(2), 56–62.

Mokuau, N.F.R. (1994). Assessing the responsiveness of health services to ethnic minorities of color. *Social Work in Health Care, 20*(2), 23–34.

Office of Management and Budget. (1997). *Revision to the standards for the classification of federal data on race and ethnicity.* Washington, DC: Executive Office of the President, Office of Information and Regulatory Affairs.

Oncology Nursing Society. (1999). *Oncology Nursing Society multicultural outcomes: Guidelines for cultural competence.* Pittsburgh, PA: Author.

Oncology Nursing Society. (2001). *Multicultural toolkit: Moving toward cultural competence.* Pittsburgh, PA: Author.

President's Initiative on Race. (1999). *Changing America: Indicators of social and economic well-being by race and Hispanic origin.* Washington, DC: National Center for Health Statistics.

Satcher, D. (1999). The initiative to eliminate racial and ethnic health disparities is moving forward. *Public Health Reports, 114*(3), 283–287.

Schneider, E.C., Cleary, P.D., Zaslavsky, A.M., & Epstein, A.M. (2001). Racial disparity in influenza vaccination: Does managed care narrow the gap between African Americans and whites? *JAMA, 286*, 1455–1460.

Schulman, K.A., Berlin, J.A., Harless, W., Kerner, J.F., Sistrunk, S., & Gersh, B.J. (1999). The effect of race and sex on physicians' recommendations for cardiac catheterization. *New England Journal of Medicine, 340*, 618–626.

Scott, C.J. (1997). Enhancing patient outcomes through an understanding of intercultural medicine: Guidelines for the practitioner. *Maryland Medical Journal, 46*(4), 175–180.

Shi, L. (1999). Experience of primary care by racial and ethnic groups in the United States. *Medical Care, 37*, 1068–1077.

Smith, D. (1999). *Health care divided; race and healing a nation.* Ann Arbor, MI: University of Michigan Press.

Tervalon, M., & Murray-Garcia, J. (1997). Cultural humility versus cultural competence: A critical distinction in defining physician training outcomes in multicultural education. *Journal of Health Care for the Poor and Underserved, 9*, 1117–1125.

Todd, K.H., Deaton, C., D'Adamo, A.P., & Goe, L. (2000). Ethnicity and analgesic practice. *Annals of Emergency Medicine, 35*, 11–16.

Todd, K.H., Samaroo, N., & Hoffman, J.R. (1993). Ethnicity as a risk factor for inadequate emergency department analgesia. *JAMA, 269*, 1537–1539.

U.S. Census Bureau. (2001). People who choose more than one race. *Public Health Reports, 116*, 626–627.

U.S. Department of Health and Human Services, Health Resources and Services Administration, Bureau of Primary Health Care. (1998). *Guidelines to help assess cultural competence in program design, application and management.* Retrieved July 21, 2004, from http://www.health.org/govpubs/MS500/

U.S. Department of Health and Human Services, Office of Minority Health. (2000). National standards for culturally and linguistically appropriate services in health care. *Federal Register.* Retrieved July 21, 2004, from http://omhrc.gov/clas

Williams, D., Yan, Y., Jackson, J.S., & Anderson, N.B. (1997). Racial differences in physical and mental health: Socioeconomic status, stress and discrimination. *Journal of Health Psychology, 2,* 335–351.

Yergan, J., Glood, A.B., LoGerfo, J.P., & Diehr, P. (1987). Relationship between patient race and the intensity of hospital services. *Medical Care, 25,* 592–603.

Ying, Y.W., Lee, P.A., Tsai, J.L., Yeh, Y.Y., & Huang, J.S. (2000). The conception of depression in Chinese American college students. *Cultural Diversity and Ethnic Minority Psychology, 6,* 183–195.

Workforce Diversity: Valuing and Embracing Difference

Gregory L. Crow, RN, BSN, MSN, EdD
Mary Magee Gullatte, RN, MN, ANP, AOCN®, FAAMA
Guadalupe Palos, RN, LMSW, DrPH

"Color is not a human or personal reality; it is a political reality."
James Baldwin (Bell, 1995, p. 36)

Decades ago, America was referred to as the "melting pot." This phrase, then and now, was heralding the reality that America was known as a nation willing to embrace freedom of race, culture, and creed. The belief of freedoms was so strong that it was written into the Declaration of Independence in 1776 by the Second Continental Congress: "We hold these truths to be self-evident, that all men are created equal, that they are endowed by their Creator with certain unalienable rights, that among these are life, liberty, and the pursuit of happiness" (National Archives and Records Administration, 2003).

In health care, as in society at large, the patient care environment and the workplace are melting pots. Although the melting pot analogy is widely used, you will see later in the chapter why it might not be the most accurate model. Society is a melting pot of race, color, creed, gender, sex, sexual orientation, size, ethnicity, languages, customs, communication styles, age, cultures, and socioeconomic status. There has been an evolution of attempts to forge an open acceptance to the differences that tend to divide rather than unite a people. Multiple movements attempting to bridge the gap have included the introduction of such terms as cultural awareness, cultural sensitivity, cultural diversity, and, of late, cultural competence (Husting, 1995).

The demographics of the workplace are changing and will continue to change rapidly. Almost every organization in the United States and in health care looks different today, both in terms of the employees and the positions they hold and the patient population we serve. Workforce diversity is not a matter of debate; it is a matter of fact. The increased diversity within organizations presents one of the greatest challenges and opportunities facing organizations, and only through hard work and committed leadership can the potential for benefit be realized (Sonnenschein, 1999). With growing diversity in our society, the likelihood that employees will be from different cultural backgrounds increases. As an organization becomes more multicultural, the risk for negative stereotyping and value conflict increases. Stereotyping of individuals can lead to negative results, especially if no effort is made to learn about an individual or cultural group. Galanti (2003), a nurse expert in cultural diversity, believes that generalizations and stereotyping may appear to be similar but have different functions. She contends people use generalizations to look for a common thread in the patterns, beliefs, and behaviors shared by a group, but additional information is needed to determine if a particular statement applies to a specific person.

Cultural Competence

Cultural competence is the translation of cultural sensitivity and awareness into behaviors and action that benefit the patient or family (Paniagua, 1998). Therefore, a Hispanic nurse can be as effective as an African American nurse in the assessment and intervention of African American clients as long as he or she incorporates the specific needs of the African American patient into his or her care. The nurse and patient sharing the same race and ethnicity does not guarantee the effectiveness of care.

In 1991, recognizing the need to embrace human differences, the American Nurses Association formed the Council on Cultural Diversity in Nursing Practice. The principle of this initiative was the "inclusion of people of all heritages and understandings among nurses and among nursing education, so that they may better reflect the population and better care for all those of all cultures" (Burnette, 1993).

With the current challenge in the economy and health care comes a golden opportunity to impact nursing diversity through academia, practice, and research. The demographics of the United States have changed drastically in the past 20 years. According the U.S. Census Bureau (2001), some of the most drastic changes are in the numbers of Asian and Hispanic citizens. In 1990, Hispanics made up 9% of the total U.S. population, and by 2000, this number reached 12.5%. The Asian population in 1990 was 2.8%, and this number rose to 4.2% in 2000. The western United States saw the largest increase in Hispanic and Asian populations. Across the country, the current pool of active nurses in practice and education is aging and will retire from the full-time workforce during the next 10–15 years.

The nursing workforce challenges of declining enrollment in schools of nursing and workplace shortages, coupled with the aging of the current nursing workforce, are creating a crisis. According to a July 2002 report, 30 states were projected to have RN shortages in 2000; moreover, over the next two decades, the shortage will spread to 44 states and the District of Columbia (U.S. Health Resources and Services Administration[HRSA], 2003). According to the U.S. Bureau of Labor Statistics (2004), more than one million new and replacement RNs will be needed by 2012. The bureau has identified RNs as one of the top 10 professions for job growth through 2012. The National Council of State Boards of Nursing (2004) stated that for the first time in U.S. history, the number of graduates who sat for the state licensing examination decreased by 20% between 1995 and 2003. According to the *National Sample Survey of Registered Nurses* released in February 2002 by the Division of Nursing within the Bureau of Health Professions, the average age of the working RN was 43.3 in March 2000, up from 42.6 in 1996 (U.S. HRSA, 2002). The RN population younger than 30 dropped from 25.1% in 1980 to 9.1% in 2000 (U.S. HRSA, 2002).

In the position of leadership, there is an opportunity to influence cultural competence in the workplace. Leaders need to understand that our choices, decisions, and behaviors reflect learned beliefs, values, ideas, and preferences (Kavanagh & Kennedy, 1992). As a nurse manager, it is important to realize that one cannot change what one does not acknowledge. From a position of power comes the responsibility of leadership to acknowledge the needs of a diverse workforce and to influence the organization toward acceptance. The influence of leaders can be positive or negative. Their influence permeates the workforce, top down, and they have the ability to impact givers and receivers of health care.

As you read in Chapter 1, the manager first must transform self in preparation to lead others. The manager can refuse to succumb to old prejudices, beliefs, and stereotypes about people and teach others to value the differences among people. Valuing diversity creates opportunities to mentor leadership, and it is because of our diversity that nursing will emerge stronger from the challenges that health care creates. Diversity brings a wealth of talents, ideas, approaches, experiences, skills, cultures, and languages to the workplace. The responsibility is multifold for the nurse manager and leader, including increasing diversity of staff, fostering cultural competence among all employees, facilitating leadership development among culturally diverse staff, and, above all, allowing personal and professional actions to reflect a leadership culture of valuing a diverse workforce (Husting, 1995).

Workplace Diversity

Nurses seemingly have an inherent nature to overcome adversity, but they often struggle with how best to lead, manage, or practice in a diverse workplace. Nurses are taught early to treat each patient as an individual and to respect the culture of patients. Nursing school curricula emphasize learning about diverse healthcare beliefs, values, and practices of patients and families. However, sometimes this knowledge does not transfer to the workplace with colleagues of diverse cultures. Oftentimes, accepting colleagues of various backgrounds and valuing their diversity is masked, at best, by politeness and disguised in job class differences. At its worst, unacceptance of diversity manifests as workplace passive or overt aggression and negative behaviors. Managers in public and healthcare organizations are searching for the right approach to more effectively work with increasing diversity on the job. Ivancevich (2000) called for a new agenda that encourages more collaboration between scholars and administrators, increases researcher on-site observations of workplace reactions to diversity management initiatives, and encourages more informative and rigorous case studies and more third-party evaluations of diversity management initiatives.

Workplace Demographics

Historically, our businesses, in general, and hospitals, specifically, reflected the existing power base in our country—white males were at the top and in charge. Women were generally relegated to staff roles, and people of color, both male and female, were generally found in departments such as central supply, dietary, and environmental services. This situation led to an organizational culture that was almost totally created, dominated, and maintained by those at the top. Moreover, it rarely reflected beliefs beyond the white European model.

When healthcare organizations were more homogeneous, in terms of who was in power and those who were powerless, many leaders felt it was easier to manage and lead them (Husting, 1995). However, most healthcare organizations as a whole were not homogeneous; there were subcultures. Moreover, these subcultures were generally under the radar of those in power, and their power was rarely, if ever, tapped. An enormous opportunity was missed to better the organization, expand market share, and reflect the wants, needs, and desires of the whole workforce.

In the U.S. healthcare workforce of 11.5 million, Weber (2000) reported that 77% are women and 23% are men; 15% of all healthcare employees are African American, 7% are Hispanic, and 3% are Asian or Native American. Interestingly, senior managers in healthcare organizations are still mostly white men. Weber further reported that in 2000, of the 30,000 members of the American College of Healthcare Executives (ACHE), approximately 50% were women and 50% were men. However, among the higher executive ranks, the race and gender mix shifts drastically. Among chief executive officers and chief operating officers of healthcare organizations nationwide, ACHE and the National Association of Health Services Executives reported that more that 98% are white (Weber). When confronted with the lack of minorities in hospital management positions, administrators often would respond that they wanted to hire more people of color but seldom found qualified applicants (Marquand, 2001). Diversity must be genuinely supported from the top down. The Institute of Diversity in Health Management (www.diversityconnection.com) offers help in hiring. At its Web site, healthcare employers can list management opportunities and find resumes of minority job seekers. More information can be found in Chapter 10 on culturally competent organizations.

World View, Culture, and Values

World view has been defined as the foundation for the actions and interpretations belonging to a specific group of individuals (Kagawa-Singer, 1996). Culture, on the other hand, is a tool that defines reality for its members (Oncology Nursing Society,

1999). Many groups use culture to define the acceptable way to behave in a situation while maintaining integrity and self-respect (Kagawa-Singer, 1996). Historically, the term "culture" has been used to refer to people of diverse racial and ethnic backgrounds, such as African Americans, Hispanics/Latinos, Native Americans, and Asians. However, culture does not always refer to people of color. It also may be defined by factors such as gender, age, education, and sexual orientation. In our rapidly changing pluralistic society, the concept of culture has expanded to include refugees or recent immigrants, multiracial or unmarried couples, gays/lesbians, people with certain religious affiliations, and those who are physically or mentally challenged (Lenburg et al., 1995).

In spite of our differences, certain values seem to be important across all groups in varying degrees. Values have been defined as "shared ideals which give rise to beliefs and norms of behavior around which a people or group organizes its collective life goals" (Rosado, 1994, p. 1). The nature and role of values are critical aspects of organizational outcomes, just as they are for groups. Universal values include respect, dignity, trust, and self-determination. Added to this list is how our Western biomedical model impacts organizations, employees, and patients. The biomedical model values autonomy, independence, privacy, self-control, punctuality, and patient's rights (Sonnenschein, 1999).

Two processes, acculturation and incorporation, may influence our world view. Acculturation has been defined as a process that involves change in ethnic values, customs, and norms so members of the dominant society may accept a person (Gordon, 1964; Palos, 1994). Incorporation is a process that allows an individual to preserve his or her own ethnic values while adopting selected cultural beliefs and practices of the dominant society (Andrews & Herberg, 1999). In society, some members of cultural groups choose to maintain their own norms, behaviors, and languages, whereas others decide to become as "American" as possible.

Cultural mores and norms are learned from parents, teachers, the media, and everyone and everything that was encountered while growing up. Culture is what a particular group agrees is reality, and it is the backdrop for the ways people think, feel, speak, and act. For every aspect of our culture we are aware of, there is much more we are not aware of on a daily basis. Learned culture is often automatic and goes unnoticed. For example, we are linked to our culture by the foods we eat. We often shop for, cook, and consume foods that are familiar to us. With religion, we have been acculturated to attend services at a particular structure affiliated with a denomination that likely will be passed on to the next generation through tradition. When raised in a household that favors a particular political party, we are likely to continue that affiliation into adulthood. Most experts agree that culture has at least three dimensions: (1) culture is learned, (2) various aspects of culture are interrelated, and (3) culture is shared and defines the boundaries between different groups (Sonnenschein, 1999). When applying this information to organizational culture, it is apparent that new employees, such as immigrants, must learn the existing culture and how each person, department, and work group are related and interrelated; and finally, organizational culture defines the boundaries between your organization and others. As most people in general business know, differentiating your organization from others in a positive way can lead to increased status and profits and can identify a healthcare organization as one of choice for employees and patients.

Societal Diversity Issues and the Workplace

The workplace is society in a microcosm. It tends to reflect the issues, concerns, and tensions in society at large. Some of these issues, concerns, and tensions are the impact of a multicultural society, the myth of the melting pot, multiculturalism, racial issues, sexual orientation, people with disabilities, reverse discrimination, gender issues, and the "isms" such as racism and ageism (Esty, Griffin, & Hirsch, 1995; Sonnenschein, 1999).

The "Isms"

The American culture means people with many differences must live and work together. Sometimes people get along, and sometimes they do not. The worst result of people not getting along is the "isms," which are destructive forces that tear organizations apart. Racism is perhaps the most obvious and problematic. Racial hatred has no boundaries. It affects organizations just as it affects all of society. One needs only to pick up a newspaper, magazine, or listen to the news to see how isms destroy families, friendships, communities, organizations, and nations. People who hate other people because of the color of their skin cannot work well in a diverse workplace. Most organizations have zero tolerance for racism. If a person is proven to be a racist, it is grounds for termination. However, racism is not the only destructive ism that organizations face. Sexism, ageism, homophobia, xenophobia, and other forms of hatred also tear organizations apart. As with racism, organizations cannot allow any ism to exist unchecked. Yet too often, they are not recognized (purposefully or because of ignorance) as isms by people in positions of power, and because of that lack of recognition, organizations can have a very destructive undercurrent or subculture that is in direct opposition to the desired culture. An organizational leader must be on the lookout for isms and be ready to thwart them in every form (Esty et al., 1995; Sonnenschein, 1999).

Multicultural Society

To understand societal issues and the meaning of diversity, the nurse manager must acknowledge and understand America as a multicultural society. The idea of multiculturalism evokes a negative response from many people (Morrison, 1992). They wonder why we cannot look at America and Americans as being one culture. Many wonder why people of various ethnic backgrounds desire to be called by prefixes specific to their place of origin (e.g., Mexican American, Arab American, African American), yet we are a culture made up of many diverse cultures. Diversity in simplest terms is the differences between people (Morrison; Sonnenschein, 1999). Generally, in the workplace diversity is viewed in terms of race, culture, gender, sexual orientation, age, and physical abilities. However, more recently terms like ethnicity, nation of origin, class, and religion have been included in discussions of diversity. To understand what diversity in the United States really means and what issues diversity elicits, we need to examine the metaphor that has been used for many years to define American culture—the melting pot.

The Myth of the Melting Pot

People from all over the world have come to the United States to live in and create a nation of freedoms, and no matter where you travel in this world, the United States is identified as the melting pot nation. Many have tried to create an analogy for this phrase that has been used for many generations. The "metal" melting pot seems to provide the best analogy. In a melting pot, different metals melt together over heat to form a new metal. This newly created metal is stronger than the individual metals in the pot. When the melting is accomplished, an entirely new metal is made. The new metal, composed of the different types of metals, bears no obvious trace of the different types of metal used to create it (Esty et al., 1995; Sonnenschein, 1999).

Humans cannot be manipulated like metal. In truth, humans have a strong need to maintain separate cultures for personal identity purposes. Although some Europeans have adopted the ways of the United States, have intermarried, and mostly have lost the cultures of their ancestors, others retained much of their cultural identities. Historically, many minority groups brought to the U.S. shores, some against their will, were forced to acculturate.

Multiculturalism and Cultural Relativism

Culture refers to the system of beliefs, values, customs, and institutions that create a common identity and ways of behavior for a given people (Kavanagh & Kennedy, 1992). Cultural issues abound in organizations. They include different styles of communication and behavior, misunderstandings concerning favoritism, uses of time, and family matters.

U.S. citizens who have retained their ancestral cultures have done so for a variety of reasons. Many have not been permitted to "melt" into mainstream American culture, having been excluded because of the color of their skin or the dissimilarity of their customs. However, significant numbers have retained their cultures because they wanted to. People have pride in who and what they are and in where they came from. They have maintained their cultural identities while trying to fit into American society—no easy task. Many have kept their languages. Others have maintained customs, dress, or food. Religious diversity also has thrived, further weakening the image of the melting pot. Many Americans do not want to be "melted" into one culture but do want to be a part of a larger society made up of many different cultures.

Cultural relativism refers to attitudes or other ways of doing things that may be different but equally valid. It often is debated as to whether cultural relativism is a practical and realistic philosophy for the medical world, including oncology. Some practitioners believe that cultural relativism, as an approach to diversity acceptance, has been idealized and that unquestionable acceptance of practices and beliefs may be more harmful than beneficial (Kavanagh & Kennedy, 1992).

Ethnocentrism

Ethnocentrism has been defined as the belief in the superiority of the ideas and practices of one's own racial or ethnic group, cultural practices, or lifestyle (Lenburg et al., 1995). Some theorists, however, believe that ethnocentrism is not always negative. For example, through ethnocentrism, people may develop a sense of peoplehood or group identity, which is considered a positive trait to possess (Herskovits, 1973; Ruggiero, 1973; Smedley, 1993). Ethnocentrism becomes negative when a stronger group destroys the practices or customs that a group holds of value and imposes their rule on other groups (Herskovits). For example, when a new graduate is hired by a healthcare organization, he or she comes from the particular practice culture of his or her school. The new graduate is taught that certain things are done in a particular way. Upon entering a first position, he or she is pressured, covertly and overtly, to conform to the new practice culture. This is also the case when an experienced nurse is hired.

Gender Issues

Gender communication issues also have a strong impact on organizations. Issues involving gender in the workplace include different communication styles and perceptions, equal opportunities, sexual harassment, and other kinds of discrimination, which may or may not be subtle. In employment interviews, women complain about men asking inappropriate questions concerning family, among other things. In fact, the primary model for cross-gender relationships comes from the family, but applying the family model in the workplace can result in unprofessional interactions, often involving patronizing, deferential, or sexually suggestive language and behaviors (Ivancevich & Gilbert, 2000).

Until the women's movement in the 1970s, women in business often felt undervalued and almost invisible (Hammer, 2002). In nursing, this can be especially troublesome. For much of nursing's history, nurses were expected to be the silent partner in health care. Often, nurses were expected to acquiesce to the desires of the hospital, administration, and physicians. Nursing, like many female-dominated work groups, was relegated to a subservient role.

Racial Issues and Health Care

Race, primarily defined by the public, is based in the ancestral color of skin; when, in fact, race is defined as one of the major divisions of mankind, each having distinctive physical characteristics and a common ancestry (Barnhart & Barnhart, 1991). The public definition creates a number of serious issues, both in American society and in the workplace. Respect, equality, and fair treatment are the major concerns.

Differing perspectives of racial issues is another critical concern. African Americans, for instance, often say that whites do not understand the issue of race. Conversely, whites, unlike African Americans, feel race is not as much of an issue. According to Carr-Ruffino (1999), most whites also tend to misunderstand the general situation of many people of color.

One's race and ethnic identification impact health. There are differences in mortality rates among races. The mortality rate was higher for African Americans than for whites for most of the leading causes of death for the total population in the United States in 2000 (National Center for Health Statistics [NCHS], 2004; www.cdc. gov/nchs). Also, according to NCHS, infant mortality rates for African Americans and Native Americans are the highest for all ethnic groups in the United States. Moreover, life expectancy for African Americans is lower than whites. Life expectancy for all races and both sexes is 77.2 years, yet for African Americans and both sexes, it is only 72.2 years (NCHS). It is apparent that one's race greatly impacts one's health and life expectancy.

Ageism

People create a variety of issues about age, including whether an employee is too old for a job, whether age differences create communication gaps based on the differences of life experiences, and whether any age group is shown the respect due to them. A person's age places him or her in an era (Esty et al., 1995; Sonnenschein, 1999). For nursing, the era of nurses deferring to physicians as a part of the healthcare culture has caused many problems. As nurses shed these familiar behaviors, other problems arise. When a group within an organization begins to change its behavior, that leads to a reaction from the rest of the organization. In order for nurses to be fully participating members of the healthcare team with an identified practice, physicians and administrators must evolve as well.

Sexual Orientation

As gays and lesbians increasingly make their presence known in the organization, a variety of issues develop in the workplace. Some people believe that homosexuality is immoral. Others just do not understand it. There are often tasteless and inflammatory jokes (Carr-Ruffino, 1999). Support for nontraditional families, with respect to insurance coverage, for example, is often an issue. As a society, we are much more mobile today. Nurses from larger metropolitan areas who transfer to a smaller community often find that what was acceptable in the larger community is less accepted in the smaller one. Sometimes, the tensions between gays and heterosexuals can escalate to workplace violence.

Carr-Ruffino (1999) posited that prejudice against the gay employee is more common among certain segments of the population than others, and it negatively impacts the holders and receivers of prejudice. For example, gays appear to be more accepted in larger cities as opposed to small towns. This is common, as larger cities tend to be more liberal. Moreover, in some large cities, gays have some of their rights codified into law. In San Francisco, New York, and Chicago, gay employees are afforded the same work benefits as heterosexual married couples. Additionally, 81% of lesbians and 76% of gay men fear they would be the victims of job discrimination if they "came out" at work. Woods and Lucas (1993) further noted that a central career focus for gay people is managing their sexual identity. Gays who are "in the closet" must deal with the stress of living a lie, whereas gays who "come out" must deal with people's reactions.

Carr-Ruffino (1999) listed several specific workplace barriers for gays, such as prejudice and discrimination, the sexual double standard, and treating gay people as tokens. As the gay population began to understand their political strength, they began putting pressure on employers to hire more gays in management, as well as staff jobs, and they demanded the same benefits. However, in the early years of the movement, gays were treated much like the token woman. Perhaps the best example of tokenism is Justice Sandra Day O'Connor of the U.S. Supreme Court. When she graduated from the Stanford Law School, the only job she could find was as a secretary in a law firm (O'Connor, 2003). The message was clear: Yes, we hire minorities; however, the glass ceiling is really thick. It can cost thousands of dollars to recruit an employee, and should the gay employee, much like any other minority, find discrimination, she or he might leave. When they leave the corporation, they generally inform their gay friends not to apply for work.

The sexual double standard indicates that heterosexual couples are welcome at all organizational sponsored events but gay couples are not. This type of discrimination is not overtly written into personnel policies; however, it can be as well known as any official policy of an organization. Organizations that hire one or two of whatever minority, with no intention of hiring more, often attempt to make the token employee very visible; however, they are rarely in a position of power or authority.

As a leader, you need to recognize the strengths that each of your team members brings to the organization and build on those strengths. As a practical matter, nearly all companies have business reasons for focusing attention on a problem and for spending both time and money on solving it. Companies are most likely to combat prejudice when they have an economic incentive for doing so. Issues like high turnover, sexual harassment lawsuits, and decreased productivity because of tension throughout the organization are cited as economic incentives (Carr-Ruffino, 1999; Esty et al., 1995; Sonnenschein, 1999).

Disabilities

The Americans with Disabilities Act of 1990 ensures workplace protections for people with disabilities. Several of its issues deal with physical barriers, yet many involve communication. In a workplace where work is manual, for example, deaf people complain about inequality. Non-deaf workers can talk while they work, but the deaf workers who communicate through sign language cannot because their hands are occupied. If they stop to talk with their hands, they are accused of slacking off, whereas hearing people who chat while working might be totally distracted by the conversation and are not called to task. Hearing impaired workers also do not have access to verbal office gossip. They might have interpreters for staff meetings, but that is about it. They often feel left out of the office culture (Esty et al., 1995).

Reverse Discrimination

Most of us have heard the old saying that two wrongs do not make a right. Those groups and individuals that traditionally held positions of power or were raised to believe that they should be given power based on their race, class, or education have found that their power base is eroding. The equal opportunity movement has created the new reality that they must share power. Reverse discrimination is the belief that diversity policies have gone too far and that whites face discrimination today. White men, however, still outnumber women and people of color in nearly all positions of power and still, on average, make more money than others in the same or similar position. The Federal Glass Ceiling Commission reported (1995) that 97% of Fortune 500 company senior managers were white and 95% of them male.

Leadership

Perhaps the most important diversity skills are leadership skills. There are many definitions of leadership and many leadership styles. Diversity would greatly benefit from strong leaders in positions of power. Diversity also needs everyone in every organization who sees the need for better working relationships, who sees the problems and can communicate solutions, to step forward and take on a leadership role. People need to understand diversity, take stands where needed, and inspire others.

Effective leaders help the diverse workforce in many ways. They help create awareness of both the issues of diversity and of the ways to communicate in a diverse workplace. To do this, they must be aware of the issues, be self-aware, and be open to different styles of leadership, management, and communication.

A leader also can help increase understanding among all members of the organization. A leader can help people in the organization realize their prejudices and stereotypes and stop those biases from affecting the workplace. A leader also manages conflict effectively.

One of the most important things a leader can do, no matter the style or role, is to embrace diversity (Esty et al., 1995). Many people resist diversity because they resist change. Yet diversity of the workplace is a trend that cannot be reversed, and it is creating change. Leaders need to do more than accept the change, more than accept the existence of diversity. To make diversity work, they need to be among the first to embrace it. By modeling good diversity skills and by demonstrating their respect and appreciation for differences, leaders can help others accept and value diversity. The fundamentals of embracing diversity include respect, tolerance, flexibility, self-awareness, empathy, patience, and humor (Mathews, 1998; Sonnenschein, 1999).

A leader can increase understanding among all members of the organization. A leader can help people in the organization realize their prejudices and stereotypes and stop those biases from affecting the workplace. A leader manages conflict between and among different factions within the organizations. The leader strives to create an open dialogue throughout the organization that allows issues to surface and be dealt with in an open and thoughtful manner, with the end goal of creating inclusiveness. By understanding diversity, a leader helps an organization move beyond the typical areas of diversity, such as gender and race, and focus on creating a community of people within the organization that identifies with the organization's culture as well as their own and the cultures of others (Sonnenschein, 1999).

Management Issues

Employees know that strong leadership from management is a positive force when dealing with issues of diversity. Executives must be prepared to respond to issues that diversity creates, as well as to other management issues. When there is weak leadership and management of diversity within an organization, a variety of problems and issues arise, including disruptions and low morale; limited creativity and innovation; miscommunication, misunderstandings, fear, prejudice, discrimination, disunity, and inefficiency; high employee turnover; an inability to compete in recruiting the best employees; and a weakened customer base (Esty et al., 1995; Mathews, 1998; Morrison, 1992; Sonnenschein, 1999).

Disruptions and low morale can impact any organization. Intergroup conflicts cause arguments, distrust, and hatred. Morale cannot stay high under such conditions. Productivity suffers. Limited creativity and innovation also can result from changes brought on by diversity. Diversity should enhance creativity and innovation, but too often managers fail to make good use of the diversity of skills and perspectives among their workers. The nurse manager will be expected to lead a diverse workforce to successfully achieve the organizational goals and outcomes. Issues of miscommunication, misunderstanding, fear, prejudice, discrimination, disunity, and inefficiency can arise from various causes. Leaders and managers need to create an environment in which employees feel good about coming to work. Bad communication, fear, and discrimination affect the whole organization and can interfere with the mission and destroy the team.

High employee turnover, especially among nurses, is an issue in all healthcare organizations. Attempting to attract and retain talented employees is the goal of all organizations. Employees leave nonsupportive organizations to find a work environment that is supportive. Organizations waste millions of dollars every year hiring and training new employees only to have them leave when the environment is not welcoming. If your organization finds itself unable to compete in recruiting the best employees, it could be because of the lack of acceptance of various groups within the organization. Any organization that gets a reputation for high turnover and low morale because of diversity problems will have difficulty attracting the top employment candidates. Organizations, for a variety of reasons, can find themselves suffering from a weakened customer base. As a negative reputation grows because of diversity problems or as an organization fails to recruit people with diverse backgrounds because of its reputation, the organization will limit its customer base. A company should resemble the communities it serves.

Challenge and Opportunity

The goal of a diverse workforce is to create and maintain a climate that welcomes, values, and nurtures all types of employees. Leaders in health care have a lot to learn from both the mistakes and successes found in general business. General business colleagues understand that the benefits of a diverse workforce accrue at all levels—personal, interpersonal, organizational, and financial. The business literature is replete with examples of the benefits of workforce diversity. Some of these benefits include (Carr-Ruffino, 1999; Esty et al., 1995; Morrison, 1992; Sonnenschein, 1999)

- Attracting and retaining the best available personnel
- Gaining and keeping greater market share
- Reducing costs
- Improving the quality of management
- Innovating
- Solving problems more effectively
- Increasing productivity
- Contributing to social responsibility
- Improving the bottom line.

However, these benefits are not automatic. Diversity means *challenge*. Racism, sexism, ageism, and homophobia disrupt the work environment, prevent teams from accomplishing their goals, and keep organizations from achieving their mission. Simple misunderstandings caused by cultural and other differences in behavior, work attitudes, and communication styles also create challenges in the workplace. The *opportunity* is to capitalize on the strengths that come from a diverse workforce, including new ideas and different (oftentimes better) ways of accomplishing goals (Mathews, 1998). Managing diversity has become a human resources mandate as organizations seek to maintain a competitive edge and compete successfully in a global economy (Dobbs, 1996). Hopefully the 21st century will herald the melding of race, culture, ethnicity, and creed into a unified diverse workforce, making positive differences in the profession and in the care of a diverse patient population.

The accountability of the manager and leader is multifold: (a) increase diversity of staff; (b) foster cultural competence among all employees (clinical and management); (c) facilitate leadership development among culturally diverse staff; and, above all, (d) let personal and professional actions reflect a leadership culture of valuing a diverse workforce (Morrison, 1992).

According to Esty et al. (1995), one of the biggest challenges of diversity is how it affects the management organizations. Some of the challenges include the following principles.

Management complexity: It seems easier to manage a group of similar-minded people. A homogeneous organization might appear to have less conflict. There is no need to constantly adjust managerial style, to listen to different ways of doing business, or to find new approaches to doing tasks that have always been done successfully one way.

Fairness: How can people be fair when different cultures define fairness in different ways? Diversity creates questions about fairness because of the need to create mechanisms to ensure equal access to the workplace, protect different groups against discrimination, and treat every individual equitably.

Individual differences versus unanimity: Some may think that it is easier to work with people with backgrounds similar to their own rather than to learn to work with people with different styles, understand new perspectives, and adjust to disparate attitudes.

Identity and loyalty: When people are all similar, they are confident in who they are and do not feel the need to redefine themselves. They do not wonder if they trust new people with new values or if others will back them up. They will be loyal to the organization as they have known it. Issues related to identity and loyalty were brought to the forefront following the events of September 11. In many communities, large and small, people who looked or worshipped differently than others found that their identity and loyalty as U.S. citizens were questioned. There were numerous examples of overt racism and discrimination.

Turning many of these challenges into benefits is possible. Finding new approaches to doing tasks, for instance, leads to innovation. Clear-thinking leaders with sound diversity skills can find the ways to make diversity work.

Recruitment and Retention

There are many benefits to having culturally diverse staff in the workplace. If staff and patients respect each others' cultural values and languages, there may be better communication, a more friendly environment, and healthcare structures that can meet the needs of diverse cultural groups (Cooper-Patrick et al., 1999). Strategies for the recruitment and retention of minority or culturally diverse staff include hiring minority search firms, creating fellowship programs for nurses of culturally diverse backgrounds, and tracking employee satisfaction by race, ethnicity, and gender. Other techniques include encouraging your organization to form partnerships with representatives of multicultural (ethnic) media sources, including newspapers, radio, or local television talk shows. Efforts can focus on informing community members about job opportunities and initiatives targeting specific patient populations, such as children immunizations or prostate screenings. Recruitment of nurses from countries that represent the local racial or ethnic population also may be a way to increase diversity within the workforce. For example, collaborations between Latin American countries such as Mexico or Chile and U.S. healthcare facilities along the U.S.-Mexico border have increased the number of Spanish-speaking nurses who meet the educational and clinical criteria.

Employee Diversity Education

The goals of cultural diversity training programs are to improve patient-provider and employee-employer interactions, change attitudes and behaviors of administrative and clinical staff, and, ultimately, increase cultural sensitivity, knowledge, and skills. Cultural competency programs should be a requirement for all employees, managers, and staff. These programs may be offered on a regular basis, integrated into orientation for new employees and managers, or made part of required in-service programs (similar to CPR or sexual harassment classes). Cultural diversity workshops have been developed, implemented, and evaluated for nurses working with Asian, African American, Latino, and underserved populations (Berman, Manning, Peters, Siegel, & Yadao, 1998). The researchers concluded that the model could be adapted to use in various geographic areas but that projected program outcomes may not always be achieved if participants did not work with the targeted patient populations on a regular basis.

Employee diversity education is meant to harness the power of a diverse and unified workforce. Roberson (1993) summarized it best, "The challenge to us as a profession is to seize the opportunity to grow, to learn, to understand, to expand our horizons and to creatively capitalize on what is best for the benefit of our patients, clients, staff, students and our profession" (p. 1).

Strategies for Attracting and Retaining a Diverse Workforce

For organizational success and workforce survival, nurse managers must embrace a diverse workforce and learn how to lead this force to accomplish organizational goals and achieve patient outcomes. The following strategies will be helpful to managers.

- Identify and manage personal and organizational "isms" (e.g., racism, ageism, sexism).
- Examine personal and organizational value systems.
- Be sincere about initiatives to eliminate discrimination in the workplace.
- Recognize and tear down gender and minority glass ceilings.
- Coach and mentor.
- Invest in diverse human resources.
- Be open and flexible to different ways of doing things.
- Set the standard for the top down; lead the change.
- Challenge the status quo and old norms.
- Ascribe to principles of fairness and equity (Roberson, 1993).

Both diversity and leadership skills begin by understanding what you as an individual bring to the workplace. As a nurse leader or manager, be aware of those things in your own background (beliefs, values, and practices) that might help you to do or see, or prevent you from doing or seeing, things important to your organization related to leading a diverse work team. Successful leaders and managers capitalize on their strengths and find ways to lessen or work around their weaknesses. Understand first and foremost that people communicate to the world through their actions and deeds. To communicate with confidence, leaders must know themselves very well. Lead by action, word, and deed.

Conclusion

The U.S. workforce is changing demographically, and there is a need for organizations to address these changes. In their changing roles, leaders and managers should use their power to positively influence the needed changes in organizational culture to welcome all potential employees. This requires leaders and managers to understand the interrelationship of diversity and human resource management. Organizations that introduce diversity into the workplace claim increases in productivity levels and, thus, stand to increase profits. However, handled improperly, diversity management easily can turn into a losing situation for all involved.

Diversity management is a corporate or managerially initiated strategy. It can be proactive and is based on operational reality to optimize the use of and contributions of an increasingly diverse national workforce. The improper or underutilization of a diverse workforce is not a legal issue, but it is a managerial and leadership issue. Nursing, and indeed all of health care, can greatly benefit from recruiting, training, and retaining a diverse workforce.

References

Andrews, M., & Herberg, P. (1999). Transcultural nursing care. In M. Andrews & J. Boyle (Eds.), *Transcultural concepts in nursing care* (3rd ed., pp. 308–337). Philadelphia: Lippincott Williams & Wilkins.

Barnhart, C., & Barnhart, R.K. (Eds.). (1991). *The World Book dictionary*. Chicago: World Book.

Bell, J.C. (1995). *Famous black quotations*. Chicago: Warner.

Berman, A., Manning, M.P., Peters, E., Siegel, B.B., & Yadao, L. (1998). A template for cultural diversity workshop. *Oncology Nursing Forum, 25,* 1711–1718.

Burnette, L. (1993). Cultural diversity. *Nursing Matters, 2,* 2.

Carr-Ruffino, N. (1999). *Diversity success strategies*. Boston: Butterworth & Heinemann.

Cooper-Patrick, L., Gallo, J.J., Gonzales, J.J., Vu, H.T., Powe, N.R., Nelson, C., et al. (1999). Race, gender, and partnership in the patient-physician relationship. *JAMA, 282,* 583–589.

Dobbs, M.F. (1996). Managing diversity: Lessons from the private sector. *Public Personnel Management, 35,* 17.

Esty, K., Griffin, R., & Hirsch, M.S. (1995). *Workforce diversity: A manager's guide to solving problems and turning diversity into a corporate advantage*. Avon, MA: Adam Media Corporation.

Federal Glass Ceiling Commission. (1995). *A solid investment: Making full use of the nation's human capital*. Washington, DC: Author.

Galanti, G. (2003). *Do you want to achieve cultural competence?* Retrieved November 7, 2003, from http://www.ggalanti.com/concepts.html

Gordan, M. (1964). *Assimilation in American life*. London: Oxford University Press.

Hammer, K. (2002). Breaking the lead ceiling. In D. Goleman (Ed.), *Business: The ultimate resource* (pp. 237–238). Cambridge, MA: Perseus Publishing.

Herskovits, M.J. (1973). *Cultural relativism: Perspectives in cultural pluralism*. New York: Vintage.

Husting, P.M. (1995). Managing a culturally diverse workforce. *Nursing Management, 26*(8), 26, 28–29, 32.

Ivancevich, J.M. (2000). Diversity management. *Public Personnel Management, 29,* 75.

Ivancevich, J.M., & Gilbert, J.A. (2000). Diversity management. *Public Personnel Management, 29,* 82.

Kagawa-Singer, M. (1996). Cultural systems related to cancer. In S. Baird, R. McCorkle, & M. Grant (Eds.), *Cancer nursing* (2nd ed., pp. 38–52). Philadelphia: Saunders.

Kavanagh, K.H., & Kennedy, P.H. (1992). *Promoting cultural diversity.* Newbury Park, CA: Sage.

Lenburg, C.B., Lipson, J.G., Demi, A.S., Blaney, D.R., Stein, P.H., Schultz, P.R., et al. (1995). *Promoting cultural competence in and through nursing education: A critical review and comprehensive plan for action.* Washington, DC: American Academy of Nursing.

Marquand, B. (2001). On the front lines of diversity. *Minority Nurse.* Retrieved July 22, 2004, from http://www.minoritynurse.com/features/nurse_emp/11-01-01c.html

Mathews, A. (1998). Diversity: A principle of human resource management. *Public Personnel Management, 27,* 175.

Morrison, A. (1992). *New leaders: Guidelines on leadership diversity in America.* New York: Jossey-Bass.

National Archives and Records Administration. (2003). *Declaration of Independence.* Retrieved July 21, 2004, from http://www.archives.gov/national_archives_experience/charters/declaration.html

National Center for Health Statistics. (2004). *Health United States, 2003.* Retrieved October 7, 2004, from www.cdc.gov/nchs

National Council of State Boards of Nursing. (2004). *What is behind HRSA's projected supply, demand, and shortage of registered nurses?* Retrieved October 7, 2004, from www.ncsbn.org

O'Connor, S.D. (2003). *The majesty of the law: Reflections of a Supreme Court justice.* New York: Random House.

Oncology Nursing Society. (1999). *Oncology Nursing Society multicultural outcomes: Guidelines for cultural competence.* Pittsburgh, PA: Author.

Palos, G. (1994). Cultural heritage: Cancer screening and early detection. *Seminars in Oncology Nursing, 10,* 104–113.

Paniagua, F. (1998). Cross-cultural guidelines in family therapy practice. *Journal of Counseling and Therapy for Couples and Families, 4,* 127–138.

Roberson, M.H.B. (1993). Our diversity gives us strength. *Nursing Matters, 2,* 1.

Rosado, C. (1994). *The concept of cultural relativism in a multicultural world.* Retrieved November 3, 2003, from http://www.rosado.net/articles-relativism.html

Ruggiero, V.R. (1973). *The moral imperative: Ethical issues for discussion and writing.* New York: Alfred.

Smedley, A. (1993). *Race in North America: Origin and evolution of a worldview.* Boulder, CO: Westview Press.

Sonnenschein, W. (1999). *Diversity toolkit: How you can build and benefit from a diverse workforce.* Chicago: Contemporary Books.

U.S. Bureau of Labor Statistics. (2004). *Economic and employment projections.* Retrieved October 7, 2004, from http://www.bls.gov/news.release/ecopro.toc.htm

U.S. Census Bureau. (2001). *Population change and distribution.* Washington, DC: Author.

U.S. Health Resources and Services Administration. (2003). *Projected supply, demand, and shortages of nurses, 2000–2020.* Retrieved October 7, 2004, from http://bhpr.hrsa.gov/healthworkforce/reports/rnproject/default.htm

U.S. Health Resources and Services Administration. (2002). *National sample survey of registered nurses.* Retrieved October 7, 2004, from http://bhpr.hrsa.gov/healthworkforce/reports/rnsurvey/default.htm

Weber, D.O. (2000, September/October). The lack of diversity at the top. *Health Forum Journal,* pp. 31–34.

Woods, J.D., & Lucas, J.N. (1993). *The corporate closet: The professional lives of gay men in America.* New York: The Free Press.

Retention and Recruitment: Reversing the Order

Mary Magee Gullatte, RN, MN, ANP, AOCN®, FAAMA
Evelyn Q. Jirasakhiran, MSN, RN

"Change your thoughts and you change your world." Norman Vincent Peale

For decades, efforts to maintain adequate levels of RNs in the healthcare workforce have centered on recruitment. The current workforce challenges and opportunities related to the national shortage of RNs in health care are outlined in Chapter 9. This chapter will focus on creating a culture of retention as one key strategy to decrease nurse turnover and cost. Surely the answer to RN vacancies lies in a strong and solid recruitment effort; however, once recruited, greater emphasis must be placed on retention. Consider that for every two nurses recruited, one or more could leave. Tens of thousands of dollars are spent each year on nurse advertising and recruitment strategies to hire RNs at all levels and across multiple specialties. Turnover comes at a high price to the organization and to the staff left behind who just spent weeks, physically and emotionally, precepting and acculturating the new hire in orientation and to the work environment.

Nurse managers find themselves facing an ever-challenging global nursing shortage. The current shortage of registered nurses in the United States is expected to intensify as baby boomers age and the need for health care grows (American Association of Colleges of Nursing, 2003). This shortage, to rival none in history, is sparked by a multitude of factors: aging nursing pool, fewer women choosing nursing as a career, and others outlined in Chapter 9. To meet this challenge, healthcare employers have initiated multiple strategies, from foreign nurse recruitment and sign-on bonuses to creative benefit packages, such as maid service, dry cleaning pick-up and delivery, and car washing. Although these tangible amenities are nice, they seldom result, alone, in retaining a satisfied employee (Ropp, 2003). Recruitment bonuses serve the purpose of alluring the nurse to the organization, but it is often a quick fix. Once the bonus is received, the employee, if primarily motivated by money, is out looking for the next big payday. Often these grand sign-on bonuses serve to devalue the current workforce and could have a negative effect on staff retention. At best, the sign-on bonus is a short-term fix. Nevidjon and Erickson (2001) stated that past solutions to the shortage (e.g., cash bonuses, relocation incentives) only served to redistribute the supply of nurses, not increase it. How to increase the supply of RNs will be reviewed later in this chapter.

High Cost of Turnover

In November 2003, the Institute of Medicine of the National Academies reported that nursing staff make up the largest segment of healthcare workers in the United States, accounting for 2.2.million RNs, 700,000 licensed practical or vocational nurses, and 2.3 million assistive personnel, which constitutes 54% of all healthcare providers. The national unemployment rate for RNs is at its lowest level in more than a decade, declining from 1.5% in 1997 to 1.0% in 2000 (U.S. General Accounting Office, 2001). This reflects the limited pool of experienced nurses available for employment.

A survey by the Advisory Board Company (2000b) reported that the national turnover rate among hospital staff nurses was 15%, up from 12% in 1996. A more recent report by the HSM Group (2002) indicated a nurse turnover rate in the United States of 21%. The national average salary for a medical surgical nurse is reportedly $46,832; turnover costs are up to two times a nurse's salary (Atencio, Cohen, & Gorenberg, 2003). Inherent in nurse turnover are costs associated with separation, replacement, and development of the nurse. Turnover costs include many variables: direct salary of the new hire and preceptor, education and development cost, marketing and recruitment costs, loss of productivity during orientation, and intangible cost of turnover on current staff.

The American Nurses Association staffing survey (2001) reported that 75% of nurses felt that the quality of patient care had decreased over the past two years, and 56% felt that they did not have adequate time to perform patient care. Aside from the financial impact of nurse staff turnover, there is the negative effect on the staff that has been involved in the orientation of the new member and potential adverse patient outcomes. Staff left behind may be working longer hours and take on increased patient assignments to fill the vacancy. Agency nurses may be employed as a quick fix. These temporary nurses are seldom as familiar with the patient population and may not possess the same level of skill as the organization staff. In a workforce survey commissioned by the Oncology Nursing Society, nearly 80% of the RNs surveyed cited difficulty retaining experienced nurses (Buerhaus, Donelan, DesRoches, Lamkin, & Mallory, 2001).

Creating an organizational culture of nurse retention is crucial to reducing vacancies in healthcare organizations. High nursing staff turnover and low entry of nurses into the workplace adversely affect both the healthcare organizations and patient outcomes.

Job Satisfaction

A key factor, lack of job satisfaction, is the most cited reason for staff turnover. Job satisfaction is multidimensional. In a study by Bratt, Broome, Kelber, and Lostocco

(2000), two key factors surfaced related to job satisfaction: stress and nursing leadership. Job stress and workplace tension are inherent in healthcare. The key is how they are managed. The nurse manager should be engaged in the human relations variables of the workplace. Any nurse manager with the responsibility of hiring, firing, and giving performance evaluations should have taken at least one basic human resources class (Cline, Reilly, & Moore, 2003). How is the staff relating to each other? Is there collaboration and cooperation among the nurses and other members of the team? If the answer to these questions is no, then what does the manager need to do to facilitate the communication among a diverse group of nursing staff? It is not enough to continue to relay the dire predictions of a catastrophic nursing shortage facing health care in the next decade. As nurse managers and leaders, there must be continual proactive steps to enact a culture of retention while leveraging the vision of being an employer of choice and a healing organization, which places the value and worth of an individual as prime mission-sensitive goals.

Sengin (2003) identified 10 attributes that contribute to job satisfaction in acute care hospitals based on frequency and consistency of appearance in the literature. The attributes include (a) autonomy related to independence within professional practice, (b) interpersonal communication and collaboration within the workplace with supervisors, subordinates, and members of the healthcare team, (c) professional practice—the opportunity for specialization and professional care delivery modes, (d) administrative/management practices—this attribute relates to organizational structure and culture, (e) status/recognition—the value of nursing within the organization; (f) job/task requirements—meaningfulness and variety of work, (g) opportunity for advancement/promotion, (h) working conditions/physical environment—includes staffing and scheduling, workload/patient assignment, equipment, and resources, (i) pay—competitive salary and benefit package, and (j) fairness—centered around treatment related to employment decisions in the workplace.

Fundamentally, individuals choose a career in health care to make a difference in the lives of others. When the organization fails to meet employee expectations because of hectic and often failed organizational systems, the employee is left unsatisfied and unfulfilled. Figure 12-1 compares the percentage of employees in health care versus the general population whose expectations are not being met. Often cited in the literature is the notion that nurses perceive being involved in decision making as a very significant variable in job satisfaction (Gleason-Scott, Sochalski, & Aiken, 1999). This involves decisions impacting clinical practice as well as personal decisions related to staffing and scheduling. Involving staff at a high level in policy and procedure development as well as in self-scheduling will score high on the retention scale.

Culture of Retention

The human relations efforts of managers toward staff are key to cohesion and commitment and creating a culture of retention in the workplace (Wagner & Huber, 2003). Health systems also must pay attention to the retention of nurse managers.

Figure 12-1. Percentage of Employees Whose Expectations Are Not Being Met

Note. From *In Our Hands: How Hospital Leaders Can Build a Thriving Workforce* (p. 28), by American Hospital Association, Commission on Workforce for Hospitals and Health Systems, 2002, retrieved February 7, 2004, from http://www.aha.org/aha/key_issues/workforce/commission/ InOurHands.html. Copyright 2002 by American Hospital Association. Reprinted with permission.

The first-line managers are often the glue that holds the hospital together (Parsons & Stonestreet, 2003). Gone are the days of the head nurse or nurse manager responsible for a small nursing unit and a core group of staff. Over the past decade, the scope and breadth of the nurse manager's responsibilities have spanned multiple units and, in some cases, across multiple hospital networks, with an increased number of culturally diverse employees. There have been human resource issues and increased demands from upper level management to recruit and retain a viable nursing workforce amid mounting national and international nursing shortages. First-line managers are assuming greater work responsibility often without formalized support or development for the expanded roles. Although there are reports of nurse managers being the reason for staff turnover, they are also the reason for staff retention. Leadership of strong nurse managers is the key to staff satisfaction and retention (Cullen, 1999). Thorpe and Loo (2003) reported that the retention of first-line nurse managers requires top level organizational attention to providing adequate resources, training, and development as well as a supportive work environment.

When a nursing unit has a high retention rate, one would wonder, "What is the secret?" There is not one answer to this question. As shown in literature and research studies, a combination of retention strategies may work for a unit depending on the areas needing short- and long-term solutions, which could be any of the following: autonomy, salaries, schedules, credibility gap, and professional respect (Nevidjon & Erickson, 2001). Some general retention strategies used at healthcare organizations were compiled under "Best Practices in Retention" (Advisory Board Company, 2000a). The following strategies may be familiar to you or might help strengthen a system you already have in place.

1. **Cultivate an interesting and accepting culture.** This comes from the top leadership of the organization and trickles down to the manager. A manager who understands diversity and promotes an atmosphere where everyone can be engaged in working together in harmony will get a lot of mileage from staff. Nurse managers who are seen by their staff as always displaying a positive attitude, no matter how stressful and challenging a day can be, will find that it rubs off on staff when positive comments are heard from patients and staff from other departments. Retention is maintained in a culture where nurses feel they make a difference, their talents are tapped, and their contributions are acknowledged. To make the work environment interesting, staff can be competitive and join hospital-sponsored contests, such as holiday decorating contests, which promote teamwork and bolster morale. They also can submit entries to contests by nursing magazines such as "The Best Nursing Team Contest" sponsored by Advance for Nurses. Activities that bring pride to a unit foster teamwork and, most of all, retention.

2. **Implement professional clinical/career ladders.** This opportunity gives the nurse autonomy and a sense of accomplishment and value, as well as a way to impact personal earnings based on the level achieved in the clinical/career ladder.

3. **Develop flexible work arrangements.** Empower staff to participate in self-scheduling; make the full-time benefited positions less than 40 hours a week (32 or 36 hours). Staff is able to schedule around work and personal activities to afford them flexibility to balance work and home. With guidance and directions from the nurse manager, this is a major gain for the staff to feel empowered to have some control over their work schedule. For this to work, it requires some give and take on the part of the staff.

4. **Offer encouragement, praise, and recognition.** Making employees feel that they are valued by the organization often is revealed as one of the highest reasons for retention. A manager who gives immediate recognition for a job well done often will find the employee striving to do better and better. A pat on the back always works, as it makes the employee know that you care and that you are paying attention. Depending on the situation, some praise is better given on a one-to-one basis and other times in front of an audience. Sharing letters of compliments written to senior administrators from patients and family and posting thank you cards from patients and their families are examples of recognizing staff for quality care.

    Another form of recognition comes from staff themselves sharing praises given by employees from other departments or from patients. Hospitals have their own programs for recognizing employees who go the extra mile. At Emory Healthcare, a program called "I just noticed you doing something special" allows patients, visitors, and employees to write on a card any exceptional action that an employee did. The card is faxed to the patient relations office, and a quarterly drawing for a customer service award gives the employee a chance to win a cash prize. Individual organizations will have ways of recognizing and rewarding employees to express value and appreciation. These activities should be encouraged. Every unit has its own way of recognizing staff: an employee of the month/quarter award, a casual dress day, and celebrating various holidays and staff special occasions. A good idea is to engage the physicians of a unit to donate prizes for employees of the month/quarter and for the staff to do special things for other members of the healthcare team, including physicians, social workers, and pharmacists. Branham (2001) reported that many managers believe that employee retention is primarily tied to money, but in survey after survey, financial compensation is only one of many factors employees cite as a reason to seek or leave an employer.

5. **Encourage direct manager-to-employee communication.** According to Ribelin (2003), nurses do not leave hospitals, they leave managers. In an interview conducted by a manager of her own unit, staff nurses were asked what they like in a manager. Being approachable came to their minds right away. A manager with an open door policy who allows them the opportunity to voice concerns or express appreciation is another characteristic they liked. Getting back with employees and following up on their concerns shows that the manager listens. Often a manager can be overwhelmed with paperwork, deadlines, or meetings and is unable to meet with staff on a regular basis. Meeting with staff face-to-face at least every month allows them to ask questions about new policies or changes in practice that may come to them in memos or announcements. You can tell the difference with a staff who is well informed and those who are not by looking at compliance on different audits done either by their own unit or by other departments.

    A staff that is well informed will most likely work to show fiduciary responsibility when it comes to the unit budget related to supplies or staffing. Making time to meet with staff is something that must be emphasized with managers. One staff meeting a month that covers only a certain shift will not do. Expecting the staff to come in on their days off to attend staff meetings has not worked. The manager must be flexible to meet the needs of the staff and schedule several meetings that will cover all shifts, including weekends. A manager who has frequent face-to-face communication with staff will reap the rewards of a high-performing unit.

6. **Competitive compensation and benefits.** Even though salary is not the number one reason for retention, it does come up somewhere along the line. Most young nurses are lured by higher paying institutions or those who offer sign-on bonuses. Unlike their more experienced counterparts, benefits do not seem to retain younger nurses. Nurses with less than one year in the profession are more likely to quit their jobs (Reilly, 2003). The future is too far for them to imagine, and they do not want to think of retirement money or benefits such as tuition reimbursement. They want to see the money that comes in their paychecks now, either because they have a student loan to repay, a new apartment to furnish, or a new car payment. Hospitals, therefore, have to compete with salaries within the metro area. It then becomes imperative that hospitals conduct an ongoing market survey of compensation. It is also important for compensation specialists to make sure that nurses with longevity are not paid less than new hires. On exit interviews of operating room nurses (Nissen, 2003), a nurse was humiliated when she found out she was training someone who was making $2 more an hour. This could be vital in retention. Nurses should be paid for the professional service that they provide (Holcomb & Kornman, 2002). Most nurses who try to balance their

professional and personal lives will stay with hospitals that offer services such as child care, dry cleaning, car washing, housekeeping, and banking (Neuhauser, 2002).

7. **Develop mentoring and preceptorship programs.** Nurses with less than one year in the profession are most likely to quit their job, making it critical that veteran nurses lend support to their rookie colleagues (Reilly, 2003). Emory Hospitals in Atlanta take pride in their residency programs for new graduates in the oncology, operating room, critical care, emergency room, and medical-surgical fields. The residency programs vary in length from six months to a year. The specialty residency combines classroom learning with precepted skills and leadership development. New graduate nurses as well as novice specialty nurses are transitioned to their role as professional or specialty nurse with confidence and less anxiety.

8. **Streamline paperwork.** Nurses are reportedly spending more and more time documenting/charting and cite this as a dissatisfier. Nurse executives should find ways and resources to support computerized/electronic documentation.

Retention Reflects Leadership Style

The management skills and attributes of the nurse manager enhance job satisfaction, sustain organizational commitment, and encourage retention (Boyle, Bott, Hansen, Woods, & Taunton, 1999). Managers are critical components in building a strong workforce (Ribelin, 2003). It is essential that the nurse manager be fully engaged with staff. The manager is the key player in advocating and implementing a culture of workplace retention. Managers often struggle with accomplishing all the goals set by the organization while wearing multiple hats and trying to maintain balance and energy. Grove (1995) wrote that the single most important aspect of managerial output is the organizational unit under the supervision or influence of the manager. Output is more than the sum of daily activities around achieving objectives; it is actual outcomes achieved based on project goals. These outcomes are not achieved by "I" but through a "**T**ogether **E**veryone **A**chieves **M**ore" attitude, headed by a dynamic and visionary leader who can get things done through and with others.

One strategy to assist the manager in achieving the desired organizational goals is to leverage the activities needed to achieve the outcome. Leverage is the measure of increased power of purposeful action to achieve movement (Barnhart & Barnhart, 1991, p. 1204). Leverage can be positive or negative. An example of positive leverage is the manager who delegates (an essential aspect of a successful manager) with clear direction and effectively communicates expectations, timelines, and outcomes. On the other hand, an example of negative leverage is a manager who pretends to delegate but continues to micromanage the delegated tasks. This negative leverage stifles employee growth potential, which leads to underdevelopment and dissatisfaction of the employee and does not bode well for the organization under the leadership of such a manager. The leadership style of the nurse manager should reflect flexibility, responsibility, efficiency, customer-focused innovation, and profitability (Ribelin, 2003).

The nurse manager should strive for consistency and regularity in management style and approach, manage and disseminate information, and facilitate communication and collaboration through consultation and consensus with subordinates and senior management. Keep your pulse on the activities within the organization through personal contact with employees. Manage by walking around. Do not get caught up day-after-day laboring over countless e-mails and telephone conversations and neglect contact with grassroots staff. Do not underestimate the value of physical presence to the frontline staff. Leverage your actions to achieve desired organizational outcomes. Remember to take care of the people who take care of the patients.

Nurse Manager Retention

As a nurse leader and manager, ask for what you need in terms of formal development and education to maximize effectiveness in your role. It is recognized, although not often acknowledged, that the first-line manager provides the glue that holds the hospital together. The question that is often not asked is where is or who provides the glue that holds the nurse manager together? In a study by Parsons and Stonestreet (2003), six themes were recorded in interviews with nurse managers related to factors that contribute to their retention: (a) communication—ability of their boss to listen and provide guidance, effective communication, clear expectations, and feedback, (b) administrative management philosophy—included an opportunity to participate in decision making and empowerment to manage, (c) effective administrative systems—availability of and access to resource management systems, meaningful orientation and professional development systems, and manager compensation systems, (d) successful personal practices—balance in life and work, (e) quality of care—the ability to support systems and processes to deliver quality patient care and safety, and (f) retention—79% of the nurse managers participating in the study verbalized plans to remain in their roles. However, they reported that they would leave their job when they could no longer ensure quality of care because of staffing shortages.

With these factors in mind, it is important for the first-line manager as well as the senior administrative manager to mentor and develop staff at all levels. The job satisfiers and motivators are often the same regardless of job title.

Employer of Choice

If the revolving door of recruitment and turnover could be stopped or slowed down, the vacancy rate for a given institution would be significantly curtailed. So what is this retention culture anyway? Retaining highly skilled staff in the workplace is coveted as silver and gold. The goal in the workplace for the managers and leaders is to become known in the healthcare and business sector as the healthcare employer of choice. That is to say, the institution is the one magnet workplace that people in the local area and people looking to work in the area want to seek employment. The responsibility for creating that environment of job satisfaction and sense of value, worth, and family lies, in large part, with the manager, backed by the senior level management. The healthcare leadership is responsible for creating an organizational culture and must adopt a "culture of caring." Within this culture of caring are employee expectations coupled with commitment to integrity, value, compassion, respect, recognition, and truth. Kouzes and Posner (1999) wrote on the principles and practices that support the basic human need to be appreciated and valued for contributions.

Recruitment

Word of the seriousness of this current and future nursing shortage has reached a large audience outside of the nursing profession. This interest has brought new stakeholders into the mix to partner with professional nursing organizations to preserve the health care of Americans. Because of the magnitude and complexity of the nursing shortage, there has been an outpouring of interest and support from the private sector and corporate and governmental agencies offering to partner with professional nursing organizations by employing short- and long-term strategies to eliminate the nursing shortage. Recruitment into the nursing profession brings a quagmire of issues, challenges, and opportunities unlike any other.

There is also heightened awareness that strategies and solutions of the past will not meet with past successes. A key reason for this revelation is that the changing demographics such as age distribution and multigenerational issues are impacting retention of nurses as well as recruitment into the nursing profession. In a report by Kimball and O'Neil (2002), a key recruitment strategy should be to focus on recruiting a more diverse nursing workforce, with both ethnic and racial minorities as well as men. In 2000, men constituted 5.4% of the RN pool in the United States, up from 2.7% in 1980 (Sagon, 2003). Figure 12-2 depicts the percent of women in healthcare careers and shows an actual decline between 1989 and 1999—an opportunity to recruit more men into nursing. Figures from the U.S. Census Bureau (2000) and Health Resources and Services Administration (HRSA) (2001), outlined in Figure 12-3, show the racial composition (African American, Hispanic, and American Indian/Alaskan Native) of the U.S. population versus the percentage that are RNs. This figure illustrates a need to recruit a more diverse RN workforce and to meet the changing demographics of a more diverse patient population. The new nurse workforce will need to be recruited from the population who is younger than 30, which is more diverse and will create an even greater dislocation, in the future, if nurses from this current generation are not successfully recruited into the profession (Kimball & O'Neil, 2002). Other recruitment challenges lie in the plethora of labor force options for women and the multigenerational issues of the generation X employee. A more detailed discussion of the multigenerational issues can be found in Chapter 2.

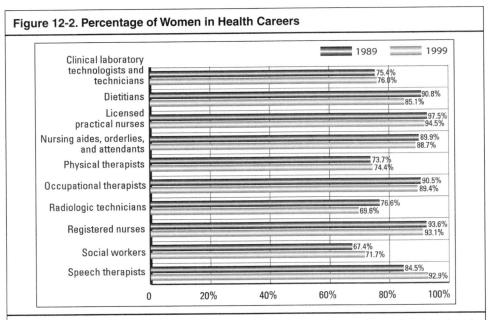

Figure 12-2. Percentage of Women in Health Careers

Note. From *In Our Hands: How Hospital Leaders Can Build a Thriving Workforce* (p. 48), by American Hospital Association, Commission on Workforce for Hospitals and Health Systems, 2002, retrieved February 7, 2004, from http://www.aha.org/aha/key_issues/workforce/commission/InOurHands.html. Copyright 2002 by American Hospital Association. Reprinted with permission.

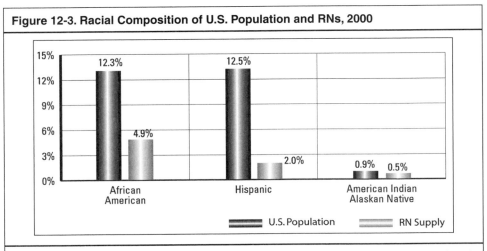

Figure 12-3. Racial Composition of U.S. Population and RNs, 2000

Note. From *In Our Hands: How Hospital Leaders Can Build a Thriving Workforce* (p. 47), by American Hospital Association, Commission on Workforce for Hospitals and Health Systems, 2002, retrieved February 7, 2004, from http://www.aha.org/aha/key_issues/workforce/commission/InOurHands.html. Copyright 2002 by American Hospital Association. Reprinted with permission.

Some of the multiple negative indicators affecting retention also impact recruitment (see Figures 12-4 and 12-5). It is important to offer long-term retention incentives for the applicant seeking employment within your organization as well as current employees you desire to retain.

Figure 12-4. Nurse Recruitment Strategies

- Sell the organization and unit (do not make false promises or paint a false picture).
- Create a shared vision.
- Market the image of nursing.
- Improve the work environment.
- Offer nurse internship and residency programs for novice nurses into a specialty.
- Develop institutional nurse reentry education and training programs.
- Recruit retired nurses to form the basis for a professional mentoring corps.
- Make the interview work for you.
- Develop an in-depth orientation program to attract new graduate nurses.
- Form some community alliances with local schools; visit on career days; give interactive health presentations; sell nursing to the next generation; talk about the rewards of nursing, service, and healing.
- Foster relationships with nursing students and faculty.
- Create a learning and mentoring environment for nursing students.
- Go to local nursing schools and provide a pizza luncheon to students during final examination week.
- Offer an educational program and skills fair for faculty at local schools of nursing.
- Offer recruitment fairs on-site and offer tours of specialty areas.
- Offer an on-site National Council Licensure Examination review course for new graduates waiting to take the State Board Examination.
- Offer recruitment incentives to new hires and current staff.
- Offer service cancelable student loan repayment packages.
- Conduct prompt follow-up with applicants to schedule interviews and facility tours.
- Add a personal touch when calls come in from prospective applicants; put the "human" back in human resources.
- Find a way to personally respond to inquiries of available positions, especially if there is an on-line application process.
- Provide a hassle-free interview encounter; facilitate parking; and avoid applicant waits and delays when it is a scheduled interview.
- Value workplace diversity.
- Partner with local specialty and diverse nursing organizations.
- Offer competitive salary and benefit packages.

Specialty Nurse Recruitment

The past two decades have witnessed an erosion of specialty, disease, or symptom-based nursing units and, in some cases, services. These units or services often were small and were sacrificed to the administrative budgets as administrators struggled with balancing healthcare revenues and expenses. The philosophy of 'no margin, no mission' was likely in the forefront of decision making to downsize and, in some cases, eliminate specialty units such as oncology in areas across the country.

Figure 12-5. Nurse Retention Strategies

- Value and respect staff.
- Break down any caste system.
- Empower staff to be involved in decision making that directly affects their work and practice.
- Support shared governance within the workplace.
- Provide timely coaching and counseling.
- Recognize and reward high performers.
- Use progressive discipline to remove poor performers who consume too much time and have a negative effect on overall staff morale.
- Work with staff to create unity and harmony and promote a sense of teamwork.
- Treat staff like adults; they do not need a mother or father.
- Establish open and honest communication.
- Treat staff fairly.
- Embrace and teach corporate values.
- Offer educational development.
- Conduct a skills fair annually for all clinical staff.
- Provide paid time off for continuing education.
- Offer residency or internship programs in specialty areas.
- Offer scholarships or percent reimbursement for formal career education.
- Develop leadership opportunities for staff.
- Be a mentor.
- Assign a consistent preceptor to the new orientee.
- Adjust patient assignments of the preceptor to allow ample time for teaching.
- Create a learning organization.
- Implement RN clinical/career ladders.
- Maintain functional and state-of-the-art equipment for staff.
- Provide appropriate staffing.
- Seek volunteers when overtime is needed.
- Listen and take immediate action regarding workplace concerns from staff.
- Offer self-scheduling.
- Offer flexible work hours and/or job sharing.
- Offer competitive compensation and benefits.
- Offer a package that includes health, education, and retirement benefits.
- Take ownership for retention in your area of responsibility.
- Engage staff in taking ownership for workplace retention.
- Encourage collaborative relationships between physicians and nurses.
- Provide challenging work opportunities for professional growth.
- Work with multigenerational issues.
- Inject some spontaneity in the staff work day with FUN.
- Celebrate successes (e.g., high patient satisfaction scores) with simple things such as pizza or an ice cream treat, theater tickets, a spa day, or a fitness center membership.
- Decorate your unit during holidays and enter contests if sponsored by the institution.
- Enter your unit in contests such as "Best Nursing Team Contest" sponsored by a nursing magazine.
- Write articles about your unit for celebrations and recognitions received and publish it in your institution's newsletter.
- Conduct exit interviews and make personnel and/or environmental adjustments as needed.

As patient care services for some diagnoses shifted to ambulatory services, the demand for the oncology beds in community hospitals felt the decline in census and inpatient revenue, forcing tough decisions. The units were reconfigured usually for medical-surgical beds, and staff that remained gave up their specialty identity. Another cost-cutting measure across many hospitals, academic and community, was to downsize master's prepared advanced practice nurses (nurse practitioners as well as clinical nurse specialists). The loss of these experts along with the dissolving of the specialty unit had the potential to impact quality cancer care (Lamkin, Rosiak, Buerhaus, Mallory, & Williams, 2001; Satryan, 2001).

Recruitment and education of specialty nurses is often more challenging and expensive than recruiting for generalist nurses. The specialty nursing expertise is generally obtained on the job, all the more reason to make every effort to retain the experienced specialty nurses, whether oncology, critical care, emergency department, or operating room. Offering internship and residency programs in areas of specialty nursing will serve to attract generalist nurses and new graduate nurses to the specialty. Partner with local specialty nursing organizations as a means to offer networking opportunities to the new specialty nurse.

Professional, Public, and Private Partnerships

The U.S. Department of Labor (2004) projected a 27% increase in the need for nurses nationwide from 2002–2012. There have been a number of initiatives launched over the past five years that have focused on reversing the nursing shortage. Groups that participate with partnering professional nursing organizations include the Robert Wood Johnson Foundation, Johnson & Johnson (Campaign for Nursing's Future), American Hospital Association, federal government (Nurse Reinvestment Act Legislation), and HRSA, just to name a few. These multifaceted initiatives have begun to make an impact. In June 2003, the U.S. Department of Health and Human Services announced awards of $3.5 million in grants to promote diversity in the nursing workforce. These funds are earmarked to support disadvantaged students, including those from racial and ethnic minorities who are underrepresented among RNs.

Remember the projection is that there will be in excess of a million nurses needed within the next seven years. The work is not finished. Look within your community for opportunities to bolster the image of nurses and promote nursing to all as an honorable and sustaining profession.

Reach out to youth in schools and youth organizations to promote nursing as a career choice. Offer to mentor a young student who expresses interest in the profession. Bring them into your work setting for a day. Share with them the rewards of a career in nursing.

Recruiting Internationally

When American healthcare organizations recruit internationally, it impacts the nursing shortage in a global way. Foreign nurses often are attracted to the higher standard of living, earnings potential, and many other benefits of working in America, leaving their home healthcare system with fewer nurses. However, Christmas (2002) pointed out those organizations investigating foreign nurse recruitment should first focus internally on retention initiatives prior to making a commitment to recruit from abroad. There are numerous strategies involved in planning to recruit an international nursing pool.

The manager must be attuned to the needs of the foreign nurse prior to and after recruitment. These needs include fit within the culture of the organization, language, socialization, support structures, licensure, working or permanent resident visa, and financial resources. When a hospital decides to recruit foreign nurses, a designated person from nursing administration may be assigned as the point person to work hand in hand with human resources. The hospital may choose to send a nurse manager and a nurse recruiter from human resources to go to the foreign country or countries of choice to personally interview applicants. Applicants can come from an agency in that country or an agency based in the United States that has its pool of applicants in that foreign country. A contract between the hospital and the agency of choice must be signed before the process begins. A hospital also may choose to interview by phone the applicants chosen by the agency, provided a resume is on hand. Once the interview is done, a contract is offered to the foreign nurse by the hospital representative or the designated agency. Necessary paperwork must be submitted by the applicant to process the visa application. Paperwork must include copies of passing TOEFL (Test of English as a Foreign Language) results, a passing CGFNS (Commission on Graduates of Foreign Nursing Schools) certificate or result, or a passing NCLEX–RN (National Council Licensure Examination for Registered Nurses) result, transcript of records, letters of recommendation, and a contract with the sponsoring hospital. An application to the Bureau of Citizenship and Immigration Services together with the application for Alien Employment Certification must be filled out by the hospital designee. An approval or denial letter will be sent to the hospital official who signed the petition. If the petition is approved, paperwork will be forwarded to the U.S. embassy where the applicant resides. The embassy will notify the nurse of the approval and a list of requirements prior to the interview date, when the appropriate visa is given. Once the nurse receives the visa, flight schedules can be arranged by the recruitment agency or a travel agency chosen by the hospital. Depending on the type of visa applied for, the process can take from several months (for working visas) to two years (for permanent resident visas). Prior to the nurse arriving in the United States, someone from the hospital (usually human resources) will be responsible for arranging housing. It is a good idea to identify nurses in the organization to serve as their adoptive sisters to orient them to the country and show them around their new environment. Transportation to and from the hospital must be arranged if their housing is not within walking distance. A good thorough orientation will be key to successful integration into the system. A warm welcome from the nurses and other employees within the hospital will help early adaptation to the new workplace. Foreign nurses have been known to stay with the hospital that recruited them as a sign of gratitude and loyalty. The majority of foreign nurses have become very successful in their careers and have proven to be great assets to their adoptive healthcare institution.

The advent of the nursing shortage extends beyond the borders of the United States. In a recent publication on ethical issues in the recruitment and retention of graduate nurses, Johnstone and Stewart (2003) reported on mounting concerns in Australia that by the year 2010, Australia will face a shortage of 40,000 nurses. As a consequence of this concern, one Australian state has given rise to a computer match service. This service, a recruitment strategy aimed at matching new graduate nurses across participating healthcare organizations, is challenged to distribute the nurses equitably within this Australian state. Reports of unethical recruiting strategies by healthcare facilities in the region has drawn criticism of the tactics used by some to entice nurses away from one employer to another. Unfortunately, the new nurses are not finding the promises being kept by the employer once they change from one job to another; hence, the nurses are left feeling unsupported, cheated, and disillusioned (Johnstone & Stewart).

The concerns of nurse leaders in Australia seem to mirror many of the same issues and challenges facing healthcare organizations and nurse leaders in America. Recruiting and retaining new and experienced nurses is critical to the survival of the healthcare system, patient care, and safety.

Conclusion

Adopting a culture of retention is key to organizations maintaining adequate staffing levels to meet the complex care needs of patients. It is imperative that employees feel empowered, in control of their own performance, and willing to help move the organization to achieve its strategic goals (Trofino, 2003). Nurse managers must be actively engaged in implementing strategies to promote job satisfaction and retain a viable workforce of RNs. Engage staff in assessing the work environment and culture of retention. Work within your individual circle of influence to make a difference in reducing turnover and promote a culture of retention. The recruitment strategy should be one of bringing new people into the profession, not merely relocating nurses who are already employed. Ensure that your organization is committed to being an employer of choice for current and future nurses.

References

Advisory Board Company. (2000a). *Best practices in retention. Executive summary.* Washington, DC: Author.

Advisory Board Company. (2000b). *The nurse executive center. The nurse perspective: Nurse job satisfaction and turnover.* Washington, DC: Author.

American Association of Colleges of Nursing. (2003). *Nursing shortage fact sheet.* Retrieved February 7, 2004, from http://www.aacn.nche.edu

American Nurses Association. (2001). *Nurses concerned over working conditions, decline in quality of care, ANA survey reveals* [Press release]. Retrieved August 26, 2004, from http://www.nursingworld.org/pressrel/2001/pr0206.htm

Atencio, B.L., Cohen, J., & Gorenberg, B. (2003). Nurse retention: Is it worth it? *Nursing Economics, 21,* 262–268.

Barnhart, R.K., & Barnhart, C.L. (1991). *The world book dictionary.* Chicago: World Book.

Boyle, D.K., Bott, M.J., Hansen, H.E., Woods, C.Q., & Taunton, R.L. (1999). Managers' leadership and critical care nurses' intent to stay. *American Journal of Critical Care, 8,* 361–371.

Branham, L. (2001). *Keeping the people who keep you in business.* New York: American Management Association.

Bratt, M.M., Broome, M., Kelber, S., & Lostocco, L. (2000). Influence of stress and nursing leadership on job satisfaction of pediatric intensive care unit nurses. *American Journal of Critical Care, 9,* 307–317.

Buerhaus, P., Donelan, K., DesRoches, C., Lamkin, L., & Mallory, G. (2001). State of the oncology nursing workforce: Problems and implications for strengthening the future. *Nursing Economics, 19*(5), 1–11.

Christmas, K. (2002). Invest internationally. *Nursing Management, 33*(11), 20–21.

Cline, D., Reilly, C., & Moore, J.F. (2003). What's behind RN turnover? *Nursing Management, 34*(10), 50–53.

Cullen, K. (1999). Recruitment, retention and restructuring report: Strong leaders strengthen retention. *Nursing Management, 30*(5), 27–28.

Gleason-Scott, J., Sochalski, J., & Aiken, L. (1999). Review of magnet hospital research. *Journal of Nursing Administration, 29,* 9–19.

Grove, A.S. (1995). *High output management.* New York: Vintage Books.

Health Resources and Services Administration, Division of Nursing. (2001). *National sample survey of registered nurses.* Washington, DC: Author.

Holcomb, S., & Kornman, C. (2002) A decent proposal. *Nursing Management, 33*(1), 39–40.

HSM Group. (2002). The 2002 acute care hospital survey of RN vacancy and turnover rates for 2000. *Journal of Nursing Administration, 32,* 437–439.

Institute of Medicine. (2003). *Substantial changes required in nurses' work environment to protect patients from health care errors.* Retrieved February 7, 2004, from http://www4.nationalacademies.org/news.nsf/isbn/0309090679?OpenDocument

Johnstone, M.J., & Stewart, M. (2003). Ethical issues in the recruitment and retention of graduate nurses: A national concern. *Contemporary Nurse, 14,* 240–247.

Kimball, B., & O'Neil, E. (2002). The evolution of a crisis: Nursing in America. *Policy, Politics and Nursing Practice, 2*(3), 180–186.

Kouzes, J.M., & Posner, B.Z. (1999). *Encouraging the heart.* San Francisco: Jossey-Bass.

Lamkin, K., Rosiak, J., Buerhaus, P., Mallory, G., & Williams, M. (2001). Oncology Nursing Society workforce survey part I: Perceptions of the nursing workforce environment and adequacy of nurse staffing in outpatient and inpatient oncology settings. *Oncology Nursing Forum, 28,* 1545–1552.

Neuhauser, P. (2002). Building a high-retention culture in healthcare. *Journal of Nursing Administration, 32,* 470–478.

Nevidjon, B., & Erickson, J. (2001). The nursing shortage: Solutions for the short and long term. *Online Journal of Issues in Nursing, 6,* 1–17.

Nissen, S. (2003). Practical steps for boosting staff retention. *OR Manager, 19,* 18–19.

Parsons, M.L., & Stonestreet, J. (2003). Factors that contribute to nurse manager retention. *Nursing Economics, 21,* 119–126.

Reilly, P. (2003). Trying to keep their own. *Modern Healthcare, 33,* 17.

Ribelin, P. (2003). Retention reflects leadership style. *Nursing Management, 34*(8), 18–19.

Ropp, A.L. (2003). Are sign-on bonuses an effective recruitment and retention strategy? Writing for the CON position. *American Journal of Maternal/Child Nursing, 28,* 291.

Sagon, E. (2003). Nursing recruiters tailor pitch to men. *Arizona Republic.* Retrieved July 15, 2003, from http://www.azcentral.com/arizonarepublic/business/articles/0715nurses15.html

Satryan, M. (2001). The oncology nursing shortage and its impact on cancer care services. *Oncology Issues, 16*(1), 21–23.

Sengin, K. (2003). Work-related attributes of RN job satisfaction in acute care hospitals. *Journal of Nursing Administration, 33,* 317–320.

Thorpe, K., & Loo, R. (2003). Balancing professional and personal satisfaction of nurse managers: Current and future perspectives in a changing health care system. *Journal of Nursing Management, 11,* 321–330.

Trofino, J. (2003). Power sharing: A strategy for nurse retention. In H. Feldman (Ed.), *The nursing shortage: Strategies for recruitment and retention in clinical practice and education.* New York: Springer Publishing.

U.S. Census Bureau. (2000). *Profiles of general demographic characteristics, 2000.* Washington, DC: Author.

U.S. Department of Labor. (2004). *2004–05 editions of the Occupational Outlook Handbook and the Career Guide to Industries available on the Internet.* Retrieved August 18, 2004, from http://www.bls.gov/news.release/pdf/ooh.pdf

U.S. General Accounting Office. (2001). *Nursing workforce: Emerging nurse shortages due to multiple factors.* Report to the chairman, Subcommittee on Health, Committee on Ways and Means, House of Representatives. Retrieved February 25, 2004, from http://www.gao.gov/new.items/d01944.pdf

Wagner, C.M., & Huber, D.L. (2003). Catastrophe and nursing turnover. *Journal of Nursing Administration, 33,* 486–492.

Recommended Web Sites to Visit

American Hospital Association Commission on Workforce for Hospitals: www.aha.org/aha/key_issues/workforce

American Nurses Association: www.nursingworld.org

Bureau of Labor Statistics: www.bls.gov

Forum on Healthcare Leadership: www.healthcareforum.org

Historically Black Colleges and Universities: www.doi.gov/hrm/black.html

Johnson & Johnson's Campaign for Nursing's Future: www.discovernursing.com

Leapfrog Group: www.leapfroggroup.org

Male Nurse Magazine: www.malenursemagazine.com

Minority Nursing Associations: http://ninr.nih.gov/ninr/research/diversity/minority_assoc.html

National Alaska Native American Indian Nurses Association: www.nanaina.com

National Association for Equal Opportunity in Higher Education: www.nafeo.org

National Association of Hispanic Nurses: www.thehispanicnurses.org

National Black Nurses Association: www.nbna.org

National Coalition of Ethnic Minority Nurse Associations: www.ncemna.org

National League for Nursing: www.nln.org

Nurses for a Healthier Tomorrow: www.nursesource.org

Oncology Nursing Society: www.ons.org

Philippine Nurses Association of America, Inc.: www.pnaa03.org

Transcultural Nursing Society: www.tcns.org

Assistive Personnel

Diane M. Otte, RN, MS, OCN®

Dramatic and varied changes in the healthcare environment since the early 1990s have necessitated the development of many creative ways to deliver patient care. The nursing shortage, an aging nursing workforce, managed care with economic rationing, cost-containment concerns at both the federal and state levels, increased patient acuity, a growing elderly population, and shortened hospital stays have become normal (McClung, 2000; Spencer, 2001). The number of people entering nursing programs has been declining steadily as many more employment options with less physical demands have opened up for women (McClung; Van Cleave & Scherffius, 2002). Unfortunately, this lack of adequate healthcare resources has developed at a time when there are also heightened patients' needs.

One of the most controversial ways of dealing with these changes, especially in hospital acute care settings, has been increasing the use of lesser-paid assistive personnel (AP). The use of AP dates back to the delivery of health care in the 1950s and includes titles as varied as their roles and responsibilities in the healthcare setting (nursing assistants, medical assistants, team associates, nurse technicians, nurse aides, patient care assistants, telemetry and cardiovascular technicians, and orthopedic and operating room technicians) (Rosen, 1999; Tuttas, 2003).

Nursing care delivery models evolved over the years and include functional nursing (early to mid-20th century), team nursing (1970s–1980s), and primary nursing (1980s–1990s). The functional model of nursing care delivery involved each staff member being assigned a set of tasks and used a variety of personnel. Team nursing used a group of staff (RN, LPN, AP) working together to provide total care to an assigned group of patients. These two models were more task oriented and reduced the amount of direct care provided by the RN (Krapohl & Larson, 1996). In the 1980s, team nursing evolved into primary care as a preferred nursing model that reinforced the professional autonomy and accountability of the RN (Kopishke, 2002). With a primary nursing model, the RN coordinates the plan of care. As the primary nursing model emerged, the use of AP decreased (Munroe, 2003).

Managed care, capitated payment, and balanced budget acts forced hospitals to redesign nursing and cut costs because of declining reimbursement and patient stay limitations. Skill mix and staffing ratios began to change as hospitals searched for alternative solutions to meet patients' needs despite budget-driven cuts in RN positions. Ultimately, this redesign culminated in the addition of caregivers at the bedside who are less skilled and nurses who were unprepared to manage and direct the care of AP (Kopishke, 2002).

The nursing shortage means there are fewer newly graduating nurses to meet current and future needs (Tuttas, 2003). The optimal skill mix for RNs and other workers such as AP remains debatable. California enacted the first law mandating minimum nurse/patient staffing ratios for all acute care and psychiatric hospital units in 1999. This is a controversial direction for states because some experts believe that staffing must remain flexible and adjustable according to contributing factors (Zimmerman, 2000). In this wave of rapid healthcare reform, patient safety also has become a major consumer awareness focus (Kido, 2001). Concerns about the quality of patient care have been raised with the utilization of AP in acute care settings, especially because AP are being asked to perform increasingly complex tasks (Kido, 2001; Lange, 2002). Research to determine optimal skill mix and patient outcomes with AP utilization is essential (Kido).

Anthony, Casey, Chau, and Brennan (2000) examined congruence between RN and AP perception of nursing practice. The study attempted to describe how different nursing team members viewed 10 factors associated with nursing practice models. The findings showed inconsistent sharing of views on aspects of nursing practice. The authors suggested a greater emphasis be placed on work group function and consistency of views between the team members (Anthony et al.).

Definitions

A universally accepted description of AP does not exist. Many different titles are included in the AP definition (Spencer, 2001). Many organizations and settings have developed and created unique positions to fill gaps that exist in staffing. A variety of roles for AP are seen in these settings ranging from the traditional unit assistant to technical and patient care models (McClung, 2000).

Clear knowledge of definitions related to the role of the AP in healthcare settings is essential. Distinguishing between direct care and indirect patient care activities and defining delegation and supervision as it relates to AP are critical to providing safe patient care within legal and regulatory parameters. Medvec et al. (1996) offered a glossary to clarify terms related to AP (see Figure 13-1).

Figure 13-1. Glossary of Terms

Accountability: The state of being responsible, answerable, or legally liable for an action.

Assignment: The downward or lateral transfer of both the responsibility and accountability of an activity from one individual to another. The lateral or downward transfer must be made to an individual with the skill, knowledge, and judgment to perform the activity. The activity also must be within the individual's scope of practice.

(Continued on next page)

Figure 13-1. Glossary of Terms *(Continued)*

Assistive Personnel: An individual who is trained to function in an assistive role to the RN in the provision of patient care activities as the RN delegates. The term includes, but is not limited to, nurses' aides, orderlies, corpsmen, office receptionists, medical assistants, medical technicians, and nursing assistants.

Competency: Having the requisite abilities or qualities to complete a task, skill, or action based on set standards of performance.

Delegation: The transfer of responsibility of an activity from one individual to another while retaining accountability for the outcome.

Direct Patient Care Activities: Activities that assist the patient in meeting basic human needs within any setting. These activities include assisting the patient with feeding, drinking, ambulating, grooming, toileting, dressing, and socializing. Responsibilities may involve the collecting, reporting, and documenting of data related to the above activities. These data are reported to the RN, who uses the information to make clinical judgments about patient care. These activities can be performed by assistive personnel in certain, but not all, situations.

Indirect Patient Care Activities: Activities that are necessary to support the patient and his or her environment and only incidentally involve direct patient contact. These activities assist in providing a clean, efficient, and safe patient care milieu and typically encompass chore services, companion care, housekeeping, transporting, and clerical, stocking, and maintenance tasks. Assistive personnel perform these activities in certain, but not all, situations.

Predictable Care: Care activities performed when the patient's condition is stable with predictable outcomes.

Responsibility: Moral, legal, or mental accountability.

Skill Mix: Percent or numbers and types of licensed and unlicensed staff who provide patient care.

Supervision: The active process of directing, guiding, and influencing the outcome of an individual's performance of an activity. Nursing supervision generally is categorized as on-site (the nurse is physically present or immediately available while the activity is being performed) or off-site (the nurse provides direction through various means of written and verbal communication but is not physically present).

Unpredictable Care: Care activities performed when the patient's condition is unstable with unpredictable outcomes.

Note. Based on information from American Nurses Association, 1992.
Note. From "Assistive Personnel: Their Use in Cancer Care—An Oncology Nursing Society Position Paper," by B.R. Medvec, J.L. Pelusi, D. Camp-Sorrell, P. Kleinschmidt, L. Krebs, and K. Mooney, 1996, *Oncology Nursing Forum, 23,* p. 651. Copyright 1996 by the Oncology Nursing Society. Reprinted with permission.

Consumers may not be aware of the increasing use of AP in many settings. Oftentimes consumers are confused by the nontraditional dress of nurses and other healthcare workers. Lange (2002) investigated patients' abilities to identify licensed nurses versus AP. She found that satisfaction with nursing care was not predicted by the patients' knowledge of name or title. Titles are not standardized across settings, name badges often list only a first name, and dress codes no longer are enforced that distinguish nurses and AP. The researcher also observed that caregivers rarely identified themselves by name and did not state their job title to patients. In healthcare settings, there are many blended tasks, making it more difficult for patients and family members to distinguish the licensed care providers.

American Nurses Association Position

The American Nurses Association (ANA) developed a position statement in 1992 that recognized the support services provided by AP to the RN (ANA, 1992). The position delineated the belief of the ANA about how AP should be used and placed the responsibility for implementation of standards for appropriate AP utilization on the nursing profession. Individual nurses are responsible for implementing the standards of practice.

The ANA position statement clarified professional nursing delivery and those activities that can be delegated. ANA has identified two different groups of activities for AP. The first group of activities involves providing direct patient care and meeting basic needs of patients, such as dressing, feeding, ambulating, and grooming. The second group involves indirect patient care activities such as housekeeping, transportation, and supply maintenance functions (Rosen, 1999).

The ANA position has served as a model for other specialty organizations to develop position statements unique to this issue. ANA opposes licensure for AP as well as establishing a scope of practice that could ultimately formalize the role of the AP and confuse the AP role with professional nursing (ANA, 1996; Thomas, Barter, & McLaughlin, 2000). Work by the ANA on the AP issue continues.

Oncology Nursing Society Position

The Oncology Nursing Society (ONS) originally developed and published a position statement about the role of AP in 1997 (ONS, 2001). Since that time, it has been revised and re-approved by the Board of Directors in 2000 and 2002. The current ONS position statement is shown in Figure 13-2. The ONS position remains consistent with the ANA position that asserted ". . . the control and monitoring of assistive personnel in clinical settings be performed through the use of existing mechanisms that regulate nursing practice" (ONS, 2002).

State Board of Nursing Practice Guidelines

Two primary methods for regulating AP practice exist. The first is regulation at individual facilities, and the second is regulation through state government. States can mandate certification or state licensure or regulate practice through state registration (Kopishke, 2002). Each state Nurse Practice Act defines the legal scope of nursing in that state. These acts identify nursing activities that cannot be delegated: nursing process (assessment, diagnosis, planning, intervention, and evaluation), requirements of specialized skills, and expert knowledge or professional judgment (Kido, 2001). It is the responsibility of every nurse to become familiar with the state Nurse Practice Act and rulings related to tasks that AP can perform (Sheehan, 2001). Sheehan also suggested that a facility policy, procedure, and job description review with RNs is critical because nurses maintain responsibility for all delegated tasks.

Figure 13-2. ONS Position on the Use of Assistive Personnel in Cancer Care

The Oncology Nursing Society (ONS) supports the collaborative role of RNs with members of the multidisciplinary team in the provision of quality cancer care regardless of the clinical setting. ONS recognizes that assistive personnel can make significant contributions in cancer care delivery systems. Cancer care settings may include individuals who are trained to function in an assistive role to oncology nurses in the provision of direct and indirect activities as delegated by the RN.

ONS supports the American Nurses Association (ANA) (1996) position that the control and monitoring of assistive personnel in the clinical setting should be performed through the use of existing mechanisms that regulate nursing practice. Typically, this includes the state board of nursing, institutional policies, and external agency standards. ONS also supports the ANA position that any nursing intervention that requires independent specialized nursing knowledge, skill, or judgment cannot be delegated.

It is the position of ONS that
The repetitive performance of a common task or procedure that does not require the professional judgment of an RN may be delegated to assistive personnel. To delegate is to transfer a selected nursing task to a competent individual. The nurse retains the accountability for the delegation.

Tasks may be delegated that
- Frequently recur in the daily care of a client or group of clients.
- Are performed according to an established sequence of steps.
- Involve little or no modification from one client care situation to another.
- May be performed with a predictable outcome.
- Do not inherently involve ongoing assessment, interpretation, or decision making that cannot be logically separated from the procedure(s) itself.

RNs maintain accountability for
- Validating competency of assistive personnel.
- Ongoing client assessment.
- Ongoing supervision of assistive personnel.
- Evaluation of the client's response to care.
- Interpretation and decision making regarding client care.

Background
The growing cost of health care has increased the need for efficient care delivery models that decrease the financial risk for healthcare organizations and healthcare practices. Many organizations and regulatory agencies are evaluating the types of work that must be performed to ensure quality care. To achieve quality care, ONS understands that a multidisciplinary approach must be used. This means that in the provision of nursing care, the oncology nurse will utilize the services of assistive personnel in cancer care.

Issues that affect licensure, regulation of nursing practice, oncology practice standards, and patient care outcomes require ongoing nursing research. Additional research also is needed to determine the appropriate provider mix and to define cancer care delivery systems that ensure optimal clinical outcomes and cost-effective care for individuals with cancer.

Note. From "The Use of Assistive Personnel in Cancer Care," by the Oncology Nursing Society, 2002, *Oncology Nursing Forum, 29,* p. 1382. Copyright 2002 by the Oncology Nursing Society. Reprinted with permission.

Role of Assistive Personnel in Various Work Settings

Hospitals

Hospital systems and work settings ranging from ambulatory, palliative care, hospice, home care, assisted living, and skilled nursing facilities have developed and implemented roles/positions utilizing AP. Job descriptions in each setting identify titles, detail duties and responsibilities, report relationships, and list expected competencies. In reality, however, the oversight of and utilization of AP remains challenging given the nursing shortage. Helpful considerations prior to using AP include evaluation of how the task may affect patient safety, the stability and acuity of the patient, the nature and complexity of the task, technology necessary to perform the task, and any infection control or safety issues involved (Sheehan, 2001).

Standing, Anthony, and Hertz (2001) reported results of a qualitative study examining narratives of nurses related to patient outcomes after delegation of activities to AP. Negative outcomes were associated with improper directions and improper follow through of protocol. Because nursing ultimately has the authority to delegate, nurses must increase their competence with delegation and supervision and ensure the responsible and safe care of patients (Standing et al.). Nurses also need to develop user-friendly tools to guide them, especially in communicating effectively, team building, and finding constructive ways to hold AP accountable as contributing members of the healthcare team. Using AP may bring about positive results with greater time efficiency and RN job satisfaction. With nursing eliminating non-nursing activities such as housekeeping and clerical functions, a greater focus on quality patient care can result (Rosen, 1999).

Assisted Living

Assisted living settings also face issues related to supervision and delegation of nursing services (Munroe, 2003). Medication management, observation for adverse drug reactions, and staff education are significant needs in these environments, and RNs can function in a comprehensive role to meet these needs (Munroe).

Spellbring and Ryan (2003) developed a medication administration training program in Maryland that led to statewide regulations related to medication administration by AP in assisted living. The AP involved were taught to administer medications by mouth to residents who were not capable of taking their own medications. Eye drops, inhalers, patches, and other topical preparations were included as well. An RN performs the monitoring functions for these staff (Spellbring & Ryan).

Home Care

The use of AP in home care settings has been in place for decades. Marrelli (2003) suggested that home care can serve as a model for how work can be delegated to AP with proper training and supervision. In this model, nurses serve as case managers and develop the standardized tools and protocols that are evidence based and individualized, while AP actually provide the care in the home setting. She also supported training advanced specialty aides to be used for patients with chronic obstructive pulmonary disease and stroke. In these situations, AP assist the patient with supportive care (after the nurse teaches the patients breathing exercises), progressive muscle relaxation, communication, and mobility.

Another program that deals with the nursing shortage and focuses on AP use involves creating a community partnership approach for young, multicultural, bilingual teenagers who complete training to become certified nursing assistants. Ultimately, these individuals may continue with formal nursing education and become professional nurses (Hunter-Yates et al., 2003).

The use of AP and the legal and professional risks involved continue to be a major concern for nurses in any work setting. Nurses need to understand what and when to delegate and become familiar with their state Board of Nursing guidelines and state Nurse Practice Act, which govern the use of AP. Nurses also must consistently inform superiors of and clearly document any incompetent performance by AP (Cady, 2001).

Orientation, Training, Skills Validation, and Continued Competency

The role of the nurse manager in initial hiring of AP staff is critical. Selection of the individual who has an interest in the clinical area, understands the job responsibilities, and is committed to working collaboratively with other staff is essential. In some settings, the interview process may include a representative team of RNs and AP already working in the clinical area. The nurse manager must continue involvement in the orientation and training of AP as well as the performance evaluation of these individuals. Generally, this is accomplished through an orientation or competency checklist that must be completed within a designated timeframe (see Figures 13-3 and 13-4). Other RN staff may be responsible for completing this checklist with AP, but the nurse manager maintains ultimate accountability for a successful hire, orientation, ongoing training, and overall satisfactory performance of AP in the clinical area.

The orientation for AP typically lasts six to eight weeks (Spencer, 2001) but can vary from setting to setting. The AP role, responsibilities, and qualifications should be delineated in the job description. Competency-based performance appraisals must be maintained. Ongoing training is essential to broaden knowledge and skills (Spencer). Lange (2002) believed that standardizing AP education and training is essential for patient safety. Delineating the RN role and visibility through dress, readable nametags, identification at the time care is provided, and education of the public about the role of nursing may impact the public impression of nursing and help distinguish between the RN and AP.

Figure 13-3. Fairview University Medical Center Nursing Assistant Core Competency Example

Name:_____   Dept/Unit:_____

Job Title:_____   Manager:_____

Core Competencies	Learning Strategies	Method of Verification/Initial (Initial each task as completed or write NA if not applicable.)	Completion of Core Competency— Date/Initial
Equipment/tube safety/maintenance and repair	Attends PBDS and Para Day 2 Works with a preceptor	Preceptor confirms ability to safely manipulate the following equipment within the scope of NA role and follow FUMC's procedure to repair equipment. • Oximeter • O_2 • Foley catheter • Jackson Pratt • Chest tubes • NG tube • Gastrostomy tube • Ostomy tube	_____
Communicates effectively with patients, staff, and visitors	Attends NEO, PBDS, Para Day 2 Works with a preceptor	Preceptor confirms the ability to perform the following • Respects patient confidentiality data • Keeps RN informed of changes in patient's status • Writes concise and pertinent change of shift report. • Demonstrates customer service • Promptly answers call lights.	_____
Role in emergency	Attends PBDS, NEO, Para Day 2 Works with a preceptor Current in BLS, emergency cart, other equipment	Preceptor confirms ability to • Identify potentially urgent situations • Summon help in emergency • Stay with patient • Run errands as directed by RN • Obtain emergency equipment • Attend FUMC's BLS class in accordance with FUMC's policy.	_____
Blood products	Attends Para Day 2 Works with a preceptor Reviews "Blood Administration Packet"	Preceptor confirms ability to • Promptly pick up blood product from blood bank/tube system • Promptly delivers blood product to unit • Notify appropriate RN.	_____

(Continued on next page)

Figure 13-3. Fairview University Medical Center Nursing Assistant Core Competency Example *(Continued)*

Core Competencies	Learning Strategies	Method of Verification/Initial (Initial each task as completed or write NA if not applicable.)	Completion of Core Competency— Date/Initial
Narcotics	Works with a preceptor	Preceptor confirms ability to • Receive a narcotic from pharmacist • Promptly hand deliver the narcotic to a RN, LPN, or unit pharmacist.	_____
Demonstrates ability to provide patient care, adjusting approaches to coincide with the developmental levels of adolescence, adult, and geriatric population	Works with a preceptor	Preceptor confirms ability to adjust patient care to meet the developmental needs of the patient.	_____

Additional comments:

_____

_____

_____

_____

I have completed my core competency assessment process and attached supporting paperwork.

Employee signature: _____ Date: _____

Preceptor(s) signature/initials

Primary preceptor: _____ Date: _____

(Continued on next page)

Figure 13-3. Fairview University Medical Center Nursing Assistant Core Competency Example *(Continued)*

Manager Review:
All the core competencies/effective behaviors have been regularly demonstrated during this orientation period.
_____ Yes/Competence demonstrated. This document verifies completion of the following:

_____Core competencies for the NA

_____Unit-specific care competencies/unit addendum if applicable

_____ No/Competencies not fully met. (Specify reason below.)

_____Employee has not completed parts of the process.

_____Additional development needed (action plan implemented).

Manager signature: _____ Date: _____

Reminder for the manager: When this sheet is completed, file all orientation documents in the employee's file. Record on the "Completion of Orientation" form and send to Organizational Learning. For questions regarding this process, contact your learning specialist.

Legend:
BLS = Basic life support
FUMC = Fairview University Medical Center
NA = Nursing assistant
NEO = New employee orientation
NG = Nasogastric tube
Para = Paraprofessional
PBDS = Performance-Based Development System

Note. Figure courtesy of Fairview University Medical Center. Used with permission.

No national standards exist in the United States for training AP employed in acute care hospitals. Other agencies such as Medicare-certified skilled nursing facilities and home health agencies have national standards (Thomas et al., 2000). A recent study of state and territorial boards of nursing looked at issues related to AP. A 77% overall response rate (41 states) was achieved with responses to AP use addressing (a) use in acute care hospitals, (b) state regulations and guidelines, (c) standardized curriculums, (d) regulatory definitions, and (e) complaints or inappropriate delegation and AP use. There were a number of differences between state and territorial boards of nursing in the area of regulation and guidelines governing supervision of AP. There also were no clear plans being made by most states to establish a standardized AP curriculum (Thomas et al.). This puts the responsibility on clinical nurse experts to provide input on the development of AP orientation, educational requirements, training, and evaluation.

Figure 13-4. Emory University Competency Monitoring Process

Name: _____Title: _____

Unit: _____

Name of Activity/Procedure/Equipment Use:_____

Vital Signs—Pulse, Respirations, Blood Pressure

Initial Competency Checklist

Required Component Actions

Pulse

1. State sites most commonly chosen for taking pulse:
   A. Radial artery—at thumb side of wrist just above radial artery. It is the most common site because it is easily accessible and convenient for both the nurse and the patient.
   B. Temporal artery—just above and to the outer side of the outer canthus of the eye
   C. Mandibular notch—at the outer angle of lower jaw just above facial artery
   D. Dorsalis pedis artery—on instep of foot
   E. Carotid artery—on either side of the neck, directly in front of the ear lobe
   F. Femoral artery—in the groin, between the anterior superior spine of the ileum and the symphysis pubis, just below the inguinal ligament

2. Assist patient into a comfortable position—sitting or lying pulse rate is affected by posture. Pulse is higher when in standing position.

3. Take pulse when temperature is being taken.

4. Use first three fingertips of the right hand to compress artery, using just enough pressure to make pulse beat distinct and not enough to obliterate pulse wave. Never use thumb to check pulse, because thumb pulsation may be confused with patient's pulse.

5. Count pulsation in the artery for one-half minute and then multiply times two to obtain full minute's rate. Check pulsation for full minute if irregularity is noted. If pulse is irregular, extremely rapid, or very weak, an apical pulse should be taken because all apical beats may not be transmitted or felt at radial artery.

6. Make note of any irregularities in rate, regularity, force, and tension.

7. Record pulse.

Respirations

1. After counting pulse, allow fingers to remain over radial artery while respiration is counted. Patient should not become aware that his breathing is being counted or it may alter usual rate.

2. Respiration is counted by observing the rise and fall of the chest for one-half minute and multiplying times two, to give a full minute's rate.

3. A complete cycle of inspiration and expiration constitutes one act of respiration. If respiration is irregular or very slow, count it for one full minute.

4. Make note of any irregularities in rate, rhythm, regularity, and depth.

5. Document respirations, making note of any irregularities.

Blood Pressure

1. Identify necessary equipment used to perform blood pressure.

(Continued on next page)

Figure 13-4. Emory University Competency Monitoring Process *(Continued)*

2. Provide a private, quiet, relaxed atmosphere as much as possible.

3. Assist patient to allow position of comfort, recumbent or sitting with forearm relaxed and supported. Blood pressure is normally affected by posture.

4. Apply sphygmomanometer cuff over brachial artery above the elbow, placing the compression bulb side over the brachial artery. Cuff should be free of air when applied.

5. Apply cuff snugly and smoothly.

6. By digital palpation, locate the pulsation of the brachial artery. Blood pressure is determined by the brachial artery.

7. Place stethoscope over the artery where pulsation is felt. Accurate readings are possible when stethoscope is directly over artery.

8. Close valve of inflation bulb and inflate cuff until pulsation of the brachial artery is obliterated.

9. Release the pressure slowly and evenly by turning the valve screw on the inflation bulb until pulse sounds are heard. The rubber tubes of the stethoscope and air pump should not contact each other, or rubbing sounds will interfere with hearing systolic and diastolic sounds.

10. Observe the dial or mercury column and note the reading on sphygmomanometer where you first hear the pulse sound. The reading at this point is the systolic pressure. Systolic pressure is that point at which the blood in the brachial artery is first able to force its way through against the pressure exerted on the vessel by the monometer.

11. Continue to release the pressure slowly until there is a definite change in the pulse sound. When the sound changes, that is the diastolic pressure. (The diastolic pressure may be recorded at the last sound heard as pressure is released from the cuff.) Diastolic pressure is that point at which the blood flows freely in the brachial artery.

12. Allow pressure to fall to zero and remove from arm.

13. Document findings and report any irregularities.

Expected Standard Performance: 100% of all applicable items on checklist.

25 out of total 25

Verified by: _____ Title: _____

Date: _____

Note. Figure courtesy of Emory University Hospital. Used with permission.

Implementing standards for AP training and education may have a positive effect on patient outcomes (Kido, 2001). Winchester (2003) believed that APs are in a unique position to make significant contributions to patient care because of the extensive amount of time they spend with the patient, especially in settings such as assisted living, nursing homes, and palliative care. Specialized training in communication skills using role-playing and videos is recommended (Winchester).

Wagner, Schiech, and Dell (2003) described an oncology nursing assistant development program designed to increase utilization of AP throughout the organization, to ensure the AP have appropriate skills to function effectively, and to promote more effective use of the RN. The curriculum complies with state requirements, is standardized, and is presented in a formal manner. A competency list was created and an evaluation method for competency determined. RNs were also taught and coached through the same key educational topics, which included role and function of AP, communication skills, infection control, safety, patient rights, respiratory care, nutrition, pain, team building, conflict resolution, negotiation, delegation, and a number of other topics. The authors noted positive outcomes since the start of the program, with improvement in the AP turnover rate and a decrease in the vacancy rate. Improved communication and morale of AP and an increase in RN job satisfaction also have been noted.

Van Cleave and Scherffius (2002) described a training program developed for operating room (OR) aides. Classes in teamwork, leadership, body mechanics, and training specific to the OR were included and followed with competency testing. The authors felt that this program was effective in keeping the OR functioning and reducing costs as well as providing quality, experienced care (Van Cleave & Scherffius).

Tuttas (2003) suggested the selection and training of lead nursing assistants (LNAs) with a separate pay scale and job description to eliminate some of the ongoing challenges that RNs and AP face. There may be a significant number of individuals who are motivated to pursue this position. These individuals can then take on more responsibility and follow up with other AP on their units. The LNA reports to the charge nurse and functions under the supervision of the RN (Tuttas). Tuttas further suggested that the "team enforcement model" may serve as a quality improvement methodology. When individuals are being held accountable for their actions on a daily basis, there is peer pressure to perform. The LNA will likely have a patient assignment but is responsible for ensuring that tasks are completed, breaks are monitored, and productivity is maintained for other AP. This model has many potential benefits, including an enhanced teamwork atmosphere, advancement opportunities, higher work ethic standards, and potential recruitment and retention incentives for professional nurses (Tuttas).

The National Board for Certification of Hospice and Palliative Nurses has developed a specialty certification for AP providing palliative care in a number of settings. Individuals taking this examination are required to have documentation of 2,000 hours of patient care experience with RN supervision. A minimum of two years of practice as an AP in hospice or palliative care settings is recommended. Recertification every four years also is required. The credential awarded to AP is Certified Hospice and Palliative Nursing Assistant (CHPNA) (Martinez, 2003). Ersek (2003) described the *Core Curriculum* developed to assist AP in preparing for this certification exam. Teleconferences, CD-ROMs, computer-based interactive teaching programs, and teaching guides also are available or planned.

Delegation

RNs must have the ability to delegate and communicate effectively with AP (Kido, 2001). Kopishke (2002) detailed five rights to delegation taught to RNs in New York: right task, right circumstances, right person, right direction/communication, and right supervision. Effective delegation, however, has many barriers. Keeling, Adair, Seider, and Kirksey (2000) suggested tips for successful delegation (see Table 13-1).

Table 13-1. Tips for Successful Delegation		
Tip	**Approach**	**Example**
Assess skills of assistive personnel (AP).	Ask open-ended questions that elicit responses other than "yes" or "no."	"How do you measure the amount of liquid consumed with meals?"
Match tasks to skills.	Become familiar with training programs for AP. Review orientation materials to determine what has been included in training.	"Describe what you have been taught in your training program and orientation." "Tell me what you would report back to me related to any changes in vital signs."
Communicate clearly.	Clearly describe the task to be performed, the expected outcome, and the time period for completion. Remember that tone of voice, rate of speech, and body language can influence the communication. Establish eye contact.	"Please take vital signs as soon as we finish report, and let me know immediately if any patient has a temperature above 100°F."
Listen attentively.	Encourage a response to any direction given or questions asked. Ask the individual to repeat the instructions given. Observe body language, tone of voice, and rate of speech. Assist AP to organize and prioritize tasks.	"Let's go over your patient list and determine what is most important to accomplish first." "Tell me what supplies you will need to provide care to this patient."
Provide feedback.	Offer feedback about performance, whether positive or needing improvement.	"Thank you for checking those vital signs and letting me know about the elevated temperature." "I should have been more clear and let you know that you need to tell me immediately about any temperature above 100°F."

Note. From "Appropriate Delegation," by B. Keeling, J. Adair, D. Seider, and G. Kirksey, 2000, *American Journal of Nursing, 100*(12), pp. 24A, 24C, 24D. Copyright 2000 by Elsevier. Adapted with permission.

Job Satisfaction and Retention

Parsons, Simmons, Penn, and Furlough (2003) examined satisfaction and turnover for AP in long-term care facilities. They found that the relationship with residents was the major reason AP stay on the job. Involvement in work-related issues and the opportunity for professional growth enhancement are also key to job satisfaction

(Parsons, Simmons, Penn, & Furlough). Bowers, Esmond, and Jacobson (2003) also studied turnover of AP and found that the AP perception of being unappreciated and undervalued by the organization contributed significantly to turnover. Kupperschmidt (2001) suggested the use of recruitment strategies such as realistic job previews, which provide pertinent information about job expectations and result in fewer surprises, ultimately resulting in better retention. A realistic job preview is a "balanced presentation of all relevant (positive, neutral, and negative) and favorable and unfavorable job-related information" (Kupperschmidt, 2002, p. 280). Asking newly hired AP to describe their expectations in terms of patient care tasks, workload, interpersonal relationships, and performing frequent follow-up is one strategy to improve employee satisfaction and retention rates (Kupperschmidt, 2001, 2002). Discussion with AP on a regular basis results in realistic job expectations, satisfaction with the organization, enhanced personal commitment, and enhanced coping strategies to deal with stressful conditions. Some healthcare facilities have developed AP career ladders, patterned after RN ladders, as a vehicle for growth, increased earnings, and retention. Wagner et al. (2003) described a clinical ladder system for AP with three levels: Level 1: AP demonstrates competency in performing basic skills; Level 2: AP demonstrates competency in performing selected advanced skills; and Level 3: AP is enrolled in and has successfully completed at least one semester in a school of nursing and demonstrates advanced technical skills, critical thinking abilities, and effective communication skills.

Cost Effectiveness of Utilizing Assistive Personnel

McClung's (2000) review of studies conducted to look at the cost effectiveness of AP utilization showed mixed results, with some reporting savings, others being budget neutral, and still others showing an increase in cost. There is a critical need for ongoing research to look at AP models across settings, geographic regions, and within clinical specialties to measure both cost effectiveness as well as safety and quality outcomes for patients (McClung). Research related to the effect of nursing staff mix and patient outcomes with AP use is essential. This research will provide information to determine how to improve training and education for AP (Kido, 2001). Clear articulation by the RN—name, title, and duties—may help patients understand the role of the RN and create a more visible role for nursing (Lange, 2002). Kupperschmidt (2002) believed that AP "who are competent, satisfied with their work situation, and have relatively stable work histories can be a major benefit to their organizations" (p. 280). She further recommended effective retention and use of competent AP to achieve quality patient care.

Krapohl and Larson (1996) reviewed literature surrounding AP utilization and made recommendations that are still applicable today. Delivery models incorporating AP still need to be evaluated in order to predict the effects on the quality of patient care, patient and nurse satisfaction, cost effectiveness throughout the entire system, and productivity.

Bernreuter and Cardona (1997a, 1997b) surveyed and critiqued studies related to AP from 1975 to 1997 and found there was only minimal evidence to support greater patient or job satisfaction with fewer or no AP. There were a number of problems associated with the literature studied: lack of standard terminology and role definition for AP, inadequate sampling, incomplete reporting of statistical analyses, problems with instruments, and failure to control variables. The authors further suggested the development of strategies to improve AP supervision: delegation, decreasing nonproductive time, documentation of objective measures of care and health outcomes, and political involvement of nursing to bring standardization to the forefront (Bernreuter & Cardona, 1997b).

Conclusion

The use of AP is likely to continue across all healthcare settings. Each practice setting will need to determine how these providers of direct patient care are developed, trained, utilized, and evaluated. The need to continue to examine AP supervision and productivity is evident. A review and modification of current job descriptions will be necessary for the nurse to ensure competency, evaluate skill, and ensure quality and safety of patient care related to AP team members.

Nursing must continue to define the nursing role, regardless of setting, to determine how these providers of direct patient care are utilized. If this does not happen, other professionals will determine this (Munroe, 2003). Becoming and staying familiar with the literature, being aware of the role of AP, understanding the legalities of nurse-delegated tasks, and legislative changes are essential to deal with the ever-changing environment (Kopishke, 2002).

Beyers (1999) believed that nursing care delivery will be provided very differently in the future and will be driven by people who have the knowledge to perform. Improvement and innovation will be facilitated through readily shared information and insights. Increased flexibility that matches patient requirements for care and caregiver styles will become the new norm. Information technology will support new ways to define competencies, measure performance, and provide feedback. Best practices will become automatic. Nurses must realize their personal and professional potential to deal with the future. Fralic (2000, pp. 212–213) offered lessons that can serve as a guide for all nurses.

- There is no single right way to staff for patient care.
- Effective planning for staffing is never accomplished as a process in isolation.
- Experimentation and innovation are essential.
- Decision support systems for staffing are required.
- Measurement systems are mandatory.
- Consider the short-, mid-, and long-term consequences of any action planned.
- Best-care scenario: The right number and the right composition of consistent, well-prepared nursing staff.

Providing optimal and safe patient care is the ultimate goal of all AP and nurses working in health care.

References

American Nurses Association. (1992). Position statement: *Registered nurse utilization of unlicensed assistive personnel.* Washington, DC: Author.

American Nurses Association. (1996). *Registered professional nurses and unlicensed assistive personnel* (2nd ed.). Washington, DC: American Nurses Publishing.

Anthony, M.K., Casey, D., Chau, T., & Brennan, P.F. (2000). Congruence between registered nurses' and unlicensed assistive personnel perception of nursing practice. *Nursing Economics, 18,* 285–293, 307.

Bernreuter, M.E., & Cardona, S. (1997a). Survey and critique of studies related to unlicensed assistive personnel from 1975 to 1997, Part 1. *Journal of Nursing Administration, 27*(6), 24–29.

Bernreuter, M.E., & Cardona, S. (1997b). Survey and critique of studies related to unlicensed assistive personnel from 1975 to 1997, Part 2. *Journal of Nursing Administration, 27*(7/8), 49–55.

Beyers, M. (1999). Impact of today's redesign initiatives on tomorrow's delivery of health care. In D.J. Weaver (Ed.), *Patient care redesign. Lessons from the field* (pp. 179–188). Chicago: Health Forum.

Bowers, B.J., Esmond, S., & Jacobson, N. (2003). Turnover reinterpreted. CNAs talk about why they leave. *Journal of Gerontological Nursing, 29*(3), 36–43.

Cady, R. (2001). Legal issues surrounding the use of unlicensed assistive personnel. *American Journal of Maternal/Child Nursing, 26*(1), 49.

Ersek, M. (2003). HPNA educational resources for nursing assistants. *Home Healthcare Nurse, 21,* 498.

Fralic, M.F. (2000). Epilogue: Closing lessons. In M.F. Fralic (Ed.), *Staffing management and methods. Tools and techniques for nursing leaders* (pp. 211–213). San Francisco: Jossey-Bass.

Hunter-Yates, S., Bline, K., Bird, C., Bresnahan, E., Couper-Noles, R., Cutler, S., et al. (2003). Start out: Building healthcare careers for minority teenagers. *Journal of Continuing Education in Nursing, 34*(3), 116–121.

Keeling, B., Adair, J., Seider, D., & Kirksey, G. (2000). Appropriate delegation. *American Journal of Nursing, 100*(12), 24A, 24C–24D.

Kido, V.J. (2001). The dilemma. *Nursing Management, 32*(11), 27–29.

Kopishke, L.R. (2002). Unlicensed assistive personnel: A dilemma for nurses. *Journal of Legal Nurse Consulting, 13*(1), 3–7.

Krapohl, G.L., & Larson, E. (1996). The impact of unlicensed assistive personnel on nursing care delivery. *Nursing Economics, 14*(2), 99–110, 122.

Kupperschmidt, B.R. (2001). UAPs: To have and to hold. *Nursing Management, 32*(3), 33–34.

Kupperschmidt, B.R. (2002). Unlicensed assistive personnel retention and realistic job previews. *Nursing Economics, 20,* 279–283.

Lange, J.W. (2002). Patient identification of caregivers' titles: Do they know who you are? *Applied Nursing Research, 15*(1), 11–18.

Marrelli, T.M. (2003). Restorative care and home care: New implications for aide and nurse roles? *Geriatric Nursing, 24,* 128–129.

Martinez, J.M. (2003). Hospice and palliative care specialty certification for nursing assistants. *Home Healthcare Nurse, 21*(3), 193–194.

McClung, T.M. (2000). Assessing the reported financial benefits of unlicensed assistive personnel in nursing. *Journal of Nursing Administration, 30,* 530–534.

Medvec, B.R., Pelusi, J.L., Camp-Sorrell, D., Kleinschmidt, P., Krebs, L., & Mooney, K. (1996). Assistive personnel: Their use in cancer care—An Oncology Nursing Society position paper. *Oncology Nursing Forum, 23,* 647–651.

Munroe, D.J. (2003). Assisted living issues for nursing practice. *Geriatric Nursing, 24,* 99–105.

Oncology Nursing Society. (2001). The role of unlicensed assistive personnel in cancer care. *Oncology Nursing Forum, 28,* 17.

Oncology Nursing Society. (2002). *The use of assistive personnel in cancer care.* Retrieved October 14, 2003, from http://www.ons.org/publications/positions/AssitivePersonnel.shtml

Parsons, S.K., Simmons, W.P., Penn, K., & Furlough, M. (2003). Determinants of satisfaction and turnover among nursing assistants. The results of a statewide survey. *Journal of Gerontological Nursing, 29*(3), 51–58.

Rosen, L.F. (1999). The changing face of staffing—UAPs. *Today's Surgical Nurse, 21*(3), 39–40.

Sheehan, J.P. (2001). AP delegation: A step-by-step process. *Nursing Management, 32*(4), 22.

Spellbring, A.M., & Ryan, J.W. (2003). Medication administration by unlicensed caregivers. A model program. *Journal of Gerontological Nursing, 29*(6), 48–54.

Spencer, S.A. (2001). Education, training, and use of unlicensed assistive personnel in critical care. *Critical Care Nursing Clinics of North America, 13*(1), 105–118.

Standing, T., Anthony, M.K., & Hertz, J.E. (2001). Nurses' narratives of outcomes after delegation to unlicensed assistive personnel. *Outcomes Management for Nursing Practice, 5*(1), 18–23.

Thomas, S.A., Barter, M., & McLaughlin, F.E. (2000). State and territorial boards of nursing approaches to the use of unlicensed assistive personnel. *Journal of Nursing Administration's Healthcare Law, Ethics, and Regulation, 2*(1), 13–21.

Tuttas, C. (2003). Decreasing nurse staffing costs in a hospital setting: Development and support of core staff stability. *Journal of Nursing Care Quality, 18*, 226–240.

Van Cleave, C., & Scherffius, J.A. (2002). Filling the void created by reductions in nurse staffing. *AORN Journal, 75*, 829–831, 833–834.

Wagner, J.S., Schiech, L., & Dell, D.D. (2003, October). Oncology nursing assistant development program. *Hematology/Oncology News and Issues*, pp. 25–29.

Winchester, T.A. (2003). Teaching communication skills to nursing home certified nursing assistants. *Geriatric Nursing, 24*, 178–181.

Zimmerman, P.G. (2000). The use of unlicensed assistive personnel: An update and skeptical look at a role that may present more problems than solutions. *Journal of Emergency Nursing, 26*, 312–317.

Interviewing and Selecting the Right Candidate

Margaret A. Bloomquist, SPHR
James N. Thomas, PhD
Mary Magee Gullatte, RN, MN, ANP, AOCN®, FAAMA

"A right judgment draws us a profit from all things we see." William Shakespeare

This chapter will focus on the critical role that behavior-based interviews play as part of an effective personnel selection system. Personnel selection is perhaps the most important function that a nurse manager performs. It represents a significant investment in time and resources for the leader, the team, and for job candidates. Furthermore, development and use of an effective selection system yields solid returns—productive employees who enjoy their jobs and contribute to the achievement of departmental and organizational goals.

Although most managers realize that personnel selection is a critical management function, many admit to feeling uncomfortable when they have to interview job applicants. Hiring managers learn all too frequently that the "perfect candidate" lacks necessary skills or is a poor "fit" with the job, the team, or the organization. Poor productivity, morale problems, excessive training expenses, high turnover, equal employment opportunity complaints, and labor disputes are a few of the unpleasant outcomes of ineffectual selection procedures, but these mistakes also impact the organization's bottom line. By some accounts, the cost for every individual hiring "mistake" easily exceeds the annual salary of the employee (Fisher, Schoenfeldt, & Shaw, 1990).

Given the importance and costs associated with personnel selection and more frequent needs to fill vacancies driven by a highly skilled and mobile, job-hopping workforce, organizations need an effective selection system that identifies people who are capable and willing to work for the recruiting organization. Job fit for the employee and employer is crucial to staff satisfaction and retention. Although there is no foolproof hiring method, following the proven strategies and techniques included in this chapter will give hiring managers the skills and confidence they need to identify and select the right candidate for the job (including selection of internal staff for promotions and transfers). The purpose of personnel selection is to identify one or more qualified candidates from a pool of applicants to be given bona fide job offers based on pre-established criteria (either formal or informal).

Importance of Effective Selection

Personnel selection provides the organization with perhaps its most precious resource—human capital. In many organizations, this represents the single biggest cost to the enterprise. Furthermore, the skills and capabilities of the workforce have a direct impact on the ability of the organization to meet performance objectives (e.g., patient satisfaction, safety, treatment outcomes). Although the importance of employee selection may appear self-evident, many managers invest precious little time and energy preparing for and performing this vital function. Healthcare organizations pay the price in poor performance, low morale, and high turnover. Nurse managers also bear the burden as they spend inordinate amounts of time and energy filling a never-ending stream of vacancies, providing remedial training, mediating disputes, or counseling team members who have performance problems. Many of the problems could be significantly reduced if more attention was given to hiring the right fit for the job and environment on the front end.

Basic Requirements for an Effective Selection Process

An effective selection process must meet several basic requirements. It must provide an accurate assessment of a candidate's ability and willingness to perform the target job; it must be perceived as fair and equitable to job candidates; and it must be practical. To qualify as "practical," the users (i.e., hiring managers) must be willing and able to perform their required roles. Generally, selection systems that fulfill these requirements are comprised of multiple tools, techniques, or procedures that are carefully sequenced to ensure maximum effectiveness and efficiency.

Typical Selection Procedures

The selection procedure normally has four steps in the process: application/resume screening, preliminary interview, in-depth interview, and additional selection tools, which will be discussed in more detail in this section (Fisher et al., 1990).

Application/resume screening: Candidates most frequently enter into a selection system by completing a job application or by submitting a resume. Application blanks request information about education, work history, and skills. Resumes leave the choice of what information to provide to the candidate, but they typically include the same sort of information. Factual information obtained from these tools (e.g., degrees, dates of employment) can be objectively verified and can be used to determine if candidates meet minimal job requirements. They also provide a means for prioritizing candidates who may have "preferred" qualifications. (Application blanks should be reviewed prior to use to ensure that they comply with applicable federal and state employment laws.)

Preliminary interview: Sometimes known as a "screening" interview, this technique can be used to gather information not provided on the application or resume and determine if a candidate meets minimum qualifications for the position (i.e., education and experience). Screening interviews also may be used to gather information about critical skills and job fit. Preliminary interviews may be conducted face-to-face or via the telephone.

In-depth interview: The "in-depth interview," usually conducted face-to-face, is used to collect more detailed information related to knowledge, behaviors, and job fit. In-depth interviews usually involve a two-directional flow of information: interviewers *get* information from the applicant while they *give* information about the position and the organization. Often the flow of information to the candidate is subtle, with candidates being very attentive to the tone and treatment afforded to them during the process.

Additional selection tools: Some selection systems include more sophisticated components such as testing and simulations. These tools provide a means of obtaining in-depth skill information. When used, care should be taken to ensure that the content and administration are standardized and job related. Common tests and simulations include cognitive ability tests, keyboarding skills assessments, software skill assessments, and medication administration simulations.

Selection System Prerequisites

Effective interviews and, indeed, any effective selection system should be based on a foundation that includes the following.

Job description: Most positions in a healthcare setting have a general job description that outlines job responsibilities and work activities. A comprehensive job description also should identify minimum education and experience requirements, behavioral/skill requirements, physical demands, and the work location. Some job descriptions also indicate pay grades/ranges and other information that may be of use to hiring managers and job candidates.

Position success profile (see Figure 14-1): A position profile, or success profile, provides information about the personnel requirements for the job (e.g., required skills, motivational fit profile) beyond that contained in a typical job description. If available, the success profile provides a more complete understanding of hiring criteria than does a typical job description, which only provides information about job tasks and administrative details, such as work location, work hours, and compensation.

Figure 14-1. Patient Care Professional Success Profile Elements

Adaptability: Maintaining effectiveness when experiencing major changes in work tasks or the work environment; adjusting effectively to work within new work structures, processes, requirements, or cultures.

Care Management: Serving as an agent for the patient within the healthcare setting; identifying key relationships in the area of patient care management; understanding the relationship between assessments, interventions, and patient responses; allocating task responsibility to appropriate others to maximize patient care.

Continuous Learning: Actively identifying new areas for learning; regularly creating and taking advantage of learning opportunities; using newly gained knowledge and skill on the job and learning through their application.

Communication: Clearly conveying information and ideas through a variety of media to individuals or groups in a manner that engages the audience and helps them understand and retain the message.

Emotional Stamina: Maintaining stable performance under pressure or opposition (such as time pressure or emotional strain); handling stress in a manner that is acceptable to others in the organization; operating with vigor, effectiveness, and determination over extended periods of time; dealing effectively with others in an antagonistic situation.

Initiative: Taking prompt action to accomplish objectives; taking action to achieve goals beyond what is required; being proactive.

Job Fit: The extent to which activities and responsibilities available in the job are consistent with the activities and responsibilities that result in personal satisfaction; the degree to which the work itself is personally satisfying.

Organization and Coordination: Establishing courses of action for self and others to ensure that work is completed efficiently.

Patient Education/Health Promotion: Supporting, explaining, and instructing patient and patient's family (significant other, care giver) in understanding the clinical procedures and equipment used to facilitate optimum health status. Promoting the lifestyle changes required of the patient and the patient's family to achieve optimum health status.

Patient Loyalty and Satisfaction: Effectively meeting customers'/patients' needs; building productive patient relationships; taking responsibility for patient satisfaction and loyalty.

Performance Standards: Setting high standards of performance for self and others; assuming responsibility and accountability for successfully completing assignments or tasks; self-imposing standards of excellence rather than having standards imposed.

Problem Solving: Identifying and understanding issues, problems, and opportunities; comparing data from different sources to draw conclusions; using effective approaches for choosing a course of action or developing appropriate solutions with ambiguous or incomplete information; taking action that is consistent with available facts, constraints, and probable consequences; making timely decisions.

Safety Intervention: Having knowledge of conditions that affect patient, self, and/or employee safety under normal conditions and conditions that occur in crisis situations. Skilled in identifying conditions that might cause health or safety hazards and taking action to remove such hazards. Understands all aspects of providing a safe environment for patient, self, and/or others.

Sensitivity: Taking actions that indicate a consideration for the feelings and needs of others; being aware of the impact of one's own behavior on others; and interacting with others in a way that gives them confidence in one's intentions and those of the healthcare organization.

(Continued on next page)

Figure 14-1. Patient Care Professional Success Profile Elements *(Continued)*

Teamwork: Working effectively and cooperatively with others; establishing and maintaining good working relationships.

Technical/professional knowledge and skills: Having achieved a satisfactory level of technical and professional skill or knowledge in position-related areas; keeping up-to-date with current developments and trends in areas of expertise.

Integration of system components (see Table 14-1): Successful patient care providers possess a complex mix of technical knowledge, behavioral skill, and motivational attributes that allow them to thrive in a very demanding work environment. No simple tool, or brief interview, will provide a hiring manager with all of the information required to assess a candidate and reach a hiring decision. Therefore, effective selection processes include several elements, each designed to work in concert with the other, to efficiently gather the required insights about candidates and support selection decision making. For the system to work effectively, hiring managers need to know what steps have been taken to screen candidates prior to interviews, what information was obtained, and how their interview(s) will contribute to a comprehensive understanding of the candidate's overall suitability for the job in question. A selection system design grid (see Table 14-1) is a useful way to convey this information.

In addition to thoughtful design, a selection system must include a set of rules and procedures for moving applicants through the process. This ensures that all candidates are treated fairly and appropriately; all candidates are given the same opportunities to demonstrate their qualifications related to the job. Well-designed procedures also enable an organization to evaluate large numbers of applicants efficiently and economically, maximizing the contributions of hiring managers, recruiters, and stakeholders. A "systems" approach to personnel selection is particularly important in tight labor markets because those organizations with well-designed systems will be able to quickly identify and render offers to highly qualified talent. They also can quickly screen out and reject candidates who do not meet requirements without allowing them to clog up the selection pipeline.

Training for screeners and interviewers: Even the most elegantly designed system requires skilled "operators." Conducting employment interviews, in particular, requires a complex skill set that must be learned and practiced, such as clinical competencies (e.g., CPR, IV administration). Interviewers must be thoroughly familiar with job requirements, must have excellent questioning and listening skills, must be familiar with common rating errors and biases, and must be excellent communicators. Unfortunately, many hiring managers give little attention to the development and maintenance of these skills.

Legal considerations: The personnel selection function has been affected by a multitude of federal and state statutes over the past 50 years (e.g., Civil Rights Acts, the Age Discrimination in Employment Act, the Americans with Disabilities Act) (see *Uniform Guidelines on Employee Selection Procedures* [1978] for more detailed information regarding legal requirements). Failure to comply with legal requirements for fair and appropriate treatment of job candidates can create significant liability for the organization. It also can create public relations nightmares that can compromise the ability to recruit and attract qualified job candidates to the organization. As a result, all selection system participants, interviewers in particular, should have a basic understanding of the legal constraints imposed on the interview process. Although a comprehensive review of legal issues is beyond the scope of this chapter, the overriding principle behind most statutes is that all information requested from job candidates must be relevant to the knowledge, skill, and ability requirements for the job and that membership in any protected class (e.g., race, national origin, religion, sexual orientation) cannot be allowed to impact selection decisions. Interviewers should use an interview guide, or script, that has been designed to comply with these requirements.

Table 14-1. Patient Care Professional—Interview Coverage Grid			
Success Profile Element*	Resume Review	HR Manager (Screening)	Hiring Manager (Expert)
Job fit	X	X	X
Communication	X	X	X
Technical knowledge	X		X
Problem solving			X
Teamwork		X	
Adaptability		X	
Initiative		X	
Organizing and coordination		X	
Care management			X
Customer loyalty and satisfaction		X	X
Performance standards			X (Optional)
Emotional stamina			X (Optional)
Patient education/health promotion			X (Optional)
Safety intervention			X (Optional)
Continuous learning			X (Optional)
*Success profile elements are listed in order of priority.			
Note. Based on information from Emory Healthcare, 2004.			

Legal considerations also affect note taking, record keeping, and reporting. Each organization should have clearly defined guidelines for these aspects of the selection function, and interviewers must follow these guidelines consistently.

Screening Applicants

The goal of screening is to filter out candidates who do not meet the position's minimum requirements. It also allows prioritization of candidates who meet the requirements of the position (i.e., qualified versus highly qualified). As the first step in the selection process, screening serves as one of the most important components of the process; yet, many managers and human resource professionals spend too little time carefully defining standards and implementing procedures to ensure that all candidates are consistently evaluated.

Another common screening problem involves a misunderstanding of purpose. Recruiters or hiring managers attempt to read too much into the limited information provided on a resume or application and behave as if they are making final hiring decisions. They spend excessive time poring over the details, reading between the lines, and making assumptions about skills and capabilities. This wastes time and leads to evaluation errors. Screening should be simple, straightforward, and consistent. Later steps in the process are better suited to gaining deep insights into candidates' capabilities and motivations.

Typical screening criteria include education/credentials, work experience, technical knowledge, work history, and career advancement. Criteria can be used as "knock-outs" or as "preferred attributes" used to prioritize candidates. Other factors also may be considered, including frequency of job changes without career advancement (commonly referred to as "job hopping"); gaps in employment history; years of experience; certifications; achievements and awards; salary history; resume writing and organization skills; and creativity in resume preparation or presentation. Reviewers should take care not to overvalue resume quality or creativity, because many job candidates employ professional resume consultants to help them "polish" their submission.

Screening for minimum qualifications is commonly performed by a human resource professional. Hiring managers also may wish to review resumes, particularly if there has been little effort expended to clearly articulate and gain alignment around screening criteria. However, even when criteria are well established, hiring managers can add value to the screening process by reviewing candidates' technical credentials and work experience.

Behavioral Interviewing Basics

Although a "systems" approach to personnel selection generally yields the best results, the most common selection system component is the interview. Well-designed and consistently implemented structured behavioral interviews can be the single greatest contributor to personnel selection success of the organization (McDaniel, Whetzel, Schmidt, & Maurer, 1994).

Goal of the interview: The overall goal of the behavioral interview is to gain detailed information that allows selection decision makers to determine the extent to which the candidate meets or exceeds the requirements established in the success profile. More specifically, effective interviews typically focus on the following key areas: technical knowledge, behavioral competencies, and job fit.

Most professional-level healthcare jobs require people to have highly specialized knowledge. In many cases, required knowledge cannot be easily or quickly acquired; therefore, a qualified candidate must already have successfully completed specialized training in the area and/or developed the critical knowledge and expertise through previous experience. Although some evidence of technical knowledge can be gleaned from the screening process, the interview allows hiring managers to determine how well time in the classroom or time on the job has translated into actual technical competence.

Although technical knowledge is critical to success, other skills and abilities often determine who will be a high performer or a mediocre underachiever. Behavioral skills that support high performance must be evaluated in the interview because they are difficult, if not impossible, to evaluate based on application/resume information alone. Behavioral interviews allow evaluators to gather information about a wide variety of skills, including teamwork, decision making, planning and organizing, and adaptability, to name a few. An effective interviewer gathers examples from the candidate's past experience that demonstrate how he or she responded to job requirements and achieved significant work objectives.

The third focus of an effective behavioral interview involves "fit." Fit is the extent to which a job candidate is likely to find the job, the organization, and the work location compatible with his or her own motivations and preferences. Although fit often is overlooked, gathering information about the candidate's willingness to do the job is as important as knowing whether the person is capable of doing the job (i.e., has the technical knowledge and skills required). Ensuring good fit is critical in efforts to improve retention and foster a climate of engaged, high-performing staff members.

There are several other important functions served by an interview. Interviews allow candidates to gain information about you, the job, and the organization. In a tight labor market, interviewers who recognize the importance of this two-way information exchange use the opportunity to make a positive impression and appropriately "sell" the opportunity to candidates. This can make the difference between a successful recruiting campaign and a high percentage of rejected job offers.

Basic Tenets of Behavioral Interviewing

Several basic tenets govern the behavioral interviewing process and outcomes. First, behavioral interviews are based on a simple premise—past behavior predicts future behavior (Byham, 1995). During a behavioral interview, candidates are asked questions that require them to give specific examples of how they actually responded to work or life situations in the past. Questions are carefully crafted to elicit behavioral examples that relate to skills required in the target job. When interviewing experienced candidates, the behavioral examples provided by candidates may involve similar, or even identical, situations like those encountered by job incumbents. However, the process works just as well with inexperienced candidates as long as the questions are adapted appropriately.

Although conceptually quite simple, there is ample research evidence to demonstrate that this approach yields superior results when compared to other interviewing formats, including situational/hypothetical questioning, stress interviews, or unstructured interviews (Janz, 1989; McDaniel et al., 1994; Motowidlo et al., 1992; Pulakos & Schmidt, 1995). Opren (1985) compared the effectiveness of a behavioral interview approach to the more common "unstructured" job interview. Interview ratings were compared to job performance measures collected one year after completion of the interviews. Behavioral interview scores were significantly correlated with measures of job performance ($r = .48$, $p < .05$ when using supervisor ratings of job performance as the criterion and $r = .61$, $p < .05$ when using objective measures of sales performance), but ratings from unstructured interviews failed to predict either measure of job performance. Campion and Campion (1994) evaluated the relative effectiveness of situation/hypothetical questioning versus experience-based behavioral questioning. The use of behavioral, experience-based questions resulted in a more effective prediction of job performance than did the use of hypothetical/situational questions ($r = .51$, $p < .05$ for behavioral questioning versus $r = .39$, $p < .05$ for situational questions). In a more comprehensive meta-analysis of validity studies looking at the employment interview, Weisner and Cronshaw (1988) reported an average validity coefficient of $r = .60$ for structured behavioral interviews. This study was based on research with more than 7,500 subjects. (By comparison, validity coefficients for other selection approaches, including cognitive testing, personality testing, or simulations, typically range between $r = .25$ to $r = .45$.)

Second, the "interview" is for data gathering/collection. To make an accurate decision, interviews must avoid evaluation bias and rating errors. A behavioral interview process addresses these considerations by breaking down the interview process into several discrete steps. What most observers recognize as the "interview" is the step that involves collection of information, but it does not involve evaluation. "Instant" evaluation, although quite common in everyday human experience, decreases interviewer effectiveness because interviewers do not objectively seek facts. Rather, they steer the conversation or attend to data that confirm their snap judgments, often completely unaware that they are falling victim to rater errors.

Another important aspect of data collection involves note taking. Reliance on memory to capture behavioral data is notoriously inaccurate. Poorly documented interviews give the first and last applicants the advantage, simply because they are remembered better than the ones in between. If interviewers fail to accurately note behavioral information obtained during the interview, they will be unable to effectively evaluate the candidate's responses when called upon to do so.

Third, analysis and evaluation occur after the interview. Once the discussion with the candidate is concluded, interviewers review the behavioral examples obtained during the interview and evaluate the quality and frequency of behavior against job requirements. Often, interviewers are required to share behavioral data with other interviewers, decision makers, or stakeholders and reach consensus about a candidate's suitability for the target job. This ensures that all data are carefully considered and it allows for checks and balances to prevent one interviewer's biases, either positive or negative, from compromising the integrity of the decision-making process.

Preparing for the Interview

A successful interview requires careful preparation. Well-executed interviewing systems provide interviewers with a tool that contains everything needed to prepare for and conduct the interview. Figure 14-2 provides an example of a tool, an interview guide. The guide outlines appropriate preparation steps that interviewers should complete before meeting with candidates.

- Become familiar with the position.
- Review the success profile for the target position.
- Review the interview guide and interview questions.
- Review the candidate resume/application.
- Modify the plan/revise interview guide, if appropriate.

Interview Discussion

Build rapport and describe the process: The best questioning technique can fail if the interviewer focuses only on collecting the candidate's information and ignores the candidate's personal needs (e.g., feel important, be treated with dignity and respect, be seen as competent). Job seekers can be insecure about their qualifications, sensitive about negative information they provide, and hypercritical about their performance in the interview.

Effective interviewers build and maintain rapport to create an environment that encourages open dialogue. This approach to interviewing yields complete information and gets past candidates' attempts to conceal or minimize information that highlights deficiencies. Building and maintaining rapport also helps create a positive impression with candidates, leaving them with the feeling that they were treated fairly. These candidates are more likely to accept a job offer and, even if unsuccessful, have a good word to say about your organization.

The early portion of the interview also provides a good opportunity to overview the interview process; to clarify key requirements of the job; and to allow the candidate to gain more information about the organization.

Review of education and work history: This is an opportunity to build on the data provided in the resume/application; fill in the gaps on education and employment history; and gain insights into technical skills and experience. This also allows the interviewer to tailor questions later in the interview. This section of the interview should be brief and should build on information already obtained. Do not require candidates to "rehash" information already provided on application forms or resumes to compensate for poor interviewer preparation.

Behavioral questions: The majority of an interviewer's time is spent asking behavioral questions and recording candidates' responses. The goal of this portion of the interview is to gather complete behavioral data points. When doing so, it is important to get the whole story—the situation or task in which the candidate acted, what he or she did in response to the situation (the action or behavior), and the results of these actions. An easy way to remember the goal of this section is to use the acronym "STAR" to describe a complete behavioral example (Byham, 1995).

Figure 14-2. Hiring Manager Interview Guide for Patient Care Professional

Hiring Manager Interview Guide for Patient Care Professional
Interview Name
Candidate Name
Interview Date
Preparation Checklist Review application materials and other material relevant to qualifications associated with the position.
Prepare to conduct the Key Background Review, if included. Note any jobs/experiences on which you are unclear or would like more information. Note any gaps in employment.
Prepare the Planned Behavioral Questions section. Review the dimension definitions and key actions. Modify questions to better fit the candidate's experience. Decide if the order of the questions should be changed; develop additional questions, if necessary.
Prepare the Motivational Fit question page(s), if included. Review the Job Fit definition and significant facets. Review the Location Fit definition and characteristics. Compare the location characteristics to the candidate's information, and mark which ones you will explore during the interview. Modify the questions to find out possible matches/mismatches between job facets and location characteristics and the candidate's preferences.
Estimate the time needed to cover each section of the Interview Guide.
Outline for Opening the Interview Greet the candidate, giving your name and role in the interviewing process.
Explain the purpose of the interview: To acquaint interviewer and candidate. To learn more about the candidate's experience and qualifications for the job. To help the candidate understand the position and the organization.
Describe the interview plan: Briefly review experiences in the current job. Ask questions to get specific information about those jobs/experiences. You may ask additional questions if necessary to get as much information as possible. Provide information about the position and organization. Answer candidate's questions about the position and the selection process. Point out that you both will get information needed to make good decisions. Indicate that you will be taking notes.
Make the transition to the Key Background Review.
(Continued on next page)

Figure 14-2. Hiring Manager Interview Guide for Patient Care Professional
(Continued)

Key Background Review

Educational background: (Only seek information about education experiences completed within the last five years, those that have special relevance to the role, or those not adequately described in the candidate's resume or supporting materials.)

Graduate school: _____Yrs. ___ Degree/Major _____ GPA ___ out of ___
College: _____Yrs. ___ Degree/Major _____ GPA ___ out of ___
Technical training: _____Yrs. ___ Degree/Major _____ GPA ___ out of ___
High school:_____Yrs. ___ Degree/Major _____ GPA ___ out of ___
Other education/training: _____Yrs. ___ Degree/Major _____ GPA ___ out of ___

Job experience: _____ Dates: _____

What were your major responsibilities/duties? Any change in responsibilities?
_____
_____
_____
_____
_____
_____
_____
_____
_____
_____

What did/do you like best about the position? What did/do you like best?
_____
_____
_____
_____
_____
_____
_____
_____
_____
_____

Why did you (or why are you planning to) leave?
_____
_____
_____
_____
_____
_____
_____
_____
_____
_____

(Continued on next page)

Figure 14-2. Hiring Manager Interview Guide for Patient Care Professional *(Continued)*

Technical/Professional Knowledge—Having achieved a satisfactory level of technical and professional skill or knowledge in position-related areas; keeping up with current developments and trends in areas of expertise.

Key Actions

Understands technical terminology and developments

Knows how to apply a technical skill or procedure

Knows when to apply a technical skill or procedure

Performs complex tasks in area of expertise

Planned Behavioral Questions

What experience have you had with _____ (a technical procedure, diagnostic equipment, or some other technically challenging aspect of the job)? Give an example that shows your level of expertise.

Describe a situation or assignment that challenged your skills as a _____. How did you manage the situation?

Describe how you have gone about learning a new technical task.

Situation/Task	Action	Result

Communication: _____

_____

Technical/Professional Knowledge Rating: _____

(Continued on next page)

Figure 14-2. Hiring Manager Interview Guide for Patient Care Professional (Continued)

Problem Solving—Identifying and understanding issues, problems, and opportunities; comparing data from different sources to draw conclusions; using effective approaches for choosing a course of action or developing appropriate solutions; taking action that is consistent with available facts, constraints, and probable consequences.	**Key Actions** Identifies issues, problems, and opportunities Gathers information Interprets information Generates alternatives Chooses appropriate action Commits to action Involves others

Planned Behavioral Questions

Tell me about a recent problem you uncovered in your job at _____? What sources of information did you use to identify this problem?

Describe the most complicated patient care–related problem you have had to deal with in the last year. How did you identify the problem and what did you do to resolve it?

Sometimes, despite our best efforts, we are unable to come up with a solution to an issue or problem. Give me an example of a work-related issue you tried to resolve, without success.

Situation/Task	Action	Result

Communication: _____

Problem Solving Rating: _____

(Continued on next page)

Figure 14-2. Hiring Manager Interview Guide for Patient Care Professional
(Continued)

Teamwork—Working effectively and cooperatively with others; establishing and maintaining good working relationships.	**Key Actions** Establishes good interpersonal relationships Subordinates personal goals Volunteers assistance

Planned Behavioral Questions

Working with others involves some give and take. Describe a time when you worked out an agreement with a peer or team member. What did you do?

Describe a time when you had to work together with new, or unfamiliar, team members to provide care to a patient. (How did you determine each team member's roles and responsibilities? How did you ensure that team members each did their fair share?)

Interacting with others can be challenging at times. Tell me about the greatest difficulty you faced with trying to get along with peers, team members, or others at work. How did you handle the situation?

Situation/Task	Action	Result

Communication: _____

_____

Teamwork Rating: _____

(Continued on next page)

Figure 14-2. Hiring Manager Interview Guide for Patient Care Professional *(Continued)*

Care Management—Serving as an agent for the patient within the healthcare setting; identifying key relationships in the area of patient care management; understanding the relationship between assessments, interventions, and patient responses; allocating task responsibility to appropriate others to maximize patient care.	**Key Actions** Understands connections Shows patient advocacy Knows how and when to apply interventions Shares appropriate responsibilities Provides support without removing responsibility Stays informed

Planned Behavioral Questions

Often we must collaborate with others (physicians, coworkers, different shifts) in order to follow the patient's critical pathway. Can you think of a time when you have done this? (What did you do?)

Tell me about a time when you recognized that a patient was not responding to a plan of care (either medical or nursing). (What did you do?)

Tell me about a time when a patient's complaint of pain or discomfort was a symptom of an undetected problem. (What was the situation? What did you do?)

Situation/Task	Action	Result

Communication: _____

Care Management Rating: _____

(Continued on next page)

Figure 14-2. Hiring Manager Interview Guide for Patient Care Professional *(Continued)*

Patient Loyalty and Satisfaction—Effectively meeting patient needs; building productive patient relationships; taking responsibility for patient satisfaction and loyalty.	**Key Actions** Uses key relationship principles Acknowledges the person Clarifies the current situation Meets or exceeds needs Confirms satisfaction Takes the "heat"

Planned Behavioral Questions

Describe a time when you had to ask numerous questions and listen carefully to clarify the exact nature of an internal/external customer's problem or need.

Sooner or later, we all have to deal with a patient/physician/other department who makes unreasonable demands. Think of a time when you had to handle an unreasonable request from an internal or external customer. (What did you do?)

Describe a time when you provided outstanding customer service to a patient, physician, or member of another department. (How did you know that your efforts delighted the "customer"?)

Situation/Task	Action	Result

Communication: _____

_____

Patient Loyalty and Satisfaction Rating: _____

(Continued on next page)

Figure 14-2. Hiring Manager Interview Guide for Patient Care Professional *(Continued)*

Job Fit—The extent to which activities and responsibilities available in the job are consistent with activities and responsibilities that result in personal satisfaction; the degree to which the work itself is personally satisfying.

Many opportunities for:
Achievement, practical results, relationship building, challenging work, details

Few opportunities for:
Entrepreneurialism, commission, compensation, travel

Planned Behavioral Questions

[Achievement] Tell me about a time when you had difficult goals in your work. How satisfied/dissatisfied were you with that?

[Details] Tell me about a job you have had that required high attention to small details. How satisfied/dissatisfied were you with that, and why?

[Commission] What pay structures have you had (i.e., set wages or part of wages based on commission/incentive performance)? How satisfied/dissatisfied were you with the compensation structure(s) and why?

When Satisfied/Dissatisfied	What was Satisfying/ Dissatisfying	Why was it Satisfying/ Dissatisfying

Communication: _____

Job Fit Rating: _____

Interview Close

Final Checklist
Introduce the buy-time question.
"I'm going to ask a question that I'd like you to think about for a few minutes before answering. While you're thinking, I'll review my notes to see if there is other information that I need. The question is: What strengths do you have that we haven't talked about?"

Review notes.
While the candidate is thinking about the question, review your notes to identify any area where more information is needed or information needs clarification.

Ask any additional questions based on the review of your notes.
Additional questions

(Continued on next page)

Figure 14-2. Hiring Manager Interview Guide for Patient Care Professional (Continued)

Ask for the candidate's answer to the buy-time question.
Buy-time answer

Position/Organization/Location
Provide information on position, organization, or location. If you are the last interviewer, check the candidate's understanding of these areas. (Note anything that appears to match or conflict with the candidate's stated motivations and preferences.)
Give candidate the opportunity to ask questions. (Note the questions asked here.)

End the interview.
Explain next steps in selection process.
Thank the candidate for a productive interview.

Post-interview Instructions
Complete each step after the interview.
1. Identify complete STARs throughout the Interview Guide.
2. Categorize STARs into appropriate dimensions.
3. Indicate whether each STAR is effective (+) or ineffective (-).
4. Consider the weight of each STAR according to its recency, impact, and similarity to the target job.
5. Determine the rating for each dimension. Record it on the line in the lower right corner of each page.

Use the following scale:
1   Much less than acceptable
2   Less than acceptable
3   Acceptable
4   More than acceptable
5   Much more than acceptable

Additional ratings:
N   No opportunity to observe or assess
W   Weak/want more data (e.g., 4W)
5H   Too high

6. Evaluate the applicant's behavior in the following observable dimension(s).

Review your notes and determine whether the applicant's behavior in each dimension's key actions was effective (+), neutral (/), or ineffective/absent (-).

Then, use the scale from step 5 above to rate the applicant's behavior in the dimension(s). Write the rating on the line provided.

Communication—Clearly convey information and ideas through a variety of media to individuals or groups in a manner that engages the audience and helps them understand and retain the message.

_____   Organizes the communication
_____   Maintains audience attention
_____   Adjusts to the audience
_____   Ensures understanding
_____   Adheres to accepted conventions
_____   Comprehends communication from others

Communication Rating: _____

Note. Copyright 2003, Development Dimensions International, Inc. All rights reserved.

It is important for the interviewer to get specifics—not generalities, theoretical answers, or opinions. Detailed behavioral examples give interviewers confidence that they have a true picture of how candidates respond to situations and allow for accurate evaluation of job requirements. Effective interviewers display considerable skill in probing and follow-up questioning to overcome some candidates' tendencies to avoid providing behavioral responses to even the most carefully crafted questions.

Evaluating fit: Effective interviewers move beyond the evaluation of capability and gather information about candidates' motives and preferences to allow them to evaluate motivational compatibility with the job and organization. "Motivational fit" can be divided into three separate elements: fit (the extent to which activities and responsibilities available in the job are consistent with the activities and responsibilities that result in personal satisfaction); organization fit (the extent to which an organization's mode of operation and values are consistent with the type of environment that provides personal satisfaction); and location fit (the extent to which geographic location is compatible with personal needs and preferences) (Byham, 1995). Questions designed to address fit differ slightly from those designed to elicit behavioral data points. "Fit" questions seek information about when the candidate was satisfied or dissatisfied; what were they doing to cause the satisfaction or dissatisfaction; and what, specifically, was satisfying or dissatisfying? "Fit" questions often are interjected throughout the interview as follow-ups to behavioral questions, but they also may constitute a separate set of questions (see Figure 14-2).

Closing the interview: This phase of the interview allows candidates to ask questions, but it also provides an opportunity for savvy interviewers to gain additional information about the candidate. For example, are all of a candidate's questions related to compensation, or does she or he ask about work unit culture, performance standards, or access to in-service training? These questions reveal much about the motivations and preferences of the candidate. Another important element of the closing phase of the interview involves a discussion of next steps. Interviewers should be prepared to provide details and accurate information about how and when candidates will be notified of results. Interviewers also should review any required next steps in the selection process.

Post-Interview Activities

As previously noted, the interview process is made up of several components. After the dialogue with a candidate concludes, interviewers can begin the analysis and evaluation portions of the process. Key activities completed by interviewers in this stage are as follows.

Analyze the interview data by first identifying and classifying relevant data points. (It is important to remember that not all data collected are relevant to job requirements.) Once relevant data points are identified, interviewers can evaluate individual success profile elements (e.g., decision making, technical knowledge, teamwork, job fit). Evaluating each dimension separately helps avoid common rating errors, such as halo and central tendency, and contributes to the accuracy of the process.

Data integration involves the pooling, or sharing, of behavioral data across interviewers. Often, integration may include stakeholders who did not conduct interviews but who have a stake in the outcome or require involvement in the decision-making process. (Nothing prevents stakeholders from accurately evaluating the behavioral data provided by interviewers as long as interviewers faithfully record data provided by candidates.) Data integration ensures that candidate information is fairly evaluated and helps decision makers align around evaluation standards. It also provides a mechanism to hold interviewers accountable for following prescribed processes while conducting their individual interviews. Finally, integrating data from multiple interviews allows selection decisions to be based on a larger pool of data, which allows for development of a more complete and accurate candidate profile. With respect to behavioral interviewing, "the whole is greater than the sum," the power of the process comes from interviewers sharing the information they collect and basing judgments on all available data, not just their own.

Making the decision: Where candidates are plentiful or recruiting efforts are highly effective, it is not uncommon to have more than one candidate who meets or exceeds job requirements. When faced with this situation, the behavioral interviewing approach allows decision makers to consider the profile of each candidate across all dimensions and place a higher value on more critical requirements before making a final hiring decision. In other cases, none of the candidates interviewed may meet requirements in all areas, and decision makers may be tempted to lower standards under pressure to fill long-standing vacancies. The candidate profile available from a behavioral interviewing process allows decision makers to make informed decisions about who might respond best to training and development efforts. Ideally, these decision makers can re-energize the recruiting function and hold out for acceptable candidates.

In addition to decision making, several other post-interview system components should be noted. Interviewers should provide their human resources department with required documentation (e.g., interview notes, data integration discussion summary, final hiring decision). These records may be required to support equal employment opportunity data reporting and audits. Candidates given job offers also should be scheduled into post-interview activities, such as medical examinations, criminal background checks, and reference checks.

Different Applications of Behavioral Interviewing

The different applications of behavioral interviewing are outlined as follows.

Screening Interview

Screening interviews follow the same general process as that listed earlier, but they are generally short and focused on a small number of job requirements. The length of a screening interview may vary from 20–45 minutes and often includes a review of technical experience, job history, basic fit (e.g., compensation range, geographic requirements), and several behavioral questions. The screening interview can be conducted by a recruiter, a human resources generalist, or a hiring manager, and it can be conducted face-to-face or via telephone.

Manager Interview

The length of a hiring manager interview generally runs 45–75 minutes and includes in-depth questions concerning technical competencies, more detailed investigation of "fit," and a thorough assessment of key behavioral competencies.

Multiple Interviews

The length of individual multiple interviews should be approximately 30–60 minutes and can include questions such as those included in the hiring manager interview. Multiple interviews allow for additional information to be collected from a larger pool of interviewers and allows for development of a more complete candidate profile. It also allows critical success factors to be covered by interviewers with special expertise in those areas (i.e., allow a technical expert to gather information about technical knowledge). If multiple interviews are planned, each interviewer should be provided with an interview guide tailored to this approach to ensure that candidates are not asked the same questions by different interviewers. Planning the interview schedule and coordinating the interview plan are critical to success.

Panel Interviews

A panel interview generally is longer than an individual interview, often running 90–120 minutes, and includes questions concerning technical competencies, motivational fit, and key behavioral competencies. Panel interviews allow for greater participation in the data collection process and provide "backup" for inexperienced interviewers. Although widely used, this approach is less efficient (in terms of data gathered per unit of interviewer time spent) and must be carefully coordinated. Panelist selection and panelist preparation are critical to maintain structure and rapport during the interview. Poor planning and preparation can turn this process into an "inquisition" that yields incomplete data and leaves candidates with an unfavorable impression of the organization.

Evaluating Success of the Interview Process

With any business process, a selection system must be carefully monitored and managed to ensure its long-term effectiveness. These monitored processes include

1. Importance of evaluation: You cannot improve what you do not measure, so take the time to evaluate the effectiveness of the process. What worked? What did not work? What could have worked better?
2. Measure the process: Ask questions of those involved in the selection process. Was the process efficient? Was I (the interviewer) able to gather relevant information? Were the tools provided useful, and did they add value to the process?
3. Measure outcomes: Ask questions. Did the process yield valuable information that supported selection decision making? Did the new hires have the skills to perform the job? Did the new hires perform successfully on the job (or in initial training)? What was short-term retention (first year)? Did the process support

achievement of workforce diversity objectives? Did the process allow the organization to comply with equal opportunity obligations?

4. Measure candidate satisfaction with the process. Ask questions. How was the selection experience from the candidate's perspective (ask candidates)? Did we receive any negative feedback or have negative candidate reactions to our selection process?

Gather and complete your evaluation data for incorporation into the process the next time. Remember there is always opportunity for improving the process.

Remember there is no foolproof method for hiring employees (including selection of internal staff for promotions and transfers). However, using the proven strategies, techniques, and tools provided in this chapter will give hiring decision makers more confidence and improve the accuracy of hiring decisions. No other investment in human resource systems or processes will provide a better return than improving the effectiveness of your interview process.

References

Byham, W.C. (1995). *Targeted selection.* Pittsburgh, PA: Development Dimensions International.

Campion, M.A., & Campion, J.E. (1994). Structured interviewing: A note on incremental validity and alternative question types. *Journal of Applied Psychology, 79,* 998–1002.

Emory Healthcare. (2004). *Emory Healthcare grid for patient care positions.* Atlanta, GA: Author.

Fisher, C.D., Schoenfeldt, L.F., & Shaw, J.B. (1990). *Human resource management.* Boston: Houghton Mifflin.

Janz, T. (1989). The patterned behavior description interview: The best prophet of the future is the past. In R.W. Eder & G.R. Ferris (Eds.), *The employment interview: Theory, research, and practice* (pp. 158–167). Newbury Park, CA: Sage.

McDaniel, M.A., Whetzel, D.L., Schmidt, F.L., & Maurer, S.D. (1994). The validity of employment interviews: A comprehensive review and meta-analysis. *Journal of Applied Psychology, 79,* 599–616.

Motowidlo, S.J., Carter, G.W., Dunnette, M.D., Tippins, N., Werner, S., Burnett, J.R., et al. (1992). Studies of the structured behavioral interview. *Journal of Applied Psychology, 77,* 571–587.

Opren, C. (1985). Patterned behavioral description interviews versus unstructured interviews: A comparative validity study. *Journal of Applied Psychology, 70,* 774–776.

Pulakos, E.D., & Schmidt, N. (1995). Experience-based and situational interview questions: Studies of validity. *Personal Psychology, 48,* 289–308.

Uniform Guidelines on Employee Selection. (1978). *Federal Register, 43,* 38290–38315.

Weisner, W.H., & Cronshaw, S.F. (1988). A meta-analytic investigation of the impact of the interview format and the degree of structure on the validity of the employment interview. *Journal of Occupational Psychology, 61,* 275–290.

Employment Laws and Regulations

Adair D. Maller, MA, SPHR

"To be persuasive, we must be believable. To be believable, we must be credible, to be credible, we must be truthful." Edward R. Murrow (Washington, 1999, p. 25)

Nurse managers face a complex web of employment laws and regulations designed to protect employee rights and prevent illegal discrimination in the workplace. The increased likelihood in recent years that employers will face legal challenges regarding their employment decisions has compelled them to give greater scrutiny to decisions to hire, fire, promote, pay, and train employees. Legal compliance has become a business necessity in the face of the large awards many plaintiffs seek in their discrimination claims. A challenge to nurse managers is to effectively navigate this legal minefield when hiring, managing, and dismissing staff. This chapter is designed to provide the nurse manager with core information on employment laws and regulations. The references at the end of this chapter provide additional in-depth content.

It is difficult to keep up with the employment laws at the federal, state, and local levels, along with the numerous interpretations from courts and government agencies. However, core management principles and practices essential to fair and legal employment programs serve as guidelines for astute managers.

Discrimination

Every employment decision involves making a distinction among individuals. The difficulties arise when the distinction is based on illegal criteria such as race, age, sex, color, religion, national origin, disability, or veteran status. An employment practice becomes discriminatory when it denies fair employment or equal opportunity to all applicants or employees, regardless of whether they are in a protected classification.

Disparate treatment is the theory of discrimination in which the employer treats individual applicants or employees differently on the basis of specific characteristics (listed earlier). Disparate or adverse impact refers to discrimination in which the employer uses an employment procedure (such as a specific test) that is facially neutral, yet works to the disadvantage of members of a specific protected classification. The employer does not have to "intend" the discrimination of a protected individual or group for the action to be illegal and, if challenged, will have to demonstrate that they used lawful, job-related criteria to make the employment decision (Fisher & Phillips, 1999).

Employment Laws

Chief among the federal laws governing the employment arena, broadly applying to most employers, is Title VII of the Civil Rights Act of 1964. This landmark legislation prohibits discrimination on the basis of race, color, national origin, sex, and religion (U.S. Department of Labor, 1964).

Title VII prohibits an employer with 15 or more employees from discriminating against an individual with respect to hiring, discharge, compensation, promotion, classification, training, apprenticeship, or other terms and conditions of employment on the basis of an individual's race, color, national origin, religion, and sex (including pregnancy, childbirth, or related medical conditions). The U.S. Equal Employment Opportunity Commission (EEOC), along with the federal courts, enforce Title VII's requirements (U.S. EEOC, 1997).

Decades later, the Civil Rights Act of 1991 greatly extended Title VII's coverage and provided for jury trials and increased available damages. This statute's enhancements for sexual harassment and sex discrimination cases prompted a rise in sex discrimination claims in the past decade. Sex-based discrimination also is outlawed in the Equal Pay Act of 1963, which prohibits pay differentials based on sex. Based on these federal laws, employers are required to pay male and female employees equally for jobs with substantially equivalent work requiring equal skill, effort, and responsibility under similar working conditions.

Similar protections to the disabled are extended in the Rehabilitation Act of 1973 and later by the Americans with Disabilities Act (ADA) of 1990. To be considered "disabled" under the ADA, an individual must have a physical or mental impairment that substantially limits one or more major life activities, have a record of such an impairment, or be regarded as having such an impairment. A qualified individual with a disability is one who can perform the "essential functions of the job" with or without "reasonable accommodation."

The Age Discrimination in Employment Act of 1967, with its various amendments, prohibits discrimination on the basis of age for all individuals older than 40 years of age. In addition, as is the case with each of these other federal laws, this legislation prohibits retaliation against age claimants. Age claims filed with the EEOC have risen sharply in the last few years as a result of increased layoffs and our aging population.

Executive orders 11246 and 11375 are the source for major regulations for affirmative action. They require that government contractors not discriminate on the basis of these protected classifications and require government contractors to take affirmative steps to ensure that individuals are employed without regard to their protected status. In addition, contractors must recruit members of protected classifications for jobs where they have been previously excluded, and noncompliance can result in the loss of government contacts. The regulations are outlined in Revised Order No. 4 issued by the Office of Federal Contract Compliance Programs of the U.S. Department of Labor.

In addition to these federal laws and regulations, most states have specific anti-discrimination laws that apply to employers operating in those states. Prudent employers are familiar with these laws as well.

Hiring Practices

Effective hiring practices necessarily focus on hiring the best qualified candidates. Of equal importance to the nurse manager should be the objective to avoid legal traps in the web of employment legislation. Managers who base their hiring decisions on job-related criteria will be in the best position to discourage or defend challenges of discrimination.

There are many things a nurse manager can do to effectively avoid discrimination claims in the hiring process. The recruiting program can reach out to a variety of sources for job candidates to ensure equal opportunity and access. Recruitment materials can portray diverse job candidates. The employer's application should request information that is strictly job-related. Selection criteria must be job-related; pre-employment testing and assessments require standardization and validation; and the selection process should be consistently and fairly used for all job candidates to avoid charges of preference or discrimination (Fisher & Phillips, 1999).

The employment interview is one of the most common selection tools in the hiring process, yet it is fraught with legal pitfalls to the unwary manager. There are areas of inquiry in an employment interview (and on the application) that a hiring manager always should avoid (Nail & Scharinger, 1998). A structured, job-based interview guide and process helps avoid unacceptable inquiries such as the ones found in Table 15-1.

Negligent Hiring

If an employee injures someone during the course of his or her employment, the employer may be subject to a state law negligent hiring claim. For example, a hospital may be sued because one of its employees assaults or harms a patient or a member of a patient's family. The claim may be successful if the employer failed to reasonably investigate the background of the employee prior to hire and the accused employee is later found to have a criminal history of assault.

Table 15-1. Unacceptable Employment Inquiries

Topic	Inquiry
Age	Except to ensure that the individual is 18 years of age or older, age is a Bona Fide Occupational Qualification (BFOQ).
Race or color	There are no acceptable questions for race or color.
National origin/citizenship/place of birth	It is acceptable to ask applicants if they are eligible to work in the United States.
Marital status	It is acceptable to ask if an applicant's records are under a different name.
Religion	It generally is not acceptable to ask about religious preference.
Child care/number of dependents	Avoid questions about these topics that are primarily directed to female applicants and are not job-related.
Housing	Questions about where applicants live or if they own their home can be discriminatory.
Credit record	It is specifically unlawful to discriminate against job applicants or employees with a history of bankruptcy.
Arrest record	It is permissible to ask about a job applicant's criminal history of convictions for felonies.
Physical data	It is not acceptable to ask an applicant about physical limitations or an applicant's weight or height.
Medical background/workers' compensation	Job-related medical examinations and certain disability-related inquiries are only acceptable following the acceptance of a conditional job offer. Managers should consult human resource professionals or legal counsel for specific advice prior to making post-offer disability-related inquiries.
Military service	Questions about an applicant's military training or education related to the job are acceptable.

It is advisable to include several steps of investigation into the background of an applicant in the hiring process to avoid potential negligent hiring claims. Criminal and consumer background checks may be lawfully conducted on applicants, with appropriate applicant authorization and full compliance by the company with the Federal Fair Credit Reporting Act, as well as applicable and specific law. Potential employers should rely only on records of relevant convictions and not on arrest records when making adverse employment decisions based on criminal activity. Careful, thorough references from previous employers can be another excellent source for verifying an applicant's background. It is advisable to verify education and to question gaps in an applicant's background.

Employee Rights

Various federal and state employment laws grant numerous employee entitlements or rights in all aspects of the employment relationship. With the wide publicity of successful court challenges, employees increasingly demand their rights in the workplace. It is important for employers to delineate employee and management rights in their employee publications, policy handbooks, and employee relations programs.

Attendance and Time Off

Employees certainly consider their need for leave or time off to be an entitlement and challenge employers' absence management programs. With the passage of the Federal Americans with Disabilities Act (ADA) in 1990 and the Federal Family and Medical Leave Act (FMLA) in 1993, an employer's lawful ability to limit employee absenteeism and requests for time off from work for illness-related issues was greatly restricted. Employers easily fall into legal traps created by the interplay and contradictions of ADA, FMLA, and state workers' compensation laws. However, nurse managers can employ good absence management practices that are consistent with these laws, provided they are in policy format, widely communicated, and consistently applied. A clear, uniformly enforced absenteeism policy also may help establish that attendance is an essential function of many jobs in health care for ADA purposes (Fisher & Phillips, 1999).

Family and Medical Leave Act

The basic rights of employees under FMLA to take time off from work to care for themselves, their child at birth, adoption, or during a qualifying illness, or for other specific family members who are ill are generally known. However, the pitfalls in this legislation are not so well understood. FMLA is taking on increasing importance in employment-related litigation. It is imperative that all managers understand and comply with FMLA and related leave laws.

FMLA requires covered employers (employers who employ 50 or more employees within a 75-mile radius) to provide eligible employees with up to 12 weeks of unpaid leave during a 12-month period for specific situations. FMLA ensures that employee's benefits are maintained and their jobs protected during the qualifying leave. Employers also are prohibited from retaliating or otherwise discriminating against employees who exercise their rights to FMLA leave.

Not all employees are entitled to FMLA provisions. Eligible employees should have worked for their employer for at least 12 cumulative months at the date beginning the leave and should have worked at least 1,250 hours during the preceding 12-month period. A part-time employee must be working at least 24 hours per week to meet this minimum number of hours. Eligible employees may take the leave for the birth of a child or for the placement of a child with the employee for adoption or foster care, for their own serious health condition, or to care for a spouse, child, or parent with a serious health condition as certified by a healthcare provider (Tysse, 1993).

A challenging area of this law is identifying covered "serious health conditions." When an employee is home ill with influenza, for example, it is not always clear if his or her time off is covered by FMLA. FMLA defines as serious any illness, injury, impairment, or physical or mental condition that involves either inpatient care (hospitalization) or continuing treatment by a healthcare provider and a period of incapacity of at least three consecutive calendar days or a regimen of continuing care such as chemotherapy. If the employee's flu symptoms develop into pneumonia or are complicated by another condition, his or her healthcare provider is likely to provide the required FMLA medical certification.

Employee notice obligations under the FMLA are minimal; when leave is foreseeable, such as for a pregnancy, employees are required to provide their supervisors with 30 days advance notice. Typically, the leave for serious illnesses is not foreseeable, and the employee must provide notice "as practicable." A more serious challenge for the employer is the requirement for notifying employees of their rights. FMLA procedures require that employers specifically designate the employee's time off as FMLA and advise them of their rights and obligations under this law. Once an employer is aware of a potentially FMLA qualifying event, the employer is required to notify the employee of their rights to job-protected leave. Employers also should adopt specific procedures for requesting that applicable employees obtain certification of the need and duration of the leave from their healthcare provider and provide a confidential review of the medical information. For sample notices and forms, see Appendices B–F.

The FMLA regulations require only unpaid leave; however, many employers require employees to use company-provided paid leave concurrently with the unpaid FMLA leave. This is allowed under the FMLA. Once the paid leave is exhausted, the FMLA leave is changed to unpaid leave. The leave can legally be used intermittently, stretched out over weeks and months to total 12 weeks. It is important that employers publish their policies about the coordination of the leave provisions and apply them consistently across the workforce.

Workers' Compensation

Workers' compensation is a workplace accident insurance program that provides medical and income benefits to employees injured on the job. The workers' compensation system is regulated by states whose legislatures establish systems and procedures to compensate injured workers. Workers' compensation laws are state-specific and can vary widely. In addition, most states have laws that prohibit discrimination or retaliation against individuals for filing workers' compensation claims (Rogers, 1994).

For employers to comply with the applicable state workers' compensation laws, it is critical for management to establish procedures for employees to report all injuries, even those that appear to be minor, to their supervisor. For health care, this covers needle sticks and lifting injuries, in particular. Initially, injured employees should complete an incident form and should be assessed for treatment, often by an employee health nurse. For serious injuries, employees should be referred to panel physicians listed on required postings for follow-up care and treatment. Workers' compensation systems also will provide for income benefits for time lost from work for the seriously injured or ill employee.

Controlling the incidents and spiraling costs of workers' compensation is primarily a responsibility of direct supervisors and managers. The nurse manager can actively reduce workers' compensation costs in the healthcare work site. Nurse managers should provide all employees with accurate, up-to-date job descriptions detailing their duties and train all employees to be safety conscious in the workplace. Include safety compliance on job descriptions and employee evaluations. It is vital that all supervisors clearly require employees to report workplace injuries immediately and follow up with human resources to coordinate compliance with overlapping requirements under ADA and FMLA.

Dismissal/Termination

The traditional at-will doctrine in the United States means that the employer and the employee enter into the employment relationship expecting that their relationship could be terminated at any time, for any reason, or for no reason at all. The doctrine of "at will" employment is accepted in some states, although eliminated by state law in other states (known as "right to work states"). Even among those non- "right to work states," the doctrine of "at-will" employment has been slowly eroding as a result of the increased legal challenges in the workplace. Today, if a manager dismisses an employee, there are likely to be objections and threats of a lawsuit if the employee feels their "rights" and "due process" were overlooked in the dismissal.

The fundamental requirements for fair and defensible disciplinary action are documentation and consistency. It is imperative for employers to apply consistent standards to their discipline and discharge practices for all groups of employees. However, consistency with established policies is always balanced with a review of the employment record of the employee, understanding of any extenuating personal problems that led to the employee's actions, and a review of the reasonableness of the action (Falcone, 1999).

Effective discipline and discharge procedures require documentation (see Appendices B–F). Carefully prepared disciplinary documents are persuasive evidence of an employer's efforts to be fair and offer due process. Too often employers are afraid to discharge employees because they fear subsequent litigation, or they have not taken the time for documenting the actions. Essential steps in an effective and defensible discipline and discharge process are found in Table 15-2.

Table 15-2. Steps in a Discipline and Discharge Process	
Step	**Action**
1	Establish clear expectations for employees, including job expectations in a job description, company policies in the staff handbook, and posted rules or policies in memoranda or staff meetings.
2	Document all problems with specific, objective, and factual information.
3	Communicate directly, honestly, and constructively with employees at each stage in the disciplinary process. Follow up performance problems with timely coaching, counseling, and progressive discipline discussions.
	(Continued on next page)

Step	Action
| Table 15-2. Steps in a Discipline and Discharge Process *(Continued)*	
4	Include the perspective of other relevant employees or individuals in the investigation process related to the alleged performance problem, after giving the employee a chance to present his or her side of the story.
5	Do not wait until ready to discharge an employee to first advise the employee of performance issues.
6	Be consistent in personnel disciplinary actions and be sure that all employees are consistently held to the appropriate performance standards.
7	Establish a process for an "appeal" of the disciplinary decision, as this grievance opportunity might avoid formal administrative charges or expensive litigation.

A discharge that is a surprise to the healthcare employee is one that likely did not follow these recommendations, and "surprise" discharges increase the likelihood of expensive litigation. Before an employee is discharged for poor performance, the manager should be able to answer the questions in Figure 15-1 affirmatively.

Figure 15-1. Managerial Questions Prior to Discharge Process

- Was the performance expectation established and documented with the employee?
- Was the standard consistently applied to all employees in the work group?
- Was the employee properly assessed, trained, and coached?
- Did the employee have sufficient time to correct and improve performance?
- Is there sufficient supporting documentation of the performance problem, as well as adherence to these steps?

It is important that employees be treated with dignity in the disciplinary process. Too often employees deserving of disciplinary action contest with outside litigation because they are angry about their treatment. Discharging a difficult employee in anger can result in unintended consequences. Discharge and disciplinary actions are never easy, but they are less disruptive when the manager gives the employee opportunities to be fairly heard, treats all with respect, and provides appeal options. It is recommended that employers employ a process to remove an employee from the workplace while postponing the decision to terminate for a few days to conduct a review of all the facts (Fisher & Phillips, 1999).

Equal Employment Opportunity Employer

The first step in filing a lawsuit alleging discrimination is the filing of a charge of discrimination on the basis of a protected classification with the EEOC. Before disgruntled employees or applicants can sue an employer in court for alleged violations of a federal law prohibiting illegal discrimination claims, they must have their allegations reviewed by the EEOC and receive a "Notice of Right to Sue" from the government agency (U.S. EEOC, 1997). It is therefore critical that all employers take the filing of an EEOC charge very seriously, thoroughly investigate the accusations, and provide a formal response to the EEOC with help of counsel.

Under federal protections, an employee has the right to file a "Notice of Charge of Discrimination" with the EEOC within 180 days of the alleged discriminatory action (U.S. EEOC, 2004). The employer must receive a copy of the allegations, which is provided by the EEOC. What follows is typically a long process for investigating the claims. The employer's first step is to prepare the company's response to the charge, referred to as the "statement of position," and provide related documentation to the EEOC investigator. Typically, the investigator reviews this statement with the charging party and may investigate further by asking additional questions of the employer or conduct an on-site investigation or fact-finding visit in which the investigator interviews key witnesses. At the conclusion of the process, the EEOC investigator will either attempt to settle the dispute or will end the investigation by making his or her determination concerning whether discrimination exists and providing the employee a Notice of Right to Sue. In some rare (but often newsworthy) cases, the EEOC will decide to litigate a case in federal court on behalf of the charging party.

Prompt response and investigation of the allegations by the employer provide a chance for early resolution. The investigation is normally conducted by the human resources department or by an attorney, with careful attention to confidentiality, impartiality, and thorough fact finding. If it is concluded during the investigation that unlawful discrimination occurred, the employer has an early chance to correct the matter and settle the charge. It is also important for the employer to avoid retaliation with an employee who has filed a charge (as such retaliation is illegal, pursuant to the anti-discrimination laws) and conduct the investigation above reproach.

Labor Law and Employee Grievances

The National Labor Relations Act (NLRA) protects an employee's right to organize for union representation and prohibits discrimination against employees who engage in organizational activities. The NLRA mandates the right of employees to join unions and bargain collectively with their employer on matters concerning working conditions such as compensation, hours of work, benefits, and various workplace issues. Employers are specifically prohibited under this legislation from interfering with employees' rights under the law and can be charged with an "unfair labor practice" reviewed by the governing board, the National Labor Relations Board (NLRB), for any such perceived interference. The NLRB holds hearings; decides the merits of charges brought by employees, unions, or employers; and prescribes remedies when violations of the NLRA are found (U.S. Department of Labor, 2003).

Nurse managers need to recognize that labor law provisions also can apply to nonunion workforces. Nonunion employees who engage in "concerted activities," such as a group of two or more employees who protest a workplace practice, cannot be dismissed for staging the protest. Similarly, there have been contradictory decisions by the NLRB about the rights of nonunion employees to have representation in an interview meeting held to obtain information from the employee as part of an investigation (but not a disciplinary meeting). Check with counsel or human resources before proceeding with an investigatory meeting if employees insist on a witness (Bland & Knox, 2000).

Employee grievances and complaints arise in union and nonunion workplaces alike. The collective bargaining contracts in unionized workplaces have traditionally been the source for established grievance procedures to resolve workplace disputes. The union contract spells out the specific grievance procedure for represented employees with little flexibility. The multi-step process generally begins with a written grievance submitted to a supervisor and ends with lengthy mediation or arbitration. In nonunion workplaces, there is an even greater need for structured processes to resolve workplace issues.

Managers in nonunion environments have more latitude to create and set out their complaint procedure, preferably in employee policies (Blankenship, 2002). These written procedures also will incorporate progressive steps, starting with meeting with immediate supervisors and moving through subsequent steps with specified time frames. The primary objective of every step in the process is to provide a fair and impartial opportunity for both parties to resolve their issues and avoid costly litigation.

Both union and nonunion work environments are increasingly turning to alternative dispute resolution (ADR) programs to reduce the time and expense of employee grievances. A number of different types of ADR are available for internal use in a company, such as arbitration, peer review panels, mediation, and ombudsmen (Gamlen & Sommer, 2000). In arbitration, disputing parties present their cases in an adjudicatory process to a third party hired to hear the dispute and render a binding decision. In contrast, the resolution presented in mediation is nonbinding, and the primary role of the third party is to facilitate communications between opposing parties. Another adjudicatory process is a peer review process that replaces the external arbitrator or mediator with a panel of company managers and employees. An organization with an ombudsman program designates a neutral individual to investigate and resolve complaints between parties in the organization. The EEOC also offers mediation and arbitration services to resolve discrimination claims.

One of the by-products of an effective grievance or ADR process is improvement in the skills and performance of managers. Nurse supervisors, aware that their decisions and actions are subject to review by next steps in a complaint process, will be more responsive and attentive to their employees' concerns and ensure that their actions are fair and consistent.

Nurse managers work in an increasingly complex workplace made more complicated by the web of laws and regulations governing their actions with employees. The successful nurse manager recognizes that investing the time and energy necessary to create a compliant workplace does not get in the way of his or her core job but *is* a key part of the job. Without time-consuming and costly litigation interfering in their roles as clinical managers, they have more time to devote to their professional responsibilities. It is imperative that the nurse manager have working knowledge of the national labor laws as well as the employment laws of the state in which they practice. This knowledge will aid the manager in practicing fair labor standards.

References

Bland, T.S., & Knox, D.P. (2000). *The employee's right to a representative during an investigatory interview.* Retrieved October 24, 2003, from http://www.shrm.org/whitepapers/documents/61709.asp

Blankenship, W.A. (2002). *Handling grievances in a non-union environment.* Retrieved September 27, 2003, from http://www.shrm.org/hrresources/whitepapers_published/CMS_00081.asp

Falcone, P. (1999, June). *Mastering progressive discipline and structuring terminations.* Paper presented at the Society for Human Resources Management Annual Conference, Atlanta, GA.

Fisher & Phillips LLP. (1999). *Employment discrimination.* Atlanta, GA: Author.

Gamlen, C., & Sommer, R. (2000). *Developing an alternative dispute resolution program.* Retrieved September 27, 2003, from http://www.shrm.org/hrresources/whitepapers_published/CMS_00079.asp

Nail, T., & Scharinger, D. (1998). *Guidelines on interview and employment application questions.* Retrieved October 10, 2003, from http://www.shrm.org/hrresources/whitepapers_published/CMS_000341.asp

Rogers, B. (1994). *Occupational health nursing: Concepts and practice.* Philadelphia: Saunders.

Tysse, G. (1993). *So you think you understand the family and medical leave act?* Retrieved September 13, 2001, from http://www.shrm.org/whitepapers/documents/defalt.asp?page=61565.asp

U.S. Department of Labor. (1964). *Title VII, Civil Rights Act of 1964.* Retrieved July 30, 2004, from http://www.dol.gov/oasam/regs/statues/2000e-16.htm

U.S. Department of Labor. (2003). *Major laws and regulations enforced by the Department of Labor.* Retrieved July 30, 2004, from http://www.nlrb.gov/nlrb/home/default.asp

U.S. Equal Employment Opportunity Commission. (1997). *Laws enforced by the EEOC.* Retrieved July 30, 2004, from http://www.eeoc.gov/policy/laws.html

U.S. Equal Employment Opportunity Commission. (2004). *Filing a charge of employment discrimination.* Retrieved August 31, 2004, from http://www.eeoc.gov/charge/index.html

Washington, G. (1999). *Attitudes of success.* Glendale Heights, IL: Great Quotations.

Labor Relations and Collective Bargaining

16

Mary Dee McEvoy, PhD, RN, AOCN®

A major role of managers is the development of relations with those who labor or work for them. The American Heritage Dictionary (1994) defined labor as "physical or mental exertion, a specific task, work for wages . . . to strive painstakingly" (p. 467). Relations is defined as "a logical or natural association between two or more things; the connection of people by blood or marriage; kinship" (American Heritage Dictionary, p. 695). Indeed, the emphasis for nursing leaders should be on the development of relationships, because it is often the lack of relationships, or trust in those relationships, that leads to collective bargaining efforts. Often, managers view collective bargaining efforts of their staff as problematic, a "we" versus "them" type of mentality. However, it is the relationship between the nurses and the managers that allows creative problem solving in the realm of patient care to flourish. In health care, issues of importance to the worker include wages, benefits, job security, and the work environment itself. The manager who understands the needs of nurses and tries to create an environment conducive to quality patient care will reap the benefits in strong, healthy staff relationships.

Collective bargaining provides a structure for employees to negotiate with their employing institution on issues of importance to them. Historically, collective bargaining has been perceived as appropriate for blue-collar workers or industrial workers around such issues as wages and benefits. Professionals, such as nurses, were viewed as providing a service to society and interested only in quality patient care issues and, as such, were above collective bargaining. The debate of the appropriateness of professionals such as nurses to organize in a union was waged in the 1970s and 1980s. Today, the debate is somewhat irrelevant because there are unionized healthcare options for healthcare workers; nurses, pharmacists, and other professionals are unionized. In contract negotiations, the nurse manager plays a key role in supporting the staff and interpreting and implementing the contract fairly. This chapter will provide an overview of the role of nursing leadership in a collective bargaining healthcare environment.

The National Labor Relations Board (NLRB), an independent federal agency created by Congress to administer the National Labor Relations Act (NLRA), governs relations between employers and employees in the United States. The purpose of the NLRA is to "define and protect the rights of employees and employers, to encourage collective bargaining, and to eliminate certain practices on the part of labor and management that are harmful to the general welfare" (NLRB, 1997, p.1). The act was created to decrease employee strife, thus enhancing the full production of work in the United States. The government is interested in the full production of work because it is essential to U.S. commerce and the welfare of America. Originally intended for the private industrial sector, in which the smooth flow of commerce would be disrupted in the presence of worker strife, the NLRA was amended in 1974 by Public Health Law 93-360 to allow healthcare organizations to bargain collectively. Thus, the NLRA outlines the rights of employees, collective bargaining, unfair labor practices of employers, and unfair labor practices of labor organizations. The NLRB, charged with overseeing the implementation of the act, has published a guide, which is available on its Web site (www.nlrb.gov). This document provides the nurse manager with a broad understanding of the laws governing the rights of workers. Figure 16-1 outlines the laws that drive employee and employer relations.

Figure 16-1. Laws Related to Collective Bargaining	
National Labor Relations Act (NLRA) 1935	Governs relations between employees and employers in the private sector Gives employees the right to bargain collectively and to strike Defines unfair labor practices Creates the National Labor Relations Board
Taft/Hartley Labor Law 1947	Defines supervisory personnel according to specific functions (hire, fire, promote, transfer, lay off, discharge, discipline)
Public Health Law 93-360 1974	Amended the NLRA to include nonprofit hospitals and other healthcare institutions Added longer rules for notifications of intent if no agreement is reached (60 days) and longer notification of intent to strike (10 days)

Employee and Employer Rights

The rights of workers are outlined in the NLRA and include the right to self-organize, form a union, bargain collectively, and strike. Workers also have the right to refrain from such activities. The act delineates conditions under which strikes are deemed unlawful. Unfair labor practices of both employers and unions are given. Threatening employees with loss of jobs or benefits if they organize into a union is an example of an unfair labor practice of an employer. Picketing in ways that prevent nonstriking employees from entering the institution, violence on the picket lines, and threats to nonstriking employees are all unfair practices of unions. The NLRA also outlines the pragmatic requirements for strikes such as timing of strike notice and collective bargaining activities. Management rights include the right to direct the workforce, hire and discharge employees, and establish shifts and working conditions.

Union Organizing

Work situations that cause employees to contemplate formal union organization usually relate to the overall feeling of being treated unfairly. Because nursing is a profession, reasons for unionization also relate to inadequate control over the practice of nursing. Roberts, Cox, Baldwin, and Baldwin (1985) surveyed 2,000 nurses regarding their feelings toward unionization. They found three categories related to a propensity to unionize: benefits, salary, and working conditions. Numerof and Abrams (1984) stated that the primary source of dissatisfaction includes limited autonomy in the nursing role, lack of communication with management, exclusion from decision making, and compensation. Finally, Clark, Clark, Day, and Shea (2000) found that nurses with a negative perception of climate were more likely to vote for a union. In this study, a negative climate was correlated with restructuring and mergers. These studies demonstrate the essential role of managers in the creation of an environment conducive to nursing practice.

Thus, lack of understanding by supervisors, lack of clear communication about institutional changes, lack of sound personnel policies, lack of appropriate working conditions, and lack of competitive wages and benefits all make employees feel that the institution is not concerned with their welfare and make them susceptible to the organizing efforts by unions. The current state of constant change in healthcare organizations makes employees feel particularly vulnerable, leading to an increase in activity related to unionization. Only 17% of the nation's 2.2 million nurses belong to unions, thus providing a ripe area for union activity (Greene, 1998). In a study of 387 union certification elections conducted by the NLRB from January 1999 to December 2001, 60% of the unions won the elections (Palthe, 2003). Thus, it can be anticipated that union organizing will continue and, indeed, accelerate as employees in healthcare institutions continue to feel dissatisfied with their environment of care.

The American Organization of Nurse Executives (1993) outlined the steps that managers can take to create a healthy work environment, thus decreasing the likelihood of unionization. These steps include emphasizing staff retention, empowering caregivers to provide quality patient care, making sure that personnel roles and responsibilities are clearly understood, instituting fair methods for evaluating employees, disciplining and rewarding employees, recognizing employees as valuable assets, supporting them in their work, and ensuring that nurses have a voice in decision making.

Astute nursing leaders will recognize signs of union activity, including an increase in the number of complaints, unexplained changes in staff attitude and confrontations with managers, rumors, employees congregating outside the institution either before or after work, and the use of words such as "power" and "employee rights" (American Organization of Nurse Executives, 1993). According to the NLRA, institutions are not permitted to retaliate against employees who engage in union activities, nor are they permitted to interfere with union organizing. However, managers are permitted to tell their staff how they feel about unions and how unions would affect the hospital. Figure 16-2 lists actions that managers may take when they suspect union organizing efforts. Managers who recognize behaviors that indicate potential union activities should report those to their directors and chief nursing officer. They, in turn, will report it to the human relations professionals in the institution, who will monitor the activity closely for any violations related to the NLRB. Costello (2002) suggested that institutions perform a "vulnerability" audit to examine how vulnerable they are to union activity. He suggested examining employee satisfaction measures and addressing those areas that need improvement.

Figure 16-2. Nurse Manager Behaviors Related to Union Activity

Permitted	Not Permitted
• Share personal views regarding the effect of unions on the hospital. • Emphasize the goals of the institution. • State the hospital is opposed to unionization. • Question the effect the union will have on patient care. • Share your experiences with unions. • Point out the risks of unionization.	• Make threats or promises to staff regarding unionization. • Retaliate in any way against staff.

Note. Based on information from American Organization of Nurse Executives, 1993.

Collective Bargaining

Healthcare institutions that are unionized operate under a union contract that is negotiated on a regular basis. The contract covers salaries, fringe benefits, and working conditions. These issues are negotiated between management and the union representatives. Contract negotiations often are adversarial, with each side taking a position on an issue and negotiating until both sides give in a little and an agreement is reached. This method is called positional bargaining. Recognizing that positional bargaining is often contentious and has harmful effects on long-term relationships, other methods have begun to emerge. Fisher, Ury, and Patton (1991) stated that arguing over position produces unwise agreements because more attention is paid to the position itself rather than the underlying consensus, is inefficient, and endangers ongoing relationships. They offered an alternative method of negotiation called principled negotiation, in which the focus is on the principles to be negotiated.

In principled negotiation, one must separate the people from the problems, focus on interests rather than positions, generate a variety of possibilities before deciding what to do, and base the result on an objective standard. In separating the people from the problems, it is important to pay attention to perception, emotion, and communication. For example, you must refrain from blaming the other side for your problems, put yourselves in their shoes, discuss each other's perceptions, and be sure that each side has a stake in the outcome. It is important to understand and recognize everyone's emotions and refrain from reacting to emotional outbursts. In principled negotiation, the focus is on interests not positions. The authors (Fisher, Ury, & Patton, 1991) stated that the most powerful interests are basic human needs such as security, economic well-being, a sense of belonging, recognition, and control over one's life. Often behind opposed positions lie shared interests. The challenge rests on finding these shared interests and focusing on them. Next, options are generated for mutual gain. In this phase, it is important to separate inventing and creating options from deciding on an option. Finally, when a decision is made regarding an option, objective criteria should be established for evaluation.

Conceptually, the positional method of bargaining is on one end of the collective bargaining spectrum, and the principled method is on the other end. The Federal Mediation and Conciliation Service (FMCS) recognized that there is a large area between the two spectrums and developed two additional methods (Brommer, Buckingham, & Loeffler, 2003). The model of principle-based negotiation that the FMCS used was called the PAST model (Barrett, 1996) and included four areas: principles, assumptions, steps, and techniques. The principles are to focus on interests rather than personalities or positions, find a mutual gain, and use a fair method to determine outcome. The assumptions, steps, and techniques further define this model. However, the FMCS mediators identified several negative aspects of this model, including the vagueness of the issues that were placed on the table, the burden of identifying unlimited options for each issue, and the propensity for dealing with economic issues that last after relationships have been built. They developed two variations on the principle method: modified traditional bargaining and enhanced cooperative negotiation. The model closest to the traditional positioning model is enhanced cooperative negotiation, in which the focus remains on issues rather than positions. The issues are prepared, proposals for managing the issues are developed and exchanged with each party, and, only then, traditional bargaining begins.

The human resource experts in the institution will decide the method of contract negotiation. However, even if positional negotiation is the method chosen, the ideas underlying principled negotiation are useful. Looking beyond the position to the interest will be helpful in determining the core issues for each of the negotiators. Open and frank discussion assists in identifying mutual interests. Often, nurses can communicate and resonate about quality of care in a shared way. Identifying the issues that impact quality of care is important for all parties in a negotiation. Demonstrating respect for all sides and all people in the negotiation process will facilitate the development of long-term relationships. It is helpful to remember that you will be working with the other side as you implement the contract that is finally signed. A beneficial, trusting relationship is important in implementation.

As a manager, you may be part of the negotiation process. The chief nursing officer of the organization, in consultation with the human resources expert, will make decisions on who is part of the negotiating team. If selected as a member of the team, it is important to prepare for negotiations by knowing the contract fully, familiarizing yourself with the issues that have been important to the staff since the previous negotiations, and familiarizing yourself with the negotiating team. One of the most important aspects as a member of the negotiating team is self-awareness.

Be aware of how you respond to stress and emotion. Negotiations can generate strong emotions in all parties involved. It is important to be aware of your response to the emotions and learn to objectify the issues. The author of this section recalled a personal experience of sitting at the negotiating table. The setting was the traditional method of each side being on opposite sides of the table. The union side was presenting an argument for a position, and the author embarrassingly stepped in with, "OK, we understand that . . . let's move on." The leader of the other side invited the author to join them on their side of the table. Thankfully, it was seen as a funny faux pas, and everyone laughed, thus releasing some tension. However, it also was a learning moment in which the author learned the importance of being patient with the process. It is important that the team is cohesive on the issues, and time must be taken for the development of this cohesiveness. Contract negotiations require considerable time and commitment. Be mindful of the energy required to take those steps you need to take to create energy, such as exercising and getting rest and relaxation.

Cela (1989) outlined three phases of negotiations. The first phase is establishing the bargaining climate, including the time schedule and routine. The union also presents their proposals or issues in the first phase. The second phase involves clarification of the intent of the proposals. The third phase involves the introduction of proposals from management. The meetings that follow focus on negotiating the proposals, with ultimate agreement on language for the contract. Many individual meetings occur outside the formal process as input is sought from the leadership team and data are gathered.

One of the most important parts of the contract, yet often overlooked, is the section on management rights. It is usually one of the last sections and is often quite short. Many of the areas delineated in the NLRA are included in this section, such as directing and assigning duties to the workforce. There are statements regarding discontinuing or reorganizing departments. The importance of this section cannot be underestimated, as it retains the right of leaders to define and carry out the mission of the institution. Nurse leaders should be fully aware of this section.

Managers not directly involved in the formal negotiations still have a role to play in the process. It is important that you attend to employee morale issues and concerns. Rumors may abound relating to what is happening at the bargaining table, and managers must continue to focus on patient care. Remember the primary mission of nursing is relating to patient care. Immersing oneself in patient care activities can help the staff and management forget the tension and conflict related to bargaining.

Strike

The NLRA requires that all parties bargain in good faith, but the law does not require that all parties reach an agreement. When agreement cannot be reached, a strike becomes inevitable. The law requires that the union give formal notice of intent to strike. FMCS must be kept informed of the progress of negotiations and of intent to strike. As outlined in Public Health Law 93-360, the Health Care Act of 1974, the intent to strike notice in healthcare institutions must be given 10 days prior to the strike. This requirement permits the organization to develop and institute plans for the continuation of patient care during the strike. FMCS pays close attention to the striking institution and the impact of the strike on the health and welfare of the community served by the striking institution. This role is important because the health of the community must be preserved.

Nurses do not take the decision to strike lightly. Forfa (1987) asked five nurses, who handled a strike differently, their opinions of what caused the strike. The nurses cited anger, powerlessness, lack of being seen as professionals, understaffing, and poor wages. The nurses who returned to work during the strike did so out of lack of money. All parties suffer economically during a strike. Nurses risk loss of pay, insurance coverage, and the threat of being replaced. They also suffer the risk of being unable to return to work, as the institution may need to downsize to accommodate changes in occupancy during a strike. There may be a transition period before full census is reached, thus impacting the closure of units and the need for fewer staff. The institution suffers economic loss as well with the need to implement a strike contingency plan. Additionally, the census will certainly drop, as patients are reluctant to seek care at a healthcare institution experiencing a strike.

The chief nursing officer and other leaders in the organization will begin strike contingency planning long before a 10-day notice of intent to strike. Forman and Powell (2003) outlined five areas that need to be addressed in a good strike plan. They include patient care, safety and security, access to/from the facility, deliveries, and communication. The essential areas of patient care need to be identified by the senior leaders in the organization. Will some services be closed? Is a decrease in census expected, thus mandating closure of patient care areas? How will the staffing plan change? Will additional staff be brought in from outside agencies to supplement the nonstriking staff? How will these relationships be managed? Will volunteers be useful? Safety and security is a major concern. Access to the institution is limited and entrances are closed. How is the safety of the staff ensured? How is the working staff protected from the effects of the picketers?

Supplies are stored long before a potential strike to reduce the need for deliveries. If deliveries are needed, consideration must be given to the type of deliveries. For example, truck drivers might not cross picket lines in sympathy to the strikers. Thus, alternate methods of deliveries will need to be considered. Developing a strike contingency plan is costly in terms of actual dollars (storing supplies, reserving additional staff through agencies that service strikes) and in terms of the time required of all to develop the plan itself. It may feel strange to bargain in good faith coincident with developing a strike contingency plan.

Leading during a strike is one of the most difficult assignments of a nurse manager. Tensions are high and rumors are rampant. Vacations are cancelled, and all non-bargaining unit staff are expected to work over and above normal operating procedures. Through the fatigue and stress, the manager must lift the morale of those who are working while reassuring patients that they are receiving quality patient care. This is a most difficult time for patients with cancer. Figure 16-3 outlines some of the behaviors needed by a nurse manager during a strike. They depend on consistent and timely health care. Patients will be concerned that they will not get their treatment at the right time and that they might not get the right treatment, as nurses will be stressed and tired. Patients and family might feel abandoned by the nurses whom they have come to trust and afraid that they will not be cared for if they have an emergency. Symptom management often occurs through telephone calls and triage. The response time to phone messages may be prolonged, thus causing additional stress for the patients and families. The manager will need to constantly reassure patients that they will be given the best health care possible, while supporting both the striking nurses and nonstriking staff.

Figure 16-3. Nurse Manager Behaviors During a Strike

- Communicate clearly and often.
- Manage by walking around.
- Show appreciation to all caregivers.
- Be charismatic and energetic.
- Be supportive of strikers as well as nonstrikers.

Note. Based on information from Forman & Powell, 2003.

Attention must be given to relationships when the striking nurses return to work. Relationships between those who chose to work and those who chose to strike will be strained. Additionally, members of the team who are not nurses, such as aides, clerks, and other professionals, may be resentful and angry with the striking staff. They may have lost out on vacations and time off, missed family events because of the need to work and, undoubtedly, suffered stress and fatigue. Teamwork will begin at a new and different place after a strike. The rebuilding of all members of the team will require astute attention. Special help may be needed from experts in team building, such as specialists in organizational development. The nurse manager must listen and develop plans for intervention in order to begin a new unit of care.

Implementing the Contract

After the contract is signed, the next phase is implementation during the life of the contract. There may be dramatic changes or subtle ones. Changes in the type of shifts would be a major change in the contract. There is never total consensus on the issues agreed upon in negotiations. Thus, if shifts are changed from an 8-hour model to a 12-hour model, there will be some nurses who are in favor of the change and others who are not. Every nurse's life changes in some way when the hours of work are changed. Home responsibilities must be altered and negotiated. Thus, not only must the manager perform the labor-intensive work of creating the actual shift plan, but the emotions of the staff also must be managed. There will be happiness and relief alongside anger and resentment. All must be managed to implement the changes mandated in the contract.

Contracts provide guidance in how to handle disputes between employees and employers. It is essential that all managers handle the disputes according to contract guidelines. Personnel policies should be handled fairly and consistently. Unfairness and lack of consistency lead to grievances. When employees feel that they have been treated unfairly or the terms of the contract have been violated, they have the right to file a grievance.

The method for handling grievances is outlined in the contract. The grievance process usually consists of several steps in order to provide the opportunity for all parties to settle the dispute before resorting to mediation or arbitration. It is essential that the manager learn the grievance process outlined in the contract and become skilled in its implementation. Do not be reluctant to ask for assistance in this area. The human relations department may have specific classes in this area and also provide individual consultation. Julius (1988) provided guidance on the grievance process. He explained that the following information should be obtained.

- The article of the contract that has been violated
- In what way has the article been violated?
- What are the facts relative to the violation?
- What is the interpretation given to the contractual language and why?
- What is the resolution that is being sought?

In hearing a grievance, many of the recommendations given during the process of negotiation apply. For example, it is important to listen to the issue rather than the emotion surrounding the position. Consider the situation as objective information and view it objectively. It is crucial to settle the grievance consistently with other similar grievances. This can be difficult if the institution is large and there are many people who are the grievance officers. In that case, someone in human relations is responsible for keeping the facts and settlements of grievances consistent.

Grievances can move through several steps and still remain unresolved. In that situation, the next move is either mediation or arbitration. In mediation, an objective third party listens to the sides of the dispute and assists each side in understanding the positions and issues of the other side, usually in separate meetings. Mediation is not binding. Arbitration, on the other hand, is a binding process. In arbitration, a third party, the arbitrator, is assigned to resolve the dispute. Because the decision is binding, the decision to go to arbitration is a serious one involving many people in the organization. In most cases, human resource experts and legal counsel will participate in this decision with the chief nursing officer. The human resource specialist will consider the policies and procedures of all areas and departments in deciding to support the decision to arbitrate. The legal counsel will consider the likelihood of winning the case and the data needed to support the case. Nurse managers are key players during arbitration. The case is presented in a legal manner, and the manager will be guided through the process with the legal experts. A great amount of time and energy is devoted to this process, and support is needed for the managers undergoing arbitration.

Summary

Labor relations and collective bargaining can be viewed with disdain or embraced as a challenge. Because there are laws that govern the relationship between the employer and employee, it is essential that the nurse manager learns them and keeps informed of new developments. Figure 16-4 provides a list of resources for the nurse manager. Developing respect for the history of the labor movement and the fundamental purpose of the laws will serve to mitigate the feelings of anxiety and frustration that may arise relating to labor relations. A healthy work environment is built on a foundation of healthy relations with a common purpose: the provision of quality nursing care.

Figure 16-4. Internet Resources	
National Labor Relations Board (NLRB)	• www.nlrb.gov • Provides a guide to the National Labor Relations Act • Provides educational papers on labor issues
Federal Mediation and Conciliation Service	• www.fmcs.gov • Provides information on conflict management • Provides educational papers on collective bargaining and mediation
Healthcare Advisory Board Nursing Executive Watch	• www.advisory.com • "On Our Watch: Labor Relations" • Weekly electronic newsletter with information on strikes
American Hospital Association (AHA)	• www.hospitalconnect.com • Provides resources and information on hospitals and quality of care • Studies commissioned by the AHA are available as resources. • Statistics and data are available.
American Organization of Nurse Executives (AONE)	• www.aone.org • Provides resources and information for nursing leaders
Nursing Management	• www.blackwell-synergy.com • Department of Recruitment and Retention • Serves as a legal checkpoint
Journal of Nursing Administration	• www.lww.com • Workforce issues • Assists in management development
JONA's Healthcare, Law, Ethics and Regulation	• www.jonalaw.com • Provides legal briefs
AONE Voice of Nursing Leadership	• www.aone.org • Provides management tips for nurse leaders

References

American heritage dictionary (3rd ed.). (1994). New York: Dell Publishing.
American Organization of Nurse Executives. (1993). When work redesign prompts unionization activity. *Nursing Management, 24*(9), 36–38.

Barrett, J. (1996). *P.A.S.T. is the future—A model for interest-based collective bargaining that works!* (5th ed.). Falls Church, VA: Jerome Barrett and Sons.

Brommer, C., Buckingham, G., & Loeffler, S. (2003). Cooperative bargaining styles at the FMCS: A movement toward choices. Retrieved February 2, 2004, from http://www.fmcs.gov

Cela, M. (1989). Management rights in a unionized hospital. *Nursing Management, 20*(2), 82, 84.

Clark, D.A., Clark, P., Day, D., & Shea, D. (2000). The relationship between health care reform and nurses' interest in union representation: The role of workplace climate. *Journal of Professional Nursing, 16,* 92–96.

Costello, M. (2002). *Latest wave in organizing, agitating by unions likely to continue for years.* Retrieved January 24, 2004, from http://www.ahanews.com/ahanews/hospitalconnect/search/article.jsp?dcrpath=AHA/NewsStory_Article/data/AHANEWS2B63&domain=AHANEWS

Fisher, R., Ury, W., & Patton, B. (1991). *Getting to yes: Negotiating agreements without giving in* (2nd ed.). Boston: Houghton Mifflin.

Forfa, L. (1987). Strike: More than 2 sides. *American Journal of Nursing, 87,* 17–19.

Forman, H., & Powell, T. (2003). Managing during an employee walk-out. *Journal of Nursing Administration, 33,* 430–433.

Greene, J. (1998). Nurses' aid. *Hospitals and Health Networks, 72*(12), 38.

Julius, D. (1988). Managing in a unionized setting. *American Operating Room Journal, 48,* 1145–1150.

National Labor Relations Board. (1997). *Basic guide to the National Labor Relations Act.* Washington, DC: U.S. Government Printing Office. Retrieved January 5, 2004, from http://www.nlrb.gov

Numerof, R., & Abrams, M. (1984). Collective bargaining among nurses: Current issues and future prospects. *Health Care Management Review, 9,* 61–67.

Palthe, D. (2003). Union certification elections in nursing care facilities. *Health Care Management, 22,* 311–317.

Roberts, R., Cox, J., Baldwin, E., & Baldwin, J. (1985). What causes hospital nurses to unionize? *Nursing Forum, 22,* 22–30.

Performance Appraisals

Catherine Glennon, RN, BC, CNA, MHS, OCN®

"Performance appraisals are like seat belts. Everyone agrees they are a good idea, but lots of people find them awkward to use." (Grote, 1998, p. 52)

Performance appraisal, or evaluation of employees, is a process in which the performance of the employee is evaluated against standards. The process of assessing performance existed long before formal systems of evaluation were developed. Albrecht (1976) described how the Chinese instituted a civil service system in which all male citizens were tested prior to filling governmental leadership positions as early as 1000 BC. With the advent of tests and appraisal systems to assist with placing and maintaining men in appropriate positions during World War II, organizations adopted a philosophy and developed tools to begin formal evaluation processes in the United States. Job descriptions for nurses were in place as early as 1887, as shown in Figure 17-1 (Swansburg, 2002a). Much progress has been made in nursing since that time, as reflected in job descriptions today. However, even then the duties were clearly articulated and written in an objective language.

Figure 17-1. Excerpts From an 1887 Job Description of a Bedside Nurse

In addition to caring for your fifty patients, each bedside nurse will follow these regulations:
- Daily sweep and mop the floors of your ward; dust the patient's furniture and windowsills.
- Maintain an even temperature in your ward by bringing in a scuttle of coal for the day's business.
- The nurse's notes are important in aiding the physician's work. Make your pens carefully; you may whittle nibs to your individual tastes.
- The nurse who performs her labors, serves her patients and doctors faithfully and without fault for a period of 5 years will be given an increase by the hospital administration of $0.5 a day, providing there are no hospital debts that are outstanding.

Note. Based on information from Swansburg, 2002a.

Components inherent in a performance appraisal system are performance standards, job analysis, job description, job evaluation, and work classification. Each of these components are rigorously reviewed and analyzed by the hiring manager with the assistance of a human resource department or specialist. This process is required to develop the job description, in which an employee will be expected to perform outlined activities. Therefore, the actual appraisal is the comparison of existent job performance against the predetermined standards.

Organizations incorporate their mission and philosophy in the performance appraisal. Managers are accountable to operationalize the mission. Employees are accountable to understand the appraisal process. The philosophy of an organization will determine the method of evaluation—the degree by which the employee, or others besides the manager, will be involved in the review. Priorities defined by leadership should be evident in the categories outlined in the appraisal tool in addition to the ranking or weight associated with each performance factor.

Performance appraisal is a process, ongoing and dynamic, not just an annual event. This process serves as a mechanism to improve performance of the employee and thus ensure quality within the institution and the profession. It correlates with positive outcomes for the patients by ensuring safe, competent care.

There are many methods of completing performance appraisals. In the past, salary or merit increases were based on years of longevity or service regardless of the individual employee performance. Currently, most salary increases are in some way tied to productivity and performance of an employee. This makes it even more critical that biases are eliminated so the employee is not jeopardized. Regardless of the appraisal system selected, inherent in each method are rater biases and errors of the evaluator that distort the appraisal. The most common are the "halo effect" (judging the whole of a person's performance by some single aspect) and leniency (rating all performance areas too high in order to avoid creating ill will). Swansburg (2002a) outlined additional rater biases.

- "Horns"—Personal feelings causing negative effects
- Leniency-stringency error—Rater assigns extreme ratings of either poor or excellent.
- Similar-to-me error—Rater rates according to how he or she views himself or herself.
- Central tendency error—All ratings are at the middle of the scale.
- First impression error—Rater views early behavior that may be good or bad and rates all subsequent behaviors similarly.
  Grohar-Murray and DiCroce (2003) further described some biases.
- Problem distortion—When a single, poorly observed performance weighs more than good performances that went unobserved
- Sunflower effect—Rater grades everyone in the group the same based on overall group performance.
- Guessing error—Rater guesses about performance rather than recording that it is unknown.
- Rater temperament effect—Reflects variances in the degree of importance different raters assign to the same attribute

Performance Appraisal Systems

Manager Appraisal

Top-down or manager performance evaluations tend to be the most common and most effective because they involve the assessment of an employee by a direct manager.

Top-down reviews are most useful when given by the immediate supervisor—someone who works with that employee every day and knows his or her strengths, weaknesses, and areas for improvement. The manager review becomes less effective when given by a human resources manager or a remote supervisor who only has secondhand knowledge of work performance. This top-down process is very efficient because the evaluator collects the necessary data and input he or she feels are required. The method is not reliant on others to contribute, as with the peer review process. An offshoot of the manager performance appraisal is called a matrix review, where multiple managers rate the same employee. This is a good choice when the employee works for multiple managers or engages in various fixed-time length projects. One manager should be accountable for the appraisal and be known by the employee. All evaluators must know the behavior and performance of the appraisee to be accurate in their assessment. Therefore, the manager who works more directly with the employee should be the formal evaluator in the matrix approach and will incorporate the contributions and feedback of the other managers involved.

Self-Appraisal

Self-appraisal provides the appraisees an opportunity to construct a self-assessment that can highlight the discrepancies between how they see themselves and how their coworkers and managers view them. Self-appraisals are based on the idea that an employee is the most familiar with his or her own involvement and dedication. Optimally, employees assess their flaws and weaknesses so that they may be discussed with management and improvements can be made.

Most employees believe instinctively that they are performing at a level that is above average. According to Rondeau (1992), four out of five individuals feel they are performing at an above average level at the time of appraisal. Many individuals may not see their own faults or may not honestly assess themselves. Therefore, the appraisal should be directly correlated with desired performance in relationship to the objectives of the manager or organization. To reduce the amount of discrepancies this process may cause, self-appraisals should be used alongside other methods of performance appraisals, such as manager appraisal and peer review. Baruch (1996) discussed that discrepancies between self and other performance appraisal sources could be due to different appraisal methods, lack of objective measures, and employee concerns regarding the link between pay and performance. According to Grote (1998), managers should require employees to set goals for what they are going to do in the next year to make the organization more efficient, service-oriented, client-friendly, and admirable. After an individual self-evaluates and receives feedback from others, including peers and supervisors, the employee can assess areas of overlap and discrepancies in performance. This usually motivates appraisees to examine the areas that others feel they need to improve and to set goals for future development. Roberts (2003) described a governmental organization process and noted that participatory performance appraisal is an essential component of a fair and ethical evaluation of an employee's performance ". . . for employee career success, self-esteem and mental health" (p. 95).

The primary benefit of self-appraisal is that the employees have an opportunity to voice their thoughts, highlight their work behaviors, performance, and achievements, and define future goals and aspirations to succeed in the position or profession. It demonstrates to employees that their insight and feedback are valuable and that the manager is listening to the employee (see Figure 17-2).

Figure 17-2. Self-Evaluation Form

SELF EVALUATION OF_____, RN

DATE_____

This evaluation is for _____Mid-year _____Annual _____Other

Please attach additional information if necessary to answer the following. Information pertains to performance since last evaluation.

1. Major achievements since last evaluation:

2. Areas of your performance you would like to improve:

3. What additional skills, resources, or knowledge would help you more effectively perform your job or enhance your skill opportunities?

4. Define goals (specific final outcomes to be obtained) and objectives (specific steps to be taken to reach goals) that will be targeted by next evaluation:

We have discussed this self-evaluation on _____ (Date)

Signature_____, RN

Signature_____, RN Manager

Peer Review

Peer review is a process through which employees assess the performance of peers against predetermined standards. Clinical and interpersonal practices are evaluated as well as professional development. Subjectivity on the part of the manager decreases if observations and feedback include more than the supervisor's. Also, contact with the employee and direct observation by the manager may be limited because of varying shifts and responsibilities. By empowering staff to assess the peers with whom they work closely, the manager can deliver more comprehensive and objective reviews to his or her staff. Hotko and Van Dyke (1998), Roper and

Russell (1997), and Vuorinen, Tarkka, and Meretoja (2000) concluded that peer review develops professional leadership and autonomy and is a means of promoting nurses' professional development in collaboration with peers. This often takes place within the framework of a preceptorship, clinical ladder program, and performance evaluation. Peer reviews often have a high level of worker acceptance and involvement; they tend to be stable, task-relevant, and accurate. By helping peers to understand each other and by airing concerns in a nonthreatening manner, peer reviews may help individuals perform better as a team. For the organization, this means higher performance. For the employees, this means a better place to work and less frustration, resulting in decreased costs and employee turnover. It also may help people to concentrate less on politics or working around people and to focus on their assigned work. Employees are able to participate in activities that are traditionally management roles, and this aspect has empowered staff to expand their professional responsibilities and maintain a sense of ownership (Parks & Lindstrom, 1995; Roper & Russell, 1997).

The manager or organization defines tools and processes. The tools for capturing required information usually are developed or adapted by each institution or, perhaps, each nursing area or unit. Evaluation elements and operational definitions are developed. A checklist, statements using a Likert scale, and a narrative form are all versions that can be used. See Figure 17-3 for an example of a form that reflects a

---

Figure 17-3. Peer Review Form

Name of employee being assessed_____

Reviewer's name_____ Date_____

Provide feedback <u>with examples</u> using expected behaviors and expected job results.

Please rate the following using this scale

1. Customer Service

   1 ------------------------ 2 ----------------------3------------------------4--------------------------- 5
Does not meet   Meets   Exceeds
Example:

2. Quality/Skill Level

   1 ------------------------ 2 ----------------------3------------------------4--------------------------- 5
Does not meet   Meets   Exceeds
Example:

3. Initiative

   1 ------------------------ 2 ----------------------3------------------------4--------------------------- 5
Does not meet   Meets   Exceeds
Example:

4. Self-directed

   1 ------------------------ 2 ----------------------3------------------------4--------------------------- 5
Does not meet   Meets   Exceeds
Example:

(Continued on next page)

Figure 17-3. Peer Review Form *(Continued)*

5. Dependability

1 ------------------------ 2 ----------------------- 3--------------------------4--------------------------- 5

Does not meet   Meets   Exceeds

Example:

---

6. Team Player

1 ------------------------ 2 ----------------------- 3--------------------------4--------------------------- 5

Does not meet   Meets   Exceeds

Example:

---

7. Productivity

1 ------------------------ 2 ----------------------- 3--------------------------4--------------------------- 5

Does not meet   Meets   Exceeds

Example:

---

8. Judgment/Decision Making

1 ------------------------ 2 ----------------------- 3--------------------------4--------------------------- 5

Does not meet   Meets   Exceeds

Example:

What is this employee doing well? What could this employee do to improve?

Additional feedback:

Return to nurse manager by _____

---

combination. The process may be individual feedback or in the form of a committee where each colleague is evaluated by the formal team based on established criteria. Committee structure and assignments vary by institution. The committee may either deliver the evaluation to the nurse themselves or convey outcomes so the manager can deliver feedback. Individual feedback may be obtained from a nurse chosen at random or specifically selected by the nurse or manager to be evaluated; usually it is a combination of both. This method also may include other nursing personnel such as licensed practical nurses/licensed vocational nurses or assistive personnel. Peer review is compatible with shared governance models of professional practice as a means of evaluating and improving standards of practice and enhancing accountability at the practice level.

Peer reviews may work best if all parties know that the reviews will not be used for setting pay, promotions, or disciplinary actions; this promotes open and honest feedback. It will not be successful if the employees do not have the maturity or desire to handle peer review responsibilities or if management does not support such an initiative. However, a peer review system with the power to give promotions, raises, or disciplinary actions is workable in some businesses, if supported by leadership and if the employees have been educated regarding how to deliver constructive feedback and other integral elements.

Criterion-Based Review

Criterion-based assessments are job-specific tools developed through empirical research carried out on a number of selected occupations. They provide competency profiles and overall job suitability scores with predictive validity. This validity is achieved by comparing assessment scores with actual job performance criteria, using benchmark organizations for each occupation. An overall job suitability score, based on these competency profiles, gives an accurate and reliable portrait of the candidate. Performance tools either encompass behavioral observations or graphic rating scales. Tziner, Kopelman, and Livneh (1993) noted when the behavioral observation method was used, there were consistently higher levels of goal clarity and pinpointing a precise course of action needed to accomplish the goals, producing acceptance and commitment. The specificity of the performance review and the ability to review progress against specific job-related goals also affect acceptance and commitment to the goals by the employee. Graphic rating scales are prone to establishing generic or unclear goals, with less commitment to the outcome (Tziner et al.). An example of a goal for a nurse to become more knowledgeable in a specific area of clinical practice would be "To broaden knowledge in designated specialty" (graphic rating) versus "To become an active member of the professional nursing organization and achieve certification in specialty within year" (behavioral observations).

Other criteria that can be measured are traits and personal characteristics and results (Sullivan & Decker, 2001). The first type is not used frequently because of the shift in relying on traits such as stability or ability to handle stress because they are not helpful in developing employees and can be discriminatory. Results-oriented appraisal is used frequently; employees know in advance what is expected and objectives are quantifiable and easily measured. A third approach, used by most healthcare organizations, is a combination: productivity combined with various types of criteria. In addition to results that were attained, the employee is evaluated in terms of personal characteristics and behaviorally specific criteria.

Swansburg (2002a) discussed other rating methodologies that are less common, such as the team evaluation consensus. Direct comparisons are made with other employees or with performance benchmarks using multiple raters, usually two to eight, including peers and supervisors. Behavior anchorage rating scales are specific descriptors of good, average, and poor performance for each job aspect using key job elements. The task-oriented performance evaluation system concentrates on job tasks rather than behavior; however, it is behaviorally based because it measures accomplishments, and task elements are evaluated by statements that support an excellent, good, average, weak, or unacceptable rating.

Merit-Based Review

The employee merit recommendation should be directly tied to the most recent performance evaluation, based on clearly defined goals and objectives previously established by the employee and supervisor. The objective is to associate merit results to job performance criteria, where weighted evaluation measures are established. If performance has substantially changed since the most recent evaluation, additional supporting documentation should be submitted with the merit recommendation. The merit portion of the system seeks to evaluate performance criteria that employees control and maximize the use of objective data over opinion. The weight of each component correlates with the importance of the function; in some roles, they may all be equal. An example for the role of nurse manager might be to ensure the provision of competent and quality nursing care to identified patient population (20%), maintain current knowledge and skills for clinical practice and professional growth (20%), leadership and communication (20%), peer/customer service (25%), and teamwork/dependability (15%). The total percentage always equals 100. After determining the score for each of the evaluation measures for each employee, the scores are added to obtain an overall score. Performance zones, such as "above average," "average," and "needing improvement" are established, and the overall score is normalized to place an employee in the appropriate performance zone from which the determination of a merit increase is made. Employees receive a documented explanation of the merit system, notification of the merit increase (percent change, dollar change, new salary), and a summary report (total points received, performance position, comments). Merit raises increase fixed costs as they are added to base pay. Bonuses, by contrast, are not added to base pay but are an additional amount of money usually received in a lump sum, which must be earned every year. Bonuses hold down fixed costs while providing staff incentive in performance.

Equity is an important factor to acknowledge in the merit-based review. In addition to performance, merit increases should acknowledge equity among others functioning in the same job description and performance level. A new graduate nurse does not have the experience and breadth of knowledge base as a senior nurse. If the employee reports to different managers, the evaluation tool must be objective so that performance can be measured equitably among different managers. When salary is directly impacted by the performance review, equity and objectivity are key factors.

360-Degree Appraisal

The concept of 360-degree performance appraisals, also known as multisource rating systems, is relatively new to healthcare organizations and gaining in popularity across the nation. This type of evaluation program is focused on providing the employee with constructive feedback aimed at improving performance and developing skills. In a 360-degree appraisal system, individuals evaluate themselves in addition to receiving an evaluation from other organizational members. Individuals receive feedback from their supervisor, peers, subordinates, and customers, thus creating a 360-degree effect for all employees involved in the process. Each review is collected at a central point, summarized, and given to the manager or other objective evaluator to review in a conference with the employee. Although some organizations have used this type of evaluation process for purposes of pay raise determinations, 360-degree evaluations are commonly implemented as a constructive feedback system in which the primary focus is to improve performance regardless of pay raise incentives. The weight of the feedback from each rater group for the performance review is determined by the organization; usually the feedback from the immediate supervisor is dominant (see Figure 17-4).

Figure 17-4. Peer and Upward Performance Feedback

Instructions: Please think of the following team member as you describe this individual according to the items that follow. (Complete all that you can.)

Evaluatee: _____ Evaluator: _____

○ Peer
○ Upward

1. Always	2. Often	3. Occasionally	4. Never

① ② ③ ④   1. Demonstrates a realistic understanding of his or her role and account-abilities

① ② ③ ④   2. Demonstrates objective and fact-based judgments

① ② ③ ④   3. Collaborates effectively with other team members

① ② ③ ④   4. Makes the team goal a higher priority than any personal objective

① ② ③ ④   5. Demonstrates a willingness to devote whatever effort is necessary to achieve team success

① ② ③ ④   6. Willing to openly share information, perceptions, and feedback

① ② ③ ④   7. Demonstrates high standards of excellence

① ② ③ ④   8. Stands behind and supports team decisions

① ② ③ ④   9. Demonstrates courage of conviction by directly confronting important issues

① ② ③ ④   10. Responds constructively to feedback from others

11. What strengths does this person bring to the team?

_____
_____
_____
_____
_____
_____

12. What might this individual do to contribute more effectively to the team's success?

_____
_____
_____
_____
_____
_____

Note. Adapted almost in its entirety from Team Excellence evaluation tool by Frank LaFasto, Senior Vice President of Organizational Effectiveness, Cardinal Health, and Carl Larson, Professor Emeritus, University of Denver. Used with permission.

The success of 360-degree appraisals relies heavily on managerial strategic planning and a focus on developmental feedback for appraisees and anonymity for appraisers. Any 360-degree coworker biases can skew results. Mark Vruno (2001), staff writer for *Insight Magazine,* defined the following means to eliminate unwanted biases while completing a 360-degree appraisal: One should ". . . ensure raters' anonymity for more accurate feedback; hold the reviewee accountable for results by focusing on specific examples of what he or she did, rather than what the rater thinks; and foster an organizational climate where matters of performance are taken seriously, including an appeal mechanism wherein people are treated fairly and respectfully"

(Vruno, 2001, p. 1). Wimer (2002) noted that if any group contains fewer than five people, it allows feedback recipients to take an educated guess about the feedback source and anonymity is absent.

As is common with any performance appraisal system, there are strengths and weaknesses involved with the 360-degree process. Antonioni (1996) noted that managers indicated approximately 25% of the appraisal feedback they received was expected positive feedback, 30% unexpected positive feedback, 20%–30% expected negative feedback, and 15%–20% unexpected negative feedback.

Antonioni (1996) outlined the following five positive outcomes of the 360-degree performance appraisal system.

- Increased awareness of appraisers' expectations
- Improvements in work behaviors and performance
- Reduction of "undiscussables"—appraiser's feeling about the appraisee's undesired behaviors
- Increase in periodic informal performance reviews
- Increase in management learning

Antonioni noted a major deficit was the great reliance on rating scale data because it does not provide the appraisee with useful information regarding others' expectations of them. Written, descriptive feedback is invaluable. Employees often are appraised using a rate scale, ranging from "needs improvement" to "exceeds expectations." A narrative section should be included to provide appraisers an opportunity to add additional comments that the rate scale might not have included and the appraisee with written feedback that is constructive and beneficial for improvement. Without a clear understanding of expectations, the employee is less able to take constructive action to change unsatisfactory behaviors. It is suggested in the literature and from managers who use this system that an employee commonly receives feedback from multiple individuals, which generally is a minimum of three peers, one supervisor, and three subordinates. This process is successful in obtaining performance feedback because employees receive information from all directions—up, down, and lateral. However, it can be an administrative challenge to collect and collate results, thus an expensive process until the manager clearly defines the steps. In some organizations, the 360-degree appraisal is reserved for senior administrative level employees.

The outcome of this diversified information is enhanced self-awareness, which potentially improves performance. It is assumed that by increasing the number of rater sources, the amount of relevant information available to the ratee also increases. Greguras, Ford, and Brutus (2003) assessed which rater sources ratees attend to and found that supervisory feedback was valued more than peer or subordinate viewpoints. A participant in the study stated, "The only thing that matters is the supervisor's perception. . . . While it's nice to please everyone, self-preservation must be primary" (Brutus, p. 356). Fox and Klein (1996) noted peer evaluations tend to be the most generous, with scores of the supervisor toward the middle.

The 360-degree evaluation is a useful process for the evaluation of personnel at the management level. It differs from alternative performance appraisal systems because managerial positions receive performance feedback from their subordinates. One benefit involved with this type of appraisal system is that managerial staff is anonymously evaluated by their subordinates, often causing lower level employees to feel as though they can voice their opinions without being reprimanded. Employees are given the chance to constructively assess the strengths and weaknesses of their supervisor in order to highlight supervisory assets and flaws that might have otherwise gone unnoticed or unchanged. Another strength often associated with this system is the fact that subordinates are able to access their managers, thus involving them not only in the feedback process but also in the professional growth of the manager. Subordinates are given the chance to have direct input on the job performance of individuals who direct the organization; thus, a sense of responsibility and integration in the organization is felt when they are allowed to provide insight.

Management by Objectives

Management by objectives is a performance appraisal strategy that values objectivity and quantitative measurement and assesses the institution or company-wide input of an employee. It is a management philosophy that can be tied into evaluation of employees. First promoted by Peter Drucker, it is a results-oriented technique traditionally used for motivating employees (Swansburg, 2002b). It is a potent device for this type of action because of its effectiveness in providing a basis for facilitating employee problem solving, goal setting, and achievement. Management by results is another strategy whereby outcomes are evaluated as opposed to the input. The extent to which management by objectives is successful depends upon the degree to which performance objectives are quantifiable, the degree to which the employee work is independent, and the predominance of an organizational culture that stresses high involvement by the employee (Rondeau, 1992).

According to Levinson (2003), the ideal management by objectives system is intended to measure and judge performance, to relate individual performance to organizational goals, and to clarify both the job to be done and the expectations of accomplishment. Levinson described the ideal process that should proceed in five steps: (1) individual discussion with the subordinate's superior, (2) establishment of the employee's short-term performance targets, (3) meetings with the superior to discuss the employee's progress toward targets, (4) establishment of checkpoints to measure progress, and (5) discussion between superior and subordinate at the end of a defined period to assess the results of the subordinate's efforts. Typically, top management sets its corporate goals for the coming year. Managers then are asked to develop their divisional goals, reflective of the goals of the organization.

Management by objectives can be most successful when goals are set to be completed over a reasonable period of time, which allows employees to fulfill the goals sufficiently. Research suggests that in some areas of work, such as an internal audit department, management by objectives combined with some form of rating checklist are the most commonly used appraisal techniques (Schweiger & Sumners, 1994). If used with another appraisal tool, management by objectives can be used to accomplish more long-term goals, whereas another tool, such as peer review, can be used to evaluate and track performance during shorter time periods. Individuals should set their own goals and then review them with their superior. The goal review should be used as a counseling session to ensure that employees are aligned with what their managers expect from them. Employee objectives should be reflective of their individual desires for job growth and personal growth. Objective goals should be set so that most employees can realistically fulfill requirements while restricting all employees from receiving extraordinary bonuses. For example, in an ambulatory care setting, the number of customer calls, time spent on the phone, and total abandoned calls might measure the performance of a triage or appointment nurse. Quantitative data that are reflective of the performance of the nurse are collected, and the nurse may be rewarded for spending less time on the phone with patients or decreasing the total amount of hang-ups, while maintaining quality and integrity of the phone encounter. The ability of the employee to achieve these goals against measurement criteria, combined with a summary of all evaluations, can be used for a complete assessment of performance (Schweiger & Sumners, 1994). Typically, employees who are not successful at implementing the goals of the institution or manager will not receive their yearly bonus or might receive less than expected.

Although management by objectives can provide both employees and supervisors with quantitative and objective data, there are some disadvantages associated with this system. Because the design of this appraisal system thrives on objective, measurable data, it can be difficult to measure characteristics and competencies that reflect personal interest or nursing compassion. Levinson (2003) stated that management by objective systems can overlook personal objectives, and no objectives will have significant power if they do not embody and reflect the "underlying dreams, wishes, and personal aspirations" (p. 110) of the individual. In a sense, when greater emphasis is placed on measurement and quantification, it is more likely that immeasurable elements will be overlooked and may even be viewed as nonproductive. Employees may feel as though they are being used to earn money for the institution instead of themselves and that their immeasurable qualities and attributions are not important or valued.

Pay for Performance

Pay for performance is a model in many progressive institutions. No longer is longevity or years of employment the factor for pay increases. Instead, it is now based on individual and or team performance. In this model, there is alignment of the goals throughout all levels of the organization. With an increasingly global market, companies, including healthcare organizations, are cognizant that lower costs are key to survival. This includes employee compensation so that the stakeholder can remain competitive. The Balanced Budget Act and prospective payment systems have posed fiscal limitations in the healthcare setting. Kadlec (2003, p. 53) noted across-the-board pay increases in business are rare today; companies are being forced to focus on "getting the right dollars to the right people."

Pay for performance, or variable pay, can take many forms, such as a merit increase to base pay, annual bonus, stock options, gain sharing, profit sharing, contingent pay, or other financial incentives. Hewitt (2003) found 77% of surveyed organizations currently have at least one type of variable pay plan in place: (a) business incentives (59%)—awards employees for a combination of financial and operational measures for company, business unit, department, plant and/or individual performance; (b) special recognition (55%)—acknowledges outstanding individual or group achievements with small cash awards or merchandise, such as gift certificates; (c) individual performance (47%)—rewards based on specific employee performance criteria; and (d) stock ownership (32%)—rewards stock to professionals who meet specific goals. This is consistent with data gathered in 2002, which showed that 80% of organizations offered variable pay compared to 59% in 1995. Furthermore, the study noted spending on variable pay for salaried exempt employees decreased to an average of 8.8%of payroll in 2003 and is projected at 9% for 2004. This is a decrease from variable pay spending of 10.8% of payroll in 2001 and 10% in 2002. The Enron incident demonstrated the negative side of pay for performance where stock options and related income distorted executive and employee decisions (Risher, 2002). However, Risher noted at the same time that the Enron case clearly confirms that pay can motivate behavior. The American Nurses Association (ANA) noted 25% of U.S. hospitals have some type of gain sharing program for staff nurses (ANA, 1998b).

Financial increases are based on the organization's success and the individual's or team's contribution to that success as indicated by their overall performance rating. Succinct objective goals for the organization are developed. These goals are used by the department, division, unit, or area to develop specific goals. The last step in the process is to link individual performance with the department and unit goals so that, ultimately, all are striving effectively together to contribute to the mission and common goals of the organization. Guthrie and Cunningham (1992) described the Quaker Oats plant initiative that is referred to frequently in pay for performance literature and concluded two criteria critical for success: (a) the organizational climate is open and characterized by high levels of trust, and (b) the management style is participative.

Risher (2002) described three theories of motivation that explain the impact of pay for performance: (a) equity theory—employees tend to compare their input or effort with that of coworkers and use that as basis for evaluating merit increase and bonuses; they want to be paid equitably, (b) expectancy theory—employees behave in ways they expect will be rewarded; rewards are simply consistent, and (c) reinforcement theory—behavior that is reinforced is likely to be repeated.

Performance standards are based on achievement of goals instead of on the traditional job activities, which often can cause a misalignment between the institution or departmental goals and individual expected job results. Good performance will be rewarded financially, and the organization is rewarded by meeting its mission. If the department does not meet its goals, the performance ratings of the individuals in the department should not reflect that they individually met goals.

A challenge in this model is the integration of the organization's goals into measurable outcomes at the individual level. Barela and Lee (2000) noted aligning incentives among disparate healthcare workers is inherently difficult because incentives are not consistently aligned clinically, philosophically, or financially. In creating a high-performance environment, it is imperative that the supervisor collaborates with staff members as they define expected job results. Outcomes and results are the basis of this approach as opposed to input or activities. See Table 17-1 for an example of each used in health care, and note the difference or degree of objectiveness in statements.

This model negates perceived inequity in the system where one employee feels he or she is rewarded the same as the next employee, even though he or she feels that he or she contributed or achieved more. With objective, precise standard categories of behaviors defined, all employees will be evaluated equally, and those who demonstrate exceptional performance will be rewarded. This method enables employees to know how they are impacting the bottom line and enables employers to measure program or organization success.

Table 17-1. Outcomes and Results Model Examples	
Input	Outcomes
Reengineer costs.	Lower staff RN overtime by 5%.
Improve patient satisfaction scores.	Zero complaints; recognized formally by patients submitting compliment forms
Assist RN to consider career path.	Achieve clinical ladder progression by 60% of RN staff.
Improve collaboration.	Coordinate monthly lab task force to research problems and improve service.

Professional Nurse Portfolio

The portfolio method is a more recent approach used by healthcare management for several purposes, including annual performance appraisals. Professional portfolios are already being used for formative assessments in the revalidation of physicians in practice, evidence for clinical ladder progression in nursing, and the human resources portion of a Joint Commission on Accreditation of Healthcare Organizations (JCAHO) survey. The portfolio contains all necessary documentation that meets JCAHO standards, such as age-specific competencies (Brooks & Madda, 1999). In the United Kingdom, this method is used by nursing regulatory bodies for maintenance and verification of continuous nursing practice for licensure. According to Jasper (2001) and Krystof (1996), a personal nursing portfolio allows nurses an opportunity to organize and present a complete synopsis of their professional accomplishments over the past year or specified time frame. This process allows the nurse to be an active participant in the evaluation process. At the time of the formal evaluation, the nurse and manager review the portfolio, which outlines accomplishments and mutually set goals in areas that require improvement.

According to Trossman (1999, p. 1) the portfolio is a "comprehensive document completed by the nurse that details the current state of their practice, background, skills, expertise and, perhaps most importantly, a working plan for professional growth." Particularly applicable to nursing and other professions that require certification and updating licensure, portfolio appraisals allow each nurse to demonstrate how performance appraisal goals have been met or exceeded (Meeks, Hayes, Stahlhammer, & Zeaphey, 1995). Portfolios also provide an individual with the opportunity to maintain an updated, written representation of his or her competencies and assessments. Employees value portfolio development because they have a mobile representation of their professional accomplishments, often used for interviewing and hiring purposes, similar to a resume. Employers value portfolio appraisals because they appreciate the vested interest and work of the package of evidence the nurse presents, and they are handing over some of the responsibility of maintaining and updating records to the employee. Documents are amassed during the evaluation period to reflect job description and performance appraisal standards. These documents then are presented to the manager before the performance appraisal meeting (Brooks & Madda, 1999). Managers can determine if the nurse has updated all of his or her certifications, continuing education, and competency requirements. However, one of the challenges is to quantify minimum requirements for an acceptable portfolio. This can be difficult when trying to distinguish pay rates for increments of performance with ratings of exceeds, meets expectations, or needs improvement.

As stated earlier, not only can portfolios include community service, professional endeavors, and involvement in outside healthcare activities of the nurse (Meeks et al., 1995), but they also contain information on plans for future development, aspirations, and mobility. In the current healthcare environment, where it is increasingly common for nurses to change jobs throughout their career, this format enables nurses to have readily available a tool reflecting their potential value to employers by emphasizing transferable skills.

No-Surprises Appraisal

Performance appraisals can be extremely stressful for the evaluator and evaluatee. To reduce the amount of stress an appraisee feels, a no-surprises policy should be implemented; the content of an appraisal should never surprise the employee (Smith, 2003). Topics or circumstances that were not addressed during the performance evaluation period with ongoing informal or formal feedback should not appear in the formal performance appraisal. When a no-surprises policy is used, employees and managers tend to feel less anxiety associated with the review, and a stronger rapport is made between the appraisee and appraiser. Managers should base appraisals on recent incidents. Incidents in the past that have not occurred again within this appraisal time frame should not resurface.

Regulations and Factors Governing Appraisals

In addition to the evaluation tool and process used, there are other key factors that must be considered when developing a successful appraisal system that directly impacts the structure and outcomes of the performance appraisal. These factors include legal guidelines, accreditation standards, professional standards, and institutional policy.

Legal

In the healthcare setting, human resources require an appraisal process to meet legal and accreditation standards. There must be standardization of forms and process to support objective performance ratings if a performance appraisal were challenged by the labor relations board or before a court of law. For example, consider an employee who sued for being "wrongfully" terminated. If the termination was because of his or her documented poor performance, lack of competency, or not meeting job and professional standards, the employer must be able to demonstrate fairness, consistency, and accuracy of the process. Because performance appraisals have played an important part in the outcome of legal challenges, it is critical that managers implementing and administering performance appraisals are well versed in the legal parameters associated with this process. Flynn (2001) reinforced that performance evaluations based on objective criteria are more likely to reduce legal challenges, in addition to a focus on behaviors rather than attitude. Martin and Bartol (1991) reviewed cases where decisions regarding promotions, discharges, layoffs, and merit pay placed the performance appraisal at the center of conflicts and misunderstandings between subordinates and superiors.

Accreditation Standards

To meet accreditation standards, such as JCAHO, a healthcare organization is required to provide the right number of competent staff to meet patient care needs. JCAHO's competence assessment (Human Resource Standard 3.20) states, "The organization periodically conducts performance evaluations" (JCAHO, 2004, p. HR-9). This applies to both hospital and ambulatory settings. The rationale for this standard explains that evaluation of performance is an ongoing process for providing positive and negative feedback to staff, students, or volunteers who provide care, treatment, and services. Formal performance evaluations may be conducted concurrently with competency assessments. JCAHO stated that performance appraisals are required to keep the organization's human resource documentation current and complete. The processes of this accreditation body are clearly defined. For example, JCAHO outlined the following processes to be met in order to fulfill the standard.

- Provide an adequate number of staff.
- Provide competent staff.
- Orient, train, and educate staff.
- Assess, maintain, and improve staff competence.

JCAHO addressed performance frequently throughout their publication and provided recommendations as follows. The healthcare organization must demonstrate that a process is in place to ensure that a person's qualifications are consistent with job responsibilities and that data are collected from the selected screening indicators to identify potential staffing effectiveness issues when performance varies from expected targets, such as ranges of desired performance, external benchmarking, or improvement goals.

The healthcare organization must assess and document the ability of each employee to carry out assigned responsibilities safely, competently, and in a timely manner upon completion of orientation. Evidence that education is offered in response to learning needs identified through performance improvement and data analysis from staff surveys, performance evaluations, or needs assessments must exist.

When an employee with performance problems is unable or unwilling to improve, the organization should modify the person's job assignment or take other appropriate action. Performance evaluations are conducted periodically at time frames identified by the organization. The evaluation of performance is based on expectations as defined in the job description and through the privileging process.

Professional Organizational Standards

The development of oncology nursing as a specialty led to the development of standards of care and professional performance for nurses delivering care to this patient population. These standards of practice constitute the basic framework and basis for job descriptions, performance appraisals, and peer review, in addition to other critical elements. The Oncology Nursing Society (ONS) includes performance appraisals in the *Statement on the Scope and Standards of Oncology Nursing Practice* (Brant & Wickham, 2004). These standards provide a statement of basic competence in oncology nursing practice and support the performance appraisal process. The content of the ONS practice evaluation standard is included in Figure 17-5. Expectations and

---

Figure 17-5. Excerpt from the Statement on the Scope and Standards of Oncology Nursing Practice

Standard II. Practice Evaluation
The oncology nurse consistently evaluates his or her own nursing practice in relation to job-specific performance expectations, statewide regulatory requirements, and national oncology nursing professional standards.

Rationale
The oncology nurse is accountable to the lay public and to patients with cancer and, thus, has a responsibility to evaluate his or her practice according to regulations imposed by the work setting, the state of practice, and the professional standards established by the Oncology Nursing Society to ensure safe and competent nursing practice.

Measurement Criteria
The oncology nurse
1. Engages in ongoing performance appraisal with peers, colleagues, and management identifying strengths, weaknesses, and areas for improvement.
2. Demonstrates and documents competencies relative to specific oncology nurse roles (e.g., an ambulatory chemotherapy nurse can de-clot central venous catheters; an in-patient bone marrow transplant nurse can assess early signs of graft versus host disease within first 100 days of transplantation; a hospice nurse can recognize and manage dyspnea) and of safety initiatives (e.g., patient identification strategies, early identification of drug-related adverse effects, medication error reduction practice guidelines).
3. Establishes goals for professional development and role maturation.
4. Assists colleagues in evaluating their performance or in seeking assistance with other performance issues (e.g., substance abuse).
5. Serves as a role model or mentor for new oncology nurses.
6. Seeks and encourages oncology nursing certification.

Note. From *Statement on the Scope and Standards of Oncology Nursing Practice* (pp. 34–35), by J. M. Brant and R.S. Wickham, 2004, Pittsburgh, PA: Oncology Nursing Society. Copyright 2004 by the Oncology Nursing Society. Reprinted with permission.

---

criteria for performance of the nurse, as defined by the organization, can be found in position descriptions that reflect professional standards of practice. Grohar-Murray and DiCroce (2003) discussed the possibility that, at times, professional standards may conflict with the goals of the organization, such as in cost-containment and length-of-stay measures. Although professional standards must dominate decision making relative to patient care, nurses must remember that effective use of resources and prevention of waste is included in professional values. Communication and collaboration are important in an effort to integrate the system and partner standards with the organization's mission. Other professional nursing organizations have similar standards, such as, but not limited to, the Association of Pediatric Oncology Nurses, American Association of Office Nurses, and American Academy of Ambulatory Care Nursing.

Institutional Policies

Institutional policies will incorporate the legal, accreditation, and professional aspects into the institution's philosophy and dictate the appraisal process through human resource policy. Within these policies, parameters specific to the institution, such as type and frequency of evaluation, will be outlined for managers who will be held accountable.

Other Factors

Budget

While conducting a performance appraisal, there are various factors that impact how, when, and what the organization deems necessary to include in the process. One of the biggest concerns that all organizations must consider is the budget. The major element of a nursing budget is usually personnel. Thus, the implications of a salary increase for staff is great. To budget for the salary increases associated with performance appraisals, the manager applies the anticipated monetary increase to the number of full-time equivalents. For example, if all nurses within a unit met standards that resulted in a 5% merit increase in base pay and their average salaries were $25,000 annually, each salary would increase by $1,250 annually. This is multiplied by the number of nurses on staff, and with fringe benefits and shift differential factored in, the average expense incurred by the organization could approximate $2,000 per employee. Pay increases are factored annually into the operational budget. The monetary amount can be predicted for the upcoming year or determined after the amount of revenue is assessed for the institution at the fiscal year end.

Many organizations outline a schedule that defines the amount of salary increase to the performance appraisal grade of the employee and the position in the minimum/midpoint/maximum range for a specific job class. With this information, managers may be tempted to skew the performance rating upward to justify the amount of salary increase they want to award, rather than allowing the objective rating results to govern the salary increase. Many managers and institutions endorse a forced distribution method in which ratings of employees are distributed along a bell-shaped curve. The assumption is that there is a normal distribution of performance among a group of employees, and the majority will fall within the middle or "meets standards"; fewer will fall into the "exceed" grouping, and yet fewer will "not meet standards." This method is not applicable to small groups of employees. This process gives the manager a tool to predict budget implications. It enforces the concept that the majority of employees are successful in meeting job standards and the minority need improvement or exceed the standards. If too many employees fall in the "not meet standards" category, the manager should reevaluate the accuracy of the job standards; is the supervisor or manager expecting too much, or is there a need for staff development and mentoring for improved performance? If too many fall in the "exceeds" category, the manager should reevaluate the accuracy of the job standards; are you expecting too little? The majority should fall within the norm of meeting expectations (see Figure 17-6). To maintain budget, managers can ensure ratings will fall within defined distribution (i.e., 5%–20% need improvement, 60%–90% meet standards, and 5%–20% exceed standards). Another option is ratings can be submitted and the percentage of increases can be determined based on distribution. This option gives a manager more flexibility to evaluate performance appropriately within area of supervision. Note that the difference in amounts of pay increase per employee can be significant dependent on method and allows for an above average salary increase for exemplary performance (see Figure 17-7).

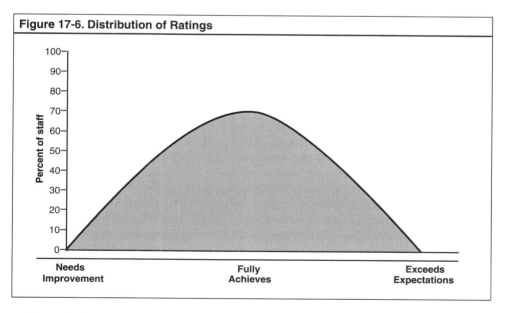

Figure 17-6. Distribution of Ratings

Organizations must manage distribution of salary increases based on the available budget. This is particularly important during times of constrained resources, while remaining competitive in the local market.

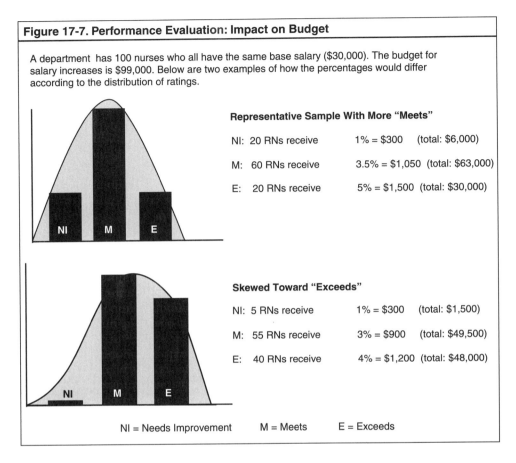

Figure 17-7. Performance Evaluation: Impact on Budget

A department has 100 nurses who all have the same base salary ($30,000). The budget for salary increases is $99,000. Below are two examples of how the percentages would differ according to the distribution of ratings.

Representative Sample With More "Meets"

NI: 20 RNs receive   1% = $300   (total: $6,000)

M: 60 RNs receive   3.5% = $1,050 (total: $63,000)

E: 20 RNs receive   5% = $1,500 (total: $30,000)

Skewed Toward "Exceeds"

NI: 5 RNs receive   1% = $300   (total: $1,500)

M: 55 RNs receive   3% = $900   (total: $49,500)

E: 40 RNs receive   4% = $1,200 (total: $48,000)

NI = Needs Improvement   M = Meets   E = Exceeds

Collective Bargaining

Nurses in collective bargaining units are evaluated according to institutional policy. An exception to the performance appraisal process as it relates to merit increases and pay for performance approaches occurs with collective bargaining or unionization of nurses. Collective bargaining for nurses has been in place for approximately 50 years. Interest in organizing stems from multiple issues faced by the nurse, such as lack of input into decisions affecting them, overtime, salary, and working conditions. One result of unionizing for the nurse may be leverage with management and input in decisions affecting his or her work environment. This leverage and respected input into decision making also can occur with an organizational supported shared governance model in a nonunion environment.

Ng and Maki (1994) examined the influence of unions on the adoption of human resource management practices in industry, ranging from hiring and promotion practices to performance appraisal methods. They studied 356 manufacturing firms and concluded that unionization is positively associated with a job posting system, formal probationary periods for new hires, and explicit criteria governing promotion. The only exception was performance appraisal where a formal evaluation was less likely to be conducted. This indicates a minimization of the importance of the performance appraisal function in union organizations because appraisal records are not considered important in pay, promotion, and layoff decisions. However, union settings are inclined to use performance appraisal in developmental and disciplinary decisions. These results indicate that trade unions are not opposed to the concept of linking pay with performance; rather, they are against such a linkage when it creates rivalry and increased pay differentials among individual employees in the same job class.

Any performance appraisal tool can be used in a unionized setting, and the evaluation process is essentially the same. However, the outcome is different as it relates to changes in pay. As annual salary increases, benefits and incentives are almost always included in the collective bargaining contract or agreement and pertains to the nursing group as a whole, not individually. Respect for long-term relationship or seniority will likely influence many human resource decisions. Thus, nurses generally are not rewarded by merit increases because of their performance but because of their contract with the bargaining unit. In general, RNs in staff positions are hourly employees and can receive annual across-the-board wage increases. In unionized settings, a step system usually is negotiated, allowing a nurse to move up a pay step on his or her anniversary date; this tends to result in nurses reaching the maximum of the pay scale. In collective bargaining contexts, RNs and their union representative are advised to scrutinize how a pay for performance system is to be approved and implemented and if it serves as a substitute for adequate base pay and annual salary increases. ANA advises the following to nurses in collective bargaining units: "The union should also share the responsibility of administering the program, ensuring there is bargaining unit control over the patient services to be measured and that the system of sharing gain be equitable. It must be clearly understood what consequences follow from unmet performance targets, with the union retaining the option to change or discontinue the program" (ANA, 1998a).

Completion of stated time intervals is noted for salary increases; performance is not an element discussed. Contracts commonly include language as follows:

Employees shall be eligible for salary increases on the first payroll period following

- Completion of the initial 26 payroll periods of continuous service
- Completion of a trial service following promotion
- Annual periods (after two bulleted items above) until the employee has reached the top of the salary range.

Salary increases shall be made upon recommendation of the employee's immediate supervisor and approval of the appointing authority. The employer shall give written notice to an employee of withholding a salary increase prior to the eligibility date, including a statement of the reason. If a salary increase is not granted on the eligibility date, the employee's eligibility date is retained no longer than 11 months. If the increase is subsequently granted within 11 months, it shall be effective on the subsequent payroll period and shall not be retroactive. Figure 17-8 is a performance appraisal section of an actual contract.

Figure 17-8. Bargaining Unit Contract Example

Performance Appraisal of Permanent Employees
This may include annual written performance appraisals for permanent employees. Such performance appraisals may be completed at least once each 12 months after an employee completes the probationary period for the class in which he or she is serving.

Performance Appraisal of Nursing Practices
Employees who provide hands-on care receive a rating from a non-registered nurse supervisor of "improvement needed" on their individual appraisal summary for nursing practices. The rating will be reviewed by a supervising RN designated by the department head or designee. This section is not to be construed as a limitation on supervisory personnel responsibility for the overall evaluation of employees.

Informal Performance Discussions
Encourage periodic informal performance discussions between employees and their supervisor to discuss work performance, job satisfaction, and work-related problems. Except when immediate action is necessary for health or safety reasons, such discussions shall be held in a private setting or sufficiently removed from the hearing range of other persons.

Personnel and Evaluation Material
Evaluation material or material relating to an employee's conduct, attitude, or service shall not be included in his or her official personnel file without being signed and dated by the author of such material. Before the material is placed in the employee's file, the department head or designee shall provide the affected employee an opportunity to review the material and sign and date it. An employee's signature shall not constitute agreement. A copy of the evaluation material shall be given to the employee.

Supervisors may keep working files on the performance and conduct of employees to provide documentation for matters such as, but not limited to, probation reports, performance appraisals, training needs, MSA reviews, bonus programs, adverse actions, employee development appraisals, or examination evaluations. An employee and/or his or her authorized representative may, upon request, review the contents of his or her file with his or her supervisor.

Note. Based on information from California State Employees Association, 2001.

Performance Appraisal Process

The evaluation process serves as a source of information to the employee, the manager, and the human resource department. The manager uses the information for decisions regarding educational needs, functioning level of staff, promotions, salaries, and other related human resource matters. Human resources uses the information to ensure equity and compliance with labor laws. The employee uses the information for assessment of current performance and as a means to set individual goals that enhance him or her personally in the profession or job and contribute to the effectiveness and overall improvement of the employer or institution.

Performance appraisals are an ongoing process, not a one-time event. It is not a day of reckoning or an annual task for the manager with only recent descriptions of employee performance and events in the manager's memory but a reflection of ongoing contributions by the employee in a two-way exchange of information between evaluator and evaluatee. It is an assessment of the employee's performance compared to the description of expected performance, which is defined in the job description. It reflects concrete, observable behaviors. The overall process with four succinct points of evaluation—interview, probationary period, performance appraisal at defined intervals, and the annual performance appraisal—is illustrated in Figure 17-9.

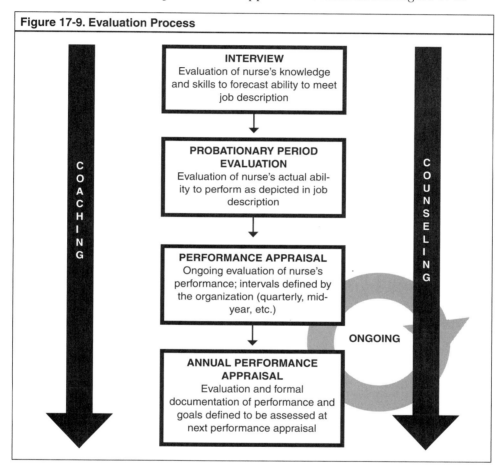

Figure 17-9. Evaluation Process

COACHING

INTERVIEW
Evaluation of nurse's knowledge and skills to forecast ability to meet job description

PROBATIONARY PERIOD EVALUATION
Evaluation of nurse's actual ability to perform as depicted in job description

PERFORMANCE APPRAISAL
Ongoing evaluation of nurse's performance; intervals defined by the organization (quarterly, mid-year, etc.)

ONGOING

ANNUAL PERFORMANCE APPRAISAL
Evaluation and formal documentation of performance and goals defined to be assessed at next performance appraisal

COUNSELING

Interview

The evaluation process begins at the employee interview. Effective communication is established between the employer and employee, later the evaluator and evaluatee, at the interview session (Rondeau, 1992). It is at this time the hiring manager describes the position the candidate is pursuing. Elements of the job are thoroughly discussed, and the individual's knowledge and skills are assessed. The manager describes key job elements and competencies and reinforces what is critical to the success of the unit, program, or project. The manager clearly defines priorities and what the employee will be held accountable for in this position and within a specific area or division for which the applicant is applying. Bernardin, Cooke, and Villanova (2000), Hochwarter, Witt, and Kacmar (2000), and Hough and Oswald (2000) discussed their research in which personality constructs and job performance are correlated. This information can serve as a guide to managers as they assess applicant characteristics that are prone to success in certain positions and work environments. Hough and Oswald discussed contextual performance, which is a relatively new and multifaceted job performance construct also know as organization citizenship behavior—behavior that will benefit in employees, the organization, and the work itself. The authors support that this construct is as important as task performance and should be assessed in potential hires at the time of interview. Ultimately, the job description defines the overall desired contribution to patient care that is expected of the employee; this may be through direct patient care or indirect activities of education, research, or management. The performance appraisal is in direct correlation of the job description. Concrete, observable behaviors are outlined in the job description and evaluated in the performance appraisal, all of which are discussed at the initial interview.

Probationary Period

The behaviors required for the position that were assessed at the interview initially are evaluated at the probationary period, usually within a range of 90 days to 6 months of employment. During the probationary period, the employee or employer may cease the working relationship without repercussion. If the performance is not acceptable, the probationary period is extended or the employment is terminated. The period should only be extended if there is a reasonable expectation that improvement is possible and desired by the employee. If the nurse's performance is acceptable as related to the job description, then, at this face-to-face encounter, the nurse is released from the probationary period and is a full member of the staff. The frequency of evaluations is reviewed at this time, with the next date clearly stated.

Frequency

After this initial evaluation, the timing of the next appraisal will depend on the policy of the institution or agency of employment and can be at any point in time or frequency but is usually quarterly, every six months, or annually. If it is a role that requires frequent job requirement changes or assessment, the evaluation process may be at more frequent intervals. Less formal opportunities for discussing performance are useful to keep both nurse and manager apprised of current performance and are useful coaching sessions. Some employers complete annual performance appraisals on all employees at the same time of the year (i.e., by June 30, the end of their fiscal year, or any designated time), usually correlated with the institution's positive financial status so that merit increases can be paid in the fiscal year. Another common time is the anniversary of the employee's hire. This will require the manager to complete evaluations on an ongoing basis, with the deadlines determined by employees' anniversary dates. Either way is acceptable; however, the employee must know in advance how often and when he or she will be formally evaluated, by what method, and by whom.

The manager is accountable for establishing the environment for quality patient care. This includes a comprehensive orientation followed by ongoing education to enhance the employee's ability to stay current in job requirements. Metcalf (2001) discussed the use of the performance appraisal, in addition to development activities, clinical workshops, seminar presentations, and participation in courses and higher education programs, as an important method to analyze development and progress made by new graduate nurses. The performance appraisal process facilitates communication between the nurse manager and novice nurse as strengths, achievements, and clinical competence are discussed. The manager must ensure the employees are working in an environment conducive to exceptional performance by allowing them the time and tools to complete the job. The institution's leadership is accountable for ensuring the evaluator is properly educated in the concept of evaluation and the process of completing performance appraisals, including the role of coach and counselor throughout the year. Managers must have the skills to be focused, nonbiased, fair, and objective. By far, the most important skill needed is excellent interpersonal skills. The manager must demonstrate respect and value for the employee.

Time

When deciding the frequency of the performance assessment, the institution must keep in mind the most valuable resource of both the manager and employee: time. Performance appraisals that are completed accurately take proper planning and time. Collection and assessment of information relating to performance and documentation of the outcomes and manager's goals are time consuming. The employee may be required to perform a self-appraisal with supportive data, outcomes, and goals. Contributions from both employer and employee require the valued commodity of time. If peers or other raters are included in the process, this must be factored in as well. To expedite this, a number of methods may be used, including ratings and checklists. Sufficient time should be allocated to deliver the evaluation. It should not be done in a hurried or haphazard manner. This scheduled time will demonstrate to the employee the importance of this process and his or her value to the supervisor and the institution. It also will encourage an exchange of information when the supervisor and the employee are not distracted by other commitments or duties. The importance of the process will be diminished if the feedback that the employee receives is inaccurate or rushed.

If additional data are needed for the review, the forms should be simple enough that they aid the reviewer and manager in quantifying or qualifying personal judgment related to employee performance. This can include peer feedback, audits, and checklists. Performance improvement initiatives, which are an evaluation on a broader scope of patient care and outcomes, are determined by priorities of the manager and team. Data collected for performance improvement frequently reflect individual contributions by team members, such as medical record documentation. These data can be included in the performance appraisal of the employee and are likely to be correlated with patient outcomes.

Coaching and Counseling

Coaching and counseling should occur throughout the year as part of the appraisal process. As a coach, the manager engages in activities to keep abreast of the performance of the employee. The coach praises positive performance and suggests means to improve negative behaviors or performance; a nonjudgmental attitude is essential. Consistent and ongoing coaching will eliminate any surprises in the annual appraisal and can prevent formal discipline by early intervention. It demonstrates the availability, support, and commitment of the manager to the team. Counseling involves a direct face-to-face interaction for the purpose of advising and assisting the employee. Even though it is not synonymous with discipline or reprimands, it unduly has a negative connotation. It can be a positive encounter that establishes an effective relationship between the manager and employee. Both of these interventions are precursors to the formal evaluation and require adequate time to ensure success. At the time of formal performance appraisal, the manager is in the role of a coach and gives feedback in a constructive manner. A manager must take the time to discuss areas of performance that fall below expectations by identifying discrepancies, with concrete examples, between actual performance and expected performance. There is an explanation of criticisms and areas for improved performance interjected with compliments and concrete examples of positive behavior, which will be encouraged to continue. Career counseling and recognition by management of the employee's future can be a part of the dialogue. The outcome of this encounter should be mutual goal setting, which will benefit both the manager and employee.

Summary

The performance appraisal process reflects the philosophy of the organization and encompasses different systems and tools. However, the basis of each is the same: evaluation of employee performance against predetermined standards. It is a process, not solely a form or tool. The tool is not an end in itself but rather a method for development of the employee and a means to support the mission of the organization. It is key that the evaluator and evaluatee understand that the performance appraisal is much more than the form or paper where the documentation exists; it is a dynamic process. It is further essential that this not be a time of surprise or "I caught you doing something wrong" for the employee. Instead, it should be a time of mutual reflection of work behavior, performance, and goal attainment. This should be a time to praise strengths and focus on setting strategies for performance improvement for the coming year.

References

Albrecht, S. (1976). Reappraisal of conventional performance appraisal systems. In B.J. Stevens, I.G. Ramey, C.M. Bidwell, D.J. Froebe, S.T. Hegyvary, P.A. Chamings, et al. (Eds.), *Quality control and performance appraisal* (pp. 53–59). Wakefield, MA: Contemporary Publishing.

American Nurses Association. (1998a). *Health care and nursing workforce issues in the United States.* (March, 1999). Retrieved November 9, 2003, from http://www.nursingworld.org/readroom/nti/mar99.htm

American Nurses Association. (1998b). *RNs and pay-for-performance: The right prescription?* Retrieved September 10, 2003, from http://www.nursingworld.org/dlwa/wages/wp8.htm

Antonioni, D. (1996). Designing an effective 360-degree appraisal feedback process. *Organizational Dynamics, 25*(2), 24–38.

Barela, T.D., & Lee, C.A. (2000). Aligned incentives are easier said than done. *Surgical Services Management, 6*(5), 11–13.

Baruch, Y. (1996). Self performance appraisal vs. direct-manager appraisal: A case of congruence. *Journal of Managerial Psychology, 11*(6), 50–66.

Bernardin, H.J., Cooke, D.K., & Villanova, P. (2000). Conscientiousness and agreeableness as predictors of rating leniency. *Journal of Applied Psychology, 85,* 232–234.

Brant, J., & Wickham, R. (2004). *Statement on the scope and standards of oncology nursing practice.* Pittsburgh, PA: Oncology Nursing Society.

Brooks, B.A., & Madda, M. (1999). How to organize a professional portfolio for staff and career development. *Journal for Nurses in Staff Development, 15,* 5–10.

California State Employees Association. (2001). *Bargaining Unit 17—Registered Nurses.* Retrieved September 5, 2003, from http://www.calcsea.org/csd/bargaining/unit17/contract99-01/unit17-13.html

Flynn, G. (2001). Getting performance reviews right. *Workforce, 80,* 76–77.

Fox, J., & Klein, C. (1996). The 360-degree evaluation. *Public Management, 80,* 20–22.

Greguras, G.J., Ford, J.M., & Brutus, S. (2003). Manager attention to multisource feedback. *Journal of Management Development, 22,* 345–361.

Grohar-Murray, M.E., & DiCroce, H. (2003). *Leadership and management in nursing.* Upper Saddle River, NJ: Prentice Hall.

Grote, D. (1998). Painless performance appraisals focus on results, behaviors. *HR Magazine, 43,* 52–58.

Guthrie, J.P., & Cunningham, E.P. (1992). Pay for performance for hourly workers: The Quaker Oats alternative. *Compensation and Benefits Review, 24*(2), 18–23.

Hewitt. (2003). *Hewitt Study shows record lows for salary increases in 2003 with only slight improvement slated for 2004.* Retrieved August 17, 2004, from http://was4.hewitt.com/hewitt/resource/newsroom/pressrel/2003/09-09-03.htm

Hochwarter, W.A., Witt, L.A., & Kacmar, K.M. (2000). Perceptions of organizational politics as a moderator of the relationship between conscientiousness and job performance. *Journal of Applied Psychology, 85,* 472–478.

Hotko, B., & Van Dyke, D. (1998). Peer review: Strengthening leadership skills. *Nursing Management, 29*(4), 41, 44.

Hough, L.M., & Oswald, F.L. (2000). Personnel selection: Looking toward the future—Remembering the past. *Annual Review of Psychology, 51,* 631–664.

Jasper, M. (2001). The role of nurse manager in ensuring competence—the use of portfolios and reflective writing. *Journal of Nursing Management, 9,* 249–251.

Joint Commission on Accreditation of Healthcare Organizations. (2004). *Management of human resources. Comprehensive accreditation manual for ambulatory care.* Oakbrook Terrace, IL: Author.

Kadlec, D. (2003). Where did my raise go? *Time, 161*(21), 44–54.

Krystof, L. (1996). Quality evaluations made easy and meaningful. *Journal of Nursing Care Quality, 11*(2), 6–8.

Levinson, H. (2003). Management by whose objectives? *Harvard Business Review, 81*(1), 107–116.

Martin, D.C., & Bartol, K.M. (1991). The legal ramifications of performance appraisal: An update. *Employee Relations Law Journal, 17,* 257–286.

Meeks, A., Hayes, T., Stahlhammer, S., & Zeaphey, M. (1995). Evaluation by portfolio. *Nursing Management, 26*(8), 72–74.

Metcalf, C. (2001). The importance of performance appraisal and staff development: A graduating nurse's perspective. *International Journal of Nursing Practice, 7,* 54–56.

Ng, I., & Maki, D. (1994). Trade union influence on human resource management practices. *Industrial Relations, 33*(1), 121–135.

Parks, J., & Lindstrom, C.W. (1995). Taking the fear out of peer review. *Nursing Management, 26*(3), 47–48.

Risher, H. (2002). Pay-for-performance: The keys to making it work. *Public Personnel Management, 31,* 317–332.

Roberts, G.E. (2003). Employee performance appraisal system participation: A technique that works. *Public Personnel Management, 32*(1), 89–97.

Rondeau, K.V. (1992). Constructive performance appraisal feedback for healthcare employees. *Hospital Topics, 70*(2), 27–34.

Roper, K.A., & Russell, G. (1997). The effect of peer review on professionalism, autonomy, and accountability. *Journal of Nursing Staff Development, 13*(4), 198–206.

Schweiger, I., & Sumners, G.E. (1994). Optimizing the value of performance appraisals. *Managerial Auditing Journal, 9*(8), 3–7.

Smith, M.H. (2003). Empower staff with praiseworthy appraisals. *Nursing Management, 34*(1), 16–17.

Sullivan, E.J., & Decker, P.J. (2001). *Effective leadership and management in nursing.* Upper Saddle River, NJ: Prentice Hall.

Swansburg, R.C. (2002a). Performance appraisal. In R.C. Swansburg & R.J. Swansburg (Eds.), *Introduction to management and leadership for nurse managers* (pp. 592–616). Sudbury, MA: Jones and Bartlett.

Swansburg, R.C. (2002b). The directing (leading) process. In R.C. Swansburg & R.J. Swansburg (Eds.), *Introduction to management and leadership for nurse managers* (pp. 383–392). Sudbury, MA: Jones and Bartlett.

Trossman, S. (1999). The professional portfolio: Documenting who you are, what you do. *The Oklahoma Nurse, 44*(2), 21–22.

Tziner, A., Kopelman, R.E., & Livneh, N. (1993). Effects of performance appraisal format on perceived goal characteristics, appraisal process satisfaction, and changes in rated job performance: A field experiment. *Journal of Psychology, 127,* 281–291.

Vruno, J.J. (2001, October/November). Do you measure up? *Insight Magazine.* Retrieved July 30, 2003, from http://www.insight-mag.com/insight/01/10-11/col-6-pt-1-WorkForce.htm

Vuorinen, R., Tarkka, M., & Meretoja, R. (2000). Peer evaluation in nurses' professional development: A pilot study to investigate the issues. *Journal of Clinical Nursing, 9,* 273–282.

Wimer, S. (2002). The dark side of 360-degree feedback. *TD, 56*(9), 37–42.

Lifelong Learning and Continuing Competency

Joan Such Lockhart, PhD, RN, CORLN, AOCN®, FAAN
Mary Magee Gullatte, RN, MN, ANP, AOCN®, FAAMA

"Invest in the human soul. Who knows, it might be a diamond in the rough."
Mary McLeod Bethune (Washington, 1999, p. 7)

Continuing competence is a key indicator of professionalism and is a mechanism by which the nursing profession is accountable to the public for its services (American Nurses Association [ANA], 2000). Professional nurses are ultimately responsible for developing and maintaining their own clinical competency, but employers, professional nursing organizations, credentialing bodies, providers of educational activities, and regulatory agencies also share in this charge (ANA, 2000; 2003).

The commitment of the RN to lifelong learning and continuing competence is emphasized in the "Standards of Professional Performance" outlined by ANA (2004a). Measurement criteria for this performance standard include behaviors that provide evidence of the self-directedness of the nurse, not only in identifying his or her own learning needs but also in participating in learning activities that contribute to continuing competency. These activities should contribute to the current clinical practice and professional issues of nurses. Nurses also are expected to maintain documentation as evidence of their continuing competency.

Similar expectations for RNs, including advanced practice nurses (APNs), are documented through standards developed by the Oncology Nursing Society (ONS) (1996, 2003) and other professional organizations for nurses working in specialties such as critical care and the operating room. The responsibility for continuing competency, assumed by employers of professional nurses and the role of nurse managers, will be addressed further and serve as the focus of this chapter.

Framework for Nursing Professional Development

Nurses are expected to actively engage in learning activities during their professional careers in order to develop and maintain their clinical competence (ANA, 2000, 2004a). This devotion to continuing competence necessitates a long-term commitment by nurses to become involved in lifelong learning activities (Brunt, 2002). Learning opportunities that support professional development of nurses include three separate, yet overlapping areas: academic education, continuing education, and staff development (ANA, 2000). Figure 18-1 depicts these three domains that comprise a "Framework for Nursing Professional Development." This framework emphasizes continuing competence and lifelong learning with the ultimate goal of quality patient and nursing care (ANA, 2000).

Figure 18-1. Framework for Nursing Professional Development

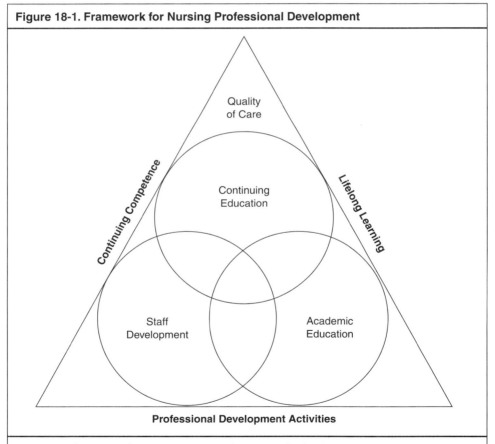

Professional Development Activities

Note. From *Scope and Standards of Practice for Nursing Professional Development* (p. 5) by American Nurses Association, 2000, Washington, DC: American Nurses Publishing. Copyright 2000 by the American Nurses Publishing. Reprinted with permission.

Academic Education

The first domain of this framework, *academic education,* includes undergraduate or graduate coursework completed at institutions of higher education, such as a university or college (ANA, 2000). These credits may or may not result in a formal degree or certificate.

Continuing Education

Continuing education (CE) includes learning activities designed to enhance the knowledge, skills, and attitudes of professional nurses (ANA, 2000). CE activities can positively impact outcomes related to patient care and professional careers. CE activities can range from formal, structured educational offerings to self-paced, independent learning formats.

Staff Development

Staff development, the third domain of this professional framework, consists of learning activities that focus on the assessment and development of competencies that are linked to a role or position assumed by nurses within a specific work setting (ANA, 2000). Employers often sponsor staff development activities for their clinical staff, thereby contributing to their shared responsibility for assuring the public of quality care provided by clinically competent employees (ANA, 2000). Although staff development activities are tailored to the learning needs of nursing staff that are hired by a specific employer, many of these educational offerings can have a positive impact on the performance of nurses employed in a variety of work settings.

In addition to serving as a domain in the framework for professional development, the term "staff development" is also viewed as a "systematic process of assessment, planning, development, and evaluation that enhances the performance or professional development of health care providers and their continuing competence" (National Nursing Staff Development Organization [NNSDO], 1999, p. 1). Staff development, as viewed in this process, will be described later in this chapter as it relates to the role of the nurse manager at the unit-based level.

The clinical competency of professional nurses through staff development is a primary concern for employers in healthcare organizations and will serve as the focus of this chapter. The nurse manager's role related to clinical competency and staff development for the unit-based clinical staff (nurse, assistive personnel) will be emphasized.

Staff Development and Continuing Competency

Staff development is conceptualized as one of three areas (see Figure 18-1) (ANA, 2000). Specific learning activities within staff development can be further organized into three components: orientation, in-service education activities, and CE (see Figure

18-2) (ANA, 2000). Although each of these three categories serves a specific purpose, all three contribute to the continuing competency of professional nurses. It is also important to recall that portions of staff development overlap with the academic education and CE domains (see Figure 18-1).

Figure 18-2. Key Components of Staff Development
• Orientation • In-service education • Continuing education
Note. Based on information from American Nurses Association, 2000.

Orientation

During the orientation portion of staff development, nurses receive information they need to carry out their designated roles and responsibilities within a specific work setting (ANA, 2000). Nurses attend orientation when they are initially hired into a healthcare organization and also attend orientations at a later time, when they assume a new position or role within that same organization. This latter example is the case for nurses who are cross-trained to function on other patient care units and for nurses who are promoted to leadership positions that require them to develop new and unfamiliar skills.

Although an orientation program primarily focuses on assessing, validating, and developing the competencies and critical thinking skills of newly hired employees, this program also helps socialize new employees to the culture of the workplace (ANA, 2000). New employees learn about the values of the organization and how they can become a contributing member (ANA, 2000). Although organizations may use various approaches in scheduling, designing, and implementing their orientation programs, the programs typically include information about the agency's philosophy, goals, policies and procedures, and specific performance expectations (ANA, 2000).

Most orientation programs pair experienced staff nurses with new orientees in a preceptor arrangement (Bumgarner & Biggerstaff, 2000). Staff nurses in the role of preceptors also are teamed with nursing students from affiliating schools of nursing in select nursing courses who have clinical experiences with the organization. Regardless of the situation, preceptors should be carefully selected, developed, acknowledged, and evaluated by the organizations (Bumgarner & Biggerstaff).

In-Service Education Activities

The second component of staff development, called in-service education offerings, also fosters the continuing competency of professional nurses (ANA, 2000). Unlike orientation programs, in-service education offerings focus on specific learning needs and are usually brief sessions, lasting 30 to 60 minutes. In-service education sessions are scheduled and presented a variety of ways, including formal centralized programs, informal unit-based sessions, or self-paced independent learning packages.

For example, an in-service education offering may introduce nurses employed on a medical oncology unit to a new IV catheter they will be using with patients on their clinical unit. During this in-service education session, the nurses may learn key features of the catheter and have an opportunity to practice using this new catheter with a model arm. Another example may be a new antineoplastic therapy or clinical trial to be implemented on the unit or in the ambulatory clinic. The same education strategies would apply.

Continuing Education

The CE component of staff development also attempts to strengthen staff's continuing competency. Although CE has been described as a separate entity, a portion of CE lies within both academic education and staff development (see Figure 18-1). For example, a CE activity for nurses employed by a healthcare agency may be a chemotherapy course sponsored by the agency or by a professional nursing organization. This course consists of formal evaluation based on program objectives. CE programs often offer formal CE credits obtained through a professional nursing organization.

Competency and Continuing Competence

Because ensuring continuing competency is a primary aim of staff development activities, it is important to understand what competencies are and how they are determined within the healthcare context. The Joint Commission on Accreditation of Healthcare Organizations (JCAHO) (2003) defined competency as the "determination of an individual's capabilities to perform up to defined expectations" (p. 347). Continuing competence is the "ongoing professional nursing competence according to level of expertise, responsibility, and domains of practice as evidenced by behavior based on beliefs, attitudes, and knowledge matched to and in the context of a set of expected outcomes as defined by nursing scope or practice, policy, code of ethics, standards, guidelines, and benchmarks that ensure safe performance of professional activities" (ANA, 2000, p. 23). The ultimate goal of competency and continuing competency is safe, quality patient care.

Healthcare organizations assess the competencies of nurses and other workers upon hire and at appropriate intervals during their employment. In most organizations, the initial assessment of competencies occurs during the orientation period. In fact, some agencies use an orientation program that is entirely competency based. The development and ongoing validation of select competencies often occur yearly using various means of staff development, such as formal and informal in-service education activities and CE offerings.

Competency-based orientation programs focus on core competencies that nurses are expected to demonstrate at the end of the orientation (Alspach, 1996). Core competencies often are prioritized in order of their risk, volume, and problem (Cooper, 2002). For example, properly suctioning a patient with a tracheostomy tube may be a high-risk, high-volume competency assessed and developed during orientation for nurses assigned to a head and neck oncology or pulmonary thoracic unit. Methods used to identify and strategies to assess and validate clinical competencies of nurses will be discussed later in this chapter.

Organizational Commitment to Staff Development

Organizational commitment to staff development is key to ensuring a competent healthcare workforce and quality patient care (Brunt, 2002). Creating a culture in the work setting that supports lifelong learning and continuing competency requires that individuals who hold leadership positions within these organizations be dedicated to this goal. Nurse managers play a vital role in developing this learning environment on a unit-based level and in supporting the professional development of their clinical staff.

Agencies That Accredit Healthcare Organizations

Employers share responsibility in assuring the public that the healthcare workers they employ provide competent nursing care (ANA, 2000). This obligation is made explicit by agencies that accredit healthcare organizations.

For example, the JCAHO strives to "continually improve the safety and quality of care provided to the public" by establishing accreditation standards that address the competence of healthcare workers (JCAHO, 2003, p. ii). Healthcare organizations seeking accreditation need to comply with these specific standards. Staff competence is particularly addressed in the human resource standards of the JCAHO accreditation manual (JCAHO). These standards require that staff competence be "assessed, maintained, demonstrated, and improved continually" (p. 244) through offerings, including orientation, in-service, and other education and training programs (JCAHO). Organizations are expected to track and analyze data related to staff competence and learning needs. Promoting compliance with these competency standards is an integral part of the role and responsibilities of nurse executives (administrators and managers) who help support an organization's mission and goals (JCAHO). Accreditation and compliance is addressed in more detail later in Chapter 25.

Scope and Standards for Nurse Administrators

ANA's *Scope and Standards for Nurse Administrators* emphasizes the importance of competence and professional development within healthcare organizations and hold nurse executives accountable for ensuring the competence of their nursing staff (ANA, 2004b). This commitment to staff development and professional nursing development extends to the unit-based level where nurse managers are expected to work collaboratively with members of the healthcare team to attain this important goal (ANA, 2004b). Nurse managers also assume overall responsibility for facilitating clinical experiences provided to affiliating nursing students (ANA, 2004b).

Benefits of Staff Development

Staff development activities, in addition to being included in accreditation standards and professional standards, are associated with positive outcomes such as job satisfaction and retention of nurses (Williams, Sims, Burkhead, & Ward, 2002). In this report, exit interviews conducted with staff revealed that the primary reason for nurses leaving an organization was dissatisfaction with their orientation.

Smith-Miller (2003) reported benefits of in-service training on the nursing care provided to otology patients after surgery. In this study, nurses who received in-service training significantly improved their perceived ability to provide quality patient care and use specialty support services.

The Role of the Nurse Manager and Staff Development

Nurse managers, as unit-based leaders within healthcare organizations, are responsible for ensuring that patients on their clinical unit receive safe, quality care from a competent nursing staff (ANA, 2004b). For this reason, nurse managers need to understand the staff development process (and activities) and its positive influence on the lifelong learning and continuing competence of nursing staff. Managers play an important role in not only ensuring a competent staff but in supporting the development of nursing staff through various educational offerings and nursing standards (ANA, 2000).

Nurse managers need to clarify their specific responsibility for staff development within the planning, organizing, staffing, directing, and controlling functions they assume for a clinical unit (ANA, 2000, 2002). The nurse manager's role in staff development may vary among healthcare organizations and often is influenced by available human and fiscal resources.

Recent decades of social, political, and economic changes forced many healthcare agencies, such as hospitals, to rethink the work of their organization and restructure (Avillion, 1998; Lockhart, 2004). Many centralized nursing staff development departments (NSDDs) that previously assumed primary responsibility for staff development activities were downsized or eliminated as separate departments. Priorities were reexamined, and the responsibility for staff development shifted within these organizations. As a result, many staff development responsibilities were decentralized and delegated to others within the organization. Staff development activities are now shared on a unit-based level by various individuals, such as nurse managers, clinical coordinators, APNs, or clinical staff nurses. In some instances, the leaders of some NSDDs retained core management functions and oversight regarding staff development within the organization.

Regardless of the approach used to deliver staff development services to nursing staff within a healthcare organization, it is important for nurse managers to obtain an organizational perspective of staff development to continue these initiatives seamlessly at a departmental or unit-based level. Nurse managers need to understand who makes decisions and what individuals are involved in the staff development and clarify their specific roles and responsibilities. Although nurse managers do not have direct control over certain variables affecting staff development, they do have choices regarding management styles and level of involvement in unit-based continued competency and personal learning (Cline, Reilly, & Moore, 2003). Figure 18-3 illustrates the six primary roles traditionally assumed by nurse educators in NSDDs: educator, facilitator, change agent, consultant, researcher, and leader (ANA, 2000).

Figure 18-3. Major Roles Assumed by Nursing Professional Development Educators		
• Educator • Facilitator	• Change agent • Consultant	• Researcher • Leader

Note. Based on information from American Nurses Association, 2000.

Nurses who assume new staff development responsibilities should receive education and training in this specialty in order to function effectively (Lockhart, 2004). Although nurses may possess clinical or management expertise, they do not necessarily have competencies in staff development (Brunt, 2002). Therefore, it is important to incorporate professional development to strengthen these competencies, and this should be an integral part of a staff development plan for an organization.

The Gullatte Clinical Practice Staff Development Model

The Gullatte Clinical Practice Staff Development Model(see Figure 18-4) will serve as the organizing framework in discussing the key features of staff development (Gullatte, 1998). This model is based on application in a medical oncology unit at an academic medical center. It also reflects the steps described in the systematic process of staff development (NNSDO, 1999) and the nursing process: assessment, planning, implementation (development), and evaluation. Each of these steps will be discussed within the context of orientation, in-service education activities, and CE offerings. Because the responsibility for staff development may vary among organizations, the roles of both nurse educators in the NSDD and nurse managers will be mentioned. Figure 18-5 provides examples of staff development responsibilities that may be assumed by nurse managers.

Assessment

The first phase of the staff development process includes a systematic assessment of learning needs that are specific to the targeted learners. This stage includes conducting an inventory of both human and fiscal resources (e.g., fees, time, materials, additional staffing to cover duties while unit staff members attend in-service, space). Each of these steps will be discussed in more detail in the following sections.

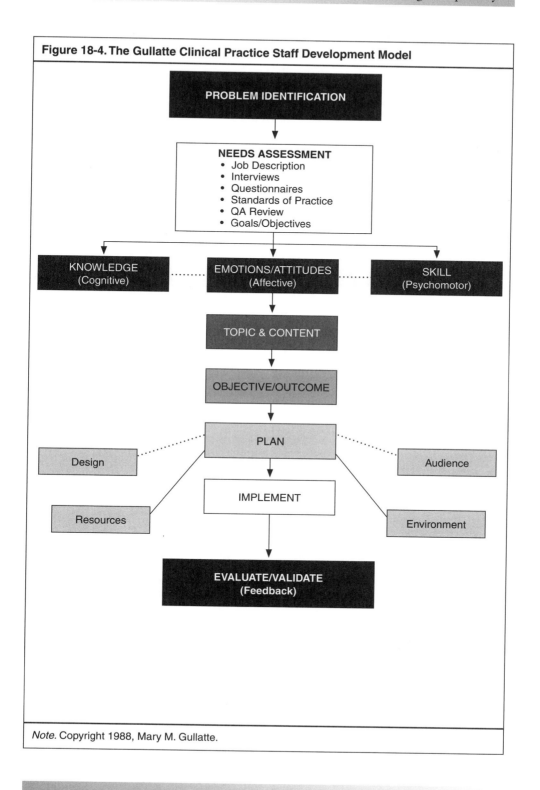

Figure 18-4. The Gullatte Clinical Practice Staff Development Model

Note. Copyright 1988, Mary M. Gullatte.

Figure 18-5. Staff Development Responsibilities That May Be Assumed by Nurse Managers

Assessment
- Assess learning needs.
- Determine resources.

Planning
- Provide resources.
- Develop collaborations.
- Design comprehensive staff development plan for the unit.
- Select preceptors.

Implementing
- Monitor plan.
- Develop and present an educational offering.
- Mentor staff in career development.
- Serve as role model.
- Serve as a preceptor.
- Provide resources (fees, time, additional staffing, materials, space).
- Prepare preceptors.
- Delegate staff development to appropriate staff.
- Provide staff with recognition for accomplishments.

Evaluating
- Assist in evaluating outcomes of the staff development plan.
- Determine cost effectiveness.
- Provide evaluation feedback on performance outcomes.

Learning Needs of Individuals

Assessing the learning needs of nurses is an essential step in the staff development process (NNSDO, 1999). Nurse managers play a significant role in this stage by collaborating with staff development educators and other individuals. The learning needs of nursing staff can be determined through both formal and informal sources, depending on the specific learner. For example, a formal written needs assessment may be conducted with nursing staff to identify learning needs they themselves perceive. Likewise, incident reports dealing with medication errors that occurred on a clinical unit offer a less structured means of determining learning needs (Brunt, 2002). Figure 18-6 lists possible sources from which learning needs of clinical RNs can be determined.

Organizations use a variety of strategies to capture the learning needs of nursing staff. For example, some employers survey their employees using a written questionnaire. This approach provides learning needs from the perspective of the targeted learner. In addition to these prescribed learning needs, it is important to determine ascribed learning needs that arise from other sources both within and external to the healthcare organization.

Hopkins (2002) described a tool used by nurse managers and clinical nurse specialists to evaluate the cognitive learning needs of RNs regarding their supervision of nursing assistants. Findings were used to guide educational activities aimed to strengthen these knowledge deficits.

Figure 18-6. Possible Sources for Assessing the Learning Needs of Professional Nurses

Internal to the Organization
- Survey of learning needs from staff perspective (questionnaires, focus groups)
- Assessment tools produced commercially
- Outcomes of individual performance appraisals
- Incident reports
- New or changed policies, procedures, and documents
- Results of quality assurance reports
- Observation on the clinical unit
- Patient satisfaction surveys
- Unit-based outcomes related to patient care (e.g., infections, readmission rates)
- Exit interviews
- Outcomes of staff development activities (orientation, in-service, continuing education)
- New or changed technology in clinical setting

External to the Organization
- Professional standards of practice and professional performance
- Professional outcomes for education and nursing practice
- Professional and healthcare trends and issues
- Recommendations from accreditation and regulatory agencies

Although conducting a needs assessment on a yearly basis is a logical strategy to determine staff learning needs, it is essential that assessment and validation of learning needs continue on a formal and informal basis throughout the year. New learning needs should be included, as appropriate, in the overall staff development plan on an ongoing basis.

Learning Needs of Groups

Although assessing the learning needs of nurses and other healthcare workers is vital in staff development, it is possible to anticipate the general learning needs of nurses based on their membership in a particular group. For example, newly hired novice nurses with less than a year of experience may need additional support during their orientation in making the transition from student to professional nurse. On the other hand, more experienced nurses may require assistance in adjusting to a more familiar role upon hire but within the context of a new setting or clinical specialty.

Cultural Diversity and Learning

Nurse managers employed by healthcare organizations in the United States are encouraged to develop a team of healthcare workers that reflects the current and future cultural diversity of the patient population for whom they provide nursing care (Davidhizar, Dowd, & Giger, 1998). The cultural background of these workers is an important factor to consider not only when assessing learning needs but in developing educational programs to help these learners be successful in their jobs.

Although heterogeneity or differences exist within designated ethnic/racial/cultural groups, researchers have developed transcultural models that can be used to guide the assessment of learning needs of individuals from diverse cultures. For example, Giger and Davidhizar (1999) developed a model that consists of six interrelated factors that need to be examined when conducting a cultural assessment: communication, personal space, time, social organization, environmental control, and biological variations. Figure 18-7 lists each of these six elements. Although all of these elements are critical, it is important to realize that communication is at the forefront of this model.

Figure 18-7. Select Concepts in Giger and Davidhizar's Transcultural Assessment Model

Communication
- Means of connecting people with one another through oral or written communications, gestures, facial expressions, body language, space, or other symbols

Space
- Extension of the body; discomfort is experienced when it is invaded; defined by culture

Social Organization
- Sociocultural behaviors learned; reflective of culture, environment, and lived experiences

Time
- Developing an awareness of the concept of time to the individual

Environmental Control
- Ability of a person to understand what one can and cannot control

Biological Variations
- Existence/nonexistence of biocultural differences in individuals based on race/ethnicity

Note. Based on information from Giger & Davidhizar, 1999.

Davidhizar et al. (1998) focused on the education of the culturally diverse student entering nursing. These nurse researchers pointed out that cultural behavior, or how one acts in certain situations, is socially acquired rather than genetically inherited. Individual core values found among culturally diverse students included values that supported smooth interpersonal relations with others, such as sensitivity, respect, loyalty, generosity, a sense of belonging, cooperation, tolerance, and accommodation of others. These, in some way, differed from the core values espoused by European Americans, which included values such as honesty, truthfulness, straightforwardness, self-assuredness, self-confidence, and self-motivation. These core values among both groups of students affect learning and the learning environment (Pacquiao, 1995).

Regardless of the model used to examine the learning needs of individuals from diverse backgrounds, it is important to recognize that differences in beliefs, core values, and behaviors exist not only among individuals and groups but also within the same individual and group under various circumstances. It is important that nurse managers directly communicate with each staff member and assess his or her unique learning needs through open discussion with the staff member. Nurse managers need to be objective and inclusive in matters concerning individuals in their healthcare team and support the success of each individual in their work environment.

In addition to considering the learning needs of individuals from diverse backgrounds, it is also important that nurse managers help their clinical staff strengthen their skills in working with diverse coworkers and in caring for patients from diverse backgrounds. For example, Lockhart and Resick (1997) described an experiential educational model they used to help nurses gain an understanding of cultural concepts needed for their professional role as a caregiver and coworker.

Resources for Staff Development

Nurse managers play a vital role in determining the human, fiscal, and environmental resources available for staff development. Care should be taken to determine who assumes primary responsibility for these services on a unit-based level.

Adequate human resources may include determining if there are appropriate numbers of qualified staff nurses who can serve as preceptors for newly hired graduate nurses and RNs during orientation. In healthcare organizations with more decentralized, unit-based staff development services, nurse managers need to determine which nurses possess particular skills and can assume the new role of unit-based educator with further education and training.

Siehoff (2003) described a Staff Educator Model that was implemented in her acute care facility where 23 staff nurses were selected to function in the role of staff educator RNs. These nurses were responsible for coordinating the unit-based staff development needs of clinical staff on their respective clinical units and were allotted two days per pay schedule to fulfill this role. Experienced nurse educators in the agency's clinical education department mentored these RNs and provided them with instruction and guidance in this new educator role. Staff educators reported many aspects of this role as rewarding, such as sharing ideas and collaborating with colleagues. Most of the RNs who evaluated this experience cited time constraints as a major barrier in this educator role.

In assessing human resources for staff development, managers should consider creative partnerships that can be developed and can contribute to the goals of staff development. For example, joint faculty appointments arranged between healthcare organizations and academic institutions may serve as a potential source of educational support for staff on the clinical unit while fulfilling faculty practice needs (Beitz & Heinzer, 2000). It may be possible to share limited resources by planning educational offerings with staff on more than one clinical unit (Lockhart & Bryce, 1996).

Directors of staff development and faculty, who comprise a consortium of 20 healthcare agencies and academic institutions called the Boston Collaborative Group, work collaboratively and share their resources for educating preceptors (Frame et al., 2002). The primary purpose of this collaboration is to provide innovative cost-effective educational offerings.

Nurse managers need to determine both direct and indirect costs associated with using unit-based staff, such as staff nurses, clinical coordinators, or APNs, for staff development purposes. These expenses may include educating and training these nurses for their new role, added wages or benefits, and replacement for direct patient care services. Nurse managers need to consider not only the costs of sending staff to educational programs external to the organization, such as travel and conference fees, but also indirect costs associated with replacing these staff for patient care needs. Nurse managers also need to consider other environmental resources for staff development purposes, such a space, equipment, and services (e.g., duplication costs).

Planning

After assessing the learning needs and resources needed for staff development on the clinical unit, it is essential to collaborate with others involved in the process and incorporate findings into a comprehensive staff development plan for the clinical unit. This plan should be organized, yet flexible enough to allow for the introduction of new learning needs or changes. It is also important that this plan be shared with nursing staff involved in the plan.

Unit-Based Staff Development Plan

Regardless of the method used to collect data related to staff learning needs, these data collected should be carefully organized and analyzed by those individuals involved in staff development. For example, learning needs (topics) should be prioritized in order of importance, with those needs of great urgency and frequency placed first. Although it may not be possible to meet all the learning needs requested, care should be taken to determine which needs are most important for patient care and other priorities. Resources to meet each of these specific learning needs, such as available speakers or existing programs, can be designated to the staff development areas of orientation, in-service education, and CE programs.

Lockhart and Bryce (1996) described a method they used to assess the learning needs of nurses from several specialty patient units. They developed a comprehensive staff development plan that prioritized learning needs, shared resources among various clinical units, and identified existing human resources to meet these learning needs. Part of this plan included teaching clinical nurses how to develop and present unit-based in-service education sessions.

Budget Needs

After developing the staff development plan, a budget needs to be created based on the projected human and fiscal resources identified. These expenses may be the responsibility of the manager of the NSDD or the clinical unit.

Documentation and Record-Keeping System

Similar to patient care activities, an important responsibility for staff development is establishing a comprehensive documentation and record-keeping system (ANA, 2000). These records should be easily retrievable for quality assurance, evaluation, and regulatory or accreditation purposes. For example, the State Department of Health may request to review unit training logs to prove that quarterly radiation in-services are conducted for therapists and dosimetrists in a radiation oncology department.

Developing Teaching and Learning Plans

Following the development of an overall staff development plan for the unit, individuals involved in teaching may need support in developing teaching and learning plans to serve as a guide or blueprint for their specific educational offering. Primary components of a teaching and learning plan include specific and measurable, learner-centered behavioral objectives that learners are expected to demonstrate, a brief outline of the content that needs to be addressed for the learner to meet the objectives, teaching strategies and audiovisuals that will be used in the offering, and the methods to evaluate learner outcomes.

Educators need to consider that people learn through different mechanisms such as listening, writing something down to be committed to memory, reading and re-reading information, or repeatedly attempting to perform a task until it is mastered. Bloom (1956) described how to write educational objectives for cognitive (dealing with recall or recognition of knowledge and the development of intellectual abilities), affective (changes in interest, attitudes, and values, and the development of appreciations), and psychomotor (motor skill) domains. For example, the stated objectives for an educational session may focus on the learners' knowledge of a topic (e.g., main mechanism of action in select chemotherapy drugs), whereas other objectives may emphasize their psychomotor skills (e.g., learning to start an IV in a patient's arm) or their affective domain (e.g., reactions and emotions associated with caring for patients following disfigured facial surgery for head and neck cancer). Regardless of the objective, presenters need to ensure that their teaching strategy and evaluation method match the stated objective in order for the learner to be successful.

Developing an Evaluation Plan

Prior to implementing a unit's staff development plan, develop a method of evaluating various aspects of the plan in advance. Consider evaluating not only the designated learning outcomes and satisfaction of learners, but include input from educators and managers. Remember to track changes in the performance of learners as evidenced by many of the sources used in the initial assessment phase, such as performance appraisals, incident reports, patient satisfaction surveys, and other documents. Evaluating the cost of staff development in light of its benefits also should be part of the overall evaluation plan.

Competency-based evaluation of learners usually is conducted as a baseline during orientation and continues on a regular basis to ensure continuing competency (JCAHO, 2003). Although many organizations use written exams and observations with skills checklists during simulations, approaches that measure the learners' actual performance in the clinical setting should be promoted (Bradley & Huseman, 2003).

The design and testing of an innovative competency program was described by Bradley & Huseman (2003), who used a direct observation approach to verify the competencies of nurses regarding pain management. Trained RNs as unit-based validators evaluated the performance of nurses at the bedside in a pain episode with patients. Review of the nurses' respective documentation also was included. These

RN validators relied on written guidelines that were derived from a pain protocol that was implemented at their agency. Educators developed six measurable competency statements based on this protocol, along with matching criteria for each competency. Criteria included measures of the nurses' cognitive, psychomotor, critical thinking, and interpersonal skills. Validators selected action plans to remedy competency statements unmet by some learners.

Zink and Robertson (2000) described the value of clinical paths as a method to evaluate nurses' competencies in an integrated delivery system. Nurse managers used these clinical paths as a framework for outcome-driven care, to evaluate nurses' skills and competencies, and to identify educational opportunities (Zink & Robertson).

Implementation

Implementing the staff development plan should follow the assessment and planning phases. Implementation not only includes presenting educational offerings using creative teaching strategies appropriate for adult learners, but managing the logistics for providing these activities.

Creative Teaching Strategies

Staff should be encouraged to use a variety of creative and active teaching strategies, such as posters, skills fairs, nursing grand rounds, self-learning packets, and simulations, when implementing unit-based staff development activities. For example, Jones, Jasperson, and Gusa (2000) described a gaming strategy they developed to test the knowledge level of neurointensive care nurses regarding the cranial nerves. These learners preferred the tool—the Cranial Nerve Wheel of Competencies—to paper and pencil examinations traditionally used to assess their competencies.

Bumgarner and Biggerstaff (2000) developed an orientation pathway based on a patient-centered approach to guide newly hired nurses and their preceptors in patient care activities, foster critical thinking skills, and apply the nursing process. This pathway also decreased reality shock experienced by new nurses during orientation and improved nurse retention and job satisfaction.

Adult Learning Principles

Regardless of the phase of staff development, it is important that everyone involved in staff development understands and incorporates principles of adult learning not only in educational offerings but through daily interactions with learners. According to these teachings, adults, such as nurses who participate in staff development activities, learn in a different manner than children or adolescents (Knowles, 1980, 1990). Educators of adults need to consider the following key factors when providing or guiding instruction. Adult learners need to

- Understand the purpose, pros, and cons of participating in an activity before they are inclined to do it (Knowles, 1990).
- Be self-directed learners and rely on their past life experiences in the learning process.

- Perceive a need to learn.
- Be motivated by their internal drive for self-esteem, an improved life, and job satisfaction.

Finally, an adult's way of learning is task-, life-, or problem-centered, rather than subject-centered, as in adolescents.

Applying these principles of adult learning to the new GN, experienced RN, or nursing assistant can be a challenge for nurse educators and nurse managers. For example, these adults should understand the need for staff development and the impact it may have on their clinical competency and performance in patient care. Active teaching strategies should be used in educational activities that provide for self-directedness and application of prior life experiences.

The learning environment should be one of open discussion and sharing of ideas, with the educator serving as a facilitator of learning.

Evaluation

Evaluation should include everyone involved in staff development and should reflect follow-up on progress toward the stated outcomes. The overall impact of the staff development program on the unit, department, and healthcare organization should be considered. The results of the evaluation plan should be discussed, with revisions made in future educational opportunities as needed.

Summary

Assuring the public that they receive safe, quality care by competent nursing professionals is a primary responsibility of individual professional nurses, and is shared with their employers, professional nursing organizations, and regulatory agencies. Continuing competency and lifelong learning through staff development are two mechanisms for attaining this goal. Nurse managers play a significant role in assessing the learning needs and resources available for staff development and in planning for adequate implementation and evaluation. Nurse managers are essential in creating a work environment that promotes learning and professional development.

References

Alspach, J.G. (1996). *Nursing staff development: Strategies for success* (2nd ed.). St. Louis, MO: Mosby.

American Nurses Association. (2000). *Scope and standards of practice for nursing professional development.* Washington, DC: American Nurses Publishing.

American Nurses Association. (2002). *Nursing's agenda for the future.* Washington, DC: American Nurses Publishing.

American Nurses Association. (2003). *Nursing's social policy statement* (2nd ed.). Washington, DC: Author.

American Nurses Association. (2004a). *Nursing scope and standards of practice.* Washington, DC: Author.

American Nurses Association. (2004b). *Scope and standards for nurse administrators* (2nd ed.). Washington, DC: Author.

Avillion, A.E. (1998). *The redesign of nursing staff development.* Pensacola, FL: National Nursing Staff Development Organization.

Beitz, J.M., & Heinzer, M.M. (2000). Faculty practice in joint appointments: Implications for staff development. *Journal of Continuing Education in Nursing, 31,* 232–237.

Bloom, B.S. (1956). *Taxonomy of educational objectives: Handbook I: Cognitive domain.* New York: David McKay.

Bradley, D., & Huseman, S. (2003). Validating competency at the bedside. *Journal for Nurses in Staff Development, 19,* 165–173.

Brunt, B. (2002). Creating and using staff development standards. *Journal of Nurses in Staff Development, 18,* 213–217.

Bumgarner, S.D., & Biggerstaff, G.H. (2000). A patient-centered approach to nurse orientation. *Journal of Nurses in Staff Development, 16,* 249–256.

Cline, D., Reilly, C., & Moore, J.F. (2003). What's behind RN turnover? *Nursing Management, 34*(10), 50–53.

Cooper, D.C. (2002). The "C" word: Competency. In K.L. O'Shea (Ed.), *Staff development nursing secrets* (pp. 175–184). Philadelphia: Hanley & Belfus.

Davidhizar, R., Dowd, S.B., & Giger, J.N. (1998). Educating the culturally diverse healthcare student. *Nurse Educator, 23*(2), 38–42.

Frame, K.B., Ballantyne, M.J., Haussler, S.C., McLaughlin, P., Kudzma, E.C., Murphy, J.M., et al. (2002). A collaborative model: Twenty healthcare agencies and academic institutions share resources to educate preceptors. *Journal for Nurses in Staff Development, 18,* 185–193.

Giger, J.N., & Davidhizar, R.E. (1999). *Transcultural nursing: Assessment and intervention* (3rd ed.). St. Louis, MO: Mosby.

Gullatte, M.M. (1998). *Gullatte clinical practice staff development model.* Unpublished.

Hopkins, D.L. (2002). Evaluating the knowledge deficits of registered nurses responsible for supervising nursing assistants: A learning needs assessment tool. *Journal for Nurses in Staff Development, 18,* 152–156.

Joint Commission on Accreditation of Healthcare Organizations. (2003). *2003 hospital accreditation standards: Accreditation policies, standards, intent statements.* Oakbrook Terrace, IL: Author.

Jones, A.G., Jasperson, J., & Gusa, D. (2000). Cranial wheel of competencies. *Journal of Continuing Education in Nursing, 31,* 152–154.

Knowles, M.S. (1980). *The modern practice of adult education: From pedagogy to andragogy.* Chicago: Follett Publishing Company.

Knowles, M.S. (1990). *The adult learner: A neglected species* (4th ed.). Houston, TX: Gulf Publishing Company.

Lockhart, J.S. (2004). *Unit-based staff development for clinical nurses.* Pittsburgh, PA: Oncology Nursing Society.

Lockhart, J.S., & Bryce, J. (1996). A comprehensive plan to meet the unit-based education needs of nurses from several specialty units. *Journal of Nursing Staff Development, 12,* 135–138.

Lockhart, J.S., & Resick, L.K. (1997). Teaching cultural competence: The value of experiential learning and community resources. *Nurse Educator, 22*(3), 27–31.

National Nursing Staff Development Organization. (1999). *Strategic plan 2000.* Pensacola, FL: Author.

Oncology Nursing Society. (1996). *Standards of oncology nursing practice.* Pittsburgh, PA: Author.

Oncology Nursing Society. (2003). *Statement on the scope and standards of advanced practice nursing in oncology* (3rd ed). Pittsburgh, PA: Author.

Pacquiao, D. (1995). Multicultural issues in nursing practice and education. *Issues, 16*(2), 4–12.

Siehoff, A.M. (2003). Staff educator RNs: Delivering unit-based education to bedside caregivers. *Journal for Nurses in Staff Development, 19,* 313–316.

Smith-Miller, C.A. (2003). Utilization and perceived benefits of postoperative otology in-service training for inpatient nurses. *ORL-Head & Neck Nursing, 21*(2), 9–10, 12–17.

Washington, G. (1999). *Attitudes of success.* Hong Kong: Great Quotations.

Williams, T., Sims, J., Burkhead, C., & Ward, P.M. (2002). The creation, implementation, and evaluation of a nurse residency program through a shared leadership model in the intensive care setting. *Dimensions of Critical Care Nursing, 21,* 155–161.

Zink, J., & Robertson, S. (2000). Clinical integration and nursing leadership across an integrated delivery system. *Seminars for Nurse Managers, 8,* 26–30.

Mentoring: Promoting the Development of Nurses

Marilyn K. Bedell, MS, RN, OCN®

"As iron sharpens iron, so does one person sharpen another." Proverbs 27:17

Nursing continues to be in a state of transition with specialization occurring in clinical, administrative, and academic settings. As nurses specialize, they need guidance and help to grow and to develop new cognitive, clinical, and technical skills. Many nurses who are in leadership positions are concerned about the development of novice nurses and nurses in the process of making career transitions. How does a nurse learn the skills needed to succeed in the profession and in his or her specialty? How do we keep nurses in the profession? How do we develop nursing leaders? Mentoring is one mechanism that can promote the development of nurses who will succeed and contribute to the profession. It is critical that nurses in positions of leadership within an organization learn about mentoring and how to use it as a tool to develop the next generation of nurse leaders.

Mentoring

Similar to nursing and management, mentoring is a science and an art. Mentoring is a process in which you are guided, taught, and influenced in your chosen profession. It is a relationship between a novice and an experienced professional. The experienced professional guides, counsels, and critiques the novice, thereby teaching professional survival skills and methods to specialize and advance in the profession.

Mentoring is not a new concept. According to Greek mythology (Homer, 1792/1991), Mentor was a loyal friend and wise advisor to King Ulysses. The king entrusted the care and training of his son to Mentor. Mentor was responsible not only for the professional skill development of the king's son, but was responsible also for the development of his social, religious, and personal talents. Mentor's comprehensive influence on the development of the king's son was to become an integral part of what became known as mentoring in medieval trade guilds. Over time, numerous words have been used to describe a mentor (see Figure 19-1).

Figure 19-1. Words Used to Describe a Mentor

• Investor	• Guardian	• Problem solver
• Teacher	• Supporter	• Sponsor
• Leader	• Coach	• Career counselor
• Motivator	• Door opener	• Challenger

The role of a mentor is to develop the unique abilities of each person in a way that is not detrimental to others. Thus, the mentor helps the protégé feel safe and comfortable asking questions, asking for advice, or talking through a situation.

Mentors should not be confused with helpful peers or role models. Peers may be able to help a person to learn by sharing experiences but are unable to warn them of potential professional problems or issues. They may be unable to offer guidance around obstacles. Role modeling is often a one-way relationship. There is no commitment from the role model to guide and counsel. It tends to be a passive process in which a person watches and then copies the model. Role modeling relies on imitation and does not encourage the development of the unique qualities of the individual. No formal discussions occur to verify why the role model performed a certain way in a specific situation (Bidwell & Brasler, 1989).

Establishing a Mentoring Relationship

To establish a true mentoring relationship, the protégé and mentor each need to make an equal contribution. The protégé must have qualities that support investment of time and energy from a mentor. As a leader, you should be looking for someone who has the following qualities: demonstrates competence, shows a desire to learn, takes initiative, and is willing to help you achieve your goals.

As a mentor, you will be required to demonstrate to your protégé that you are competent, accountable, and committed to let the protégé grow to a level of his or her ability. This may entail the protégé "outgrowing" you during the process.

Nurses may wonder why they should become a mentor. According to Hollister (2001), if done correctly, mentoring will help nurse leaders to (a) enhance their own clinical, educational, research, and/or administrative skills; (b) develop and retain talent in their organization; (c) gain support for important initiatives; (d) bridge the gap between generations; and (e) create a legacy. Creating a legacy may be one of the most important things a leader can do. To be remembered for facilitating the growth and development of other nurses would be a long-lasting reward for the mentor.

Stages of Mentoring

Pilette (1980) described four stages of mentoring: relationship building (introduction), questioning (facilitative, confrontive), information (advice, networks), and transition (motivation, initiative), which were further refined by Cohen (1999).

During the relationship building stage, a person is invited to be, or asked to be, a protégé. Once the relationship is set, the protégé is encouraged to think and dream about his or her career as a whole. The mentor may see skills and potential that are not visible to the protégé. It is a time when goals are established. The role of the mentor is to nurture the relationship.

As the protégé moves into the questioning stage, he or she may begin to have worries that he or she will not be able to meet the goals and expectations that have been set. The mentor then works with the protégé to ensure that the goals are still realistic and able to be accomplished. Plans and timelines are generated for meeting goals. Plenty of time is given to discussing issues and concerns. The mentor pushes the protégé to generate potential solutions to problems. A mentor works to facilitate projects and opportunities. At this point, the mentor should consider when there is a need to confront problems and give honest feedback.

The information stage is a time for the mentor to establish effective communication networks for the protégé. The protégé learns how to maneuver in the organization. The protégé is given broader responsibility. The mentor provides advice and access to various professional networks.

Finally, in the transition stage, the protégé becomes self-assured and self-reliant. The protégé requires less supervision and guidance from the mentor. The protégé remains motivated to grow professionally and often takes the initiative to seek out new opportunities independently. At this point, the formal mentoring relationship may terminate. Often the outcome of a mentoring relationship is a lifelong friendship.

Mentoring and Business

During the late 1970s and early 1980s, business literature began to focus on mentor/protégé relationships as a means to develop executives. Many executives attributed their success in business to a supportive mentor relationship (Roach, 1979). Levinson, Darrow, Klein, Levinson, and McKey (1978) suggested that to develop professionally, you need the help of a strong, seasoned mentor. They have described five major roles for a mentor that still hold true: teacher, sponsor, host, exemplar, and counselor.

As a teacher, the mentor works to enhance the intellectual development of the protégé. In the sponsor role, the mentor will look for new professional opportunities that will help the protégé grow and develop professionally. The mentor conveys information about professional expectations, customs, resources, and the social structure of the organization; this is the host role. An exemplar is an admirable person because he or she seems to instinctively know the right thing to do and the right way to do it. An exemplar acts as a role model and encourages questions about his or her own practice. As a counselor, the mentor supports, advises, and gives feedback. This may be one of the toughest roles for the mentor. There is the need to honestly critique the performance of the protégé. Without this direct feedback, the protégé may not grow and develop to his or her full potential.

Creating a Mentoring Environment

Highly motivated nurses need an environment that supports their professional growth and development. Mentoring relationships can be used as a means to create such an environment. Nurse leaders must strive to become mentors. Prestige and satisfaction as a professional come from helping nurses grow and develop professionally.

Mentors are needed during transition points in a career. Benner (1984) described the framework of moving from novice to expert in nursing. Often, mentors are needed when you are a novice or an advanced beginner in a clinical, administrative, research, or academic position. During these stages, it is helpful to have the support of a competent, proficient, or expert practitioner to guide your professional development.

A nurse mentor should be able to relate to the issues that confront a nurse who is learning a new job and learning to navigate in the organization. Helping the protégé learn about the "politics" of the organization, the administrative structure, and the culture are key to learning how to succeed in a new work environment.

In addition, the professional role is just one of the roles a nurse must prioritize and play. It often is hard to balance the multiple roles a nurse must fulfill every day such as nurse, spouse, parent, friend, child, sibling, student, and professional society member. Mentors can help the nurse find the proper balance needed to meet the various challenges these roles will entail.

Creating opportunities for younger nurses to succeed and advance and providing them with support and encouragement can be the most significant roles available to a leader in nursing. Mentors can help a nurse develop a strong professional identity. They can support the development of intra-professional relationships based on mutual respect and trust. Mentors can teach the fine art of networking. A large circle of colleagues allows access to many new and creative opportunities.

Nurses who have made it to the "top" must be careful not to pull the ladder up behind them. Nurses must realize that clout comes from the prestige of those whom you help to grow professionally. A nurse may feel that he or she has made it on his or her own and may find it hard to understand the importance of helping others. Professional support makes career growth easier for everyone. Getting to the top of a ladder is easier if you have strong support underneath and on each side of you. When the manager is perceived as being a capable leader and works to develop other capable leaders, leadership will be sustained at all levels in the organization.

Skills Needed for Mentoring

As a mentor, the nurse leader needs to be able to set the vision, believe in the protégé's capabilities, show genuine interest, find time to commit to the relationship, and be sensitive to needs of the protégé (Shaffer, Tallarico, & Walsh, 2000). The mentor must remember that the role is an extremely important and influential one. The mentor is potentially in a position of power. Lee (2000) reminded us that truly successful mentors do not use power, but rather use empowerment to help the protégé become creative and productive. Through empowerment, legitimate power is achieved and maintained.

Starting the Relationship

According to Murray (2002), early on in the mentoring relationship, the mentor should work with the protégé to answer the following questions. What are the expectations and outcomes desired by the protégé and the mentor? Is there a philosophic match between the mentor and the protégé? How can the protégé demonstrate that he or she is committed to the relationship? What sort of orientation to the relationship will be required? What will it take for us to be effective? Why do we want to do this? How can our skills be applied to this work? How long do we think this will take?

It is important to lay the groundwork for the relationship early. The mentor needs to work with the protégé to make sure that they (a) set goals, (b) agree to the commitment of time and energy needed to make the relationship work, (c) determine factors that will help them build a trusting relationship, (d) establish benchmarks that will indicate that progress is being made, (e) determine what will be different as a result of this relationship, (f) understand the talents they each have that will help make them successful, and (g) decide what will happen if either finds the relationship is not working for either the mentor or the protégé (Lanser, 2000; Moscinski, 2002).

Lanser (2000) described traits of successful mentors. The author indicated that you must be able to commit time and energy to the relationship; adhere to commitments given to the protégé; listen without judging, but listen to questions and provide guidance while not offering solutions; and provide constructive feedback that is objective and easy to hear.

A mentor needs to be flexible and permit the relationship to grow, develop, and change course as needed. As a mentor, you need to know what you can offer, be willing to make an offer, and then move forward to work toward mutual goals. Through this relationship, the goal should be to promote autonomy while providing honest feedback, encouragement, and support.

Mentoring Outcomes

If mentoring is done well, the following outcomes should be achieved. The protégé should progress in his or her career, be empowered to achieve results, expand his or her professional knowledge, and fully understand the social and political structures he or she resides in. More importantly, if mentoring is done well, the outcome is a generation of talented and competent new leaders who will be willing to mentor others.

Mentoring Resources

Both the American Organization of Nurse Executives (AONE) and the Oncology Nursing Society (ONS) have developed tools to help nurse leaders learn more about mentoring. AONE has two mentoring publications that are available on its Web page: "A Handbook for Professional Advisors/Mentors" (www.hospitalconnect.com/aone/docs/handbook_mentors.doc) and "A Handbook for Those Who Wish to Be Advised/Mentored" (www.hospitalconnect.com/aone/docs/handbook_mentees.doc). These handbooks include a variety of ideas and resources for establishing a mentorship program. In addition, they provide guidance to both mentors and protégés on how to establish and sustain a successful mentoring relationship.

ONS is committed to the development of nurse leaders and nurse mentors. Its Leadership Development Institute is focused on developing nursing leaders both within ONS and within their home organizations. The emphasis is to prepare future nursing leaders for influential roles in cancer care. ONS invests in the individual nurse for the collective good of the nursing profession. At its core is the importance of the concept of mentoring.

In addition, ONS, through the ONS Foundation, has provided many opportunities for writers and researchers to be mentored by other well-seasoned writers and researchers who are ONS members. The dyads work together to complete publications and research projects. The novice is guided and taught the skills necessary to complete the assigned project.

ONS has developed a powerful video and booklet series that focuses on mentoring, *Power of Presence* (Nevidjon, 2001). The video is titled "Mentorship: Our Commitment to Our Future." The tape focuses on the role an oncology nurse can play in nurturing nurses new to oncology into their specialty.

Celebrations and Final Thoughts

Throughout the mentoring process, the mentor should look for celebratory moments. Milestones should be formally acknowledged and achievements marked with joyful celebrations. Being able to reflect on the process helps us to better understand and value overcoming major barriers to complete something of worth. Nothing is grander than to see a colleague achieve a dream and to know you played a significant part in making it happen. Nurse leaders must be committed to developing the next generation of nurses. Competent leaders are needed to take us forward in this complex, complicated, and demanding healthcare environment. Nurses must get excited and focused on designing the care environment of the future. Nurses must be at key leadership tables to advocate for patients and nurses. The role of the nurse leader is to make sure nurses are prepared to mentor and grow. The rewards of mentorship will leave a lasting legacy for the next generation of nurses.

References

Benner, P. (1984). *From novice to expert: Excellence and power in clinical nursing practice.* Menlo Park, CA: Addison-Wesley.

Bidwell, A.S., & Brasler, M.L. (1989). Role modeling versus mentoring in nursing education. *Image: Journal of Nursing Scholarship, 21*(1), 23–25.

Cohen, N.H. (1999). *The manager's pocket guide to effective mentoring.* Amherst, MA: HDR Press.

Hollister, L.R. (2001). The benefits of being a mentor. *Healthcare Executive, 16*(2), 49–50.

Homer. (1792/1991). *The odyssey of Homer.* New York: Oxford University Press.

Lanser, E.G. (2000). Reaping the benefits of mentorship. *Healthcare Executive, 15*(3), 18–23.

Lee, L.A. (2000). Buzzword with a basis: Motivation, mentoring and empowerment. *Nursing Management, 31*(10), 24–28.

Levinson, D.J., Darrow, C.N., Klein, E.B., Levinson, M.H., & McKey, B. (1978). *The seasons of a man's life.* New York: Alfred A. Knopf.

Moscinski, P. (2002). Take charge of your mentoring experience. *Healthcare Executive, 17*(4), 62.

Murray, R.B. (2002). Mentoring: Perceptions of the process and its significance. *Journal of Psychosocial Nursing, 40*(4), 44–51.

Nevidjon, B. (Ed.). (2001). *The power of presence.* Pittsburgh, PA: Oncology Nursing Society.

Pilette, P. (1980). Mentoring: An encounter of the leadership kind. *Nursing Leadership, 80*(60), 23–24.

Roach, G.R. (1979). Much ado about mentors. *Harvard Business Review, 57*(1), 14–15.

Shaffer, B., Tallarico, B., & Walsh, J. (2000). Win-win mentoring. *Dimensions in Critical Care Nursing, 19*(3), 36–38.

CHAPTER 20

Workplace Reengineering, Reorganization, and Redesign

Patricia Stanfill Edens, RN, MS, MBA, FACHE

"He who upsets a thing must know how to rearrange it." African proverb

Workplace reengineering, reorganization, and redesign are responses to internal and external factors exerting influences on the organization in this dynamic healthcare environment. The most aggressive application in the workplace is reengineering. Hammer and Champy (1994), the founders and leading proponents of reengineering, defined the process as the fundamental rethinking and radical redesign of process to achieve dramatic improvements in critical, contemporary measures of performance, such as cost, quality, service, and speed. Reengineering is the design of a completely new process, whereas variations on reengineering can deliver enhancement or improvement in an existing process or a response to an external stressor. Reorganization and redesign are less aggressive in scope than reengineering and may involve reconfiguring an existing structure or process similar to what may be involved in total quality management rather than starting from scratch. The manager operating in the current healthcare environment can expect to face a need for workplace reengineering, reorganization, and redesign in the future and must be prepared both professionally and personally for its impacts.

The Driving Force for Workplace Reengineering, Reorganization, and Redesign

No business can be stagnant and expect to survive. An ongoing transformation process is the norm, and when business does not evolve with the environment, failure results. Hospital business activity is influenced by a variety of internal and external forces. Factors may include changes in reimbursement, a shortage or excess of labor, changes in the political landscape, the economy, and others. Managers must be cognizant of the environment in which they function in order to anticipate and recognize the need for change and for facilities to remain viable entities.

External Forces

Organizations are currently analyzing trends in the healthcare environment as external factors come to bear on facilities. The current hospital environment can expect a flat-to-obvious decline in inpatient volumes over the next 5–10 years because of less invasive technologies and surgeries and a smoothing of demand, too, as more seniors maintain a healthy lifestyle, including prevention and screening measures leading to early detection and lower acuity interventions. The transition from inpatient- to outpatient-driven strategies will keep the higher acuity patient in the inpatient setting with a need for more intensive care beds and fewer traditional inpatient accommodations. Consumer cautiousness related to cost of insurance, co-pays, and pharmaceuticals leads to fewer voluntary admissions in both inpatient and outpatient areas (Advisory Board, 2003).

The outpatient areas can expect a surge in volume as inpatient admissions are averted, but the reimbursement to the facility is significantly lowered. Emerging technologies have the potential to drive more change as technologies such as positron emission testing can avert surgical interventions by indicating malignancy in advance of or in place of biopsy prior to surgery. A continued rise in physician- or company-owned specialty hospitals and outpatient centers will siphon patients from the traditional hospital setting, leading to a decline in both census and revenues as patients in the hospital facility generally become more acute and provide lower margins. Mergers, acquisitions, and closures of facilities also impact both inpatient and outpatient volumes as patient duplications or absence of services result (Advisory Board, 2003).

Changes in reimbursement are external factors with significant implications for volume shifts in the traditional hospital facility. With their higher overhead costs, hospitals often lose managed care contracts to outpatient imaging centers or physician offices or to other better-managed organizations willing to provide care at a lower price. Managed care organizations (MCOs) are influenced by the purchasers of their product to deliver a lower cost of care. Business, the underwriter of health care for much of the population, demands that the MCO negotiate lower rates to keep down the business premium cost. Business also is offering to its employees graduated payment plans based on services selected. Many employees are selecting lower premiums leading to higher co-pays, which may be more difficult for the hospital to collect. Coupled with changes in managed care costs are the dramatic fluctuations in government-sponsored reimbursement, such as Medicare and Medicaid. Annually, the centers for Medicare and Medicaid attempt to drive down the reimbursement to both hospital and nonhospital settings. Of recent note has been the move to restructure physician office reimbursement (lowering reimbursement) that may lead to an influx of chemotherapy patients from the physician office outpatient setting back into the hospital outpatient setting. This type of movement would require a significant change in the hospital, as most do not have sufficient infusion center capacity to handle this influx.

Being sensitive to the external forces that may influence a facility is important, but these same forces may translate to internal impacts, which are equally important. For example, there are influencing factors that are difficult to segment into external or internal forces on a consistent basis. Cultural impacts external to the facility can come from a shift in demographics in the market. A large foreign or indigent population shift may cause internal forces that necessitate the need for translators or accommodations to the cultural needs of this population. Societal needs in the community may influence hospitals both externally and internally. A hospital losing money on obstetrics may not be able to close the service if they are the only provider in the community. Although the internal need is to close the service in order to save dollars, the external need is greater to keep the service. External forces may lead to internal influences or may stand alone as a rationale for change. Once external forces are considered, the nurse manager should consider internal forces.

Internal Forces

Probably the most influential internal force impacting facilities is lowered margins, as reimbursement has steadily declined over past years. Arguably, lowered reimbursement is external to the facility in most instances, but the use of dollars can be determined as an internal factor that must be managed. As wages increased because of staff shortages and technology costs increased with price increases from vendors, profits in the hospital were consumed. The use of dollars in service delivery decisions (e.g., cardiology versus oncology) has significant internal ramifications. Coupled with weakened infrastructure in the facility and sociopolitical factors within the management structure of the organization, these declining fortunes of the hospital industry beg for redesign. Drucker (1993) described the incongruous economic realities of industry that translate well to health care. In most industries, when volume grows, profitability also grows. It is hard to understand why rising demand does not always equate to enhanced performance of the healthcare entity. Looking from the most obvious financial impacts, whether internal or external, to less obvious influences supports the need of the organization for change.

The culture and history of the organization can influence responses to factors interpreted as threatening within the facility. The internal climate that exists within a facility can determine the ability of the staff to accept change in a positive manner. Poor morale, lack of trust, and a feeling of disengagement with the organization are internal factors that influence the organization's ability to reform and succeed. If staff reductions are the immediate response to internal threats without a clear plan of action, staff may not trust the organization to appropriately handle future events. Downsizing, whether through eliminated positions, department outsourcing, or layoffs, is an unfortunate trend in health care and often leads to more detrimental effects than it prevents. A secretive senior management also may lead to distrust on the part of employees as opposed to an open communication model in which staff are kept apprised of events that may impact their future.

A thorough and ongoing assessment of external and internal factors exerting an influence on the organization is expected of senior leadership to define a proactive plan of action in anticipation of strategic threats. By developing and implementing a plan of action in advance of anticipated negative events, corrective measures may be initiated. Whether it is the development of a strategic plan or a process improvement study, forward-thinking organizations are defining an action plan to respond to their environment in a positive manner, which is designed to accomplish their goals. Strategic planning follows a well-known process of setting goals and defining implementation plans based on previous activities, a next step, so to speak. In contrast, reengineering is radical redesign implying a major upheaval within the facility. By carefully defining a strategic approach to workplace reengineering, reorganization, and redesign and incorporating the influences of external and internal factors, the process may be better managed, leading to a more positive outcome on the facility and employees.

Change in the Organization

In the popular guide to change, *Who Moved My Cheese*, a line in the book stated, "I keep doing the same things over and over again and wonder why things don't get better" (Johnson, 1998, p. 43). The need for change in the organization can be generated from external pressures, such as reimbursement declines, or internal pressures, such as a failure in process like slow turnover times in surgery leading to surgeon dissatisfaction. Consistently doing things the same way without considering either system weaknesses or external impacts dooms the organization to failure, at the worst, or to mediocrity, at best. The organization will not get better unless the managers are willing to risk change.

If planned or unplanned change occurs in an organization, the manner in which it is handled can dictate success or failure. Regardless of source, "a change imposed is a change imposed" (Johnson, 1998, p. 91). Leading change within an organization requires an ability to clearly state vision and direction and the ability to involve all parties and motivate them to accomplish the plan. Knowledge of change theory assists the leader in effecting change in a positive and timely manner. The implementation of a strategic plan or a workplace redesign implies a change in the status quo. The primary goal of the manager is to educate employees so that they know what to expect as change occurs in the organization. The pace of change in the healthcare environment can be rapid. The ability of an organization to respond to both internal and external influences and implement a strategy to respond without self-destructing is critical to survival. Organizational change takes a toll on the people within the organization. Involving them in the process of change can mitigate some of the stress of change.

Pollard (2001), in a two-year study of 98 women and 86 men, determined that the lowest mental well-being (self-reported) occurred right before reorganization. Physiologic measures such as blood pressure readings and total cholesterol reached their highest levels, again, prior to reorganization. Both managers and employees must acknowledge that change is stressful to the point of physical symptoms. Pollard further stressed time for self, appropriate nutrition, exercise, and verbalization to supportive people as strategies to manage the stress of change (Pollard). Managers should be cognizant of their employees' need to ventilate but should not be reactive to their comments. Managers also should consider verbalization to supportive people but not necessarily to peers and never to subordinates.

Leaders of change in an organization may not always be the managers. Lack of managerial leadership may result in negative consequences, such as staff turnover, union discussions, and poor morale that impacts patient care. To control the environment, managers must communicate clearly to employees and develop an open communication model. Employees must be able to verbalize that change is occurring and comprehend the impact of this change on the organization, their department, and on themselves. If employees cannot understand the need for reactive change because of external factors, the facility will not survive. Managers must have the trust of their employees on an ongoing basis and well in advance of change in order to bring forth the agenda necessary to direct the facility through uncertain or difficult times. Educating staff to current global and local market factors on an ongoing basis is one way to ensure that change in response to external factors does not come as a total surprise.

Leading Change

Leading change is the ability to motivate others to achieve a set of goals and objectives. In a progressive organization, senior leadership may request a contingency plan for continuing inpatient declines or staffing vacancies. The manager may be asked to define a plan that incorporates the mission and vision of the organization while addressing the need to cut costs or deal with impending staff shortages. Change leadership requires creative thinking, the ability to appropriately influence others, an ability to see beyond the job description, and a flexible attitude. It also requires an ability to see the global picture for the industry and the facility so that a fair allocation of human, financial, and clinical capital occurs. It is crucial to involve the staff in decision making after first explaining the purpose of the planning exercise. If the manager does not have the trust of the employees, this will be the most difficult step in the change process, as the employees will perceive change as negative and threatening rather than as a way to enhance the performance of the facility. The goal for the manager is to be able to effect change without a loss of employee trust. If change is not managed well, employee resistance will lead to failure of the effort, turnover of staff, negative impact on the quality of patient care, and decline in productivity.

Change management requires an agent to manage the process. If senior management demands a change in patient satisfaction scores, and the employees do not understand what they can do to accomplish this task, it is the responsibility of the manager to become the change agent to reconcile the request of senior management with actions that the employee can understand. For employees, these actions might include introducing themselves upon entering the room, explaining their role, and always asking if there is anything else the patient needs before departing. In a more global sense, finances—savings or increases in revenue, personal or professional needs, patient's needs, or organizational needs dictate change priorities.

Averting Conflict Related to Change

Conflict may occur as a result of change. Conflict management strategies are integral skills for the manager. A simple strategy is education of the staff. Informing subordinates as to why change is necessary in advance of the action is a positive approach that often will circumvent the conflict that may arise if change is not managed well. Staff acceptance rather than the potential for sabotage is a direct result of understanding why change is occurring. Managing change through the organization correctly enhances the potential for organizational success. One strategy to implement change is to involve the individuals who are impacted. An interactive change management approach rather than a reactive approach when confronted with change is preferred. Managers who create a culture that encourages staff to challenge the existing environment will seldom face the need for redesign, because the constant assessment for change will lead to a progressive organization.

Change within a healthcare organization is inevitable, given the dynamics of the environment. Individuals must learn to adapt, most appropriately with the assistance of management. Recognizing that change can be beneficial to a facility, managers must be prepared with a strategy and plans. Although the pace may be rapid, the prepared manager can determine the best plan to bring the agenda of change forward without negatively impacting the organization. Planning is the key to controlling change.

Strategic Planning, Visioning, and Reengineering

Change in the organization may flow from the strategic planning process or from the vision of the leadership. It may be incremental as annual goals are achieved. It differs from reengineering in that it assumes a baseline level of performance that is not detrimental and determines the strategy needed to move the enterprise forward. If an organization is operating well in its environment, strategic planning may be all that is indicated to guide the enterprise. However, strategic planning may be an annual event that consumes time and effort with minimal outcome effect in an organization. An understanding of the strategic planning process can serve as the foundation for a reengineering or redesign effort. An in-depth review of strategic planning and marketing is covered in Chapter 22 of this book.

Successful managers write a concise plan of action that evolves from the mission statement of the facility, internalize the plan so that it guides the process of work for the stated time period, and accept ongoing evaluation and revision as integral parts of the stated strategy. Managing the work process based on a carefully developed strategy is far superior to reacting to repeated episodic events. Reaction rather than planned action will create stress in the organization. Strategy development must consider flow of work and end-point outcomes rather than measuring task completion. The ability to visualize and model the future is the essence of leadership. Strategic planning is interdependent, collective, and multiplicative in the organization as departments and service lines define their individual strategies, which ultimately must roll up to accomplish the overriding strategy of the organization. It generally has a defined beginning and end that equate to the fiscal year of the facility.

For strategic planning to be successful, senior management must have a clear vision of what the organization should be in order to accomplish its obligations to the consumer of provided services. This vision must clearly state, for example, that the facility must meet the healthcare needs of the community in which it resides. Being able to describe the vision of management guides the development of the plan and encourages the buy in of the employees. Hospital Corporation of America (HCA), a for-profit healthcare provider with 197 hospitals and 80 ambulatory surgery centers in 23 states, places much emphasis on its vision, mission, and values statement. Employees are educated annually to its content and are expected to incorporate it into their daily actions, and managers are expected to incorporate its elements into their management of their business enterprise, including the strategic planning process. The corporate leadership of HCA defined strategic initiative for the company, but then each facility and its managers adapt that strategy to the local market in order to meet both local and corporate goals. Strategic plans for all facilities are based on the 12-month fiscal year of the parent company, and incentive compensation is partially based on successful implementation of the plan measured against expected outcomes.

Once a clear understanding of the overriding vision and mission is shared, the manager must begin to conceptualize the actions needed to achieve the goals of the organization. Strategic plans generally begin at the senior management level, and then departments or service lines are expected to expand on their specific contribution to the overall completion of the plan. Following this premise will allow an analysis of the situation that prevents an inappropriate strategic plan that can have long-term negative consequences. As noted by Clancy (2003), "the results of poor decisions often do not appear until years later" (p. 343).

A strategic plan should be dynamic and ever changing, evolving as it is implemented. Just as a plan of care for a patient is revised as the patient's condition improves, the strategic plan should be monitored and adjusted as the plan is implemented. Flexibility in implementation is the key to successful strategic accomplishment. A plan is written with a strong foundation of evidence, but often the constraints of the real-life situation require adaptation and change in order to accomplish the goal. Using a SWOT (strength, weakness, opportunity, threat) analysis or an analysis of the service life cycle will provide a comprehensive foundation for the strategic plan (Ginter, Swayne, & Duncan, 2002). The ability to adapt and reorient the direction of the strategy is the key to organizational survival. Often though, the strategic plan is not sufficient to reorient the direction of the organization, and a more sweeping change is indicated.

The need for a more aggressive reengineering of the organization may originate from a variety of sources. As data are gathered for the strategic planning process, management may realize that the organization is no longer working efficiently and effectively. Planning a strategy to reorient the existing situation and perhaps move forward a bit will not suffice. A major overhaul is indicated at times. The rationale for this may be new competition, lack of systematic planning in past years leading to stagnation, or mismanagement. Regardless of the cause, reengineering may be indicated. Timing of reengineering is situational or opportunity dependent. It may occur midyear and cross into the next fiscal year.

Wolper (1999) believed that health care would continue to face the external pressures of mergers, consolidations, changes in patient volume and type, and reimbursement, leading to the need for a more sophisticated delivery system. Hospitals that find themselves with a negative net income may come to the realization that the status quo is not working. A department may not be delivering sufficient work for its cost. All are examples where reengineering may be indicated. Reengineering evolved primarily in the manufacturing sector, and to reinvent the existing healthcare model, managers looked for assistance from industrial engineers. Forward thinking managers believed that industrial engineering could benefit hospitals, so they brought in industrial engineers, called them management engineers, and tasked them to assist in process redesign. Management engineering in health care employs engineering principles to work flow processes, patient needs, cost per unit of service, and staffing in an attempt to achieve cost efficiencies and effectiveness. Reengineering begins with a blank sheet of paper, with the only known fact being what the outcome should be when the process is implemented.

Applying quantifiable principles in health care is not a new concept, but incorporating clinical staff participation increases the likelihood of success. For example, management engineers in one facility developed a productivity measurement system for radiation therapy without clinical staff input, resulting in all procedures carrying the numeric value of one. This value of one for a procedure was the same regardless of the time or effort involved. As reimbursements declined, productivity measures were tightened, resulting in major difficulty in attainment for the department. The problem was that a 15-minute daily treatment was given the same productivity value as a two-hour radiosurgery procedure, which consumed much more staff time. Staff reductions without rationale also can create chaos. If housekeeping staff is eliminated, patient rooms become less clean, nurse workloads increase, and both nurse and patient satisfaction decrease. Unfortunately, in many instances, nursing has become the position to which eliminated tasks from other departments are given. Management engineers in conjunction with clinical staff can collaboratively define the skill mix to deliver an optimal outcome. Alone, neither group has the skill set to deliver success. If one only knows that the outcome is to decrease labor costs without regard for the work that still must be done, failure is a given. If a manager does not have access to management engineering support, the following reengineering measures will provide initial direction to a reengineering approach to a task.

Reengineering Measures

Management engineers tend to use quantifiable indicators, whereas clinicians tend toward qualitative measures. For example, a clinician might describe the appetite of the patient, whereas a management engineer will define caloric intake. Being able to identify a task and determine the measure of success requires the ability to complete a productivity analysis. Managers may be expected to reengineer a process or task as part of their job responsibilities. The following steps provide the nurse manager, without the support of a management engineer, with a guide to conduct an initial productivity analysis (Wolper, 1999).

The first step is to determine if the process or task is necessary. Why are you doing what you are doing? Is it because nurses always have been assigned to the task of giving baths since the inception of primary care? If it is determined that the task is necessary, then define the objective and the outcome. For example, if the objective is to decrease labor dollars per man-hour, could a different skill mix deliver greater hours of care at a lower cost without sacrificing care quality? Secondly, the manager should gather data such as staff hours, patient load, patient satisfaction, staff satisfaction, and outcomes on the unit or on a comparable unit. Involve the staff or other appropriate parties, and brainstorm around the topic of how might the unit decrease labor dollars per man-hour without suggesting any ideas to the group. Allowing free and open discussion may stimulate ideas that the manager had not considered. This may be all that is necessary to quantify what can be done to enhance productivity, define an action plan, and implement it.

Tools used in reengineering measures include smoothing, quality control, benchmarking, and, in some instances, statistics that may be incorporated into the analytical process to further validate the reengineering process. Tools to measure reliability or validity are useful as the level of management expertise develops. Recognition of bias in the analysis is also important. For example, the manager who favors an employee even though his or her performance is not up to par can invalidate a productivity analysis because workloads are not equal. Another approach with application to reengineering is smoothing. Given a set of tasks, are all completed in the morning and none left for other times in the day? Implementing something as simple as spreading patient care tasks among staff at varying times of the shift can reduce workload. Not all baths have to be given in the morning. Patients who usually bathe in the evening may prefer that to a frantic morning bath in between procedures and trips to radiology. Smoothing also can refer to management levels. Are multiple layers of management really necessary, or can fewer levels accomplish the same work and free up labor dollars? Clinicians often are promoted based on their clinical skills, when in reality, management skills are critical to the success of the organization. Once management skills are enhanced, they can be applied across the organization regardless of the clinical expertise of the individual.

Quality control is another management engineering tool that may be useful to the manager. By setting indicators and measuring on a scheduled basis, the manager can take corrective action before a situation gets out of hand. In the example given previously, reviewing labor dollars per man-hour each payroll period would prevent costs from escalating because corrective action can be taken promptly. Conforming to set labor hours or skill mix is similar to manufacturing standards, ensuring all widgets are alike over time. If policies are followed, outcomes should be the same to the point that patient variables allow. Benchmarking is another tool that is useful in quantifying performance measures between processes or facilities. A manager in a health system interested in comparing volume, revenue generated, and length of stay between facilities in the network could develop a comparison table (see Table 20-1) to benchmark the facilities against each other. By identifying the best performer, the manager can delve more deeply into what the facility is doing to provide more net revenue per case or shorten the length of stay.

Table 20-1. Five-Hospital Comparison

	Hospital A	Hospital B	Hospital C	Hospital D	Hospital E
FTEs	765	800	550	850	245
Lic beds	201	250	200	150	219
Beds srv	188	210	185	150	171
Pop	117,000	260,000	250,000	108,000	275,400
Est. cases	515	1,144	1,100	475	1,211
# cases	145	226	150	117	114
Tot chgs	1,856,597	3,403,766	3,027,752	2,259,375	2,032,809
Chg/case	12,804	15,061	20,185	19,311	17,832
Net rev	924,959	1,447,781	917,336	894,691	779,298
Net rev/case	6,379	6,406	6,116	7,647	6,836
Tot LOS	662	1,007	636	640	584
LOS/case	4.6	4.5	4.2	5.0	5.0

Too often, healthcare providers say they provide good quality care, when, in fact, this is a nebulous description unless it can be quantified. Is quality defined as timeliness and accuracy of medications or a decrease in the nosocomial infection rate? Is it monitored over time? Are measures implemented to take corrective action? Whether it is called quality assurance, total quality improvement, benchmarking, or quality control really is not the issue. The issue is to define indicators, track them over time, and be prepared to take corrective action to deliver the optimal outcome.

Reengineering implies a much more involved process, beginning with a blank slate and defining new actions that may or may not include any of the current activities. Implementing an organizational redesign may be less complex but uses many of the same principles.

Implementing Organizational Redesign

In the current work environment, success is enhanced if work is defined by processes, not tasks. Management structure often is cross-departmental, as middle managers assume responsibilities for multiple services within an organization. The development of service line management was a first attempt at a matrixed approach to management, rather than the more traditional hierarchical approach. As service line positions expand over several nonrelated clinical areas, the manager must find similarities in process. The move from function to process requires an education to the expectations of the role, whether management or staff (Clancy, 2003).

To redesign a job requires a shift in focus from a task, or group of tasks, to a focus on the process of work. The first step is to identify available resources that can be used to explore options. For example, a cross-functional team may come together to enhance the registration process of the outpatient with cancer who arrives twice a week in the infusion center. Having the right people involved, or on the bus, and knowing where to drive it are the keys to success (Collins, 2001). The patient should not have to wait in line in the hospital admitting and registration department at every visit. Team members from admitting, billing, the infusion center, pharmacy, and other involved departments may be empowered to redesign the process.

In one facility, the group decided to register the patient initially and have the registration staff available on call if any information changed. The patients were educated to the new process, told it was to save time and inconvenience for them, and involved in the responsibility of keeping registration information up to date. This process was not a new one to the organization because it was similar to how a patient receiving radiation is managed over four to six weeks of therapy. Any changes are electronically updated in the patient's file by the infusion center receptionist, and a copy of any changes in the insurance card is sent to registration and billing by the patient's nurse. The work redesign ultimately reengineered the process to be more patient friendly and stabilized the flow of scheduled patients who appeared at their appointment times without delays. The new process continues to be monitored to determine if correct registration and billing information is being captured. To date, the redesigned process is working for the patient and the center.

If the registration process is considered for reengineering, as opposed to redesign, the team basically is instructed to begin the redesign process with a clean slate with no discussion of existing procedure or activities. The team leader may begin the discussion by defining the desired end point and then asking the team to decide how to achieve that goal. Participants in the group must be empowered to reengineer the process after being informed of any constraints on the activity. Although it is preferred that no conditions are put on the initial discussion, this constraint may not be feasible. For example, if adding employees is not an option, team members should be informed in the initial stages of the discussion. The team leader might start the discussion by asking members of the group to define all the pieces of the admission process that need to be addressed without regard to existing procedures. By charting steps in the process, the group may visualize redundancy, bottlenecks, or immediate opportunities for productivity improvements. In a reengineering exercise, participants are not in a mode that protects the status quo or restricts creativity, rather it allows them to freely define best-case scenario.

Reengineering a process may take more time than restructuring an existing process but often provides greater benefit to the organization. A manager can redesign a bad process to be marginally improved, but reengineering is free of preconceived steps in the process. Reengineering, ultimately, may validate that the existing process is acceptable, but if that occurs too often, then opportunities are not being selected appropriately for review.

Once consensus is reached and the appropriate management review is complete, implementation occurs. Certainly major organizational changes may need to be tested before roll out to the entire facility. Depending on the process, a pilot may be indicated to validate the implementation plan (Sultz & Young, 1999). For example, electronic physician order entry may be piloted on one unit or with a single physician group to allow operational feedback to validate the theoretical process proposed by the team.

For redesign to be successful, regardless of the method used, several issues are pertinent. The team must be selected carefully to represent the skill set and knowledge base necessary to achieve the desired outcome. A management briefing related to the internal and external factors that may impact the efforts of the team is desirable, as team members may need an update on the current influences to be considered. Providing clear direction, guidance, and respect for the opinions of all team members and timelines for group work should precede any address of the topic. Because teams are cross-functional, cross-departmental, and may involve a variety of job positions, education of participants to the responsibility of team membership will contribute to the desired result.

Employee Readiness and Support

Empowerment of employees is the single most critical component of effective change in the organization. The methods managers use—total quality management, reengineering, right sizing, restructuring, and turnarounds—routinely fall short because they fail to alter behavior (Kotter, 1996). Although managers often say they empower their employees, in reality, they are afraid to give power to people, which is the true definition of empowerment. Kotter believed that organizational transformation will not occur unless many employees participate in the process. Removing the fear factor by giving permission to speak freely is the true essence of empowerment.

Numeroff (1985) described a more realistic view of how power is given: "If you give a mouse a cookie, then he'll ask for a glass of milk. He'll want to look in a mirror to make sure he doesn't have a milk mustache" (pp. 1–3). The book espouses that the more you give the mouse, the more he asks for, ultimately leading to his young host's exhaustion. Managers tend to hold back from involving employees in the process of management out of the fear that staff will ask for even more control. Employees are ready to assist in the redesign of work; it is the management team that needs to be encouraged to change from a traditional management structure to one of shared governance.

Strategies for Success

Managers who are challenged to reengineer, reorganize, or redesign the workplace can be ensured success by incorporating several simple management principles. Establishing the appropriate management tone in the workplace far in advance of any needed intervention is key. Creating a climate conducive to open communication and safety in challenging the status quo is most important. Employees encouraged to share opportunities and issues in advance of collapse can protect the organization from the need for redesign or reengineering. A simple, timely comment from an employee that the patients do not seem happy with the registration process can mitigate major patient dissatisfaction. Correcting small issues before they metastasize is the best strategy. It is natural for change to occur, whether expected or unexpected. Change can only surprise you if you do not expect it (Johnson, 1998). By allowing employees a safe place to verbalize their thoughts, change becomes a natural evolution rather than an unexpected crisis.

A coaching style of management is another success strategy for the manager. Think of the legendary football coaches who inspired their teams to greatness, and draw from their example. You will succeed in inspiring your staff to achievements far greater than if you just manage by mandate. Encourage a shared governance model where staff take increasing responsibility for their actions, and they become engaged and are more willing to do what it takes to achieve success in their workplace. Educating employees to expectations and providing team-building strategies contribute to success in the workplace. If employees can be rewarded or provided incentives for their actions, it reinforces the importance that the organization places on staff participation. A simple question of "Here is where we are; where would we like to be?" may be all it takes to achieve success when those closest to the issue drive the solution. As nurse managers take on greater span of control, it is imperative that staff become self-directed and motivated. Operational excellence must be driven bottom up, not top down. Wise managers know they are only as effective as their weakest employee. Coach employees to their highest level of performance, and managerial success will be enhanced.

Creating a climate for innovation is another management practice that will encourage success. "An agile company turns out innovative products and services and anticipates disruptive events . . . rather than reacting when it may already be too late" (Nohria, Joyce, & Roberson, 2003, p. 49). Encouraging proactive development of services and strategies by staff based on knowledge of the healthcare environment only will invigorate the organization. The organization that protects the status quo ultimately will fail in its mission to provide quality patient care. The care provided five years ago in health care is outdated. Without encouraging innovation, the manager will be guilty of delivering less than optimum care.

Managers must develop a skill set that will serve them as they continue their management careers. Many of the topics in this chapter require management knowledge, not clinical expertise. Because many managers in the healthcare setting come from a clinical background, management knowledge may be lacking. As we do our patients a disservice if we are not clinically prepared, we do our employees and organization an equal disservice if we lack skills necessary for success. Formal courses such as an MBA program, continuing education, and self-study will provide additional education to the manager and will contribute to personal growth and success.

Recognizing that change is inevitable, the manager can develop the skills needed to manage it, encourage staff to communicate in advance of chaos, and, ultimately, be able to lead and intervene in workplace reengineering, reorganization, or redesign. The knowledge that no situation is unmanageable is reassuring as managers are asked to do more with less, manage multiple departments, and are expected to deliver quality care and retain a strong, viable workforce. With a team effort led by knowledgeable, capable, and competent leadership, the workplace can survive and prosper despite any challenge.

References

Advisory Board. (2003, Fall). *Softening of demand? Advisory Board assessment of emerging volume concerns.* Retrieved January 12, 2004, from http://www.advisory.com/members/default.asp?contentid=37766&program=14&collectionid=932

Clancy, T. (2003). The art of decision making. *Journal of Nursing Administration, 33,* 343–349.

Collins, J. (2001). *Good to great: Why some companies make the leap and others don't.* New York: HarperBusiness.

Drucker, P.F. (1993). *Innovation and entrepreneurship: Practice and principles.* New York: HarperBusiness.

Ginter, P.M., Swayne, L.E., & Duncan, W.J. (2002). *Strategic management of health care organizations* (4th ed.). Malden, MA: Blackwell Publishing.

Hammer, M., & Champy, J. (1994). *Reengineering the corporation: A manifesto for business revolution.* New York: HarperBusiness.

Johnson, S. (1998). *Who moved my cheese? An amazing way to deal with change in your work and in your life.* New York: G.P. Putnam's Sons.

Kotter, J.P. (1996). *Leading change.* Boston: Harvard Business School Press.

Nohria, N., Joyce, W., & Roberson, B. (2003). What really works. *Harvard Business Review, 81*(7), 43–52.

Numeroff, L.J. (1985). *If you give a mouse a cookie.* New York: HarperCollins.

Pollard, T.M. (2001). Changes in mental well-being, blood pressure and total cholesterol levels during workplace reorganization: The impact of uncertainty. *Work & Stress, 15*(1), 14–28.

Sultz, H.A., & Young, K.M. (1999). *Health care USA* (2nd ed.). Gaithersburg, MD: Aspen Publishers.

Wolper, L.F. (1999). *Health care administration* (3rd ed.). Gaithersburg, MD: Aspen Publishers.

CHAPTER

▓▓▓▓▓▓▓▓▓▓▓▓▓▓▓▓▓▓▓▓▓▓▓▓▓▓▓▓▓▓▓▓

21

Writing a Business Plan

Linda J. Shinn, MBA, RN, CAE

"What the future holds for us depends on what we hold for the future. Hard-working 'todays' make high-winning 'tomorrows.'" (Holler, 1995, p. 20)

Business planning is the process for implementing the strategic direction of an organization. It is the "who, what, by when, and at what cost" of achieving the mission and goals of the organization. In a healthcare environment characterized by economic turbulence, more government regulation, mounting costs, demand of investors for transparency in allocation of organizational resources and a return on investment, and greater consumer demand for services, business planning is a must.

This chapter defines business planning, explains its importance for oncology nurses, explores how it might be used in practice, outlines the elements of a business plan, and identifies resources to assist the oncology nurse in developing a business plan.

A well-crafted and fully utilized business plan is a
- Map for achieving strategic goals
- Communications tool
- Financial resource
- Performance evaluation instrument.

Map for Achieving Strategic Goals

According to Williams (2003), "a strategic plan is the roadmap that organizations, whether for profit or not for profit, use to
- Stay focused on their mission.
- Set priorities.
- Foster growth and development" (p. 71).

Synchronous with the strategic plan, the business plan is a tool to allocate resources (i.e., human, fiscal, and technologic) to implement the strategic plan. It is a document that can be used to track organizational progress, evaluate and celebrate that progress, and make midcourse corrections. A business plan also can help organizational leaders hold people accountable for how resources are managed and how work is done. The elements of a business plan appear later in this chapter.

Communications Tool

As a communications tool, the business plan can be used in a variety of ways. The plan can be used to explain to a board of directors, employees, supervisors, investors, clients, suppliers, consultants, elected officials, media, the community, and others what an organization is and does. It is a document from which an organization can build its annual activity report or other report of accomplishments.

Often there will be two versions of the business plan, an internal version and an external version. An external version must be consistent with the internal version but generally omits the "who" and may be more selective in financial information shared. The external plan usually is created for an audience outside an organization (e.g., investors, consumers, media). For investors, the version will be focused on what this audience wants (e.g., description of the product or service for which funding is sought), need for product or service, competition, projected expenditures and revenue, and anticipated return on investment. For consumers, it would focus on products and services, with a heavier emphasis on access. For the media, the content will be focused on promotion. An external version would be in lay terms and not full of jargon or acronyms specific to a business or profession.

An internal rendition of a business plan will be more specific to those inside an organization (e.g., employees, board of directors). Technical terms or terms unique to the industry or profession (e.g., oncology) may be used. An organization's internal operation will be outlined in greater detail.

In addition, the business plan can serve as a reporting mechanism. It can be used to prepare an annual report or other report of accomplishments. It can be used to provide progress reports to investors, boards of directors, employees, and other stakeholders.

Financial Resource

A business plan often is used to lure investors to finance a new business venture. For example, a group of physicians might develop a business plan for the creation of an outpatient surgical center. A group of oncology nurse managers might develop a business plan for the creation of a cancer center. An existing business might use a business plan to secure dollars for a new product or service. A hospital might develop a business plan for a satellite facility in a nearby community.

A business plan is a key part of an organization's financial portfolio. It is the detail of how the group plans to acquire and spend its money and allocate other resources, a barometer of how things are going, and a key to the likely success or failure of a new venture or the sustainability of current operations.

Performance Evaluation Instrument

A business plan can serve as an accountability tracking tool and evaluation mechanism. Managers at every level of an organization can set performance goals based on the business plan and monitor progress according to the plan's requirements. Progress and performance can be measured against the plan. Midcourse corrections can be made.

The Importance of Business Planning

Entrepreneurs have historically "flown by the seat of their pants" when developing a new business. For many years, healthcare institutions were operated by intuition with little attention to formal planning. In the 1960s and 1970s, healthcare organizations, hospitals in particular, began to plan more carefully for the future, often as a result of state and federal requirements. Early planning focused on infrastructure, such as buildings and equipment. Later, legislators, professional societies, and healthcare planners began to look at the need for manpower (e.g., physicians, pharmacists, nurses) and drafted plans for numbers of educational programs, internships, and residencies. Incentives were developed to lure providers (e.g., nurses, physicians) into underserved areas.

Zuckerman (2000) stated that businesses outside of healthcare institutions have long used growth in market share and improvement in financial performance to track the success of strategic planning. To date, however, only a few providers have used these indicators to measure the effectiveness of their strategic initiatives. Business and strategic planning will become more important at every level in health care as emphasis on efficiency, outcomes, and the bottom line increases. By setting a strategic direction and implementing practical business planning, an organization can take a critical, objective look at what is being done in the organization; how it serves the customer; the return on investment in human, fiscal, and technologic resources; what has obsolesced; and what is needed in the future.

Professional groups such as the Oncology Nursing Society engage in routine planning, analyzing trends, making assumptions about the future, and setting strategic goals. A business plan is created that outlines the tactics for achieving the goals, the timeline required, and the resources needed. The business plan is a yardstick against which progress can be measured.

Much is accomplished in business and health care today through partnerships, strategic alliances, and joint ventures. Collaboration with others requires an understanding of plans for the future (e.g., strategic, business). Cooperative efforts also may necessitate joint business planning.

Business Planning for Nurse Managers

The current healthcare environment requires nurses to have knowledge of the business of health care. As nurses seek an ever-increasing role in decision making in health care, an understanding about the marketplace, including information about trends, competitive analysis, marketing, sales, production, finance, and evaluation (i.e., the business plan) is a must. Two examples illustrate this point. The average senior nursing officer in an acute care hospital is responsible for 822 full-time employees and a $90 million budget (Nicholas, 2003). These responsibilities necessitate a plan for deployment of resources and an allocation of personnel (i.e., the business plan).

Palliative care programs, whether at home or in the hospital, result in significant savings in end-of-life care. Such savings augur for development of hospital-based palliative care programs (Ford, 2003). Making a case for palliative services requires information about the market to be served, the competition, risks, opportunities, revenue and expenditures, personnel, and sales (i.e., the business plan).

Zagury (2003) pointed out that the application of the basic components of the nursing process—assessment, planning, implementation, and evaluation—are the same for the development of a sound business plan. For years nurses have applied the nursing process to those in their care or under their supervision. Whether a nurse executive, nurse manager, nurse practitioner, or staff nurse, nurses can take these skills and apply them to the business of health care for the benefit of their institution and for career development.

Enlightened employers are engaging employees in all aspects of the business by providing ongoing information about the organization's vision, mission, goals, finances, challenges, and opportunities. Understanding basic business planning can help nurse managers make sense of the information, contribute to the future of the organization, and manage a myriad of changes. A comprehensive business plan can be an important accessory to the nurse manager requesting additional resources, including physical, fiscal, technologic, and human.

Elements of a Business Plan

This section provides the nurse manager with a review of the elements of a business plan.

Executive Summary

An executive summary is the first element of a business plan. It should be a persuasive synopsis of the plan. The executive summary highlights the objectives of the company, the product or service proposed, the marketplace to be served, and a concise account of resources (human, fiscal, and technologic) needed for achievement.

Answering the questions identified in each of the areas below can guide the nurse manager in creating a business plan. Such a plan can be used to launch a new healthcare program, product line, or center.

1. The organization (description)
   - What is the mission, purpose, goals, of the organization (i.e., the strategic plan)?
   - What is the history?
   - Who are the principals (senior executives)?
   - What is the authority of the principals?
   - What is the work experience of the principals?
2. The business (i.e., program, service, or product to be offered)
   - What is the service or product to be offered?
   - Who will the customers be?
   - Where will the service or product be made?
   - When will the service or product be available?
3. The marketplace (national, regional, state, local)
   - Who are the competitors?
   - How have they been successful?
   - What are their weaknesses?
   - How is the proposed product or service distinctive from that of the competition?
   - What is already available in the market?
   - Who are the potential customers?
   - What is the customer profile?
   - What do the customers need?
   - How is the competition failing to meet the need?
   - What is the potential market share?
   - How will the potential customers be told about the product or service?
4. Risks and opportunities (new program, service, product)
   - What are the barriers to entering the market?
   - What are the market trends?
   - What are the strengths and weaknesses of the offering?
   - What is the life cycle of the service or product?
     - Growth
     - Decline
   - What assets does the company have/lack?
     - Personnel
     - Technology
     - Funds
5. Financing
   - What will the product/service cost?
     - To develop (capital investment)
     - To maintain
   - What is included in the cost?
   - What is the up front investment required?
   - What investment is required in the long term (i.e., a three- to five-year forecast)?

- What is the anticipated cash flow, profit, or loss?
- Who are the potential investors?
    - The private sector (e.g., foundations)
    - The public sector (e.g., government)
- A balance sheet, income statement, and break-even analysis also should be included.
6. Sales (marketing)
    - What is the market plan (i.e., how will customers be reached, prospects identified, sales or use generated)?
    - What tactics will be used?
    - What is the distribution plan?
    - Who are the sales representatives?
    - What is the budget for sales?
    - How does this budget compare with that of competitors?
7. Production
    - What will be the expenses to produce the product or service?
    - How will the product or service be produced (e.g., equipment, facilities, staffing, purchasing)?
    - How will the product or service be maintained?
    - What patents, trademarks, or copyrights are required?
    - What permissions for use of the work of others are required?
8. Human resources
    - What will be the qualifications, including experience of personnel?
    - What number of personnel will be needed?
        - Short term
        - Long term
    - Will personnel be employed, leased, or donated?
    - What will be the responsibilities of personnel?
    - How will personnel be held accountable?
    - What will the conditions of work be?
    - What compensation and benefits will be required?
    - What external resources will be available?
        - Legal counsel
        - Consultants
        - Insurance
        - Investors
        - Bankers
        - Board of directors
9. Evaluation (measures of success)
    - What are the benchmarks for success?
        - Customer
        - Sales
        - Financial
        - Competition
        - Share of market
    - What if the product or service is a failure?

- Rescue
- Regroup
- Redesign
- Withdraw
10. Risk management
   - Crisis management plan including a succession plan for senior management
   - Insurance
   - Legal

Appendices

Several supporting documents should be included as appendices to a business plan. The type of documents will depend upon the product or service offered and how it will be financed. Typical addenda include
- Legal documents (e.g., articles of incorporation, bylaws)
- Resumes (of owners, administrators, and other key personnel)
- Organization chart
- Job descriptions
- Pro forma budget
- Credit information
- Quotes, estimates
- Letters of support.

Planning Resources

There are a myriad of resources to help with business planning. Commercial Web sites offer tutorials and templates, some for a fee. College and university schools of business offer business planning seminars. Some universities offer small business incubators, a place where plans can be developed, implemented, and nurtured; for example, Howard University, Washington, DC, has a Small Business Development Center. The Small Business Administration is an organization that exists to help maintain and strengthen the nation's economy by aiding, counseling, assisting, and protecting the interests of small businesses. It devotes a portion of its Web site to business planning and offers print materials on the subject.

Planning resources also may be available at the workplace. The finance department or business office is a good place to start. The chief financial officer in any organization is a key player in business planning. Large healthcare systems may employ a full-time strategic planner. These people can be tapped for help in developing a business plan. Human resource departments also may provide guidance on planning, as they are often pivotal in the planning for and deployment of personnel.

Professional associations such as the Oncology Nursing Society, American Organization of Nurse Executives, Chamber of Commerce, or American Management Association can be good resources. These organizations may have articles on business planning and can provide information about their experiences in business planning. They also can serve as a resource for experts or consultants on business planning.

The Review and Revision of a Business Plan

The pace at which the world moves requires constant attention to strategic and business planning. Plans are not static and require quarterly review to be sure the organization is on course. Plans should be updated at least annually to reflect changes in the marketplace, resources, and timelines. Stakeholders of the organization (e.g., personnel, board of directors, investors, creditors) should receive an annual report of progress, including accomplishments and information on any midcourse corrections made.

Summary

The business plan is an important device in helping an organization achieve its mission and goals. It is a multipurpose tool when carefully designed and fully utilized. It takes time, thought, and tenacity to build. It is a document that nurses can use in understanding the business of health care and the affairs of their employers. It is also a process that nurses can use to make the case for a new program, product, or service for those in their care or their employ. It is a must for nurses who may be starting a new business, inventing a program or product, or bringing an idea to the marketplace.

References

Ford, K.R. (2003). Business planning for palliative care. *Oncology Issues, 18*(1), 40–41.

Holler, W.E. (1995). *Thoughts on leadership*. Chicago: Triumph Books.

Nicholas, L. (2003). *Hug your CNO!* Retrieved October 29, 2003, from http://lhaonline.org/Publications/presentation/LyonPP/2003/06-13-03.htm

Williams, P. (2003). Strategic planning. In L.J. Shinn (Ed.), *Conversations in leadership of professional nursing associations*. Pensacola, FL: Pohl Publishing.

Zagury, C. (2003). *How to develop a business plan*. Retrieved August 27, 2003, from http://nsweb.nursingspectrum.com/ce/ce250.htm

Zuckerman, A. (2000). Leveraging strategic planning for improved financial performance. *Healthcare Financial Management, 54*(12), 54–58.

CHAPTER 22

Cancer Program Strategic Planning and Marketing

Joseph M. Spallina, FAAMA, FACHE

"It takes vision and courage to create—it takes faith and courage to prove." (Young, 1995)

This chapter will review the principles and practices of healthcare program strategic planning and marketing with a focus on cancer. Review of the strategic business planning chapter will enhance the understanding of the principles discussed in this chapter. If the world remained constant, there would not be any need to plan. The primary purposes of planning are to remain viable and on course and to achieve established goals in a dynamic environment. The concept of planning has universal applicability, whether we are planning a family vacation, a new consumer product, or the future of a clinical program and healthcare enterprise.

Strategic Planning and Marketing Defined

In his book *Management: Tasks, Responsibilities, Practices,* Drucker (1973) discussed strategic planning in the context of an entrepreneurial skill. He first described what strategic planning is **not**. Drucker's proposed solution is a little difficult to understand. He wrote "The essence of planning is to make present decisions with knowledge of their futurity" (p. 119). The concept of the *futurity* of today's decisions and the outcomes they will have over time requires the following approach: (a) conceptualize the future based on a reasonable set of assumptions; (b) assume risk in making assumptions about the key characteristics of the future; and (c) assume risk when selecting a decision from among a number of alternatives (or solution set) that is intended to lead to the desired goal.

For strategic planning to be successful, the decisions we make today (and the assumptions, processes, and risk parameters that we use to make those decisions) must lead us to our stated future goals. The ultimate goals for cancer programs are

(a) provision of quality services, (b) growth, development, and the ability to serve and respond to community need, and (c) long-term financial survival.

Although Drucker's (1973) book was written more than 30 years ago, the techniques and leadership theory described in the book apply to today's cancer programs and cancer program leaders. Many articles and books have been written addressing the topic of strategic planning in health care. However, few of these writings address clinical program or cancer program strategic planning.

Planning and Marketing

Richard Bode (1993) authored a little-known yet wonderful and heart-warming book titled *First You Have to Row a Little Boat*. Bode wrote about his life and how he learned to steer through its challenging and unpredictable nature. With the wind to his sails and as the captain of his ship, Bode described how he braved the elements and mastered the ability to pick his own course in life and achieve his desired goals.

The analogies and lessons described by Bode are applicable to cancer program strategic business planning. As in life, where we are not in total control of our fate, the same is true with cancer programs. We are not in total control of the environment in which the program operates. If left to their own, cancer programs will float in the direction of the prevailing currents. There is no certainty that such a course will ensure success.

Hospital leadership must decide if developing and maintaining a current strategic business plan for its cancer program provide value. One can argue that without a sense of direction, you end up as someone else's lunch or lost at sea!

More recently, leaders in the healthcare industry are exploring the strategy of building strong clinical programs to ensure the overall strength of their healthcare enterprise. In most healthcare enterprises, cancer programs are identified as a priority for growth. Strong clinical programs (and, in this case, cancer programs) are dependent on strong hospital and specialist relationships. The strength of these relationships correlates directly with the extent to which the hospital and cancer program physicians are integrated.

All cancer programs today are faced with a common set of questions: (a) How is our market changing, and what will it look like in the future? (b) What will the competition look like in the future (Will oncology groups grow? Will they consolidate and gain market power? Will for-profit firms enter our market?)? (c) Where should the cancer facility be located (e.g., hospital, freestanding cancer centers)? (d) What role should our cancer program have in the future market (grow or not grow, remain at our current location or move)? (e) What should our strategies be for managing effective physician relationships? (f) What kind of business relationship should the hospital have with the medical and radiation oncologists in the future market to maximize oncology referrals (Should we enter into any joint ventures with the physicians and, if so, for which services?)? (g) Should our program establish a relationship with an academic cancer program? If so, for what purpose? (h) Will we be able to afford new technologies in the future? What criteria do we use to assess which technologies we acquire, and what impact will they have on our growth and viability? (i) What process should we use to explore market and cancer program physician relationship opportunities and to reach agreement with physicians on specific strategies and investments? (j) How should we market our cancer program? On what basis? How do we measure the results of our marketing investments?

The answers to these and many other questions have tremendous implications for the future success of a cancer program. To answer these questions, hospitals must decipher future trends. What is clear is that (a) cancer program margins for both hospitals and physician practices will continue to decline. More efficient operations and growth are required to offset these trends and for programs to remain viable. (b) There is greater competition for patients with cancer in the market and a greater level of competition between hospitals and cancer program physicians. In many markets, this competition is leading (or has led) to a shift of market power and revenue from the hospital to the oncology practice. (c) There is little room for error in cancer program strategies and investments. (d) The business models that hospitals and cancer program physicians have used are quickly becoming obsolete. The new models will require closer working and equity-based relationships between hospitals and cancer program physicians. (e) Cancer programs must market and differentiate themselves beyond aspects of service, high touch, and technology. (f) Cancer program marketing must involve cancer program physicians.

Determining how to develop successful cancer program strategies (both strategic/market and marketing) using a process that involves both hospital representatives and cancer program physicians is a fundamental question that many organizations are struggling with today. The absence of strategies (and implied absence of leadership) leaves the cancer program vulnerable and threatens its future viability. Leadership's responsibility, both at the hospital executive level and cancer program management level, is to ensure that (a) strategies exist and they are current; (b) strategies are based on a reasonable set of assumptions about the market (both now and in the future), the role of cancer program physicians, the cancer program's role in the market, and the oncologist/hospital relationship; and (c) progress on implementing the strategies is reviewed routinely.

Successful cancer programs will demonstrate strong leadership that motivates and guides cancer program physicians and staff to an agreed upon vision according to a set of strategies and goals that define a course to growth.

Key Stakeholders: Participants, Roles, and Process

Clinical program strategic plans are by their very nature a component of the hospital's overall strategic plan. Readers should become familiar with their hospital's strategic plan and planning process and understand where the cancer program strategic business planning and plan fits into that process. For the purpose of this chapter, assume that the cancer program strategic plan is an extension and supportive element of the hospital strategy.

The key constituency groups to include in the cancer program business planning process should represent all service and business aspects of the cancer program, including (a) physicians who represent the leadership (formal or informal) of the cancer program physician staff (e.g., medical oncologists, radiation oncologists, surgeons, gastroenterologists), (b) cancer program administrative leadership, (c) hospital oncology nursing leadership, (d) hospital planning and business development, (e) hospital leadership (optional; inclusion is a function of the strategic planning issues at hand and the cancer program politics).

Leadership's responsibilities in cancer program business planning and marketing are ongoing. Hospital executives and cancer program leaders must work collectively and communicate in a timely, efficient fashion on an ongoing basis. Cancer program leadership responsibilities in the strategic business planning and marketing processes include ensuring that strategic and marketing planning responsibilities are clear and unambiguous among all parties involved. This includes defining specific leadership responsibilities and the work schedule in the planning processes, agreeing on the participants and the roles of the participants in the planning processes, agreeing on data and information requirements, being responsible for analyses, and ensuring timely review and approval of the findings and conclusions from the analyses.

At the onset, cancer program and hospital leadership have to address whether a fundamental change in direction for the program is required or formulative improvements (fine tuning) in strategies and direction are required.

Continuous monitoring of the environment and market served by the cancer program must occur. Attention must be paid to (a) changes in the nature of the competition (e.g., new competitors, oncology practice consolidation/mergers/joint ventures), (b) new technologic developments, (c) significant changes in reimbursement, laws, and regulations for oncology services, (d) market opportunities, and (e) monitoring of oncologists/hospital relationships and interest in ease of practice improvements and joint ventures.

Once the current and future key characteristics of the environment have been identified, program and hospital leadership must work with cancer program physicians to create a meaningful vision, strategic direction, and a framework for growth.

Incorporating responsibilities for executing strategies into individuals' annual performance plans is essential for successful implementation. Routine (e.g., quarterly) review and discussion of progress on strategies and the implementation plan is essential. These discussions will allow for (a) the identification of solutions to obstacles to maintain the direction and pace of the plan and strategy implementation and (b) to ensure that the strategies contribute to the defined program goals and determine if formulative change (e.g., midcourse corrections) is required.

Essential Components of a Strategic Plan

For the purpose of this chapter, cancer program strategic plans are composed of three distinct and sequential phases (sets of activities). In phase I, the situation, capabilities, and opportunities analyses must answer two fundamental questions: Where are we now? and What opportunities are available to ensure cancer program viability? In phase II, formulating strategic direction answers the questions: Where are we going? and How are we going to get there? Phase III, which focuses on execution planning and ongoing review, answers the questions Are we getting there? and How do we know if we are getting there?

The primary objectives of the first phase are to (a) serve as the foundation for developing a future cancer program vision, (b) formulate a conceptual framework of the future environment (market, competition, technology, reimbursement, hospital/physician relationships) in which the cancer program will operate, (c) identify potential points of partnership with cancer program physicians, (d) identify potential market and technology opportunities, and (e) identify key issues that must be resolved if the strategic plan is to be successful and if the cancer program is to remain viable.

In the second phase, establishing the strategic direction for the cancer program must be completed. This includes (a) formulating the future cancer program vision. The vision statement must take into consideration what the future environment will look like and how it will look different from the current environment and the cancer program's role in the future environment; and (b) achieving the vision through strategies that cancer programs and hospital leadership will use to interact with the environment as they steer the program to the future vision.

The third phase focuses on (a) establishing priorities among the strategies, (b) planning the tactics for priority strategies, (c) estimating resource requirements (capital, annual operating, staff time) and assessing the financial impact of the recommended strategies, (d) establishing metrics for successful strategy implementation and incorporating the metrics into the organization's performance metrics and annual management performance and professional development plans, (e) establishing a review process to determine progress on the plan and the mechanisms for reporting and discussing progress throughout the organization, and (f) reviewing the plan routinely and updating the plan, as required. (Please refer to Chapter 21 for a detailed description of the strategy and business planning process.)

The Marketing Plan

The marketing planning process encourages cancer program leaders to introspectively evaluate the current cancer program position, focus on target market segments, establish strategic direction and market strategies, and develop a discipline that enables the program to achieve its desired position in the market. A marketing plan is a set of strategies and budget (resource allocation) directed to specific "target markets" for the expressed intent of increasing an organization's market share and profitability. Successful marketing plans and goals should lead to increased financial performance and differentiate the program in the market.

The marketing plan is a subset of the strategic plan, and, therefore, the marketing planning process is similar to the strategic planning process. The cancer program's marketing plan or goals address only four specific, yet essential, components of a cancer program. These four key areas, more commonly referred to as the marketing mix or the "four P's", establish clarity in the strategies and success in marketing the cancer program. They include (a) product (e.g., key cancer program services), (b) place (the markets served by the program and the distribution channels to reach the target markets), (c) promotion (advertising and publicity for key services and program segments), and (d) price (charges, managed care contracts, global billing arrangements, and niche arrangements).

Understanding which services will provide the greatest return and contribute the most to growth is an essential requirement to start the marketing plan or establish marketing goals. For example, clinical expertise, unique features of the cancer center facility, the oncologists themselves, and new and/or state-of-the-art equipment are important program characteristics to market and accentuate to target audiences. Although most organizations understand the value of the plan's outcomes, they often launch into developing a plan without considering some very basic assumptions.

Is this a hospital-focused plan? Contemporary cancer program marketing plans must go beyond marketing the hospital and must market physician practices that distinguish the program in the community. Physician leaders should be an integral part of the marketing plan development phase.

What are we marketing? Traditional marketing plans emphasize program promotion. Successful plans will continue to include program promotion but also will focus on (a) program differentiation and leadership in the market, (b) competitive cost position, (c) quality position, and (d) referring physician relationships.

Is there interest in pursuing hospital/physician integration? In today's market, most healthcare experts agree that increasing levels of integration are needed between hospitals and physicians to survive competitive threats and remain attractive to payors. The level of integration that can be achieved for a particular program depends on the extent of managed care development and existing hospital/program physician relationships.

Is there market demand for cancer program services? As consolidation occurs in healthcare markets and managed care influences demand, organizations must consider whether their cancer programs can remain viable and competitive.

Is there commitment to pursuing a marketing plan? There must be buy-in for the development of a marketing plan from both the hospital and physician practices, or the plan will never reach its full potential.

Target Market Segments

Once the marketing position assessment and related market analyses are completed, the wealth of data and information will provide the basis to identify the key target market segments served by the cancer program. These segments typically include (a) referring physicians (primary care and specialists), (b) communities and the public, (c) payors, and (d) vendors.

Once the segments are initially defined, further refinement in defining them is required. The market analysis will guide this continued definition. For example, two communities might be identified in the market analysis where the cancer program is underperforming. Further analysis, might reveal that in one community, the cancer program does not have strong community visibility and awareness by the residents at large. By contrast, in the other community, the key factor attributable to low market performance is the inability to negotiate a managed care contract that is favorable to the hospital.

Use of the market analysis data and findings is a continued effort to probe, segment, and discover why gaps in performance exist. The gaps identified represent strategies that are initially developed.

Developing the Marketing Plan

The strategic plan recommendations (e.g., the direction and pace of the strategies, program growth) will determine if a cancer program marketing plan is required. If development of a marketing plan is recommended as a strategy in the strategic plan, a formalized plan should be prepared immediately following the completion of the strategic plan. If development of a plan is not included as a recommended strategy, the strategic plan must include key marketing strategies, at a minimum.

Development of a marketing plan (see Figure 22-1), similar to the development of a strategic plan, requires skill, experience, and expertise. In many instances, hospitals will not have the staff with expertise to adequately prepare a marketing plan. If hospital planning and marketing staff do not possess this required skill set, external assistance will be required to expertly prepare the marketing plan.

The marketing planning process relies on the strategic planning database and analyses. To begin the formal process of developing a marketing plan, program leadership should proceed with initiation activities that establish coordination of the project. A steering committee should be formed to guide the process and ensure its completion. Participants on the committee may vary from organization to organization but should include program physician leaders, hospital leadership, program administrative leadership, and marketing and planning services representatives. All members of the committee must be introspective and provide guidance in developing strategies and establishing priorities throughout the planning process.

Other tasks that should be completed during the initiation activity include (a) develop a schedule, (b) establish the approval process for the plan, (c) establish a communications process to update key constituents about progress on developing the plan, (d) collect appropriate data and information, and (e) conduct personal and confidential interviews (primary research) with primary care, program physicians, and other members of the medical staff (as required) to gain insight into perceptions of the current and future role and position of the cancer program.

Activity I: Marketing Issues and Opportunities Identification

The goal of activity I of the planning process is to identify marketing issues and opportunities for the program through primary and secondary research. This activity

Figure 22-1. Planning Process to Develop a Cancer Program Marketing Plan

	Activity I	Activity II	Activity III	Activity IV
	Marketing Issues and Opportunities Identification	Marketing Strategy Development	Marketing Budget and Action Plan	Marketing Plan Approval and Presentation

Outputs	• Market analysis and research
	• Marketing position assessment
	• Discuss key opportunities and critical planning issues.
	• Marketing segments identified
	• Discuss and agree on key hospital/cancer program physician alignment requirements.
		• Future cancer program mission, vision, and market positioning statements
		• Marketing strategies
		  - Product
		  - Place
		  - Promotions
		  - Price
			• Finalize marketing strategies.
			• Action planning
			  - Objectives and metrics
			  - Priorities
			  - Responsibilities
			  - Resource requirements
			    * Capital
			    * Annual operating
				• Executive summary
				• Key resource requirements
				• Year I implementation requirements
				• Metrics
				• Key organizational priorities and responsibilities
				• Presentations for marketing plan approval

Working Sessions	*	*	*	*

Note. Figure courtesy of Arvina Group, LLC. Reprinted with permission.

is composed of a number of important research-based tasks. By comprehensively assessing a program's capabilities, an organization develops an understanding of key programmatic competencies and vulnerabilities.

The four P's (product, price, promotion, and place) are assessed to determine their relative strength in the market and within the marketing mix. This assessment takes into account many of the analyses and findings from the strategic plan. The capabilities assessment should include a review of the facility's capacities cost and quality position, hospital/physician relationships, referring physician relationships, managed care relationships, and technology capabilities. Conducting primary research with a program's past patients and family members, as well as patients and family members served by competitor programs, is a key process to discover important facts.

The external market assessment helps programs realize how they compare to major competitors and how attractive they are to payors and the public in terms of price, quality, market share, and access. At a minimum, this assessment should include market share assessments for new cancer cases, radiation therapy cases, and inpatient oncology admissions by cancer site (ICD-based analyses). The market share assessment should be completed by zip code or county level, depending on the planning requirements of the program. Additional assessments should include development of a market position assessment that provides an overview of the marketing mix and the program's position in the market by examining the traditional four P's of marketing (see Figure 22-2).

Figure 22-2. Sample Cancer Program Marketing Position Assessment

Marketing Mix	Cancer Program Position Assessment Summary			
	Strong	Medium	Weak	Comments
Product	X			Distinctive quality, regional reputation. Product is defined based on cancer program services offered.
Price		X		Price competitiveness/cost position improving; based on severity-adjusted charges. Continuing development of package pricing.
Promotion			X	Very little specific to the program.
Place		X-County	X-Regional	Recently, some physicians expressed concern about market erosion at the service area periphery. Market strategies for other than ABC County should focus on specific communities and strengthen the secondary and tertiary service areas.

Note. Figure courtesy of Arvina Group, LLC. Reprinted with permission.

An evaluation of comparative cost and quality position (among key competitors) using severity-adjusted data should be completed. Additional analyses must include a regional assessment of the need for medical and radiation oncologists and surgeons in selected subspecialties, an estimate of future demand for cancer program services given alternative scenarios for managed care and competitor development, and an assessment of existing outreach initiatives and identification of potential future targets.

The outputs of activity I will identify key challenges that the program must address to grow and key opportunities for growth. The findings, in combination with each other, begin to simulate the program's future potential and marketing direction as it moves into the next phase of strategy development.

Completion of the analysis serves as the platform to critically assess the cancer program marketing mix. Each program will have its own unique position relative to the four P's. Analyzing the assessment will highlight the key marketing issues that must be addressed in the marketing strategy development.

Activity II: Marketing Strategy Development

The marketing strategy development activity is the most critical stage of the planning process. Many organizations get bogged down at this point in "analysis paralysis," and little strategy emerges. Ultimately, strategy development based on comprehensive data analysis and solid research will ensure a more successful marketing plan and implementation process.

To begin the strategy development process, a positioning statement should be developed. This statement, which complements the organization's mission and vision statement, succinctly states what the cancer program will look like in the future. Although the positioning statement will change over time, it establishes agreement on the future program direction.

Once program leadership has approved a positioning statement (typically established as part of the strategic planning process), target market segments must be finalized. Plans that fail to be segment-specific are generally unfocused. Program leaders are learning that in highly competitive cancer markets, developing market segment-specific strategies is essential.

Once the positioning statement and target market segments are established, marketing and organizational strategies must be defined that will enable the organization to capitalize on opportunities identified in activity I. The strategy development process challenges many programs, with strategies often focusing on internal capabilities. Strategies are mechanisms that a program can employ when interacting with its environment to move to a different position. Following a few simple guidelines can facilitate cancer program leadership in successful strategy development: (a) avoid developing tactics or actions as strategies, (b) develop marketing strategies that address key issues and opportunities, (c) continue to build programmatic strengths and address key vulnerabilities, (d) make sure that strategies are identified for the priority target segments, (e) ensure that strategies help move the cancer program closer to its agreed upon future position as delineated in the positioning statement, and (f) consider using multidisciplinary strategy work groups to draft strategies (around specifically assigned issues or topics) and to present draft strategies to the steering committee.

Activity III: Marketing Budget and Action Plan

To proceed with activity III, the steering committee must agree on the strategies established in activity II and develop an implementation plan. This activity focuses on the logistics of making the strategies come to life and identifying the following information: (a) specific actions that must be implemented to successfully achieve the strategy, (b) priorities and completion dates for these actions, (c) individual accountability for each priority, (d) resource requirements for each action and strategy, and (e) the mechanism to review and measure progress on achieving the strategies and how improvements will be quantified.

This information will be developed for each strategy (or group of strategies) in the implementation plan. The steering committee and hospital leadership should approve a final version of the implementation plan.

Activity IV: Approval and Presentation of the Marketing Plan

The final activity is to obtain formal approval for the plan and present it to key constituents. For organizations that have involved a broad spectrum of participants in development of the plan and have kept organization leaders, physician leaders, and board members apprised of the plan's intent, the activity should proceed smoothly. Typically, refinements to the plan will be identified as a result of the presentation process and will be incorporated to strengthen the plan.

Executing the Marketing Plan: How to Ensure That Real Change Occurs

Producing the Right Results

Marketing plans often can be characterized as being too resource intensive and unaffordable to implement, with the anticipated end result producing little change. To ensure that the plan produces the desired results, cancer program leaders must consider a number of important factors.

Develop strategies that differentiate the cancer program. Failure to differentiate the cancer program in any market is an invitation to encourage the public to support the competition.

Provide high-quality, cost-effective services. Cancer programs must scrutinize their product and price position early in the development of a marketing plan.

No amount of creative strategies in a marketing plan can compensate for a cancer program with services that fail to adapt to market demand and cost positions that are noncompetitive.

Gain commitment prior to initiating planning. Cancer programs must have organization and physician leadership commitment to the development and implementation of the plan. This commitment must include assurances that financial resources are available for implementation.

Ensure involvement of cancer program physician and administrative leadership. Both program physician and administrative leaders must work together to develop the plan and execute its implementation. Marketing plans will fail without adequate support and participation by these groups.

Provide adequate information system support. The structuring of the marketing plan and monitoring of the plan's progress relies heavily on access to accurate and current data.

Set realistic, achievable goals. When planning implementation of the marketing strategies, cancer programs are better off trying to accomplish less and building momentum by truly achieving their goals than trying to do too much or taking a shotgun approach to implementation.

There are many caveats that organizations will encounter throughout the development and implementation of cancer marketing goals and plans. The most successful plans are based on solid research that identifies the needs of the market not only from a demand, technologic, and clinical perspective, but also from a business, image, and pricing perspective. Only when this full range of needs is identified and segmented will marketing strategies bring about the changes needed to sustain and improve the market position of cancer programs.

Developing the Marketing Campaign

A marketing campaign may or may not be required to support the marketing plan or goals of the cancer program. The magnitude of the cancer program marketing issues that must be resolved and the nature of the marketing strategies to resolve these issues will determine the requirements for a campaign.

A marketing campaign is a concentrated and focused set of marketing activities targeted at selected segments and is designed to deliver a specific message. Development of the marketing campaign would include the following considerations: The marketing campaign itself would be identified as a priority strategy in the marketing plan or goals; hospital marketing and communications specialist/staff or an advertising firm would be assigned primary responsibility to direct and design the campaign. The design needs to address the timing for the key marketing activities in the campaign, and the marketing medium (e.g., radio, television, outdoor advertising, publications, direct mail) that will be used (based on the message that is intended, the market segment targeted, and the marketing issue to be resolved). The selection of the marketing medium will be determined by the communications message that is intended and the marketing budget. A budget must be established to finalize the campaign, and a monitoring and measurement process must be established (as part of the campaign design) to gauge actual against expected outcomes and relate outcomes to campaign costs. The target markets or markets are identified. The desired marketing outcome (e.g., low public awareness, few referrals from primary care physicians whose practices are remote from the cancer center) needs to be reaffirmed from the market position assessment. A shotgun marketing approach is inconsistent with the essence of marketing and with the concept of a marketing campaign. Collateral material, if required, needs to be designed and approved by cancer program and hospital leadership. A detailed rollout plan is prepared specifying a critical pathway of events for the campaign, individuals who are responsible for each element of the campaign, and a completion date for each activity and resource budget.

Marketing campaigns are expensive, complicated, and require significant effort and support. Their use must be measured against the changes in the market place cancer program and the ones hospital leadership is trying to achieve. When designed and executed successfully, a marketing campaign can make a tremendous contribution to enhance cancer program market share.

Requirements for Success in Cancer Program Planning and Marketing: The Imperative for Professional Management Development

There are two evolving trends in health care that conflict and create a significant challenge for the industry. The aging of the population contributes to the increased demand for healthcare services and, in particular, those offered through clinical programs (e.g., cancer, women's, orthopedics). As these trends evolve, many hospitals are moving toward a product line or modified product line management structure to manage these growing programs. Additionally, the healthcare industry is experiencing a critical shortage of qualified managers while it concurrently expands the span of control of its management and executive teams to minimize overhead costs.

As span of control increases, the industry has managers and executives with responsibilities for multiple clinical programs, and less time is spent in the direct management of these programs. Management time focuses on resolving crisis and issues, and little, if any, time is spent on entrepreneurial and business development activities.

Regardless of the reasons behind these disturbing industry trends, healthcare organizations and professional societies will have to take a leadership role *today* to train and guide the professional development of *tomorrow's* clinical program managers. Organizations that fail to recognize this requirement or fail to act on it will struggle with the success of their clinical programs and will not maintain a sustainable competitive advantage. As organizations plan the future skills requirements for their clinical program managers, they will have to take into account the capabilities and expertise available throughout the organization.

Leadership Requirements for Future Cancer Programs

Spallina (2002) described design guidance that healthcare organizations and professional societies might consider in addressing the clinical program management shortage and other issues they should take into consideration (see Figure 22-3).

Figure 22-3. Cancer Program Leadership Requirements

- Clinical and operations expertise
- Services and technology evaluation and design
- Organizational management
- Financial and business planning, evaluation, and management
- Quality assessment process design and management
- Information systems management
- Strategic planning
- Physician relations management
- Marketing and promotions
- Facility programming and planning

Clinical and operations expertise. This is an important component of a solid foundation for clinical program management but not the only requirement for tomorrow's clinical program managers' skill set. Clinical research will become an increasingly important activity in clinical programs as new biologic and genomic solutions are designed for the diagnosis and treatment of disease.

Services and technology evaluation and design. This skill requirement, along with clinical and operations expertise, historically comprised the majority of skills required for clinical program managers. Contemporary clinical program managers will require a far more expansive set of skills and expertise, as described later.

Organizational management. Active physician involvement is essential to any successful clinical program. In one form or another, clinical programs are developing "boards" to guide the development of program policy, strategies, and financial priorities. It typically is the responsibility of the clinical program manager to manage the agenda for "board" activities and follow up on "board" discussions and decisions.

Financial and business planning, evaluation, and management. Successful clinical programs will increasingly be run as businesses (i.e., mimic for-profit environments). The new tools of the future will focus on cash flow and clinical program financial feasibility analyses and will include financial and operational simulation/modeling, return on investment analyses, and multivariant scenario analyses.

Quality assessment process design and management. Quality assessment and process improvement will continue to be essential tools to successfully manage and contain costs (e.g., margin management, competitive financial position) in clinical programs. The manager's skills must include design capabilities to modify the processes as new technologies are introduced and must be able to manage the process to ensure that mechanisms are in place for active monitoring and implementation of corrective action, when required.

Information systems management. Vast quantities of clinical, financial, and performance data will be available from a variety of internal and Web-based sources. The role of the clinical manager is to ensure that these data are converted into meaningful information and routinely used in the management and planning of the clinical program. Information will be rolled up and provided on a routine basis in the form of "dashboard indicators" to guide management of operations and program direction.

Web-based resources (analysis tools, clinical information repositories, results reporting, and data configuration) are becoming increasingly available for clinical programs. The clinical program manager will become the designer to integrate internally managed data and information with Web-based solutions.

Strategic planning. The aging of the population will accelerate the demand for healthcare services at a pace that will exceed healthcare organizations' ability to respond successfully. Successful programs will have clearly defined and well-executed strategies and business relationships (not necessarily equity-based joint ventures) with program physicians.

Physician relations management. Successful clinical programs are dependent on the involvement of program physicians in the planning and execution of program strategies. Clinical programs are evolving as business platforms for hospital and physician goal alignment. The clinical program manager serves as the healthcare organization's lead individual to understand and manage these relationships.

Marketing and promotions. Strategic plans will serve as the basis for clinical program marketing. Clinical program managers will guide and lead the development of marketing plans and execution of those plans. These strategies will direct the use of limited resources in differentiating and promoting the program in the community among its competitors.

Facility programming and planning. Increasing demand for healthcare services will require expansion in capacity and facilities. Future clinical program facilities will reflect an increasing outpatient orientation and an increased occupancy/use of space by physician practices.

After 2010–2015, facilities will have to reflect the increasing use of new biologic and genomic solutions in health care. The design of these facilities will likely have very different requirements than clinical centers that are being planned and built today. The transition to new and different clinical solutions at a time when the aging of the population is peaking and the demand for healthcare services is accelerating further complicates the facility planning process.

Successful facility planning will be distinguished by award-winning design, plans that identify *today* the direction and potential location/zones for *tomorrow's* facility expansion, and operational planning that is integrated into the facility design, anticipates future expansion, and leads to cost efficiencies. These plans also will successfully address the transition (in operations and facilities) from clinical solutions, as we know them today, to new biologic and genomic tools.

Clinical program managers will lead and direct a multidisciplinary team of physicians, nurses, managers, facility planners, operations experts, and scientists. The planning process will be linked to the leadership structure of the program (i.e., program "board" involvement and approval) and will allow little room for error or opportunity to correct mistakes in future years.

Summary

With knowledge of these leadership requirements and a shrinking base of experienced managers, healthcare organizations and professional societies have little choice in their approach to prepare for the leadership development challenges of the future. Organizations will focus leadership development, training, and continuing management education on integrating business tools and skills into clinical program management.

The complexities of managing clinical programs will continue to grow in the future as the number of qualified managers is expected to diminish. Healthcare organizations and academic programs will modify existing management and leadership courses and will develop clinical program management training tracks. Healthcare providers that create solutions to this management imperative will maintain their competitive edge in the challenging times that will greet the industry in the future.

References

Bode, R. (1993). *First you have to row a little boat*. New York: Warner Books.

Drucker, P. (1973). *Management: Tasks, responsibilities, practices*. New York: Harper & Row.

Spallina, J.M. (2002). Clinical program leadership: Skill requirements for contemporary leaders. *Journal of Oncology Management, 11*(3), 24–26.

Young, O.D. (1995). *Thoughts on leadership*. Chicago: Triumph Books.

Accreditation: A Method for Measuring Compliance

Patti L. Owen, MN, RN

"Ideals are like stars: We never reach them, but like the mariners of the sea, we chart our course by them." Carl Schurz (Washington, 1999, p. 73)

The accreditation of healthcare organizations has long been a fundamental component of national efforts to ensure high-quality care. Merriam-Webster (2004) defined accredit as "giving official authorization or approval to" and "to recognize as conforming to a standard." Ensuring compliance to standards and preparing for accreditation surveys are fundamental responsibilities of nursing management. The purpose of this chapter is to provide a historical overview of accreditation; discuss the concept of continuous survey readiness; describe the benefits of accreditation; and provide a description of four accreditation organizations common to cancer program leaders.

Overview of Accreditation

Healthcare quality cannot be discussed without recognizing national efforts to measure quality of care. Dalrymple and Scherrer (1998) noted that accreditation has served as a method for measuring and enhancing quality in many different aspects of contemporary life. The fundamental principles of accreditation can be applied to a variety of entities such as schools, summer camps, nursing homes, or healthcare organizations. Accreditation standards are established to reflect current practice and expectations. Recognized as the foundation of an accreditation system, *standards* are defined as accepted measures of comparison for quantitative or qualitative value (*Webster's II,* 1994). In the healthcare industry, standards are expectations that are used to assess organizational compliance.

Typically, external peer review ensures that standards for patient care are defined and supported by organizational processes and procedures. External review by an accrediting organization validates the compliance of internal processes. Scrivens (1997) listed the traditional characteristics of accrediting organizations as (a) a focus on processes/procedures, (b) written standards, (c) assessment of compliance with standards by trained surveyors with healthcare experience, (d) scoring based on degree of compliance, (e) voluntary participation, (f) confidential findings, and (g) an independent board conducting the process.

In the 1980s, accrediting organizations began to move away from the traditional model of reviewing organizational policies and procedures to measuring outcomes. This shift caused the healthcare industry to develop methods for measuring the results of care rather than just the plans for care. The new focus on outcomes required healthcare accrediting organizations to revise their approach to measuring quality. An example was the new approach taken by the Joint Commission on Accreditation of Healthcare Organizations (JCAHO). The *Agenda for Change* was a movement from quality assurance to a continuous search for quality improvement (Scrivens, 1997).

Over time, the model of continuous quality improvement (CQI), grounded in the principles of the quality gurus Deming, Crosby, and Juran (Scrivens, 1997), gained acceptance within the healthcare industry well into the 1980s and 1990s. Accreditation systems developed approaches that would incorporate the principles of CQI within a structure compatible with external review. In addition, the model of patient-centered or patient-focused care required new tools for evaluation of clinical activities. Standards were revised to measure direct performance or outcomes, rather than administrative structures or capability for delivering quality care (Scrivens, 1997). In general, accrediting organizations have and will continue to adapt their approach to meet the current understanding and beliefs about the most effective methods for determining quality in health care.

Commitment to Continuous Readiness

Another recent change related to accreditation is the survey preparation process. There is growing consensus among accreditation and healthcare organizations that the best method for survey preparation is continuous readiness. Hengesbaugh (JCAHO, 2003), chairman and public member of the JCAHO Board of Commissioners, stated, "Readiness for a survey at any time is a logical extension of the accredited organization's commitment to continuous improvement." The goal is to focus on continuous improvement practices for quality care rather than doing so on an intermittent basis by incorporating standards into the daily processes of the organization and demonstrating a sustained level of compliance.

A proactive, planned approach to accreditation surveys involves maintaining compliance to current externally established standards. Smeltzer and Vrba (1991) described the process of preparation through a method of understanding the standards, developing tools to monitor ongoing compliance with the standards, educating the staff regarding the standards, and ensuring performance is in compliance with the standards. Through a similar, yet more extensive approach, Jackson, Kuehn, Watkins, and Gilliam (1994) demonstrated the effective use of mock surveys in preparing for an accreditation survey.

Jackson et al. (1994) began the preparation for accreditation with a review of results from prior surveys. Identification of deficiencies was used to create an action plan to ensure survey readiness. The action plan identified applicable standards, desired outcomes for compliance, responsible change agents, and targeted completion dates. Next, education was provided to nursing leaders in an effort to prepare them as effective change agents, expand their awareness of the purpose and process of the accrediting organization, and demonstrate that the standards are achievable and reflect external expectations for health care.

Following a mandatory education workshop, a mock survey was held to measure compliance to standards and increase staff awareness of the survey process. The survey process included developing tools, preparing mock surveyors, and conducting the mock survey. Following the mock survey, a formal summation conference was held to provide departments with feedback on their performance. Outcomes of the mock survey resulted in an increased staff comfort level with the survey process, monitoring tools, data regarding compliance to standards, leadership development, team building, and networking.

Incorporating compliance with standards into daily practice is good management and ensures ongoing quality care. As such, survey time becomes less stressful and an opportunity for nurses to "show off" their performance and outcomes (Smeltzer & Vrba, 1991). The key to compliance is creativity. The use of examples and suggestions found in manuals from consultants and colleagues is recommended.

Overall, nursing leaders are responsible for survey preparation in a proactive rather than reactive manner. The benefits of continuous readiness far outweigh the negative aspects of short-term preparation. A short-term or "ramp up" approach to accreditation surveys often leads to significant costs, a crisis mode of operation, and significant stress and/or anxiety among staff members (Simpson, 1994). Furthermore, the gains often are not sustained over time. Instituting an approach of continuous readiness will increase the benefits and decrease the costs of accreditation.

Benefits of Accreditation

Overall, accreditation is valuable in helping an organization to improve organizational performance. Although each accreditation organization lists specific benefits that are unique to its function, several general benefits can be applied to accreditation. For a healthcare organization, accreditation by an external agency demonstrates a commitment to quality care and quality improvement; defines methods of achieving standards through guidelines, policies, and procedures; provides an objective evaluation of organizational performance; provides a mechanism for staff education; serves as a recruitment tool; and serves as a "seal of approval" or a recognized measure of quality care for consumers (managed care/insurers/employers/patients/community).

More specifically, each accreditation organization lists specific benefits inherent in its goals. For example, the American College of Surgeons Commission on Cancer (CoC) described benefits such as the ability to network with quality cancer programs and the availability of free marketing through a partnership between CoC and the American Cancer Society (American College of Surgeons Commission on Cancer [CoC], 2002). Similarly, JCAHO, from a broader scope and larger client base, listed benefits such as expediting third-party payment, meeting certain Medicare requirements, and often fulfilling state licensure requirements (JCAHO, 2004). Healthcare organizations must determine the value of each accreditation based on organizational goals and the cost/benefit ratio.

Accreditation Organizations

There are four accreditation organizations in which oncology leaders often participate: (a) JCAHO (see Table 23-1), (b) American College of Surgeons CoC (see Table 23-2), (c) American College of Radiology (see Table 23-3), and (d) the Foundation for the Accreditation of Cellular Therapy (FACT) (see Table 23-4). A general description of each organization is provided. Although the survey processes and standards associated with each organization are continuously evolving, charts are provided with current information, including eligibility, key elements, survey process, potential outcomes, and resources.

Joint Commission on Accreditation of Healthcare Organizations

Since 1951, JCAHO has provided accreditation services to healthcare organizations in the United States (JCAHO, 2003). JCAHO is the most widely used accrediting organization and, therefore, is recognized nationally as the leader among accrediting organizations (Roberts, Coale, & Redman, 1987). Currently, JCAHO accredits more than 16,000 organizations in the United States and many other countries (JCAHO, 2003).

In 1999, JCAHO communicated a new vision for accreditation in an effort to enhance the credibility and relevance of the accreditation process as well as create a model that is more data driven, less predictable, more cost effective, and more individualized to the organization. Beginning in 2004, the new accreditation model, "Shared Visions—New Pathways," will be based on the following goals: (a) shift focus from JCAHO survey preparation to continuous operational improvement in support of safe, high-quality care, (b) decrease costs related to survey "ramp up," (c) reduce documentation burden to focus more on critical patient care issues, and (d) focus survey in areas specific to individual organizations (JCAHO, 2003).

Table 23-1. JCAHO Accreditation Program

Organization	Eligibility	Key Elements	Survey Process	Potential Outcomes	Resources

Joint Commission on the Accreditation of Healthcare Organizations (JCAHO)	• All types of healthcare organizations meet the following requirements:
	  - Located in the United States or its territories or, if outside, meets designated criteria
	  - Assesses and improves the quality of its services
	  - Identifies the services it provides, indicating which services it provides directly under contract or through some other arrangement
	  - Provides services addressed by JCAHO's standards
		• Patient-focused functions
		  - Ethics, rights and responsibilities
		  - Provision of care, treatment, and services
		  - Medication management
		  - Surveillance, prevention, and control of infection
		• Organization functions
		  - Improving organizational performance
		  - Leadership
		  - Management of the environment of care
		  - Management of human resources
		  - Management of information
		• Structures with functions
		  - Medical staff
		  - Nursing
			• Three-year survey cycle
			• Survey process
			1. Begin periodic performance review (PPR) 15 months into accreditation.
			2. Complete application.
			3. Provide data for the priority focus process (PFP).
			4. During on-site visit, organization's compliance will be evaluated on
			  - Tracing the care delivered to patients
			  - Verbal and written information provided to JCAHO
			  - On-site observation and interview by surveyors
			  - Documents provided by the organization.
				1. Accredited
				  - Compliance with all standards
				  - Successfully addressed all requirements for improvement within 90 days* after survey
				2. Provisional accreditation
				  - Organization fails to address requirements for improvement within 90 days* after survey.
				3. Conditional accreditation
				  - Organization is not in substantial compliance with standards. An on-site, follow-up survey is required.
				4. Preliminary denial of accreditation
				  - Justification to deny accreditation related to level of noncompliance
				  - Decision is subject to appeal
				5. Denial of accreditation
				  - All review and appeal opportunities have been exhausted.
					• Web sites—www.jcaho.org and www.jcrinc.com
					• Publications—a variety of manuals, books, periodicals, software, and other products can be found listed on the Web site.
					• Education—more than 200 seminars on over 75 topics are offered each year. Call customer service at 877-223-6866.
					• Consulting—comprehensive consulting and customer education services are offered to all types of healthcare organizations. For consulting services, call 630-268-7400.
					• The Continuous Survey Readiness (CSR) Program—a process of ongoing consultation and education that takes place locally. For more information, call 630-268-7452.

(Continued on next page)

Table 23-1. JCAHO Accreditation Program (Continued)

Organization	Eligibility	Key Elements	Survey Process	Potential Outcomes	Resources
Joint Commission on the Accreditation of Healthcare Organizations (JCAHO) (cont.)			• Unannounced surveys will begin in 2004 for organizations that volunteer. • In 2006, all accreditation resurveys will be unannounced.	6. Preliminary accreditation - Organization demonstrates compliance with selected standards. * To be changed to 45 days in 2005	

Note. From *CAMH: 2004 Comprehensive Accreditation Manual for Hospitals* (pp. 1–2, 15, 21, 26), by the Joint Commission Resources, 2004, Oakbrook Terrace, IL. Copyright 2004 by the Joint Commission on Accreditation of Healthcare Organizations. Reprinted with permission.

Table 23-2. American College of Surgeons Commission on Cancer Accreditation Program

Organization	Eligibility	Key Elements	Survey Process	Potential Outcomes	Resources
American College of Surgeons (ACS) Commission on Cancer	• Hospitals • Free-standing treatment facilities • Healthcare networks • Initial requirements include - Key elements are in place for one year	• Clinical services—provides state-of-the-art services along the continuum of care for patients with cancer	• Three-year survey cycle • Survey guidelines 1. Complete or update Web-based survey application record 30 days prior to on-site inspection. 2. Provide documentation related to cancer committee activity and compliance to standards 2 weeks (14 days) prior to on-site survey.	• 36 standards • Outcomes include 1. Full approval—no deficiencies 2. Three-year approval with contingency—one to seven deficiencies	• Survey-related resources/tools are available on the Cancer Programs page of the ACS Web site at www.facs.org - Survey-related resources - Cancer program tracking tools

(Continued on next page)

Table 23-2. American College of Surgeon's Commission on Cancer Accreditation Program (Continued)

Organization	Eligibility	Key Elements	Survey Process	Potential Outcomes	Resources
American College of Surgeons (ACS) Commission on Cancer (cont.)	- Reference date established; cancer registry database has two complete years of data and one year of follow-up data. - Participates in a consultative evaluation of cancer program - Meets standards - Submits data to National Cancer Database.	• Cancer committee—leads program through setting goals, monitoring activity, and evaluating patient outcomes and improving care • Cancer conferences— provides a forum for patient consultation and professional education • Quality improvement program—mechanism to evaluate and improve patient outcomes • Cancer registry—provides data to monitor quality of care/patient outcomes	3. Payment of survey—mail invoice within 30 days of survey. 4. Prepare for on-site visit. Surveyor will - Review documentation to determine compliance with standards. - Review 25 medical records to evaluate American Joint Committee on Cancer staging by managing physician, pathology reports, and quality of abstracted data. - Meet with a member of administration, cancer committee chair, cancer liaison physician, and cancer registrar. Surveyor may request meetings with other members of the cancer care team. - Hold a wrap-up session to discuss strengths/weaknesses and provide suggestions to correct deficiencies. • Award notification—8–12 weeks following survey.	3. Nonapproval— eight or more deficiencies 4. Approval deferred (valid only for new programs).	- Other cancer program resources

Note. Based on information from American College of Surgeons Commission on Cancer, 2003.

Table 23-3. American College of Radiology Accreditation Program

Organization	Eligibility	Key Elements	Survey Process	Potential Outcomes	Resources

American College of Radiology (ACR)	• Radiation oncology facilities/ programs
	• Single-site facilities
	• Multi-site facilities
		• Clinical care—third party, objective peer review and evaluation of patient care
		• Documentation—treatment planning and treatment records
		• Personnel qualifications/ staffing levels
		  - Radiation oncologist
		  - Medical physicist
		  - Radiation therapists/ simulation staff
		  - Dosimetrist
		• Equipment—Quality Management Program and verification of performance
		• Continuous Quality Improvement Program
		  - Chart review
		  - Morbidity/mortality
		  - Internal outcomes studies
		  - Individual physician peer review
		  - Patient satisfaction
		  - New patient conferences
		  - Port film review
		  - Chart rounds
			• Three-year survey cycle
			• Survey guidelines
			1. Complete application.
			  - Treatment and equipment information
			  - Staffing levels and qualifications
			  - Patient census data
			  - Physics quality, assurance/quality, control documentation
			  - Self-assessment documentation from physicians
			  - Response to identified deficiencies from ACR standards checklist
			2. Submit data for case review.
			  - List of patients treated over a 12-month period prior to survey
			  - ID numbers/physician initials of 10 patients for selected sites: breast, prostate, lung, head/neck, and other sites
			  - Preliminary case self-assessment peer review data collection forms on 10 patients
			3. Prepare for on-site survey. Surveyor will
			  - Verify application information.
			  - Tour facility.
			  - Interview chief of radiation oncology, physicists, administrator, and other key personnel.
			  - Collect information on quality assessment/quality improvement program.
			  - Collect/assess medical and dosimetry/physics data and documentation.
			• Final report will be provided in 8–12 weeks.
				• Full accreditation
				• No accreditation with specific recommendations
				• Facilities providing satisfactory responses to recommendations may be granted a three-year accreditation.
					• Survey-related resources/tools are available on the ACR's Web site at www.acr.org
					• Contact ACR's Radiation Oncology Practice Accreditation Program at 888-726-8956.

Table 23-4. Foundation for the Accreditation of Cellular Therapy Program

Organization	Eligibility	Key Elements	Survey Process	Potential Outcomes	Resources

Foundation for the Accreditation of Cellular Therapy (FACT)	• Clinical Transplantation Program
	• Hematopoietic Cell Collection Facility
	• Hematopoietic Progenitor Cell Laboratory
		• Clinical program—facilities and staff meeting FACT standards
		• Safety requirements—programs must minimize risks to health and safety of employees, volunteers, patients, and donors.
		• Transplant team—a dedicated team, including program director
		• Competency—specific training and competency of physicians and staff
		• Quality management—written quality management plan that covers all aspects of transplant program
			• Three-year survey cycle
			• Survey guidelines
			1. Program submits registration form and survey fee.
			2. Program submits checklist documentation and fee.
			3. FACT staff reviews submissions and obtains missing documentation.
			4. On-site inspection is scheduled, and inspectors review application program.
			5. Prepare for on-site inspection. Inspectors will
			  - Conduct initial interview.
			  - Inspect all sites; complete checklist.
			  - Conduct exit interview with review of key findings.
			6. Inspection team submits completed reports to FACT office for review.
			7. FACT board makes accreditation decision.
			8. Program director is notified of accreditation decision within 12 weeks.
			9. Program corrects deficiencies if needed.
				1. Full accreditation
				2. Few, minor deficiencies and/or variances
				  • Full accreditation requires the following:
				  - Documented correction of deficiencies
				  - Satisfactory response to all variances from recommendations.
				3. Major and systemic deficiencies
				  • Full accreditation requires:
				  - Documented correction of all deficiencies
				  - Satisfactory response to all variances from recommendations
				  - Satisfactory completion of a focused reinspection.
					Additional information is available on the FACT Web site: www.factwebsite.org

Note. Based on information from the Foundation for the Accreditation of Cellular Therapy (www.factwebsite.org).

Several components of the new JCAHO accreditation process are noteworthy. First, beginning in 2004, organizations will submit an electronic application and receive a customized list of applicable standards for which they are responsible based on the types of services and care settings submitted. Second, in an effort to reduce redundancy, numerous standards will be deleted or consolidated, and a new format will streamline the survey process. Third, a self-assessment process, called a periodic performance review, will be introduced in 2004. Every 18 months, organizations will be required to perform a review of all applicable standards and report corrective actions to JCAHO for those standards not being met. Similarly, JCAHO announced plans to conduct all regular accreditation surveys on an unannounced basis starting in 2006. "The new accreditation process, 'Shared Visions—New Pathways,' creates the expectation that each accredited organization be in compliance with 100% of the Joint Commission's standards 100% of the time," said Dennis S. O'Leary, JCAHO president (O'Leary, 1997). Fourth, JCAHO will implement a priority focus process. This new process will focus the accreditation survey in areas specific to the individual organization. A Web-based application integrates hospital-specific presurvey data. Overall, the priority focus process will enhance customization of the accreditation survey for the healthcare organization. Finally, a new approach will be implemented for complex organizations surveyed under more than one accreditation manual. A generalist surveyor will survey common standards that apply to more than one setting or program (e.g., hospital, home care, long-term care) at one site. At the same time, specialist surveyors will survey programs that have specialty standards only pertaining to that specialty program. This process will reduce redundancy in the survey and reduce time and costs associated with surveyors.

The transition to the new survey process must be planned. An accreditation transition timeline will help an organization to prepare for the new process (see Figure 23-1). The timeline example plots the activities of the new 2004 JCAHO accreditation process over a 39-month time frame. Sharing the timeline with the organization as well as providing education about the new process are important responsibilities of nursing leadership. As a leader among accrediting organizations, JCAHO will serve as a model for continuous compliance.

American College of Surgeons: Commission on Cancer Approvals Program

An estimated 80% of all newly diagnosed patients are treated in cancer programs accredited or approved by the American College of Surgeons CoC (2002). In 1922, the American College of Surgeons established the CoC as a consortium of professional organizations "dedicated to reducing the morbidity and mortality of cancer through education, standard setting, and the monitoring of quality care" (American College of Surgeons CoC, 2004b). The commission's approvals program serves as the accrediting body for healthcare facilities that are committed to providing quality patient care in all cancer care arenas, including prevention, early diagnosis, pretreat-

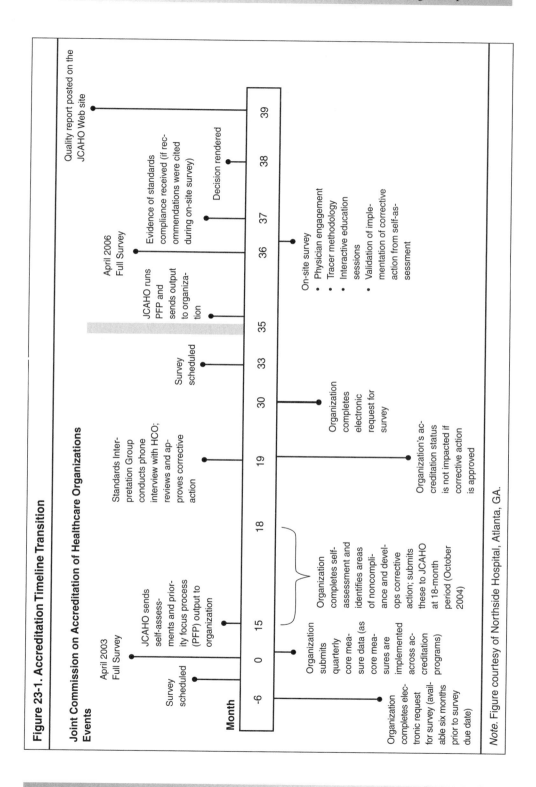

Figure 23-1. Accreditation Timeline Transition

Joint Commission on Accreditation of Healthcare Organizations

Note. Figure courtesy of Northside Hospital, Atlanta, GA.

ment evaluation, staging, treatment, rehabilitation, ongoing surveillance, support services, and end-of-life care.

The *Cancer Program Standards 2004* (American College of Surgeons CoC, 2004a) provides the structure and requirements of cancer programs seeking approval or accreditation. The standards support four primary components of the approvals program: a multidisciplinary cancer committee, cancer conferences, evaluation of quality outcomes and approvals, and a cancer registry. These primary components, coupled with a full scope of clinical services, comprise the elements required for approval. As with many standards of accrediting organizations, the CoC standards were reviewed and revised recently in response to a number of factors. These factors include the desire to move beyond structure and process as measures of quality and the need to redefine and measure quality cancer care.

As such, the new standards have a greater focus on the quality of tumor registry data, patient outcomes, and quality improvement. Additional changes include standards that provide rationale and are more measurable; do not duplicate requirements of other organizations (e.g., JCAHO); are tailored to address the unique needs of an organization based on size and services; and are more flexible. The survey process was updated to allow an online survey application, a pre-assessment of cancer program activity resulting in a survey focused on areas for improvement, and a new requirement of annual updates to the CoC.

The annual update concept supports the movement toward continuous compliance. Although a three-year survey cycle will remain, annual updates will ensure ongoing compliance. CoC approval is awarded to those programs committed to and compliant with the multidisciplinary, quality patient care standards set forth by the CoC.

American College of Radiology

The American College of Radiology (ACR) is the accrediting organization for radiation oncology. ACR is the primary professional organization of radiologists, radiation oncologists, and clinical medical physicists in the United States with more than 30,000 members (ACR, 2004). The accreditation process is designed to be educational and promote quality.

Compliance with the ACR "Standards for Radiation Oncology" is central to accreditation by the ACR Radiation Oncology Accreditation Program. The ACR standards are guidelines that attempt to define principles of practice associated with high-quality care. The goals of the program are to provide an objective peer review; recognize quality radiation oncology practices; identify opportunities for improvement in practice and patient outcomes; and provide a referral list for patients (ACR, 2003).

The accreditation process includes an assessment of personnel, equipment, treatment planning and treatment records, and quality control procedures. A comparison is made of these key elements to a database of ACR accredited facilities, a national database for staffing and equipment ratios, the ACR "Standards for Radiation Oncology," and other professional guidelines. A one-day on-site survey is conducted by board certified radiation oncologists and board certified medical physicists.

Foundation for the Accreditation of Cellular Therapy

In comparing the history of accrediting organizations discussed in this chapter, FACT is the most recent. In 1996, FACT (then called the Foundation for Accreditation of Hematopoietic Cellular Therapy), was established as a nonprofit organization for voluntary accreditation in the field of hematopoietic cell therapy (FACT, 2003). As the first accreditation organization to establish standards for clinical transplant programs, the goals of FACT are to promote high-quality patient care and laboratory performance.

A clinical transplant program is defined by the following criteria: geographic proximity; a single program director; common staff training, protocols, and quality assessment; integrated clinical team; and a cell collection and processing facility that meets FACT standards. Program size is also a consideration in that a defined number of transplants must be performed annually to obtain and maintain accreditation. Accreditation for either allogeneic or autologous transplant programs requires 10 new patients of that type each year (FACT, 2002).

Compliance with the FACT standards provides the basis for accreditation. The standards provide an infrastructure for all phases of collection, processing, and transplantation. The "Standards for Hematopoietic Progenitor Cell Collection, Processing & Transplantation" include the following: terminology and definitions, clinical program standards, cell collection standards, and cell processing standards (FACT, 2002). The accreditation process includes a written application and an on-site survey by trained inspectors highly experienced in the field. The application checklist is derived from the standards, completed by each facility, and reviewed by the inspector during the survey. Finally, the FACT Board of Directors reviews findings and makes accreditation decisions (FACT, 2002).

Summary

Accreditation is an important indicator of quality for healthcare organizations. Accreditation provides a method of measuring compliance with standards that have been established and accepted by the healthcare industry. Over the past two decades, accrediting organizations have shifted the focus from procedures and structure to performance and outcomes. The need for continuous survey readiness is becoming an expectation of organizations seeking and maintaining accreditation. Ensuring compliance to standards and continuous survey readiness are expectations of nursing leadership. As such, oncology leaders need to demonstrate a thorough knowledge and understanding of applicable standards and implement plans that ensure continuous compliance.

References

American College of Radiology. (2003). *ACR radiation oncology accreditation program frequently asked questions*. Retrieved October 25, 2004, from http://www.acr.org/s_acr/doc.asp?CID=590&DID=8062

American College of Radiology. (2004). *About the American College of Radiology*. Retrieved October 25, 2004, from http://www.acr.org/s_acr/sec.asp?CID=2561&DID=17606

American College of Surgeons Commission on Cancer. (2002). *Proposed revisions to CoC cancer program standards*. Retrieved May 21, 2002, from http://www.facs.org/cancer/coc/proposedchanges.html

American College of Surgeons Commission on Cancer. (2003). *List of cancer program standards*. Retrieved August 1, 2003, from http://www.facs.org/cancer/coc/newstandards.html

American College of Surgeons Commission on Cancer. (2004a). *Cancer program standards 2004*. Retrieved August 1, 2003, from http://facs.org/cancer/coc/programstandards.html

American College of Surgeons Commission on Cancer. (2004b). *What is the Commission on Cancer?* Retrieved August 30, 2004, from http://www.facs.org/cancer/coc/cocar.html

Dalrymple, P.W., & Scherrer, C.S. (1998). Tools for improvement: A systematic analysis and guide to accreditation by the JCAHO. *Bull Medical Library Association, 86*(1), 10–16.

Foundation for the Accreditation of Cellular Therapy. (2002). *Standards for hematopoietic progenitor cell collection, processing and transplantation* (2nd ed.). Omaha, NE: Author.

Foundation for the Accreditation of Cellular Therapy. (2003). *FACT accreditation general information*. Retrieved October 6, 2003, from http://www.unmc.edu/Community/fahct/About_FACT.htm

Jackson, K.S., Kuehn, P.L., Watkins, K.C., & Gilliam, J. (1994). Mock survey: Methodology for measuring compliance and facilitating change. *Journal of Nursing Administration, 24*(1), 34–39.

Joint Commission on Accreditation of Healthcare Organizations. (2003). *Ambulatory care advisor: Unannounced triennial surveys to begin in 2006*. Retrieved June 27, 2003, from http://www.jcaho.com/accredited+organizations/ambulatory+care/advisor/2003issue1/unannounced+surveys.htm

Joint Commission on Accreditation of Healthcare Organizations. (2004). *Joint commission accreditation*. Retrieved September 6, 2003, from http://www.jcaho.org/htba/index.htm

Merriam-Webster. (2004). *Merriam-Webster online dictionary—accredit*. Retrieved September 29, 2003, from http://m-w.com/cgi-bin/dictionary?book=Dictionary&va=accredit

O'Leary, D. (1997). Needed: Competition between accreditors? An interview with Dennis O'Leary, M.D. *Managed Care, 6*(12), 35–40.

Roberts, J., Coale, J., & Redman, R. (1987). A history of the joint commission on accreditation of hospitals. *JAMA, 258*, 936–940.

Scrivens, E. (1997). Putting continuous quality improvement into accreditation: Improving approaches to quality assessment. *Quality in Health Care, 6*, 212–218.

Simpson, S. (1994). JCAHO standards: Options and opportunities. *Seminars for Nurse Managers, 2*, 218–223.

Smeltzer, C.H., & Vrba, P.D. (1991). Standard compliance: The process and art of preparation. *Journal of Nursing Administration, 21*(4), 45–54.

Washington, G. (1999). *Attitudes of success*. Glendale Heights, IL: Great Quotations.

Webster's II new riverside dictionary. (1994). Itasca, IL: Riverside Publishing.

Quality and Process Improvement

Colleen L. Corish, RN, MN, OCN®
Margaret L. Anthony, RN, MSN, CNOR
Casey T. Liddy, MHA

"An organization's performance of important functions significantly affects the quality and value of its services." (Moses, 2003)

The Institute of Medicine (IOM) (1999) found that as many as 98,000 people die every year from needless healthcare errors. It brought to light the fact that there needs to be a focus on quality throughout the entire industry, from the federal government to the bedside nurse (Agency for Healthcare Research Quality [AHRQ], 2001). The current quality movement in health care parallels the wake up call that the U.S. manufacturing industry experienced in the 1980s when they realized that the Japanese were leading the world in manufacturing. Quality in American industry was thought to be unnecessary. America was a burgeoning world superpower after World War II, and American industry was a major factor in the allied victory. In fact, many of the principles of the quality gurus were developed from the processes that were implemented to make the American wartime industry so strong. They were the best in the world, so why would they need to improve?

At the end of the war, Europe and Japan were in major need of rebuilding. Two major American quality experts, W. Edwards Deming and Joseph M. Juran, aided in the reconstruction of Japan. These men went to teach the Japanese how to improve quality and rebuild their manufacturing capability. Philip B. Crosby went on to expound on the earlier work of Deming and Juran in his book *Quality Is Free* (1979). Twenty-first-century health care is experiencing the same awakening that manufacturing experienced in the 1980s, and health care is turning to the same "quality gurus" who reconstructed Japanese and American manufacturing. The objective of this chapter is to present the principles and tools of quality management and their application in healthcare safety and quality.

Quality Gurus

This section will summarize the work of the leading quality gurus, their processes, and application to healthcare quality management.

W. Edwards Deming

William Edwards Deming is widely credited as the father of quality improvement (QI). He was born in Sioux City, IA, on October 14, 1900. He enrolled in the University of Wyoming at Laramie in 1917 and graduated in 1921 with a BS in electrical engineering. He later went on to earn his MS and PhD in mathematical physics from the University of Colorado and Yale University, respectively. He was invited to Japan in 1950 by the Union of Japanese Scientists and Engineers (JUSE) to help postwar Japan rebuild and improve their industrial infrastructure. His work was so influential that JUSE created the Deming Prize, which is still awarded to companies and individuals (W. Edwards Deming Institute, 2001).

Deming's teachings turned Japan into a world leader in the manufacturing of automobiles and electronics in less than 30 years. His teachings were adopted by American industry in the 1980s and are still in use (Voehl, 1995).

Deming's 14 Points

Figure 24-1 summarizes Deming's 14 Points, which were published in his classic book *Out of the Crisis* (1982). This process is the basis for what we know today as Total Quality Management (TQM) and Continuous Quality Improvement (CQI). This process is not specific to any one industry or sector but is a universal approach to improving quality.

Figure 24-1. Deming's 14 Points of Quality Improvement

1. Create constancy of purpose toward improvement of product and service.
2. Adopt the new philosophy.
3. Cease dependence on mass inspection.
4. End the practice of rewarding business on the basis of price tag alone.
5. Improve constantly and forever the system of production and service.
6. Institute training on the job.
7. Institute leadership.
8. Drive out fear.
9. Break down barriers between departments.
10. Eliminate slogans, exhortations, and targets for the workforce.
11. Eliminate quotas and management by objective. Substitute leadership.
12. Remove barriers that rob people of pride of workmanship.
13. Institute a vigorous program of education and self-improvement.
14. Put everybody in the company to work to accomplish the transformation.

Note. Based on information from Deming, 1982.

One might ask how a system that was designed to improve quality in manufacturing could make an impact on the healthcare system. Deming expands on his 14 points and applies his theory to healthcare services and gives examples of quality problems that healthcare organizations could track to improve quality. Nurse managers knowledgeable of the Joint Commission on Accreditation of Healthcare Organizations (JCAHO) will find his list to be very familiar (Figure 24-2). This list shows how ahead of his time Deming was, because anyone who works in health care is currently tracking some or all of those indicators to measure quality. Some of his points are encapsulated in the JCAHO National Patient Safety Goals.

Figure 24-2. Quality Problems in Health Care

- Incorrect dosages of drugs to patients
- Wrong drug given
- Improper administration of drug
- Number of toxic reactions observed to drugs given
- Number of incomplete medical records
- Number of unnecessary surgical procedures performed
- Number of surgical complications
- Number of transfusion reactions

Note. Based on information from Deming, 1982.

Control Charts

Deming, being a mathematician by training, relied on statistical process control to track QI. Control charts are often the primary tool used to detect variation in a process and are considered more sensitive in detecting variation than a run chart. This is the basic tool that a manager can use to predict the future performance of a process or monitor how a change has impacted a particular process.

A control chart (Figure 24-3) is a graphic display of a process over time and consists of an upper control limit, a lower control limit, and the process mean. If a data point falls outside the upper or lower control limits, the process is described to be "out of control." A control chart does not tell you what is wrong with the process; it is merely a signal that additional analysis is needed.

Plan-Do-Check-Act

Many healthcare organizations are using a QI process that was developed by Walter A. Shewhart in 1939 that was introduced to the Japanese by Deming and has been referred to by many since as the Deming Cycle. The Plan-Do-Check-Act (PDCA) is a process that is used to help organizations identify a process that needs to be improved, plan the intervention that will hopefully improve the process, implement the intervention, check to see what the outcomes of the intervention were on quality, and then act on the data (Deming, 1982). Another hybrid developed is FOCUS-PDCA, where FOCUS is find a process, organize a team, clarify your current knowledge of the process, uncover the root cause, and start the PDCA cycle (Medical Risk Management Associates, 2003). All of these models provide the same element: steps that guide an individual or a group through the improvement process. These models tell us how to go about making change. It took the Japanese nearly 30 years to become the world leader in manufacturing in the 1980s, and it has taken American industry nearly as long to catch up. The healthcare industry is still in the beginning stages of adopting and using the teachings of these quality gurus to improve the care process.

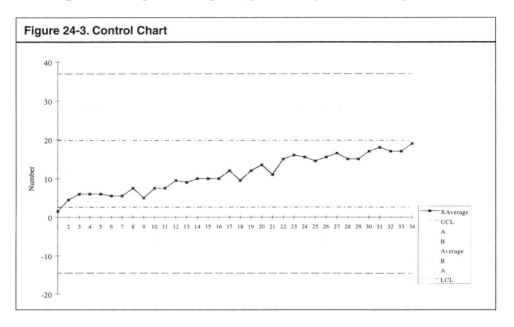

Figure 24-3. Control Chart

Joseph M. Juran

Joseph Moses Juran was born December 24, 1904, in Braila, Romania. In 1909, his father moved to America in search of a better life for himself and his family. The family reunited in the United States in 1912. Throughout school, Juran was an overachiever who eventually ended up nearly three years ahead in school compared to others his age. In 1924, he graduated with a BS in electrical engineering from the University of Minnesota and began working for Western Electric Company, part of Bell Telephone. He was assigned to the inspection department of the Hawthorne Works plant in Chicago. This is where Juran would have his first exposure to his life's work in statistical process control (Juran, 1964).

Juran remained with Western Electric through the Great Depression and during that time used the extra time that came with reduced work hours to pursue a law degree at Loyola University. He continued to move up within Western Electric until 1941, when he went to Washington, DC, with the Lend-Lease Administration. There he worked on critical processes to speed important shipments to allied countries that were essential to the war effort. He began to study and write on the subject of statistical process control. The demand for his services grew rapidly, and he was invited to travel to Japan to present to JUSE in 1954, shortly after Deming (Juran, 1964).

Control and Breakthrough

Juran (1964) stated that managers must do two things: stay in complete control to maintain the status quo, and make changes to "break through" to a higher level of performance. This is a delicate balancing act, and, in some ways, it is difficult to comprehend because these two concepts seem to contradict each other. Should we stay the same or change? Juran stated that managers must do both. Although managers ensure the quality of daily operations, they must work toward changing the system to make it better (Juran, 1964).

The Juran Trilogy

Juran proposed that following the Juran Trilogy would assist in ensuring quality processes. The Trilogy is Quality Planning, Quality Control, and Quality Improvement. This expands on his theory of Control and Breakthrough, which was referenced previously. Juran believed that following this process would lead to better outcomes. Under each heading (see Figure 24-4) are lists of steps that will lead the organization toward QI (Juran, 1989).

The Juran Trilogy illustrates the general steps needed to achieve QI. The nature of this process, like Deming's, can be applied to any industry or situation to set up and direct QI efforts.

Figure 24-4. The Juran Trilogy

Quality Planning	Quality Control	Quality Improvement
Determine who the customers are. Determine the needs of the customers. Develop product features that respond to the customers' needs. Develop processes that are able to produce those product features. Transfer the resulting plans to the operating forces.	Evaluate actual quality performance. Compare actual performance to quality goods. Act on the differences.	Establish the infrastructure needed to secure annual quality improvement. Identify the specific needs for improvement—the improvement projects. For each project, establish a project team with clear responsibility for the project to have a successful conclusion. Provide the resources, motivation, and training needed by the teams to • Diagnose the causes. • Stimulate establishment of a remedy. • Establish controls to hold the gains.

Note. Based on information from Juran, 1989.

The Pareto Principle

The Pareto Principle is a very simple yet very profound concept. Juran wanted management to look at "the vital few and useful many" (Juran, 1964). This is best illustrated by using an example. The director of quality wants to reduce medical errors. Where does she start? She could look at all the medical errors, but that could be too much to get her arms around in one project. The Pareto Principle, now widely called Pareto analysis, would take all of the medical errors and group them into categories. These categories would be displayed to show their percentage as it relates to the whole. For example, the results could show that 35% of the errors were related to medications. This may still be too large a project to tackle. She could repeat the Pareto analysis to break down all errors related to medications to find where in the medication process the errors occurred. This could show that 25% of the errors were related to administration. This would help to determine where to begin to improve the rate of medical errors by starting where one could make the most difference.

This tool is very effective in helping managers narrow down the project to an acceptable level. The QI process is just that—a process, and the most important part is to start with a project and goals that are attainable. No one can solve world hunger in one project, and no one can fix all the quality problems in one project. Many times a manager is faced with what appears to be an insurmountable problem. Breaking the issues down into manageable projects can be facilitated by the use of the Pareto chart (see Figure 24-5).

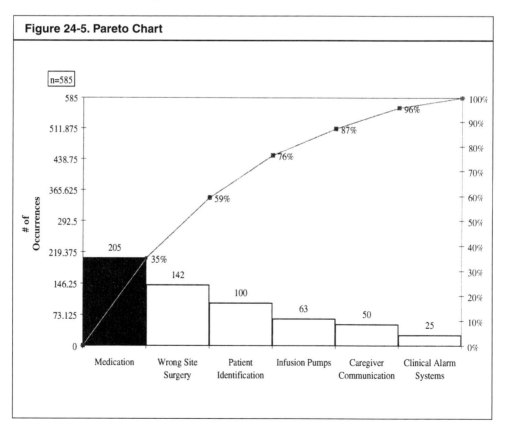

Figure 24-5. Pareto Chart

Philip B. Crosby—Zero Defects

Philip B. Crosby was born on June 18, 1926, in Wheeling, WV. He worked for many companies throughout his life in the field of quality management. Most notably he worked for Martin-Marietta, where he developed the drive for "zero defects" (Crosby, 2002).

Crosby's most widely known work was *Quality is Free*, which was published in 1979 just prior to the quality movement of the 1980s in America. He began by stating that, "Quality is free, it is not a gift, but it is free. What costs money are the unquality things—all the actions that involve not doing jobs right the first time" (Crosby, 1979, p. 1). The costs of redoing what should have been done the first time are where QI practices really make the difference. He also uses a 14-step process to accomplish QI goals (see Figure 24-6).

Figure 24-6. Crosby's 14 Steps to Quality Improvement

1. Management commitment
2. Quality improvement team
3. Quality measurement
4. Cost of quality evaluation
5. Quality awareness
6. Corrective action
7. Establish an ad hoc committee for the zero defects program.
8. Supervisor training
9. Zero defects day
10. Goal setting
11. Error cause removal
12. Recognition
13. Quality controls
14. Do it over again.

Note. Based on information from Crosby, 1979.

Crosby proposed that managers need to be involved in quality as much as their employees are. Many quality programs call for managers to support the QI process, but he did not think that was nearly enough. Without management participation, quality programs are doomed to fail (Crosby, 1979).

Quality Reports and Monitoring

Juran listed the seven quality control tools that he believed were necessary for QI, and these tools are now widely used in industry around the world to aid in quality programs (Juran, 1989). The control chart and Pareto chart have been referred to previously; below are some of the other important quality tools.

Cause and Effect Diagram

Kaoru Ishikawa developed the cause and effect diagram to help managers begin to think about the root causes of quality problems that they are experiencing (see Figure

24-7). It is used to brainstorm all possible opinions about what is causing the issue. Frequently used categories in health care are procedures, equipment, environment, and people. This leads directly to further investigation of the possible causes by using the other quality tools mentioned in this chapter. A manager would take the cause that he or she believes is the most probable cause of the problem, and use the PDCA cycle or control chart to further study the problem (Skymark Corporation, 2003a).

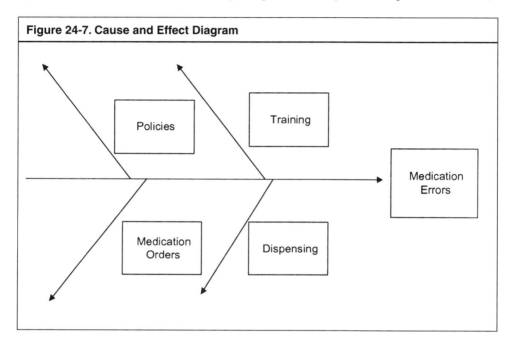

Figure 24-7. Cause and Effect Diagram

Scatter Diagram

A scatter diagram is helpful in determining trends and patterns in data. It is also able to show the relationship between two different variables. A trend line is plotted to show positive, negative, or no correlation. This is used in many organizations to determine the relationship in staffing indicators to see if there is a correlation. For example, worked hours and patient satisfaction are tracked as separate data elements, but a scatter diagram will compare those two data points and show a possible relationship (Skymark Corporation, 2003b). In Figure 24-8, nine months of patient satisfaction scores are charted against the worked hours for the month. This chart shows a slightly negative relationship, which means that patient satisfaction scores are lower as worked hours increase.

American health care has the best care that money can buy in terms of technology and science. So why do we need to improve? As shown by the IOM report (1999), we are lagging behind the rest of the world when it comes to outcomes. A major change in health care is over the horizon. The Baby Boomer generation (birth years 1946–1964) is expected to raise the demand for health services along with ushering a new focus on service quality. This generation is accustomed to getting value out of the products they buy, and they expect the same out of the healthcare industry. The federal government is also beginning to take notice. Medicare and Medicaid are having financial difficulty because of ever-rising healthcare costs coupled with the increasing demand for health services. At their current pace, it is going to be difficult, if not impossible, to continue on this path. Patients and payors alike are looking for healthcare providers to prove that they can provide quality services.

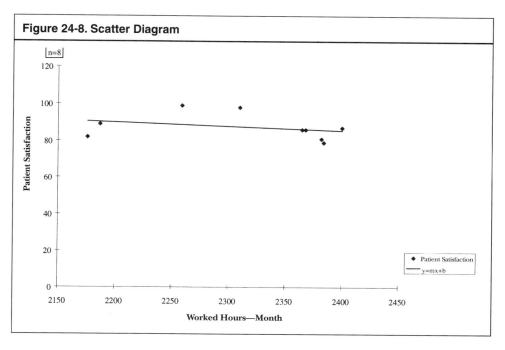

Figure 24-8. Scatter Diagram

Leading Staff Toward Performance Improvement

"Performance improvement" (PI) is the all-encompassing term that is used to describe processes that ensure quality of care for patients. It moved into prominence within the healthcare industry in the early 1990s because of rising concerns about the costs of health care in the United States. The response from the healthcare industry was to design performance measures that would contain costs as well as address quality. IOM defined quality care as "the degree to which health services for individuals and populations increase the likelihood of desired health outcomes and are consistent with current professional knowledge" (Jennings & Staggers, 1999, p. 19). Initially, QI in health care belonged to administration or to the manager. It was a method used to improve the way things were done at a particular healthcare facility. Health care then gravitated more toward the models used in industry by changing the focus from the management level to the staff or individual level. Attaining higher levels of quality was redirected to the people who work within an organization and improving their performance by altering the processes they were using. The healthcare industry also realized that the perception of quality lies with the stakeholder, and that performance measures should be designed to focus on the view of the specific group. According to Jennings and Staggers, "the challenge remains to examine structural components of quality carefully to determine which, if any, make a difference in the delivery of quality care" (p. 21).

Although the level of focus was redirected, healthcare organizations require that their leaders remain committed and involved in PI efforts. The goals, mission, and core values of the organization must be mirrored in the processes that are changed or improved at the departmental level. PI is also driven at some level by legal, regulatory, and accreditation organizations. For example, JCAHO stated that the goal of the improving organization performance function is to ensure that the organization designs processes well and systematically monitors, analyzes, and improves its performance to improve patient outcomes (Moses, 2003, p. 16). Value in health care is the appropriate balance between good outcomes, excellent care and services, and costs. To add value to the care and services provided, organizations need to understand the relationship between the perception of care, outcomes, and costs and how processes carried out by the organization affect those three issues. An organization's performance of important functions significantly affects the quality and value of its services (Moses, 2003).

JCAHO typically looks at how an organization designs its PI processes, how it monitors performance through data collection and analysis, as well as how it sustains improvement. Although JCAHO does not require that an organization use any specific model or program, it does require that there is a model in place and all members of the organization are able to speak to it and what it accomplishes for them. (See Chapter 23 for more information on accreditation.)

The importance of involving the customer in PI cannot be overlooked. In health care today, it is the patient, the ultimate consumer, who drives change within our system. The consumer is the judge and jury of health care because he or she experiences the good and the bad things firsthand. Jennings and Staggers (1999) noted that for processes to improve, the process must first be seen through the eyes of those who are using it. Healthcare systems must learn to view quality of care from the patient's perspective and develop performance measures that make sense to patients as well as to administrators and healthcare professionals, such as nurses (Jennings & Staggers). Nurses have long provided leadership in health care for QI and have worked diligently to develop a history of quality measurement research that has become invaluable documentation of outcomes related to patients.

Building a successful PI program also means establishing standards and guidelines to be used within the organization. It means that each member who has a stake in the process must be involved and have assigned responsibilities. It is important to remember that management is not the primary stakeholder in a PI program; they are responsible for overseeing the activities and ensuring adherence to standards and policies. Key components that the PI lead teams should have are (a) representation from a cross-section of staff, (b) strong performers—those who seek accomplishment should be team members, (c) team members—should have the respect of their peers,

(d) staff-driven program with clear expectations, and (e) a team leader—an expert who will guide and facilitate the team.

The team leader needs to be able to decide when to intercede and when to step back and allow the team to proceed on its own. Helping the team to understand the process, measuring the outcomes, and communicating the findings should be the focus of the leader's role. Managers need to realize that with PI, the staff is the most valuable resource they can have. These are the people who work in the system every day and have most likely already discovered methods to work around the barriers. They also intimately understand the needs of the patients whom they work with on a daily basis and have access to that all-important customer perspective (Sims, 2003).

Through research, it has been identified that there are often gaps between evidence and practice. According to Davis et al. (2003), "knowledge translation can draw on people from many disciplines, including informatics, social and educational psychology, organizational theory, and patient and public education, to help close the gap between evidence and practice. Knowledge translation is set within the practice of health care and focuses on changing health outcomes using evidence-based clinical knowledge" (p. 33). The lead team may be responsible for managing further organizational change by reviewing PI processes and also competencies, policies, and procedures, thus providing a mechanism for knowledge translation within an organization.

Members of the organization own its processes and are responsible for the variations and changes that the processes undergo. To move improvements forward through the organization, the process owner assumes responsibility to submit his or her information as completely as possible to the lead team for its input and evaluation. The lead team members can determine priorities by assigning priority levels to a process. They determine if additional people need to be involved and determine the end recipients of the information regarding the process change. The lead team develops a schedule or timeline for "rolling out" the information and then is responsible to do so as scheduled. This includes soliciting approval/information from appropriate groups as necessary. The lead team then assists with dissemination of the information once the process is evaluated.

Team members need to be given the authority to carry out plans that are developed. If the structure of the organization does not allow for this, the team should be given access to those within the organization that can move the process forward. The program should identify the channels of communication to report results and findings throughout the organization. Information sharing allows those at the staff level to not only be a part of the process but also to claim ownership of the process and its conclusions. Communicating results to the rest of the organization not only keeps other members informed but may allow others to avoid the same process errors that already have been identified. Managers and administrators can use the information to move the organization forward and make futuristic decisions. Supporting staff as they plan, implement, measure, and evaluate the changes that they make through the PI process will allow them to assume direct responsibility for the differences that they make in their everyday work environment.

Since moving the focus of PI, it has been more of a challenge for managers to "pass the baton" and let the staff take the lead with developing and communicating process changes. Managers may feel left out of the loop and may not be up to date on all changes taking place throughout the organization. One method of implementing this change is to develop a management council. The council may be comprised of nurse managers from all clinical settings within the organization. The goals of the council may vary depending on the organization and its practice settings, but, ultimately, the focus is to allow the managers to be aware of practice changes that may affect their area and improve quality of care across the continuum. Processes that impact patient care may be the issue that the council can address on a regular basis, such as patient education tools, ancillary services, policies, procedures, and protocols. The management council can be a useful tool to bridge staff PI initiatives and management input (Murray & Broad, 2002).

Improvement of Quality Through Policies and Procedures

Policies involve action and usually are a statement that expects a specific action to be completed. It sets the boundaries for activities and describes the actions that are to take place in a certain scenario. A procedure can easily be defined as a set of general steps used to complete an action; a procedure usually describes how a policy is to be carried out. Nurse managers can be either the designer of the policy or the facilitator of the policy development.

Nurses have made valuable contributions to developing and moving the concept of "best practices" forward in the healthcare setting. A process to develop evidence-based policies is being used as nursing utilizes the concept of evidence-based practice so that policy and practice remain congruent. Nurse managers should be familiar with evidence-based policy design, as they may be the source of the evidence needed to facilitate policy development. There may be evidence to support as well as contradict using a specific procedure, and it becomes essential to sort out what is opinion or historical practice and what is based on true research. For practice areas where true research data are absent, it may be more appropriate to use QI data. Evidence that is based on expert opinion only is considered last because it is not data-driven. Nurse managers must understand the scope of the problem and be able to develop measurable goals that are feasible to the situation during the planning stage of developing an evidence-based policy. "Evidence-based policies should have focused goals that lead to measurable, standardized outcomes. All segments of organizations involved in a change of policy may believe that they are meeting the same goals, but unless terms and goals are similarly defined, the actual data collected may differ significantly, and the outcomes will be diverse" (DePalma, 2002, p. 58). Desired outcomes for evidence-based policies should be developed at the planning stage and allow for evaluation of the policy. Developing evidence-based policies requires definitive evidence for planning, implementation, and evaluation of the results. Nurse managers should have the expertise that these steps entail and should be the primary facilitators in this process.

The traditional method of policy development often leads organizations to develop policies and procedures in a disjointed method. One department develops a policy and procedure, and another department develops the same one with a slightly difference slant. There is decreased quality and patient satisfaction when there is not consistency throughout the organization, as well as possible legal ramifications. As noted by Paige (2003), "the Joint Commission no longer bases standards on distinct departments or disciplines. Instead, it emphasizes overriding professional boundaries and constructing a collaborative approach to delivering patient care" (p. 46). To ensure maintenance of consistent practice wherever a patient goes within a healthcare organization, policies and procedures must be standardized. JCAHO also stated "the principle of one level of quality care when patients with the same nursing care needs receive comparable care throughout the hospital, which is provided through the use of uniform policy and procedures" (Paige, p. 46). Using facility-wide policy and procedures will ensure a defined process for review, revision, and dissemination of the revised documents.

One of the first steps in the development of facility-wide policies and procedures involves the design of a generic template. The creation of a generic template that can be used by multiple areas or departments will ensure that all policies will have the same look and all of the same components. A standard format usually involves the following: (a) identification of the committees or people that approve or authorize the policy, (b) the department from which the policy originated, (c) the manual the policy belongs in and any cross-references that are needed, and (d) signature approval of the policy.

Specific time frames for review of the policies need to be established and maintained. Any review data need to be documented and be retrievable when requested. A timely review process keeps the policies current and up to date and ensures that the organization is current with any regulatory changes or requirements.

Nurse managers may find that keeping policy and procedure manuals current and up to date becomes a mundane task that does not provide the relevant information that their staff require for day-to-day operations. Manuals with outdated content and inconsistent information will not be adequate resources and will not allow for the information sharing that the manuals were intended for. With progression toward an electronic medical record, it has led to the conversion of policy manuals from paper to computer. Converting paper manuals to an online version will assist staff in locating the most up-to-date policies and also will allow the entire organization access at any one time. Using an online format will maintain a consistent format and template for the policies and a master list of all policies available. A process for reviewing and updating the information can be developed; interdisciplinary teams can review policies through e-mail and send responses to a team leader to facilitate changes. The organization will need to continually assess the status of the online manuals to ensure easy location and retrieval for all users. Online systems can allow for "real-time" changes to be made; this requires the system to alert the users that a change has been made. This also requires the organization to continually assess this process and keep the online information flowing to the staff.

PI initiatives are clearly linked to the design and review of policies and procedures. Once a change in a process is made and the stakeholders are comfortable with the change, it is time to move the process on and look at the policies and procedures that encompass the changed process. Because change is best facilitated with consistent communication, remember to include everyone involved—patients, too! Organizations need to review their policies and procedures to determine their value to the patient. If a policy or procedure is not providing benefit to the patient, it should be revised or discarded. All of the individuals who are involved in changing a process must be a part of the marketing so that the change is accomplished in a positive manner. Management must stand behind their employees as they identify opportunities to improve care and service to their patients. Employees who are taught to seek out opportunities to improve service and their work environment will have a distinct advantage as they help design the future goals and measures of excellence within their organization through the use of PI.

Competency and the Impact on Quality Outcomes

How do institutions ensure competency in the performance of initiatives? How do healthcare professionals determine the best clinical decisions? Historically, nursing as a profession has established competency through rote testing and return-demonstration. Even in the field of medicine, the old adage "see one, do one, teach one" is how physicians describe some of their competency training. Most caregivers have heard about the many safety issues in the healthcare settings. Are issues regarding the lack of a safe healthcare system and less than optimal quality outcomes based on poor training? AHRQ (2001) stated,

> Patient safety has become a major concern of the general public and of policymakers at the State and Federal levels. This interest has been fueled, in part, by news coverage of individuals who were the victims of serious medical errors and by the publication in 1999 of the IOM's report *To Err is Human: Building a Safer Health System.* In its report, the IOM highlighted the risks of medical care in the United States and shocked the sensibilities of many Americans, in large part through its estimates of the magnitude of medical error–related deaths (44,000 to 98,000 deaths per year) and other serious adverse events. The report prompted a number of legislative and regulatory initiatives designed to document errors and begin the search for solutions. But Americans, who now wondered whether their next doctor's or hospital visit might harm rather than help them, began to demand concerted action.

With access to the Internet and other sources of information, patients, family members, and other members of the lay public are becoming more informed and savvy about what constitutes excellence in care. Most people seeking health care commonly use the terms evidence-based practice, best practices, and positive clinical outcomes.

Models of care using evidence-based practice need to be based on competencies that have been tested with various QI or PI methods. In developing competencies for the delivery of quality care, multiple aspects that impact care must be considered. Deutschendorf (2003) stated, "Future care delivery models must take into consideration the changes in patient characteristics, financial constraints and clinic trends, to succeed in achieving positive financial and clinical outcomes" (p. 52). The unit-based nurse leaders (UBNLs) who have administrative responsibility for a clinical unit or area are ultimately responsible for overseeing the training of the staff. He or she may designate education and training to a unit educator, advanced practice nurse (APN), or clinical nurse specialist (CNS), but UBNLs are accountable for ensuring that the staff performs with competence and expertise, which is extremely challenging! Because of financial constraints and other factors, many institutions do not hire APNs or CNSs to augment the administrative responsibilities of UBNLs. Institution-based educational departments often have a "bare bones" budget and usually oversee orientation and minimum "extra" educational offerings. It is further noted that, "Opportunities for educational activities, other than mandatory competency testing, often are limited, as nurses are unable to leave the patient care units" (Deutschendorf, p. 54).

Institutions have various methods of verifying competency. Testing, checklists, return-demonstration, and competency-based orientation manuals are some methods used. But, are these methods rigorous enough? Do they ensure that team members are learning from evidence-based best practices? Or are competencies done in this manner because it has "always been done this way"? Bradley and Huseman (2003) published an article that discussed the shortcomings of current competency testing for nursing staff. They applied a model of validation to improve documentation of pain assessment and management. The results of their initiatives concluded that, "Educators are walking away from the reams of check-off sheets and embracing key competency statements that encompass the elements of competency. They are moving away from learning objectives toward application of competencies. Moving staff up the competency ladder from the lower rungs of knowledge onto the upper rungs of application involves finding the right competency statements and defining the process" (pp. 172–173). UBNLs must embrace new methods of establishing competency. The more validated a competency, the more able the UBNL and educators are to ensure consistency of application. Even if UBNLs have educators and APNs, they must be informed about the competency process. If an employee is unable to learn or maintain a competency, it will be the UBNL's responsibility to ensure accountability, develop a plan for improvement, or institute disciplinary action. By using validated competencies that employ various QI and PI methods, quality standards of care can be developed.

Development of Standards of Care

McAdams and Montgomery (2003) noted that the reason institutions use PI measures is to improve the standard of care delivered to patients and families. Institutions may participate in both internal and external PI or "benchmarking" activities to establish standards of care. Many forms of benchmarking occur in healthcare settings. Tran

(2003) stated, "Commonly confused with market research, benchmarking isn't simply comparing one hospital to another. It involves measuring the performance of an existing process, which enables managers to target improvement efforts that eventually yield best practices" (p. 19).

As many UBNLs and oncology clinical team members are aware, patients with cancer experience many challenging and, at times, painful side effects. Some of these side effects result in physical and/or emotional pain. Many people reading this chapter are familiar with terms such as severe diarrhea, intractable nausea and vomiting, and significant fatigue. Over the past few years, more emphasis has been focused on the causes and treatment of neuropathic pain in the oncology population. One example of a QI initiative to improve a standard of care for patients with cancer involved the Neuropathic Pain (NP) project funded by the Oncology Nursing Society Foundation and Purdue Frederick. The study took place between June 1998 and May 2000 and used the FOCUS-PDCA methodology. According to the Medical Risk Management Associates' (2003) Web site, FOCUS-PDCA is "a systematic method for improving processes. Through FOCUS-PDCA, knowledge of how a process is currently performing to meet customer needs and expectations is used and test process changes. The purpose of these process changes is to improve the product or service from the customer's viewpoint."

In 2002, members of the NP project team (Smith, Whedon, & Bookbinder, 2003) wrote an article that highlighted detailed examples of each section of the FOCUS-PDCA process. It was a good example of how nurse-led QI projects can lead to positive changes in clinical practice. Another QI project involving a chronic illness was documented in an article about reducing insulin medication errors. Heatlie (2003) noted the following about the nurse who practices at the bedside: "The bedside nurse has become the primary provider of diabetes patient education. The nurse who is not knowledgeable enough about the care of the patient with diabetes cannot be expected to engage in appropriate critical thinking during the patient's hospitalization and provide the patient with quality educational preparation for self-management of a complex healthcare regimen" (p. 94). The findings in this article also can be extrapolated to apply to the often-complicated management needs of the patient with cancer.

Oncology UBNLs are well aware of the focus on high-alert medications as a major safety initiative in all settings that deliver care to the cancer population. Patients with cancer often receive multiple "high-alert" agents because of co-morbidities and side effects caused by treatments. Agents such as insulin, cardiac drugs, narcotics, and, most notably, chemotherapy require intense double checks and monitoring when administered. "Healthcare organizations are faced with an increased demand to improve patient care by preventing medication errors" (Heatlie, 2003, p. 93). In 1995, a tragic situation occurred that involved the delivery of high-dose chemotherapeutic agents, which resulted in the development of a very recognized standard of care for the administration of chemotherapy. A patient at the Dana-Farber Cancer Institute received an overdose of a chemotherapeutic agent (Connor, Ponte, & Conway, 2002). The patient eventually died from the overdose. Somewhat as a result of this error, a standard of care involving multiple double checks by MDs, pharmacists, and nurses has evolved for the administration of chemotherapy. This standard is used by most institutions at the present time.

UBNLs can be the initiators and leaders of QI/PI processes in their areas as well as for the institution. All team members, both professional (RNs, MDs, APNs) and nonprofessional (nurse assistants, unit secretaries, transporters), can be part of initiatives that lead to the establishment of quality standards of care. These team members must feel a "buy in" to the process. Team members will want to know what "outcomes" they can expect if they participate in the initiative. MDs may want quality care initiatives to be determined by data and information and demonstrated on control charts. Nurses may want to know how quality initiatives will afford them more time to interact with their patients. Nursing assistants may ask how the initiatives will help them to prioritize their care delivery. The expectations for each of these groups are understandable and even predictable.

Because of the many advances over the past 20 years, the delivery of care for many patients has dramatically evolved. Patients with cancer no longer have a hospital stay or an outpatient visit. These patients now experience a continuum of care. To maintain high quality and consistent standards of care for these increasingly acute and complex patients, it is key to have excellent communication between both professional and nonprofessional caregivers. Lynn and Goldstein (2003) noted that, "In reality, the various programs do not communicate with each other, nor do they take responsibility for measuring and achieving excellent care across settings. No one measures outcome, determines patterns of care, or provides feedback"(p. 816). Instilling the importance of outcomes and quality in the establishment of standards of care is where the UBNLs could have the most impact. Oncology clinical team members care for patients with a varied range of problems. The more consistent and validated the approach to care, the more predictable the outcomes for the patients.

Earlier in the chapter, several founders of QI and PI were highlighted. Each of these individuals used different models to establish quality outcomes. Over the years, these models have been applied "as is" or adapted and revised to meet the needs of various business settings and institutions. Many of these models have been used in healthcare settings. Based on the discussion in this chapter, it is clear that focused initiatives can be "tailored" to meet the needs of a specific institution, initiative, and/or patient population. This chapter also discussed examples of focused quality initiatives that resulted from active inquiry (e.g., peripheral neuropathy project) or negative outcomes (e.g., chemotherapy incident). The remainder of this chapter will discuss an institution-based focused initiative.

A Focused Initiative—IMPROVING the "Homegrown" Way

At the Medical University of South Carolina (MUSC) in Charleston, a "homegrown" process improvement model has been developed. For many years, the institution followed Deming's FOCUS-PDCA model for QI; however, after identifying that the organization had opportunities to improve in the evaluation and monitoring of change, the IMPROVE model was developed (see Table 24-1).

At MUSC, the IMPROVE model has been used to demonstrate the development of an "oncology dashboard." This dashboard was developed so that many individuals from different areas—leadership, finance, clinical services—could evaluate the financial performance of the different oncology service lines. Members of the oncology leadership team identified (I) that we were lacking a resource to evaluate financial performances. After approximately three years of work on the project, a dashboard that is both easy to read and accurate has been developed. The project is being written up in the IMPROVE format to demonstrate how we will be using the information to impact decision making at the institution. For several years, the leadership team worked with the director of Decision Support Systems to figure how to "mine" the correct data from our repositories to measure (M) performance. During the development of the dashboard, we identified many reasons (P) why certain service lines were more profitable and why other services either were extremely expensive or simply lost money. We are now in the process of sharing the information and determining a course of action (R) based on the data. After we complete the plan of action, we will enact the remaining letters of the IMPROVE model—operationalize, validate, and evaluate. Individuals responsible for both clinical and financial performance can now review the information from the dashboard to assist in making decisions on how to allocate hospital, research, and grant-funded resources.

Table 24-1. IMPROVE Model

Steps	Rationale	Helpful "Tips"
Identify the problem or opportunity.	The opportunity or problem statement is a brief, clear description of the issue studied. What is the problem?	Narrow the scope; do not try to solve "world hunger." What are you trying to accomplish? What is the goal?
Measure (data collection).	Select performance indicators that demonstrate that the change is an improvement. If you do not set a goal, then how will you know when you get there?	Use clear measurable goals. Examples: Reduce rate of hospital-acquired pneumonia by 50%. Collect data to identify the root cause. Tools: Flow chart, Pareto, focus groups, surveys, control charts Stretch goal: Will reach 100% of goal over time
Problem analysis	What are the most likely causes responsible for the opportunity/problem? Is it recurrent?	How was the cause of the problem identified? Direct observation is frequently the most helpful, but often overlooked, tool. Examples: literature, opinion of the local experts, direct observation, and data
Remedy the cause.	Potential solutions for the problem should be based on effectiveness and reasonably instituted.	Solutions may be evidence-based practice, best guesses of those with knowledge of the issue, literature review, benchmarking, and expert opinion. May use education plus one of the following: automate, standardize, checklist, and redundancy. Remember that unless the change is "hardwired" into the organization, it will not be sustained.

(Continued on next page)

Table 24-1. IMPROVE Model *(Continued)*		
Steps	**Rationale**	**Helpful "Tips"**
Operationalize your plan.	Implement the solutions.	Do what you said you were going to do. Consider a small limited pilot of your solutions prior to wide-scale implementation. Those involved in the process should be involved in the implementation (include area leaders).
Validate the effectiveness of your intervention.	Did the process work? Compare before and after.	This is the monitoring that occurs throughout implementation. Tweak based on observation and measurement.
Evaluate for change and sustained improvement. *Note.* After implementing a project using the IMPROVE model, it is important to review the lessons learned.	Ongoing monitoring will determine if change is needed.	Identify a plan for monitoring for sustained improvement over time. Assign team/individual responsible for ongoing monitoring. Graphically display identified measures; add narrative to describe change.
Note. Table courtesy of the Medical University of South Carolina. Used with permission.		

This focused quality initiative will impact many aspects of the cancer program. Eventually, the dashboard will be revised to include information about clinical pathways, standards of care, and focused financial projects that will have a positive impact on both quality and financial outcomes. It is the first dashboard developed at this institution and is therefore a model for future projects for other service lines. UBNLs from all of the oncology settings at MUSC will be involved in the revisions and implementation of the outcomes from this IMPROVE project.

It is the intent of this chapter to give an overall view of QI and PI processes and how UBNLs can impact the initiation of focused initiatives. Nurses have exposure to many situations where QIs could be initiated. In her article on palliative and end-of-life care, Reb (2003) discussed how nurses' involvement in developing and implementing quality initiatives has had a positive impact on coordinating care for patients. Reb was very clear when she said, "Nurses should strive to improve care for those who are most vulnerable in society, including children, the elderly, the poor, minorities, and those with chronic illnesses. Healthcare professionals and policymakers should work now to make a difference in the lives of those they care for who are approaching the end of life" (p. 47). But, she also recognized that more initiatives should be implemented and outcomes evaluated. The increased pressure on UBNLs in regard to educating and maintaining a competent clinical team that is able to focus on high-quality initiatives has been highlighted. Deutschendorf (2003) stated, "Novice nurses, inadequate staffing by nurses, severity of illness, lack of expert resources, lack of supervision by qualified nurse managers, and the inappropriate use of guidelines for nursing practice all contribute to the underlying causes of failure to rescue" (p. 53). QI initiatives are difficult for nurses to implement. They need guidance, coaching, and support to sustain quality outcomes. "Given the direction in utilization of process improvement methodologies (how to plan, implement, measure, and evaluate changes made) and support as needed throughout the process, they [nurses] can make dramatic differences in many aspects of their work environment" (Sims, 2003, p. 75). The work is even more challenging because of the current state of the nursing workforce. Because of staffing shortages, novice nurses, and the lack of specialty units, standards of care need to be developed to assist in quality outcomes for the patients. Sims also noted that the leader must "step back and let the team members direct the work to be done. Her role became that of coach, helping them to gain an understanding of how to lead the process improvements, how to implement the changes, and how to measure outcomes to demonstrate the staff's success and communicate to others" (p. 75). UBNLs are the key and the ongoing link to success of quality initiatives and the outcomes that result.

References

Agency for Healthcare Research Quality. (2001, July). *Making health care safer. A critical analysis of patient safety practices: Summary*. Rockville, MD: Author. Retrieved September 14, 2003, from http://www.ahrq.gov/clinic/ptsafety/summary.htm

Bradley, D., & Huseman, S. (2003). Validating competency at the bedside. *Journal for Nurses in Staff Development, 19,* 165–173.

Connor, M., Ponte, P., & Conway, J. (2002). Multidisciplinary approaches to reducing error and risk in a patient care setting. *Critical Care Nursing Clinics of North America, 14,* 359–367.

Crosby, P.B. (1979). *Quality is free.* New York: McGraw-Hill.

Crosby, P.B. (2002, January). *Biography: Philip B. Crosby.* Retrieved August 30, 2004, from http://www.philipcrosby.com/pca/C.Articles/articles/year.2002/philsbio.htm

Davis, D., Evans, M., Perrier, A., Rath, D., Ryan, D., Sibbald, G., et al. (2003). The case for knowledge translation: Shortening the journey from evidence to effect. *BMJ, 327,* 33–35.

Deming, W.E. (1982). *Out of the crisis.* Cambridge, MA: Massachusetts Institute of Technology, Center for Advanced Engineering Study.

DePalma, J. (2002). Proposing an evidence-based policy process. *Nursing Administration Quarterly, 26(4),* 55–61.

Deutschendorf, A.L. (2003). From past paradigms to future frontiers: Unique care delivery models to facilitate nursing work and quality outcomes. *Journal of Nursing Administration, 33,* 52–59.

Heatlie, J. (2003). Reducing insulin medication errors: Evaluation of a quality improvement initiative. *Journal for Nurses in Staff Development, 19,* 92–98.

Institute of Medicine. (1999). *To err is human: Building a safer health system.* Washington, DC: Author.

Jennings, B., & Staggers, N. (1999). A provocative look at performance measurement. *Nursing Administration Quarterly, 24*(1), 17–30.

Juran, J.M. (1964). *Managerial breakthrough: The classic book on improving management performance.* New York: McGraw-Hill.

Juran, J.M. (1989). *Juran on leadership for quality: An executive handbook.* New York: The Free Press.

Lynn, J., & Goldstein, N. (2003). Advance care planning for fatal chronic illness: Avoiding commonplace errors and unwarranted suffering. *Annals of Internal Medicine, 138,* 812–818.

McAdams, C., & Montgomery, K. (2003). Narrowing the possibilities: Using quality improvement tools to decrease competence assessment overload. *Journal for Nurses in Staff Development, 19,* 40–46.

Medical Risk Management Associates. (2003, February). *Employee quality tools to enhance patient safety.* Retrieved September 14 and December 18, 2003, from http://www.sentinel-event.com/focus/ppframe.htm

Moses, K. (2003). Journey to excellence: Performance improvement in ambulatory surgery. *SSM: Surgical Services Management, 9*(2), 16–22.

Murray, M., & Broad, J. (2002). Separate but united: Integrate quality care across multiple settings with a management council. *Nursing Management, 33*(8), 35–37.

Paige, J. (2003). Solve the policy and procedure puzzle. *Nursing Management, 34*(3), 45–48.

Reb, A. (2003). Palliative and end-of-life care: Policy analysis. *Oncology Nursing Forum, 30,* 35–50.

Sims, C. (2003). Increasing clinical, satisfaction, and financial performance through nurse-driven process improvement. *Journal of Nursing Administration, 33,* 68–75.

Skymark Corporation. (2003a). *Kaoru Ishikawa: One step further.* Retrieved December 18, 2003, from http://www.skymark.com/resources/leaders/ishikawa.asp

Skymark Corporation. (2003b). *Scatter plots.* Retrieved December 18, 2003, from http://www.skymark.com/resources/tools/scatter_plots.asp

Smith, E.L., Whedon, M.B., & Bookbinder, M. (2003). Quality improvement of painful peripheral neuropathy. *Seminars In Oncology Nursing, 18*(1), 36–43.

Tran, M. (2003). Take benchmarking to the next level: Research best practice status by heeding operational strengths and weaknesses. *Nursing Management, 34*(1), 18–24.

Voehl, F. (1995). *Deming: The way we knew him.* Delray Beach, FL: St. Lucie Press.

W. Edwards Deming Institute. (2001). *Biography of W. Edwards Deming.* Retrieved September 28, 2003, from http://www.deming.org/theman/biography.html

Legal and Risk Management Issues

Marilyn Jones-Bradshaw, MBA, MN, RN, CCS

In an ever-increasing litigious society, healthcare providers have seen an explosive increase in the number of medical malpractice and product liability (including medical equipment and drug products) cases. A 2003 U.S. Department of Health and Human Services report stated that jury awards and settlements in 1991 amounted to 298 payments of $1 million or more as reported to the National Practitioner Data Bank; in 2002, there were 806 payments (Adams, 2003). Approximately 70%–80% of all cases filed against doctors are dismissed (Coble, 2003), which can be interpreted that these cases should not have been brought forth. Litigation costs will continue to rise as class action lawsuits target health plans, pharmaceutical companies, physicians, nurses, and hospitals.

To prevent windfall judgments, numerous states, lawmakers, physicians, healthcare entities, and professional healthcare organizations are pushing and lobbying for tort reform with a cap on noneconomic and punitive damages. In March 2003, the U.S. House of Representatives passed a tort reform plan backed by President George W. Bush. The plan called for a $250,000 limit on noneconomic "pain and-suffering" damages; a cap on punitive damages at two times economic damages; a three-year statute of limitations on complaints; damage payments allocated by actual negligence; disclosure to juries of other sources of compensation to injured plaintiffs, such as their insurance coverage; and a limit on lawyers' contingency fees to 15% of damages above $600,000 (Tucker, 2003).

In the past, it was the physicians, facilities, and/or manufacturers that were the main targets of these lawsuits, and they bore the full weight of the publicity and cost of the litigation. As the role and practice of nurses expanded over the years, nurses were frequently added as codefendants in medical malpractice lawsuits. The nurse manager may encounter issues related to violation of patient care and professional practice standards, medication errors, medical errors, medical equipment malfunction, product liability, inadequate and/or inappropriate staffing, workers' compensation, and other risk management issues. Nurse managers should have a working knowledge of legal issues, risk prevention, and risk management principles, and educate staff regarding risk prevention and safe nursing practices. National and specialty nursing organizations, such as the American Nurses Association (ANA), the Oncology Nursing Society (ONS), and others, have adopted scope and standards of practice for nurses. The ANA published an indexed version of the *Nursing: Scope and Standards of Practice* (ANA, 2004), and ONS published the *Statement on the Scope and Standards of Oncology Nursing Practice* (Brant & Wickham, 2004).

This chapter outlines aspects of legal and risk management issues that nurses should be aware of in their day-to-day practice. The nurse who reads this chapter will become aware of common legal terminology, the legal process that he or she may encounter with legal proceedings, and malpractice prevention measures. The nurse also will become aware of risk management principles and prevention. The chapter will introduce ethical issues the nurse may encounter in the clinical setting.

Legal Terminology and Definitions

The nurse manager may be called upon to prepare staff or personally engage in the review of medical records, compile medical information regarding a potential or actual malpractice case, and may work with legal counsel in interpreting the events that occurred. If the nurse manager is involved with potential or actual medical litigation, it is important that the nurse manager has a clear understanding of common legal terminology. A glossary of frequently used legal terms is presented in Figure 25-1.

Figure 25-1. Legal Terminology and Definitions

Term	Definition
Assault	The threat or use of force on another that causes that person to have a reasonable apprehension of imminent harmful or offensive contact (Garner, 2001; Law.com, n.d.).
Attorney-client relationship	A privileged relationship in which communications between attorney and client are confidential and cannot be disclosed without the client's consent (O'Keefe, 2001).
Attorney work product	Any type of preparation by the attorney on behalf of his or her client, including thought processes and mental opinions (O'Keefe).
Battery	The use of force against another, resulting in harmful or offensive contact (Garner).
Breach	Violation or infraction of a law or obligation (Garner; Gullatte, 1998). Breach can be the act of failing to perform one's agreement, breaking word, or otherwise actively violating one's duty to another (Law.com).
Civil	Of or relating to private rights and remedies that are sought by action or suit, and distinct from criminal proceedings (Garner).
Complaint	The initial pleading that starts a civil action and states the basis for the court's jurisdiction, the basis for the plaintiff's claim, and the demand for relief (Garner).

(Continued on next page)

Figure 25-1. Legal Terminology and Definitions *(Continued)*

Term	Definition
Damages	Money claimed by, or ordered to be paid to, a person as compensation for loss or injury (Garner). There are several types of damages, such as those that were caused by the injury, and include items such as medical and hospital bills, ambulance charges, or loss of wages. General damage items may include pain and suffering, future problems and crippling effect injury, loss of ability to perform various acts, shortening of life span, anguish, and loss of companionship (Law.com).
Defamation	The act of harming the reputation of another by making a false statement to a third person (Garner).
Defendant	A person sued in a civil proceeding or accused in a criminal proceeding (Garner).
Deposition	A witness's out-of-court testimony that is reduced to writing for later use in court or for discovery purpose (Garner).
Discovery	The act or process of finding or learning something that was previously unknown (Garner).
Expert	A person who, through education or experience, has developed skill or knowledge in a particular subject, so that he or she may form an opinion that will assist the fact-finder (Garner).
False imprisonment	A restraint of a person in a bounded area without justification or consent (Garner).
Fraud	A knowing misrepresentation of the truth or concealment of a material fact to induce another to act to his or her detriment (Garner).
Interrogatories	A written question submitted to an opposing party in a lawsuit as part of discovery (Garner).
Invasion of privacy	An unjustified exploitation of one's personality or intrusion into one's personal activity, actionable under tort law and sometimes under constitutional law (Garner).
Judgment	A court's final determination of the rights and obligations of the parties in a case (Garner).
Jury	A group of persons selected according to law and given the power to decide questions of fact and return a verdict in the case submitted to them (Garner).
Legally incapacitated person	A person, other than a minor, who is permanently or temporarily impaired by mental illness, mental deficiency, physical illness or disability, or use of drugs or alcohol to the extent that the person lacks sufficient understanding to make or communicate responsible personal decisions or to enter into contracts (Garner).
Libel	A defamatory statement expressed in a fixed medium, especially writing but also a picture, sign, or electronic broadcast (Garner).
Loss of consortium	A loss of the benefits that one spouse is entitled to receive from the other, including companionship, cooperation, aid, affection, and sexual relations (Garner).

(Continued on next page)

Figure 25-1. Legal Terminology and Definitions *(Continued)*	
Term	**Definition**
Malpractice	An instance of negligence or incompetence on the part of a professional. To succeed in a malpractice claim, a plaintiff also must prove proximate cause and damages (Garner; Gullatte). To prove malpractice, there must be testimony of an expert as to the usual standard of care applied to a particular act or conduct that is claimed to be malpractice and testimony of the expert that the professional did not meet that standard (Law.com).
Negligence	The failure to exercise the standard of care that a reasonable prudent person would have exercised in a similar situation; any conduct that falls below the legal standard established to protect others against unreasonable risk of harm, except for conduct that is intentionally, wantonly, or willfully disregardful of others' rights (Garner; Gullatte).
Plaintiff	The party who brings a civil suit in a court of law (Garner).
Pleading	A formal document in which a party to a legal proceeding (especially a civil lawsuit) sets forth or responds to allegations, claims, denials, or defenses (Garner).
Preponderance of evidence	This is the burden of proof in most civil trials in which the jury is instructed to find for the party that, on the whole, has the stronger evidence, however slight the edge may be (Garner).
Proximate cause	The cause that directly produces an event and without which the event would not have occurred (Garner).
Punitive damages	Damages awarded in addition to actual damages when the defendant acted with recklessness, malice, or deceit (Garner).
Relief	The redress or benefit, especially equitable in nature (such as an injunction or specific performance), that a party asks of a court (Garner).
Request for production	In pretrial discovery, a party's written request that another party provide specified documents or other tangible thing for inspection and copying (Garner).
Slander	A defamatory statement expressed in a transitory form, especially speech (Garner).
Standard of care	In the law of negligence, the degree of prudence that a reasonable person should exercise. Specific professional practice standards are established for physicians and nurses to practice for various specialties (Garner).
Statute of limitations	A statute establishing a time limit for suing in a civil case based on the date when the claim accrued (as when the injury occurred or was discovered) (Garner).
Subpoena	A writ commanding a person to appear before a court (Garner).
Tort	A civil wrong for which a remedy may be obtained, usually in the form of damages (Garner).
Trial	A formal judicial examination of evidence and determination of legal claims in an adversary proceeding (Garner).

Tort Procedures and an Overview of the Litigation Process

Most of the lawsuits that nurses may be involved in will fall under *tort* law. Tort is a civil wrong resulting in injury to a person or property. A tort case is brought about when the injured person seeks compensation for a wrong done (Bagley, 1995). *Negligence* and *malpractice* lawsuits usually are under the jurisdiction of civil law and tort procedures. The nurse manager or nursing staff may be called upon to review and compile the medical facts of a potential case, be called as a witness (as someone who can verify or refute allegations in the case), or, worst-case scenario, be named as a defendant. It is important that nurse managers know the steps involved in bringing any negligence or malpractice cases to trial.

Initiation of a Civil Suit and Statute of Limitation

The parties involved in a lawsuit are the *plaintiff* and the *defendant*. One of the first considerations in going forth with a lawsuit is to determine if the *statute of limitation* has expired. The plaintiff usually has a finite period of time from the alleged injury to file a lawsuit. Statute of limitation varies from state to state.

Filing of the Lawsuit

The plaintiff brings about the action by filing a *complaint* with the specific allegations in the appropriate court against the defendant. The complaint will identify the parties to a suit, include the cause of action, and state the demand for damages. Usually the patient/plaintiff will file one or more of the following: negligence, malpractice, wrongful death, wrongful birth, defamation, assault and battery, false imprisonment, loss of consortium, emotional distress, or intentional indifference (Monarch, 2002). The complaint is served to the defendant, and the defendant then will have a specific amount of time to *answer* the complaint and each allegation. After the defendant answers the complaint, the answer is served to the plaintiff, and the complaint is filed with the court with jurisdiction over the case.

Discovery

Discovery is the step involving gathering evidence, documentation, and information to support or defend the parties' positions. There are several tools used in the discovery phase. *Interrogatories* are written questions that the opposing parties need to answer. *Depositions* are written or oral questioning of each party that might have knowledge about the facts of a case and usually are taken before a court reporter. *Request for production* of documents can be for items such as medical records, x-rays, educational records, billing records, and personnel files. An *independent medical examination* also can be a discovery tool (Monarch, 2002).

An exception to the discovery rule is the *work-product rule* and the *attorney-client privilege*. The work product rule protects information that the attorney collects in the course of preparing for the case. The attorney-client privilege protects communication between the attorney and the client.

Trial

There are several components to a *trial* (Monarch, 2002).

- Selection of the jury
- Opening statement by the plaintiff's attorney and then by the defendant's attorney
- Presentation of the evidence by the plaintiff's counsel and then the defendant's counsel
- Motion for directed verdict by either attorney
- Closing arguments by the defendant's attorney and then by the plaintiff's attorney
- Instructions to the jury by the judge
- Jury deliberations
- Jury verdict
- Appeal

Negligence Issues in the Nursing Environment

Nursing negligence may be a basis for bringing about a civil lawsuit. Nursing negligence occurs when the nurse fails to do as a reasonable and prudent nurse would do under the same or similar situations (Gullatte, 1998). For the plaintiff to win a negligence claim, four elements need to be proved. The first element is the existence of a *duty* and a *standard of care* for which the nurse is held. The nurse-patient relationship provides the framework for the duty, and the patient is dependent upon the nurse to provide the standard of care. The second element is a *breach* (violation) of the duty and/or standard of care. When the nurse fails to conform to the standard of care, there is a breach of duty. The third element is *causation*. It must be proven that the breach of duty caused the injury. The last element is *damages*. The patient must prove that damage or injury occurred as a result of the negligent act (Guido, 2001).

The nurse encounters multiple day-to-day issues and untoward events that may lead to negligence claims. The nurse must stay constantly aware and operate within the boundaries of the appropriate standards of care, policies, procedures, and protocols.

HIPAA, Patient Privacy, and Patient Confidentiality

The most significant legislation to ensure patient privacy is the Health Insurance Portability and Accountability Act (HIPAA) of 1996. This law mandates that patient information is secured and that policies, procedures, and technologic protections are in place to maximize patient privacy and prevent the unauthorized disclosure of any information that would identify the patient (Monarch, 2002). All covered entities were required to be compliant by April 14, 2003, or face the penalties imposed. For misuse of patient data, the fine could be $250,000 plus jail time (HIPAA, 2004). To be compliant, a covered entity must

- Review the access employees have to protected information, and determine the "minimum necessary" access.
- Develop specific policies and procedures regarding HIPAA requirements.
- Provide training for current and all future employees on those policies and procedures.
- Appoint a privacy officer to monitor the practice's HIPAA compliance.
- Provide a Notice of Privacy Practices to all patients.
- Obtain HIPAA-compliant agreements with all business associates.
- Get a signed authorization every time patient information is released per request of a client.
- Implement new procedures to provide patients access to their information.

In the medicolegal setting, claims for invasion of privacy can arise against the nurse. These claims can stem from allegations of the nurse inappropriately using the plaintiff's name or likeness, the nurse making an unreasonable and extremely offensive invasion upon the patient or his or her personal affairs, or the nurse placing the patient in a false light in the public eye (O'Keefe, 2001). A claim of breach of confidentiality can arise if wrongful disclosure of a patient's private information is done without his or her authorization (Monarch, 2002). The oncology nurse is privileged to a vast repository of knowledge about the patient's cancer and condition. It is vital that this duty of privacy and confidentiality be strictly adhered to and all institutional policies and procedures are followed.

Informed Consent

The patient with cancer may undergo many diagnostic tests, invasive procedures, surgeries, and a host of other medical treatments and clinical trials that would require informed consent. Informed consent is not simply the patient saying "yes" and signing a piece of paper. Informed consent requires that the patient be informed of the diagnosis, procedure/treatment, who will perform the procedure/treatment, and the benefits, risks, options, and alternatives to the recommended medical treatment. If a patient refuses an ordered medical procedure and/or treatment, the nurse must inform the physician and document all information related to this refusal (O'Keefe, 2001). The physician or managing provider is ultimately responsible for obtaining the informed consent.

Additionally, the patient must be competent to give an informed consent. Competency involves the patient being an adult or an emancipated minor or mature minor, conscious, and uncoerced. Allegations of assault and battery can arise out of failure to obtain informed consent (O'Keefe, 2001). The nurse has a professional and ethical obligation to ensure that informed consent for healthcare tests, procedures, and treatment occurs. It may be necessary to administer a Test of Functional

Health Literacy in Adults (TOFHLA), especially as it relates to a more diverse patient population. TOFHLA is designed and used to measure functional health literacy in healthcare settings of both numeric and reading comprehension. This test uses actual health materials such as prescription bottle labels and appointment slips. It is further designed to determine the understanding of materials needed for patients' health care or healthcare education (Parker, Baker, Williams, & Nurss, 1995).

Medication Administration

Administration of hazardous drugs in medical treatment is not unique to oncology nursing. Many cytotoxic agents such as antineoplastic agents are very toxic and require meticulous calculation of dosage and safe administration. It is the position of ONS that cytotoxic agents be administered by competent oncology healthcare professionals who are knowledgeable regarding the cytotoxic agents and who are clinically competent in verifying the dosage and in the administration of these drugs as well as monitoring and educating the patient and family about expected side effects and management (ONS, 2002). Failure to do so may result in irreparable harm and/or death to the patient (Frank-Stromborg & Christensen, 2001). Wrongful death and malpractice cases can be a result of medication errors resulting from inappropriate administration of antineoplastic agents.

In recent years, hospitals and other medical facilities have initiated a number of intensive process improvement measures to improve patient safety and reduce medication errors. Even though more hospitals are reporting and analyzing medication errors, in 2002, more errors resulted in harm to patients. The data from a 2002 report on medication errors in U.S. hospitals issued by U.S. Pharmacopoeia's MedMARx program summarized 192,477 medication error reports (up from 105,603 in 2001) submitted by 482 hospitals and healthcare facilities. The study indicated that the majority of reported errors were caught and corrected before they adversely affected patients. However, around 3,000 errors resulted in some patient injury, and there was a significant increase in the percentage of injuries likely to result in permanent harm (Wechsler, 2003).

Preventive measures such as computerized physician order entry, bar code medication administration, IV medication error-prevention software, single-dose packaging, and up-to-date medication information at the point of care are being used to prevent medication errors. Oncology nurses can greatly decrease their risk of malpractice lawsuits by being knowledgeable about all drugs administered and following the minimal standard: give the right drug, give the right dosage, and give to the right patient, by the right route, at the right time (O'Keefe, 2001). ONS offers a general and advanced certification for oncology nurses; more information on national certification can be found on its Web site (www.ons.org).

Failure to Provide for Patient Safety

Many patient safety initiatives in healthcare organizations were formed in response to the 1999 report from the Institute of Medicine (IOM), which estimated that up to 98,000 people die each year in America's hospitals as a result of medical mistakes that are preventable (IOM, 1999). The IOM report sparked a flood of action in health policy by a range of healthcare advocacy/regulating groups. Established regulators such as the Joint Commission on Accreditation of Healthcare Organizations (JCAHO) and Medicare Peer Review Organizations have developed new patient safety requirements. The federal Quality Interagency Coordination Task Force is attempting to produce a thorough federal approach to medical safety improvement. The nonprofit National Quality Forum also is working with insurers, states, and the federal government on these issues. The Agency for Healthcare Research and Quality (AHRQ) is formulating expert evaluations of cost-effective safety practices (Mello, Studdert, & Brennan, 2003). Hospitals and other healthcare facilities are under intense pressure and scrutiny to meet these patient safety initiatives.

A safety organization that generates a lot of activity is The Leapfrog Group, based in Washington, D.C. The Leapfrog Group is a consortium of more than 150 public and private organizations that provide healthcare benefits. It represents 34 million healthcare consumers. The Leapfrog Group works with medical experts throughout the United States to identify problems and propose solutions that it believes will improve hospital systems that could break down and harm patients. This safety group decided to focus on three practices that have great potential to save lives by reducing preventable mistakes in hospitals. These practices are Computerized Physician Order Entry (CPOE), Evidence-based Hospital Referral (EHR), and ICU Physician Staffing (IPS) (Leapfrog Group, n.d.).

With CPOE, the physician enters orders into a computer rather than writing them on paper, and the prescription can be automatically checked against the patient's current information for potential mistakes or problems. EHR is the system for ensuring that patients with high-risk conditions are treated at hospitals with characteristics shown to be associated with better outcomes. The IPS initiative is based on data that suggest a high intensivist staffing level in the ICU is an important factor to consider when choosing a hospital if a doctor expects that a patient is likely to stay in an ICU during his or her hospitalization (Leapfrog Group, n.d.).

Failure to Follow Standards of Care

Standards of care are established through licensing authorities, professional organizations such as ONS, and healthcare providers' policies and procedures. The oncology nurse can be liable for failure to adhere to nursing standards of care (Brent, 2001).

Failure to Document Patient Care

Medical record documentation is an essential tool in patient care and has numerous important usages. It serves to document care provided and is a communication tool used by all healthcare providers involved in the care of the patient. Third-party payors use the medical records in billing and paying for services rendered. Documentation is also important in defending litigation in which negligence is alleged. Documentation can be your best defense. All aspects of patient care, monitoring, and follow-up must be recorded in the medical record (Brent, 2001).

Frequent Allegations in Negligence Lawsuits Involving Nurses

The list below is a summary of frequent allegations that involve nurses in negligence/malpractice lawsuits (Austin, 2003; Gullatte, 1998). These suits most often resulted from failure of the nurse to

- Adequately document patient care.
- Monitor the patient.
- Initiate treatment in an appropriate and timely fashion.
- Follow physician orders.
- Notify the physician.
- Identify abnormal signs and symptoms and respond appropriately.
- Identify and rule out potential problems.
- Identify high-risk patients.
- Convey discharge instructions.
- Follow facility procedure.
- Report questionable care or substandard medical practices.
- Ensure patient safety.
- Use medical equipment and supplies safely.
- Administer medication correctly.
- Provide adequately trained staff and adequate supervision.

All of these acts of negligence are avoidable if the nurse acts with prudent judgment and in the best interest of patient safety and quality care.

Legal Issues With Student Nurses

Student nurses are vital to the future of nursing to replenish a shrinking nursing pool. They are entrusted with the care of patients under the close supervision of an RN who is either a direct agent of the healthcare facility or who is a designee of the school of nursing. Even though they have not graduated, student nurses are held to the standard of a competent professional nurse when performing nursing duties, and they are liable for any negligent acts. The student nurse is acting as an agent of the hospital or other facility, even if this relationship is only as an affiliation (Pozgar, 1993).

The Impaired Nurse

Healthcare professionals are a microcosm of society. As reflected in society, chemical dependence afflicts a number of healthcare colleagues. The challenge is to balance the safety and quality of care for patients with an interest and concern for the nurse. If the nurse manager has reasonable cause or certainty that a nurse has a chemical dependency problem, the manager must confront the nurse with the gathered facts and outline the options, which may include treatment and reinstatement after successful treatment (*Nurse's Legal Handbook*, 2000). As nurse manager, it is imperative that you have an understanding of the nurse practice act in the state in which you practice. State Boards of Nursing policy and procedures vary by state.

Although chemical dependence is grounds for disciplinary action under state licensure statutes, more than 37 states offer programs to provide rehabilitative, nondisciplinary interventions. Such programs are either voluntary, with no threat of referral to disciplinary authorities, or coercive, with punishment withheld as long as the impaired nurse takes part in a rehabilitation program. The highest percentages of nurses suspected of impaired practice are reported to nursing peer assistance programs, employer assistance programs, state boards of nurse examiners, and state hospital associations. Most impaired nurses are reported to the state boards of nurse examiners. Some states require those who desire to retain a license to practice professional nursing to sign sworn statements of current sobriety or fitness. Other states allow reporting to nursing peer assistance programs instead of reporting to state boards of nurse examiners (Blair, 2002).

Malpractice Prevention

Prevention is the key in avoiding malpractice lawsuits. Measures that may be taken by the nurse include the following (Austin, 2003).
- Communicate with the patient in a timely, sincere manner.
- Educate patients in all aspects of their care.
- Comply with all governing standards of care.
- Appropriately supervise care.
- Adhere to the nursing process.
- Document patient care.
- Provide frequent and timely follow-up.

Risk Prevention and Management

Risk management is an internal systematic program aimed at reducing preventable injuries to patients, employees, and visitors and reducing financial losses of the facility through risk identification and evaluation processes, risk analysis, and risk control measures (Brent, 2001). Risk prevention and management is the responsibility of all employees. The nurse manager and other RNs will be at the frontline in making the risk management program a success. Risk prevention is the key in improving quality care as well as reducing risk. Some key risk prevention strategies for reducing professional liability exposures and lawsuits are listed (Austin, 2003).
- Create realistic policies and procedures.
- Create realistic expectations.
- Ensure that questions are answered completely.
- Alleviate the patient's anxiety.
- Allow the patient to express anger.
- Develop a strong relationship with the patient and the family.
- Recognize most common signs of malpractice.
- Minimize consequences.
- Establish good documentation.
- Handle patient complaints effectively.

The Incident/Occurrence Report

The incident or occurrence report is an internal institutional reporting, monitoring, and trend-analyzing tool. When an untoward actual or potential event occurs, the staff should follow the institutional policy and procedures for reporting. Immediate monitoring and appropriate follow-up on the status of the patient are crucial. The nurse and risk manager also must investigate the incident and maintain an atmosphere of trust and caring with the patient. Serious or life-threatening incidences must be reported immediately to the facility's legal counsel for their input and guidance (Austin, 2003).

The incident report should not be punitive. The staff may perceive that these reports are used by managers to punish them, and this perception leads to under-reporting of incidents. Other factors that may lead to poor reporting are the perception by staff that incident reporting has no constructive value and fear that the incident will result in legal action against them in the future (Dunn, 2003). Education of staff by the nurse manager and the risk manager regarding the purpose of incident reporting is vital.

Recent laws are emphasizing more reporting of medical errors. The Consolidated Appropriations Act of 2001 includes the Patient Safety and Errors Reduction Act, which incorporates many of the recommendations of the IOM report. This law calls for study and carrying out of error-reduction systems and safe practices by providers and gives organizations certain legal protections to encourage reporting and collection of error information. Under the provisions of the patient safety law, AHRQ is to establish a confidential National Patient Safety Database of reported medical events (includes sentinel events, adverse events, and "close calls") to be used entirely for research on improving the quality and safety of patient care (Cavanaugh, 2001).

AHRQ will identify and evaluate public and private sector patient safety reporting systems, certify organizations that will collect and analyze information on medical errors, and help healthcare providers assess it. If providers follow AHRQ guidelines, data obtained during the analysis of medical errors will be treated as confidential and protected from disclosure (Cavanaugh, 2001).

A number of states have laws that protect the incident report against disclosure in the event of medical negligence litigation. The reasoning for this is to allow the facility to identify problems and take corrective measures to improve patient care. Legal counsel must review these incident/occurrence reports that record breaches in the standard of care or injury to a patient, visitor, or staff. There must be no mention of an incident report in the medical record. However, the staff must document objectively what happened; what assessment, intervention, treatment, and follow-up occurred; and what was the outcome for the patient (Austin, 2003).

Regulatory and Private Agencies' Influence on Risk Management

There are a number of governmental and private sector agencies that have a significant impact on institutional risk management programs and quality of patient care. These regulatory agencies set standards, policies, and/or procedures for the institution to abide by, and failure to do so may result in sanctions against the institution, such as fines, penalties, loss of accreditation, loss of reimbursement, and other punitive measures. Increasingly, the consumer uses these agencies' report cards on the quality and safety performance of the institution to determine where to seek health care.

Department of Health and Human Services

The U.S. Department of Health and Human Services (DHHS) is the government's primary agency for protecting the health of all Americans and providing vital human services, especially for those who are least able to help themselves. DHHS, which is located at the national and state levels, includes a wide variety of programs, such as medical and social science research, ensuring food and drug safety; Medicare (health insurance for elderly and disabled Americans) and Medicaid (health insurance for low-income people); preventing an outbreak of infectious disease, including immunization services; and improving maternal and infant health (U.S. DHHS, 2003). Consumers can report healthcare safety and care concerns directly to DHHS.

The Centers for Medicare and Medicaid Services

The Centers for Medicare and Medicaid Services (CMS) is a federal agency within DHHS. The primary programs for which CMS is responsible are Medicare and Medicaid, both of which directly impact healthcare facilities (CMS, 2003). Medicare is a national health insurance program and covers approximately 55% of elder health care in the United States. Medicaid pays for medical assistance for certain individuals and families with low incomes and resources and covers 12% of elder health care (Blatt, 2002). For healthcare institutions to receive payment from Medicare and Medicaid, they must meet the conditions of participation.

Occupational Safety and Health Administration

The Occupational Safety and Health Administration (OSHA) is an agency under the U.S. Department of Labor, and its mission is to ensure safe and healthful workplaces in the United States. OSHA's current goal is to reduce workplace fatality rates by 15% and workplace injury and illness rates by 20% by 2008. All healthcare facilities must adhere to OSHA's safety guidelines (OSHA, 2003).

OSHA is very concerned with worker exposure to hazardous drugs such as antineoplastic cytotoxic medications, anesthetic agents, antiviral agents, and others. These hazardous medications are capable of causing serious effects, including cancer, organ toxicity, fertility problems, genetic damage, and birth defects. OSHA published safety guidelines for the safe handling and disposal of hazardous drugs, which include cytotoxic antineoplastic agents (OSHA, 2003).

OSHA mandates that workplaces have a written Hazard Communication (HAZCOM) Program to ensure that employers and employees know about work hazards and how to protect themselves in order reduce the incidence of chemical source illness and injuries. Material Safety Data Sheets (MSDSs) also are required in work facilities. Chemical manufacturers and importers must obtain or develop a MSDS for each hazardous chemical they produce or import. Distributors are accountable for ensuring that their clients are provided a copy of these MSDSs. Employers must have an MSDS for each hazardous chemical they use (OSHA, 2003).

Regulatory Influence of State Government

States have the power to regulate healthcare providers through licensure or certification as well as through the enforcement or requirement of the federal-state Medicaid program. Medicaid is a cooperative federal and state program for the poor. The states apply federal standards and use federally approved survey instruments in inspecting Medicaid facilities (Blatt, 2002; CMS, 2003).

Joint Commission on Accreditation of Healthcare Organizations

JCAHO is an independent, not-for-profit organization that provides accreditation to U.S. hospitals and healthcare facilities and is working to achieve high patient safety standards. As of January 1, 2004, all JCAHO-accredited hospitals and healthcare facilities are required to implement JCAHO's 2004 National Patient Safety Goals. These patient safety goals will have a significant impact on institutions' risk management programs. JCAHO's 2004 National Patient Safety Goals focus caregivers on a variety of patient safety issues, specifically (JCAHO, 2004a)
- Improve the accuracy of patient identification.
- Improve the effectiveness of communication among caregivers.
- Improve the safety of using high-alert medications.
- Eliminate wrong-site, wrong-patient, and wrong-procedure surgery.
- Improve the safety of using infusion pumps.
- Improve the effectiveness of clinical alarm systems.
- Reduce the risk of healthcare-acquired infections.

Healthcare consumers can report to JCAHO, through its Web site, any quality of care concerns that they may have about a healthcare organization. JCAHO (2004b) addressed all complaints that relate to quality of care issues within the scope of its standards that include issues such as patient's rights, care of patients, safety, infection control, medication use, and security. Dependent upon the issue, JCAHO (2004b) will
- Conduct an unannounced, on-site evaluation of the organization.
- Ask the healthcare organization to provide a written response to the complaint.
- Incorporate the complaint in the quality-monitoring database that is used to continuously track the performance of healthcare organizations over time.
- Review the complaint at the time of the healthcare organization's next scheduled accreditation survey if it is scheduled in the near future.

Ethical Issues Regarding Death and Dying

The oncology nurse may encounter numerous ethical issues regarding extremely sensitive subject matter such as the right to die, euthanasia, and assisted suicide. There are no easy answers to these complex issues, and many hospitals have established ethics committees to facilitate dialogue and establish policies regarding these matters. The oncology nurse must be aware of the ethics committee and how to access it as needed.

Hospital ethics committees have three basic functions: developing hospital policies on ethical matters; educating staff, patients, family, and the community on ethical issues; and consulting with the interdisciplinary healthcare team, patient, and family on difficult decisions (Powell, 1998). Consults are obtained from ethics committees on issues such as consent and patient autonomy, declining and withdrawing treatment, biomedical research/investigational compliance, right to die, mental health treatment, organ donation, and contraception.

The staff and nurse manager can access the ethics committee regarding areas of concern by reviewing the hospital's policies on ethics and following those guidelines. Hospital administrators, chaplains, social workers, and nursing administrators also can direct the staff to the ethics committee.

Advance Directives

The Patient Self-Determination Act of 1990 provided the federal law that mandated that healthcare facilities inform a patient of the right to have a living will and durable powers of attorney for health care. Nurses are instrumental in educating the patient regarding these advance directives, which are legal documents that express the wishes of the patient regarding healthcare situations in the event the individual is no longer capable of giving informed consent. One such advance directive is the *living will.* The living will is a document that lists under what circumstances, such as terminal illness, a patient desires certain decisions be made on his or her behalf. These directions usually involve circumstances when life-sustaining treatment, such as food, fluid, and cardiopulmonary resuscitation, is to be withheld so that the patient may die in as much dignity and peace as possible (O'Keefe, 2001).

The medical durable power of attorney for health care allows the patient to name another person to be the decision maker in the event the patient becomes functionally impaired and unable to do so. If the patient cannot make an informed decision, then the substitute decision maker can do so (O'Keefe, 2001).

Euthanasia

Euthanasia is an action or inaction that is planned to result in an easy, painless, or good death (O'Keefe, 2001). Ethical issues regarding euthanasia usually involve active and passive euthanasia. Active euthanasia is when the healthcare provider facilitates the patient's death through some direct intervention. One form of active euthanasia is assisted suicide in which a person, usually a physician, provides the patient with the resources to end his or her life. The most famous cases of assisted suicide in recent times involved Dr. Jack Kevorkian, in which he actively assisted patients in the state of Michigan (O'Keefe).

Case Studies

Patient Confidentiality and Duty of Care

In March 1987, Marianne New received treatment for medullary thyroid carcinoma, a genetically transferable disease. In 1990, Heidi Pate, the plaintiff and adult daughter of New, was diagnosed with the same condition. Pate filed a lawsuit against New's physicians (defendants) alleging that the physicians should have informed her of the genetically transferable nature of the disease. Pate also claimed that early testing and preventive actions could have been taken. Pate alleged that as a result of the physicians' negligence, she suffered from advanced medullary thyroid carcinoma. The physicians' attorneys moved to dismiss the lawsuit for failure to state a cause of action. The defendants alleged that no professional relationship existed between Pate and the physicians; therefore, there was no duty of care (Blatt, 2002).

Human genetics in oncology can involve a number of difficult issues, especially when a hereditary or genetic condition threatens the well-being of others in the patient's family. Legal, social, and ethical issues can arise. One issue, in this case, involved the duty of care by the physician to the children of a patient to warn the patient of the genetically transferable nature of disease for which the physician was treating the patient. The issue of duty of confidentiality also comes into play in this case. When is it allowable to breach patient confidentiality? The ultimate ruling in this case was that when a prevailing standard of care creates a duty that is clearly for the benefit of certain recognized third parties, and the physician knows of the existence of those third parties, the physician's duty includes those third parties (Blatt, 2002). Therefore, in this specific case, the duty of the physician to inform should have extended to the children.

Wrongful Death and Failure to Follow Standards of Care

Wrongful death claims are filed by the survivors of patients who allege that the death of the patient was due to the negligence of the healthcare provider and/or facility. In 1987, Mr. Manning was admitted to the hospital with diagnoses of end-stage chronic obstructive pulmonary disease, hypoxemia, and increased carbon dioxide retention. Manning was ordered supplemental oxygen, by a nasal cannula, and he had a do-not-resuscitate order in place. During transportation of Manning to a private room, the nurse failed to provide the supplemental oxygen citing proximity between the current room and the private room. Manning stopped breathing during the transport, and the staff started CPR. Upon arrival of the physician, resuscitative measures were stopped because of Manning's "no code" status. The family sued the hospital and two nurses. One nurse was found not negligent, but the other nurse involved in the move was found negligent in transferring the patient without supplemental oxygen. The family was awarded $184,800 in damages (Monarch, 2002).

Summary

As nurse manager, it is important to have a broad base understanding of areas of risk and vulnerability inherent in health care. Equipped with this knowledge, the nurse manager can direct the nursing staff to be proactive in meeting patient care needs and providing for patient safety. In today's litigious society, the nurse manager should educate staff regarding legal, ethical, and risk management issues that may impact their practice. A proactive preventive approach to identifying and correcting potential risks is vital in the healthcare environment. Conducting a Failure Mode Effect Analysis to analyze potential problem areas early would involve taking a look at patient care treatments and/or interventions that may be a combination of high risk, high volume, and/or problem prone. The nurse manager then would use process improvement strategies to go through process steps to see where there is a potential for a process failure and take the necessary corrective action to prevent such an error. This is key to being proactive in patient safety management. Nurses at all levels must continue their critical role as patient advocates, educators, and competent clinicians in an ever-changing healthcare medical-legal environment.

References

Adams, D. (2003). HHS joins call for national tort reform. *American Medical News, 46,* 13.

American Nurses Association. (2004). *Nursing: Scope and standards of practice.* Retrieved January 26, 2004, from www.ana.org or www.nursingworld.org

Austin, S. (2003). Managing risk. In S. Austin (Ed.), *Five keys to successful nursing management* (pp. 342–380). Philadelphia: Lippincott Williams & Wilkins.

Bagley, C. (1995). *Managers and the legal environment: Strategies for the 21st century.* St. Paul, MN: West Publishing Company.

Blair, P. (2002). Report impaired practice—stat. *Nursing Management, 33*(1), 24–25.

Blatt, D.L. (Ed.). (2002). *High court case summaries* (4th ed.). Eagan, MN: West Group.

Brant, J.M., & Wickham, R.S. (2004). *Statement on the scope and standards of oncology nursing practice.* Pittsburgh, PA: Oncology Nursing Society.

Brent, N.J. (2001). *Nurses and the law: A guide to principles and applications.* Philadelphia: Saunders.

Cavanaugh, M. (2001). New regulations focus on medical errors. *RN, 64*(4), 71–72, 74.

Centers for Medicare and Medicaid Services. (2003). *Facts about CMS.* Retrieved January 26, 2004, from http://www.cms.hhs.gov/researchers/projects/APR/2003/facts.pdf

Coble, Y.D., Jr. (2003). Act now as medical liability reform gains momentum. *American Medical News, 46,* 16.

Dunn, D. (2003). Incident reports—Their purpose and scope. *AORN Journal, 78,* 45–46, 49–61, 65–70.

Frank-Stromborg, M., & Christensen, A. (2001). Legal issues in chemotherapy administration. In M.M. Gullatte (Ed.), *Clinical guide to antineoplastic therapy: A chemotherapy handbook* (pp. 281–295). Pittsburgh, PA: Oncology Nursing Society.

Garner, B. (Ed.). (2001). *Black's law dictionary: Second pocket edition.* St. Paul, MN: West Group.

Guido, G.W. (2001). *Legal and ethical issue in nursing* (3rd ed.). Englewood Cliffs, NJ: Prentice-Hall.

Gullatte, M.M. (1998). Legal issues influencing cancer care. In J.K. Itano & K.N. Taoka (Eds.), *Core curriculum for oncology nursing* (pp. 734–739). Philadelphia: Saunders.

Health Insurance Portability and Accountability Act. (2004). *Federal HIPAA regulation mandates.* Retrieved January 24, 2004, from http://www.hipaaps.com/what.html

Institute of Medicine. (1999). *To err is human: Building a safer health system.* Retrieved February 9, 2004, from http://www.iom.edu/includes/DBFile.asp?id=4117

Joint Commission on Accreditation of Healthcare Organizations. (2004a). *National patient safety goals for 2004 and 2005.* Retrieved January 24, 2004, from http://www.jcaho.org/accredited+organizations/patient+safety/npsg.htm

Joint Commission on Accreditation of Healthcare Organizations. (2004b). *Report a complaint about a health care organization.* Retrieved January 24, 2004, from http://www.jcaho.org/general+public/public+input/report+a+complaint/index.htm

Law.com. (n.d.) *Assault.* Retrieved February 28, 2004, from http://dictionary.law.com/default2.asp?typed=assault&type=1

Leapfrog Group. (n.d.). *Survey results.* Retrieved February 8, 2004, from http://www.leapfroggroup.org

Mello, M., Studdert, D., & Brennan, T. (2003). The Leapfrog standards: Ready to jump from marketplace to courtroom? *Health Affairs, 22,* 46–59.

Monarch, K. (2002). *Nursing and the law: Trends and issues.* Washington, DC: American Nurses Publishing.

Nurse's legal handbook (4th ed.). (2000). Springhouse, PA: Springhouse Corporation.

Occupational Safety and Health Administration. (2003). *OSHA's 2003–2008 strategic management plan goals.* Retrieved January 26, 2004, from http://www.osha.gov/pls/oshaweb/owadisp.show_document?p_table=NEWS_RELEASES&p_id=10214

O'Keefe, M.E. (2001). *Nursing practice and the law: Avoiding malpractice and other legal risk.* Philadelphia: Davis Company.

Oncology Nursing Society. (2002). *Education of the professional RN who administers and cares for the individual receiving chemotherapy and biotherapy.* Retrieved January 26, 2004, from http://www.ons.org/publications/positions/EducationOfProfessionalRN.shtml

Parker, R.M., Baker, D.W., Williams, M.V., & Nurss, J.R. (1995). The test of functional health literacy in adults: A new instrument for measuring patients' literacy skills. *Journal of General Internal Medicine, 10,* 537–541.

Powell, L. (1998). Hospital ethics committees and the future of health care decision-making. *Hospital Materiel Management Quarterly, 20,* 82–101.

Pozgar, G.D. (1993). *Legal aspects of healthcare administration* (5th ed.). Gaithersburg, MD: Aspen Publishers.

Tucker, W. (2003). Legal malpractice. *The Weekly Standard, 8,* 18–19.

U.S. Department of Health and Human Services. (2003). *HHS: What we do.* Retrieved January 26, 2004, from http://hhs.gov/news/press/2002pres/profile.html

Wechsler, J. (2003). Medication error reporting rises. *Pharmaceutical Executive, 23*(12), 26.

CHAPTER 26

Program Development in a Veterans Healthcare System

Carol J. Thompson, RN, MSN, AOCN®, CS
Connie Hampton, MSN, RN, FNP

The Department of Veterans Affairs provides competitive health care for the veteran population. This chapter will give the novice nurse manager an overview of the Veterans Health Administration (VHA) cancer program and its commitment to becoming the number one healthcare provider for the veteran population. This integrated healthcare system provides acute medical, surgical, and psychiatric care and both primary and specialized outpatient services with almost all major specialties and subspecialties represented. VHA provides health care to more than an estimated 25.6 million veterans (Department of Veterans Affairs, 2003b). There are approximately 120 Veterans Affairs (VA) medical centers diagnosing and/or treating patients with cancer across the United States. According to the American Cancer Society (2004), cancer will claim more than 563,700 American lives in 2004. The Department of Veterans Affairs has an estimated 175,000 veteran patients with cancer (Department of Veterans Affairs, 2003b). As the veteran population ages, there will be an increase in the number of patients diagnosed with cancer. Approximately 35,000 new cases of cancer occur in VA patients each year, and cancer is the second leading cause of death among veterans (Department of Veterans Affairs, 2003b).

Congruent with the development of hematology and oncology as a specialization in the practice of medicine, the VHA has developed programs in cancer care. The VHA provides veterans with the benefit of receiving the most current therapies as well as the best practice based upon clinical research processes and findings. The VHA understands that cancer is a varied and complex collection of diseases with many causes and clinical characteristics, and for this reason, the VHA identified that this disease requires a formal plan of action, which was named the National Cancer Registry. This cancer program ensures that users of the veterans healthcare system have easy access to consistently high-quality cancer prevention, detection, and treatment services (Department of Veterans Affairs, 2003b). This strategic plan is composed of 12 objectives. According to the VHA, the strategic objectives are to

1. Ensure that the quality of VA cancer care meets or exceeds accepted national standards of practice.
2. Improve cancer patients' access to care.
3. Provide appropriate cancer management expertise to each patient as promptly as possible.
4. Provide for the continual monitoring and improvement of outcomes of therapy.
5. Provide clinically useful prevention, screening, and early detection services.
6. Improve the quality of life of patients with cancer.
7. Provide compassionate and humane care that clearly demonstrates respect for the patient's dignity.
8. Ensure that the care provided derives from shared decision making between the patient and treatment personnel.
9. Ensure that through its clinical research activities, VHA continually builds upon current knowledge, contributes to the national research base, and provides for state-of-the-art preventive, diagnostic, and therapeutic interventions.
10. Ensure patient access to promising interventions.
11. Contribute to the common good by establishing a national model for a systematic approach to the problem of cancer.
12. Ensure that suitable and timely patient-centered end-of-life care is made available when appropriate.

The cancer strategy identified and defined several elements to be addressed by each facility. These elements serve as a blueprint for cancer management and care from diagnosis to end of life for all VA facilities and include prevention, screening, clinical practice recommendation, clinical investigation and research, tumor registry, and continuing care/terminal care.

Eligibility and Reimbursement

The primary factor in determining a veteran's eligibility to receive VA healthcare benefits is "veteran status." Veteran status is established by active duty service in the military, naval, or air service and a discharge or release from active military service under other than dishonorable conditions (VHA, 2004). In October 1996, Congress passed Public Law 104-262, the *Veterans' Health Care Eligibility Reform Act of 1996*. This law made the way for the creation of a medical benefits package—a standard enhanced health benefits plan available to all enrolled veterans (VHA, 2004). This package emphasizes preventive and primary care, offering a full range of outpatient and inpatient services. The VA's goal is to ensure the quality of care and service the veteran receives is consistently excellent in every location, in every program. The VA is required by law to bill any and all insurance companies used by non–service connected veterans. Non–service connected means that the condition being treated did not occur during the veteran's military tour. If the condition being treated was documented and identified during the time of service, the patient is considered to be service connected.

Cancer care is expensive, and reimbursement is important to the VHA. The VHA has a three tiered co-payment system that divides each service into one of three categories. The first category is primary care. All primary care visits require a $15 co-payment. This amount may be paid at the time services are rendered or may be billed to the patient. The second category is specialty clinics. The patient is charged a $50 co-payment. The last category is no co-payment designation, meaning that there are no fees for the patient. The eligibility department assesses the veteran's financial status and military service to determine what fees are to be charged. Veterans are not required to pay co-payments recommended by their insurance provider. Non–service connected veterans with an income and assets over the yearly amount required by the VA will pay a $7 prescription co-pay for a 30-day supply of medication. Service-connected veterans with less than a 50% service connection also may be required to pay for prescriptions for non–service connected conditions. These moneys are used to offset the increasing costs of medication and maintain high-quality care. All funds collected are returned to the local VA facility.

Regulatory Commissions

The undersecretary heads the VHA and is responsible for the operation of the nation's largest integrated healthcare system. This position is nominated by the president of the United States and is confirmed by Congress. Congress regulates the Central Cancer VHA, and, because of this, federal law supercedes state and local law. With a medical care budget of more than $22 billion, the VHA employs approximately 180,000 healthcare professionals at 163 hospitals, more than 800 community and facility-based clinics, 135 nursing homes, 43 domiciliary vocations, 206 readjustment counseling centers, and various other facilities (VHA, 2004). In addition to its medical care mission, the veterans healthcare system is the nation's largest provider of graduate medical education and a major contributor to medical and scientific research. The Central Cancer Registry for the VA identifies and uses the guidelines of the National Cancer Institute (NCI), American College of Surgeons, American Joint Committee on Cancer, and several other organizations. According to the National VA Cancer Registry, all VA facilities must pursue membership in the NCI cooperative group program or the Community Clinical Oncology Program or its affiliate memberships. Comprehensive cancer center designations are awarded to VA facilities that meet the American College of Surgeons Commission on Cancer established standards. The multidisciplinary Commission on Cancer sets standards for quality cancer care delivery and surveys hospitals to assess compliance (American College of Surgeons, 2003). Forty-five VA facilities have successfully met the criteria to receive designation as comprehensive cancer centers. Such facilities have an effective tumor registry department, interdisciplinary tumor board meetings, and cancer committee meetings. The cancer committee membership is compiled of physician's representatives from medical oncology, surgery, diagnostic radiology, pathology, and hospice/palliative care, nursing, administration, social work, and quality management. The cancer committee is the core team of specialized professionals designated by the director of each facility for planning, initiation, and evaluation of cancer activities. Veterans are able to access the intranet to assess which facilities have successfully been designated as comprehensive cancer centers.

Care and Services Provided

The VHA incorporates its comprehensive integrated healthcare system in providing excellence in healthcare value, service as defined by its customers, education, and research through an organization that is held accountable to the population it serves.

A variety of federal benefits are available to the veteran. Services covered under special authority are adult day health care, dental care, domiciliary care, emergency care in non-VA facilities, homeless programs, nursing home care, readjustments counseling through veteran centers, sensory-neural aids, sexual trauma counseling, and care at non-VA facilities through shared agreements (VHA, 2004).

The VHA provides leadership in the provision of specialty programs such as long-term care, psychiatry, acute care, intensive care, cardiac care, surgical procedures, spinal cord injury centers, clinical research, oncology, and blood and marrow stem cell and solid organ transplants. Women veteran program managers are available through each VA facility. Such program managers ensure that all VA facilities in the network provide service either on site or through a referral system using other VA centers or community resources. Primary care, preventive health screening, gender-specific care, such as cervical and reproductive health screening encompassing pregnancy and infertility evaluation, and evaluation for osteoporosis and treatment are services available for female veterans through the VHA (National Commission on VA Nursing, 2001).

Late in 1995, the VHA initiated a transformation of a hospital-based system into a healthcare system (Stevens, Holland, & Kiser, 2001). With a movement toward providing primary and ambulatory care to its veterans, the VHA developed strategies to provide coordinated continuous care within an integrated healthcare system. As a result, 22 geographically located Veterans Integrated Service Networks (VISNs) were developed that encompass 1,200 facilities, including 773 ambulatory and community-based clinics, 206 counseling centers, 132 nursing homes, and 172 hospitals (VISNs, 2002). Health promotion and disease prevention became an increased focus in healthcare provision. Improving access to care, creating a seamless healthcare delivery system, improving patient safety, and documented healthcare quality are part of the initiative in redesigning the delivery of care in the VHA (Stevens et al.).

Along with the redesign was the effort to work more closely with the Graduate Medical Education Department. Approximately 9% of U.S. residency training positions are funded by the VHA. One-third of all residents receive training within the VA healthcare system. The medical training programs are part of the culture of the VA healthcare system and an essential part of the care provided (Stevens et al., 2001).

Program Development

The remainder of this chapter will focus on the development of a cancer program within a VHA facility. All programs need to begin with a strategic plan. This plan will outline the need and scope of services to be provided within the identified program. Program plans include staffing and budgeting as well as issues related to customer satisfaction.

Strategic Planning

In formulating a plan for the development of a cancer program, the following elements must be considered.
1. Service to be provided, programs/sections supported, areas of excellence, and challenges to the program
2. Performance measures
3. Projected workload and full-time equivalents that are based on a standardized acuity system and Decision Support System (DSS) mapping, IV equipment and construction needed. Program-specific business plans are evolving; specialty services have not been tasked to develop business plans. Facilities have developed strategic plans that encompass business plans. The leadership council develops these strategic plans in strategic planning sessions. Nurse managers have input to nursing leadership and collaborate with upper management in the implementation of strategies to achieve organizational goals. More information related to generalized healthcare strategic planning is included in Chapter 22.

Within a cancer program, the manager needs to operationalize the following aspects of care in line with the VHA standards: staffing, budgeting, and ensuring standards of clinical practice throughout the trajectory of illness.

Clinical Practice

The VA recognizes the importance of using evidence-based standards in providing best practices to its patients. Recommendations must be valid, reliable, and frequently reviewed and revised as new information becomes available. All of this information must be easily accessible to the clinician. For these reasons, the recommendations contained in the Physician Data Query (PDQ) database, provided by NCI and made available through the National Library of Medicine, represent the standards of care to be provided in the VA and are designated as the VA national care guidelines. PDQ is a result of a comprehensive review by national cancer experts and is based upon objective data according to the strength of evidence (Department of Veterans Affairs, 2003b). This is done carefully. All PDQ information is available 24 hours a day electronically.

Staffing and Budgeting

Congress determines the budget for the VHA. All VISNs identify shared mission, vision, and value statements that guide institutional activity and reflect the national mission. A DSS has been developed to guide budgets based upon workload statistics. The purpose of the system is to collect accurate cost, revenue, and workload data for the submitting of proposals, performing clinical projects, and justification of staffing and funding (Department of Veterans Affairs, 2003c).

The DSS is an information system that supports and promotes effective resource stewardship and the highest standards in patient care in the VHA. DSS is an electronic database and set of tools for data reporting and analysis. This database provides patient care data and enables state-of-the-art activity-based costing, clinical quality, and productivity analysis. The data then are used for budget forecasting and resource/staffing justification. The DSS unit is responsible for communicating information to service chiefs and assisting them in managing their areas. Product line managers and service chiefs are responsible for providing needed data for periodic processing.

Nurse managers are not responsible for developing unit-specific budgets but should staff their respective units appropriately so that care to patients is provided safely and efficiently. Staffing for the oncology area is based upon the unique needs of providing cancer care reflective of the scope of care provided. Nurse-patient ratios are guided by an acuity system, which incorporates the administration of antineoplastic agents, and supportive care issues necessary for patients with cancer. Because of the complexity of care required for the patient with cancer, these patients are given the maximum acuity score to allow for additional staffing.

Clinical Investigation

Clinical trials provide an avenue for the VA to make available to veteran patients new preventive, diagnostic, or treatment options, which may become the standard of future care. They also represent the only reliable process to acquire objective data suitable for the provision of efficient and cost-effective patient care. Increased participation in clinical trials by VA patients will be accomplished in accordance with the Interagency Agreement (IAA) as of January 1, 2000. This agreement is among the VA, NCI, and all VISNs facility directors, clinical managers, and chiefs of staff are expected to be familiar with the IAA document (Department of Veterans Affairs, 2003b). The purpose of this agreement is to increase the access of eligible veterans to all phases of NCI-sponsored clinical trials and to provide VA clinical researchers with expanded opportunities to participate in clinical cancer research (Department of Veterans Affairs, 2003a). The NCI/VA agreement covers a large range of NCI clinical trials, mainly prevention, diagnostic, and treatment studies. These studies are significant because of the scientific results that may lead to future advances in cancer care. Most patients with cancer enter these studies in hope of being cured, increasing their life span, and contributing to research. Only mandatory veterans are eligible.

Congress identified mandatory veterans as service-connected veterans, determined by the VA, with a service-connected problem who were prisoners of war, exposed to radiation and herbicides, are receiving VA pension, are eligible for Medicaid, or are non–service connected with incomes of $21,001 a year or less if single with no dependents or $25,204 a year or less if married or single with one dependent, plus $1,404 for each additional dependent (Hill, 2004).

Tumor Registry

The tumor registry is a formal means of tracking patient care and outcomes and is a critical element in any cancer program (Department of Veterans Affairs, 2003b). This tracking system provides important epidemiologic, staging, demographic, survival, and other clinical data. The VA National Tumor Registry facilitates and compiles incidence statistics, comparison of systemwide outcomes with national standards, analysis of specific therapies and outcomes, evaluation of prevention practices, and planning for resource allocation. There is also a component that provides analytical reports and resource allocation planning. According to the national VA cancer strategy, all VA medical centers must establish a tumor registry and provide reports to the central registry.

Continuing Care and Terminal Care

The professional and ethical obligation of VA providers does not end when all efforts are found to be unsuccessful. The clinician should never state that there is no more that can be done for the patient. Although cure may not be possible, dignified, comfortable care free of anxiety, pain, and suffering will be provided (Department of Veterans Affairs, 2003b). VA clinicians are encouraged to use a systematic approach for the care of terminally ill patients and their families. National guidelines and research-based outcomes are used to facilitate a smooth transition into palliative care. Every VA medical treatment facility is to provide or have a formal relationship with organizations providing hospice care; those relationships must ensure that hospice services are made available to every appropriate VA patient with cancer when the need so arises (Department of Veterans Affairs, 2003b). Pain management is of critical importance, and for this reason, all VA facilities must have an evidence-based protocol for pain management.

Rehabilitation

Rehabilitation is another integral component of cancer care. The VA requires that in designated comprehensive cancer centers, rehabilitation services must be made available for both inpatient and outpatient veterans. This treatment can, at a minimum, be provided through the use of physical, occupational, recreational, and speech therapy services. All VA facilities must provide rehabilitation or must provide appropriate rehabilitation referrals to be considered a comprehensive cancer center (Department of Veterans Affairs, 2003b).

Customer Satisfaction and Risk Management

The VHA encourages its patients with cancer to report any concerns with their care. This is encouraged upon admission. Each patient is given a booklet entitled *Patient Rights and Responsibilities*. This booklet contains information on what type of care the VA has committed to provide, its pledge to keep all information confidential, and that the patient has the right to participate in his or her care and the complaint process. The VHA encourages patients to file complaints concerning care in written form. This information is given to a customer service representative or directly to the director of the facility. The nurse manager often is contacted regarding any patient concerns and will conduct a fact-finding interview at the unit level and address patient/family concerns. The patient and/or family members are consulted as part of fact finding. The nurse manager is to address all patient complaints in a timely manner. Issues are addressed, and interventions are sought to support the patient and his or her family so that the cancer experience is supported. Quality management then reviews the allegations, and another fact-finding investigation is conducted. Based on facts, quality management may decide that a root cause analysis must be conducted. Root cause analysis is defined as an approach to eliminate the recurrence of undesirable events. The findings from the root cause analysis are used to make changes in the system or healthcare process. The results are not used for disciplinary purposes. Quality management may identify the need for a formal investigation, called an administrative board of investigation. The facility director appoints the members of this group. This process is conducted in a confidential manner, and the testimonies received are obtained under oath. The group listens to all versions of the complaint and is tasked to make recommendations. Disciplinary action, if recommended, is based on facts found and may be in the form of a written counseling, suspension, and/or termination. Quality management reviews all recommendations, making additions as indicated.

On minor occasions, a patient may file lawsuits against the federal government—not the VHA. This process is called a tort claim. Tort claims are medical malpractice lawsuits filed against the federal government. Physicians, nurses, and other credentialed, privileged, and appointed staff cannot be individually named in a tort claim because of immunity. This does not mean that the nurse or physician cannot be reported to his or her state licensing board. VHA regional counsel reviews the tort claims, and a peer review is conducted. Once the tort claim is settled, the facility is given a notice with the amount allocated to the patient. The situation then is sent for an external peer review. If the practitioner is deemed negligent, he or she is reported to the National Practitioner Data Bank.

Practice Concerns

As with other healthcare systems, the VHA is concerned with the care provided to its patient population and with promoting quality healthcare outcomes. One goal of the VHA is to develop an esprit de core of nursing staff: VA nursing is a dynamic, diverse group of honored, respected, and compassionate professionals. The VA is the leader in the creation of an organizational culture where excellence in nursing is valued as essential for quality health care to those who have served America (National Commission on VA Nursing, 2003). The Commission on VA Nursing's objective is to provide advice and make recommendations to Congress and the secretary of Veterans Affairs regarding legislative and organizational policy changes to enhance the recruitment and retention of nurses in the department.

Oncology nurses in the VHA follow standards of care developed by national organizations such as the Oncology Nursing Society (ONS), NCI, and the American Nurses Association. All guidelines must be evidence based. The professional nurse is required to attend an introductory chemotherapy course and to remain up to date on past and current antineoplastic agents to maintain his or her chemotherapy competence. These classes are developed by oncology certified nurses and follow ONS course guidelines. Structured preceptor programs for oncology nurses include didactic courses in administering chemotherapy and providing care to patients who have received chemotherapy. Upon completion of didactics and competency validation, mentoring of the new oncology nurse continues. Nurse managers are responsible for monitoring progress through structured orientation programs and mentoring processes. As with other nurses from different treatment facilities or sites, the VA nurses access professional organizational memberships, attend off-station education meetings, and engage in informal and/or support groups to maintain their professional and personal caregiver needs.

It is important to advance the knowledge and skills of nurses providing care for patients with cancer. As treatment options continue to transform, program development must embrace and promote an environment that supports continuous learning and mentoring. Additional cancer care/services provided to the veterans include bone marrow transplantation, chemotherapy, surgical therapy, brachytherapy, biotherapy, radiation therapy, symptom management, and palliative and hospice care. The VA's core values support the education needs of staff and patients so that the best care is provided to the veterans and their families. Additionally, respect and ethical concerns as core values espoused by the VHA for the veteran and his or her families act as guideposts in decision making for staff interactions with patients and families, maintaining them as core members in team planning when considering various options during the process. Interdisciplinary planning of care is an expectation of the continuum of care provided to the veteran with cancer.

Nurse managers responsible for the care of patients with cancer provide the leadership in developing programs. The nursing staff functional statement reflects the competency level of nurses providing direct care. The VHA has committed significant resources and expertise to support the nurse with the diverse learning needs to support patients with cancer. Nationally, the VHA uses an Employee Education System (EES) for education and training (Rick, Kearns, & Thompson,

2003). Included with the EES priority are the ongoing mandatory education requirements and regulatory training (Rick et al.). The VHA has used advances in technology and developed visual and interactive learning, with feedback approaches for mandatory education for nurses. This implementation of desktop learning has provided nurses with greater feedback and offers the nurse manager opportunities for better use of resources to support nursing educational needs. The VHA has identified recruitment and retention of nursing staff as essential concerns in providing optimal care to the veterans. The influx of specialized care has increased the concern for the development and retention of specialized nursing staff. The VHA recognizes nursing as the structural support to provided care, and without nursing, many services would not be provided and care would be significantly compromised (VISN, 2002). Concerns for retention have caused VHA nurse leaders to develop focus groups that target nursing recruitment and retention as desirable nursing service goals (VISN). It has been the aim for nurses to be more involved in decision making and to feel valued and to work in clean, safe environments while receiving adequate compensation for services provided. The VA has been proactive in meeting the national nursing shortage through several initiatives.

The VA Learning Opportunities Residency (VALOR) program resulted in the hiring of newly qualified graduate nurses. The initiative provided the outstanding student with an opportunity to develop clinical competency while enrolled in school. The VHA has a clinical faculty associate position to support clinical teaching on the medical/surgical units. This initiative also required the position to support student nurse technicians who had been hired during the student's non-school hours, such as during summer or winter break. A special pay provision offers incentive toward employment because they are already oriented to the VA and its practice requirements, so they may be hired from one to three steps above the entry level established for new graduates.

Conclusion

This chapter was intended to provide the reader with a general overview of the structure and process of the VHA, its nursing structure and responsibilities, and its commitment to excellence in oncology care. The VHA ensures that all oncology care provided is obtained from evidence-based research and clinical trials. All cancer care programs are to adhere to the National VA Cancer Registry. These guidelines are the blueprints for a successful cancer program in the VHA. Because the VHA is a branch of the federal government, it is a very complex healthcare system requiring the knowledge of laws and directives. All of the laws and directives make management in the VHA challenging and exciting. It is the responsibility of the oncology care manager to maintain current knowledge of all cancer regimens. Maintaining a current knowledge base ensures that the veteran population will have safe, up-to-date health care. The VHA is committed to be the number one provider of health care for the veteran population.

References

American Cancer Society. (2004). *Cancer facts & figures.* Atlanta, GA: Author.

American College of Surgeons. (2003). *What is the Commission on Cancer?* Retrieved January 6, 2004, from http://www.facs.org/cancer/coc/cocar.html

Department of Veterans Affairs. (2003a). *Interagency agreement between the Department of Veterans Affairs and the National Cancer Institute for a partnership in clinical trials for cancer.* Retrieved October 26, 2004, from http://www1.va.gov/cancer/docs/NCI_VA_2000.doc

Department of Veterans Affairs. (2003b). *National cancer strategy.* Retrieved January 4, 2004, from http://www1.va.gov/cancer/docs/NationalCancerDirective.doc

Department of Veterans Affairs. (2003c). *VA heart of Texas health care network* [Memorandum 10N17-00-18]. Washington, DC: Author.

Hill, C. (2004, January 29). *Interview with insurance specialist.* Atlanta, GA.

National Commission on VA Nursing. (2001). *Veterans Commission on VA Nursing.* Retrieved January 4, 2004, from http://www1.va.gov/ncvan

National Commission on VA Nursing. (2003, July). *Department of Veterans Affairs.* Paper presented to VHA nursing leadership, Washington, DC.

Rick, C., Kearns, M., & Thompson, N. (2003). The reality of virtual learning for nurses in the largest integrated health care system in the nation. *Nursing Administration Quarterly, 27*(1), 41–57.

Stevens, D., Holland, G., & Kiser, K. (2001). Results of a nationwide Veterans Affairs initiative to align graduate medical education and patient care. *JAMA, 286,* 1061–1066.

Veterans Health Administration. (2004). *VHA health benefits & services.* Retrieved October 26, 2004, from http://www1.va.gov/health_benefits

Veterans Integrated Service Networks. (2002, January). *VISN 22: Report from RN recruitment & retention workgroup.* Paper presented at Nurse Recruiter's Working Group Executive Summary, Dallas, TX.

Radiation Oncology Management

Frances Cartwright-Alcarese, RN, MS, AOCN®

In 2003, an estimated 1.33 million individuals will be diagnosed with cancer in the United States, of which approximately 60% will require radiation therapy as a component of their care (Simmonds, 2003). Skin cancer is the most common cancer, followed by prostate, lung, colon, rectum, and urinary bladder in men and, in women, cancers of the breast, lung, colon and rectum, and uterine corpus. Radiation therapy is used definitively to cure some cancers without additional therapies. In addition, it is used in the adjuvant setting as part of a carefully orchestrated plan of care involving both surgery and medical oncology. This chapter will provide a description of the clinical, technical, and financial operations of a radiation oncology department. A more in-depth discussion can be found in a comprehensive radiation oncology textbook (Dow, Bucholtz, Iwamoto, Fieler, & Hilderley, 1997; Watkins-Bruner, Moore-Higgs, & Haas, 2001), as well as in the manuals, reviews, and studies that are cited in the related sections.

Types of Care/Services Provided

Radiation therapy causes differential cell killing of malignant cells over normal cells, leaving much of the normal tissue intact after completion of treatment. The goal of radiation therapy is to cure, control, palliate, or prophylactically treat the disease. Curative intent is the aim when the disease is confined to a local or regional site, and the expectation is that the radiation dose will completely eradicate the tumor. Radiation in the definitive setting is used in oropharyngeal, laryngeal, esophageal, brain, anal, bladder, and prostate cancers to preserve the normal anatomy and function while curing patients of their cancer. Control intent is to slow down and/or delay disease progression. Palliative intent is to decrease symptoms resulting from the tumor(s). In the palliative setting, radiation is a well-tolerated intervention that can treat both bone and soft tissue of metastases in a relatively short interval. Prophylactic radiation is given to prevent cancer growth in high-risk sites, such as cranial radiation in small cell lung cancer. Total body irradiation (TBI) can gain access to sanctuary sites within the body where chemotherapy is often ineffective and can aid in the treatment of hematologic disorders. Less frequently, radiation therapy is used to treat benign conditions related to or caused by uncontrolled tissue growth and/or inflammatory cell infiltration (DeLaney, 2003).

Radiation is used pre-operatively in rectal, esophageal, and lung cancer to shrink tumors and sterilize the surrounding stroma to increase the chances of a successful resection. Radiation is used postoperatively in many head and neck cancers, brain cancers, and breast, stomach, and rectal cancers to decrease the risk of a local recurrence.

Radiation Dose. The modern radiation reporting dose is the Gray (Gy), which is 100 rad of dose, or the centiGray (cGy), which is the same value as the rad (1,000 cGy = 1,000 rad). Historically, the Roentgen (R) was used as a unit of radiation exposure as measured in air, whereas the rad, or radiation absorbed dose, was used to quantify the dose absorbed by a patient's tissues.

Ionization Radiation. Ionization radiation occurs when energy is transferred to a particle causing a release of ions, or charged particles. Both photons and electrons of varying energy are used to cause ionizations within the cancerous tissues. The ionizations cause the formation of oxygen radicals in the cell. These radicals react with the DNA molecule causing both double stranded and single stranded breaks in the DNA. The double stranded breaks are considered the lethal injury for most cells. Because cancer cells are going through their cell cycle abnormally, cancer cells are more likely to have mis-assortment of genetic material when they attempt to undergo mitosis. The radiation dose is delivered using different radiation fraction sizes to take advantage of the known radiobiologic properties of various cell types. For example, squamous cell cancers of the oropharynx are known as a group to decrease their cell cycle length as the radiation treatment progresses; radiation dose is delivered twice a day, or accelerated fractionation, to prevent the adverse effects of the tumor's repopulation during the course of treatment. Radiation is cumulative, and damage continues for a period of time after radiation treatments are completed. This is an important concept for patients who are undergoing radiation therapy treatments to understand when describing the timing of side effects.

Radiosensitivity. Radiosensitivity refers to how the tissue responds to radiation but is not an indication of radiocurability. For example, a tumor can be radioresistant but radiocurable because the tissue and critical structures that need to be included in the field can tolerate the high dose needed. Several factors modify the biologic injury induced by radiation therapy and thus impact treatment response. Oxygen has been found to enhance the effects of ionizing radiation by aiding in the production of cell damage via radiation-induced free radicals (Kumar, Mocharnuk, & Harrison, 2000).

Radiation is commonly given concurrently with chemotherapy with a curative intent. For example, cisplatin (cis-platinum, CDDP, platinum, Platinol® [Bristol-Myers Squibb, New York, NY]) is used for locally advanced head and neck tumors. Cisplatin and fluorouracil (5-FU, Adrucil® [Sicor, Irvine, CA]) are combined and given concurrently for esophageal, stomach, and rectal cancers. Fluorouracil and mitomycin (mitomycin-C, Mutamycin® [Bristol-Myers Squibb]) are used concurrently for anal cancers. There are a number of innovative combinations being tested in both single institutions and multicentered trials, which may prove to be of benefit in the coming years.

Radiation and Delivery Systems

Advances in both treatment-planning software and radiation delivery systems have resulted in new strategies both to increase the radiation dose and to decrease the radiation treatment field while preserving efficacy, resulting in less injury to normal tissues.

Cobalt-60. A cobalt-60 radiotherapy unit is still used by some radiotherapy departments. It is an extremely reliable machine because it relies on a radioactive isotope, cobalt-60, to produce therapeutic radiation and can be used on most patients requiring palliative treatments and patients with relatively superficial tumors. However, the dose rate is lower compared to the linear accelerator, and as the cobalt decays, less radiation is delivered, thus lengthening the treatment time. The cobalt source must be replaced every five to six years.

Linear Accelerator. The linear accelerator is considered essential to any department because it produces high-energy photon and electron beams, capable of great precision in dose delivery. The linear accelerator moves on a gantry that is capable of moving 360 degrees around the patient to deliver sophisticated three-dimensional (3-D) therapy plans.

Three-Dimensional Conformal Radiation. 3-D conformal radiation is a treatment planning strategy using 3-D data acquired from either a computed axial tomography (CAT) scan or magnetic resonance imaging (MRI) to generate a digital reconstruction of the target volume and the surrounding critical structures. Using this information, blocks and beam modifiers are used to treat the 3-D object while sparing as much normal tissue as possible.

Intensity-Modulated Radiation Therapy (IMRT). IMRT is considered an improved form of 3-D conformal radiation. Using the principals of 3-D conformal therapy, IMRT allows the radiation oncologist to produce very complex distributions of radiation around critical and historically dose-limiting structures, such as the spinal cord and optic nerves.

Stereotactic Radiosurgery (SRS). SRS, performed by a linear accelerator or gamma knife unit, is a noninvasive procedure that delivers a high dose of radiation to a tumor-targeted area of the brain. It often is used instead of surgery to eliminate brain metastases. Other indications are for therapy of brain tumors and arteriovenous malformations in the brain. Law, Mangarin, and Frankel-Kelvin (2003) provided an in-depth discussion of the SRS procedure, reviewed possible side effects, and discussed the role of the radiation oncology nurse.

Brachytherapy. Brachytherapy is the use of a sealed radiation source (within a container) that delivers a prescribed dose to a well-defined space. Brachytherapy sources are either used via intracavitary insertion or interstitial insertion. An intracavitary source is inserted into a body structure, such as a cervix, vagina, or esophagus. An interstitial source is inserted directly into the tumor (e.g., prostate seed implant, base of tongue implant). Beyond these distinctions are dose rate considerations. Low dose rate implants usually are given over a period of several days to months, and high dose rate implants are given during a few minutes. Patients with temporary implants are radioactive while the source is in place. Permanent implants are radioactive until the source decays. The amount of time the patient remains radioactive depends on the radioactive source used (Watkins-Bruner et al., 2001). Abel, Dafoe-Lambie, Butler, and Merrick, (2003); Devine and Doyle (2001); Gosselin and Waring (2001); and Hogle, Quinn, and Heron (2003) provided an excellent discussion of brachytherapy procedures, nursing implications for treatment outcomes, and quality-of-life issues for breast, prostate, head and neck, and gynecologic cancers.

Unsealed Sources. Radiation oncology departments sometimes use unsealed radioactive isotopes. The most common example is iodine (^{131}I), which is primarily administered for primary and metastatic thyroid cancer. Strontium (^{90}Sr) is an isotope administered for bone metastases. It is delivered as a single injection, usually on an outpatient basis. Phosphorous (^{32}P) is an isotope administered intraperitoneally in the management of ovarian cancer. Because isotope therapy is unsealed, body fluids are contaminated. For the first week, it is usually necessary to maintain body fluid precautions.

Radiation Therapy Plan of Care

The planning and delivery of radiation therapy is a team effort that requires collaboration and coordination among the radiation oncologist, medical and surgical oncologists, physicist, dosimetrist, radiation oncology nurse, radiation therapist, and radiation safety officer. The radiation oncologist determines the dose to be delivered to the treatment field, indicating critical structures that need to be blocked, and the number and frequency of fractions to be delivered. The medical physicist and dosimetrist, using these parameters, develop treatment programs to calculate the dose distributions within the treatment field. The radiation therapist, under the direction of the radiation oncologist, delivers the radiation treatments according to the treatment plan by preparing the patient and the equipment daily as prescribed. Although the radiation oncology nurse is not directly involved in the treatment planning and delivery of radiation, he or she is responsible for essential aspects of the patient's care throughout the treatment process, and this care will greatly influence optimal outcome.

Consultation. A consultation is provided to the patient and family when radiation therapy is being considered as a treatment option. The consultation includes history and physical examination, review of previous tests and laboratory studies, discussion of the diagnosis, stage of disease, current health status, and efficacy of radiation therapy as an option. Other treatment options, including research protocols, along with the risks and benefits of each, should be included in the discussion. The radiation oncology nurse provides an in-depth discussion of the self-care activities that need to be maintained throughout the course of treatment.

Informed Consent. The radiation oncologist, prior to beginning any aspects of treatment planning, must obtain informed consent. The *Practice Guideline on Informed Consent—Radiation Oncology* (American College of Radiology [ACR], 2003b) requires that the physician inform the patient of the following: "(a) the nature of the patient's diagnosis and intended treatment; (b) reasonable treatment alternatives; (c) potential side effects, common complications, and benefits of treatment; and (d) potential consequences of refusal of treatment" (p. 527). The radiation oncology nurse ensures that the patient and family have an understanding of the treatment goal, the course of treatment, short- and long-term side effects, and alternative treatment options. The practice guideline also requires informed consent be obtained for "(a) external beam irradiation, including any tattoos given or photographs taken; (b) brachytherapy procedures; (c) administration of conscious sedation; and (d) any experimental therapy, which also requires Institutional Review Board (IRB) approval" (ACR, 2003b, p. 526). The radiation oncology nurse, preferably at this time but prior to the start of treatment, assesses the patient's knowledge and understanding of the informed consent, the treatment plan, side effect occurrence, and management strategies.

Simulation. The simulation is a procedure conducted on a machine that mimics the treatment capabilities of the actual treatment unit, but it is not capable of delivering radiation therapy. It is performed to determine the treatment field and to identify sensitive organs in the treatment field using x-rays and films. Structures and/or organs that do not need to be included in the treatment field are blocked by using lead alloy blocks, IMRT, 3-D conformal radiation, or similar technologies. Blocks, molds, casts, masks, and immobilization devices are used to ensure that the desired position is replicable, that the tumor field is maintained, and critical structures are protected. The radiation oncologist then writes the prescription plan that must be accurately replicated with each radiation treatment. To determine that the treatment plan can be replicated for each treatment, a setup is conducted. A setup consists of taking a port film or x-ray of the area to be treated, prior to the first radiation treatment, to ensure that the treatment is given as planned. A port film is taken regularly during the course of treatment (usually weekly). The *ACR Practice Guideline for Radiation Oncology* (ACR, 2000) indicated a port film must be taken at least every other week. Port films must be approved by the radiation oncologist prior to the first treatment and reviewed weekly.

Chart Rounds. Weekly chart rounds are held and usually include the radiation oncology team (radiation oncologist, radiation oncology nurse, radiation therapist, physicist, dosimetrist, and, whenever possible, the nutritionist, and social worker). During this meeting, port films, total dose delivered, and patient response are evaluated. The radiation oncology nurse discusses any issues with self-care, lab work, chemotherapy schedule, if applicable, and other indicators that may predict the patient's ability to complete the treatment without treatment interruptions.

On-Treatment Visits. On-treatment visits are conducted weekly for patients who are receiving a full course of radiation therapy. The radiation oncologist and the radiation oncology nurse see the patient. During this time, treatment response, acute side effects, and lab work are evaluated. Acute side effects occur within the first 90 days from the start of treatment. To ensure consistent assessment, acute side effects are graded by using either the *Radiation Therapy Patient Care Record: A Tool for Documenting Nursing Care,* a tool developed by the Radiation Oncology Special Interest Group (SIG) (Catlin-Huth, Haas, & Pollock, 2002) of the Oncology Nursing Society (ONS), or the Acute Radiation Morbidity Scoring Criteria developed by the Radiation Therapy Oncology Group (RTOG) (2003a). Early side effects are related to cell loss or death, inflammation, and edema. Side effect prevention/ management strategies are reinforced. Except for fatigue and anemia, which are expected, and significant systemic effects of radiation therapy (Magnan & Mood, 2003), side effects are site specific (Dow et al., 1997). The timing and severity of these effects will vary with the site being treated, total dose delivered, the presence of concurrent or induction chemotherapy as well as how well the side effects are managed. Bruner, Haas, and Gosselin-Acomb (2005) provided an excellent review of side effects and nursing care for the patient receiving radiation therapy. Many patients need to be seen by the radiation oncology nurse daily or twice daily for nursing care (e.g., patients with head and neck cancer receiving twice daily radiation treatments [hyperfractionization] requiring oral irrigation, patients requiring wound care in the treatment field, new tracheotomies requiring suctioning). This care is essential to the successful completion of the course of therapy. Patients on a short course of radiation therapy will be seen periodically to determine treatment response. For example, a patient receiving a two-week course of treatment for bone metastases may be seen daily to determine treatment response (e.g., pain relief). The radiation oncology nurse assesses patients in pain and collaborates with both the radiation oncologist and referring physician to ensure that pain management is optimal. In the case of patients receiving TBI, the radiation oncology nurses' role includes monitoring the patient's tolerance to treatment so that supportive care is planned and to communicate immunosuppressive precautions to the healthcare team and to the patient and family caregivers.

Follow-Up Care. Follow-up visits are conducted at specified time intervals after the patient completes the course of radiation therapy to assess tumor response, late side effects, and treatment sequelae. The radiation oncology nurse continues to monitor for side effects, complications, and issues of survivorship. Late side effects occur greater than 90 days to years post-radiation therapy. To ensure consistent assessment, late side effects are graded using the Late Radiation Morbidity Scoring Criteria (RTOG, 2003b). Late side effects are related to stromal changes. Bruner et al. (1998) provided an excellent review of late complications associated with radiation therapy.

Essential Networking

Oncology Nursing Society. ONS, a national organization of more than 30,000 RNs and other healthcare professionals, is dedicated to excellence in patient care, teaching, research, and education in the field of oncology. Information about ONS is available online (ONS, 2004). The Radiation SIG was established in 1989 to carry out the aims of ONS in the specialty field of radiation (ONS, 2003). The Radiation SIG has and continues to develop and implement strategies to address and enhance education, professional and patient resources, and leadership development in radiation oncology. Information and access to these resources are available online (ONS, 2003).

American College of Radiology. ACR is a nonprofit professional society composed of radiologists, radiation oncologists, and clinical medical physicists in the United States. ACR describes its primary purposes as follows: "(a) advance the science of radiology; (b) improve radiologic services to the patient; (c) study the socioeconomic aspects of the practice of radiology; and (d) encourage continuing education for radiologists, radiation oncologists, medical physicists, and persons practicing in allied professional fields" (ACR, 2003a). Consensus-driven practice guidelines and technical standards for radiation oncology practice are developed and revised as needed.

American Society of Clinical Oncology (ASCO). ASCO's membership is comprised of clinical oncologists, healthcare professionals, oncology nurses, and other healthcare practitioners who specialize in all fields of oncology, including medical, hematology, radiation oncology, surgery, and pediatrics (ASCO, 2003). Clinical practice guidelines and patient guides are available online.

American Society for Therapeutic Radiology and Oncology (ASTRO). ASTRO's mission is to advance the practice of radiation oncology by promoting excellence in patient care, providing opportunities for educational and professional development, promoting research and disseminating research results, and representing radiation oncology in a rapidly evolving socioeconomic healthcare environment. An associate membership is available to nurses. More information is available on its Web site (ASTRO, 2003).

Radiation Therapy Oncology Group. RTOG (2003c) is a national cancer study research group funded by the National Cancer Institute that is comprised of 250 major research institutions nationally and in Canada. RTOG, since 1968, has developed protocols that involve radiation therapy, either alone or in conjunction with surgery and/or chemotherapy, for the diagnosis and therapy of brain, breast, head and neck, lung, gastrointestinal, genitourinary, and gynecologic cancers. Quality-of- life indicators also are examined in these studies. The RTOG newsletter includes new studies, open studies, citations of recently completed published studies, and new patient education information.

National Comprehensive Cancer Network (NCCN). NCCN practice guidelines in oncology are the recognized standard reference for appropriate practice. These guidelines are site specific and are posted on the Web with the latest date and version number (NCCN, 2003).

Diseases/Sites Treated With Radiation Therapy

It is beyond the scope of this chapter to include all of the cancers treated with radiation therapy. Major cancers are briefly described below. Information about clinical trials related to radiation oncology can be accessed through RTOG. Comeau-Lew (1997) provided a discussion of major childhood cancers treated with radiation therapy.

Lung Cancer. Radiation therapy and chemotherapy are principle treatments in inoperable, unresectable, and potentially resectable lung cancer. RTOG clinical trials continue to examine escalating radiotherapy doses to achieve improved disease control.

Breast Cancer. Five to six weeks of external beam radiation therapy followed by a boost to the tumor bed remains the standard treatment for women treated with conservative surgery (excision of the tumor with clean margins and preservation of the breast). Brachytherapy is being examined for partial breast irradiation, with rows of catheters or the mammosite device to treat the lumpectomy cavity (Hogle et al., 2003). Postmastectomy radiation is considered for women who present with risk factors associated with local-regional recurrence (i.e., tumor size, number of positive lymph nodes, estrogen-receptor status, number of recovered lymph nodes) (NCCN, 2003). NCCN recommends that women with T3 tumors and/or four or more positive axillary lymph nodes receive postmastectomy radiation therapy.

Prostate Cancer. In its early, clinically localized stage, prostate cancer is treated with either radical prostatectomy or external beam radiotherapy. Patients with favorable features are treated with permanent seed or temporary high dose rate brachytherapy. For patients with advanced disease, the combination of brachytherapy and external beam radiation is used or external radiation by itself.

Head and Neck Cancer. In its early stage, head and neck cancer is treated definitively with surgery or radiation therapy (external beam and/or brachytherapy), whereas advanced tumors are treated with surgery combined with adjuvant irradiation. Some advanced tumors are treated with concurrent chemo-radiation therapy using an accelerated hyperfractionated treatment schedule.

Esophageal Cancer. Radiation therapy in combination with chemotherapy and/or surgery is an important treatment for esophageal cancer. A variety of clinical trials seek to identify new treatment strategies to improve survival.

Gastrointestinal Cancer. Many gastrointestinal malignancies are treated with adjuvant pre- or postoperative radiotherapy. Standard treatment for locally advanced disease is chemotherapy and irradiation.

Gynecologic Cancer. The primary treatment for early-stage cervical cancer is usually surgery. Radiation therapy is used if an unexpected poor prognostic factor is found at surgery. In patients with advanced cervical cancer, the standard of care is concurrent chemotherapy and radiation therapy using both a course of external beam irradiation and brachytherapy.

Central Nervous System Cancer. Radiation therapy is used to treat primary malignant and metastatic brain tumors alone or in combination with surgery. It is also used to treat benign tumors that have recurred or had an incomplete resection to prevent or inhibit the growth of the tumor. It can be used with a curative intent, to control tumors, or for palliation.

Regulatory Commissions and Practice Organizations

There are a number of agencies and groups that enforce regulations that mandate a safe working environment and/or equipment safety that address practice issues; many are necessary for third-party billing.

Nuclear Regulatory Commission (NRC). NRC regulates the licensing of radioactive sources produced in nuclear reactors and the safety of the general public and healthcare workers (NRC, 2003).

Americans with Disabilities Act (ADA). ADA is an act from the U.S. Department of Justice system that helps to prevent discrimination against individuals with disabilities, including a cancer diagnosis (U.S. Department of Justice, 2003).

Occupational Safety and Health Administration (OSHA). The OSHA Act of 1970 ". . . assures safe healthful working conditions for working men and women; by authorizing enforcement of the standards developed under the Act; by assisting and encouraging the States in their efforts to assure safe and healthful working conditions; by providing for research, information, education, and training in the field of occupational safety and health; and for other purposes" (U.S. Department of Labor, 2003).

Joint Commission on Accreditation of Healthcare Organizations (JCAHO). JCAHO is an independent, not-for-profit organization that evaluates and accredits more than 16,000 healthcare organizations and programs in the United States. JCAHO is the nation's predominant standard-setting and accrediting body in health care (JCAHO, 2003).

Radiation Safety

The radiation safety officer is responsible for monitoring and maintaining the safe use of radioactive substances. ACR (2003b) described in its guidelines activities that are included in this role.
(a) Maintain a roster of all individuals involved with radioactive sources, distribute and monitor film badges that measure staff radiation exposure, and report and follow up on these reports.
(b) Collaborate with the radiation oncology nurse to provide education to staff caring for inpatients receiving brachytherapy, isotopes, and intraoperative radiation.
(c) Participate in the development and revision of policies and procedures and standards of care related to radioactive substances.
(d) Participate in inspections conducted by regulatory agencies.

The radiation oncology nurse collaborates with the safety officer and other members of the team to integrate radiation safety into the education plan. It is essential that the radiation oncology nurse have an understanding of the principles of time, distance, and shielding to provide patient care, educate patients, and educate staff caring for patients receiving radiation therapy.

Principles of Time, Distance, and Shielding

The sum of time spent at varied distances from the radiation source will influence the total radiation absorbed. Because the closer the individual is to the source the greater radiation exposure, time spent close to the source should be limited. The general recommendation is no more than 30 minutes per 8-hour shift (Dunne-Daley, 1994).

Because the amount of exposure decreases at greater distances from the source, care should be given from the greatest point of distance possible. The radiation exposure is inversely related to the distance from the radiation source. The amount of radiation exposure decreases as the square of the distance from the radiation source increases. Therefore, distance is the single most significant factor that can be used to decrease a caregiver's exposure to radiation. The general recommendation for visitors is to be positioned six feet from the source (Dunne-Daley, 1994).

A lead shield is positioned to act as a barrier between the source and the caregiver and visitors. Used properly, the shield provides an additional protective barrier. Not used properly, it gives a false sense of security.

The radiation oncology nurse can use the principles of time, distance, and shielding to explain to the patient and family why the patient is alone in the room when receiving external beam radiation, or why staff and family limit their visits when patients are receiving brachytherapy procedures. The radiation oncology nurse plays an essential role in educating the staff regarding these principles and works with the nursing team to plan direct care activities so they can be performed with limited visits. It is important that the nurse assesses the patient prior to the brachytherapy procedure to ensure that there are no underlying conditions that would make it difficult or impossible to undergo this procedure. The radiation oncology nurse instructs the patient and family prior to the procedure that although the nurse will limit his or her time, appropriate, safe care will be rendered. The patient and family are instructed that visits will be limited to specified short periods of time, and that it may be helpful for the patient to bring crafts, books, or other items that will help the time go faster. When the patient and family are well informed, they are less likely to feel uncared for or isolated.

Staffing and Budgeting

Minimum nursing staffing requirements were first suggested and published by ACR (Bruner, 1990). Since that time, ONS has published the third edition of the *Manual for Radiation Oncology Nursing Practice and Education*, a guideline for radiation oncology nursing practice (Bruner et al., 2005). These manuals serve as useful tools that define the nurse's role and lend support to budgeting nursing positions; however, several factors, beginning in the 1990s, lead to the reduction of nursing positions in radiation departments. The delivery of radiation therapy treatments is rapidly becoming more complex. Although advanced technologies may improve clinical outcomes, their implementation requires more complex treatment planning and lengthened treatment delivery time, with a resultant increased need for radiation oncologists, dosimetrists, physicists, and radiation therapist resources. This competes with the increasing demand for nursing resources, which are not directed at the actual treatment planning and delivery, but are essential in ensuring that the caring aspects of physical, psychological, and social outcomes are optimal.

When considering staffing requirements of a radiation department, it is important to analyze the workload according to the patient population treated and their specific needs. When reviewing staffing needs, factors that need to be considered, in addition to general staffing guidelines, are (a) the percent of patients treated with curative, control, palliative, and prophylactic intent; (b) diagnoses, stage of disease, and related acuity of patients treated; (c) implementation of new technologies;

and (d) attention to quality of life needs related to the above mentioned factors. There is a need to examine the impact that nursing care has on patient outcome in radiation oncology. Outcomes that can be measured include number of treatment delays, severity of side effects, inpatient admissions, length of stay, and other costly interventions (Moore-Higgs et al., 2003b). It is also important, when considering staffing and budgeting, how much of nursing resources are being consumed with non-nursing functions. Moore-Higgs et al. (2003a) using a descriptive design, collected data from 281 licensed radiation oncology nurses to identify specific role functions. The investigators reported that in addition to performing administrative, clerical, patient care, and research activities and a strong educator role, the majority of radiation oncology nurses performed non-nursing tasks, such as stocking rooms, cleaning rooms and equipment, and completing forms. Using radiation oncology nursing resources in this manner is costly and inappropriately uses valuable nursing expertise better spent on the care of the patient.

Practice Concerns

The radiation oncology nurse needs to stay up to date with new information regarding patient education as well as advances in the treatment of patients with cancer requiring radiation therapy. The third edition of the *Manual for Radiation Oncology Nursing Practice and Education* (Bruner et al., 2005) comprehensively outlines education and practice content of the role of the radiation oncology nurse and includes assessment and teaching tools.

"Standards of Care" pertain to professional nursing activities performed by the radiation oncology nurse using the nursing process. The overall goal is to influence patients and families' overall health, well-being, and quality of life across the radiation therapy continuum. "Standards of Professional Performance" describe a competent level of behavior in the professional nursing role. Both standards of care and of professional performance are intended to provide a framework for radiation oncology nursing services. The reader is encouraged to supplement these standards with additional resources. For example, organizations described earlier under the section "Essential Networking" provide resources that can be accessed for up-to-date information related to the treatment and management of the patient receiving radiation therapy.

Aspects of Care: Adult. Muscari Lin (2001b) presented radiation therapy case studies, each followed by multiple-choice questions, which validate the radiation oncology nurses' understanding of the material so that optimal, effective physical, psychological, social, and educational outcomes can be achieved. This chapter includes current references for additional reading.

Aspects of Care: Pediatric. Comeau-Lew (1997) presented developmental aspects of illness from infancy through adolescence with nursing interventions, followed by interventions to manage radiation therapy–related side effects.

Aspects of Care: Support Resources. The radiation oncology nurse should be familiar with institutional and community resources to ensure that the patient has access to support resources. The reader is encouraged to access local, regional, and national cancer-related support resources that may be helpful to patients undergoing radiation therapy and their family members, which include support groups, one-on-one counseling, education and financial aid, and cancer-related events. For example, the American Cancer Society (ACS) has a variety of support resources that address the physical, psychological, social, and educational needs of patients with cancer and their families. Its Web site includes national, regional, and local activities (ACS, 2003).

Moore-Higgs et al. (2003b) suggested the use of practice guidelines, critical pathways, performance improvement clinical indicators, standards, and policies and procedures so that clinical, service, and financial outcomes can be measured.

Standards/Guidelines. The radiation oncology nurse can use the guidelines provided in the *Standards of Oncology Nursing Education: Generalist and Advanced Practice Levels* (Jacobs, 2003a) and the standards described in the *Statement on the Scope and Standards of Advanced Practice Nursing in Oncology* (Jacobs, 2003b) to integrate the aspects of nursing into the overall radiation oncology program. ACR's "Practice Guidelines for Radiation Oncology" (2000) described the activities that are integral to a radiation therapy quality assurance program. This document includes, but is not limited to, a detailed description of the following: treatment process, qualifications and responsibilities of personnel, patient and personnel safety, educational program, quality improvement, and documentation (ACR, 2003a). ACR develops and revises practice guidelines as the science of radiation therapy continues to advance. These guidelines are consensus driven and are approved by the Commission on Quality and Safety as well as the ACR Board of Chancellors, the ACR Council Steering Committee, and the ACR Council.

Continuous Performance Improvement. The radiation oncology department uses core measure data to identify critical processes and to develop performance improvement activities that will improve outcome. It is important to identify aspects that influence quality of patient care and to ensure that services are rendered in the most cost-effective manner possible. The operations of a radiation oncology department provide a framework that supports the patient care activities and will impact patient satisfaction and financial effectiveness. Lara (1997) included the following processes in daily operations: staffing, registration, scheduling, chart maintenance, transcription, filing, and database entries. Muscari Lin (2001a) listed details of the care delivery process as wait times (i.e., routine and those produced by inefficiencies) and determining decision points (i.e., those points at which judgments regarding how to proceed need to be made). Including these aspects, while using Muscari Lin's (2001a) suggestion to use a flow process with sticky notes and poster board to track each step, provides a process by which a corrective action plan can be developed by the interdisciplinary team based on specific problems identified. It is important to monitor the outcome of the action plan to evaluate if improvements are optimized and ongoing and if there is a need for change.

Hospital-based radiation oncology departments use performance measurements consistent with JCAHO standards (2003). Joint Commission Ambulatory Care Accreditation is available for radiation oncology clinics. Lara (1997) described the process improvement challenges and opportunities present in a radiation oncology department.

Care Maps/Critical Pathways. The care map identifies specific patient care needs and details planned interventions focusing on patient outcome. The radiation oncology nurse is in a pivotal position to work collaboratively with the interdisciplinary team to identify the patients' needs and to plan interventions. Care maps may provide an optimal alternative to the traditional nursing care plan because the patient follows a planned course of radiation therapy, with a range of predictable care management needs and expected outcomes. Bieck, Haller, Kugel, Price, and Fieler (1997) discussed the development and implementation of care maps in radiation oncology and described how care maps relate to quality improvement and nursing research.

Documentation. Documentation of nursing assessment, nursing interventions, and evaluation of patient outcomes are included in the patient's treatment record. The *Radiation Therapy Patient Care Record: A Tool for Documenting Nursing Care* (Catlin-Huth et al., 2002) provides instructions and tools to standardize the documentation of nursing care provided to patients receiving radiation therapy. Included in this care record are the initial nursing assessment/database form (see Figure 27-1), the patient medication record (see Figure 27-2), documentation of radiation therapy patient care (see Figure 27-3), assessment parameters (see Figure 27-4), and documentation of teaching and instructions (see Figure 27-5). Each set of instructions and tools are treatment-site specific. Using this patient care record provides an opportunity to standardize grading of radiation toxicities and improve consistency in reporting outcomes of nursing interventions. These outcomes can be correlated to the timing and intensity of toxicity-related treatment interruptions, completion of treatment, and hospitalizations, which may negatively impact the patient's and family caregivers' physical, psychological, social, spiritual, and financial aspects of caring, as well as, in some cancers, compromise clinical outcomes. For example, mucositis, pain, dysphagia, and interference with eating and chewing are major treatment complications experienced by individuals treated with radiation therapy to the head and neck. Multiple strategies to manage oral complications have been examined with varied results. Using the tools described previously provides an opportunity to standardize the documentation of the assessment, incidence, severity, and timing of side effects and patient adherence to strategies identified to manage side effects and outcomes.

Quality of Practice and Performance. The *Statement on the Scope and Standards of Advanced Practice Nursing in Oncology* (Jacobs, 2003b) described standards that provide a framework by which the quality of practice and performance can be measured and quantified. This document includes six standards of care with measurement criteria and seven standards of professional performance with measurement criteria that can be useful for developing job descriptions, describing competency requirements, defining roles, and measuring and evaluating clinical performance.

In the *Manual for Radiation Oncology Nursing Practice and Education*, Bruner et al. (2005) included a competency checklist, which is useful as an evaluation tool both for the beginner radiation oncology nurse and as a useful annual evaluation tool (see Figure 27-6).

Because treatment for the patient with cancer is based on the outcome of clinical trials, it is important that the radiation oncology nurse be up to date in and participate in research. It is essential that the care of the patient with cancer be evidenced based and that research be conducted in areas where this is lacking (e.g., quality of life, symptom management).

Consultation and Collaboration. Radiation oncology nurses provide consultation to nurses and healthcare providers regarding the healthcare needs and nursing care of the patient with cancer undergoing radiation treatment.

Figure 27-1. Radiation Therapy Initial Nursing Assessment/Database

Patient _____ MR#/RT# _____ Radiation Oncologist _____ Date ___

Diagnosis _____ Prefers Appointment in: AM _____ PM _____

VITAL SIGNS			
Temp:	Pulse:	Resp:	O_2 Sat:
BP:	Height:	Weight:	Pain (0-10) ____Site ___ Describe:_____

HISTORY OF PRESENT ILLNESS

Chief complaint:

Prior radiation therapy? ____No ____Yes, site treated _____ Facility _____
Prior chemotherapy?   ____No ____Yes, last treatment _____ Facility _____
Prior hormonal therapy? ____No ____Yes, last treatment _____ Facility _____

CURRENT MEDICATION / ALLERGIES

See Patient Medication Record

PAST MEDICAL HISTORY	
Medical:	Surgical:
Transfusion hx:	Family cancer hx:

SOCIAL HISTORY / HABITS

Lives with _____	Transportation _____
Tobacco ____Yes, Pack year history _____ ____No ____Quit _____	ETOH ____ Yes, freq _____ ____ Quit _____

Sleep hx:	Insomnia ____Yes ____No None _____	Difficulty getting to sleep	Difficulty maintaining sleep	Early AM awakening

REVIEW OF SYSTEMS

Constitutional	Fatigue level 0-4 ____	Fevers ___Yes ___No	Night sweats ____Yes ___No	Weight loss ____No ____Yes, ___lb / ___months
Eyes	Vision blurred ___Yes___No	Blind ____Yes ___No	Requires:	Glasses ____Con
Ears, Nose, Mouth, Throat	Hearing loss ____Yes ___No (Circle) R / L / Both sides	Difficulty swallowing ____Yes ___No	New lumps ____Yes ___No Location:
		Dentures ____None ____Upper ____Lower	Dental condition ____Good ____Fair ____Requires consult
	Hearing aide(s) ___Yes ___No		
Cardiovascular/ Respiratory	Heart attack ____Yes ___No	Cough ___Yes ___No	Orthopnea ___Yes___No
	Stroke ____Yes ____No	Dyspnea __Yes __ No	# pillows req _____
	Angina ___Yes ___No	O_2 @ ____L/min	Hemoptysis ___Yes ___No
	Pacer ___Yes ___No		Other:

(Continued on next page)

Figure 27-1. Radiation Therapy Initial Nursing Assessment/Database *(Continued)*

REVIEW OF SYSTEMS (CONTINUED)			
Gastrointestinal	Nausea ___Yes ___No	Ulcers ___Yes ___No	Dyspepsia ___Yes ___No
	Vomiting ___Yes ___No	Diarrhea ___Yes ___No	Blood in stools ___Yes ___No
	Constipation ___Yes ___No	Hemorrhoids ___Yes ___No	Feeding tube ___Yes ___No # ___cans of ___/day
Genitourinary	Dysuria ___Yes ___No	Frequency ___Yes ___No	Urinary incontinence ___Yes Type ___ ___ No	Vaginal itching ___Yes ___No
	Hematuria ___Yes ___No	Urgency ___ Yes ___No		Vaginal discharge ___Yes ___No Describe ___
Integumentary	Rashes ___Yes ___No Location:	Sores ___Yes ___No Location:	Edema ___Yes ___No Location:	Alopecia ___Yes ___No Location:
	Healing incision ___Yes ___No Location:	Vascular access ___R / L Port / CVC ___ R / L PIC / PICC Last flush: ___	Other:	
Neurologic/ Psychiatric	Oriented x ___ spheres	Headaches ___Yes ___No Depression ___Yes ___No	Vertigo ___Yes ___No	Syncope ___Yes ___No
	Memory ___Good ___Fair ___Poor	Seizures ___ No ___Yes, freq ___	Learning preference: ___Written ___Verbal___Video Barriers ___Yes ___No Specify ___	
Allergic/ Immunologic	Auto immune disorder ___Yes ___No Type ___	Seasonal allergies ___Yes ___No	Other:	
Musculoskeletal	Arthritis ___Yes ___No Location:	Weakness ___Yes ___No	Balance difficulty ___Yes ___No	Assistive device:
	ROM ___Normal ___Decreased in R / L UE ___Decreased in R / L LE	At Risk to Fall ___Yes ___No	ADL ___No limits ___ Needs dressing assistance ___ Needs meal assistance	Other:

Patient has problems with ____Child care ____ Spiritual issues ____ Financial issues ____Transportation
Specify:
_____
_____

Other concerns:
_____
_____
_____
_____

_____(____)   _____(____)   _____(___
Signature   Initials   Signature   Initials   Signature   Initials

Note. From *Radiation Therapy Patient Care Record: A Tool for Documenting Nursing Care* (pp. 13–14), by C. Catlin-Huth, M. Haas, and V. Pollock, 2002, Pittsburgh, PA: Oncology Nursing Society. Copyright 2002 by the Oncology Nursing Society. Reprinted with permission.

Figure 27-2. Patient Medication Record

PATIENT _____ MR#/RT# _____ DATE _____

PATIENT MEDICATION RECORD

Allergies_____

Pharmacy_____ Telephone_____

CHEMOTHERAPY

NEOADJUVANT (N) CONCURRENT (C)		DRUGS	LAST COURSE	FUTURE COURSE(S)	MEDICAL ONCOLOGIST
N	C				
N	C				
N	C				
N	C				

MEDICATIONS

DATE (PTA = prior to admission)	MEDICATION	DOSE	ROUTE	FREQ	DC'D	SAMPLES	REFILLS Amt Dispensed/ # of Refills/ Date Refilled/Initials

_____ ( ) _____ ( ) _____ ( )
Signature   Initials   Signature   Initials   Signature

(Continued on next page)

Figure 27-2. Patient Medication Record *(Continued)*

MEDICATIONS AND IV FLUIDS GIVEN IN DEPARTMENT DURING TREATMENT

DATE	TIME	MEDICATIONS AND IV FLUIDS	DOSE	ROUTE AND LOCATION	RESPONSE	INITIALS

_____   (   )   _____   (   )   _____
Signature   Initials   Signature

Note. From *Radiation Therapy Patient Care Record: A Tool for Documenting Nursing Care* (pp. 15–16), by C. Catlin-Huth, M. Haas, and V. Pollock, 2002, Pittsburgh, PA: Oncology Nursing Society. Copyright 2002 by the Oncology Nursing Society. Reprinted with permission.

Figure 27-3. Radiation Therapy Patient Care Record—Breast

PATIENT _____ MR#/RT# _____ DATE _____

RADIATION THERAPY PATIENT CARE RECORD—BREAST

Site		Surgical Procedure
Histology		Recurrence (Y / N) Location
Grade/Stage		Genetic Counseling (Y / N)
ER/PR Status		Protocol
HER-2 Status		Other
Menopausal Status		

ASSESSMENTS									
Dates									
(cGy or Gy) / Fx									
Comfort Alteration KPS									
Fatigue									
Pain Location									
Pain Intensity									
Pain Intervention									
Effectiveness of Pain Intervention									
Hot Flashes/Flushes									
Nutrition Alteration Anorexia									
Weight									
Skin Alteration Skin Sensation									
Radiation Dermatitis									
Mucous Membrane Alteration Drainage									
Drainage Odor									
Lymphedema Upper Arm (____ cm above elbow)	RT								
	LT								
Lymphedema Lower Arm (____ cm below elbow)	RT								
	LT								
Emotional Alteration Coping									
Sexuality Alteration									
Injury, Potential Bleeding/Infection	Date								
WBC									
Hemoglobin/Hematocrit									
Platelets									
Vital Signs TPR									
BP									
Other									
INITIALS									

Note. From *Radiation Therapy Patient Care Record: A Tool for Documenting Nursing Care* (pp. 15–16), by C. Catlin-Huth, M. Haas, and V. Pollock, 2002, Pittsburgh, PA: Oncology Nursing Society. Copyright 2002 by the Oncology Nursing Society. Reprinted with permission.

Figure 27-4. Assessment Parameters and Common Toxicity Criteria: Radiation Therapy Patient Care Record—Breast

COMFORT ALTERATION

Karnofsky Performance Score (KPS)
100%   Normal, no complaints
90%   Can perform normal activity, minor signs of disease
80%   Can perform normal activity with effort, some signs of disease
70%   Cannot do active work, but can care for self
60%   Requires assistance, but can meet most needs with assistance
50%   Requires considerable assistance and frequent medical care
40%   Disabled, requires special care
30%   Severely disabled, hospitalization indicated
20%   Very sick, supportive hospitalization needed
10%   Moribund, fatal processes progressing rapidly

Fatigue (ONS scale)
1   No fatigue
2   Mild fatigue
3   Moderate fatigue
4   Extreme fatigue
5   Worst fatigue

Pain Location
Write, in the box, the location of pain.

Pain Intensity
Record the patient's subjective rating of degree of pain, with ratings ranging from 0 (no pain) to 10 (severe pain).

Pain Intervention[c]
0   None
1   Over-the-counter medications
2   Nonsteroidal anti-inflammatory agents or non-opioids
3   Opioids
4   Adjuvant medication (e.g., neuroleptics [amitriptyline, carbamazepine])
5   Complementary and/or alternative methods

MUCOUS MEMBRANE ALTERATION

Drainage[c]
0   Absent
1   Present

Drainage Odor[c]
0   Absent
1   Present

EMOTIONAL ALTERATION

Coping[c]
0   Effective
1   Ineffective

Effectiveness of Pain Intervention[c]
0   No relief
1   Pain relieved 25%
2   Pain relieved 50%
3   Pain relieved 75%
4   Pain relieved 100%

Hot Flashes and/or Flushes[a]
0   None
1   Mild or no more than 1 per day
2   Moderate and greater than 1 per day
3   —
4   —

NUTRITION ALTERATION

Anorexia[a]
0   None
1   Loss of appetite
2   Oral intake significantly decreased
3   Requiring IV fluids
4   Requiring feeding tube or parenteral nutrition

SKIN ALTERATION

Skin Sensation[b]
0   No problem
1   Pruritus
2   Burning
3   Painful

Radiation Dermatitis[a]
0   None
1   Faint erythema or dry desquamation
2   Moderate to brisk erythema or patchy moist desquamation, mostly confined to skin folds and creases; or moderate edema
3   Confluent moist desquamation $\geq$ 1.5 cm diameter and not confined to skin folds; pitting edema
4   Skin necrosis or ulceration of full-thickness dermis; may include bleeding not induced by minor trauma or abrasion

SEXUALITY ALTERATION

0   Absent
1   Present

The cited parameters were established by
[a]National Cancer Institute (NCI) Common Toxicity Criteria, Version 2.0
[b]Radiation Therapy Oncology Group (RTOG), Version 2.0 or the RTOG SOMA Scales
[c]Oncology Nursing Society Radiation Documentation Tool Workgroup

Note. From *Radiation Therapy Patient Care Record: A Tool for Documenting Nursing Care* (pp. 15–16), by C. Catlin-Huth, M. Haas, and V. Pollock, 2002, Pittsburgh, PA: Oncology Nursing Society. Copyright 2002 by the Oncology Nursing Society. Reprinted with permission.

Figure 27-5. Teaching and Instructions—Breast

PATIENT _____ MR#/RT# _____ DATE _____

TEACHING AND INSTRUCTIONS—BREAST

	DATES/ INITIALS	METHOD	EVALUATION	PLAN	COMMENTS
General Care Nutrition					
Social Service					
Discharge Care					
Referrals					
Site-Specific Simulation					
Initial Treatment					
Side Effects					
Pain Intervention					
Menopause Symptom Management					
Skin Care					
Lymphedema Management					
Prevention/Other Breast Self-Exam					
Lymphedema Prevention					
Smoking Cessation					
Osteoporosis Prevention					
Genetic Counseling					

Method Codes
A = Personal session
B = Family conference
C = Booklet (specify)
D = Demonstration
E = Audio/video resource

Evaluation Codes
UE = Unable to evaluate (explain)
V = Verbalizes concept accurately
D = Demonstrates skill accurately
R = Needs review
NR = Not receptive to learning at this time (explain)

Plan Codes
RC = Reinforce concept
RD = Return demonstration
LOM = Learning objective met
RF = Referral to other healthcare givers (specify)

SOCIAL INFORMATION

Lives With (specify relationships)

Agency in Home
Durable Medical Equipment in Home
Transportation
Prescription coverage
Other

_____ ( ) _____ ( ) _____ ( )
Signature   Initials   Signature   Initials   Signature   Initia

Note. From *Radiation Therapy Patient Care Record: A Tool for Documenting Nursing Care* (pp. 15–16), by C. Catlin-Huth, M. Haas, and V. Pollock, 2002, Pittsburgh, PA: Oncology Nursing Society. Copyright 2002 by the Oncology Nursing Society. Reprinted with permission.

Figure 27-6. Clinical Practicum Evaluation Tool

	Satisfactory		
	Yes	No	N/A
Consultation, Simulation, and Treatment Planning Phase			
1. Identifies self and nursing role to patient			
2. Checks patient identification			
3. Verifies that informed consent has been obtained			
4. Obtains nursing history and assessment			
5. Identifies patient's physical and psychosocial needs			
6. Assesses patient's literacy level and ability to learn			
7. Teaches patient and family about general and site-specific side effects of radiation therapy and self-care measures			
8. Solicits questions to be sure patient and family understand teaching			
9. Explains treatment protocols appropriate to patient (e.g., external beam radiation, brachytherapy, radiosensitizers, radioprotectors, hyperfractionation, total body irradiation, combined modality therapy)			
10. Reinforces discussion of appropriate clinical trials and assists in informed consent process			
11. Documents individualized plan of care			
12. Communicates plan of care to patient, family, and radiation therapy team			
Treatment Phase			
1. Assesses patient for general side effects of treatment (e.g., fatigue, skin changes)			
2. Assesses patient for acute site-specific or modality-specific side effects of treatment (e.g., alopecia, mucositis)			
3. Initiates measures to manage general side effects (e.g., dry desquamation, moist desquamation, anorexia)			
4. Initiates measures to manage site-specific side effects (e.g., mucositis)			
5. Teaches self-care measures to manage side effects of treatment			
6. Alerts patient to report potentially dangerous or uncomfortable symptoms immediately to nurse or physician			
7. Monitors patient's psychological status and coping skills			
8. Explains procedures and answers patient's questions			
9. Documents patient's response to treatment and symptom management			
11. Institutes appropriate radiation safety precautions			
12. Consults and collaborates with other members of the healthcare team. Demonstrates effective communication skills			
13. Refers patients as needed to appropriate specialists (e.g., dietitian, pain management team, sexual counselor)			
14. Discusses discharge instructions with patient and family			
Follow-Up Phase			
1. Assesses patient for late effects of treatment			
2. Teaches or reinforces appropriate self-care measures			
3. Assesses patient for symptoms of recurrent disease			
4. Monitors patient's psychological status and coping skills			
5. Consults and collaborates with other members of the healthcare team as needed			
6. Checks appropriate laboratory and diagnostic data			
7. Reinforces need for patient to continue to report potentially dangerous or uncomfortable symptoms immediately to nurse or physician			
8. Evaluates and documents long-term response to therapy and side effects			
9. Refers patients as needed to appropriate specialists (e.g., dietitian, pain management team, sexual counselor)			
10. Instructs patient in cancer prevention and early detection measures			

Note. From *Manual for Radiation Oncology Nursing Practice and Education* (3rd ed., pp. 10–11), by D.W. Bruner, M.L. Haas, and T. Gosselin-Acomb (Eds.), 2005, Pittsburgh, PA: Oncology Nursing Society. Copyright 2005 by the Oncology Nursing Society. Reprinted with permission.

The radiation oncology nurse collaborates with the radiation oncologist, the physicist, and the radiation safety officer to include updates in radiation oncology as well as the concept of time, distance, and shielding into the education plan.

The radiation oncology nurse provides education to the staff that cares for patients receiving radiation implants. Because the same nurses may not always be caring for these patients, this education should be repeated each time a procedure is scheduled.

Staff Development: Role Development

The role of the nurse in radiation oncology has expanded to include care of the patient receiving external beam radiation, brachytherapy, intensity-modulated procedures, and proton beam programs. Bruner et al. (2005) described the scope of practice for the radiation oncology nurse.

> The radiation oncology nurse is a registered professional nurse who functions independently and interdependently with the radiation oncology team in providing quality patient care. The radiation oncology nurse provides clinical care, education, and consultation. The radiation oncology nurse may participate in the leadership roles of clinician, educator, consultant, and/or researcher. Using an evidence-based model of practice, the radiation oncology nurse will provide assessment, diagnosis, outcome identification, planning, implementation, and evaluation, focusing on the continuum of care to support the patients receiving radiation therapy, their families, and caregivers.
>
> It is recommended that minimal education for the radiation oncology nurse is a baccalaureate degree in nursing. Preferred nursing experience should include 2 years of oncology nursing; alternately, a 6–12 month didactic and clinically based preceptorship is highly recommended. Oncology nursing certification also is recommended.
>
> The advanced practice nurse (APN) in radiation oncology is a master's or doctorally prepared nurse with specialized knowledge and skills acquired through study and supervised practice. Regardless of certification requirements, all oncology APNs must be licensed in their state as an RN and are subject to that state's legal restraints, regulations, and privileges for recognition and licensure of advanced practice nursing (Jacobs, 2003). (p. 3)

Moore-Higgs et al. (2003a) provided a discussion of the literature that began defining the role and qualifications of the radiation oncology nurse during the past two decades. Using a descriptive design, they collected data from 281 licensed radiation oncology nurses and reported administrative, clerical, patient education, and research responsibilities. These investigators found that the role of the radiation oncology nurse varied based on the treatments and technology available, the population that is being served, and the staffing resources available, as well as the awareness of the importance of the role.

The ONS Radiation SIG provides a forum for the nurse to collaborate with his or her colleagues to develop and implement strategies to ". . . promote excellence in oncology nursing by improving the quality of care delivered to patients receiving radiation treatment through research, education and exchange of information" (ONS, 2003). ONS provides a voluntary credentialing process for the oncology nurse to become certified as an Oncology Certified Nurse (OCN®) or Advanced Oncology Certified Nurse Practitioner (AOCNP™)/Advanced Oncology Certified Clinical Nurse Specialist (AOCNS™). The radiation oncology nurse who becomes certified as an OCN or AOCNP/AOCNS substantiates that he or she has met all of the eligibility criteria and has mastered the knowledge to provide competent oncology nursing care. The nurse working in radiation oncology is challenged with staying up to date with the advances in the knowledge of radiation biology along with the rapid technologic growth. The radiation oncology nurse should stay current by attending conferences, participating in continuing education programs, and reading the literature.

Legal Issues

The privacy rule, issued as a result of the Health Insurance Portability and Accountability Act (HIPAA) of 1996, developed national standards to protect individuals' medical records, claims, and other personal health information (U.S. Department of Health & Human Services, 2003). The covered entities (insurers, group health plans, providers, clearing houses) and their business associates are required to train all staff on these privacy policies and procedures. Radiation oncology departments are responsible for ensuring that the entire team participates in initial HIPAA training and ongoing updates.

Informed Consent

The informed consent process follows federal guidelines and the institution's own regulation process. The practice guideline on informed consent concerning radiation oncology requires consent be obtained for "(a) external beam irradiation, including any tattoos given or photographs taken, (b) brachytherapy procedures, (c) administration of conscious sedation, and (d) any experimental therapy, which also requires Institutional Review Board (IRB) approval" (ACR, 2003b, p. 526). The role of the radiation oncology nurse during the consent process is that of patient educator and patient advocate. The nurse is responsible for the patient's and family's understanding of the information presented, including purpose of the treatment, clinical trials available (including aim and alternate treatments), and risk versus benefit (discussion of treatment goal [i.e., cure, control, palliation] versus acute and late side effects) (Bruner et al., 2005).

Reimbursements

Reimbursement levels for radiation therapy services along with most cancer services have decreased; however, some radiation therapy codes have increased. The proposed rule for ambulatory payment classifications was reported in August 2003. Because of the differential impact of these reimbursement changes, all radiation therapy services need to be examined in planning beyond 2004. The radiation oncology nurse as well as administrators, billing managers, physicians, radiation therapists, dosimetrists, physicists, patient accounting staff, and financial service professionals should have an understanding of the new and changing CPT/HCPCS/ICD-9 coding and usage rules planned for 2004 and beyond. Recognizing common coding mistakes, the use of modifiers and proposed modifiers, especially for outpatient hospital procedures and freestanding centers, and a basic understanding of coding scenarios of specialty procedures, such as IMRT, SRS, 3-D, and brachytherapy, are essential.

Abbey (2001) provided a discussion of maintaining an effective reimbursement system that can be applied to radiation therapy delivered in the hospital-based programs, paid under Medicare Part A, or the freestanding centers or private practices, paid under Medicare Part B. It is essential that the financial manager of the radiation therapy department stay up to date with regulatory changes, which can drastically change the reimbursement of hospital-based versus freestanding radiation therapy.

Patient Billing

Codes for services associated with the technologic and medical components of treatment are listed in the *Current Procedural Terminology* (American Medical Association, 2003). Estimated or established costs of equipment, supplies, operations, salaries, and workloads associated with individual codes need to be considered to evaluate true revenue and productivity. Mills, Spanos, Jose, Kelly, and Brill (2000) provided a description of the complexity of technical and professional billing associated with radiation oncology, exemplifying the resources that are involved in providing radiation oncology services with a rationale to defend costs. For radiation oncology, there is separate payment for diagnostic procedures such as simulation, port films, guidance under ultrasound, isodose planning, dosimetry, simulation, physics, treatment, devices, brachytherapy and seeds, radioelement applications, therapeutic nuclear procedures, special procedures, and facility fees associated with visits. This payment is made for the technical component of services only. Professional fees are billed on the HCFA 1500 form, and global billing will be discontinued.

Abbey (2001) pointed out that it is essential that staff members who are responsible for making entries into the charge master understand the financial significance of the entries. This is very pertinent to radiation oncology, where there are a varied number of technical components and complex cases. Ensuring that a "user friendly" system is in place is also essential.

Business Plans

The development of a business plan is essential for the establishment of a new radiation therapy program or expansion of an existing one. A business plan is a written document that clearly defines the goal of the program and outlines the methods for achieving them. Business plans generally consist of the following key components.
- Definition and description of the program/service (if an existing program, include current utilization statistics)
- Industry trends
- Analysis of the market
- Financial projections and requirements

Because radiation therapy is a fixed-cost business, the goal is to increase patient volumes while carefully managing and evaluating how staffing resources are being used. Key success factors in developing a radiation oncology business plan include an overall market analysis that incorporates the department's current situation, accessible target areas not being captured, and a review of what resources would be needed to capture that population in terms of staff expertise, staff availability, technology, and marketing. An analysis of competition in regard to these possible resource investments is necessary, as well as review of key competitive capabilities and competitive weaknesses.

Program Definition/Description

This section should include a narrative description of the proposed new program or expansion of an existing program. Key factors driving the need for the program should be highlighted. Historical statistics need to be gathered and analyzed that include the annual new radiation treatments and patient characteristics (e.g., diagnoses, stage of disease, referring physician). These statistics will need to be tracked on an ongoing basis once the program is operational.

Industry Trends

Patients and current and potential referring physicians view new technology as an essential characteristic of a state-of-the-art radiation oncology department. IMRT is rapidly being adopted by many centers. Because of the rapid development in radiation oncology technology, the depreciation time frame may be considerably lessened. The need to recruit new staff and/or the time and resources needed to train staff to manage new technology is an essential part of the business plan. As indicated in the section entitled "Reimbursement," the payor, using different reimbursement systems, can greatly impact the profitability of a radiation therapy program. These factors must be included in the business plan.

Market Analysis

If the business plan is for an existing program that seeks to expand, measurement of current market share is useful. Internal utilization statistics for a defined market can be compared to total numbers for that same geographic area if available. These statistics provide an indication of existing business that might be captured. Statewide databases operated by health departments, hospital associations, or other related entities often have such statistics available. Alternate data sources include proprietary databases that have been compiled through analysis of insurance claims. These statistics can be compared to the same characteristics of the institutions/catchment area as an indicator of missed target opportunities at the home site. The information technology department is a good resource to assess opportunities to obtain these data. Some examples include the hospital's tumor registry and the statewide utilization databases (e.g., SPARCS data set in New York State). It is important also to track major cancers treated with radiation therapy to show which cases generate the greatest radiation therapy profit.

Financial Requirements/Projections

The financial section of the business plan should include projected volume, associated revenue, and expenses. Volume projections generally are based on a number of factors, including unmet demand, overall market size and projected market share shifts, and related incidence and prevalence.

Expenses should include an estimate of capital and operating expenses. Capital expenses generally include equipment and construction, whereas operating expenses include staff salaries and fringe benefits, office and medical supplies, equipment maintenance, and other expenses necessary to operate the program.

Summary

Radiation oncology remains a major modality of cancer treatment. As advances in technology and delivery systems continue to evolve, along with treatment strategies that improve the efficacy of radiation therapy, it is important for the nurse in radiation oncology to remain the expert. The nurse in radiation oncology is in a pivotal position to advance education, research, and clinical care in this exciting field. The radiation oncology nurse manager plays a leading role in the operations related to care of the individual receiving radiation therapy.

References

Abbey, D.C. (2001). Designing and maintaining an effective chargemaster. *Healthcare Financial Management, 55*(3), 50–55.

Abel, L., Dafoe-Lambie, J., Butler, W.M., & Merrick, G.S. (2003). Treatment outcomes and quality-of-life issues for patients treated with prostate brachytherapy. *Clinical Journal of Oncology Nursing, 7,* 48–54.

American Cancer Society. (2003). *ACS homepage.* Retrieved December 5, 2003, from http://www.cancer.org/docroot/home/index.asp

American College of Radiology. (2000, January 1). *ACR practice guidelines for radiation oncology.* Retrieved December 4, 2003, from http://www.acr.org

American College of Radiology. (2003a). *ACR homepage.* Retrieved December 4, 2003, from http://www.acr.org

American College of Radiology. (2003b). *ACR practice guideline on informed consent—Radiation oncology* (pp. 525–528). Retrieved December 4, 2003, from http://www.acr.org/

American Medical Association. (2003, November). *Current procedural terminology.* Chicago: Author.

American Society of Clinical Oncology. (2003). *ASCO homepage.* Retrieved December 5, 2003, from http://www.asco.org

American Society for Therapeutic Radiology and Oncology. (2003). *About ASTRO.* Retrieved December 5, 2003, from http://www.astro.org/about_astro/governance/mission.htm

Bieck, P., Haller, M., Kugel, K., Price, L., & Fieler, V. (1997). Care maps in radiation oncology. In K.H. Dow, J.D. Bucholtz, R. Iwamoto, V. Fieler, & L. Hilderley (Eds.), *Nursing care in radiation oncology* (2nd ed., pp. 401–420). Philadelphia: Saunders.

Bruner, D.W. (1990). Report on the Radiation Oncology Nursing Subcommittee of the American College of Radiology Task Force on Standards of Development. *Oncology, 4*(8), 80–81.

Bruner, D.W., Haas, M.L., & Gosselin-Acomb, T. (Eds.). (2005). *Manual for radiation oncology nursing practice and education* (3rd ed.). Pittsburgh, PA: Oncology Nursing Society.

Catlin-Huth, C., Haas, M., & Pollock, V. (Eds.). (2002). *Radiation therapy patient care record: A tool for documenting nursing care.* Pittsburgh, PA: Oncology Nursing Society.

Comeau-Lew, C. (1997). Pediatric cancers—The special needs of children receiving radiation therapy. In K.H. Dow, J.D. Bucholtz, R. Iwamoto, V. Fieler, & L. Hilderley (Eds.), *Nursing care in radiation oncology* (2nd ed., pp. 316–351). Philadelphia: Saunders.

Delaney, T.F. (2003). Radiation therapy's other role. *Advance for Imaging and Oncology Administrators, 13*(10), 69–70.

Devine, P., & Doyle, T. (2001). Brachytherapy for head and neck cancer: A case study. *Clinical Journal of Oncology Nursing, 5,* 55–58.

Dow, K.H., Bucholtz, J.D., Iwamoto, R., Fieler, V., & Hilderley, L. (1997). *Nursing care in radiation oncology* (2nd ed.). Philadelphia: Saunders.

Dunne-Daley, C. (1994). Education and nursing care of brachytherapy patients. *Cancer Nursing, 17,* 434–435.

Gosselin, T.K., & Waring, J.S. (2001). Nursing management of patients receiving brachytherapy for gynecological malignancies. *Clinical Journal of Oncology Nursing, 5,* 59–64.

Hogle, W.P., Quinn, A.E., & Heron, D.E. (2003). Advances in brachytherapy: New approaches to target breast cancer. *Clinical Journal of Oncology Nursing, 7,* 324–331.

Jacobs, L.A. (2003a). *Standards of oncology nursing education: Generalist and advanced practice levels* (3rd ed.). Pittsburgh, PA: Oncology Nursing Society.

Jacobs, L.A. (2003b). *Statement on the scope and standards of advanced practice nursing in oncology* (3rd ed.). Pittsburgh, PA: Oncology Nursing Society.

Joint Commission on Accreditation of Healthcare Organizations. (2003). *Setting the standards for quality in health care.* Retrieved December 5, 2003, from http://www.JCAHO.org/accredited+organizations/svnp/svnp_index.htm

Kumar, P., Mocharnuk, R., & Harrison, L.B. (2000, March 13). *Adverse effects of anemia on radiation therapy and quality of life.* Retrieved December 5, 2003, from http://www.medscape.com/viewprogram/584_pnt

Lara, A.E. (1997). Continuous process improvement: One department of radiation oncology's experience. In K.H. Dow, J.D. Bucholtz, R. Iwamoto, V. Fieler, & L. Hilderley (Eds.), *Nursing care in radiation oncology* (2nd ed., pp. 365–370). Philadelphia: Saunders.

Law, E., Mangarin, E., & Frankel-Kelvin, J. (2003). Nursing management of patients receiving stereotactic radiosurgery. *Clinical Journal of Oncology Nursing, 7,* 387–392.

Magnan, M., & Mood, D.W. (2003). The effects of health state, hemoglobin, global symptom distress, mood disturbance, and treatment site on fatigue onset, duration, and distress in patients receiving radiation therapy. *Oncology Nursing Forum, 30,* 33–39.

Mills, M.D., Spanos, W.J., Jose, B.O., Kelly, B.A., & Brill, J.P. (2000). Preparing a cost analysis for the section of medical physics—Guidelines and methods. *Journal of Applied Clinical Medical Physics, 1*(2), 76–85.

Moore-Higgs, G.J., Watkins-Bruner, D., Balmer, L., Johnson-Doneski, J., Komarny, P., Mautner, B., et al. (2003a). The role of licensed nursing personnel in radiation oncology part A: Results of a descriptive study. *Oncology Nursing Forum, 30,* 51–58.

Moore-Higgs, G.J., Watkins-Bruner, D., Balmer, L., Johnson-Doneski, J., Komarny, P., Mautner, B., et al. (2003b). The role of licensed nursing personnel in radiation oncology part B: Integrating the ambulatory care nursing conceptual framework. *Oncology Nursing Forum, 30,* 59–64.

Muscari Lin, E. (2001a). Administrator/coordinator role. In E. Muscari Lin (Ed.), *Advanced practice in oncology nursing* (pp. 377–394). Philadelphia: Saunders.

Muscari Lin, E. (2001b). Radiation therapy. In E. Muscari Lin (Ed.), *Advanced practice in oncology nursing* (pp. 119–135). Philadelphia: Saunders.

National Comprehensive Cancer Network. (2003). *Guidelines for the treatment of breast cancer.* Retrieved December 5, 2003, from http://www.nccn.org/physicain_gls/toc.heml

Nuclear Regulatory Commission. (2003). *Homepage.* Retrieved December 12, 2003, from http://www.nrc.gov/

Oncology Nursing Society. (2003, November 18). *Radiation Special Interest Group.* Retrieved December 5, 2003, from http://radiation.ons.wego.net/?v2_group=0&p=4918

Oncology Nursing Society. (2004). *ONS online.* Retrieved December 5, 2003, from http://www.ons.org

Radiation Therapy Oncology Group. (2003a). *Acute radiation morbidity scoring criteria.* Retrieved December 5, 2003, from http://www.rtog.org/members/toxicity/acute.html

Radiation Therapy Oncology Group. (2003b). *Late radiation morbidity scoring criteria.* Retrieved December 5, 2003, from http://www.rtog.org/members/toxicity/late.html

Radiation Therapy Oncology Group. (2003c). *Protocols.* Retrieved October 16, 2003, from http://www.rtog.org/index.html

Simmonds, M.A. (2003). Cancer statistics, 2003: Further decrease in mortality rate, increase in persons living with cancer. *CA: A Cancer Journal for Clinicians, 53*(1), 2–3.

U.S. Department of Health & Human Services. (2003, August 4). Office for Civil Rights— HIPAA. *National standards to protect the privacy of personal health information.* Retrieved December 7, 2003, from http://www.hhs.gov/ocr/hipaa/

U.S. Department of Justice. (2003, July 23). *ADA regulations and technical assistance materials.* Retrieved December 5, 2003, from http://www.usdoj.gov/crt/ada/publicat.htm

U.S. Department of Labor. (2003, December 11). *OSHA homepage.* Retrieved December 12, 2003, from http://www.ohsa.gov/

Watkins-Bruner, D., Moore-Higgs, G., & Haas, M. (2001). *Outcomes in radiation therapy: Multidisciplinary management.* Sudbury, MA: Jones & Bartlett.

Ambulatory Care Management

Anne M. Ireland, RN, MSN, AOCN®
Virginia R. Martin, RN, MSN, AOCN®

The current healthcare delivery system has created a new highly competitive marketplace where economics influence many healthcare decisions. The health system has historically been based on a medical model, with more emphasis on acute care rather than preventive care. Some of the many changes in health care include a shift from acute to ambulatory care, from primary to preventive care, from a fee for service to a managed care insurance system, and, simultaneously, there have been major advances in the treatment of chronic health problems (American Academy of Ambulatory Care Nursing [AAACN], 1997a). New available treatments are adding to life expectancy and productive years. The healthcare industry has shifted, as a result of these influences, from a hospital-centered system to one focused on the outpatient system. Ambulatory care always has been organized around the physician's delivery of reimbursable clinical care to the individual who seeks out care when ill, which resulted in a physician being in control of the ambulatory system (Haas, Hackbarth, Kavanagh, & Vlasses, 1995). Today, that influence has shifted as a result of all the changes in health care.

The specialty of oncology care has moved from the inpatient to the outpatient setting. It is estimated that 85%–95% of oncology care takes place in the outpatient area (Martin, 1996; Shirkman, Cloutier, Tittle, Massaro, & Munroe, 1999). Complex technology and treatments and the management of crises or adverse effects once dealt with only in the inpatient setting now occur in outpatient settings. These changes have profoundly affected both the nurse and the patient. Additionally, current positive trends in oncology include a longer survival time for patients with cancer and the development of supportive medications, affording the opportunity for outpatient management.

The ambulatory patient population has changed and has new characteristics along with changes in the healthcare system. A major patient advantage of ambulatory care is that it is potentially less disruptive; people are able to maintain their jobs and family life and have more control in this setting. Today, ambulatory patients are as diverse as inpatients in their clinical presentations, and the ambulatory criterion is no longer exclusive to the patients cared for in this setting. Acuity has changed, and an increased number of patients with chronic illnesses have complex treatments in this setting. Patients are informed consumers because of the wide availability of media coverage and data available regarding health issues (Hastings, 2001). The consumers not only want access to health care but also want it at a reasonable cost and quality. Each ambulatory patient has a constituency of family members and/or concerned others who may be involved in his or her care between visits, especially given the wide practice of early hospital discharge.

The nursing roles in ambulatory care have not been immune to the changes in health care or in the ambulatory patient population. Nursing in this setting has developed into a specialty practice. AAACN was founded in 1978 as an association with the purpose of targeting ambulatory nurse leaders. Today, AAACN is an association of professional nurses who identify ambulatory care practice as essential to the continuum of high-quality, cost-effective health care. The mission of AAACN is to advance the art and science of ambulatory care nursing practice. The major issue confronting nurse leaders in ambulatory care is being able to articulate and demonstrate the value nurses contribute to the specialty. The ambulatory nursing manager has many challenges to support the staff roles, develop new programs, accommodate volume and acuity changes, and continually strive toward quality improvement initiatives.

Factors Influencing Ambulatory Care Practice

Ambulatory care delivery is affected by four types of factors: environmental support, support services, patient related, and personnel (Martin & Xistris, 2000). How the office or practice space is designed, what hours of operation exist, computer information systems or operating systems used, and the types of services offered are all environmental factors. Whether the ambulatory setting has a laboratory on site or uses an off-site facility, how the medical records are kept, transportation support services, supplies, housekeeping, and environmental maintenance and repair are support services critical to the delivery of care. The types of patients (medical, surgical or radiation, adult or pediatric), the volume, the acuity, and the telephone call systems or other systems used for care are the patient-related factors. The personnel factors include the types of staff employed, the skill mix of the staff, and the support services, such as social work, rehabilitation, pharmacy, and nutrition care. Close coordination of all these factors influences the amount of disruption a patient experiences.

Types of Care/Services Provided

There are six broad categories of ambulatory practice settings in the United States: university hospital-based, community hospital-based, health maintenance organization clinics and services, solo or physician group practices, federal government health systems, and the community and freestanding centers (AAACN, 1997a; Haas et al., 1995; Martin & Xistris, 2000). In the past, the university/hospital outpatient departments were set up to fulfill the mission of academic centers. Now that focus includes the need for a flow of patients to fill beds. Community hospital outpatient departments were traditionally a charitable function for the community. Today they may include surgery centers, cardiac rehabilitation, drug and alcohol programs, work-site health promotion programs, hospice and community health programs, urgent care centers, and infusion centers. The physician group or private practice remains the principal mode by which physicians provide ambulatory services. Today, that group includes alignments into larger groups or affiliations with hospitals rather than the solo private practice groups of the past. Health maintenance organizations provide a stated range of services to a defined population through prepayment of a fee. These are care systems, and the focus is on prevention and maintenance. The federal programs were mandated to serve specific populations, such as the veterans, and were, until recently, free of charge to those members.

Oncology outpatient care can be delivered in any of the settings described. The services typically available for patients with cancer include prevention, screening, and detection; medical/hematology oncology; chemotherapy; surgical oncology, including outpatient surgery; radiation therapy; blood component therapy; patient and family education; financial counseling; discharge planning referral; nutrition support; group/individual counseling; physical therapy/rehabilitation; supply and prescription procurement; survivor services; and symptom management (Houston & Houston, 1993; Lamkin, 1994). Medical oncology or hematology oncology practices often are located separate from radiation or surgical oncology practices. However, some centers, for example, National Cancer Institute (NCI)-designated comprehensive cancer centers and community cancer centers, may contain all three modalities or a combination of two of the oncology services. Some examples of ambulatory oncology practices may include chemotherapy and transfusion therapy centers, day hospitals, freestanding clinics, radiation treatment centers, outreach or network programs, clinics for screening and prevention of cancer, and genetic screening programs. Complementary therapy programs may be offered within chemotherapy infusion centers and provide such programs as acupuncture, relaxation therapy, specialized nutrition counseling, and/or massage therapy. Clinical research is found most often in the office or academic setting.

Ambulatory Care Nursing Role

The historic role of the staff nurse in ambulatory care is the "traffic cop." Verran's publication in 1981 of the taxonomy of the domain of ambulatory nursing practice was the first in a series of efforts to define and describe ambulatory nursing practice. Barhamand (1991) detailed the role, benefits, and realities of the office-based oncology nurse. The author concluded that the office-based oncology nurse functioned as a multifaceted, independent practitioner in much of his or her daily role. The majority of the nurse's daily responsibilities fell into four categories: nursing-related activities, administrative duties, clerical-related activities, and ancillary activities. The most frequently reported nursing-related tasks were managing telephone calls and providing psychological support for the patient. Within the nursing-related tasks, Barhamand classified the tasks as routine (vital signs, height, weight), midlevel (venipuncture, mixing chemotherapy), requiring special skills (venous access devices, electrocardiograms), or requiring a higher level of independence (facilitating a support group).

In 1992, the Oncology Nursing Society (ONS) conducted a national survey designed to address the salary, staffing, and professional practice patterns in ambulatory oncology settings. Nursing activities reported from this study included patient and family teaching; care of catheters, ports, and pumps; patient assessments; treatment delivery; toxicity management; and facilitating support groups.

Porter (1995) has presented the notion that nurses function in one of two ways in an ambulatory oncology practice model: as a complement or as a substitute. The "nurse as complement" performs activities to assist a physician in the medical care of a patient. The nurse's responsibilities revolve around fulfilling the physician's requirements for assistance with patient care. In this practice setting, the nurse's job description will support the notion of nurse as complement by focusing on task-based functions and will not delineate expectations for professional practice. The "nurse as substitute" performs similar tasks and functions to meet similar needs as the physician. In collaborative practice settings, the nurse has an expanded role that includes nursing assessment, patient counseling, and side effect management. The nurse can function independently from the physician, coordinating and managing the care of a select group of patients on a daily basis. Porter stated this level of performance requires that the nurse have a "comprehensive understanding of oncology, immunology, community health, and critical care, as well as expert competency and leadership as direct caregiver, educator, manager, collaborator, and researcher" (p. 22).

There are eight core dimensions of the current clinical practice role in ambulatory care: enabling operations, technical procedures, nursing process, telephone communications, advocacy, teaching, care coordination, and expert practice (Hackbarth, Haas, Kavanagh, & Vlasses, 1995). Nurses practice autonomously but with a high degree of interdisciplinary focus, as the entire healthcare team is needed in care delivery. The healthcare team members may include any of the following: physicians, nurse practitioners, physician assistants, RNs, licensed practical nurses, medical assistants, nursing assistants, and receptionists.

The managers are challenged to minimize role overlap with practitioners, using the best mix of staff in the most cost-efficient manner. RNs frequently are targeted for reduction in numbers because of cost, and yet patient acuity is rising, and there is a need for highly trained RNs to handle this acuity.

AAACN (1997a) supported a survey to describe the scope and dimensions of the staff nurse in the ambulatory setting and hypothesized on future developments that would affect this role. The authors identified "core dimensions" of the ambulatory nurse's role as well as tasks that could be delegated to others (Hackbarth et al., 1995; Haas, 1998). The core dimensions are listed in Figure 28-1. A survey of the ambulatory care nursing role reported that nurses spent significant amounts of time enabling clinic operations and procedures (e.g., setting up rooms, searching for space and equipment, transporting clients, collecting specimens) and less time performing tasks that required a nurse (e.g., patient teaching, advocacy, telephone triage) (Haas

& Hackbarth, 1995; Hackbarth et al.). Less time was spent on complex dimensions such as care coordination and expert practice. The barriers to performing these higher-level skills included lack of time, lack of support staff, excessive paperwork, administrative blocks to clinical practice, excessive number of patients, lack of monetary resources, and physician resistance (Haas & Hackbarth, 1995; Hackbarth et al.). Lack of adequate space was another barrier. Without adequate exam rooms, space for files and teaching materials, or access to a telephone and computer, nurses find it difficult to coordinate and provide quality care.

Figure 28-1. Current Consensus of Role Dimensions in Ambulatory Care Nursing

- Assessment and triage
- Prevention
- Clinical procedures
- Collaboration
- Care management
- Patient education
- Advocacy
- Telephone practice
- Communication and documentation
- Outcome management
- Protocol development and use

Note. Based on information from Haas, 1998.

ONS completed a survey in 2002 to further delineate the roles and responsibilities of the ambulatory/office nurse in oncology. The survey included questions related to salary and credentials, staffing systems, areas of delegation, legislative involvement, and level of activity within the ONS organization. Survey results will be published in 2004 and should assist in providing a current view of the role of the ambulatory oncology nurse.

In 1998, AAACN convened a "think tank" to develop a conceptual framework for ambulatory care nursing. The group identified 61 core areas of knowledge and skills and categorized them under three roles, which are a part of ambulatory care nurses' practice daily. The role components are the organization/system role, the professional role, and the clinical nursing role (Haas, 1998, 2001).

Today, the ambulatory care nurse is more noted for rapid assessment skills and develops long-term relationships with patients and families (Haas, 2001). AAACN provides a definition of today's ambulatory care nursing practice (see Figure 28-2). The role of the ambulatory nurse is complex and multifaceted. Now, more than ever, the nurse must possess in-depth knowledge of select diseases and their management, common or expected side effects, and acute toxicities requiring urgent intervention. RNs must possess strong consistent clinical judgment, confidence in decision making, and must be able to communicate effectively (Hastings, 2001). The ambulatory care nurse has to respond to high volumes of patients while dealing with issues that are not always predictable. Clinical decisions have to be made with less data. There is a shift in collaborative relationships in ambulatory care; the staff nurse is seen more as a coordinator and manager of care and less as a direct implementer (Hastings).

Additionally, the nurse must be a skilled educator, patient advocate, collaborator, and manager if he or she is to navigate the complex systems to ensure quality patient care; all this in times of fiscal constraints and reimbursement struggles. Ambulatory nurses, in conjunction with the institutions where they are employed, must begin to study and report outcome data supporting the role of the ambulatory nurse and the value they bring to the healthcare team.

Figure 28-2. American Academy of Ambulatory Care Nursing Definition of Ambulatory Care Nursing

Ambulatory care nursing takes place on an episodic basis, is less than 24 hours in duration, and occurs in a single encounter or a series of encounters over time. Ambulatory care nurse-patient encounters take place in health care facilities as well as in community-based settings, including but not limited to schools, workplaces, and homes. The focus of ambulatory care nursing services encompasses use of cost-effective ways to assist patients in promoting wellness, preventing illness, and managing acute and chronic diseases to effect the most attainable positive health status over the patient's life span.

Ambulatory care nursing includes those clinical, management, educational, and research services provided by registered nurses for and with individuals who seek care and assistance with health maintenance and/or promotion. These individuals engage predominantly in self-managed health activities or receive care from families with or without assistance from community-based agencies outside the institutional setting.

Note. From *Ambulatory Care Nursing Administration and Practice Standards* (p. 19), by the American Academy of Ambulatory Care Nursing, 2004, Pitman, NJ. Copyright 2004 by the American Academy of Ambulatory Care Nursing. Reprinted with permission.

Models of care delivery in the ambulatory setting have evolved along with the changes in health care. The consumer initiates the care and expects a high level of care to be delivered. Three categories of consumer concerns are access, reasonable cost, and quality care (Haas, 2001). Nursing models of care delivery are classified in three major categories: facilitating access to care, direct intervention, and care coordination (Mastal, 2001).

The manager must prepare staff for these challenges of ambulatory care nursing delivery. The process of orientation is the manager's responsibility for the nurse transitioning into ambulatory care. Practice differences are the change in control; a general sensory overload; a lack of shift start and end; daily changes in expected workload; and difficulty planning time and controlling the pace of work. Customer service skills and flexibility also are needed in this setting, with patient and family satisfaction always a part of the care plan. Coordinating care is the most important challenge in care delivery. It is important to note that control remains with the patient and family; the visits are short; and alternate communication devices, such as the telephone, are used as a part of care delivery (Haas, 2001).

The nurse manager must recognize the ambulatory care nurse has a great deal of autonomy. The manager may be the administrator for several practice settings, and direct time with staff may be limited. In some practices, the staff nurse will report directly to the physician or a clinic manager who is not a nurse. The staff nurse may be the only nurse in a practice setting. The nurse manager, if present, will have the opportunity to help the staff to develop skills to direct and guide other professional team members and supervise assistive personnel. The manager supervising assistive personnel needs to know the role expectations and their level of competence, allocate time for supervision, keep communication open, and provide feedback.

The nurse manager is responsible for the quality of care delivered. The concept of quality of care is grounded in the integration of standards of practice. Standards define and guide practice. AAACN established the first national guidelines or standards of ambulatory care nursing (see Figure 28-3). These standards are intended to be used with other specialty standards depending on the practice setting (AAACN, 2004).

Figure 28-3. American Academy of Ambulatory Care Nursing Ambulatory Care Nursing Administration and Practice Standards

- **Standard I: Structure and Organization of Ambulatory Care Nursing**—Professional ambulatory care nursing is provided within an environment that supports the nurse to provide quality patient care that is caring, efficient, effective, and evidence-based.

- **Standard II: Staffing**—An adequate number of ambulatory care nurses are available to meet the patient care needs for the practice setting and maintain a safe and caring work environment.

- **Standard III: Competency**—Professional ambulatory care nurses demonstrate technical, critical thinking, and interpersonal skills necessary to complete their expected job responsibilities.

- **Standard IV: Ambulatory Nursing Practice**—The nursing process is the foundation used by professional ambulatory care nurses in making clinical decisions as they assess and identify patient health status, establish outcomes, and plan, implement, and evaluate the care they provide.

- **Standard V: Continuity of Care**—Professional ambulatory care nurses facilitate continuity of care using the nursing process, interdisciplinary collaboration, and coordination of all appropriate healthcare services, including available community resources.

- **Standard VI: Ethics and Patient Rights**—Professional ambulatory care nurses recognize the dignity, diversity, and worth of individuals and families; respect individual cultural, spiritual, and psychological differences; and apply philosophical and ethical concepts that promote access to care, equality, and continuity of care.

- **Standard VII: Environment**—Professional ambulatory care nurses participate in a coordinated systemwide process that creates and maintains a safe, ergonomically correct, comfortable, and hazard-free therapeutic environment for patients, visitors, and staff.

- **Standard VIII: Research**—Professional ambulatory care nurses conduct and participate in clinical and healthcare research. Research findings are disseminated. Evidence-based information is used to improve health care and organizational effectiveness.

- **Standard IX: Performance Improvement**—The performance improvement process is coordinated and integrated with that of the organization and includes the continuous data collection, evaluation, and improvement of the safety, quality, and appropriateness of ambulatory care nursing. Ambulatory care nursing leaders set expectations, provide resources and training, foster communication and coordination, and participate in improvement activities. Ambulatory care nursing leaders create an environment in which patients, their families, and organizational staff can identify and manage opportunities for improvement.

Note. From *Ambulatory Care Nursing Administration and Practice Standards* (pp. 9–17), by the American Academy of Ambulatory Care Nursing, 2004, Pitman, NJ. Copyright 2004 by the American Academy of Ambulatory Care Nursing. Reprinted with permission.

Along with identification and adoption of the nursing role in the practice setting, the manager also must support the staffing mix. Staffing is the process of assessing patient care needs and determining and providing the appropriate number and mix of nursing personnel to meet patients' requirements for care and desired quality outcomes (Haas & Hastings, 2001). The staff mix chosen is influenced by the technology and complexity of therapies rendered in the setting. Visit volume is no longer a good predictor of the number and type of staff needed to care for ambulatory patients. Instead, staffing needs to be based on the number of patients and the complexity of their needs. The skill mix refers to the number and type of nursing personnel assigned to care for a population of patients (Haas & Hastings). Factors that influence staffing include the payor mix and market factors, type of patient encounter, requirements per patient encounter, interdisciplinary team function, provider-perceived needs for support staff, and use of benchmarking or comparative data to set staffing levels.

Unfortunately, staffing mix and nursing roles in ambulatory care often are questioned. Medical and nursing assistants may target RNs for reduction and replacement. At the same time, the patient acuity continues to rise, along with a need for highly trained staff. Inpatient areas have used classification systems to help them to project, assign, and justify staffing patterns based on patient requirements. Several attempts have been made in ambulatory care to develop a similar system with less success. Staffing often is based on the number of primary providers, or counts are made of the visit numbers. This does not take into account the type of visit or the identified patient need. The lack of information on ideal staffing patterns and mix is frustrating. It is imperative that research efforts focus on trying to determine what influences the quality of care, care outcomes, and patient safety in ambulatory care.

Workload, theoretically, is predicted by the appointment system, but complications can include walk-ins, urgent visits, no-shows, and overbooking. Workload refers to the amount of patient care required in a specified period of time (Haas & Hastings, 2001). Workload measures remain in development in ambulatory care. The purpose of systems is to differentiate the types of visits, the types of providers needed, and the number of nursing personnel needed. Two types of systems are prototype intensity and factor-based intensity. One of the most difficult challenges in using any system to predict workload in ambulatory care is that it cannot be used prospectively. Rather, it is used for trending based on retrospective data. An example of a trending system used to measure workload for a chemotherapy infusion center is shown in Figure 28-4.

A recent three-part series in *Nursing Economic$* detailed the development of a patient intensity system to reflect both severity of illness and the complexity of nursing service required in an ambulatory oncology research center (Cusack, Jones, & Chisholm, 2004a, 2004b; Jones, Cusack, & Chisholm, 2004). The Ambulatory Intensity System (AIS) takes into consideration the nature of patient encounters, correlating workload parameters and intensity levels with a time factor that includes both direct and indirect nursing activities. In part II of the series, Jones et al. described how AIS was integrated into the scheduling system at the authors' clinical center. Part III elaborates on the ability of AIS to assist with research allocation, critical thinking, staff development, project time, and coordination of patient care (Cusack et al., 2004b).

Figure 28-4. An Example of Workload Measurement in an Infusion Center

INFUSION ROOM STAFFING

Drug	JAN	FEB	MAR	APRIL	MAY	JUNE	JULY	AUG	SEPT	OCT	NOV	DEC	TOTAL	Length of infusion (minutes)	Level
DOXIL	17	14	12	26	18	22	15	13	24	15	14	12	202	90	4
GEMCITABINE	112	108	93	112	90	83	98	79	111	115	123	128	1,252	60	3

Sheet 2

	JAN	FEB	MAR	APRIL	MAY	JUNE	JULY	AUG	SEPT	OCT	NOV	DEC	TOTAL	Length of infusion (minutes)	Level
DOXIL	1,530	1,260	1,080	2,340	1,620	1,980	1,350	1,170	2,160	1,350	1,260	1,080	18,180	90	4
GEMCITABINE	0	0	0	0	0	0	0	0	0	0	0	0	0	60	3

Staffing Level	RN/PT ratio	Length of infusion
LEVEL 1	1:1	15
LEVEL 2	1:1	30
LEVEL 3	1:1	60
LEVEL 4	1:2	90
LEVEL 5	1:2	120
LEVEL 6	1:4	240
LEVEL 7	1:4	360
LEVEL 8	1:4	480

Formula for calculating staff/patient ratio = adding all the treatment minutes of each regimen monthly, assigning staffing level, and dividing by nursing productive time.

Other practice concerns for the manager besides the nursing role and staffing include scheduling, facility planning, space utilization, environmental management, and equipment and supplies (Angiulo & Dickey, 2001). The scheduling process is a prearranged timing of patient encounters intended to reduce the wait for both patients and providers. There are many factors related to scheduling, and some are not easy to control. The type of scheduling usually is determined by collecting data from the providers on average visit length. Then a schedule for the provider is built in a system, and follow-up patients are scheduled within the parameters set. As expected, providers are variable, and assumptions for one provider may not be practical for another. Patients also are variable, as the time of their arrival for an appointment may vary, and if other support services are going to be provided on a visit, the delay of any of those services can influence the time of arrival. Every system needs to be customized for the site it serves. A follow-up system should be built for patients who do not show, cancel, or arrive late; this will eliminate or reduce problems later. Facility planning includes factors such as location, layout and design, safety, security, a plan for emergencies, and other environmental management (Angiulo & Dickey). Space utilization of a facility needs constant oversight. As practices grow in numbers of providers and patients, the manager will spend much of the day making sure space is allocated evenly and patient flow is efficient. Safety of the environment is a major focus of practice support. Plans for hazardous waste, furnishings, and a monitoring system for medical products are just a few examples of environmental management. Some of the other areas to include in a plan for the support of the practice include security, a medical emergency plan, infection control, and preparation in the event of a disaster (Angiulo & Dickey). The manager also must manage the equipment and supplies for the center. This involves selecting, purchasing, and providing inventory control systems, monitoring storage, and charging properly for supplies utilized (Angiulo & Dickey).

Buchsel and Yarbro (2004) detailed organizational considerations for nursing leadership in physician office practices, oncology infusion centers, outpatient surgical oncology settings, radiotherapy centers, and breast cancer clinics. They stressed that consumers are looking for comprehensive, compassionate quality care, in addition to convenience, availability of services, continuity of care, and relationships with staff. They suggested that creative approaches to multidisciplinary care, along with careful planning, can ensure a successful program.

One of the ways formal communication is accomplished between the nurse and patient in ambulatory care is through the telephone. Telephone nursing practice is identified as a subspecialty in ambulatory care nursing. It is defined as nursing practice because care is provided for individual patients or defined patient populations over the telephone. Telephone outcomes include improving patient access for information, support, and coordination of care; improving responsiveness to patient and family needs; enhancing communication among professionals; providing patient and family care; expanding the responsibilities of the professional nurse within the clinic; and enhancing more appropriate use of physician time (AAACN, 1997b). Telehealth nursing focuses on cognitive function and solid professional judgment. This is a whole new body of knowledge and skill in nursing. Telemedicine, online clinics, advice nurses, or home visits by computer are some examples of the way care is provided in the telehealth specialty today.

Budgeting

The budgeting process is a plan for managing processes to attain certain goals and objectives (Noa & D'Angelo, 2001). It is built on historical perspectives, forecasts, and anticipated revenues and requires goals and objectives. The nurse manager understands the benefits of planning a budget. It promotes effective decision making, allows consideration of alternatives, specifies major assumptions, and monitors operations and productivity (Noa & D'Angelo). The most common types of budgets are capital and operating budgets. Capital budgets usually forecast or estimate capital needs for the coming year, such as replacement of major equipment or facility renovation (Noa & D'Angelo). An operating budget includes statistical, revenue, and expense budgets. A statistical budget provides measures of workload or activity for each unit or service provided (Noa & D'Angelo). An expense budget is a projection of expected costs allocated to a specific program or service based on anticipated volume of activities (such as staff salaries and medical/surgical supplies) (Noa & D'Angelo). Indirect costs are assigned, which may include things such as buildings or equipment, depreciation, or bad debt (Noa & D'Angelo). A revenue budget is a projection of expected revenues associated with a specific program or service based on volumes projected in the statistical budget (Noa & D'Angelo). For example, the manager of an infusion area would be asked each year to project, based on last year's volume, what revenues are expected in each charge category. Variance reports usually are reported monthly for the manager and provide an analysis that demonstrates actual results compared to the plan. A larger more complete analysis of the budget process helps provide reports, trends, or results back to the manager to complete the cycle.

Regulatory Commissions

The quality of care in ambulatory services is subject to external monitoring by government agencies, third-party payors, consumer groups, and the legal system of the society (Laughlin, 2001). The nurse manager is accountable to these groups and to individual patients and families to monitor the performance and measure outcomes of care delivery against standards; exercise processes for ongoing improvement; and maintain a system of checks and balances for prevention, detection, and management of problems and errors in care delivery (Laughlin). The organizations are responsible for self-assessment to reduce risks to patients, visitors, and staff; to ensure high quality of care; and to minimize legal and financial liability (Laughlin). Regulatory requirements are generated by standards of professional organizations, by federal and state legislative acts, and by requirements of official agencies representing the public and purchasers of healthcare organizations (Laughlin). Some of the agencies and acts that have regulatory requirements in ambulatory care are the Occupational Safety and Health Administration (OSHA); American with Disabilities Act (ADA); Joint Commission on Accreditation of Healthcare Organizations (JCAHO); the National

Committee for Quality Assurance (NCQA); Accreditation Association for Ambulatory Health Care (AAAHC); and state-by-state legislation and regulations.

OSHA has a set of workplace statutes that are monitored by compliance inspections. The employer is responsible for ensuring safety of employees and the public from blood-borne pathogens, for preventing the transmission of mycobacterium tuberculosis, and for communicating about potential hazards to employees and the protective measures to prevent exposure. ADA prohibits discrimination in the rendering of healthcare services or the process of employment based on a disability. JCAHO is an independent, not-for-profit organization that establishes and assesses compliance with standards of quality for healthcare services. The standards are organized into the following functional areas: patients' rights and organization ethics, assessment of patients, care of patients, education of patients and families, continuum of care, improving organizational performance, leadership, management of the environment of care, management of human resources, management of information, and the surveillance, prevention, and control of infections. Patient safety is a major focus of JCAHO. NCQA is a not-for-profit, independent organization that assesses, evaluates, and publicly reports on the quality of managed care organizations. AAAHC offers voluntary, peer-based review of the quality of healthcare services of organizations such as ambulatory care clinics, physician and dental group practices, health maintenance organizations, procedure centers, and other similar facilities. State government agencies have a variety of policy approaches for regulating health care to the public. Licensing and regulation includes state practice acts, misconduct report practices, and the storage, prescribing, and dispensing of medications.

Staff Development

Development of nursing staff within the ambulatory setting will vary based on the specialty of the practice setting. AAACN established the first national guidelines or standards of ambulatory care nursing. Figure 28-3 provides a list of the standards as revised in 2004. These guidelines can be used in most practice settings and, when used with other specialty standards and State Nurse Practice Acts, can help to guide daily practice. The established nursing practice standards should specify how nurses perform and should provide the foundation for staff development programs, required competencies, clinical career ladders, and performance appraisal systems.

In many academic and hospital outpatient settings, a nurse educator is in position to identify learning needs, develop and implement educational programs, and provide ongoing support and education of the nursing staff. In a community setting or private practice, resources may be limited. The nurses in these settings often are very resourceful and seek out the knowledge they need to understand new treatments and expected side effects. Often, the physician(s) they work with is an important source of information. Additionally, the presence of pharmaceutical representatives in their setting allows for sharing of resources that relate to any new therapy, as well as quality patient education materials for the patient and family and information related to billing and reimbursement. The presence of Internet access in most settings also has made resources more readily available.

A key component of staff development is the initial orientation to the practice setting upon hire. This varies considerably among practice settings and specialties. In 2002, the author conducted an informal survey of ambulatory oncology settings on the East Coast, revealing an average of three weeks orientation (range two to four weeks) for a new hire into an ambulatory/office oncology setting. Academic settings tended to offer a longer orientation period. Factors influencing the length of orientation required included previous experience in the specialty, previous experience in the ambulatory or office setting, and ready access to supportive resources when needed. A comprehensive orientation program includes gaining familiarity with the setting, personnel, available technology (e.g., computer scheduling program, order entry system), policies and procedures related to the services provided, emergency care management, after-hours coverage for patients and families, and competency assessments, and establishing a timeline for learning new skills required to fulfill the requirements of the position. Most settings have unique policies and procedures but often use specialty guidelines in their creation. For example, an oncology clinic may have its own procedure on chemotherapy extravasation management but will use the book *Chemotherapy and Biotherapy Guidelines and Recommendations for Practice* to support it (Polovich, White, & Kelleher, 2005).

Nurses working in specialty clinics perform specialized tasks on a daily basis. For example, many oncology nurses working in an ambulatory setting administer chemotherapy on a daily basis. Nurses in this environment must undergo a systematic process to ensure competency related to administration of chemotherapy and managing any acute reactions as well as anticipated side effects or unanticipated toxicities. Historically, most ambulatory oncology settings developed their own chemotherapy competency or had their nurses attend a training program somewhere convenient to where they lived. In 1998, ONS developed a two-day chemotherapy and biotherapy course designed to provide the knowledge required by nurses administering chemotherapy. The course is not a competency program but provides comprehensive knowledge of chemotherapeutic and biotherapeutic agents and nursing management of side effects and acute reactions. ONS recommends that this course be augmented with a hands-on clinical practicum for nurses administering chemo/biotherapy. One of the benefits of this course is that it is a standardized national course taught only by ONS chemotherapy course trainers. Therefore, if a nurse already has taken the course elsewhere, the hiring institution can be confident of the qualities of both the course content and the trainer.

Given the high level of specialization in nursing, it would seem that most nurses would be members of their specialty nursing organizations, but this is not the case. A survey of ambulatory nurse managers in 1997 revealed that 35% of them did not list membership in any professional organization (Haas & Hackbarth, 1997). The American Nurses Association's (ANA's) Web site showed that fewer than 10% of nurses in the United States are on its membership list (ANA, 2003). Given the apparent small portion of nurses who are members of professional nursing organizations, one must wonder if nurses have access to the resources and support that membership in these organizations typically brings.

Legal Issues

Patients with complex healthcare needs are commonly managed in ambulatory settings. Inherent in every patient encounter is the potential for legal liability. An area of specific concern in ambulatory care settings is the legal risks associated with telephone triage. It is estimated that an ambulatory nurse spends more than 50% of his or her time on the telephone, and a large portion of this involves providing care to patients based on their report of a particular problem (Haas & Hastings, 2001). Nurses must possess excellent assessment skills and have a vast knowledge of the multitude of possibilities of what may be happening to the patient. The key to limiting the legal liability associated with telephone calls is thorough and accurate documentation (AAACN, 1997b). Many practices use telephone triage algorithms or decision trees to guide the questions asked during the phone call and to ensure comprehensive documentation. The forms used to document the telephone call should be signed (ideally by both the nurse and the physician) and become a part of the patient's permanent record. Figure 28-5 shows an example of a telephone encounter form.

The recent publication of a telephone triage book for oncology nurses provides a much needed resource for ambulatory nurses to systematically assess patient reports of specific problems (Hickey & Newton, 2004). The text includes sections on tips for performing telephone triage, telephone assessments, legal concerns of telephone triage, and guidelines on a variety of symptoms or concerns commonly reported by patients.

Prescription refills are a frequent request from patients, and these do not necessarily arrive in the context of a visit but often as a telephone request. Whether addressed during an office visit or as a telephone request, the prescription refill should be documented in the chart with detailed information. Figure 28-6 is an example of a prescription refill form.

Documentation of treatment in the context of a planned patient visit is critically important. For example, a patient in an ambulatory clinic receiving a planned cycle of chemotherapy requires specific, thorough documentation related to laboratory results, IV access, names and dosages of drugs administered, patient response to therapy, and patient education provided. Figure 28-7 is an example of a chemotherapy flow sheet used to capture all the critical components the nurse must assess and document during the encounter. This form doubles as the billing ticket for the services provided and includes all the recommended elements detailed in the ONS *Chemotherapy and Biotherapy Guidelines and Recommendations for Practice* (Polovich et al., 2005).

Reimbursement

Reimbursement for care rendered in an outpatient, ambulatory, or private practice setting will vary based on the site of service designation of the specific practice. Areas designated as hospital outpatients are reimbursed based on ambulatory payment classifications, whereas a freestanding clinic or private practice is reimbursed based on an established fee schedule. It is critically important to understand this designation, as it determines the billing and reimbursement for all services delivered to patients from the site.

Figure 28-5. Telephone Encounter Form

Fletcher Allen Health Care   NAME: _____
Hematology/Oncology Clinic   DOB: _____
Telephone Encounter Form   MRN: _____

Attending MD: _____

Message taken by: _____

Attention: _____   RN ☐   MD/NP ☐

Date: _____   Time of call: _____

Caller: _____   Phone number to reach: _____

Phone call returned on _____ (date) at _____ (time).

ASSESSMENT: _____
_____
_____
_____
_____
_____
_____
_____

Allergies: _____

ACTION/INTERVENTION: _____
_____
_____
_____
_____
_____
_____

Time required for phone call _____ minutes

MD/NP Notified: YES ☐   NO ☐   Name of provider notified: _____

Prescription called in: YES ☐   NO ☐

Drug/Dose/Route/Frequency: _____
_____

Name of pharmacy: _____ Phone number: _____

_____
                                          Date/Signature RN

_____
                                          Date/Signature MD

Note. Figure courtesy of Fletcher Allen Health Care. Used with permission

---

Figure 28-6. Prescription Refill Request

Fletcher Allen Health Care
Hematology/Oncology Clinic
Prescription Refill Request

NAME: _____
DOB: _____
MRN: _____

Date: _____   Time of call: _____

Person calling: _____   Phone #: _____

Prescribing physician: _____

Name of medication (ASK CALLER TO SPELL FROM THE BOTTLE LABEL):

_____

_____

Dosage: _____   How often do you take? _____ times per day

pills _____   # refills _____

Pharmacy name: _____   Phone number: _____

Mailing address:

_____

_____

Called in by : _____   Date: _____   Time: _____

_____
Physician signature

REMINDER: Refill requests called in by 2 PM will be called in by end of day. Refill requests called in after 2 PM will be called in the following day.

Note. Figure courtesy of Fletcher Allen Health Care. Used with permission

---

Recent changes in federal legislation will dramatically affect reimbursement for oncology medications in both the hospital outpatient and physician office setting. Historically, mark-up on medication has been the sustaining profit for both hospital-based and private practice oncology clinics. The oncology community now will be forced to find other means to be profitable. One of the concerns about these impending changes in reimbursement is that ambulatory oncology care may be redirected back into the hospital setting, which the system is not prepared for nor are the services available in these locations at this time. The years ahead will pose many challenges around access to care, quality care, and the role of the nurse in meeting the patients' needs. Indeed, the mere survival of ambulatory, outpatient, and private practice oncology services is in question.

Figure 28-7. Chemotherapy/Biotherapy Flow Sheet

Attending MD: _____
Clinical Study # _____
Drugs Provided _____
Allergies _____
Diagnosis/CD-9 Code _____

❑ Chemotherapy Encounter (V58.1) ❑ Anemia of Neoplastic Dz. (285.22)
❑ Care Following Chemotherapy (V66.2)   ❑ Neutropenia (288.0)
❑ Nausea/Vomiting (787.01)   ❑ Thrombocytopenia (287.4)
❑ Dehydration (276.5)   ❑ Other _____

Temp/Pulse			
Resp/BP			
Height/Weight/BSA			
	Lab location _____	Lab location _____	Lab location _____
WBC/ANC			
HgB/HCT/PLTs			
Neut/Lymph/Monos			
K+/Na++			
Alk. Phos./T. Bilirubin			
AST/ALT			
Creat/BUN			
Ca++/Calc. Ca++			
PT/INR			
IV start (size, loc) (36000)			
VAD Lab draw (36540)			
Declot VAD (36550)			
Blood Return?			

	Dose/units	start	end	Init.	Dose/units	start	end	Init.	Dose/units	start	end	Init.
90780 (1st), 90781 addl.												
90782 (SC/IM)												
Hydration (sol'n)												
IV push (96408)												
Infusion (96410 / 96412)												
Clin. Study (NC)												

Notes:	❑ 99211	❑ 99211	❑ 99211
	I was directly supervised by Dr. _____ who was present in the clinic suite during this time and was directly available.	I was directly supervised by Dr. _____ who was present in the clinic suite during this time and was directly available.	I was directly supervised by Dr. _____ who was present in the clinic suite during this time and was directly available.
Primary RN:			
VAD: left or right			
Signature/Credential			

Note. Figure courtesy of Fletcher Allen Health Care. Used with permission

Payor approval or denial of a therapy for a given diagnosis and how and where the therapy is administered are often points of discussion between providers and insurance companies. Practices must have processes in place to ensure prior authorization or approval has been granted before the planned therapy being administered. In the absence of this approval, they put themselves at risk for not being reimbursed and the patient at risk for personal responsibility for the bill. Each insurance company has its own set of policies and procedures, and what is covered by one is not necessarily covered by another. The roles of a savvy business manager and an astute and knowledgeable certified coding and billing specialist cannot be underestimated and are well worth the financial investment for a practice that wants to ensure adequate reimbursement for services and medications administered.

The ambulatory nurse is challenged with securing reimbursement for nursing services rendered in a system that is medically driven. Currently, the nursing services delivered are billed as "incident to" a physician's service. This mandates that the billing provider be immediately available and physically present while the services are being delivered to the patient. Practices must have clear documentation tools in place that specify who the supervising provider was at the time of service.

Unfortunately, much of the nurse's independent daily work is not currently reimbursable. Patient management by telephone, patient education, and other activities related to care coordination are not billable services if the service is delivered by an RN. This limits nursing practice to physician supervision and does not allow for independent treatment or intervention, although these are within the nurse's defined scope of practice, particularly at the advanced practice level.

The Future

To date, the ambulatory care setting has been a positive environment for patients, their families, and the staff who work therein. The model has been successful based on attention to patient-focus, providing easy access, and ensuring the provision of quality care. Many settings have provided "one-stop shopping," which has been a significant patient satisfier.

Nurses working in ambulatory settings generally enjoy autonomous practice with a collaborating physician or team of physicians. The role of the nurse is one of colleague, with a flexible working schedule, and has a focus on continuing education and opportunities for expanding upon skill base.

Undoubtedly, ambulatory care will continue to flourish and, as more sophisticated means of patient management arise, programs will be designed to manage what now happens in hospitals in an office setting. For example, in oncology, febrile neutropenic patients are managed on an outpatient basis with daily contact for assessment and antibiotic management (Holdsworth, Hanrahan, Albanese, & Frost, 2003; Kern, 2001). Considerable debate and discussion continues over how to determine patients eligible for this novel approach (Donowitz, Maki, Crnich, Pappas, & Rolston, 2001).

Settings now manage patients with acute deep vein thrombosis in outpatient arenas (Spyropoulos, 2000). At diagnosis, the patients are referred to a hematologist who initiates therapy with low molecular weight heparin. An advanced practice nurse often performs patient education related to the diagnosis and its management and how to give subcutaneous injections. Patients then are followed daily until they have reached therapeutic levels of warfarin. Ongoing evaluation is performed to follow the prothrombin time for the duration of therapy. These are both examples of fairly low-risk problems that historically have been managed on an inpatient basis that are less expensive to deliver in an ambulatory setting and help patients to avoid several days in the hospital. The future of ambulatory care will bring more exciting professional opportunities for nurses in highly specialized areas. Advanced practice nurses will play a large part in making these opportunities patient focused, quality driven, and cost effective.

References

American Academy of Ambulatory Care Nursing. (1997a). *Nursing in ambulatory care: The future is here.* Washington, DC: American Nurses Publishing.

American Academy of Ambulatory Care Nursing. (1997b). *Telephone nursing practice administration and practice standards.* Pitman, NJ: Anthony J. Janetti.

American Academy of Ambulatory Care Nursing. (2004). *Ambulatory care nursing administration and practice standards.* Pitman, NJ: Anthony J. Janetti.

American Nurses Association. (2003). *About us.* Retrieved December 14, 2003, from http://www.nursingworld.org/about

Angiulo, C., & Dickey, E. (2001). Practice/office support. In J. Robinson (Ed.), *Core curriculum for ambulatory care nursing* (pp. 70–83). Philadelphia: Saunders.

Barhamand, B. (1991). A survey of the role, benefits, and realities of the office-based oncology nurse. *Oncology Nursing Forum, 18,* 31–37.

Buchsel, P.C., & Yarbro, C.H. (2004). Oncology nursing in the ambulatory setting (2nd ed.). Sudbury, MA: Jones and Bartlett.

Cusack, G., Jones, A., & Chisholm, L. (2004a). Patient intensity in an ambulatory oncology research center: A step forward for the field of ambulatory care, part I. *Nursing Economic$, 22,* 58–63.

Cusack, G., Jones, A., & Chisholm, L. (2004b). Patient intensity in an ambulatory oncology research center: A step forward for the field of ambulatory care, part III. *Nursing Economic$, 22,* 193–195.

Donowitz, G.R., Maki, D.G., Crnich, C.J., Pappas, P.G., & Rolston, K.V.I. (2001). Infections in the neutropenic patient—New views of an old problem. *Hematology 2001,* 113–139.

Haas, S.A. (1998). Ambulatory care nursing conceptual framework. *Viewpoint, 20*(3), 16–17.

Haas, S.A. (2001). Ambulatory care nursing specialty practice. In J. Robinson (Ed.), *Core curriculum for ambulatory care nursing* (pp. 3–15). Philadelphia: Saunders.

Haas, S.A., & Hackbarth, D.P. (1995). Dimensions of the staff nurse role in ambulatory care, part III: Nursing research to design new models of nursing care delivery. *Nursing Economic$, 13,* 230–241.

Haas, S.A., & Hackbarth, D.P. (1997). The role of the nurse manager in ambulatory care: Results of a national survey. *Nursing Economic$, 15,* 191–203.

Haas, S.A., Hackbarth, D.P., Kavanagh, J.A., & Vlasses, E. (1995). Dimensions of the staff nurse role in ambulatory care, part II: Comparison of role dimensions in four ambulatory settings. *Nursing Economic$, 13,* 152–164.

Haas, S.A., & Hastings, C. (2001). Staffing and workload. In J. Robinson (Ed.), *Core curriculum for ambulatory care nursing* (pp. 133–145). Philadelphia: Saunders.

Hackbarth, D.P., Haas, S.A., Kavanagh, J.A., & Vlasses, E. (1995). Dimensions of the staff nurse role in ambulatory care, part I: Methodology and analysis of data on current staff nurse practice. *Nursing Economics$ 13,* 89–98.

Hastings, C. (2001). The ambulatory care practice arena. In J. Robinson (Ed.), *Core curriculum for ambulatory care nursing* (pp. 16–30). Philadelphia: Saunders.

Hickey, M., & Newton, S. (Eds.). (2004). *Telephone triage for oncology nurses.* Pittsburgh, PA: Oncology Nursing Society.

Holdsworth, M., Hanrahan, J., Albanese, B., & Frost, J. (2003). Outpatient management of febrile neutropenia in children with cancer. *Paediatric Drugs, 5,* 443–455.

Houston, D.A., & Houston, G.R. (1993). Administration issues and concepts in ambulatory care. In P.C. Buchsel & C.H. Yarbro (Eds.), *Oncology nursing in the ambulatory setting* (pp. 3–19). Sudbury, MA: Jones and Bartlett.

Jones, A., Cusack, G., & Chisholm, L. (2004). Patient intensity in an ambulatory oncology research center: A step forward for the field of ambulatory care, part II. *Nursing Economic$, 22,* 120–123.

Kern, W.V. (2001). Risk assessment and risk-based therapeutic strategies in febrile neutropenia. *Current Opinions in Infectious Disease, 14,* 415–422.

Lamkin, L. (1994). Outpatient oncology settings: A variety of services. *Seminars in Oncology Nursing, 10,* 229–236.

Laughlin, C.B. (2001). Regulatory compliance and risk management. In J. Robinson (Ed.), *Core curriculum for ambulatory care nursing* (pp. 453–459). Philadelphia: Saunders.

Martin, C. (1996). Incidence of emergency visits among oncology patients receiving outpatient chemotherapy: Implications for care in a capitated market. *Cancer Control, 3,* 435–441.

Martin, V.R., & Xistris, D. (2000). Ambulatory care. In C.H. Yarbro, M.H. Frogge, M. Goodman, & S.L. Groenwald (Eds.), *Cancer nursing principles and practice* (5th ed., pp. 1641–1660). Sudbury, MA: Jones and Bartlett.

Mastal, M.F. (2001). Context of ambulatory care. In J. Robinson (Ed.), *Core curriculum for ambulatory care nursing* (pp. 31–54). Philadelphia: Saunders.

Noa, C., & D'Angelo, L. (2001). Health care fiscal management. In J. Robinson (Ed.), *Core curriculum for ambulatory care nursing* (pp. 84–95). Philadelphia: Saunders.

Oncology Nursing Society. (1992). *National survey of salary, staffing, and professional practice patterns in ambulatory oncology clinics.* Pittsburgh, PA: Author.

Polovich, M., White, J.M., & Kelleher, L.O. (Eds.). (2005). *Chemotherapy and biotherapy guidelines and recommendations for practice* (2nd ed.). Pittsburgh, PA: Oncology Nursing Society.

Porter, H.B. (1995). The effect of ambulatory oncology nursing practice models on health resource utilization, part 1: Collaboration or compliance? *Journal of Nursing Administration, 25*(1), 21–29.

Shirkman, N., Cloutier, A., Tittle, M., Massaro, T., & Munroe, D. (1999). Meeting the challenge of unscheduled outpatient visits. *Nursing Management, 30*(2), 51–53.

Spyropoulos, A.C. (2000). Outpatient-based treatment protocols in the management of venous thromboembolic disease. *American Journal of Managed Care, 6*(20 Suppl.), 1034–1044.

Verran, J. (1981). Delineations of ambulatory care nursing practice. *Journal of Ambulatory Care Management, 4,* 1–13.

Homecare Issues

Mary E. Warner, BSN, RN, OCN®
Veronica S. Stone, RN, OCN®, NMCC
Patricia E. Frank, RN, BSN, OCN®

The healthcare delivery system has experienced tremendous changes in reimbursement over the past decade. Many services formerly provided in the hospital setting have been transitioned to the home setting. The cost effectiveness of providing health care in the home has been recognized by insurance companies and other providers (Fieler & Hanson, 2000). In 1967, there were 1,753 homecare agencies; today, more than 20,000 providers deliver home care, indicating a greater need for homecare services (National Association for Home Care, 2001).

Before World War II, several generations of a family shared one home and therefore were able to provide care to one another if a member fell ill. Today, family members, especially mothers, work outside of the home. In 2003, 69% of married mothers were employed in business, creating a challenge for families with a member who required home nursing care (U.S. Department of Labor, 2004).

Hospitals have been challenged over the past decade to provide their services under curtailed reimbursement caused by the prospective payment system. Their response has been to reduce length of stay. Patients are discharged from the hospital to continue recovering at home under the care of family members. Homecare nurses are charged to provide actual care or instruct the family to ensure the implementation of the physician's plan of care (Buhler-Wilkerson, 2001). The home becomes filled with medical equipment and staffed with informal caregivers whose lives are arbitrarily restructured because they are mandated to provide nursing care. This is termed "family focused care," and nursing literature now includes the concept of "caregiver-burden" (Williams, 2002). The modern homecare nurse becomes a mediator as the technical medical world invades the formerly private retreat of the patient. Home-based patient care necessitates reorganizing a person's home to accommodate medical equipment and supplies.

The impact of change to the home environment on the identity and self-esteem of family members is not well documented. The unique skill of the homecare nurse is to help the patient and family transform their home into a "therapeutic landscape" capable of supporting the well-being of the patient while maintaining the integrity of the home and family unit (Williams, 2001). Historically, patients have traveled to special places in search of healing. They may have gone to spas for mineral-rich warm waters or to sites of supposed miracles, such as Lourdes in France, where the walls are lined with discarded crutches. Modern patients are sent home to await the homecare nurse who will bring the healing experience with him or her to the patient.

Types of Homecare/Services

Homecare agencies may be seen as "one-stop shopping" because they offer a variety of patient services. Nursing care; respiratory, speech, physical, and occupational therapy; social work and psychiatric services; and products such as oxygen and durable medical equipment can be offered to patients in their home (Silver & Wellman, 2002). Healthcare providers, including advanced practice nurses, RNs, licensed practical/vocational nurses, home health aides, and respiratory, physical, speech, and occupational therapists, offer supportive and therapeutic care through an agency. Each discipline and category requires separate provider numbers, licensing, and oversight.

Nurses can provide care in the home for patients with almost every diagnosis. Cancer; cardiac, renal, and respiratory diseases; alterations in nutrition; infection; and chronic pain are some of the healthcare needs of the homecare patient. Specialty nurses assess and manage these health problems (Humphrey, 2002a).

Nursing standards of care are set by professional organizations such as the American Nurses Association and State Boards of Nursing. Specialty organizations also have standards regarding the qualifications of nurses serving in home care (Fieler & Hanson, 2000). Educational preparation and experience can dictate the level of care provided by various personnel. The generalist nurse will function in direct patient caregiving. The advanced practice nurse may provide direct care, usually as educator and researcher or in a leadership or management role (Iwamoto, Rumsey, & Summers, 1996).

Regulatory Concerns

The homecare nurse manager must keep abreast of the local state and federal regulations governing operation of home healthcare agencies. At the federal level, the Centers for Medicare and Medicaid Services (CMS) is the source of regulations. CMS mandates structure, staffing requirements, allowable services, and reimbursement. These regulations can be found on the CMS Web site (www.cms.hhs.gov). Consumers and professionals may access the site. It is easy to navigate, and phone numbers are listed as a supplemental resource.

The Home Health Agency Manual, a publication of federal regulations, also may be accessed at the CMS Web site. The CMS manual, as printed from its Web site, is not considered an official version of the document but is useful as a reference. Each regulation has a reference number followed by one or more letters, indicating the status of the rule. For example, a rule followed by "FC" means "Final rule with comment period," indicating the time and process for further discussion of the rule.

Comments and questions can be made directly online if there are any concerns or objections to the rule.

Home Health Compare, a rating report of home health agencies, is a new CMS service available to professionals and the community. Eleven measures address specific areas of patients' functional status to gauge the effectiveness of homecare interventions. The functional status measures address improvement in the patient's activities of daily living, the mobility in the home environment, mental health improvement, and ability of the family to handle a medical emergency. Initially, these parameters were rated for a limited number of homecare agencies. CMS publishes comparison ratings, which are updated every three months, for each agency that receives Medicare and/or Medicaid payments.

Individual states license and regulate physicians, nurses, and other healthcare professionals as well as hospitals, long-term care facilities, home health agencies, and hospices. Their goal is to ensure that quality care is provided to consumers of those services. States regulate private health insurers and can mandate their coverage of various healthcare services. These mandates can vary from state to state (Sparer, 2002). Every agency must ensure that it is aware of and compliant with all state and local regulations. It is the responsibility of the nursing director to ensure regulatory compliance.

Staffing and Budgeting

Under the fee-for-service reimbursement system, agencies were paid per home visit. Therefore, productivity was measured by number of visits made per day. In October 2001, the Prospective Payment System (PPS) was extended to homecare services. Under this system, the agency is expected to perform all patient visits and care, including providing supplies, which are given for a set fee determined by Medicare and based on its analysis of patient data. These data describe the functional status of the patient and substantiate the need for homecare services. Previously, the patient's medical diagnosis was sufficient to indicate the need for services (Nowicki, 2001).

The new system of reimbursement affected home healthcare staff in several ways. Staff cannot raise revenues by making more home visits. To be profitable, the agency must provide care with *less* visits while maintaining quality of care. Staff must be re-acculturated to view increased visits as wasteful. To qualify for the highest reimbursement under PPS, the comprehensive, accurate collection of patient data by staff is more important than ever. Field staff must give a detailed description that paints a picture of the patient's needs and allows office-based "coders" to select appropriate reimbursement codes. Proper coding generates the highest payment from Medicare. Homecare nurses, who have routinely assessed patients' health status, now must learn new phraseology to support reimbursement and, subsequently, benefit their patients (Greaves, 2003). Managers can respond to these challenges by changing the care delivery model, changing the mix of personnel, and by using benchmarking as a tool to set staffing guidelines.

Changing the Delivery Model

The homecare nurse manager may be tempted to set a goal of early patient discharge from homecare services in order to be fiscally sound. Early discharge of patients from service is not recommended. Reimbursement is based on a 60-day episode of care. Patients retained on service for the full episode of care can continue to be monitored. The nurse will be able to provide early intervention if there is a change in the condition of the patient. This monitoring can be done via telephonic contact supported by appropriately spaced visits. Other team members may be used to provide high-quality, cost-effective home health care without early discharge from the homecare setting (Hollers, 2003).

Changing Mix of Personnel

One cost-saving measure in the homecare milieu mirrors that of the inpatient setting in the use of the licensed practical/vocational nurse (LPN/LVN) in providing home care. Medicare Conditions of Participation (CoP), state boards of nursing, standards of the Joint Commission on Accreditation of Health Care Organizations (JCAHO), and the Community Health Accreditation Program address this issue. Medicare CoPs allow LPNs/LVNs to assist with patient teaching of self-care techniques under the supervision of an RN. JCAHO provides guidelines for qualifications, supervision, and competency validation of licensed personnel. Individual state government regulations, which may be more restrictive, take precedence over guidelines issued by accrediting organizations (Stoker, 2003).

Benchmarking

Benchmarking, comparing your productivity to that obtained by a large number of other comparable agencies, has a role in the inpatient setting and is moving into home health care. A survey of this type identifies processes that others have used to improve their performance and allows for self-comparison. Benchmarking is a recommended tool to support implementation of change programs. When agencies with comparable demographics have achieved greater productivity, it difficult to argue that these goals cannot be achieved. This can be a motivator for staff to improve their performance (Braverman & Wright, 2002).

Practice Concerns

The major concern in the PPS environment of restricted reimbursement is how to efficiently deliver care and maintain quality patient outcomes. An appropriate area of study is to examine how managers and staff are changing their practice to meet these goals.

In a survey of readers of *Home Healthcare Nurse*, questions of the impact of PPS on nursing practice were asked. Respondents reported that they centered on educating staff, specifically on OASIS (a standard assessment data set), ICD9 coding, computer programs, and outcome-based quality improvement. Once staff have learned about these tools, it may be necessary to examine actual nursing practice for ways to gain efficiency (Humphrey, 2002b).

PPS has propelled the trend to evidence-based practice. Nursing interventions must be applied appropriately and to the greatest possible effect. One recommendation is that improved practice starts with better intake data. Efficiency can be increased by using nurses to collect all intake data and begin the OASIS data collection immediately. This would give the admission nurse more time for improved assessments and care planning. To support accurate assessments, nursing staff should be trained in ICD9 coding. Proper coding should have a positive effect on revenues and help the agency provide more nursing care (Humphrey, 2002b). Managers must be aware of research and products that reduce nurse visit time and support good patient outcomes.

The following is an excellent example of this principle in action. Homecare patients are often learning to manage diabetes. Research indicates that homecare nurses frequently were not using hemoglobin A1C (HbA1C) values in planning care for their diabetic patients.

The HbA1C test indicates the amount of glycosylated hemoglobin in the blood. Glycosylated hemoglobin is a form of hemoglobin indicating average blood glucose levels during the previous two to three months. The HbA1C should be ordered, as it is the most accurate of these tests. A finding of > 8.1% indicates that the patient's blood sugar for the past several months has been averaging > 200 mg/dl (Fischbach & Dunning, 2004).

A study of physicians' knowledge of HbA1C values showed that as their knowledge increased, their patients' HbA1C values decreased, indicating better diabetic control (Setter, Corbett, Campbell, Cook, & Gates, 2003). It is an easy extrapolation (and a good subject for a study) to predict the same results if homecare nurses increased their knowledge of HbA1C values. By sharing HbA1C results, nurses can assist their patients in tracking long-term glucose control. Their partnership may result in better patient outcomes.

Wound care is an expensive proposition under PPS because the supplies are not reimbursed separately. Agencies are challenged when caring for patients with high-volume medical supply usage (see Figure 29-1). For example, venous stasis ulcers traditionally require twice a day wet-to-dry normal saline dressing changes. Costs can mount upwards of $35,000 for 16 weeks of care. One agency performed a trial of a multilayer high compression system of care. This treatment for pressure ulcers provides compression, which assists in reestablishing venous valve function while maintaining a moist wound bed. The dressing is changed once a week. The agency has reported a case of an ulcer that healed at less cost than the reimbursement rate (Hughes, 2002). This wound care system saved expense, preserved the use of skilled nurses' time, and provided for improved patient outcomes.

Use of telephone technology can support quality care (Schroeder & DePalma, 2003). The National Aeronautics and Space Administration first developed telemonitoring to facilitate care of astronauts. This two-way television communication is used today in medical practice, prison systems, and various government agencies, including the U.S. Army. Monitors capable of recording vital signs, magnifying lenses, and a stethoscope can be placed in patient homes. The cost effectiveness of such monitoring still is being evaluated.

Figure 29-1. Current Wound Care Concepts

Wound Bed Preparation (WBP)
Essential to achieve timely wound healing
Necrotic tissue and exudate in the wound create a "burden."
Growth factors are inhibited. Interventions are not effective.
Compression dressings are believed to reduce exudate in the wound bed.
Use of WBP Decision Algorithm may contribute to faster healing.

Venous Ulcers
Ulcer size decreased with use of silver ions in a nanocrystalline form. Antimicrobial effect present only when ionized state is maintained. Silver ions are inactivated by sodium chloride. Normal saline solution (NSS) is contraindicated.

Case study
Lateral malleolus wound of the right foot in a 53-year-old male observed in April. Wound size increased with NSS wet-to-dry dressings.
Silver nanocrystalline protocol initiated on June 29.
Dressing changed every three days by client's wife. Nurse visited once a week.
Wound healed in 36 days (six weeks).

Note. Based on information from Allen, 2002; Hughes, 2002; Ovington, 1999.

Obtaining reimbursement for telemonitoring of patients is improving. Some managed care companies will negotiate contracts that include reimbursement for telemonitoring services meeting certain criteria (Schroeder & DePalma, 2003).

The use of a personal digital assistant (PDA) is recommended for home care. Nurses' use of PDAs is growing. Telephone lists, calendars, medical references, and patient teaching materials are available for quick reference. Patient data can be collected and transmitted using a PDA. This technology is costly, up to $1,000 per unit, and is rapidly improving.

Many users will soon replace their PDA for a model with the latest features. New users may want to save money by purchasing a slightly used PDA with features that would meet their needs. The credibility of any software purchased must be evaluated. Are numerical calculations done correctly? Are drug interactions and side effects accurate? All use of PDAs must comply with public policies governing patient privacy, including the Health Insurance Portability and Accountability Act (HIPAA). A secured password must be used on every PDA that stores patients' data (Hunt, 2002).

Nursing practice is steadily evolving from reliance on traditional teachings or anecdotal evidence to looking at models and standards of practice, which reflect scientific evidence. The Internet has many resources for evidence-based nursing information. Table 29-1 contains a few sites of interest for the nurse manager on evidence-based practice. Some sites may have associated fees. The agency may be associated with a hospital whose library subscribes to various Internet resources, allowing free access (Benefield, 2002).

Staff Development

Nursing staff development is discussed in-depth in Chapter 18 of this text. Staff selection and development are prime responsibilities of management. Good performance by managers will help control costs of business operations by providing competent personnel and reducing turnover. Management has an obligation to develop and maintain required skills of healthcare providers. Nurses, and all employees, are responsible for patient care and safety. Patient safety issues include knowledge of what to report to the office or when to call for help for the patient. A documented program of education, certification, and review will provide assurance that all employees are competent.

Table 29-1. Evidence-Based Practice Resources		
Organization	**Web Site**	**Description**
Joanna Briggs Institute	www.joannabriggs.edu.au/about/home.php	A free site based in Australia supporting evidence-based practice.
Cochrane Collaboration	www.cochrane.org	A free Web site developed from a 1972 textbook by Archie Cochrane in the United Kingdom.
Evidence-Based Nursing	http://ublib.buffalo.edu	A free Web site from the University at Buffalo, NY. Worth browsing for quantity of information.
National Guideline Clearinghouse	www.guideline.gov	A free site sponsored by the U.S. Department of Health and Human Services. Contains healthcare reports, including reports on disparities in American health care.
Oncology Nursing Society	www.ons.org	A free site supporting oncology nursing practice with an evidence-based resource center.
Online Journal of Clinical Innovations	www.cinahl.com/cexpress/ojcionline3/index.html	Since 1984, an online database from the Cumulative Index to Nursing and Allied Health Literature. Access fee of $40 for individuals and $100 for institutions.

A staff development program includes baseline requirements of the services provided by the agency, education that supports clinical expertise of staff, the fulfillment of credentialing requirements, and targeting of functional needs of patients and caregivers in the home.

A successful program would include a measurement of growth for staff to recognize their professional development. Orientation sessions for new employees must be supplemented by ongoing meaningful education. A concept currently being advanced in continuing education is the link between caring behaviors and competency. Being competent in giving care is recognized by patients as "caring" for them. Nurses need to be reminded of standards of care and made aware of what constitutes negligence. Failure to comply with ordinary procedures can result in negative outcomes and portray nurses as uncaring. Critical thinking is a competency that is challenging to teach and measure. Creating a class of seasoned and novice nurses focusing on case studies will allow for sharing of new knowledge and valued experience. The learning may go in both directions (Mustard, 2002). An example of a developmental skill need that is high volume and problem prone is related to venous access. Managing central venous access devices is an area of ongoing educational need for home healthcare nurses. The homecare nurse is often the only professional assessing the device and should possess a thorough understanding of the physical mechanics involved with various devices, their use, and their management.

Gorski (2002) discussed potential complications of central venous access devices that include "pinch-off" of the catheter with subsequent inability to flush. This should not occur in peripherally inserted central catheters because they are placed through a wider portion of the costoclavicular space. Catheters used for parenteral nutrition are at risk for lipid buildup that can occur when premixed solutions are stored for up to seven days in the home. Use of the 1.2 micron filter guards against this effect. The buildup of drug precipitates in central catheters is caused by failure to routinely flush these lines with 10–20 ml of normal saline solution.

More than 250,000 patients with a central venous catheter will have a catheter-related infection each year (Jackson, 2001). Unrecognized, untreated infections may lead to general sepsis and death. Homecare nurses must be knowledgeable in recognizing signs and symptoms of catheter-related infection. Most infections are acquired after placement of the device during routine use and care. Good skin preparation and frequent hand hygiene are considered the best preventives (Jackson). The competency of the nurse in managing venous access devices should be documented in his or her employment records, as reflected in agency policy (Gorski, 2003).

Another area of development for the homecare staff is cultural competency. As reviewed in Chapter 10, organizational commitment to cultural competency begins at the top of management. The homecare nurse must be aware of cultural influences on patients' responses to illness. For example, communicating pain management varies based on gender, age, ethnicity, race, and socialization for both the patient and healthcare provider. Using a tool like the Word Descriptor Scale may be a more appropriate pain measurement tool for people of some cultures rather than the widely used numerical 0–10 pain scale, with 0 meaning no pain and 10 meaning the worst pain possible (Duggleby, 2003). There is a growing expectation for healthcare providers to have an awareness of culture on response to illness. Nurses must identify their own biases to avoid imposing their cultural values on patients (Fieler & Hanson, 2000).

Care of the Caregiver

Our society readily recognizes that patients may be suffering physical and psychological pain. But what are the feelings of nurses as they provide care through the continuum of the patient's illness? Jezuit (2002) completed a study of intensive care unit nurses involved with patients at the end of life. This study identified specific characteristics described as suffering in the nurses caring for these patients. Sources of these stressful feelings in the nurses included conflict between the nurses and physicians and/or patients; the need for nurses to set aside their personal values;

nurses having personalized the patient's situation; and nurses experiencing failure of their goals for the patient. The nurses in the study refrained from sharing their feelings with peers based on a perceived lack of support at work.

Homecare nurses and other staff identify strongly with their patients. They may experience dissonance with the overall plan of care for the patient and feel powerless to change it. Obviously, peer support is less available in the home setting than perhaps in hospitals. A program of education helping staff cope with troubling situations would provide peer support and possibly result in a more productive staff (Jezuit, 2002).

Legal Issues

Liability risk is a concern for any business entity. Home health care is no exception. Issues concerning fraud and abuse, bonding, medical equipment, patient abandonment, and abuse or neglect are a few of these concerns that will be addressed in this section. The home healthcare industry has been a focus of Medicare review for fraud since the mid-1990s (Berek, Gutierrez, Stone, & Testa, 2000). Recent changes in the Medicare reimbursement system mandate that all agency personnel understand and properly interpret federal, state, and local regulations to avoid billing practices that could be misconstrued as fraudulent. Examples of fraud are charging for visits that were never made or using codes that make patients appear sicker in order to secure higher reimbursement.

New technologies offered in the home may bring new legal risks. Protocols should be well written and based on the latest research. Consult with your legal department or counsel regarding any possible liability. Review your insurance coverage in detail against your business plan for uncovered areas of liability.

Fair and equitable access to care is a concern of regulatory agencies, especially for Medicaid. Studies have shown that minority clients have received less homecare services even when their need was greater (Davitt, Kaye, Bagati, & Graub, 2001). This is especially true when coupled with a language barrier. If a patient is unable to understand care instructions, the patient may be labeled as noncompliant. The patient may be eligible for additional services but not aware because of a lack of understanding of the explanation of benefits. The patient may not know how to ask for care. Many agencies employ bilingual staff to address these issues.

Patient abandonment is a legal concern for every agency. Agencies can be held liable for patient abandonment if there is staff knowledge or speculation that the patient is being left alone for unsafe periods of time. The agency can be cited if a patient is discharged from services in a manner that would be considered abandonment by any peer organization with similar jurisdictional requirements. Document completely any patient discharge for reason other than goals met or appropriate patient demise (expected causes). Nurse managers should have an ongoing clinical pertinence review of provider documentation on all clients receiving care.

Case Study

Malpractice charges can involve negligent care or omission of care based on the standard of reasonable and customary care and according to the homecare standards of nursing practice. Example: a homecare nurse was visiting a patient for wound care and failed to take vital signs per protocol during the visit. The patient complained of having a nondescript headache during the visit. Hours after leaving the patient's home, the patient sustained a stroke. The nurse could be open to a charge of negligence for *omitting* the vital signs and not following up on the headache complaint, which may or may not have revealed a change in blood pressure, or other signs if assessed (Croke, 2003).

Charges of harassment—physical, psychological, or sexual—can occur in any business that sends personnel into private homes. Harassment policies should be developed to provide protection for patients, caregivers/family members, staff, and the agency. Abuse can take many forms, including verbal. Policies clearly defining abuse and the methods of reporting all suspected or actual abuse should be available to all staff and patients. Medical professionals have a well-known obligation to report abuse to appropriate authorities. A membership in your state homecare association also can provide resources for these issues.

Reimbursement

Costs of healthcare services originally were paid out of pocket, and large numbers of people were unable to afford care. Labor unions pushed for health insurance as far back as 1915 but were unsuccessful. The forerunner of Blue Cross was the Baylor Plan. Schoolteachers in Dallas, TX, could pay the Baylor University Hospital $6 each year and be guaranteed certain services, such as maternity services. Other plans had similar starts in the 1930s. Employers eventually became the provider of health insurance usually by contracting with a commercial insurance company.

Managed care plans have grown and diversified in areas such as how they provide access to services, control costs, and ensure quality care by their providers. These vary from indemnity plans in which all elective admissions require precertification to health maintenance organizations (HMOs), which seek to control costs by providing incentives to physicians to lower costs of care by reducing hospital admissions. New models of HMOs give physicians greater control over patients' treatments (Nowicki, 2001).

Revenues are realized by setting charges based on costs, discounting charges for individual insurers, using preset per diem rates regardless of services rendered, charging according to the diagnosis, or by capitation, which is agreeing to care for a large number of people for a set fee (Nowicki, 2001). Many homecare patients are covered by Medicare. Medicare, the federal government's payment of healthcare costs for people over 65 years of age, was legislated in 1966. Payments from Medicare for home health services are made according to the fees set under PPS. The Balanced Budget Act of 1977 created PPS, and it went into effect October 1, 2000. PPS uses the case payment system known as diagnosis-related groups. First applied to inpatient hospitals, payment was made according to expected costs for delivering care. Diagnoses such as pneumonia, cholecystitis, or acute myocardial infarction were determined to have costs within a certain range. These costs were formulated, and payment was made based not on real-time expenses but the averaged financial costs of institutions across the nation (Sparer, 2002).

This method of reimbursement has been expanded into home care. Home health resource groups (HHRGs) are used. Patient status and need for home healthcare data are derived from an initial assessment that assigns each patient into one of 80 HHRG groups. Each group provides for reimbursement based on an assumed amount of projected services to be rendered by the homecare agency. Payment is set based on this assessment. All services and supplies must be provided within this amount if the agency is to avoid a loss (Nowicki, 2001).

Medicaid, a program regulated by the federal government and administered by the individual states since 1967, provides health care only to people with very restricted income. Homecare services are covered for skilled services only. A waiver option allows states to use the funds to provide personal care, such as bathing, to reduce the need for nursing home placement of many citizens. These programs are referred to as home- and community-based services (HCBS).

Each of the 50 states has implemented an HCBS program (Nowicki, 2001). For proper coding and billing, an understanding of the Medicare Outcome and Assessment Information Set (OASIS) is essential. OASIS is a system of data collection meant to identify outcomes of the interventions provided by home healthcare personnel. OASIS is not a complete set of data about a patient. It does not include pediatric information or vital signs. OASIS data support outcome-based quality improvement and has been adopted by Medicare to verify effectiveness of the care provided to patients in the home. OASIS is compatible with electronic transmission of data. Agency computer systems need to interface with OASIS for billing and coding. Medicare has made available HAVEN®, a software program that can be downloaded free from the CMS Web site. HAVEN can be used to submit OASIS data to Medicare if you do not have access to other software that conforms to CMS electronic specifications (CMS, 2003).

Home health agencies need five forms to be completed for each admission, according to Medicare rules: the Healthcare Financing Administration (HCFA) 485, which verifies the appropriateness of the proposed home health services; OASIS on admission and discharge; a PPS form; billing and record forms; and a "Plan of Care" form. Home visits are documented on the plan of care, which contains data indicating the status of the patient, response to care, and actual plan of care. Educational needs of patients and caregivers are included in care plans under the nursing diagnosis of knowledge deficit.

The use of a laptop computer enables the nurse to directly enter data while in the home. Computer-based patient record systems need a uniform taxonomy to translate data from visits in the field into easily coded billing data. Outcomes of interventions also need to be included in this database. At least eight nursing taxonomies have been evaluated for suitability to computer use, including Nursing Outcomes Classification, Patient Care Data Set, Nursing Minimum Data Set, and Systematized Nomenclature of Medicine Reference Terminology (Saba, 2002).

Nursing documentation systems have been developed in pen and paper form and for electronic use to document care provided in home visits. Home health aides, social workers, physical or speech therapists, as well as nurses can use the Home Healthcare Classification System. This system consists of 21 care components and includes outcome codes. An alphanumeric code indicates the various components of the information needed for proper billing. Clinical pathways have been developed for direct computer entry by the nurse or office staff (Saba, 1990, 2002).

A complete understanding of the rules and finer points of coding is necessary to avoid denials. Collaboration between the homecare manager and the nurse to achieve optimum coding of diagnosis listed on the HCFA 485 is recommended. The primary diagnosis listed on the 485 should be the one requiring the most homecare services, even if it is not the most severe illness of the patient. Comorbidities should not be listed unless they have the potential to impede a positive response to treatment (Greaves, 2003).

Coding becomes difficult when an original diagnosis technically no longer exists. If a patient is being seen for postsurgical care of a cholecystectomy incision, the actual incision does not have a diagnosis. It is the result of a procedure that cured the patient's original problem. In this situation, it is better to use a symptom code. A thorough knowledge of the levels of coding is needed (Prophet-Bowman, 2003).

Some hospitals in conjunction with local universities offer certification courses for coders. The American Association of Professional Coders and the Associated Health Information Management Association offer certification by examination (Mercy Health System, 2002). Online training programs in coding are available through the American Health Information Management Association's Web site (Prophet-Bowman, 2003).

Business Plan

Chapter 21 provides an in-depth review of business plan development. This chapter will focus specifically on planning for a home health agency.

As an agency structures its business plan, many factors must be considered. A community needs assessment is a key step. A needs assessment is a survey conducted in response to a perceived need and helps to identify the population the potential business would serve. Once completed, the needs assessment guides the formulation of ideals: services needed and how to provide them.

Ideals for a proposed business are structured by learning from members of the community what they believe quality care would include. The "ideal structuring" phase could consist of simple conversation or formal interviewing of community members. A survey of community members comparing satisfaction ratings of existing services might be needed.

A comprehensive analysis of the population in your community that is most likely to use your services or make the referrals is warranted. An assessment of any available financial support funding for the services your agency would provide is essential. Knowledge of laws governing the home healthcare agency is necessary. Research federal, state, and local laws. Credentialing agencies and professional organizations offer assistance in this phase. Carefully consider legal and insurance coverage for the agency. These are monthly expenditures, but they are areas that can adversely affect your "bottom line" if the agency is faced with liability, nonpayment, or employment issues.

When selecting the support team (attorney, accountant, human resources) that will provide the expert knowledge needed, it is important to assess their knowledge and experience with your type of business.

Another area to review prior to completion of the business plan that is specific to home health care is if the agency is going to seek Medicare/Medicaid payments or rely on the private sector. If the agency is going to operate under the Medicare system, there are certain factors (location and office requirements) that impact reimbursement of services provided. Medicare dictates requirements for all of these and has them available for review with the aforementioned guidelines.

The finalized agency business plan includes a needs assessment, business objectives, a plan to meet the business objectives successfully, an outline of personnel to be employed, location, a detailed financial/legal format, a plan for quality assurance review, and a projected budget with projected revenue sources.

Summary

Home health care will be needed in the future, and the financial challenges will continue. Nurse managers must use intelligent planning, new technology in the office and field, and ongoing development of staff. Families, in their changing "home landscape" of medical equipment and therapies, need effective psychological support so they can successfully assume the new identities brought on by personal illness. Their ability to use technology and master simple and complex care skills and our ability to teach and support them are key to the future of homecare nursing.

References

Allen, J. (2002, May/June). Management of a venous leg ulcer using Acticoat antimicrobial barrier dressing. *Supplement to the Remington Report*, pp. 10–12.

Benefield, L.R. (2002). Evidence-based practice: Basic strategies for success. *Home Healthcare Nurse, 20*, 803–807.

Berek, J., Gutierrez, N., Stone, J., & Testa, L. (2000). Fraud. What is the evidence? *Care Management Journal, 2*(1), 44–53.

Braverman, C., & Wright, K. (2002, October 28). *Total turnaround: How to use national benchmarks, an operational review, and focus change strategies to totally turn an agency around.* Presented at the 21st annual meeting of the National Association for Home Care & Hospice, Salt Lake City, UT.

Buhler-Wilkerson, K. (2001). *No place like home. A history of nursing and home care in the United States.* Baltimore: The Johns Hopkins University Press.

Centers for Medicare and Medicaid Services. (2003). *HAVEN data entry software.* Retrieved September 25, 2003, from http://www.cms.hhs.gov/oasis/havensof.asp

Croke, E.M. (2003). Nurses, negligence, and malpractice. *American Journal of Nurses, 103*(9), 54–63.

Davitt, J.K., Kaye, L.W., Bagati, D., & Graub, P. (2001). Beneficiary profiles and service consumption patterns in an urban Medicaid home and community-based waiver program. *Care Management Journal, 3*(2). Abstract retrieved September 6, 2003, from http://www.ncbi.nlm.nih.gov/entrez/query.fcgi?cmd=Retrieve&db=PubMed&list_uids=12455219&dopt=Abstract

Duggleby, W. (2003). Helping Hispanic/Latino home health patients manage their pain. *Home Healthcare Nurse, 21*, 174–179.

Fieler, V.K., & Hanson, P.A. (2000). *Oncology nursing in the home.* Pittsburgh, PA: Oncology Nursing Society.

Fischbach, F.T., & Dunning, M.B. (2004). *A manual of laboratory and diagnostic tests* (7th ed.). Philadelphia: Lippincott Williams & Wilkins.

Gorski, L.A. (2002). Effective teaching of home IV therapy. *Home Healthcare Nurse, 20,* 666–674.

Gorski, L.A. (2003). Central venous access device occlusions. Part 2: Nonthrombotic causes and treatment. *Home Healthcare Nurse, 21,* 168–173.

Greaves, P. (2003). ICD-9-CM coding from a manager's perspective. *Home Healthcare Nurse, 21,* 240–248.

Hollers, F.K. (2003). Financial success: How to beat the odds. *Caring, 22*(7), 12–16.

Hughes, S.C. (2002, May/June). The cost-effective use of multi-layer high compression in home care under PPS. *Supplement to the Remington Report,* pp. 4–15.

Humphrey, C.J. (2002a). The current status of home care nursing practice—Part 1: Clinical practice under PPS. *Home Healthcare Nurse, 20,* 677–684.

Humphrey, C.J. (2002b). The current status of home care nursing practice—Part 2: Operational trends and future challenges. *Home Healthcare Nurse, 20,* 741–747.

Hunt, E. (2002). The value of a PDA to a nurse. *Tar Heel Nurse, 64*(3), 18–19.

Iwamoto, R.R., Rumsey, K.A., & Summers, B.L.Y. (1996). Scope of oncology nursing practice. In J.M. Brant (Ed.), *Statement on the scope and standards of oncology nursing practice* (pp. 5–7). Washington, DC: American Nurses Publishing.

Jackson, D. (2001). Infection control principles and practices in the care and management of vascular access devices in the alternate care setting. *Journal of Intravenous Nursing, 24*(Suppl. 3), S28–S34.

Jezuit, D.L. (2002). The manager's role during nurse suffering: Creating an environment of support and compassion. *JONA's Healthcare Law, Ethics, and Regulation, 4*(2), 26–29.

Mercy Health System. (2002). *Three new certificate programs available for the CHE healthcare organizations.* Retrieved September 24, 2003, from http://mercynet.mercyhealth.org/news/?item=470

Mustard, L.W. (2002). Caring and competency. *JONA's Healthcare Law, Ethics, and Regulation, 4*(2), 36–43.

National Association for Home Care. (2001, November). *Basic statistics about home care.* Retrieved September 25, 2003, from http://www.nahc.org/Consumer/hcstats.html

Nowicki, M. (2001). *The financial management of hospitals and healthcare organizations.* Chicago: Health Administration Press.

Ovington, L.G. (1999, December). The value of silver in wound management. *Podiatry Today,* pp. 59–62.

Prophet-Bowman, S. (2003). A primer on ICD-9-CM coding. *Home Healthcare Nurse, 21,* 384–395.

Saba, V.K. (1990). *Home health care classification (HHCC) system.* Retrieved September 25, 2003, from http://www.sabacare.com/tables678.html

Saba, V.K. (2002). *Home health care classification system: An overview.* Retrieved September 22, 2003, from http://nursingworld.org/ojin/tpc7/tpc7_7.htm

Schroeder, B., & DePalma, N. (2003). As close as the phone: Telemonitoring in home care. Retrieved September 6, 2003, from http://www.nurseweek.com/ce/ce1060a.htm

Setter, S.M., Corbett, C.F., Campbell, R.K., Cook, D., & Gates, B.J. (2003). A survey of the perceptions, knowledge, and use of A1C values by home care patients and nurses. *The Diabetes Educator, 29*(1), 144–152.

Silver, H.J., & Wellman, N.S. (2002). Family caregiver training is needed to improve outcomes for older adults using home care technologies. *Journal of American Dietetic Association, 102,* 831–836.

Sparer, M.S. (2002). Government. In A.R. Kovner & S. Jonas (Eds.), *Health care delivery in the United States* (7th ed., pp. 315–338). New York: Springer.

Stoker, J. (2003). Home care LPN utilization. *Home Healthcare Nurse, 21,* 85–89.

U.S. Department of Labor, Bureau of Labor Statistics. (2004, April). *Employment characteristics of families summary.* Retrieved October 28, 2004, from http://stats.bls.gov/news.release/famee.nr0.htm

Williams, A. (2002). Changing geographies of care: Employing the concept of therapeutic landscapes as a framework in examining home space. *Social Science & Medicine, 55,* 141–154.

Management of Hospice Services

Cynthia Braswell, RN, MS

"When my life is finally measured in months, weeks, days, or hours, I want to live free of pain, free of indignity, free of fear, free of loneliness. Give me shelter. Give me your hand. Give me your care. Give me your understanding. Give me your love. Then let me go peacefully. And help my family to understand." Anonymous

It is the role of the nurse manager to act as the patient's advocate. The nurse manager is often a key resource regarding end-of-life care. As the terminally ill patient's condition begins to decline, the nurse manager may act as the catalyst to provide information and initiate the initial assessment for hospice services. It is important for the nurse manager to demonstrate astute assessment skills and be open to discuss the patient's options with the primary care physician.

This chapter is designed to offer an overview of hospice care issues. The content provides general principles that are significant when considering hospice services for the terminally ill patient. There are numerous books and reference sources dedicated to hospice services. The nurse manager is encouraged to further examine the practice of hospice and palliative care.

Hospice Care Services

The types of care and services provided by hospice organizations are based on a concept. It is a concept whereby multiple disciplines combine efforts to focus on the quality of life of a patient who has been diagnosed with an incurable disease process. The goal is to have the best quality of life until the end of life. This includes, but is not limited to, meeting the physical, social, psychological, and spiritual needs of each patient. It is very important to clarify that the care and services provided in the practice of hospice does not enhance or deter the end-of-life process. In the United States, the term *hospice* refers to a specific programmatic model for delivering palliative care (Coyle & Ferrell, 2001).

The approach to care is to comfort, not to cure. Patients and their families that have opted to receive hospice services have made a conscious decision to abstain from aggressive treatment. The focus shifts from curative measures that were aligned with their respective diagnosis to a plan of care that is designed to maintain comfort and an optimal level of dignity. If a hospice patient and his or her family choose to return to curative treatment or therapy, they have the option to terminate hospice services. There is no penalty to resume hospice services later should the treatment outcome be less than expected.

Symptom management is the cornerstone of hospice services. Pain is the most prevalent symptom associated with the terminally ill. The management of pain is achieved after a comprehensive assessment of the patient's needs, including the patient's ability to ingest and/or absorb a medication, and any caregiver issues that might exist. Achieving a state of analgesia and/or sedation is an area that may require careful titration of a single medication or a combination of preparations. The hospice team must listen and respect the patient's description or gestures that might signal the need to make immediate adjustments in his or her pain management.

Other symptoms are associated with the terminally ill patient. They may include, but are not limited to, respiratory, gastrointestinal, neurologic, and dermatologic symptoms (see Table 30-1). Kaye (1998) named the important principles of symptom control.

- Medical expertise
- High-quality nursing care
- Full assessment
- Attention to detail
- Regular review
- Ability (and energy) to listen
- Communication skills

Hospice services may be provided in a variety of locations. Most are provided in the home of the patient or a family member. Hospice services also are provided in skilled long-term-care facilities, assisted-living facilities, or inpatient hospice units. The acuity level of the patient, the ability of the caregiver to provide appropriate care, and the availability of facilities dictate the location where care will be rendered.

Homecare hospice (not to be confused with home healthcare) is the primary site of care for terminally ill patients. In 2001, 94.5% of the days of service provided by our nation's hospices were at the routine homecare level, 4.3% were general inpatient care, 0.4% to respite care, and 0.8% of the days were continuous home care (National Hospice and Palliative Care Organization [NHPCO], 2003). Many surveys have revealed that most patients want to die at home in familiar surroundings and with the people who are most significant to them. Homecare hospice involves providing patients and their families with education, equipment, medications, and supportive care in their homes. Clinical visits by the physician, RN, social worker, chaplain, certified nursing assistant, and volunteers are conducted on an intermittent basis.

The RN case manager coordinates the frequency of the home visits. The regularity is dictated by acuity level and the individual needs of the patient and his or her family. There are specific standards that each hospice must follow to meet the regulations of a payor source. For example, Medicare, Medicaid, and private insurers have established guidelines that require the RN case manager to visit the patient a specific number of times each week. Other disciplines are required to make patient visits at specific intervals in order to meet reimbursement criteria.

Table 30-1. Symptoms Associated With Terminally Ill Patients	
Symptom	Percent
Weight loss	77
Pain	71
Anorexia	67
Dyspnea	51
Cough	50
Constipation	47
Weakness	47
Nausea/vomiting	40
Edema/ascites/pleural effusion	31
Insomnia	29
Incontinence/catheterized	23
Dysphasia	23
Bedsore	19
Hemorrhage	14
Drowsiness	10
Paralysis	8
Jaundice	8
Diarrhea	4
Fistula	1

Note. From *Notes on Symptom Control in Hospice and Palliative Care* (p. 3), by P. Kaye, 1998, Machiasport, ME: Hospice Education Institute. Copyright 1998 by the Hospice Education Institute. Reprinted with permission.

Inpatient hospice is provided to patients in one of three settings: a freestanding hospice unit, a unit based in a hospital, or in a long-term care facility. Patients who are placed inpatient are high acuity, in a crisis, and usually are there for a short period of time. The average length of stay in an inpatient hospice unit is less than two weeks. In a pain crisis, inpatient hospice meets the needs of the patient who requires close monitoring until the crisis can be controlled. The inpatient unit offers an alternative to patients who are actively dying and whose family members prefer they not die at home. The inpatient unit also offers a refuge for family members who request respite care. Inpatient services, regulations, and benefits are designed to provide short-term inpatient care for the purposes of pain control and other symptom management, diagnostic assessment, respite care, and when the needs of the patient can no longer be safely or effectively managed in the home (Kilburn, 1997).

Residential hospice is provided to patients who require a higher level of skilled care that cannot be provided in the home. These patients are not severely acute or actively dying, requiring inpatient hospice. Residential hospice also can act as a site for respite care to provide a relief for family members or to provide adult day care. These services offer an alternative to homecare for those patients with no or inadequate primary caregivers (Kilburn, 1997).

Continuous care is part of the Medicare hospice benefit. The purpose of continuous care is to maintain the severely acute patient at home. Medicare provides reimbursement for caregivers to be placed in the home on a 24-hour basis if the patient is experiencing a symptom crisis or is actively dying. Fifty-one percent of the care must be nursing related (Kilburn, 1997).

Long-term care facility hospice is provided to patients who reside in a nursing home setting. The nursing home is considered their legal residence. Thus, the same level of care that is provided to a patient in the home environment is applied to the nursing home resident. Some hospice patients are referred while residing in long-term care, whereas others may be transferred into long-term care after being admitted in a hospice program at home (Coyle & Ferrell, 2001).

Assisted living (personal care home) hospice is provided to patients who reside in an assisted living facility. The assisted-living facility or personal care home is regarded as their legal residence. Thus, the same level of care that is provided to a patient in the home environment is applied to the assisted living facility resident. Just as in other care settings, the hospice team remains the care manager in collaboration with the assisted living facility staff to advocate for patient/family palliative care goals (Coyle & Ferrell, 2001).

Direct care of the patient is implemented by the hospice interdisciplinary (ID) team. The team consists of a physician medical director, an RN case manager, a chaplain, a social worker, a certified nursing assistant, and volunteers. The role of the team is to assess the needs of the patient, design a plan of care, and implement appropriate services. The team meets at regular intervals to discuss any adjustments that need to occur to meet the needs of the patient and his or her family members. The focus of the hospice interdisciplinary team is on the quality of life until the end of life.

The physician medical director is responsible for ordering and directing the care of the hospice patient after the patient's primary care physician has certified that the patient has a terminal illness that will, with all probability, conclude the patient's life within six months. The medical director also is actively involved with continuing education of the team.

The RN case manager is responsible for assessing the needs of the patient and implementing the plan of care in conjunction with the other disciplines on the team. The case manager is continuously monitoring changes in the patient's status. As changes occur, the case manager integrates the necessary resources to meet the needs of the patient. The case manager educates the family regarding symptom management, equipment utilization, and any adjustments in the plan of care. The case manager is the family's key contact person as the patient's condition begins to decline and death becomes imminent. He or she incorporates the role of advanced clinician, educator, researcher, and consultant to families, staff, colleagues, and communities (Matzo & Sherman, 2001).

The certified nursing assistant provides direct care to meet the personal hygiene and daily living needs of the patient based on the plan of care. The nursing assistant works directly with the case manager to provide for a comfortable, safe environment. The nursing assistant has the most encounters with the patient and often alerts the case manager to changes in the patient's behavior that may warrant modifications in the plan of care. The certified home health aid may be the member of the ID team who best knows what the patient needs and may provide the most valuable input as the ID team plans care for the patient (Kinzbrunner, Weinreb, & Policzer, 2002).

The social worker assesses the social needs of the patient and his or her family. The psychosocial assessment is conducted to determine to what extent the patient and his or her family will need supportive resources. The role of the social worker is to assist the patient and his or her family with nonphysical needs. This may include, but is not limited to, counseling, assisting with financial issues, planning funeral arrangements, contacting distant family members, and acting as a nonmedical resource.

The chaplain is responsible for assessing the spiritual needs of the patient and his or her family. The services provided by the chaplain are not denomination- or affiliation-specific. It is not the role of the chaplain to replace the patient's primary clergy but to offer spiritual support and assist the social worker to meet any psychosocial needs. Although it would be ideal to receive pastoral care from one's own minister, rabbi, or priest, the majority of Americans are unaffiliated with formal religious institutions and therefore not able to directly access this vital function (Kinzbrunner et al., 2002).

The dietitian conducts a nutritional assessment and designs meal plans to support the patient's nutritional needs. Each meal plan is individualized to accommodate the physiologic status of the patient. As the patient's ability to metabolize some nutrients declines, the menu is adjusted accordingly. The dietitian is available to educate the staff, patient, and family members regarding the changes that occur with eating patterns at the end of life. Dietitians can be helpful in advising patients and families on the various alternatives that might assist in optimizing caloric intake for patients (Kinzbrunner et al., 2002).

The bereavement coordinator conducts a bereavement assessment and follows the patient's family for an extended period of time after the patient's death. They provide resources for and/or conduct regularly scheduled grief counseling sessions for family members. The loss of a loved one is often the beginning of a long road of healing for the patient's family members. The ability to cope with loss is an individualized process that requires time to develop.

The volunteer coordinator directs the services provided by a team of volunteers. Volunteer services are an active component of hospice services. More than 55% of patients and their families benefit from the time donated by volunteers (Kilburn, 1997). The volunteer coordinator and the volunteers are agents of the hospice organization. Their goal is to supplement the services provided by the other members of the ID team. They also provide administrative support and participate in community and public relations efforts.

The pharmacy plays a key role in symptom management. The pharmacy works with the hospice team to design an individualized regime and make recommendations for adjustments as the patient's level of care changes. Many pharmacies have developed creative methods to deliver medications for discomfort management during the dying process. The pharmacy may compound medications and design special formulations to resolve multiple symptoms with ease of administration. The pharmacist can advise clinicians on potential drug-drug interactions, suggest alternative therapeutic approaches to difficult symptom management problems, and educate the staff on the newer medications and therapies available for use (Kinzbrunner et al., 2002).

Durable medical equipment (DME) services are usually a contracted service between the respective DME provider and the hospice organization. Medical equipment is delivered to patients in the home environment, nursing home setting, assisted living facility, or personal care home. The ID team collaborates to determine the equipment and supplies the patient might need. The RN case manager works directly with the DME provider to ensure the necessary equipment is made available to the patient. This includes any DME and self-help devices that may be prescribed in the ID team's plan of care (Kilburn, 1997).

Physical therapy, occupational therapy, and speech therapy are additional services that are included as part of the hospice benefit. The physician medical director may order these specialized services to benefit the patient's level of functioning and quality of life. All specialized therapies participate in care planning, evaluation, and revisions as patient and family needs change (Kilburn, 1997).

Regulatory Commissions

Each state has established regulations regarding hospice licensure. Licensure is a group of laws and/or regulations developed by state authorities that delineate minimum compliance criteria for performance of functions covered under a given licensure category (Kilburn, 1997). A hospice must be state licensed to become Medicare certified and participate in public third-party reimbursement programs. Licensure is obtained after meeting the specific criteria set forth by the regulatory authorities. In states without hospice licensure, a hospice may have to hold a home health or other license or certification if providing care directly and if seeking reimbursement for hospice services (Kilburn).

Some states require a hospice to obtain a certificate of need. The certificate-of-need programs are run by state regulatory bodies; these agencies use formulas to plan the number of hospice providers that are able to operate in their respective states. Some hospices may hold multiple licenses to include nursing home or home health services. Accreditation is not required to operate a hospice organization. Though accreditation continues to remain voluntary, many organizations choose to pursue it not only to internally improve the quality of their operations and services, but also to serve as a signal to consumers, referrers, payors, and regulators that the organization meets the rigorous standards and requirements of a recognized accrediting body (Kilburn, 1997).

Staffing and Budget

NHPCO (2003) identified the most frequent staffing ratios after surveying 800 hospices. The ratio of patient to case manager is 14:1. The ratio of patient to social worker is 25:1. The ratio of patient to chaplain is 49:1. Certified nursing assistants make 5.2 visits per day. Thirty-five percent of patients in hospice care die within seven days. These statistics are the guidelines for staffing in a hospice organization. Employee-related costs are the largest budgetary line item. The revenue for salaries, benefits, and education average 43% of the operating costs of most hospice care organizations.

Practice Concerns

The perception of services provided by hospice organizations is a major concern. Death is not an option, yet the thought that every living individual will be removed from life as he or she is currently experiencing it remains one of man's greatest fears. When one is informed by a physician that all medical interventions have been exhausted, a series of emotions is unleashed. These emotions are not exclusive to the patient and his or her family but to healthcare providers as well. The issues regarding dehydration, nutrition, and overmedicating patients remains a sensitive area that is open for continued education. Many still view the accepting of hospice services as giving up.

Dispelling the myths associated with the hospice concept can greatly affect the appropriate utilization of services. Many people, including healthcare professionals, do not possess a clear understanding about the practice of hospice care. Any patient with a confirmed incurable diagnosis that makes it unlikely he or she will live beyond six months may meet the criteria to be included in a hospice program (see Table 30-2). Hospice services are not reserved for end-stage patients with cancer. Patients with any end-stage disease process can benefit from the support offered by hospice organizations.

Table 30-2. Hospice Patients Served in 2001 by Diagnosis	
Diagnosis	**Percent**
Cancer	53.6
End-stage heart disease	10
Dementia	7
Lung disease	6
End-stage kidney disease	3
End-stage liver disease	2

Note. From *Facts and Figures* (p. 5), by the National Hospice and Palliative Care Organization, 2003, Alexandria, VA: Author. Copyright 2003 by the National Hospice and Palliative Care Organization. Reprinted with permission.

An accurate understanding of hospice services will place hospice as a choice option, not as a last resort. Hospice is a continuation in the plan of care, not the end of care. The earlier the multidisciplinary team is integrated into the patient's life, the more time there is to assist the patient and the family through one of life's most challenging experiences.

Many patients have been referred to a hospice program so close to the end of their lives that they have endured unmanaged symptoms for an extended period of time. The disease process may be so advanced that there is little time to implement optimal symptom management and preserve dignity. The family member(s) and/or caregiver(s) have not received the benefits that the multidisciplinary team can offer them to prepare for their loss. Hospice referrals come late in the course of the disease. In 1995, the median length of hospice stay was only 29 days (Kabcenell, Lynn, & Schuster, 2000).

The Robert Wood Johnson Foundation (2002) funded the Last Acts Campaign to Improve Care and Caring Near the End-of-Life to conduct a 1,000-person survey to gauge opinion on the current state of end-of-life care in the United States. The study demonstrated the public's dissatisfaction with the way end-of-life care is being provided by the healthcare community. Only 11% of adults surveyed in August 2002 said that the U.S. healthcare system is doing an "excellent" or "very good" job caring for dying people; 26% said the healthcare system is doing a "poor" job.

Staff Development

An adequate number of qualified healthcare professionals is the foundation of hospice care. The practice of hospice is a unique form of health service. Professionals who opt to provide hospice services must receive specialized training and orientation. Most healthcare professionals have focused on diagnosis, disease management, and curing illness. Hospice care reverses many of the learning processes that are the basis of the healthcare educational system. The continued confrontations with the emotions associated with death and dying can challenge even the most experienced healthcare professional.

Most hospice organizations provide internal continuing education. Educational programs are usually clinical or regulatory-related programs. Hospices that participate in certification or accreditation programs are required to schedule educational offerings to meet the specific criteria set forth by the certifying body. As regulations, policies, and standards change, the staff must be updated to ensure it is meeting the requirements.

There are numerous national, state, and local hospice and palliative care professional organizations to meet the needs of each member of the ID team. The organizations center their activities on continuing education, impacting policy changes, and improving the quality of end-of-life care. Professional hospice and palliative care certification is available for physicians, RNs, and certified nursing assistants.

A physician may become board certified in palliative medicine through the American Board of Hospice and Palliative Medicine. An RN may become certified in hospice and palliative care through the Hospice and Palliative Nurses Association. A nurse must take and pass a national exam to become a certified hospice nurse (Connor, 1998). A nursing assistant may become a certified hospice and palliative nursing assistant after the completion of a comprehensive examination through the National Board for Certification of Hospice and Palliative Care. There are also organizations that provide continuing education for social workers and chaplains who work in the field of hospice.

Legal Issues

State and federal laws that impact health care and the practice of hospice are continuously evolving as hospice becomes a more prevalent care option. As legislative bodies review and change regulations, hospice organizations must respond to meet the required criteria. Hospice programs also must follow traditional business and legal guidelines. NHPCO has identified eight minimal areas to consider.
1. Incorporate and develop bylaws, articles of organization, and a governance structure.
2. Tax status—determine if your organization is for profit or 501(c)3 status.
3. Determine if a certificate of need is required by your state.
4. Determine if hospice licensure exists in your state.
5. Review Medicare regulations regarding certification and reimbursement.
6. Determine if your organization will seek accreditation.
7. Obtain liability protection.
8. Secure outside contracts that are necessary to provide services.

Reimbursement

Reimbursement for hospice services may come from a variety of sources. Medicare is the leading reimbursement source for hospices. In 2001, 91% of hospices were Medicare certified, and 74% of all hospices were accredited (NHPCO, 2003). Medicaid, health insurance programs, HMO plans, and private donations also provide funding.

The fluctuations in the economy and the shrinking healthcare dollar have placed a financial burden on some hospice organizations. Medicare reimburses the hospice provider a per diem rate for the services provided under the Medicare hospice benefit. The benefit requires physician care, nursing care, social services, spiritual counseling services, short-term inpatient care, respite care, physical therapy, occupational therapy, speech therapy, laboratory, nutritional services, and volunteers be made available to every patient. Each state Medicare office is responsible for the administration functions of the benefits.

The *Medicare Hospice Manual*, through the Health Care Financing Administration, is an important guide for hospice providers. The manual outlines the participation in the Medicare program regarding hospice services. The hospice provider must agree to meet the criteria set forth by Medicare, as well as provide an opportunity for Medicare representatives to conduct on-site inspections of the hospice organization (Centers for Medicare and Medicaid Services, 2003).

Business Plan

Hospice organizations, as with any organization, must be managed as a business. Strategic planning and sound fiscal decisions can dictate the survival of a hospice organization. The comprehensive services provided by the ID team, as well as the cost of medications, equipment, and supplies, can prove to be expensive. It is the responsibility of the hospice organization to manage a budget without compromising the quality of service. The practice of business and hospice must achieve a delicate balance during a time when healthcare services and the financing of health care are undergoing a major paradigm shift.

References

Centers for Medicare and Medicaid Services. (2003). *Hospice manual*. Retrieved September 2, 2004, from http://www.cms.gov/manuals/21_hospice/hs0-fw.asp

Connor, S. (1998). *Hospice: Practice, pitfalls, and promise*. Washington, DC: Taylor & Francis.

Coyle, N., & Ferrell, B. (2001). *Textbook of palliative nursing*. New York: Oxford University Press.

Kabcenell, A., Lynn, J., & Schuster, J. (2000). *Improving care for the end of life*. New York: Oxford University Press.

Kaye, P. (1998). *Notes on symptom control in hospice & palliative care*. Machiasport, ME: Hospice Education Institute.

Kilburn, L. (1997). *Hospice operations manual*. Dubuque, IA: Kendall/Hunt.

Kinzbrunner, B.M., Weinreb, N.J., & Policzer, J.S. (2002). *20 common problems in end-of-life care*. New York: McGraw Hill.

Matzo, M., & Sherman, D. (2001). *Palliative care nursing: Quality care to the end of life*. New York: Springer.

National Hospice and Palliative Care Organization. (2003). *Facts & figures*. Alexandria, VA: Author.

Robert Wood Johnson Foundation. (2002). *Last Acts Campaign to improve care and caring near the end-of-life*. Retrieved September 2, 2004, from http://rwjf.org/programs/infoByArea.jsp?value=End-of-Life+care&id=000006

CHAPTER 31

In Search of Nursing Excellence

Joanne M. Hambleton, RN, MSN, CNA

In 1981, the governing council of the American Academy of Nursing appointed a task force to examine characteristics of systems impeding and/or facilitating professional nursing practice in hospitals (McClure, Poulin, Sovie, & Wandelt, 1983). The task force noted that although there were severe shortages of nurses reported by facilities across the country, a number of hospitals were not experiencing any problem in nursing retention and recruitment. Several hospitals had succeeded in creating a work environment that retained nurses. The task force referred to these nursing organizations as "magnets" for professional nurses because of their ability to attract and retain qualified nurses.

This chapter will review the phenomena of the magnet hospital program. Included in this chapter will be an overview of the nursing research studies that identify and describe characteristics and outcomes associated with magnet hospitals. A summary of the process required by the American Nurses Credentialing Center's (ANCC's) Magnet Hospital Program and tips on a successful application will be presented.

The recognition of magnet hospitals prompted a national study to identify factors that helped successful nursing organizations achieve their reputations for excellence as places for nurses to work. The task force members recognized that this work would be helpful to other organizations and could be instrumental in resolving the nursing shortage. The study, *Magnet Hospitals: Attraction and Retention of Professional Nurses,* was conducted in the fall of 1981 (McClure et al., 1983). There were two main questions to be answered by the study:

1. What are the important variables in the hospital organization and its nursing service that create the "magnetism" that attracts and retains professional nurses?
2. What combination of variables produces models of hospital nursing practice in which nurses have professional and personal satisfaction that leads to successful recruitment and retention of qualified nursing staff?

This study included two group interviews, one for the chief nursing officers and one for staff nurses conducted by a task force member. The interviews included the same nine questions for each group. The interviewees were asked to respond to questions about their organizations' reputation, job satisfaction, staff nurse involvement in activities and programs, nurse-physician relationships, leadership and staff relationships, and nursing recruitment and retention. The outcome of the study was very interesting. Both groups identified the same elements as contributors to "magnetism"; this finding was independent of size or region of the country. These elements were participative management style, strong and effective leadership, decentralized organizational structure, adequate staffing, availability of clinical nursing specialists, high number of BSN-prepared nursing staff, primary nursing care delivery models, autonomy of nurses, high value on teaching, positive image of nursing, excellent orientation and continuing education programs, support for formal education, and career development programs.

The original magnet hospital study (McClure et al., 1983) identified a combination of elements that created a positive work environment within these organizations for nurses to practice. These elements identified professional nursing practice and organizational values that could be used as building blocks for designing successful nursing practice models within healthcare delivery organizations. ANCC used the information gained from this study to design its inaugural Magnet Recognition Program in 1994.

Kramer (1990) revisited the magnet hospitals in the original study to see if they were being affected by the continuing nursing shortage. The study found that they had continued to experience limited or no impact from the nursing shortage. The magnet hospitals were engaging in a variety of innovative and challenging programs. As a group, the original magnet hospitals continued to display evidence of cultures of excellence and to design successful solutions to current problems in nursing care delivery.

The Nursing Work Index (NWI) was developed from the original magnet hospital report (McClure et al., 1983). NWI has been the major instrument used for more than 20 years to measure magnetism (Kramer & Hafner, 1989). Kramer and Hafner suggested from their work that when staff nurses are in autonomous, self-governing roles, there is an increase in levels of trust in their top managers because of the top manager's willingness to listen, respond, and value and respect roles and differences that are important.

Data from nurses from the original magnet studies and from the ANCC magnet program revealed 14 characteristics that differentiated magnet organizations from non-magnet organizations. These characteristics have become known as the "forces of magnetism" (ANCC, 2003) and are fundamental requirements in the ANCC magnet program (see Table 31-1). The characteristics (forces) are considered important factors in why magnet organizations are better able to recruit and retain nurses.

Magnet Application Process

The magnet application process is defined in the ANCC's "Health Care Organization Instructions and Application Process" manual (2003). ANCC is a separately incorporated nonprofit organization through which the American Nurses Association (ANA) offers credentialing programs and services.

Table 31-1. The Forces of Magnetism: Organizational Elements of Excellence in Nursing Care

Characteristics	Description
Quality of nursing leadership	Nurse leaders in magnet organizations are perceived as being knowledgeable risk takers who fully support the philosophies associated with autonomous nursing practice. They convey a strong sense of advocacy and support for their nursing staff.
Organizational structure	Magnet organizations have flat organizational structures with unit-based decision-making models. Nursing departments are decentralized and have strong nursing representation throughout the organization's committee structures. The nursing leader serves at the executive level of the organization.
Management style	Magnet hospital and nursing administrators use a participative management style that incorporates feedback from staff at all levels of the organization. Feedback is an important value in communication and decision-making properties of magnet organizations. Nursing leaders are visible, accessible, and committed to fostering strong communication between leaders and staff throughout the organization.
Personnel policies and programs	Magnet hospitals have competitive salaries and benefits. Nurse staffing and schedules are designed to be flexible in meeting patient care and staff needs. Staff nurses are actively involved and engaged in clinical promotion activities, administrative policy development, and in unit and organization-wide programs and activities.
Professional models of care	Models of care in magnet hospitals support the role of the registered nurse as the clinical leader with the responsibility and authority to plan and coordinate care. Nurses have accountability over their own practice and responsibility for their clinical competence.
Quality of care	Nurses in magnet hospitals perceive that they are providing high-quality care. Providing quality care is seen as an organization-wide priority. Nursing leaders in magnet hospitals are viewed as responsible for developing environments where high-quality care is provided.
Quality improvement	Quality improvement and performance management are viewed as educational activities and are inherently important to maintaining quality care in magnet hospitals. Staff nurses participate in performance improvement activities and perceive these processes as contributing to improvement initiatives in their organizations.
Consultation and resources	Magnet hospitals have experts available for staff nurses to provide advice and support in handling clinical and human resources issues. These experts include advanced practice nurses as well as peer support from nurses and other disciplines who have gained expert level knowledge to assist in care planning and coordination.
Autonomy	Magnet hospital nurses are permitted and expected to practice with autonomy, consistent with professional standards established within their organizations. Staff nurses use independent judgment, within the context of multidisciplinary collaboration, in all approaches to patient care.

(Continued on next page)

Table 31-1. The Forces of Magnetism: Organizational Elements of Excellence in Nursing Care *(Continued)*	
Characteristics	**Description**
Community and the hospital	Magnet hospitals have a strong connection to the community they serve and maintain a presence through a variety of ongoing community-focused activities. Outreach programs are present in magnet hospitals to ensure strong partnerships and positive corporate citizenship activities and outcomes.
Nurses as teachers	Magnet nurses are permitted, and expected, to integrate teaching in all aspects of their patient care activities. This integrated practice is perceived by the magnet nurses as one of the activities that provide a high level of professional satisfaction within their roles as staff nurses.
Image of nursing	Magnet nurses were viewed as integral to the organization's ability to provide patient care services. The care provided by the nursing staff is perceived by other disciplines and members of the organization as an essential ingredient in the mission of their organization.
Interdisciplinary relationships	Collaboration and mutual respect are fundamental in characterizing the way disciplines work together in magnet hospitals. The value and role of respect for one another is exhibited in all members of the healthcare team.
Professional development	Magnet hospitals place a significant emphasis on orientation, in-services, continuing education, formal education, and career development. Professional growth and development are valued, as are opportunities for competency-based clinical advancement and clinical competency.

Note. From "The ANCC Magnet Recognition Program: Converting Research Findings Into Action" (pp. 106–107) by L.D. Urden and K. Monarch in M.L. McClure and A.S. Hinshaw (Eds.), *Magnet Hospitals Revisited: Attraction and Retention of Professional Nurses,* 2002, Washington, DC: American Nurses Publishing. Copyright 2002 by the American Nurses Publishing Company. Reprinted with permission.

The magnet recognition program goals (ANCC, 2003) are

- Recognize nursing services that use the *Scope and Standards for Nurse Administrators* (ANA, 2004) to build programs of nursing excellence for the delivery of patient care.
- Promote quality in a milieu that supports professional nursing practice.
- Provide a vehicle for the dissemination of successful nursing practices and strategies.
- Promote positive patient outcomes.

The magnet application process consists of four phases (ANCC, 2003): (a) application, (b) submission of written documentation and evaluation, (c) a site visit, and (d) magnet recognition decision. Each phase will be reviewed in this text.

Tips for Successful Application

The process required to identify, explain, and exhibit the necessary documentation to meet the ANCC magnet standards is intense. Reviewing the standards and creating a working group to describe how your organization meets these standards require a significant amount of time, energy, and commitment to the process. The process must include staff nurse involvement from the beginning and throughout the process. Once you achieve magnet status, you also must maintain magnet status on a continuum.

Healthcare delivery systems have unique cultures and personalities. There are many ways to describe how an organization meets the standards required to achieve magnet status. ANCC magnet organizations come in all sizes and shapes. Large and small, general or specialty, urban or suburban, the magnet standards and responses describing how an organization meets a specific standard are as varied as healthcare organizations. However, there are some general methods most organizations follow to achieve magnet status.

A magnet coordinator is required by ANCC. This role is critical to the success of an application process. The coordinator needs to be a detail-oriented individual who can successfully lead a group. The magnet coordinator should be someone who knows your organization (its culture and personality), possesses great communication skills, has good writing skills, and has a positive attitude about the organization.

The ANCC Web site (www.nursingworld.org/ancc/magnet.html) is an excellent resource for information on the magnet program. The site provides an overview of the program, contact names from all magnet-designated organizations, publications, and programs available for organizations that are interested in obtaining information from the ANCC or from individual magnet organizations. This formal and informal network can be a valuable resource to organizations seeking ideas and suggestions for ways to enhance nursing services.

The ANA Institute for Research, Education, and Consultation (IREC) holds regional workshops to assist organizations in preparing for the magnet application process. These are hosted by magnet-designated facilities to share best practice concepts and steps they used to meet the ANCC magnet standards. The workshops offer general instructional sessions as well as private consultant sessions. Individual organizations can register to have ANCC magnet surveyors answer specific questions an organization may have related to its application process. IREC consultants also can be hired by an organization to help it through the magnet application process.

Each year, a national conference is held to review the ANCC magnet accreditation processes and to share cutting-edge practice or research. Many organizations send their magnet coordinators to this conference to network with other organizations and to begin to plan their strategies for their application. Some organizations send their entire magnet team to this conference. The conference is a wonderful way to get the application process officially started or to validate work the team has started. This is highly recommended for all interested in pursuing the magnet application process.

Once the magnet coordinator has been selected, the core working group for the magnet application process needs to be formed. This group should include specialists within the organization as well as a number of staff nurses and managers. A good mix will provide diverse ideas as the standards are assessed and evidence is identified within the organization. Consider nurses in advanced practice roles (clinical nurse specialist, staff development instructors), unit managers, and staff nurses from all settings (radiation, ambulatory clinics, interventional units, perioperative areas, critical care, surgery, medical oncology). Bring in specific individuals when needed, such as nurses with expertise in research, infection control, quality management, administration, and finance, to assist with the assembling necessary for the application process.

The process begins with working group members reading and understanding the magnet program standards. Initially, the language used in the standard statements may intimidate staff. The first few meetings may seem slow in progress, but as this familiarity grows and staff become more comfortable with the process, the activity and outcomes will begin to move at a quicker pace. Meetings held at least monthly for an entire day are the most productive.

The magnet working group responsibility is to identify examples of activities throughout the organization that reflect the intent of an individual standard. The group members obtain the needed information (policy and procedure; minutes from a task force, nursing committee, or council; continuing education brochure) from individuals, committees, or written materials. These can be filed by standard number, with a concise statement explaining why this example was selected. The nursing process is integrated throughout the ANCC magnet standards.

The magnet coordinator should develop an agenda for each meeting with assignments for each member. The agenda should include an overview of the goals and assignments for that session. Each session should include a status report from each group midway through the session to share examples each group has decided to use. The entire group should assess all examples to ensure the example is valid for the particular standard. This may be the time when a group member says, "Great example, but it may work better in this standard." Mixing and matching will continue throughout the application process. The meeting should end with a summary of the session accomplishments by each group. The magnet coordinator needs to identify work to be accomplished between sessions by the coordinator or others accountable for obtaining information. This may seem like a lot of work, but the time taken in the identification of examples is critical to the success in writing the application. This is the most time-consuming aspect of the process; spending the appropriate time on the application will be rewarded with a success.

Once you have completed the "hunting and gathering" of all of the information, it is time to start the writing phase. The writing phase is where the examples are used to tell your organization's story. It is where all the effort and work of your staff come alive into a document that provides, to the surveyors, evidence of your culture of excellence, your innovative ideas, your commitment to fostering excellent nursing practice, and superior patient care. When the document is complete, the organization will take pride in its achievements.

Phase I: The Application

An organization must conduct a self-evaluation of its nursing division using the ANA's *Scope and Standards for Nurse Administrators* (ANA, 2004). There is no imposed time limit on an organization conducting its self-assessment. These standards are available to the public without requiring the magnet application manual. Following this self-assessment, if the organization decides to pursue magnet status, it must identify a magnet project director and complete an application form indicating the planned date for submission of the written documentation. An application fee (established by ANCC) must accompany the application form and is nonrefundable. The written documentation must be submitted within two years from the date of the submitted application fee and form.

Phase II: Submission of Written Documentation and Evaluation

The application requires written documentation described within the application manual (ANCC, 2003). The standards include measurement criteria for standards of care (23) and standards of professional performance (40). In addition, demographic information is collected, and an organizational overview is required. For an organization to move on to a site survey, a score must be achieved from the written documentation that is within the range of excellence. The criteria are identified within the application manual, along with the scoring and required ranges for excellence within each category. An additional application fee is sent with the written documentation, which is based upon the size of an organization.

Phase III: The Site Visit

When the written documentation achieves scores within the range of excellence, as determined by the magnet reviewers, the appraisers from ANCC schedule a site visit. The range of excellence scores is determined by ANCC for each of the 14 standards. Each range has a predetermined required score, with ranges from 40–100, depending upon the particular standard. The total range for score must be within 800–1000. Travel costs and expenses for the site surveyors associated with the site visit are the responsibility of the applicant. Mutually agreeable dates are determined, and an agenda for the visit is provided to the applicant. The purpose of the visit is to verify, clarify, and amplify the content of the written application as well as to evaluate the organization milieu in which nursing is practiced (ANCC, 2003). The appraisers will be evaluating the degree to which the "forces of magnetism" are evident throughout the organization.

Phase IV: Magnet Recognition Decision

The appraisers provide a confidential summary report of their assessment of the application and site visit to the ANCC Commission on Magnet Recognition. After reviewing the information, the commission is responsible for determining whether the organization has provided evidence of a dynamic, innovative, excellence-focused organization that possesses the forces of magnetism. After the commission votes on the applicant, the organization is contacted and informed of its decision.

The magnet status is awarded for a four-year period. Annually, each magnet-designated organization must complete interim reports to ANCC to ensure continued compliance with the magnet recognition standards. To achieve redesignation, the applicant must submit written documentation, successfully achieving scores within the range of excellence, and pass the site survey process.

Magnet Readiness

How does an organization determine if it is ready for magnet application? All organizations have some of the characteristics of "the forces of magnetism." Even if an organization is not ready to apply for magnet status, there are aspects of the magnet process that can be used to enhance care delivery and improve models of professional practice. The criteria defined by the magnet program can be used to identify values and goals within nursing organizations and healthcare delivery organizations to enhance care delivery. Many organizations adopt the magnet standards as part of a strategic goal for nursing services (Duchene, 2002; Upenieks, 2003).

Organizations interested in applying for magnet status also must participate in the National Center for Nursing Quality (NCNQ) (ANCC, 2003). NCNQ collects nurse-sensitive data to evaluate the impact of nursing care within an organization. The data elements include patient injury rates (falls occurrence); maintenance of skin integrity (pressure ulcer prevalence and occurrence); patient and nursing staff satisfaction (trending and benchmarking); skill mix (RNs, LPNs, assistive personnel); and nursing hours provided per day. NCNQ provides quarterly reports to member organizations. The reports provide opportunity for all participants to benchmark nursing units with others in this database. Organizations must participate in the NCNQ surveys prior to the submission of their written documentation.

Magnet Success

The success of the magnet program is evident by the plethora of articles and research activities surrounding magnet hospitals and their impact on nurse satisfaction and patient care. The concept of magnet hospitals has evolved based upon the research conducted over the past 20 years and the impact of the cyclical problem of the nursing shortage throughout this period as well (Urden & Monarch, 2002). Many healthcare-related boards and organizations consider magnet status the "gold standard" (American Hospital Association, 2002; McKim, 2003; Nursing Executive Center, 2000a, 2000b).

Linda Aiken, director at the Center for Health Services and Policy Research at the University of Pennsylvania, has conducted a series of outcome studies that evaluate the impact of magnet hospitals on nurse satisfaction and patient outcomes. Her work built upon the work of Kramer and Schmalenberg (1991a, 1991b) using the NWI (Aiken & Patrician, 2000). Havens and Aiken (1999) compared 39 magnet hospitals with five comparison hospitals matched on hospital characteristics for a sample size of 234 nurses. The magnet hospitals demonstrated statistically superior outcomes, including lower Medicare mortality rates and slightly better RN-to-patient ratios. ANCC-designated magnet hospitals consistently demonstrate stronger support of professional nursing practice. This was further validated by a study of ANCC-designated magnet hospitals compared with the hospitals identified from the original magnet study in 1983 (Aiken, Havens, & Sloane, 2000). The study compared whether hospitals accredited by ANCC were as successful in creating excellent nursing care environments as the original American Academy of Nursing's (1983) magnet hospitals were. The study found that the ANCC-designated magnet hospitals were successful in creating excellent environments for nurses to practice. The ANCC-designated magnet hospitals had a significantly higher ratio of RNs to patients than the original magnet study hospitals. The ANCC-designated magnet hospitals had lower burnout rates, higher levels of job satisfaction, and gave their hospitals higher ratings for the quality of care provided than the nurses from the original magnet study. This study provides validation that ANCC magnet hospital designation is a valid benchmark of nursing practice excellence and a way for consumers to identify hospitals with good nursing care.

Value of Magnet Designation

Most organizations need a year to complete the application process. The process is intense, but the reward of magnet status makes the effort justifiable. Magnet status is a symbol of excellence (Havens & Aiken, 1999; McKim, 2003). It is used by many organizations to market and communicate the success of an organization (Nurse Executive Center, 2000a). Magnet status is prominently displayed on Web sites, recruitment and marketing ads, and in written media from magnet-designated organizations.

Magnet status is becoming a recruitment tool for organizations as well. Nurses, especially new graduates, evaluate the presence of magnet hospitals when considering applying for positions. The magnet program, and the success of magnet hospitals, is becoming better known as the number of magnet-designated hospitals grows (Gasda, 2003). The American Organization of Nurse Executives has stated that it believes healthcare organizations participating in, or contemplating, a workplace redesign effort should consider what it refers to as "framing excellence in the work environment" (McKim, 2003). It is recommending that groups consider broad organizational structures and philosophical approaches to achieving organizational improvements. Magnet hospitals are included within this framework as an example of an organizational classifier for best practice.

Magnet status is a positive message for nurses and for the healthcare delivery industry. The attainment of magnet status is a way to provide international recognition for the work of nurses. Magnet hospitals are more than just great places for nurses to work. Magnet hospitals have fewer deaths per discharge (Scott, Sochalski, & Aiken, 1999) and are recommended as criteria for individuals who are evaluating local healthcare systems (Parker-Pope, 2001). Magnet hospitals also are described as employers with an exceptional commitment to helping minority nurses advance their careers (Carol, 2002). The characteristics of the magnet hospital are one of the most positive concepts that have been designed for nursing.

The magnet award is a reward for the entire healthcare organization that achieves this status. Magnet organizations provide environments where nurses can achieve excellence. Excellence in nursing means excellence in patient care, a goal everyone in health care should be seeking.

Summary

The magnet recognition and award process is built upon years of research that demonstrates that there are specific ways nursing practice can be supported. Integrating these strategies into healthcare environments, nurses and patients achieve high satisfaction and positive outcomes. Improved nurse retention, decreased patient mortality, and high patient and nurse satisfaction scores are all outcomes associated with magnet hospitals. Sustainable programs that foster and support nurses will help healthcare organizations achieve their goals of providing service excellence. Nursing leaders must embrace the magnet ideals and help their organizations create environments where nurses, support staff, and patients thrive. The magnet success stories can help us lead the way to a better future for nurses and the healthcare industry.

References

Aiken, L., Havens, D.S., & Sloane, D.M. (2000). The magnet nursing services recognition program: A comparison of two groups of magnet hospitals. *American Journal of Nursing, 100*(3), 26–35.

Aiken, L., & Patrician, P. (2000). Measuring organizational traits of hospitals: The revised Nursing Work Index. *Nursing Research, 49,* 146–153.

American Academy of Nursing. Task Force on Nursing Practice in Hospitals. (1983). *Magnet hospitals: Attraction and retention of professional nurses.* Kansas City, MO: American Nursing Publishing.

American Hospital Association. (2002). *In our hands: How hospital leaders can build a thriving workforce.* Washington, DC: AHA Commission on Workforce for Hospitals and Health Systems.

American Nurses Association. (2004). *Scope and standards for nurse administrators.* Washington, DC: American Nursing Publishing.

American Nurses Credentialing Center. (2003). *The magnet nursing services recognition program: Health care organization instructions and application process.* Washington, DC: Author.

Carol, R. (2002, Spring). Career magnetism. *Minority Nurse.* Retrieved October 29, 2004, from http://www.minoritynurse.com/features/nurse_emp/05-02-02a.html

Duchene, P. (2002). Leadership's guiding light. *Nursing Management, 33*(9), 28–30.

Gasda, K. (2003). The magnet pull. *Nursing Management, 34*(1), 41–45.

Havens, D., & Aiken, L. (1999). Shaping systems to promote desired outcomes: The magnet hospital model. *Journal of Nursing Administration, 29*(2), 14–20.

Kramer, M. (1990). The magnet hospitals: Excellence revisited. *Journal of Nursing Administration, 20*(9), 35–44.

Kramer, M., & Hafner, L.P. (1989). Shared values: Impact on staff nurse job satisfaction and perceived productivity. *Nursing Research, 38,* 172–177.

Kramer, M., & Schmalenberg, C. (1991a). Job satisfaction and retention. Insights for the 90's. Part I. *Nursing, 91*(3), 50–55.

Kramer, M., & Schmalenberg, C. (1991b). Job satisfaction and retention. Insights for the 90's. Part II. *Nursing, 91*(4), 51–55.

McClure, M., Poulin, M., Sovie, M., & Wandelt, M. (1983). *Magnet hospitals attraction and retention of professional nurses.* American Academy of Nursing Task Force on nursing practice in hospitals. Kansas City, MO: American Nurses Association.

McKim, S. (2003, July/August). Healthy work environments. Nurse leader. *American Organization of Nurse Executives,* pp. 15–22.

Nursing Executive Center. (2000a, November 10). Hospitals advertise magnet status to remain competitive in the search for nurses. *Nursing Watch.*

Nursing Executive Center. (2000b, October 27). Magnet hospitals attract national attention. *Nursing Watch.*

Parker-Pope, T. (2001, March 2). How to lessen impact of nursing shortage on your hospital stay. *Wall Street Journal,* p. D1.

Scott, J.G., Sochalski, J., & Aiken, L. (1999). Review of magnet hospital research: Findings and implications for professional nursing practice. *Journal of Nursing Administration, 29*(1), 9–19.

Upenieks, V. (2003). What's the attraction to magnet hospitals? *Nursing Management, 34*(2), 43–44.

Urden, L.D., & Monarch, K. (2002). The ANCC magnet recognition program: Converting research findings into action. In M.L. McClure & A.S. Hinshaw (Eds.), *Magnet hospitals revisited: Attraction and retention of professional nurses* (pp. 103–116). Washington, DC: American Nurses Publishing.

Nursing Information Systems

Deborah A. Houston, MS, RN, CPHIMS

As health care has become more automated over the years, the need for nursing staff to become familiar with computers and computer applications to do daily work has become more commonplace. In many institutions, nurses use computers to retrieve patient information and clinical results, enter patient data, access reference information via the Internet or their institutions intranet, request time off and schedule staff, complete employee evaluations, and a wide variety of other activities. Having basic computer knowledge has become a prerequisite for hiring in many settings. This chapter will provide an overview of information systems and technology facing nursing today. It is written with the nurse manager in mind, giving a broad overview of the topic. Texts are available that provide a more in-depth presentation of the topics discussed.

State of the Technology

Many institutions have had clinical results (laboratory values, pathology reports, radiology reports, physician transcription) available online for some time. More recently, systems to support nursing practice have developed. These systems encompass not only documentation of care given, but support the entire nursing continuum, from staffing and productivity systems to care planning, care management, and outcomes applications.

The majority of systems that support nursing are part of the basic hospital information system (HIS). HIS usually provides functionality that supports patient registration and demographics, patient billing, and documentation. In many cases, large HIS vendors also provide functionality that supports departmental processes (laboratory/pathology, pharmacy, diagnostic imaging) as well as allied health department functionality. Often patient scheduling is part of a basic HIS application.

The majority of healthcare institutions select commercial vendor products for their HIS systems. Some of the larger HIS vendors include Cerner Corporation, Eclipsys,

EPIC, IDX, Misys Healthcare, and Siemens Medical Systems. There are numerous other vendors that may support part or all of HIS functionality. These systems can support nursing practice and can be configured and built to meet the majority of nursing requirements.

In the realm of oncology-specific HIS vendors, IMPAC, iKnowMed, and OpTx provide specific oncology functionality. These systems may be in use in medical office practice settings or oncology departments of larger institutions. The systems are specifically focused to the niche of oncology, and many institutions are unable to support a separate system for this patient population. In some larger institutions, internal information technology staff has custom-built systems in lieu of purchasing a vendor-supported system. This approach may be able to provide the specific user requirements that a commercial vendor cannot deliver; however, it can be a very costly and lengthy process to develop these systems to maturity (Morris, 2002).

Business Planning for Purchasing

As institutions plan for purchase of an HIS, all user groups who will use the system should be involved in the selection process. Process analysis must be undertaken to evaluate all user needs for the new system (Smith, 2000). Nursing staff should clearly identify the minimal essential requirements to support nursing practice. For example, functionality may be present to allow the nurse to document routine assessment of patients but may not include a chemotherapy toxicity grading scale as part of the basic assessment package. In addition, awareness that no system will provide 100% of the functionality desired must be realized. A conscious decision in system selection must be a compromise to obtain the most functionality possible yet be reasonable in requests for specific or specialty items. If a nononcology focused vendor is being considered, then requiring specific oncology-related functionality to be present in the product selected may greatly limit the available applications.

One key aspect to planning for selection of an HIS system is to clearly identify needs and wants for the new system. Research systems at other institutions of similar size and type. Does the application work as anticipated? Visit HIS vendor booths at conferences, being cognizant that the vendor representatives are most often sales oriented and may not be aware of the true faults and weaknesses of the respective system. Determine if the product being demonstrated is in production or in development. Have selected vendors visit your facility and demonstrate their system, showing specific functionality required for your institution. Form a core group of participants from all areas of the institution to participate in this process and evaluate demonstrations.

Implementation of nursing systems is usually part of a larger HIS project. Budgets for the overall implementation should include nursing "subject matter experts." These staff may take the role of system analysts within the information technology (IT) department or end user staff "loaned" to IT for the project timeline. Either way, good collaboration with the user department is a necessity.

Applications to Clinical Practice

Systems used to support nursing care should include the ability to collect and display data from assessments and planning, vital signs and demographics, fluid balance, and medication administration records at a minimum. In many instances, this basic functionality can be configured to provide specific data entry screens to collect specific admission assessments, discharge planning, patient/family teaching, and other care requirements. Data collection tools that provide the ability to document toxicity grading or tolerance to chemotherapy also may be able to be configured by basic HIS vendor systems.

The change in the way nurses document work must be considered in determining the implementation sequence of nursing functionality. Therefore, in most cases, nursing departments choose to implement electronic documentation in phases. Not only does this assist in decreasing time required for training, it does not overwhelm the nursing staff by implementing all of their documentation online at one time. For example, basic vital signs documentation may be implemented first, followed by admission assessments, patient and family education documentation, then discharge summaries. Shift-to-shift assessment documentation that may take a larger amount of time by the nurse may be implemented later.

Although systems can be configured to support nursing activities, additional functionality can be provided for other members of the healthcare team. Nutritional assessments performed by nursing upon admission to the hospital can be electronically transmitted to the dietary department, signaling criteria that require intervention or further assessment by a registered dietitian. Assessment of a patient's functional status when presented to the healthcare institution can be communicated to all members of the team, identifying that the patient may be at a high risk for falls and signaling the physical therapist to perform a further in-depth assessment of need for assistive devices. Assessments by respiratory therapists can be reflected in the electronic record, demonstrating an improvement or decline in patients' respiratory status.

Overall, electronic documentation of patient status, by any member of the healthcare team, can be accessed and reviewed by all members of the team. This not only provides timely communication of information, it ultimately can prevent duplication of effort and rapid notification of patient abnormalities. Systems can be built to provide electronic notification of abnormal findings or critical laboratory values. In some instances, this notification can be relayed directly to the care provider's pager or cell phone, which can enhance the response time to deal with the abnormal or critical findings.

System Integration

As systems are implemented, integration of the entire patient record must be considered. The overall goal of electronic information systems is to provide easy access to patient information, eliminate duplication of work, and enhance communication within the healthcare team. Integration of various applications must occur to meet these goals.

In most cases, the institution's HIS provides basic patient demographic information throughout the various applications in use. This provides consistent data related to patient name, address, next of kin, or allergies. Ensuring that the various applications receive these basic patient data from the source system is imperative to keeping the systems consistent. Updates to this information, such as local phone numbers, must be made in the source system, or interfaces between the applications must be present to update in one system and have the other systems reflect the current information.

The ability of nursing documentation to automatically display data from other automated systems (laboratory results, pharmacy) and send data to other systems is an advantage of an electronic system. This eliminates the need for redundant data entry. For example, entry of allergy information into the HIS system transmits that information to the hospital's operating room information system. Inputting new allergy information determined from a reaction while the patient was in the operating room communicates that information immediately back to the main HIS system. This allows access of information by all members of the healthcare team.

Developing a Nursing Informatics Program

The practice of nursing informatics may take many forms, from planning and implementation positions, to change management, to being the conduit between information systems and user departments. In larger institutions, nursing informatics professionals may be found both in nursing departments as well as in IT.

Dependent on the intended direction of nursing informatics positions, the staff can be either a part of IT or a defined group within the nursing department. In many instances, the nursing positions found in IT tend to be more application or project dependent, functioning in roles such as project manager, clinical analyst, or support analyst. Nursing department informatics nurses may provide advisory roles, workflow analysis, and clinical direction, as well as user support. In either case, nurses working this arena are increasing in numbers, as well as in recognition. The American Nurses Association published the *Standards of Nursing Informatics* in 1994. The American Nurses Credentialing Center (1998) has provided specialty certification in this area since 1995 (Hassett, 2000).

Staffing for these programs is based on the focus of the positions. For a departmental-focused informatics program, the positions may be as few as one (a dedicated nurse informatician to act as a liaison to IT) or may be several if application support and user training is part of this group. If coverage for this service is 24 hours/7 days a week, the number of staff can be substantial. Budgeting for these positions usually is covered by operational cost centers. In some instances, if the positions are engaged in system design and configuration, capital-funding sources may be used.

When determining staff necessary to support applications during implementation, the scope of the implementation must be taken into consideration. If the support is for the initial deployment of an application or part of an application, the number of staff needed will be greater. In most cases, one support person per nursing unit or floor of nursing units for the initial few days of implementation is ideal. This level of support is needed around the clock as well. This will allow the staff to have easy access to support staff, float staff, and trainees and to provide coverage for staff that are off on the first day. Usually after two or three days of intense support, the numbers of staff can be decreased significantly.

Dependent on the presence or the ability of the institutions' IT help desk to assume the support role for applications and respond to calls, having staff available on an ongoing basis may be necessary. In most cases, this can be done on an on-call type situation, provided the support staff has access to the application being supported from home. This may require computer equipment as well as available access to the support staff at home. Access can be provided via a virtual private network connection from home or dial-up access via a computer modem. Dial-up access also may necessitate the person has a cell phone so that he or she can be on the phone with the caller and access the application at the same time. As users get more familiar with the applications in use, the calls to the support staff diminish and hopefully will only be a rare occurrence.

Information Security

Information security is intended to protect information (e.g., personal data, healthcare data, financial information, payroll information) from access by unauthorized users as well as from unintended loss of that data. Security is aimed at protecting not only the information systems themselves but also the data held within the system. System security is aimed at providing not only physical protection of systems, but also it is preventing unauthorized users from accessing applications (Young, 2000).

Physical safety factors include having uninterrupted power sources for the computer hardware (desktop personal computers as well as the main computer system that supports the applications). Nursing staff should ensure that at least one computer/monitor on each nursing unit is plugged into an emergency power outlet. In addition, a review of equipment that connects to the computer (cardiac monitors, blood pressure monitors, pulse oximeters) also should be conducted. This equipment needs emergency power access as well.

Ensuring that data entered into the HIS are backed up is a part of system security. Copies of files kept on personal computers should be backed up to disk or stored on a central computer network that is backed up by central IT. Routine storage of data from the HIS system should be managed by the IT department; however, nursing should be aware of the procedure and steps to gain access to the data if needed. In addition, a disaster recovery plan should be present. Nursing units should be aware of downtime procedures and how to revert back to paper documentation when needed. Policies and procedures on how to manage downtime should be developed. This includes policies on how many data are to be reentered into the system when it becomes available or how to document in the electronic system where data can be found that were collected during an unexpected system outage.

Data security revolves around who should have access to what data in the system. With the advent of the Health Insurance Portability and Accountability Act (HIPAA), institutions are required to comply with the auditing capability of systems as well as securing systems by information access based on the healthcare provider's role. In most cases, nursing systems may have distinct roles for the RN or licensed vocational nurse that are separate from a nursing assistant or unit secretary. Examples are that a nursing assistant may be able to document vital signs taken on a patient, but the RN must be the one to document the assessment that accompanies the abnormal vital signs.

The security of the data contained in the HIS is critical. User IDs and passwords are to be kept confidential, and policies should be in effect to prevent sharing. Support must be available 24 hours a day to assist users who forget their ID or password. Passwords also require renewal or changing on some routine basis. In most cases, staff signs an information security confidentiality statement annually or at least upon employment. This statement reinforces the institution's intention to keep data secure and deal with staff who share data or access data inappropriately.

Application of Nursing Information Systems in Practice

Use of electronic systems to provide tools to document nursing care is at the core of nursing information systems. Nursing systems can include those that provide documentation of patient care as well as those that manage the nursing staff (staffing and productivity applications and those that provide performance management).

The ability to document the assessment, planning, interventions provided, and evaluation of those interventions is key to these nursing systems. Collection and display of data obtained from nurses are available to all members of the staff. Abnormal vital signs or excessive weight gain or loss can be routed to the RN for validation. Staff can easily review data values entered on the previous shift. "Exception charting" can be implemented if the institution's documentation policies allow that type of charting.

Specialty area (operating room, intensive care unit, recovery room) documentation can be configured in most general HIS applications by additional modules. Numerous specialty vendors also provide this specific type of functionality, providing interface connections to critical care equipment (monitors, ventilators). Two of these specialty vendors are Surgical Information Systems and PICIS.

Other areas of nursing management that can benefit from automation include systems that provide staffing and productivity applications and patient acuity systems. Staff scheduling can be facilitated, including staff self-scheduling if desired. Productivity data can be collected from these systems, demonstrating staff required based on the acuity of patients versus staff hours actually worked. Patient acuity systems often are used in nursing. These systems can be found as part of a major HIS vendor's offerings, usually at a separate cost from the basic system.

Additional applications can be developed or purchased to support other nursing initiatives. Performance improvement or quality assurance activities and tracking can be facilitated by the use of automated systems. Frequently, internal IT resources build these types of applications, but numerous companies exist that also provide these services.

Summary

The need for nurses to interact with electronic systems is now commonplace in most healthcare settings. Nurses should see this change in how information is documented and delivered to others as a challenge. Once nurses are familiar with computers and electronic devices, the easier it will be to adapt to this new technology. Remember when the first automated IV pumps were introduced to nursing? Remember when the electronic thermometer became part of everyday use? Soon, we will not give a second thought to the use of a computer in our everyday care of patients. Over time, nursing systems will become more user friendly. As more nurses get involved in the field of informatics, commercial HIS vendors will be influenced to build systems that simplify the ability of the nurse to care for patients. It is only a matter of time.

References

American Nurses Association. (1994). *Standards of nursing informatics*. Washington, DC: American Nurses Publishing.

American Nurses Credentialing Center. (1998). *Informatics nurse certification catalog*. Washington, DC: American Nurses Association.

Hassett, M. (2000). Nursing informatics practice development. In M. Brady & M. Hassett (Eds.), *Clinical informatics* (pp. 113–122). Chicago: Healthcare Information and Management Systems Society.

Morris, M. (2002). Selection of oncology information systems. In M.J. Ball, C.G. Chute, J.V. Douglas, C.P. Langlotz, J.C. Niland, W.L. Scherlis, et al. (Eds.), *Cancer informatics: Essential technologies for clinical trials* (pp. 250–269). New York: Springer-Verlag.

Smith, K. (2000). Needs assessment. In M. Brady & M. Hassett (Eds.), *Clinical informatics* (pp. 15–24). Chicago: Healthcare Information and Management Systems Society.

Young, K.M. (2000). *Informatics for healthcare professionals*. Philadelphia: F.A. Davis.

Nursing Research: Current Perspectives and Future Trends

Susan M. Bauer-Wu, DNSc, RN
Mary E. Cooley, PhD, CRNP, CS
Martha W. Healey, RN, MS, FNP

Nurse managers need to have an appreciation of nursing research for a number of reasons. Recognition that nursing knowledge is not static, but ever changing and improving, is the hallmark to excellence in patient care. Supporting a practice environment that questions if the care given is the best it can be is a *win-win* for everyone: patients receive the best possible care, nursing staff is empowered and stimulated to think *outside of the box*, and they can feel assured that they are providing the highest quality of care based on evidence. Supporting an evidence-based practice environment allows nursing managers and administrators to benefit from such secondary gains as patient and nurse satisfaction, which can have a positive impact on staff retention and fiscal matters.

It is important to realize that the term "nursing research" implies two aspects: the use of research methods (conducting research) and techniques to evaluate and guide practice (utilizing research) (Norris, 1999). Involving clinical staff in nursing research activities is very important and can be accomplished in a variety of ways. Staff can team up with a nurse scientist (e.g., doctoral-prepared nurse researcher) to be the clinical experts on a study. As co-investigators, they can provide valuable insights into the patient experience and essential information about the logistics of carrying out the study. Clinical staff can partner with the nurse scientist in a mentored relationship. In this way, clinicians function as co-principal investigators who are involved in every step of the study from development, to implementation, to dissemination of findings. Nurses can play a key role in recruitment and data collection activities, which can be incorporated into usual patient care. Finally, clinical nurses are integral to the success of research utilization and evidence-based practice activities. Involving staff at this level makes research real to them and helps them to embrace practice changes that are based on research findings.

This chapter provides an overview of nursing research and its application in the clinical setting. Attention will be given to both the general nuts and bolts of conducting research as well as the use of research to guide nursing practice. The conduct and utilization of research are interdependent processes in that both processes are needed to advance the science of nursing practice. An understanding of these processes can guide nurse managers to make effective decisions about incorporating research into their clinical environments.

Basics of Conducting Research

Conducting research is quite labor and resource intensive and requires research skills and experience. Before embarking on such an undertaking, it is critical to understand the different types of research, the steps to conduct research, and the necessary resources that are required. The following section will provide a brief overview and important considerations for the conduct of research. For novice researchers who are planning to carry out a study, it is highly recommended to use comprehensive research methods textbooks as well as to team up or consult with an experienced researcher.

Although research can be performed independently, it is more likely to be successful with a research team. Each member of the team brings complementary skills and resources to collaborate on projects of shared interest. Ideally the research team is interdisciplinary, composed of members from disciplines such as nursing, medicine, statistics, immunology, psychology, pharmacology, and economics. "An interdisciplinary collaborative approach is necessary to achieve a richness of research information for the discipline of nursing" (Nies, Hepworth, & Fickens, 2001, p. 411). In successful interdisciplinary team functioning, team members rely upon and trust the contributions of other members and are likely to generate higher quality data, publications, presentations, and improved health outcomes (Nies et al.).

Research Methodology

There are three general methods for conducting research: quantitative, qualitative, and triangulation. Quantitative research generates "hard" data that are quantified numerically and are often hypothesis driven. It uses deductive logic to systematically and objectively answer questions regarding a topic about which one has some knowledge (Begley, 1996). Qualitative research, on the other hand, is inductive and exploratory and generally is not hypothesis driven (Bailey, 1997). Qualitative research methods "study things in their natural settings, attempting to make sense of, or interpret, phenomena in terms of the meanings people bring to them" (Begley, p. 122). One method is not necessarily superior to the other. The choice of which to use, quantitative or qualitative, depends upon the research questions and how to most appropriately answer them. The decision may be influenced by constraints of time and resources and the researcher's particular skills (Begley). A mixed methods approach combines quantitative and qualitative methods and is known as "triangulation." This method can sometimes provide a fuller and more accurate description of the phenomenon or population studied than a single approach (Begley). Although triangulation often adds richness and strength to the study, it also increases the complexity of the research design, requiring more time and resources. Regardless of the research method chosen, there are specific steps that generally occur when conducting research (see Figure 33-1).

Figure 33-1. Steps of Conducting Research

1. Define the clinical problem.
2. Identify the research question(s).
3. Conduct a comprehensive review of the literature.
4. Identify the conceptual framework (not always in qualitative).
5. State the purpose, specific aims, and hypotheses (if quantitative).
6. Define the study variables and determine how they will be assessed and measured (i.e., selection of instruments, if quantitative, and interview guide, if qualitative).
7. Describe the sample and data collection procedures.
8. Analyze the data.
9. Interpret the results.
10. Disseminate the findings.

When considering what method or design to use, it is important to determine the *state of the science* of the phenomena of interest. In some areas of nursing science, there is a lack of substantial rigorous evidence to guide clinical practice. Sometimes, what evidence is known comes from studies in which the sample was small or restricted to a single clinical setting or population. If this is the case, replication research can strengthen confidence in (or refute) the original findings, or it could increase generalizability beyond the original study sample(s) (Gould, 2002). Focusing on secondary data analysis is another option to consider. With secondary data analysis, the data were collected for another purpose yet are available for analysis to answer other research questions. This approach is often less expensive (and sometimes free), can be accomplished with less effort than primary data collection, and can be analyzed in less time (Nicoll & Beyea, 1999).

Defining the Problem and Identifying the Research Question(s)

Nurses in clinical practice are well positioned to identify clinical problems worthy of investigation. Many of the best research questions arise through observations and experiences in day-to-day patient care. Nurses may wonder if there is a better way to carry out a procedure or if there are innovative approaches to addressing such patient issues as symptom management. McCorkle (1990) identified four methods that a nurse can use to identify a research problem: (a) direct observations, thoughts, and experience, (b) discussion with experienced nurses, (c) reading the literature and recognizing discrepancies, and (d) evaluating a theory about a substantive field. Once a problem has been identified, the next step is to carefully analyze it to develop the research question(s) (McCorkle, p. 30).

Perhaps the most important step to performing good research is identifying the research question(s). These need to be focused, clear, and explicit. A study with an exquisite design and meticulous data collection procedures can produce meaningless findings if the research question is vague and lacks the characteristics of a good clinical research question. These characteristics can be remembered by using the mnemonic FINER: Feasible, Interesting, Novel, Ethical, Relevant (Cummings, Browner, & Hulley, 1988). Feasible means that the study is doable—there is an adequate number of eligible subjects, sufficient resources (including technology), affordable in time and money, and the project is manageable in scope (Cummings et al.). Interesting means that the investigator has a genuine interest and passion to complete this study. Clinical research can be a lengthy and laborious process, and investigators can easily drift away from completing all the steps of a study if they lose interest in the topic. Novel means that the study has the potential to provide new findings, extend previous findings, or confirm or refute previous findings. Ethical means that the study can be carried out while maintaining the best interests of the research subjects and that it does not pose unacceptable risks or invasion of privacy. Finally, relevant means that the study has a strong likelihood for advancing scientific knowledge (i.e., nursing science), influencing clinical management and health policy, and guiding future research (Cummings et al.).

Nurse-Sensitive Outcomes and Measurement

Nurse-sensitive outcome indicators "focus on how patients, and their conditions, are affected by interaction with nursing staff" (American Nurses Association, 1995, viii). In order for an outcome to be identified as sensitive to nursing, there needs to be empirical evidence linking nursing input and interventions to the outcome (Doran, 2003). Research has already generated an initial list of outcomes that have consistently been found to be sensitive to nursing care provision across the continuum of healthcare settings. These include (a) clinical outcomes related to the management of symptoms (e.g., pain, nausea and vomiting, fatigue), (b) functional outcomes associated with self-care abilities and physical and psychosocial functioning, (c) safety outcomes, which include adverse incidents and complications (e.g., decubitus ulcers, falls), and (d) perceptual outcomes related to satisfaction with nursing care and with the results of that care (Doran).

Identifying the most appropriate instruments to measure study outcomes can be challenging and time-consuming. Beck (1999) stated that "the choice of a research instrument is critical to the success of a study and the confidence that can be placed in the research findings" (p. 21). Instruments need to be both valid (measuring what it is intended to measure) and reliable (measuring the same phenomenon over time).

There are various types of validity (e.g., content, criterion, construct) and reliability (e.g., inter-rater, test-retest, homogeneity/equivalence) that need to be evaluated and considered before using an instrument. Criteria for assessing research instruments are described in Figure 33-2.

Figure 33-2. Questions for Assessing Research Instruments

I. Assessing the development of the instrument
  Did the developer identify a theoretical basis for the instrument?
  How was the instrument conceptually defined?
  How was the instrument operationally defined?
  How were the instrument items generated and refined?
  What types of validity did the developer assess? (content, criterion-related, construct)
  How were these types of validity assessed?
  Were acceptable levels of validity achieved?
  What types of reliability did the developer assess? (stability, equivalence, internal consistency)
  What were the sample characteristics of the subjects involved in the developer's psychometric testing?

II. Assessing the psychometric testing of the instrument by other researchers
  What types of samples has the instrument been used with?
  What types of reliability were assessed?
  What levels of reliability were achieved with these samples?
  What types of validity were assessed?
  What levels of validity were achieved with these samples?

Note. From "Opening Students' Eyes. The Process of Selecting a Research Instrument," by C.T. Beck, 1999, *Nurse Educator, 24*(3), pp. 21–23. Copyright 1999 by Lippincott Williams & Wilkins. Reprinted with permission.

Human Subject Considerations

It is imperative to understand issues related to the protection of human subjects and to obtain necessary training in this area before one institutes her or his first research project. An appreciation of historical issues helps to underscore the importance of human subject considerations.

At the conclusion of World War II, the unethical treatment of human subjects was revealed during the Doctors Trial of the Nuremberg Proceedings. During this trial, 20 German physicians were accused of planning and enacting the "Euthanasia Program," the systematic killing of those deemed unworthy of life. In addition, they were accused of conducting pseudoscientific medical experiments on concentration camp prisoners without their consent, many of whom subsequently died. As a result, the Nuremberg Code was established to address the necessity for voluntary consent of human subjects, the importance of due diligence to minimize risks to human subjects, and the need to allow subjects the right to terminate participation at any time (*Trials of War Criminals,* 1949–1953).

Unethical treatment of human subjects was not exclusive to World War II and Nazi Germany; it also was occurring in the United States. The Tuskegee Syphilis Study, initiated by the U.S. Public Health Service, was conducted from 1932 to 1972. The study was a nontherapeutic study examining the long-term effects of syphilis on African American men from Macon County, Alabama. The participants received incentives of medical examinations, meals, a small stipend, and burial insurance. However, none of the participants received informed consent outlining the risk related to participation. In addition, curative treatment for the disease, penicillin discovered in 1946, was withheld from these men. Press reports in the early 1970s caused the study to close, and more than 100 men had died and others suffered needlessly (Jones, 1993). The Tuskegee Syphilis Study triggered congressional hearings and initiated new laws for the protection of human subjects.

As a result of the Tuskegee Syphilis Study, the National Research Act was signed into law in 1974. This act established the National Commission for the Protection of Human Subjects of Biomedical and Behavioral Research, created regulations for the protection of human subjects, and established institutional review boards (IRBs) for any research involving human subjects. In addition, the National Commission for the Protection of Human Subjects of Biomedical and Behavioral Research met in 1976 to identify the basic ethical principles to guide research conduct involving human subjects. The Belmont Report was generated from discussions at this and subsequent meetings and serves as the gold standard regarding the ethical principles used in human subject research (National Commission for the Protection of Human Subjects of Biomedical and Behavioral Research, 1979). Its principles are autonomy—respecting people; beneficence—minimizing the risk to human subjects; and justice—distributing the benefits and burdens of research among human research subjects (National Commission for the Protection of Human Subjects of Biomedical and Behavioral Research).

IRBs are comprised of a minimum of five voluntary members (men and women, professionals, at least one community member, and one nonscientific individual). The mission of the IRB is to protect the rights and welfare of human subjects involved in research studies. Investigators using human subjects or information that can be linked to a specific individual must submit an application to their institution's IRB for approval before initiating a study. Applications for review by the IRB need to include the study proposal, a copy of the informed consent, the specific institution's application form, and any additional information that is required by the specific institution. Research studies cannot begin until an investigator receives approval by the IRB. In many institutions, it is not uncommon for this approval process to take at least two months, so this period of time must be factored into the timeline for completing the study. In addition, funding agencies require that IRB approval be received before funding is released; and, in some cases, IRB approval is required upon submission of the grant application.

Most institutions in the United States require that all key personnel involved in research receive training and certification in the protection of human research subjects. The National Institutes of Health requires such training for anyone receiving federal funding for research. The Collaborative IRB Training Initiative (CITI), conceived by the leadership of the Fred Hutchinson Cancer Center and the University of Miami, now includes more than 1,000 member institutions and provides a Web-based comprehensive selection of educational modules that can be used to satisfy institutional instructional mandates in the protection of human research subjects (CITI, 2000).

Additionally, the researcher also must consider the Health Insurance Portability and Accountability Act (HIPAA) when conducting research with human subjects. Enacted in 1996, HIPAA represents the first federal privacy standards to protect the medical records and other health information of individuals both living and deceased (U.S. Department of Health and Human Services, 2001, 2003). Healthcare providers and other healthcare entities, health insurers, and pharmacies have been required to comply with these federal standards since April 14, 2003. The standards address the use and disclosure of all individually identifiable health information.

To become more knowledgeable about the regulations surrounding the use of human research subjects and the IRB process, novice researchers may benefit from participating in educational programs, contacting members of the IRB to learn directly from them, or becoming a member of a review board. More detailed information is available on the government Web sites regarding the use and protection of human subjects in research (http://www.hhs.gov/ohrp and http://www.hhs.gov/ocr/hipaa/).

Funding

To successfully conduct research, the investigator frequently needs to obtain funding to support the salaries of those conducting the study and to pay for supplies and other associated research expenses. Determining how and where to obtain funding can be a bit daunting at first. The following section describes how researchers can begin to address the funding issue and provides several resources to begin the search for funding.

The fiscal requirements for the study and the investigators' level of expertise play a significant role in determining where the researcher should apply for funding. During the early phases of writing the proposal, it is helpful to construct a budget that realistically reflects the amount of money it will take to complete the study. The budget includes the cost for personnel, space, transportation, and supplies.

The amount of funding awarded is often on a smaller scale to novice researchers, but it expands with experience and the scope of the research project. This developmental process allows the researcher to establish a reputation within his or her discipline while providing assurance to the donors that the investigator is fiscally responsible and capable of completing proposed research projects (Malone, 1996). Each granting or funding source will have specific areas of interest, requirements, and guidelines for projects that the agency will fund. The investigator can thus determine which funding source is the best match for the proposed research project. This match will be based on the scope of the project, the researcher's level of expertise, and the criteria set forth by the granting agency.

There are numerous resources about funding available to researchers, including the researcher's institution, local and national organizations, foundations, industry, and the U.S. government. A detailed review of grant writing opportunities can be found in Chapter 34. A systematic approach will assist the researcher to determine the appropriate funding source. Using worksheets, the researcher can list requirements of a proposed study (the aims of the study, the total budget, and the proposed length of time it will take to complete the study) and funding source criteria (the amount of money granted, type of research supported, and the type of researchers supported). These worksheets will aid in determining the most appropriate match and the most likely source for successful funding (The Foundation Center, 2003).

To get started, researchers conducting pilot studies may consider applying for support from their own institution, local professional nursing associations, and local organizations or foundations. Individuals with more experience may choose to investigate national foundations, organizations, and government resources for funding opportunities. There are many books and an abundance of online resources available to assist in the search for funding (see Table 33-1).

Additional strategies to enhance the chance of obtaining funding for projects include contacting the funding source to discuss a specific proposal and asking if the project interests them; joining and becoming active in one or more nursing organizations; becoming involved in local funding organizations; networking with researchers and finding an experienced doctoral-prepared researcher to mentor, collaborate, and review your proposal; following the research application directions explicitly; and allowing plenty of time to complete the proposal and submit it on time.

The conduct of research requires knowledge and skills of research processes, time, patience, institutional support, and financial resources. A brief overview of the some of the steps in conducting research was provided as well as tips for successful implementation of clinical research studies, including development of a "good" research question, considerations for the study of human subjects, and identification of appropriate funding resources.

Research Utilization

The ultimate goal of clinical nursing research is to improve patient outcomes. Therefore, once a research project is complete, the dissemination and utilization of the findings are imperative. Unfortunately, a gap often exists between research and practice. Despite evidence that the use of research-based nursing practice improves patient outcomes and decreases the cost of care, consistent implementation of research-based practices has been a challenge in many clinical settings (Fagin, 1982; Goode et al., 2000; Heater, Becker, & Olson, 1988; Thompson, 1998). This section discusses the evolution of research utilization in nursing practice, common barriers to the implementation of research findings, and strategies that may be useful in incorporating research into the clinical setting.

Interest in transferring research findings into clinical practice became evident in nursing during the latter part of the 1970s (Horsley, Crane, & Bingle, 1978; Krueger,

Table 33-1. Funding Resources

Funding Resources	Funding	Web Site	Contact Information	Details
American Cancer Society (ACS)	Grants: $10,000+ to students, junior and senior investigators	www.cancer.org	800-227-2345	ACS is a nationwide community-based organization dedicated to eliminating cancer as a major health problem by preventing cancer, saving lives, and diminishing suffering from cancer, through research, education, advocacy, and service. Has specific grants on psychosocial and behavioral research.
American Organization of Nurse Executives (AONE)	The AONE Institute for Patient Care Research & Education is an established research seed grant program to aid the effort of AONE members pursuing research projects in the area of nursing leadership and administration. Links to additional resources are available.	www.aone.org	P.O. Box 92592, Chicago, IL 60675-2592 312-422-2800	Facilitates and supports research and development efforts that advance nursing administration practice and quality patient care
U.S. Department of Health and Human Services	Small and major research grants available through a variety of institutes and agencies	www.hhs.gov/grantsnet	200 Independence Avenue, S.W., Washington, DC 20201 877-696-6775	Internet portal to all Department of Health and Human Services funding. There are more than 300 grant programs offered.
The Foundation Center	None	http://fdncenter.org	79 Fifth Avenue/16th St., New York, NY 10003 800-424-9836	Provides online proposal writing course, databases listing grant makers information and the funding process, and links to additional resources

(Continued on next page)

561

Table 33-1. Funding Resources (Continued)

Funding Resources	Funding	Web Site	Contact Information	Details
In-house	Small grants to initiate projects. Amounts vary among institutions.	Investigator's employer		Often your own company will sponsor pilot work.
National Cancer Institute (NCI)	Small and major research grants, career awards, and training grants. Wide range of funding opportunities. Major grants generally are for senior investigators.	www.cancer.gov	NCI Public Inquiries Office Suite 3036A 6116 Executive Boulevard, MSC8322 Bethesda, MD 20892-8322	NCI conducts and supports research, training, health information dissemination, and other programs with respect to the cause, diagnosis, prevention, and treatment of cancer, rehabilitation from cancer, and the continuing care of patients with cancer and their families.
National Institute of Nursing Research	Small and major research grants, and training grants. Wide range of funding opportunities. Major grants generally are for senior investigators.	www.nih.gov/ninr/	National Institute of Nursing Research Bethesda, MD 20892-2178 301-496-0207	The National Institute of Nursing Research supports clinical and basic research to establish a scientific basis for the care of individuals across the life span.
Oncology Nursing Society	Small research and mentored grants ($5,000–$10,000/ junior and senior investigators) Major research grants ($45,000+, senior investigators)	www.ons.org	125 Enterprise Drive Pittsburgh, PA 15275 866-257-4667	Mission: Promote excellence in oncology nursing and quality cancer care
Sigma Theta Tau	Grants $2,500–$10,000 for both junior and senior investigators	www.nursingsociety.org	550 West North Street Indianapolis, IN 46202 317-634-8171	Honor society of nursing, first to fund nursing research
Additional resources	Industry: pharmaceuticals/publishing companies, local and national, foundations, societies, and associations			
Internet search engines	www.google.com, www.altavista.com, http://fundingopps2.cos.com/			

1978; Stetler & Marram, 1976). As Table 33-2 illustrates, a variety of models have evolved over time to help guide nurses in the use of research findings (Rossworm & Larrabee, 1999; Stetler, 2001; Titler et al., 2001). A common theme among all of the models is that they use a specific critical-thinking process to access and evaluate studies for utility, feasibility, and cost (White, Leske, & Pearcy, 1995). A major component of these models is a synthesis of the literature to determine whether a change in practice is warranted. In some cases, there may be insufficient research available upon which to base a practice decision. Therefore, one option may be for the clinician to conduct a research study to gain the additional evidence needed (see Figure 33-3). On the other hand, if a change in practice is warranted, implementation and subsequent evaluation of the effectiveness of the change are appropriate.

Table 33-2. Overview of Research Utilization Models

Research Utilization Model	Proposed Steps of Model
Western Interstate Colleges of Higher Education in Nursing Regional Program for Nursing Research Development (Krueger, 1978)	Gather and critique research studies. Develop a research protocol. Use change theory to implement research in clinical setting.
Conduct and Utilization of Research in Nursing Model (Horsley et al., 1978)	Identify clinical problem. Gather and critique research studies. Develop practice protocol. Test protocol in clinical setting. Decide about usefulness. Extend innovation. Implement strategies to maintain innovation.
Stetler Model of Research Utilization (Stetler, 2001)	Preparation: Select problem. Validation: Critique and synthesize research studies. Comparative evaluation/decision making: Decide whether to use findings. Translation/application: Implement research findings. Evaluation: Evaluate and make refinements.
Iowa Model of Evidence-Based Practice to Promote Quality Care (Titler et al., 2001)	Select topic based on priority of the organization. Form a team. Critique and synthesize research. Decide if there is sufficient research to guide practice. Pilot test change in practice. Decide about adopting the innovation in practice setting. Institute the change. Evaluate outcomes.
Model for Evidence-Based Practice (Rossworm & Larrabee, 1999)	Assess need for change in practice. Link problem with intervention and outcomes. Synthesize best evidence. Design a change in practice. Implement and evaluate change in practice. Integrate and maintain change in practice.

Recent research utilization models have incorporated concepts related to evidence-based practice. Although research utilization and evidence-based practice are related concepts, they are not synonymous. Research utilization is the process by which research findings become incorporated into clinical practice, whereas evidence-based practice is the conscientious and judicious use of the best available evidence to guide decision making about clinical care (Nicoll & Beyea, 2000; Sackett, Rosenberg, Grey, Haynes, & Richardson, 1996). Both processes require first finding the evidence by locating relevant data sources within the published literature, and then evaluating what evidence is found. Sources of credible information other than primary studies may be used as "evidence" in evidence-based practice. Potential sources of information may include systematic reviews of randomized trials or observational studies, case reports, consensus of national or local experts, quality improvement data, or clinical observations (Guyatt et al., 2000; Stetler, 2001). Hence, the major difference between research utilization and evidence-based practice is that evidence-based practice allows for the integration of clinical expertise and patient preferences with

Figure 33-3. Relationship Between Research Utilization and the Conduct of Research

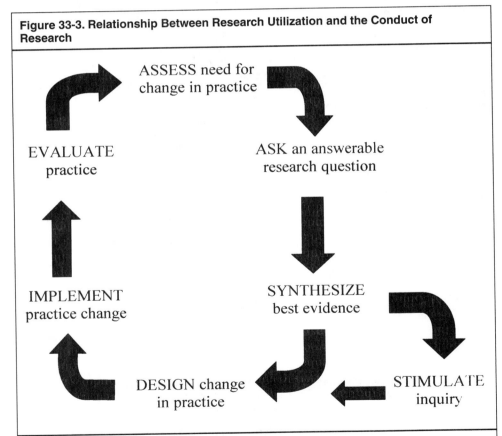

ASSESS need for change in practice

ASK an answerable research question

SYNTHESIZE best evidence

STIMULATE inquiry

DESIGN change in practice

IMPLEMENT practice change

EVALUATE practice

Note. From "Building a Foundation for Evidence-Based Practice: Experiences in a Tertiary Hospital," by E.A. Mohide and B. King, 2003, *Evidence-Based Nursing, 6,* p. 101. Copyright 2003 by the Dana-Farber Cancer Institute. Reprinted with permission.

the results of systematic research to guide practice decisions (Nicoll & Beyea, 2000; Omery & Williams, 1999).

Barriers to the Implementation of Research

Many clinical activities are based on tradition, trial and error, and expert opinion, rather than scientific evidence. Some may not be research-based simply because the research to support these practices is inconclusive or the practices have never been investigated in a systematic manner. As nursing begins to build a scientific base for clinical practice, however, a shift toward incorporating research findings into the practice setting is critical. To facilitate the transfer of knowledge gained through research, it is necessary to understand the common barriers to implementation of research findings as well as strategies that may be used to enhance adoption of research utilization activities.

Multiple studies have examined the barriers associated with research utilization, and the findings have been consistent across studies, across time, and among nurses in various roles (Funk, Tornquist, & Champagne, 1995; Retsas, 2000; Sitzia, 2001; Walczak, McGuire, Haisfield, & Beezley, 1994). Common barriers to using research evidence in practice are lack of organizational support to use research, inaccessibility of research findings, and attributes of nurses. Lack of organizational support was identified as the most important perceived barrier for not using research findings. Nurses identified that not having enough time to read and critique studies and not having adequate support to understand study findings impeded their ability to use research (Retsas; Walczak et al.). In an exploratory study, nurse managers' lack of support was associated with a lack of research utilization projects within the clinical setting (Caine & Kenrick, 1997). Similarly, another study found that clinical managers could influence research if they used their position and authority to promote the use of research in practice. Specific behaviors that support the use of research are providing resources, such as adequate staffing and training opportunities, and helping nurses overcome opposition by physicians, other healthcare providers, and administrators to conducting the proposed research (Valente, 2003).

Other common barriers cited by nurses are that research findings are difficult to read, relevant literature is not compiled in one place, and the implications for practice are not clear. Often, there may be limited research in one's area of interest and even when research is available, the quality of the research (i.e., methodologic inadequacies) may be problematic. Lastly, several studies identified that the attributes of nurses themselves can interfere with research utilization activities. Attitudes of nurses and educational level have been associated with barriers to use of research findings in practice. Not surprisingly, nurses with more positive attitudes toward research were more likely to implement research findings (Hatcher & Tranmer, 1997). Similarly, a higher level of education was associated with a higher likelihood of using research-based findings in practice (Brown, 1997). Nurses who had research coursework included within their basic nursing education reported fewer barriers to using research as compared to nurses who did not have research within their curriculum.

Strategies to Enhance Use of Research in the Clinical Setting

Nurse managers' efforts to initiate and maintain change within the clinical practice arena are always complex. The process involves changing the behavior of multiple caregivers within an organizational system. Therefore, incorporation of research utilization activities into clinical practice is best accomplished as a broad-based organizational initiative that uses a multifaceted approach (Royle & Blythe, 1998). Goode and Bulecheck (1992) identified a model for incorporating research utilization as an organizational process, which included three major building blocks: organizational commitment, a research utilization committee to facilitate change, and having a planned change process so that the change occurs in an orderly fashion.

The first building block is establishing an organizational commitment to develop a successful research utilization program. Nurse executives need to create an organizational culture that promotes inquiry and stimulates critical examination of clinical practices. The commitment to research should be explicitly stated in the organization's mission statements and reflected in job performance and merit programs. Most importantly, administrators must provide financial support for nurses' participation in research-related activities. In addition, it is essential to provide adequate resources for nurses to gain the skills needed to understand and critique research (see Figure 33-4). Potential resources include having a doctoral-prepared nurse available for consultation and collaboration in research activities, providing educational opportunities for nurses to enhance their knowledge of research, and providing access to a library or electronic databases so that nurses can perform literature searches.

Figure 33-4. Guidelines to Critiquing Research

In critiquing a study, you need to address questions such as the following:
1. Was the problem studied significant to generate or refine knowledge for nursing practice?
2. What are the major strengths of the study?
3. What are the major weaknesses of the study?
4. Was the methodology of the study sound?
5. Are the findings from the study an accurate reflection of reality or credible?
6. What is the significance of the findings for nursing practice?
7. Are the findings consistent with those from previous studies?
8. Can the study, as conducted, be replicated by other researchers?

Answering these questions requires careful examination of the problem, purpose, literature review, framework, methods, results, and findings of the study.

Note. From *Understanding Nursing Research* (p. 380), by N. Burns and S.K. Grove, 1999, Philadelphia: Saunders. Copyright 1999 by Saunders. Reprinted with permission.

Another important component of a strong research utilization program is the establishment of a research utilization or evidence-based practice committee (Fleming, Hazelett, & Brunt, 2003). It is best to have members of the committee represent a variety of clinical specialties and all types of nursing staff, such as staff nurses, nurse managers, advanced practice nurses (APNs), and a nurse scientist. A varied committee structure enables all levels of nurses to be involved in the research process and influence the adoption of change within the institution. This committee can be linked to other committees that address policies and procedures to facilitate the production of evidence-based clinical practices.

Finally, having a planned change process in place facilitates the adoption and implementation of research-based practices. Involvement of staff at all levels is critical to gather support and educate personnel about how research-based practice can improve the quality of care. Staff nurses and APNs can be instrumental in identification of patient care problems that need to be addressed within the organization. These problems can be identified through quality improvement activities and then directed toward the research utilization committee. Once the committee has synthesized the literature and made the determination of whether to change policy and procedures or to more clearly define the interventions that are in place, implementation within the system is initiated.

Several authors have advocated that APNs act as change agents for facilitating research utilization within an organization (DeBourgh, 2001; Goode & Bulecheck, 1992; McGuire, Walczak, & Krumm, 1994). APNs have skills related to the use of research and implementing change within an organizational setting. Thus, they can work collaboratively with the clinical and managerial staff and a doctoral-prepared nurse to champion research-based changes. An ideal situation is to have a nurse scientist available for collaboration and consultation regarding research-related activities within the institution. In other situations, fostering collaborative relationships through joint appointments with an academic institution may provide the support needed to develop and implement a research utilization program. Building collaborative relationships among researchers and clinicians provides the leadership, expertise, and clinical insight needed to bridge the gap between research and clinical practice.

Figure 33-5 lists other strategies for facilitating research utilization. An important strategy for transferring research into clinical practice is to ensure that research findings are communicated to clinicians in an efficient and interpretable format (Sitzia, 2000; Valente, 2003). To facilitate the transfer of research-based knowledge into a busy clinical setting, Valente (2003) developed research fact sheets on topics

---

Figure 33-5. Strategies for Promoting Research-Based Practice in the Clinical Setting

- Identify a doctorally-prepared nurse for consultation and collaboration in research-related activities.
- Encourage advanced practice nurses (e.g., clinical nurse specialists, nurse practitioners) to act as coaches for establishment of research-related activities.
- Involve all types of nurses in research-related activities.
- Establish research-related committees.
- Establish journal clubs to share reading and critique of research.
- Link quality improvement and research utilization activities.
- Implement classes that promote understanding of research utilization skills.
- Provide clinicians with research findings in an efficient and interpretable format.
- Create a forum for dialogue between researchers and clinicians.
- Develop interdisciplinary research teams with members from academic and practice settings.

that are important for clinical practice. The research-based fact sheets provide a one-page summary of key concepts related to the particular topic, explain the evidence base supporting those concepts, and list references. The fact sheets are organized around particular clinical questions such as "Why does smoking cessation need to happen?" and then presents the evidence in a concise, eye-catching colorful way that is distributed by mail to all nursing staff. Other resources for finding out about research-based practice are listed in Table 33-3.

Table 33-3. Resources for Research-Based Practice		
Resource	**Services Provided**	**Contact Information**
Agency for Healthcare Research and Quality	Access to clinical guidelines based on reviews of research evidence	www.ahrq.gov
American Society of Clinical Oncology	Practice guidelines for patients and clinicians Technology assessment Articles and resources related to practice guidelines and technology assessment	www.asco.org
Health Information Research Unit: Evidence-Based Health Informatics	Brings together quality-assessed summaries of best current studies of diagnosis, course, and management of clinical disorders	http://hiru.mcmaster.ca
The Cochrane Collaboration	Produces international guidelines based on systematic review of clinical trials Offers practical advice about how to overcome barriers in implementing an evidence-based practice (EBP) program Spanish language version available	www.cochrane.org
Critiquing research for use in nursing practice (Ida Grove, IA: Horn Video Productions, 1996)	Instructional software for teaching selected research utilization skills of reading and critiquing an article	www.fhs.mcmaster.ca/lro /newacqs_cdrom.htm
Medical Library Association	Contains a master list of Web resources for EBP Links to an EBP journal for healthcare available Tutorials on how to effectively search the literature for information	http://mlanet.org/index .html
National Comprehensive Cancer Network	Practice guidelines Oncology outcomes database Educational conferences	www.nccn.org
Oncology Nursing Society	EBP resource center Clinical guidelines	www.ons.org
	(Continued on next page)	

Table 33-3. Resources for Research-Based Practice *(Continued)*		
Resource	**Services Provided**	**Contact Information**
Virginia Henderson Sigma Theta Tau International Library	Hosts two services to support evidence-based nursing practice: The Registry of Nursing Research is an electronic research resource. *The Online Journal of Knowledge Synthesis for Nursing* publishes critical reviews of research literature for the purpose of guiding research and practice.	www.stti.iupui.edu/library
The WISDOM Centre	Provides EBP-related training via the Internet	www.shef.ac.uk/uni /projects/wrp/seminar .html#EBP

Note. Based on information from Cooke & Grant, 2002; Mast, 2000; Sitzia, 2001.

There continues to be a gap between the discovery of clinically relevant research and the application of that research into practice. Traditionally, emphasis has been placed upon the conduct of research. It is equally important, however, to translate the knowledge gained from research into practice. Thus, it is time for research utilization activities to assume a greater role in education, practice, and research activities. To date, little research has been conducted to identify effective strategies for enhancing research utilization in the clinical setting (Omery & Williams, 1999). New innovative approaches, such as using a team of interdisciplinary scholars geared toward developing and testing interventions that assist in the transfer of knowledge from research to practice, are needed to advance knowledge in this area (Estabrooks, Floyd, Scott-Findley, O'Leary, & Gushta, 2003).

Summary

This chapter has provided an overview of nursing research in the clinical setting, addressing both the conduct and utilization of research. Nurse managers can play a key role in research facilitation by supporting clinical staff and incorporating strategies to enhance nursing research activities. The conduct and utilization of research are interdependent processes, yet both are essential to advance the science of nursing practice. This point is simply summarized in the following excerpt.

> In a practice discipline like nursing, scientific knowledge is assumed to contribute to the betterment of nursing care. The mechanism of such an improvement is through more knowledgeable and better informed nurses. The assumption is that nursing research develops nursing science, which in turn is available to be used to practice nursing in better ways. (Kirkevold, 1997, p. 977)

The conduct of research requires knowledge and skills of research processes, time, patience, institutional support, and financial resources. A brief overview of some of the steps in conducting research was provided as well as tips for successful implementation of clinical research studies, including development of a "good" research question, considerations for the study of human subjects, and identification of appropriate funding resources.

References

American Nurses Association. (1995). *Nursing report card for acute care*. Washington, DC: American Nurses Publishing.

Bailey, P.H. (1997). Finding your way around qualitative methods in nursing research. *Journal of Advanced Nursing, 25*, 18–22.

Beck, C.T. (1999). Opening students' eyes. The process of selecting a research instrument. *Nurse Educator, 24*(3), 21–23.

Begley, C.M. (1996). Using triangulation in nursing research. *Journal of Advanced Nursing, 24*, 122–128.

Brown, D.S. (1997). Nursing education and nursing research utilization: Is there a connection in clinical settings? *Journal of Continuing Education in Nursing, 28*, 258–262.

Caine, C., & Kenrick, M. (1997). The role of clinical managers in facilitating evidence-based practice: A report of an exploratory study. *Journal of Nursing Management, 5*, 157–165.

Collaborative Institutional Review Board Training Initiative. (2000). *Protection of human resource subjects*. Miami, FL: Author. Retrieved September 7, 2004, from http://www.miami.edu/ctireg/

Cooke, L., & Grant, M. (2002). Support for evidence-based practice. *Seminars in Oncology Nursing, 18*, 71–78.

Cummings, S.R., Browner, W.S., & Hulley, S.B. (1988). Conceiving the research question. In S.B. Hulley, S.R. Cummings, W.S. Browner, D. Grady, N. Hearst, & T.B. Newman (Eds.), *Designing clinical research: An epidemiologic approach* (pp. 12–17). Philadelphia: Lippincott Williams & Wilkins.

DeBourgh, G.A. (2001). Champions for evidence-based practice: A critical role for advanced practice nurses. *AACN Clinical Issues, 12*, 491–508.

Doran, D.M. (2003). *Nursing-sensitive outcomes: State of the science*. Sudbury, MA: Jones and Bartlett.

Estabrooks, C.A., Floyd, J.A., Scott-Findley, S., O'Leary, K.A., & Gushta, M. (2003). Individual determinants of research utilization: A systematic review. *Journal of Advanced Nursing, 43*, 506–520.

Fagin, C.M. (1982). The economic value of nursing research. *American Journal of Nursing, 82*, 1844–1849.

Fleming, E., Hazelett, S., & Brunt, B. (2003). Ensuring success: Research by committee. *Journal of Nursing Administration, 33*, 532–537.

The Foundation Center. (2003). *The Foundation Center's user-friendly guide to funding research and resources*. (2003). Retrieved October 13, 2003, from http://fdncenter.org/learn/ufg/index.html

Funk, S.G., Tornquist, E.M., & Champagne, M.T. (1995). Barriers and facilitators of research utilization: An integrative review. *Nursing Clinics of North America, 30*, 395–407.

Goode, C., & Bulecheck, G.M. (1992). Research utilization: An organizational process that enhances quality of care. *Journal of Nursing Care Quality*, Special Report, 27–35.

Goode, C.J., Tanaka, D.J., Krugman, M., O'Connor, P.A., Bailey, C., Deutchman, M., et al. (2000). Outcomes from use of an evidence-based practice guideline. *Nursing Economic$, 18*, 202–207.

Gould, D. (2002). Using replication studies to enhance nursing research. *Nursing Standard, 16*(49), 33–36.

Guyatt, G.H., Haynes, R.B., Jaeschke, R.Z., Cook, D.J., Green, L., Naylor, C.D., et al. (2000). Evidence-based medicine: Principles for applying the users' guides to patient care. *JAMA, 284*, 1290–1296.

Hatcher, S., & Tranmer, J. (1997). A survey of variables related to research utilization in nursing practice in the acute care setting. *Canadian Journal of Nursing Administration, 10,* 31–53.

Heater, B.S., Becker, A.M., & Olson, R.K. (1988). Nursing intervention and patient outcomes: A meta-analysis of studies. *Nursing Research, 37,* 303–307.

Horsley, J., Crane, J., & Bingle, J.D. (1978). Research utilization as an organizational process. *Journal of Nursing Administration, 8*(7), 4–6.

Jones, J.H. (1993). *Bad blood: The Tuskegee syphilis experiment.* New York: The Free Press.

Kirkevold, M. (1997). Integrative nursing research: An important strategy to further development of nursing science and nursing practice. *Journal of Advanced Nursing, 25,* 977–984.

Krueger, J.C. (1978). Utilization of nursing research: The planning process. *Journal of Nursing Administration, 8*(1), 6–9.

Malone, R.E. (1996). Getting your study funded: Tips for new researchers. *Journal of Emergency Nursing, 22,* 457–459.

Mast, M. (2000). Evidence-based practice: What it is and what it isn't. *Oncology News, 15,* 1, 4–5.

McCorkle, R. (1990). Development of the research question. In M.M. Grant & G.V. Padilla (Eds.), *Cancer nursing research: A practical approach* (pp. 27–42). Norwalk, CT: Appleton & Lange.

McGuire, D.B., Walczak, J.R., & Krumm, S.L. (1994). Development of a nursing research utilization program in a clinical oncology setting: Organization, implementation and evaluation. *Oncology Nursing Forum, 21,* 704–710.

National Commission for the Protection of Human Subjects of Biomedical and Behavioral Research. (1979). *The Belmont Report: Ethical principles and guidelines for the protection of human subjects of research.* Washington, DC: OPPR Reports. A6–14. Retrieved October 29, 2004, from http://www.hhs.gov/humansubjects/guidance/belmont.htm

Nicoll, L.H., & Beyea, S.C. (1999). Using secondary data analysis for nursing research. *AORN Journal, 69,* 428, 430, 433.

Nicoll, L.H., & Beyea, S.C. (2000). Working with staff around evidence-based practice: The next generation of research utilization. *Seminars in Perioperative Nursing, 9,* 133–142.

Nies, M.A., Hepworth, J.T., & Fickens, S. (2001). An interdisciplinary team approach to nursing scholarship. *Journal of Nursing Administration, 31,* 411–413.

Norris, A.E. (1999). Thinking about the meaning of "research" in nursing. *Clinical Nurse Specialist, 13,* 76.

Omery, A., & Williams, R.P. (1999). An appraisal of research utilization across the United States. *Journal of Nursing Administration, 29*(12), 50–56.

Retsas, A. (2000). Barriers to using research evidence in nursing practice. *Journal of Advanced Nursing, 31,* 599–606.

Rossworm, M.A., & Larrabee, J.H. (1999). A model for change to evidence-based practice. *The Journal of Nursing Scholarship, 31,* 317–322.

Royle, J., & Blythe, J. (1998). Promoting research utilization in nursing: The role of the individual, organization, and environment. *Evidence-Based Nursing, 1*(3), 71.

Sackett, D.L., Rosenberg, W.M., Grey, J.A., Haynes, R.B., & Richardson, W.S. (1996). Evidence-based medicine: What it is and what it isn't. *BMJ, 312,* 71–72.

Sitzia, J. (2001). Barriers to research utilization: The clinical setting and nurses themselves. *European Journal of Oncology Nursing, 5,* 154–164.

Stetler, C.B., & Marram, G. (1976). Evaluating research findings for applicability in practice. *Nursing Outlook, 24,* 559–563.

Stetler, C.B. (2001). Updating the Stetler model of research utilization to facilitate evidence-based practice. *Nursing Outlook, 49,* 272–279.

Thompson, M.A. (1998). Closing the gap between research and practice. *Evidence-Based Nursing, 1,* 7–8.

Titler, M.G., Kleiber, C., Steelman, V.J., Rakel, B.A., Budreau, G., Everett, L.Q., et al. (2001). The Iowa model of evidence-based practice to promote quality care. *Critical Care Nursing Clinics of North America, 13,* 497–509.

Trials of war criminals before the Nuremberg military tribunals under control council law no. 10. Nuremberg, October 1946–April 1949. Washington, DC: U.S. G.P.O, 1949–1953. Testimony excerpts come from National Archives Record Group 238, M887.

U.S. Department of Health and Human Services, National Institutes of Health Office for Protection from Research Risks, Protection of Human Subjects. (2001). *Code of federal regulations.* Title 45, Part 46. Retrieved October 13, 2003, from http://hhs.gov/ocr/hipaa/privruletxt.txt

U.S. Department of Health and Human Services, Office for Civil Rights. (2003). *Standards for privacy of individually identifiable health information. Code of federal regulations.* Title 45, Parts 160 & 164. Retrieved October 13, 2003, from http://hhs.gov/ocr/hipaa/privruletxt.txt

Valente, S.M. (2003). Research dissemination and utilization: Improving care at the bedside. *Journal of Nursing Care Quality, 18,* 114–121.

Walczak, J.R., McGuire, D.B., Haisfield, M.E., & Beezley, A. (1994). A survey of research-related activities and perceived barriers to research utilization among professional oncology nurses. *Oncology Nursing Forum, 21,* 710–715.

White, J.M., Leske, J.S., & Pearcy, J.M. (1995). Models and processes of research utilization. *Nursing Clinics of North America, 30,* 409–420.

Securing Funding for Nursing Research

Janice Mitchell Phillips, PhD, RN, FAAN

Increasingly, healthcare professionals are engaged in grant writing to secure funding to support a number of patient-related activities. Gone are the days when grant writing was reserved for scholars in the academia. Now, more than ever, nurses across diverse settings are required to secure funding to support nursing research, special projects, or demonstration projects designed to improve patient outcomes. In fact, nurses who possess skill and experience in successful grant writing may enhance their marketability in certain venues. As a nurse manager, you and your staff may have a project to improve some aspect of patient care, which could be supported by a grant from the National Institute of Nursing Research (NINR), the Oncology Nursing Society (ONS) Foundation, or another funding agency. This chapter will (a) provide a beginning overview on opportunities for grant funding available through NINR at the National Institutes of Health (NIH), (b) highlight resources for use when preparing a proposal for submission to NINR, and (c) discuss practical tips for consideration before, during, and after the submission process. Special emphasis is placed on writing proposals to support nursing research aimed at improving patient outcomes and advancing nursing science. More specific information related to nursing research is reviewed in Chapter 33.

National Institute of Nursing Research

NINR, one of 27 institutes and centers (ICs) located within NIH in Bethesda, MD, has received increased recognition, visibility, and funding since its elevation from a nursing

Editor's note. This chapter is drawn from information that was current as of fall 2004. Readers are encouraged to validate statements in this chapter with the relevant National Institutes of Health and National Institute of Nursing Research Web sites to ensure that information is still correct.

research center in 1986 to an institute within NIH in 1993. "NINR supports clinical and basic research to establish a scientific basis for the care of individuals across the life-span—from management of patients during illness and recovery to the reduction of risks for disease and disability and the promotion of healthy lifestyles" (NINR, 2003). The research mission of NINR is located on its Web site (http://ninr.nih.gov/ninr).

NINR promotes interdisciplinary research to enhance a comprehensive approach to addressing a number of health issues across the life cycle, from prevention to end of life. To do so, NINR-funded researchers conduct research with individuals, families, and communities in diverse settings, including the clinical arena, home, community, and nontraditional healthcare sites. In response to the national emphasis on reducing and, ultimately, eliminating health disparities, NINR encourages research that addresses the health needs of underserved and high-risk populations. In addition, the institute supports a large number of research, research training, and career development opportunities for the junior, mid-career, and senior researcher (NINR, 2003). NINR supports meritorious research that is multidisciplinary in nature and aimed at strengthening nursing science and patient outcomes.

Role of the Program Director at NINR

Individuals seeking funding from NINR are strongly encouraged to contact the program director overseeing their particular area of interest when initiating the application process. In addition to interacting within and outside the NIH research community, the program directors at NINR serve as contact persons for researchers and can assist the researchers by identifying funding opportunities and the appropriate mechanism for funding, reviewing a two-page concept paper, and discussing review and budget issues. Each program director is responsible for an area of science. Some of the areas of science at NINR include (a) research in chronic illness and long-term care, (b) research in health promotion and risk reduction in adults, (c) research in cardiopulmonary health and critical care, (d) research in neurofunction and sensory conditions, (e) research in immune response and oncology, and (f) research in end-of-life and environmental contexts. Researchers wishing to pursue an area of science not included within any of these areas are encouraged to contact NINR to discuss their area of interest.

Program directors devote a large portion of their time communicating with researchers via the phone, e-mail, or during attendance at a number of local, regional, and national conferences. Program directors also attend meetings to present NINR funding opportunities and provide consultation to researchers. Although program directors do not have any authority with regard to funding decisions, they attend review sessions and can share with applicants the results of their review after a summary statement is released. Applications are selected for funding if they are deemed to be of scientific merit and are in concert with the institute's mission. Prior to making an award, the program directors are responsible for working with the applicant to resolve any outstanding issues, such as those regarding human subjects, the recruitment and retention of minorities, and budgetary concerns. If an application is selected for funding and an award is made to the applicant, the program director will evaluate annual progress and communicate with the principal investigator regarding issues and opportunities for additional funding and building his or her research career. The program director will collaborate with members of the grants management team to monitor the progress of the award throughout the life cycle of the grant.

Finally, program directors assist in moving the science forward by developing program announcements, collaborating with NIH staff at large, convening state-of-the-science workshops, and identifying potential areas for future research.

Funding Application

NINR currently supports three major categories of grant mechanisms: research, research training, and research career development. Table 34-1 provides an example of selected mechanisms available through the institute. A full description of all funding mechanisms is provided on the NINR Web site (www.nih.gov/ninr/research/dea/rest-type.html). Program directors at NINR can assist the investigator in identifying the appropriate mechanism when preparing his or her application. For example, the R01 mechanism may be better suited for an investigator with previous research experience and preliminary work to support the proposed study. On the other hand, an R03 may be better suited for an individual seeking funding to support preliminary work that can provide the foundation for a subsequent R01 application. Mechanisms for funding vary across the NIH campus, and thus applicants should become familiar with other components within NIH and related funding opportunities. Each mechanism has specific eligibility criteria, requirements, and deadlines.

Applicants can apply for funding in response to a program announcement (PA), a request for applications (RFAs), or as a result of an investigator-initiated idea. In brief, a program announcement is a call for applications on a particular topic that describes and gives notice to the research community of the existence of an NIH-wide extramural initiative (funding opportunities to universities, institutions, or research entities outside of the NIH community), research interest, or mechanism of support. There may be funds set aside for a program announcement (National Cancer Institute [NCI], 2002). Program announcements are usually good for a period of three years. In contrast, an RFA is a one-time call or solicitation for applications addressing a well-defined scientific area. Funds usually are set aside to support a number of applications (NCI). Both types of announcements are calls for applications that contain very specific instructions as well as contact information. This usually requires several in-depth readings to fully capture what is required to prepare a responsive application. NINR collaborates with other ICs throughout NIH to help sponsor various calls for proposals. All calls for applications are listed in the *NIH Guide for Grants and Contracts* (http://grants.nih.gov/grants/guide/index.html). Investigator-initiated applications or unsolicited applications are based on the researcher's interest and should be consistent with the NINR mission. A detailed listing of NINR's supported PAs and RFAs are listed on the institute's Web site. A few examples include

- PA-03-170   Health Promotion Among Racial and Ethnic Minority Males
- PA-03-108   NIH Small Grant Research Program (R03)
- RFA-NS-05-03   Research on Research Integrity
- RFA-CA-05-013 Reducing Barriers to Symptom Management and Palliative Care.

Table 34-1. National Institute of Nursing Research Training and Research Mechanisms and Selected Career Development Awards

Research Mechanisms

Code	Mechanism	Description	Special Features	Award Amount	Time	Receipt Dates§	National Institutes of Health (NIH) Web Site
R01	Research Project (Traditional)	To support a discrete, specified circumscribed project	Need to show expertise, preliminary work	No limit **	Up to 5 years; usually 4 years. R01s are renewable. Two revisions are allowed.	Postmark by Feb. 1, June 1, or Oct. 1 (note*)	(www.nih.gov) Grants, Grants Page, Grant Topics, Funding Opportunities, Application Forms, PHS 398, see instructions germane to the R01 grant (particularly the section on Research Plan)
R15	Academic Research Enhancement Award (AREA)	To enhance the research environment of educational institutions that have not been traditional recipients of NIH funds	Special application instructions. Modular grant procedures apply. ***	Maximum of $150,000 direct costs for the entire project***	Up to 3 years. R15s are renewable; only one revision is allowed.	Receipt dates Jan. 25, May 25, or Sept. 25 (note*)	(www.nih.gov) Grants, Grants Page, Grant Topics, Funding Opportunities, Guidelines & Policies, Funding Program Guidelines, AREA Awards
R03	NINR Small Grant Program	To provide support for pilot, feasibility, and methodology studies in specified scientific areas that will lead to an R01	Must address topic in 1 of 4 areas. Modular grant procedures apply. 10-page limit for research plan (sections a-d)	Maximum of $50,000 direct costs per year	Up to 2 years. R03s are not renewable; only one revision allowed.	Postmark by Feb. 1, June 1, or Oct. 1 (note*)	(www.nih.gov/ninr) Research Funding & Programs, DEA, OEP Extramural Resources, PAs and RFAs. (PA-02-120) July 1, 2002

(Continued on next page)

Table 34-1. National Institute of Nursing Research Training and Research Mechanisms and Selected Career Development Awards (Continued)

Code	Mechanism	Description	Special Features	Award Amount	Time	Receipt Dates§	National Institutes of Health (NIH) Web Site
Type 3	Minority supplements for high school, undergraduate, graduate, postdoctoral, or faculty	To attract minority individuals to enter biomedical and behavioral research careers	Principal investigators of existing grants (see guidelines for listing of mechanisms) may apply for supplement	Varies according to level of minority individual (see guidelines)	A reasonable period of time remaining on the parent grant, usually at least 2 years	Anytime; always speak with scientific program director prior to submission.	(www.nih.gov) Grants, Grants Page, Grant Topics, Funding Opportunities, Guidelines & Policies, Funding Program Guidelines, Research Supplements for Underrepresented Minorities
			Training Mechanisms				
F31	National Research Service Award (NRSA) Predoctoral Fellowship	To help ensure that highly trained nurse scientists are available in adequate numbers and in appropriate research areas to carry out the NINR mission	Must assure training on a full-time basis, at least 40 hours per week	$20,772 annual stipend, tuition, and fee formula amount, plus annual institutional allowance of $2,750 (may change each year)	Up to 5 years	Received by April 5, Aug. 5, or Dec. 5	(www.nih.gov/ninr) Research Funding & Programs, DEA, OEP Extramural Resources, PAs and RFAs. PAR-02-019, Nov. 26, 2001
F32	National Research Service Award (NRSA) Postdoctoral Fellowship	To provide postdoctoral research training to nurses to broaden their scientific backgrounds and extend their potential for research	Same as above. Program has high NINR priority.	Stipend based on experience: $35,568 to $51,036 tuition and fee formula amount, plus annual institutional allowance of $5,500	Up to 3 years total NRSA postdoctoral support; exceptions can be made by waiver.	Received by April 5, Aug. 5, or Dec. 5	(www.nih.gov) Grants, Research Training Opportunities, Extramural, NRSA, F32, PA-03-067, Feb. 6, 2003

(Continued on next page)

Table 34-1. National Institute of Nursing Research Training and Research Mechanisms and Selected Career Development Awards (Continued)

Code	Mechanism	Description	Special Features	Award Amount	Time	Receipt Dates§	National Institutes of Health (NIH) Web Site
F33	National Research Service Award (NRSA) Senior Fellow	To provide opportunities for experienced scientists to make major changes in research careers, to broaden scientific background, and to acquire new research capabilities	Must have at least 7 years relevant postdoctoral research or professional training and appropriate sponsor	$48,852 stipend; institutional allowance of $5,500	2 years	Received by April 5, Aug. 5, or Dec. 5	www.nih.gov; Grants, Research Training Opportunities, Extramural, NRSA, F33, PA-00-131, Aug. 28, 2000
T32	National Research Service Award (NRSA) Institutional Award	To enable institutions to make NRSA awards to individuals for predoctoral and postdoctoral research training in specified areas	Requires full-time training—40 hours/week	Predoctoral: $20,772 stipend, $2,200 training-related expenses, tuition and fee formula amount, $800 travel Postdoctoral: $35,568-$51,036 stipend, $3,850 training-related expenses, tuition and fee formula amount, $800 travel	5 years	Receipt date of May 10	(www.nih.gov) Grants, Research Training Opportunities, Extramural, NRSA, T32, PA-02-109, May 16, 2002

(Continued on next page)

Table 34-1. National Institute of Nursing Research Training and Research Mechanisms and Selected Career Development Awards *(Continued)*

			Career Development Awards				
Code	Mechanism	Description	Special Features	Award Amount	Time	Receipt Dates§	National Institutes of Health (NIH) Web Site
K01	Mentored Research Scientist Development Award	A period of additional mentored research experience to enhance the candidate's career or to gain expertise in a research area new to the candidate	Must spend a minimum of 75% effort on research and research career development.	Up to $50,000 salary plus fringe benefits; research expenses up to $20,000	3 years	Postmarked by Feb. 1, June 1, or Oct. 1	(www.nih.gov/ninr) Research Funding & Programs, DEA, OEP Extramural Resources, PAs and RFAs. PA-00-019, Dec. 2, 1999
K22	NINR Career Transition Award	A period of support to provide research training experience in the NIH clinical research laboratories and to facilitate successful transition to an extramural environment as an independent researcher	Intramural: 100% effort Extramural: Minimum of 75% effort on research career development	Up to $50,000 salary plus fringe benefits; research expenses up to $75,000	Up to 3 years intramural followed by up to 2 years extramural	Will be reannounced as an ongoing annual receipt date	www.nih.gov/ninr; Research Funding & Programs, DEA, OEP Extramural Resources, PAs and RFAs. RFA-NR-04-004, July 29, 2003

(Continued on next page)

Table 34-1. National Institute of Nursing Research Training and Research Mechanisms and Selected Career Development Awards (Continued)

Code	Mechanism	Description	Special Features	Award Amount	Time	Receipt Dates§	National Institutes of Health (NIH) Web Site
K23	Mentored Patient-Oriented Research Career Development Award	A period of mentored research experience to support the career development of investigators who have made a commitment to focus on patient-oriented research.	Must spend a minimum of 75% effort on research and research career development.	Up to $75,000 salary plus fringe benefits; research expenses up to $25,000.	3 years	Postmarked by Feb. 1, June 1, or Oct. 1	(www.nih.gov/ninr) Research Funding & Programs, DEA, OEP Extramural Resources, PAs and RFAs. PA-00-004, Oct. 8, 1999
K24	Mid-Career Investigator Award in Patient-Oriented Research	A period of mentored research to provide clinicians with protected time to devote to patient-oriented research and to act as mentors for beginning clinical investigators.	Must spend between 25%–50% of effort conducting patient-oriented research and mentoring. Must have independent research support.	Up to $83,350 salary plus fringe benefits; research expenses up to $25,000. (Based on a maximum legislative salary cap of $166,700)	3 years	Postmarked by Feb. 1, June 1, or Oct. 1	www.nih.gov/ninr; Research Funding & Programs, DEA, OEP Extramural Resources, PAs and RFAs. PA-00-005, Oct. 8, 1999

(Continued on next page)

Table 34-1. National Institute of Nursing Research Training and Research Mechanisms and Selected Career Development Awards *(Continued)*

| | | | Small Business Projects | | | | |
Code	Mechanism	Description	Special Features	Award Amount	Time	Receipt Dates§	National Institutes of Health (NIH) Web Site
R41	Small Business Technology Transfer Grant (STTR) Phase I	To provide initial support to small business concerns that team with research institutions to explore the scientific and technical feasibility of a research project with commercial applications.	–	$100,000 total costs (direct, indirect, and fixed fee)	1 year; non-renewable	Received by April 1, Aug. 1, or Dec. 1	(www.nih.gov) Grants, Grants Page, Grant Topics, Funding Opportunities, Small Business Opportunities, STTR
R42	Small Business Technology Transfer Grant (STTR) Phase II	This phase provides support for in-depth development of the activities initiated in phase I that are likely to lead to commercial products or services.	–	$500,000 total costs (direct, indirect, and fixed fee)	2 years; non-renewable	Received by April 1, Aug. 1, or Dec. 1	www.nih.gov; Grants, Grants Page, Grant Topics, Funding Opportunities, Small Business Opportunities, STTR

(Continued on next page)

Table 34-1. National Institute of Nursing Research Training and Research Mechanisms and Selected Career Development Awards (Continued)

Code	Mechanism	Description	Special Features	Award Amount	Time	Receipt Dates§	National Institutes of Health (NIH) Web Site
R43	Small Business Innovation Research Grant (SBIR) Phase I	To establish the technical merit and feasibility of proposed research or R&D efforts that may ultimately lead to commercial products/services.	—	$100,000 total costs (direct, indirect, and fixed fee)	6 months; non-renewable	Received by April 1, Aug. 1, or Dec. 1	www.nih.gov; Grants, Grants Page, Grant Topics, Funding Opportunities, Small Business Opportunities, SBIR
R44	Small Business Innovation Research Grant (SBIR) Phase II	To support in-depth development of research and development ideas for which feasibility has been established in phase I and which are likely to result in commercial products or services	—	$750,000 total costs (direct, indirect, and fixed fee)	2 years, non-renewable	Received by April 1, Aug. 1, or Dec. 1	www.nih.gov; Grants, Grants Page, Grant Topics, Funding Opportunities, Small Business Opportunities, SBIR

- § Revision dates one month later, except for R15, for which the established dates remain the same.
- * All AIDS-related research applications are due January 2, May 1, and September 1.
- ** If application proposes $500,000 or more in direct costs in any one year, must contact program staff prior to submission (NIH Guide, 5/03/96). Effective January 1, 2002, applicants must seek agreement to accept assignment from program staff at least 6 weeks prior to the anticipated submission of these applications (NIH Guide, 10/16/01). Budgets of $350,000 direct costs in any year go to advisory council for special consideration of high budgets.
- *** For further details, see the AREA Program Announcement (NIH Guide, 1/10/03) at http://grants1.nih.gov/grants/guide/pa-files/PA-03-053.html

Note. NIH has expanded its use of the Modular Grant Application and Award for grant applications with total direct costs of $250,000 a year or less. For details, please refer to the December 15, 1998, NIH Guide Notice at http://www.nih.gov/grants/guide/notice-files/not98-178.html

Table courtesy of the National Institute of Nursing Research.

Application Review and Funding at NINR

Although a detailed review on the research processs and constructing and submitting an application is beyond the scope of this chapter, a few key elements are highlighted. The reader is referred to numerous authors who provide a more detailed review related to proposal development and grantsmanship (American Nurses Association, 2001; Burns & Grove, 2001; Crain & Broome, 2000; Granger & Chulay, 1999; Harden & McFarland, 2000; Jones, Tulman, & Clancy, 1999; Kinney, 1999; NCI, 2002; Office of Behavioral and Social Sciences, 2001; Ogden & Goldberg, 2002; Phillips, 2000; Polit & Beck, 2004; Reif-Lehrer, 1995; Ross, 2001; Sandelowski & Barroso, 2003; Schilling, 2003; Throckmorton, 2002; Tornquist, 1986).

In addition to the multitude of resources located on the NIH Web site, professional and specialty nursing organizations, such as Sigma Theta Tau, the American Nurses Association, and the ONS Foundation, also provide a number of resources for research development and funding. For example, ONS through its Web site (www.ons.org) offers consultation for research ideas and mentorship for its members conducting oncology research. ONS also has identified priorities for advancing oncology nursing research. Additional sources of funding include private institutions, industry (e.g., pharmaceutical companies), and individual donors. These sources of funding often are used to help support nursing research.

The NINR Web site provides a wealth of resources and information needed for preparing and submitting an application as well as information essential for managing a grant after funding. An invaluable resource is the free online course "Research for Developing Nurse Scientists" (http://ninr.nih.gov/ninr). This online course provides a general overview on NIH guidelines related to grant preparation and management, practical tips for enhancing a research career, and key issues in conducting research, including topics such as ethical concerns, the recruitment of diverse populations in NIH-funded research, and research dissemination. The Web site also contains frequently asked questions (http://ninr.nih.gov/ninr/faq.html).

Researchers can apply to NINR for funding through a variety of mechanisms. Table 34-2 provides a selected listing of the various funding mechanisms. As depicted, there are mechanisms to support the general categories of research, research training, and research career development. These mechanisms can be used to support the research and research training and career development for the beginning to the more advanced researcher. NINR also supports a number of small business research opportunities as well as a number of initiatives focused on attracting minority individuals to enter biomedical and behavioral research careers. Researchers are strongly encouraged to contact the program director representing their area of interest at the beginning of the application process. As mentioned earlier, the program director can be very helpful in providing guidance during this phase of the process.

The preparation and submission of a competitive application requires great time, focus, diligence, and effort. When preparing an application, researchers are required to strictly adhere to the guidelines outlined in the announcement (if appropriate) and the Public Health Service grant application kit (e.g., PHS 398) and carefully review all of the guidelines and any other pertinent information outlined by the funding agency. PHS 398 serves as the roadmap for formatting an application for federal funding and must be carefully adhered to. Crain and Broome (2000) provided a grant application process-planning tool to assist researchers when submitting an extramural grant application. These authors highlighted the need for careful planning and organization throughout the entire process. Figure 34-1 depicts how a grant is tracked through NIH.

Table 34-2. Selected Standard Receipt Dates and Review and Award Cycles				
	Types of Application	**Cycle I**	**Cycle II**	**Cycle III**
Application Receipt Dates	National Research Service Award (NRSA)*	January 10	May 10	September 10
	All academic research enhancement awards, except those involving AIDS-related research	January 25	May 25	September 25
	New research grants and conference and research career awards. All (new, competing, revised, and supplemental) program project and center grants	February 1	June 1	October 1
	Competing continuation, supplemental, and revised research grants and research career awards	March 1	July 1	November 1
	NRSA (standard)**	April 5	August 5	December 5
	All AIDS-related grants	May 1	September 1	January 2
Review and Award Schedule	Scientific merit review	June–July	October–November	February–March
	Advisory council review	September–October	January–February	May–June
	Earliest project start date	December	April	July

* Institutional Award (T_{32})
** Predoctoral Fellowship (F_{31}), Postdoctoral Fellowship (F_{32})

Note. Based on information from NIH, 2004.

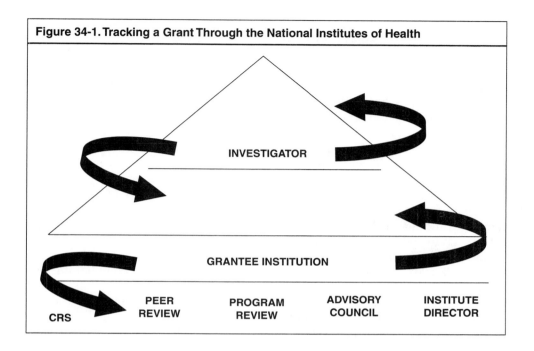

Figure 34-1. Tracking a Grant Through the National Institutes of Health

INVESTIGATOR

GRANTEE INSTITUTION

CRS

PEER
REVIEW

PROGRAM
REVIEW

ADVISORY
COUNCIL

INSTITUTE
DIRECTOR

Researchers submitting an application to NIH will need to attach a cover letter with their application highlighting their preferred assigned IC and review section. For example, if the researcher wishes to have NINR serve as the primary assignment for funding consideration, the researcher should highlight this in the cover letter addressed to the Center for Scientific Review (CSR). CSR serves as the central point of receipt for many of the applications submitted to NIH and will evaluate and triage all incoming applications (CSR, 2003). When appropriate for review of this application, researchers may request dual assignment, meaning they may request assignment for review of the application in addition to ICs within NIH who share a common interest in the proposed area of research. Similarly, the researcher will need to identify which study section he or she wishes to review the application. Depending on the topic area, an application will be assigned to a study section based on the area of science. Nursing science most often is assigned to NURS 1 NSAA: Nursing Science Adults and Older Adults and NURS 2 NSCF: Nursing Science Children and Families for review. Members of the sections include nurse researchers and researchers from diverse disciplines who have demonstrated expertise in their specialty area and a previous history of research funding. Disciplines outside of nursing can include medicine, public health, economics, sociology, psychology, and anthropology. The diverse composition of expertise on these review sections is needed to fully address the breadth and depth of applications received for review. Applications also may be assigned to other study sections that focus on behavioral and social sciences research, AIDS and related research, and risk prevention and health behavior. A full description of the various study sections is located on the CSR Web site (www. csr.nih.gov/).

Study sections at CSR review applications that are submitted in response to a program announcement according to the area of science, such as for investigator-initiated proposals. On the other hand, an ad hoc panel of experts, either within CSR or in NINR, reviews applications that are submitted in response to an RFA. An NINR study section reviews nursing research training and career development applications.

Research proposals submitted to NIH undergo a two-tiered review process. The designated study section or initial review group, either from CSR or NINR, performs the first level review. Reviewers consist of a group of experts and/or a national scientist who is actively engaged in research. Reviewers evaluate proposals according to five categories: significance, approach, innovation, investigator, and environment. Additional evaluative categories focus on the inclusion of women, minorities, and children, budgetary concerns, the protection of human subjects, and a data and safety monitoring plan. The PHS 398 provides a more detailed description of these categories and is available through the university research business office or online (http://grants.nih.gov/grants/funding/phs398/phs398.html). During the initial review, a score is assigned ranging from 1.0 (outstanding) to 5.0 (worst) in increments of 1.0 (NCI, 2002). All applicants will receive a summary statement highlighting the strengths and weaknesses of their application. A number of applications will not be reviewed at the meeting and will be deemed to be in the lower half of the applications with triage. These applications will not be scored. This is where the program director can be of assistance to the researcher in helping to interpret the summary statement and making recommendations for the amended application.

The second level of review includes an internal appraisal of applications for scientific merit and program relevance. At NINR, the National Advisory Council for Nursing Research performs the second level review.

The institute director makes the funding decision. Research proposals are funded depending on their scientific merit, availability of funds, program relevance, and council recommendation. Researchers whose application has marginal scientific merit are encouraged to contact their program director to discuss the summary statement and discuss plans for possible resubmission of an amended application. It is important to note that researchers rarely are funded with the first application. Many researchers, including the more experienced researchers, must resubmit a revised application that addresses the concerns of the reviewers. Revised applications must carefully consider all aspects highlighted by the reviewers. Kinney (1999) asserted that revised applications should do the following: (a) contain substantive improvements, (b) be responsive to all concerns identified in the summary statement, (c) contain updated information since the original submission, and (d) clearly delineate where changes have been made. O'Connell (2001) provided a discussion on the gentle art of submission and underscored the importance of peer review as an essential part of becoming a scientist.

After a grant is funded, the program director will work in concert with members of the NINR grants management team to monitor the progress of the grant throughout the funding period. Funded investigators disseminate their findings (e.g., publications, press releases) associated with the grant and share these with NINR staff and acknowledge NINR as a source of their funding in any dissemination activities. Research findings may be used in testimony to Congress, annual reports, or other documents prepared by NINR. For example, the document "Making a Difference:

NINR Research Results" provides examples of how nursing research is making a difference in advancing nursing science and improving the health and well-being of the nation. These and other informative documents are located on the NINR Web site.

Summary

This chapter has provided an introduction to securing research funding from NINR. Figure 34-2 highlights a few reminders for use when preparing a proposal for submission to the institute.

Figure 34-2. Ten Key Aspects of Proposal Development and Submission

- Assemble a team with demonstrated expertise, experience, and productivity.
- Allow more time than expected, start early, and develop a realistic timetable.
- Adhere to all instructions outlined in announcements, application packet, and by the funding agency.
- Contact the program director early on in the process.
- Construct a proposal that is based on the state of the science and potential to advance knowledge (e.g., nursing science).
- State clearly what you mean and make no assumptions on the part of reviewers.
- Become familiar with NINR (e.g., mission, previously funded grants, opportunities for research).
- Construct an application that carefully considers aspects of the review criteria (significance, approach, innovation, investigator, environment).
- Prepare an aesthetically pleasing application.
- Have your proposal pre-reviewed before submission to the funding agency.

Opportunities to identify and address a number of research priorities will continue to be identified. Ongoing nursing research will continue to be central to efforts devoted to advancing nursing science and enhancing evidence-based practice. From a program director's perspective, I have noted four key qualities among NINR's successful researchers. I refer to them as the four P's: passion, people, persistence, and productivity. Successful researchers demonstrate *passion* about their area of research and have selected research topics that are near and dear to their hearts. They have identified a cadre of *people* that mentor, motivate, and share their resources and expertise with them to help them accomplish professional and research goals. In turn, successful researchers also reach back and help other people who are interested in developing a research career. *Persistence* is key in the world of grantsmanship. Oftentimes, researchers will need to submit grants more than once to be funded. Although the receipt of a summary statement or word of an unfunded proposal may be disappointing initially, researchers try and try again. Finally, reviewers love evidence of *productivity*. Successful researchers provide evidence of their productivity through their publications and presentations. Even at the student level, it is never too early to begin to develop a habit of productivity and dissemination of findings. Individuals pursuing research careers are encouraged to explore the various opportunities for research and research career development and training opportunities provided by NINR. *Bon escriber!*

References

American Nurses Association. (2001). *Grant writing tips for nurses and other health professionals.* Washington, DC: Author.

Burns, N., & Grove, S.K. (2001). *The practice of nursing research: Conduct, critique, and utilization* (4th ed.). Philadelphia: Saunders.

Center for Scientific Review. (2003). *Referral and review.* Retrieved October 21, 2003, from http://www.csr.nih.gov/review/peerrev.htm

Crain, H.C., & Broome, M.E. (2000). Tool for planning the grant application process. *Nursing Outlook, 48,* 288–293.

Granger, B.B., & Chulay, M. (1999). *Research strategies for clinicians.* Stamford, CT: Appleton & Lang.

Harden, J.T., & McFarland, G. (2000). Avoiding gender and minority barriers to NIH funding. *Journal of Nursing Scholarship, 32*(1), 83–86.

Jones, C.B., Tulman, C., & Clancy, C. (1999). Research funding opportunities at the Agency for Health Care Policy and Research. *Nursing Outlook, 47,* 156–161.

Kinney, M.R. (1999). Seeking funding for clinical research. In M.A. Mateo & K.T. Kirchoff (Eds.), *Using and conducting nursing research in the clinical setting* (pp. 171–181). Philadelphia: Saunders.

National Cancer Institute. (2002). *Everything you wanted to know about the NCI grants process but were afraid to ask* (DHHS NIH Publication No. 02-1222). Bethesda, MD: Author.

National Institutes of Health, Office of Extramural Research. (2004). *NIH medical & behavioral research grant policies, guidelines & funding opportunities.* Retrieved September 8, 2004, from http://grants2.nih.gov/grants/oer.htm

National Institute of Nursing Research. (2003). *About NINR.* Retrieved October 21, 2003, from http://www.nih.gov/ninr/research/diversity/mission.html

O'Connell, K.A. (2001). Talking back to reviewers: The gentle art of resubmission. *Journal of Professional Nursing, 17*(6), 276.

Office of Behavioral and Social Sciences. (2001). *Qualitative methods in health research: Opportunities and considerations in application and review* (NIH Publication No. 02-5046). Bethesda, MD: National Institutes of Health.

Ogden, T.E., & Goldberg, I.A. (2002). *Research proposals: A guide to success.* San Diego, CA: Academic Press.

Phillips, J.M. (2000). Shaping a research agenda for the African American community: Issues and opportunities. *Journal of National Black Nurses Association, 11*(1), 1–3.

Polit, D.E., & Beck, T.C. (2004). *Nursing research: Principles and methods* (7th ed.). Philadelphia: Lippincott Williams & Wilkins.

Reif-Lehrer, L. (1995). *Writing a successful grant application.* Sudbury, MA: Jones & Bartlett.

Ross, H. (2001, April/May). *Where to begin the search for funding: What grant seekers need to know. Closing the Gap,* pp. 1–2. Retrieved November 1, 2004, from http://www.omhre.gov/ctg/ctg_funding.pdf

Sandelowski, M., & Barroso, J. (2003). Writing the proposal for a qualitative methodology project. *Qualitative Health Research, 13,* 781–820.

Schilling, L.S. (2003). Ten things I learned while writing my last research grant. *Pediatric Nursing, 29*(2), 150–151.

Throckmorton, T. (2002). Grant writing: Learning to climb a professional mountain. *Journal of PeriAnesthesia Nursing, 17*(3), 196–201.

Tornquist, E.M. (1986). *From proposal to publication: An informal guide to writing about nursing research.* Menlo Park, CA: Addison-Wesley.

Web Sites of Interest for Additional Information

American Nurses Foundation—http://nursingworld.org/anf/
National Cancer Institute—www.nci.hih.gov

National Institutes of Health—www.nih.gov
National Institute of Nursing Research—http://ninr.nih.gov/ninr
Oncology Nursing Society—www.ons.org
Sigma Theta Tau International—www.nursingsociety.org

Additional Resources for Grant Preparation and Management

Computer Retrieval of Information on Scientific Projects—www.crisp.cit.nih.gov

National Institutes of Health Office of Extramural Research—http://grants1.nih.gov/grants/oer.htm

NIH Guide for Grants and Contracts—http://grants.nih.gov/grants/guide/notice-files/NOT-OD-01-049.html

NIH Forms and Applications Page—http://grants.nih.gov/grants/forms.htm

Outreach Notebook for the Inclusion, Recruitment, and Retention of Women and Minority Subjects in Clinical Research—http://grants2.nih.gov/grants/policy/emprograms/overview/women-and-mi.htm

PHS 398—http://grants.nih.gov/grants/funding/phs398/phs398.html

The Original How to Write a Research Grant Proposal Application—www.niaid.nih.gov/ncn/grants/write/index.htm

Cancer Centers of Excellence

Sharon Krumm, PhD, RN

The concept of the center of excellence (COE) emerged in the 1970s, when patient volumes were essentially equated with clinical quality, and has evolved over time into a more comprehensive and clearly defined concept. Although some COEs are self-designated by their institutions, others are so designated by national associations or insurers and employer coalitions. The development of a cancer COE is a major strategic decision for a program or organization. The advantages of developing a COE must exceed the initial investment of time, capital, and other organizational assets, and there must be the organizational commitment to re-invest and sustain the center over time. The rewards or benefits accrued to a cancer COE may include increased patient referrals with direct financial benefits; increased research funding; improved education; enhanced recruitment and retention of outstanding physicians, nurses, and other staff; quality clinical outcomes; and enhanced reputation and prestige.

Defining Centers of Excellence

The definition of a COE varies with the perspectives of the organization awarding this designation. For example, a 1987 study published by Humana, Inc. (currently part of Columbia Healthcare/Hospital Corporation of America/Galen Healthcare) identified three essential elements of a COE. They included specific physician group characteristics, such as exceptional professional skills and expertise; a medical and clinical research program; and hospital facilities committed to patient care excellence, state of the art technology, and a highly competent professional nursing staff (The Advisory Board Company, 1994).

In 1994, Georgetown University School of Medicine, with support from the U.S. Department of Health and Human Services, provided this definition: "A center of excellence is a program for delivery of health care characterized by a commitment to the fundamental principle of providing the highest quality of medical care. It displays a comprehensive set of attributes and resources attesting to that commitment and evidence of outstanding performance in the management of one or more medical conditions" (The Advisory Board Company, 1994, p. 3).

This definition was later expanded as follows: "An institution, or subunit within an institution, recognized for technical performance, expansive resources, patient volume, and proven dedication to quality of care may be a center of excellence" (Meyer, 1994, p. 52).

The Advisory Board Company (1999) defined an internally designated COE as: "A center that is established and operated by a hospital and designated as a center of excellence by the operating institution due to its provision of high quality and highly specialized care. Hospitals typically use the designation as a marketing instrument, emphasizing to potential patients and payors that the hospital is committed to maintaining a quality program" (p. 2). A focus on specialized and quality care is a shared component of both of these definitions.

For insurers, COEs have a more distinct definition. High quality, low costs, and inclusion within a network of providers are components of this definition. For insurers' purposes, in addition to providing high quality and technologically advanced care, a COE offers packaged pricing for specific procedures. Therefore, COE designation usually denotes cost savings in addition to quality care (The Advisory Board Company, 1994). Insurers solicit requests for proposals to hospitals interested in COE designation for specific services.

They then use specific criteria to determine which hospitals provide high-quality care at an acceptable cost and are eligible for their designation as a COE. Figure 35-1 lists criteria that insurers may use for this determination.

Figure 35-1. Insurers' Criteria for Center of Excellence Designation

Outcome Criteria
- Average length of stay
- Infection rates
- Procedures reperformed
- Mortality rates
- Volumes

Quality Criteria
- Accreditation or certification
- Patient satisfaction surveys
- Physicians' curriculum vitae
- Physicians' performances (number of procedures annually, survival rates, cost per procedure)

Cost Criteria
- Cost per procedure
- Global case rate

Note. From *Executive Summary, Healthcare Industry Committee* (pp. 3–4), by The Advisory Board Company, 1996, Washington, DC: Author. Adapted with permission.

Although no single regulatory body or group has the authority to designate or certify a COE, some national associations may certify COEs in specific fields. The American College of Surgeons Commission on Cancer (ACoS) is one example. ACoS designates a cancer program as a comprehensive cancer program or a community hospital cancer program according to the number of patients with cancer who are treated and the services provided. The Department of Veterans Affairs confers the designation of clinical programs of excellence within eight categories throughout its hospitals. In a number of states, the state educational board is involved in the designation of COEs within academic medical centers. The board establishes the criteria and determines which programs meet its qualifications for designation as a COE.

The designation as a comprehensive cancer center by the National Cancer Institute (NCI) recognizes the achievement of specific requirements in a number of categories. In many ways, this designation meets the criteria for a COE as it represents a rigorous review, which denotes that the cancer center provides a high level of excellence in research, education, and clinical care.

In June 1994, then governor, Lorton Chiles of Florida introduced the concept of COEs into that state's health reform legislation. Within the proposed legislation, COEs were defined as "hospitals whose non-profit mission historically has been to provide health care services to the most acute and complex of patients . . . serve as teaching and research institutions . . . provide the most complex patient cases . . . provide a disproportionate share of services to the medically indigent population through charity and Medicaid programs" (The Advisory Board Company, 1994, p. 6). Federal healthcare reform, which might include COE concepts, continues to be a major topic of political interest.

COEs, regardless of how they are designated, share several common components. Among these are advanced technology; educational programs; recognition as a clinical leader by other physicians and the public; priority allocation of resources; "sufficient patient volume, staff size and revenue to warrant the name"; and use of COE name for marketing purposes (The Advisory Board Company, 1996, p. 2). Research is another shared component, especially among academic medical centers. Ronning (2003) offered the following comprehensive and contemporary definition: ". . . a center of excellence is a program that combines clinical excellence with marketing, operational and service excellence and evidences an excellent organization" (p. 6). He asserted that clinical quality is a "given" in today's environment and that "an excellent organization is the determining factor in achieving center of excellence performance and recognition."

Evolving Concepts of Centers of Excellence

With the emergence of medical specialization in the 1970s, clinical competence was the primary requirement for excellence. Competition arose between academic medical centers and young specialists as they moved out of the medical centers and into community-based practices and began marketing their practices to attract patients. Internal designation as a COE was frequently used by these specialty practices as a marketing strategy. The advent of managed care contracting and the shift to prospective payment and diagnosis-related groups in the 1980s allowed comparisons of the cost of care among providers and demonstrated that clinical outcomes for low-cost care often were comparable to those of high-cost care. Managed care companies seized the opportunity to direct patients to low-cost programs, many of which were marketed as COEs. Managed care contracts with these COEs, however, were primarily awarded based on the price or cost of care. By the mid-1990s, specialists and hospitals began to develop relationships and specialty programs, which they designated as COEs in an effort to influence insurers to refer patients to these programs. In addition to low costs and clinical quality, convenience and easy access to care were considered essential if a COE was to remain competitive in the consumer-oriented 1990s (Ronning, 2003).

Ronning (2003) proposed that COEs, in their current and more mature stage, be redefined within the context of contemporary health care and that the positioning strategy that they afford be taken into consideration by provider organizations. He proposed that COEs share common attributes (see Figure 35-2) but recognized the distinctions between the fundamental aspects shared by most programs and those found only in highly sophisticated, truly excellent programs. These attributes vary according to the various stakeholders' (e.g., payors, patients, physicians, provider/ organization partners in specialty programs) perception of excellence. For example, payors have a more limited perspective, which is primarily focused on financial performance, whereas program partners have the broadest perspective, which encompasses disease management and clinical integration. The determination of the extent and level of attainment of each attribute provides a useful framework for a systematic evaluation of a COE.

Figure 35-2. Stakeholders' Perspectives Regarding Attributes of Centers of Excellence

Payors' Perspective
- Program volume
- MD volume and specialization
- Quality
- Financial performance
- Satisfaction (patient and staff)
- Scope of services

Patients' Perspective
- Facilities
- Emergency care
- Access
- Image

Physicians' Perspective
- Physician/hospital relations
- Technology
- Research and teaching

Physicians' Perspectives, Higher Level Attributes
- Organization
- Payor relations

(Continued on next page)

Figure 35-2. Stakeholders' Perspectives Regarding Attributes of Centers of Excellence *(Continued)*

Program Partners' Perspectives
- Information systems
- Health and wellness programs

Program Partners' Perspectives, Higher Level Attributes
- Performance improvement
- Disease management
- Clinical integration

Note. From *Reinventing Centers of Excellence: Strategies for Saving and Strengthening Specialty Services* (p. 4), by P.L. Ronning, 2002, Chicago: Society for Healthcare Strategy and Market Development of the American Hospital Association. Adapted with permission.

The concept that COEs are not synonymous with inpatient care has evolved in relatively recent times. Individuals with a cancer diagnosis receive care in a number of settings across the trajectory of their illnesses. Patients move among physician offices, hospital ambulatory and infusion centers, inpatient and intensive care units, home care, and palliative and hospice care settings. Highly effective COEs provide integrated care across these settings.

The designation of a hospital as magnet by the American Nurses Association Credentialing Center does not fit the traditional definition of a COE. However, such designation confers many of the attributes attributed to COEs, including improved clinical outcomes, enhanced image, recruitment and retention advantages, and, potentially, an increase in patient referrals. A highly competent professional nursing staff has been a consistent theme for COEs since their inception. Fox Chase Cancer Center in Philadelphia was the first freestanding NCI-designated comprehensive cancer center to achieve this distinguished designation, followed by the M.D. Anderson Cancer Center in Houston, TX. Other hospitals and academic medical centers with cancer COEs, including NCI-designated clinical or comprehensive centers, more recently received this designation, whereas others are in the review process.

Realizing the Benefits and Challenges of Centers of Excellence Designation

For most organizations, there are three fundamental reasons for pursuing COE status: improved quality of care, increased referral volumes, and increased profits. Other benefits contribute to these three, including increased patient and staff satisfaction, recruitment and retention of excellent clinical and administrative staffs, and enhanced education and research. Quality of care results when carefully selected clinical programs are the focus of organizational resources and receive the commitment of clinical and administrative staffs. These clinical programs must be considered important by the community served and/or serve a significant number of potential patients to affect the community's perceptions of the program.

Multihospital systems may select one hospital as a cancer COE, knowing that achievement of this status by one hospital will reflect positively on other hospitals within the system as a result of the halo effect. Other organizations may combine two related programs as a COE to improve clinical quality in both programs. An innovative area of care, such as a specific clinical research program or innovative diagnostic procedure, may be designated a COE, although it serves only a small number of patients and does not generate a profit, because this designation enhances the hospital's overall image. When referring physicians and potential patients recognize a cancer program or hospital as excellent, there is an increase in patient referrals to the organization as a whole and specifically to the cancer program. As noted by Ronning (2003), where organizational excellence exists within a COE, increased profits are realized.

Academic medical centers benefit when a COE results in the pooling of resources to allow researchers and clinicians to more easily engage in collaborative research and patient care. Synergistic, innovative research and more effective patient care delivery are achieved for patients with cancer when they are cared for in this environment (The Advisory Board Company, 1999).

Large companies and conglomerates look to COEs to leverage their catastrophic health benefit expenses. The Leapfrog Group is one example of a conglomerate of nonhealthcare companies aggressively pushing providers to achieve high-quality, low-cost health care. Most recently, the Leapfrog Group defined specific initiatives for improving healthcare outcomes based on the Institute of Medicine's report, *To Err Is Human* (Hudon, 2003). As previously noted, insurers financially benefit by steering patients to high-quality, low-cost COEs. Patients and families benefit from improved clinical outcomes when excellence truly exists within a COE (Traska, 1989).

The challenges of achieving COE status for a clinical program are significant, more so for large healthcare systems where internal competition for resources is more intense. Physicians and hospital administrators typically initiate the process for COE designation and receive approval from their governing boards. However, in addition to receiving "local" approval, academic medical centers often must receive support from their board of regents before initiating the COE process. This approval is necessary to ensure that the COE is consistent with the scope and mission of the university (The Advisory Board Company, 1999).

Creating and sustaining a culture of excellence may be the most significant challenge for a COE. The organizations' initial strategic decisions regarding resource allocations, marketing efforts, and operational changes must be regularly and systematically reevaluated. Although some organizations designate a nonprofitable program as a COE because of the halo effect it affords, most COEs are intended to achieve increased profits. This requires effective assessment and ongoing reassessment of external and internal trends, such as competitors, population demographics, technology, physician capabilities and referral patterns, and finances. Administrators, physicians, nurses, and other clinical staff comprising a COE must sustain an inherent, passionate commitment to excellence (Ronning, 2003). Sustaining this passion must be a priority for clinical and administrative leaders and is required to overcome organizational inertia and sustain the benefits for patients, the organization, and staff.

Investing in Centers of Excellence

Organizational investments required to achieve and sustain COE status were previously identified in this chapter. These investments include an extraordinary amount of time, energy, passion, and leadership from physicians, nurses, and administrators. Financial resources include operating, capital, and marketing budgets. Resources for research and education include the appropriate and adequate allocation of staff to these services and sufficient budgets to support them. Access to services must be ensured through an efficient intake process and support for referring physicians; attention to the needs and requirements of the payors of the services must be attended to. Technology and innovation, as an impetus for designating a COE, often require significant financial and staffing resources.

Often a COE requires redesign of the organizational structure to permit a number of departments and programs to successfully collaborate. Most hospitals are organized along departmental lines, such as nursing, marketing, medicine, or surgery. Matrix structures or realignment of departments along specialty lines allow COEs to truly differentiate themselves and achieve their goals (Ronning, 2003). To be successful, the authority and responsibility for achieving clinical, programmatic, and financial goals must be invested in the clinical and administrative leaders within the COE, rather than within the more traditional departmental structure.

Human resources, including clinical, administrative, and support staff, are the most significant requirements, especially in ensuring adequate numbers and competencies. Certain staff members, such as marketing staff, may be assigned to the COE for a portion of their time, whereas others are full-time employees of the COE. New positions may be implemented to achieve programmatic goals. For example, case managers may be used to ensure high quality and efficient care for patients receiving cancer care across several settings or in highly technical areas, such as blood and marrow transplantation. Nurse case managers within a COE ensure access to appropriate care and manage care processes to ensure that targeted clinical and financial outcomes are realized (Smith, 2003).

Magnet status is not commonly considered a designation of a COE; however, it is a powerful strategy for achieving COE recognition. When nurses are committed to high-quality care and to the organization in which they work because of the environment that exists in magnet hospitals, low turnover rates reduce the cost of care, strong and effective physician-nurse collaborations promote high-quality care, and necessary changes are made more easily by a flexible professional staff. An appropriate level of nurse staffing is a consistent attribute among magnet hospitals, as is the commitment to ensuring nurses' professional development and continuing education (Hinshaw, 2002). Given the existing and projected shortage of professional nurses, attention to their work environment, compensation and advancement, empowerment regarding clinical decision making, physician relationships, and professional development are essential and require a significant organizational investment (American Association of Colleges of Nursing, 2002; American Hospital Association Commission on Workforce for Hospitals and Health Systems, 2002).

The determination of which programs to include within a cancer COE depends on several factors that are summarized in Figure 35-3.

Figure 35-3. Factors for Selecting Center of Excellence Programs

- Program assets (patient volumes, technology)
- Physician, nursing, technical, and support staff (including competencies)
- Physician leadership
- Diagnostic facilities
- Dedicated clinical facilities (inpatient, outpatient, hospice)
- Multidisciplinary teams
- Information systems
- Education: patient, public, and professional
- Research: clinical trials
- Rehabilitation services
- Emergency management services
- Image and reputation
- Payor relations
- Financial performance
- Community outreach
- Screening
- Administrative staff (including competencies)

Note. Based on information from The Advisory Board Company, 1994; Ronning, 2002.

To achieve success as a COE, sustained physician leadership and adequate numbers of specialists are required. Rethinking the definitions of excellence within existing hospital and multihospital systems and redefining the organizational structure to support COEs are required. Using the factors listed in Figure 35-3, an organization is guided in its selection of services or programs to include within a COE. For example, homecare services may be included if these services already exist with sufficient staff, leadership, a good reputation, and information systems that can be integrated with others in the COE. A COE may decide to develop a homecare program to achieve a higher level of disease management and improve clinical outcomes and satisfaction.

If determined to be necessary through marketing and financial analysis, new facilities may be built to support a cancer COE. Carefully planned facilities will be a substantial advantage to patients, families, and the public by efficiently providing multidisciplinary services and amenities across the continuum of cancer care. New facility planning also should consider labor productivity, such as the design elements of the ideal nursing unit, and flexibility to accommodate future expansion or changes in healthcare delivery. Although a new building dedicated to cancer services may enhance a COE's and organization's image, productivity, and flexibility, the true measure of its success is the realization of improved clinical outcomes and the achievement of the COE's goals, not simply a better building (Health Care Advisory Board, 2003).

Measuring Centers of Excellence Success

Recognizing that any organization may designate its cancer program as a COE, patients and oncology nurses should consider as valid only those COEs that meet the more rigid definitions and requirements discussed in the first section of this chapter. Designation by NCI as a comprehensive or clinical program is a strong endorsement of a cancer program and signifies that the program has achieved a significant level of excellence. Accreditation by ACoS is another worthy consideration.

Other programs, including private group practices, which meet rigorous criteria for excellence, warrant designation as a COE. Cancer programs that are fully integrated across care settings and along the trajectory of care represent the most sophisticated of the COEs.

By using the criteria listed in Figure 35-2, one can systematically evaluate or rate a cancer program to determine if it warrants designation as a cancer COE and to what extent it does so. Ronning (2002) suggested a weighted rating scale, where the common or fundamental criteria of volume, quality, satisfaction, scope of services, and financial performance are assigned a greater weight than the higher, more difficult level to attain criteria of disease management and clinical integration. This permits smaller programs with more limited resources and scope of services to receive full recognition for the legitimate excellence of their programs. Oncology nurses may find this evaluation approach helpful in a number of ways. It can be used for planning a COE and for evaluating an existing COE for performance improvement purposes.

Summary

Oncology nurses often are asked to recommend cancer programs to family, friends, or acquaintances; they can determine which designated cancer COEs meet the criteria for excellence and to what extent they are met. This determination also may guide an oncology nurse's decision among potential employers, as greater professional satisfaction is associated with organizations achieving a recognized high standard of excellence. Finally, attaining and sustaining cancer COE designation is not possible without the passionate leadership of oncology nurses and the highly competent care that they provide.

References

The Advisory Board Company. (1994). *Definitions of the term "centers of excellence" fact brief.* Washington, DC: Author.

The Advisory Board Company. (1996). *Executive summary, Healthcare Industry Committee.* Washington, DC: Author.

The Advisory Board Company. (1999). *Overview of centers of excellence, custom research project.* Washington, DC: Author.

American Association of Colleges of Nursing. (2002). Hallmarks of the professional nursing practice environment. Washington, DC: Author.

American Hospital Association Commission on Workforce for Hospitals and Health Systems. (2002). *In our hands: How hospital leaders can build a thriving workforce.* Chicago: American Hospital Association.

Health Care Advisory Board. (2003). Re-envisioning the acute care enterprise: Strategic considerations for capital planning and facility design. Washington, DC: Author.

Hinshaw, A.S. (2002). Building magnetism into health organizations. In M.L. McClure & A.S. Hinshaw (Eds.), *Magnet hospitals revisited: Attraction and retention of professional nurses* (pp. 83–101). Washington, DC: American Nurses Publishing.

Hudon, P.S. (2003). Leapfrog standards: Implications for nursing practice. *Nursing Economic$, 21,* 233–236.

Meyer, L. (1994). Why centers of excellence are gaining momentum. *Journal of Health Care Benefits, 3,* 52–56.

Ronning, P.L. (2002). *Reinventing centers of excellence: Strategies for saving and strengthening specialty services.* Chicago: Society for Healthcare Strategy and Market Development of the American Hospital Association.

Ronning, P.L. (2003). What to do about specialty services: Specialty hospitals, centers of excellence and the future. *Spectrum,* 5–6.

Smith, A.P. (2003). Case management: Key to access, quality, and financial success. *Nursing Economic$, 21,* 237–240, 244.

Traska, M.R. (1989). In search of centers of excellence. *Business and Health, 7*(9), 11–14.

CHAPTER 36

Advocacy and Health Policy

Ilisa M. Halpern, MPP

The words *lobbying* and *lobbyist* often bring negative images to mind for most people who live outside Washington, DC. Because of caricatures portrayed in Hollywood films and made-for-TV movies, unfavorable news reports, and scandalous examples of how money can influence policymaking, many healthcare professionals consider lobbying to be an activity for morally bankrupt, highly paid individuals and not something in which they want to engage or feel would have any benefit to them or the patients for whom they care. However, healthcare professionals—nurses in particular—are beginning to see lobbying, or health policy advocacy, in a different light; this shift is a result of recent successes of coordinated grassroots advocacy efforts that have helped advance the nursing profession and/or the interests of patients. These nurses, as citizen-lobbyists, are having an impact on policymaking at all levels of government.

The purpose of this chapter is to describe what constitutes health policy advocacy and why nurses should be actively involved in the policymaking process, to provide examples of ways in which health policy advocacy has made a difference, and to offer an overview and resources about how nurses can engage in the policymaking process. The terms *policymaking* and *policymaker* are used throughout this chapter to refer to the process by which laws, regulations, ordinances, and other public policies are created and the elected officials who are in a position to create, amend, or otherwise affect local, state, or federal policies, respectively.

Health Policy Advocacy Allows You to Turn Outrage Into Action

Every day, people have experiences that are frustrating, unbelievable, or so outrageous that they think, "How can this be? There ought to be a law!" Nurses often experience frustration in their day-to-day practice—fighting with managed care companies, facing inadequate Medicare reimbursement, and trying to cobble together adequate care for uninsured patients. Nurses need to know how to be proactive to affect health policy change rather than just being frustrated by the daily and numerous obstacles they face. Health policy advocacy means channeling this sense of outrage about poorly conceived laws, policies, and regulations, or about the absence of a law when the need for one is clear, into action. Advocates let policymakers know what they, as citizens and constituents, believe elected officials should do.

In fact, Americans have the constitutional right to tell federal legislators what concerns them. The Constitution grants individuals the "right of the people . . . to petition the government for a redress of grievances . . ." (U.S. Constitution, First Amendment). If we took the time to think about it, we all could come up with a list of grievances we would like our public officials to address. Policymakers work for the citizens; taxpayers—such as the nation's nurses—fund their salaries, health insurance, and retirement benefits. Therefore, nurses have every right to hold their elected officials accountable and to give them feedback on their job performance. After all, nurses are held accountable by their employers, so the ultimate job review you can give your elected officials is by voting to either return them to office or to end their service.

Nurses Are Natural Advocates

Nurses are professional advocates; they regularly represent and work on behalf of patients, as well as their family members and others in the healthcare system. Nurses have many competing responsibilities and priorities and every day give a lot of themselves to their patients and employer. With less and less free time, people understandably tend to choose activities that provide the most "bang for the buck." One of the historical challenges to getting nurses more engaged in the policymaking process has been the misperception that health policy advocacy takes a lot of time, requires specialized knowledge or skills, and does not make a difference in policy deliberations. The good news is that health policy advocacy does not require nurses to develop a new skill set. Read my lips: "No new skills." Rather, advocacy involves taking existing skills used in nursing and applying them in a different arena (see Table 36-1).

Health Policy Advocacy

Advocacy is defined as the support or defense of a cause and the act of pleading or arguing on behalf of another person. Despite its simple definition, advocacy is multi-faceted, and the types of advocacy activities in which nurses and nursing organizations, such as the American Nurses Association (ANA) and the Oncology Nursing Society (ONS), engage are numerous and diverse. Although many of the issues of concern to nurses can be addressed by nonprofit and private sector efforts (e.g., working to retain young nurses in the profession by developing a nurse mentoring program at a local hospital), only government action will achieve the desired changes regarding other issues (e.g., prohibiting mandatory overtime for nurses). In other cases, because of economies of scale and infrastructure or capacity issues, the government can be more efficient at certain endeavors than individual organizations.

Table 36-1. Top Ten Advocacy Myths Debunked

Misconceptions	Actuality
(1) I am too busy—there is just not enough time in the day.	Most nursing and healthcare organizations make it easy and fast to weigh in with your elected officials. For example, the Oncology Nursing Society (ONS) has a *Legislative Action Center* at www.onslac.org that allows you to send an e-mail with just a few clicks. Most of these Web-based advocacy sites provide nurses with a template letter to make it even easier!
(2) I am a nurse, not a lobbyist.	Perfect! Members of Congress are more likely to listen to you. You can provide the member with substance and valid information, as you are an expert in the field seeing real patients and working in the real world—outside of Washington, DC. You are a "legitimate voice"—not a paid lobbyist.
(3) Why should I bother? It doesn't seem to make a difference. I have written before and not received a response. When I have received a response, the letter didn't address the issue I wrote about or I totally disagreed with the views expressed.	It may not feel like it, but it absolutely makes a difference. Offices count the calls, e-mails, faxes, and mail, and they log in the opinions that are expressed and have to provide a regular report on all constituent communications to the member of Congress. If you have written and have not received a response, write or call and let the office know. Sometimes, with the volume of mail, letters get lost. Also, if you disagree with the views expressed in the letter, write again and politely repeat your request and rationale and indicate you are disappointed in the member's position on the issue. Usually if you bring it to his or her attention, you get a prompt response. Also, think about Mothers Against Drunk Driving or "Megan's Law"— tenacity and one letter from one person or family can result in one law.
(4) My member is a lost cause, or doesn't sit on the relevant committee, or doesn't care about health care.	It is still essential to weigh in so that you have gone on record with your member of Congress. You never know when an issue will resonate with him or her or his or her staffers. There are many members of Congress who were not actively engaged in healthcare issues until someone in their family became affected by a particular disease or condition.
(5) My issue is not being discussed in Congress.	Maybe that is because no one is writing or calling in about it. You can help elevate an issue to the national agenda by communicating to your policymakers about it. Sometimes it takes a grassroots movement to garner Congressional attention. People writing in with their HMO horror stories stimulated the development of the "Patients' Bill of Rights."
(6) I am not an expert in the issue you are asking me to write or call about. I know about pain management, not genetic testing.	As a nurse, you are an expert in the provision of health care, and you understand firsthand what patients need and face. Just be honest about your experience as a nurse. The template letters or talking points that your professional organization provides will take care of the rest.

(Continued on next page)

Table 36-1. Top Ten Advocacy Myths Debunked *(Continued)*	
Misconceptions	**Actuality**
(7) I cannot make it to Washington to have a meeting with my elected official.	Members and staffers will tell you that developing a relationship with your policymakers and their staffers "back at home" is more effective because you can see them in your own community. Coming to Washington is effective, but visiting the members and staff in their district offices is even better.
(8) The process is intimidating. I don't understand what a substitute amendment is, am unclear on how conference committee works, and cannot remember what a pocket veto means.	The details and nuances of the federal policymaking process are difficult to follow, but you do not need to know them all. The action alerts from your professional organization tell you what you need to know in terms of bill status and context, and the template letters include all the relevant details. Do not worry if you cannot remember your fourth grade civics class—no one can, not even members of Congress (see Figures 36-1 and 36-3).
(9) I am a Democrat and my member is a Republican, or I am a Republican and my member is a Democrat.	Increasingly, healthcare issues are becoming bipartisan. For example, passage of the Nurse Reinvestment Act had broad bipartisan support, and Democrats and Republicans worked together to craft and enact the measures. Diseases and conditions, such as cancer, heart disease, and diabetes, do not respect political party affiliation; they are unfortunately universal scourges. Policymakers realize that all patients need nursing care, irrespective of for whom they voted in the last election. Do not worry about your party affiliation; identify yourself as a voter, constituent, and a nurse. These are suitable qualifications for your views to be treated with respect. In the 106th and 107th Congresses, ideological opposites Senators Jesse Helms (R-NC) and Ted Kennedy (D-MA) joined together to sponsor the "Eliminate Colorectal Cancer Act." If a healthcare concern can unite these two policymakers, you need not worry about differing in party affiliation from your member of Congress.
(10) I already do advocacy every day at my job—I "give at the office" to my patients.	Every day, Congress makes decisions that affect your patients and your job. To protect both of your interests, you need to take action! Remember, it is easy take part online through tools such as the ONS Legislative Action Center (www.onslac.org). Taking a few minutes to send an e-mail or make a phone call can make a world of difference to the successful enactment of legislation that addresses the nursing shortage or helps reduce medical errors. Policymakers often claim that the reason for their inaction on matters is that they are not "hearing from home" on the issue. Let's not give them that excuse!

Note. From *Top Ten Advocacy Myths Debunked,* by the Oncology Nursing Society, 2003. Retrieved November 3, 2003, from http://www.ons.org/lac/pdf/10TipsMyths.pdf. Copyright 2003 by the Oncology Nursing Society. Adapted with permission.

For example, although nursing organizations can and do fund initiatives to address the nursing shortage, they have restricted resources and limited reach. However, by using some of their own resources to advocate increases in federal funding for the Nurse Reinvestment Act and other federal nursing workforce programs, the ANA,

ONS, and others in the nursing community have secured millions of dollars in federal funding to address the nursing shortage. If, instead, individual nursing organizations had used the resources allocated to advocacy and invested them directly in nursing recruitment and retainment, it would have amounted to only a few thousand dollars. By leveraging their resources at the federal level, national nursing organizations have reaped a much greater return by delivering millions of new dollars for essential nursing workforce programs that will support nurses, nurse faculty, and nursing students across the country.

Nursing organizations educate policymakers at the local, state, and federal levels; advance proactive legislation on behalf of nursing and patients; and work to defeat proposals that would have adverse effects on nursing or patients. Health policy advocacy activities offer nurses a way to let their voices be heard. (Increasingly, many nursing organizations are engaging in both types of activities: funding their own priority initiatives to address key issues of concern and engaging in health policy advocacy to affect change at the federal, state, or local levels.) Key types of health policy advocacy in which nurses can engage are

- Patient (discussed above)
- Legislative—supporting or opposing policies in the U.S. Congress, state legislatures, or city or county level councils
- Regulatory—impacting the development and implementation of rules and regulations proposed by agencies such as the U.S. Department of Health and Human Services (e.g., Health Insurance Portability and Accountability Act [HIPAA]) or the U.S. Department of Labor (e.g., workplace safety standards)
- Media—using various media forums to communicate advocacy positions to raise public awareness and affect policymakers (e.g., letters to the editor, op-eds)
- Legal—employing legal action to promote or block particular actions or hold parties responsible for malfeasance (e.g., suing the tobacco industry on behalf of individuals with tobacco-related disease).

Health Policy Advocacy Is Essential to Supporting and Advancing the Field of Nursing

During the past 20 years, more health and consumer-based organizations have incorporated advocacy into their missions and principal activities as they have seen the gains that can be attained through such initiatives. For example, the HIV/AIDS activism of the 1980s and the breast cancer movement of the 1990s are well-known, tangible examples of what organizations and communities can achieve if they choose to allocate human and financial resources to affect public policies. Both causes have benefited from increases in research and programmatic funding for efforts to reduce and prevent the incidence, morbidity, and mortality of breast cancer and HIV/AIDS. Moreover, the recent five-year coordinated, consensus effort of biomedical research entities, universities, individual scientists, healthcare providers, patient advocacy organizations, and private enterprise to secure the doubling of the budget of the

National Institutes of Health was an unprecedented success; one attainable only by the active advocacy of hundreds of organizations and thousands of individuals across the country. Nurses are beginning to realize that involvement in the public policymaking process can and does make a difference. If one understands the basics of the policymaking process, has a passion about nursing and caring for patients, and has a little time, he or she can make gains in Washington, DC, state capitols, and before city or county level councils. (The policymaking process in this chapter focuses on the U.S. Congress; however, most of what is discussed can be applied to state legislatures as well as local government. For more information about state or local government, visit the Web sites of the National Conference of State Legislatures (www.ncsl.org), the U.S. Conference of Mayors (www.usmayors.org), and the National Association of Counties (www.naco.org).

For nursing and patient care issues to begin to receive the attention, public policy response, and funding they deserve, nurses must engage in proactive and aggressive advocacy efforts to help drive the national agenda toward nurses' concerns. Increasingly, much of what nurses do and experience daily while caring for their patients is influenced directly by laws, regulations, and other policies. Every day, policymakers and elected officials take action and can positively and negatively influence issues that affect nursing practice and patient care. Lawmakers regularly make decisions that have an impact on patients, nurses, physicians, healthcare insurers, pharmacists, social workers, hospitals, and researchers, and these decisions may be made with limited substantive knowledge and understanding of the people and systems they are affecting. For example, think about the recent change in practices and policies because of the implementation of HIPAA—the federal law requiring the creation and implementation of new regulations to safeguard and keep confidential patients' health information. Most nurses would attest that although protecting patient privacy is imperative, the new federal requirements are causing significant challenges to the way they can interact with patients, families, and other healthcare providers and are proving to be extremely difficult to interpret and apply. Other top nursing concerns impacted by policymakers include the nursing shortage, mandatory overtime, staff-to-patient ratios, patient safety and prevention of medical errors, care for the uninsured and underserved, and long-term viability of the Medicare and Medicaid programs.

Without hearing directly from nurses about priority problems, recommended solutions, and illustrations of where well-meaning policy has unintended, adverse consequences (e.g., HIPAA), policymakers may fail to address such concerns, remain unaware a problem exists, or use information and expertise provided to them by others. Of particular concern is when some of their sources may not share the views or be concerned with the interests of the nursing community. One of the principal assets the nursing community has is its good name; nurses are not only constituents and voters to policymakers of a particular district or state but also are experts in a highly respected profession who provide health care to elected officials, their family members, and constituents. For example, nurses are perceived to be on the side of patients, not profits. It is because of this "white hat" reputation that nurses' opinions are well respected and welcomed by policymakers. In fact, many policymakers seek input and expertise from healthcare professionals in their communities when they need information or additional viewpoints about pending legislation or regulatory matters. For example, U.S. Senator Tom Harkin (D-IA) has a Nurse Advisory Committee through which he solicits expertise and viewpoints from a wide range of nurses throughout Iowa. Policymakers must receive such expertise and viewpoints so they are aware of the needs in their communities and the consequences—positive and negative—of changes in policy. Nurses can be valued resources to elected officials and their staff, serve to raise issues of importance, and help to craft and implement necessary solutions.

A Quick and Simple Refresher on U.S. Civics—Policymaking "101"

For most of us, the last time we really understood or remembered the nuances of how a bill becomes a law was in our elementary school civics lessons. In fact, most members of Congress and their staffers do not have much more formal education about the process; they learn on the job. You need not have a PhD in political science or public policy to become involved and bring about change in the public policy process. You only need to understand the basics (see Figure 36-1). Although the information contained here uses the U.S. Congress as the example, most state legislatures are structured and function similarly.

Figure 36-1. The U.S. Congress	
U.S. House of Representatives	**U.S. Senate**
Known as • Representative • Congressman or Congresswoman • Member of Congress • House member	Known as • Senator • Member of Congress
435 members, with a varying number of members per state The number of representatives per state depends on the state's population. (Populous states such as California have more representatives than less populous states such as Idaho.)	100 members, with two senators from each of the 50 states
Two-year terms; all 435 seats are open for election every two years.	Six-year terms; one-third of the Senate is elected every two years.
A House member represents a Congressional district, which is circumscribed by the state legislature and based on population density.	Senators represent their entire state.
	(Continued on next page)

Figure 36-1. The U.S. Congress *(Continued)*	
U.S. House of Representatives	**U.S. Senate**
House members must be at least 25 years old, a U.S. citizen for at least seven years, and a resident of the district they represent.	Senators must be at least 30 years old, a U.S. citizen for at least nine years, and a resident of the state they represent.
Congressional districts may be part of a city, multiple cities, multiple towns, or entire counties. The U.S. Constitution sets the number of House members at 435. The number of House members per state is determined by the Federal Census and is reviewed and changed every 10 years when the new census results are available. The calculation to determine the number of representatives per state is made by dividing 435 into the total population of the United States. When a state, such as Wyoming, does not have enough people to qualify for a Representative, the Constitution addresses this by stating that every state must have at least one.	
National elections are held every two years on the first Tuesday of November in even numbered years. At that time, senators whose six-year terms are expiring and all 435 seats in the House of Representatives are open for election. The presidential election is held every four years. Elections held in non-presidential election years (e.g., the 2006 election) are known as "midterm elections" because they are held in the middle of a president's four-year term.	
A "new Congress" begins in the January following a November election, lasts two years, and has two sessions. For example, the 108th Congress runs from 2003 to 2004. The first session of the 108th Congress was in calendar year 2003, and the second session of the 108th Congress was in 2004.	
When policymakers are working in Washington, Congress is referred to as being "in session." When policymakers are in their home states and districts meeting with their constituents and conducting business locally, Congress is referred to as being "in or on recess." Although the Congressional schedule is different each year, some regularly scheduled breaks, or recesses, occur each year. These usually coincide with weekends, holidays, and the election cycle. Often the time members spend at home is called a "district work period." Visiting with members of Congress and their staff is effective whether you meet with them at home or in Washington. (For more information on meeting with members and staff to discuss issues of concern, see the "How One Nurse Can Make a Difference" section of this chapter.)	

Two senators and one member in the House of Representatives represent every person in America in the U.S. Congress (except residents of Washington, DC, who are represented by a single delegate to the U.S. House of Representatives). In other words, everyone has a Congressional delegation consisting of three members: two senators and one representative.

Because the United States principally has a two-party system consisting of Democrats and Republicans, each chamber has two groups: a majority party and a minority party. The party with the greatest number of members in a chamber is considered to be the majority party, and the party with the smaller number of members is called the minority party. The few members of Congress who are not affiliated with a national political party and identify themselves as Independents typically choose a party with which to affiliate for organizational purposes. For example, U.S. Senator Jim Jeffords (I-VT) organizes with, or is counted as, a Democrat.

Key Congressional Committees for Nurses and Healthcare Issues

Like most large organizations, Congress has committees that do much of its work. Both the Senate and House have numerous standing committees; members receive committee assignments at the start of each new Congress. Unless something unusual happens (such as the death or retirement of a member in the middle of a term), committee assignments for members last an entire Congress, or two years (see Figure 36-1 for an explanation of Congress). The leadership in each respective party makes committee assignments, and the overall makeup of majority to minority members in the chamber as a whole generally determines the ratios (i.e., number of majority members to minority members). Each committee has two key leaders: a chairperson, who is a member of the majority party, and a ranking member, who is the most senior member of the minority party on the committee (see Figure 36-2).

Figure 36-2. Key Committees for Nurses and Healthcare Issues

U.S. House of Representatives	U.S. Senate
Appropriations Committee: the committee that controls the federal purse strings and determines federal funding for all government functions, from defense to biomedical research	Appropriations Committee: the committee that controls the federal purse strings and determines federal funding for all government functions, from defense to biomedical research
Labor, Health and Human Services & Education Appropriations Subcommittee (LHHS): the specialized subcommittee that determines federal funding for federal agencies, including the departments of Health and Human Services, Labor, Education, and all of their subagencies (National Institutes of Health, Centers for Disease Control and Prevention, and the Health Resources and Services Administration, which administers nursing workforce programs)	Labor, Health and Human Services & Education Appropriations Subcommittee (LHHS): the specialized subcommittee that determines federal funding for federal agencies, including the departments of Health and Human Services, Labor, Education, and all of their subagencies (National Institutes of Health, Centers for Disease Control and Prevention, and the Health Resources and Services Administration, which administers nursing workforce programs)
Energy and Commerce Committee and its Health Subcommittee: the authorizing committee with policy and oversight jurisdiction over the Medicaid program, Part B (outpatient services) of the Medicare program, and all non-Medicare and non-Medicaid healthcare issues (e.g., Nurse Reinvestment Act, National Institutes of Health, Centers for Disease Control and Prevention)	Health, Education, Labor, and Pensions: the authorizing committee with policy and oversight jurisdiction over all non-Medicare and non-Medicaid healthcare issues (e.g., the Nurse Reinvestment Act, National Institutes of Health, Centers for Disease Control and Prevention)

(Continued on next page)

Figure 36-2. Key Committees for Nurses and Healthcare Issues *(Continued)*	
U.S. House of Representatives	**U.S. Senate**
Ways and Means Committee and its Health Subcommittee: the authorizing committee with policy and oversight jurisdiction over both Part A and Part B (inpatient) of the Medicare program (shares jurisdiction over Part B with the House Energy and Commerce Committee)	Finance Committee and its Health Subcommittee: the authorizing committee and subcommittee with policy and oversight jurisdiction over the Medicare and Medicaid programs
None of the authorizing committees has appropriating power; only the House and Senate Appropriations Committees can allocate federal resources and authorize actual spending on programs.	

If your representative or either of your senators sits on one of these key committees, your participation in advocacy is even more important because these members play a key role in crafting, advancing, or defeating legislative proposals of concern to the nursing community. To learn on which committees your members of Congress serve, visit the U.S. Congress Web site managed by the U.S. Library of Congress (http://thomas.loc.gov).

Key Types of Legislation

In general, two main types of legislation exist: authorization and appropriations. An *authorizing bill* provides a federal agency with the general authority to conduct programs and obligate funds. This type of bill does not guarantee funding; rather, Congress needs to allocate funds as part of the annual appropriations budget process. For example, in August 2002, Congress enacted, and the president signed into law, the "Nurse Reinvestment Act," authorizing legislation that expanded existing federal nursing workforce programs and created new initiatives to increase recruitment and retainment of nurses at all levels of the healthcare system. By enacting this legislation, Congress authorized or permitted the spending of federal funding on such endeavors. However, unless Congress provides specific funding in the annual *appropriations bill* (in this example, the Labor, Health and Human Services, and Education funding measure referred to in Figure 36-2) that contains funding for the Nurse Reinvestment Act and its individual programs, the programs could go without financial support. For a more detailed description of the federal budget and appropriations process, view the ONS Federal Budget and Appropriations Primer at http://www.ons.org/lac/pdf/Primer.pdf.

Appropriations measures are the "checks" that Congress writes that, in essence, draw down funds from the federal treasury. Acts of Congress have created numerous programs, but some have failed to secure appropriations for their implementation and support. In such cases, in particular, it is critical for advocates to take action to help secure much-needed funding that will help enact and implement important programs.

Thousands of legislative proposals are introduced in the Senate and House during each session of Congress. However, typically fewer than 5% of the bills introduced in Congress are ever enacted into federal law (see Figure 36-3). For a descriptive diagram illustrating this process, consult "How a Bill Becomes a Law" (http://www.ons.org/lac/hptk/ch6.shtml).

Figure 36-3. How a Bill Becomes a Law

Step 1: Bill language or legislation is drafted. An individual senator or representative may develop original legislation. The president, a private citizen, a business or trade association, or an organization, such as ANA or ONS, may request that a bill be prepared and may assist in drafting or revising the proposed legislation.

Step 2: Legislation is introduced. A bill is introduced in the Senate by a sponsoring senator or in the House by a sponsoring representative and assigned a number. In the Senate, all bills start with "S" followed by a number (e.g., S 1234); all bills in the House start with "HR" (e.g., HR 5678). The bill's title, sponsors and cosponsors (i.e., members who join with the sponsor in official original support of the measure), and introductory remarks are published in the *Congressional Record* (www.gpoaccess.gov/crecord), an official account of the daily proceedings of the House and Senate chambers.

Step 3: Legislation is referred to a committee and subsequently to a subcommittee. The secretary of the Senate and the clerk of the House assign, or refer, a bill to the committee(s) with the appropriate jurisdiction. Both Senate and House committees have a number of subcommittees or smaller groups of members who focus on policy matters in particular issue areas. A bill usually is referred to the subcommittee with the most appropriate jurisdiction under the committee rules. For example, a House bill that ensures private health insurance coverage of colorectal cancer screening likely would be referred to the House Energy and Commerce Committee and subsequently referred to the House Energy and Commerce Health Subcommittee.

Step 4: Subcommittee hearing and markup are held. Subcommittees have the option to hold hearings on a bill and invite testimony from public and private witnesses. Individuals or organizations, such as ANA or ONS, may make their views known by testifying before the subcommittee, submitting a written statement to be included in the official record of the hearing, or disseminating a press statement or other materials at the hearing. Once subcommittee hearings are completed, the subcommittee may meet to "mark up" a bill, that is, to consider changes and amendments to the text of the legislation. The subcommittee members literally go through the measure, line by line, "marking it up" with the adopted changes. The members then vote on whether to report the bill favorably to the full committee. If not favorably reported, the bill usually dies.

Step 5: Full committee hearing and markup are held. Once a bill is reported to the full committee, or if the subcommittee has abdicated its jurisdiction and deferred to the full committee, the full committee may repeat any or all of the subcommittee's procedures, which include hearings, markup, and a vote. Advocates also have the opportunity to testify or otherwise express their views at the full committee level. If the full committee votes favorably on a bill, it is ordered "reported" out of committee and sent, along with the committee report, to either the full Senate or full House for consideration by all of the members in the chamber. The committee report includes the origin, purpose, content, impact, and estimated cost of the legislative proposal.

(Continued on next page)

Figure 36-3. How a Bill Becomes a Law *(Continued)*

Step 6: Floor consideration and full chamber vote are held. Once the bill is reported out of committee, it is placed on the calendar for consideration and additional debate. Prior to reaching the House or Senate floor, members of the leadership in the chamber usually discuss and determine the parameters for debate (e.g., how long the debate will last, how many amendments may be offered). Once the debate parameters have been determined, all the members bring the measure before the chamber for consideration. At this stage, the bill may be further amended, voted up or down, referred back to committee, or tabled. Should either of the two latter options occur, the bill typically dies. A majority vote is necessary for the legislation to be passed, or enacted, in a chamber. Some measures that are reported out of committee may not be brought forward to the full chamber for a vote; this could be because of a lack of time on the calendar or political factors.

Step 7: Legislation is considered in the other chamber. After the Senate or House passes a bill, it is referred to the other chamber. Each chamber considers the legislation under its respective parameters and rules. (For more information about how each chamber handles legislation, visit www.house.gov or www.senate.gov.) Many times, one chamber could pass a measure and the other may never take it up. If this occurs, the legislation usually dies.

Step 8: Legislation is sent to conference committee. To be sent to the president for signature, a bill has to pass both the House and Senate in *identical form.* If significant differences exist between the Senate and House versions of a bill, a "conference committee" may be appointed by the president of the Senate and the Speaker of the House to resolve the differences. Conference committees usually are composed of senators and representatives on the committees that originally considered the legislation. If the president of the Senate and the Speaker of the House fail to name "conferees" to the conference committee, the bill dies. If conferees are named, they meet to discuss and debate the differences between the two bills and develop uniform legislation. However, if the conferees are unable to reach agreement on a single, uniform measure, the bill usually dies.

Step 9: Uniform legislation is considered by the House and the Senate. If, however, the conferees reach agreement on the bill, the revised bill, now a uniform measure, and a conference report are sent back to the Senate and the House for a final vote. For the measure to be sent to the president, both the Senate and House must approve the compromise conference committee bill by a majority vote.

Step 10: The legislation is sent to the president. If the bill has made it this far (which is rare), the bill then goes to the president for consideration. The president has four options: (a) sign the bill, which will make it a law; (b) take no action for 10 days while Congress is in session, which also will make it a law; (c) take no action while Congress is adjourned and at the end of the second session of a Congress, which will result in the bill being "pocket vetoed," a move which in essence kills the measure; or (d) veto the bill. If the president vetoes a bill, Congress may attempt to override the veto. This requires a two-thirds vote by both the Senate and House. If either chamber fails to get a two-thirds vote, the bill is dead. If both succeed, the bill becomes law.

Note. From *How a Bill Becomes a Law,* by the Oncology Nursing Society, 2002. Retrieved November 3, 2003, from http://www.ons.org/lac/hptk/ch6.shtml. Copyright 2002 by the Oncology Nursing Society. Adapted with permission.

One Nurse Can Make a Difference; One Letter Can Result in One Law

Can one person help bring about change? Think of the woman who started Mothers Against Drunk Driving or the families that brought about Megan's Law and the Amber Alert system. Each of these family members turned tragic events into public policy triumphs. Similarly, individuals who wrote to members of Congress with horror stories about their experiences with health maintenance organizations stimulated the development and consideration of the "Patients' Bill of Rights." Other examples of how individuals have made a tangible difference include

- Women undergoing mastectomy who were discharged from the hospital the same day of surgery in the 1990s wrote and called policymakers; numerous states enacted laws banning "drive-through mastectomies."
- Nurses and patients weighing in with members of Congress with letters, e-mails, faxes, phone calls, and face-to-face meetings voicing concern about the effect of the nursing shortage on patient access to quality care in 2002 resulted in the enactment of the Nurse Reinvestment Act of 2002 (Public Law 107-205).
- Oncology nurses, oncologists, and patients with cancer called, e-mailed, and met with their members of Congress protesting the inclusion of Medicare cancer care cuts in the fiscal year 2004 Congressional budget resolution; because of this vocal protest, the cancer care cuts were removed when the budget resolution was considered in conference committee. The conference committee is the process by which members of the House of Representatives and Senate work to reconcile differences between their respective versions of a measure, with the goal being development of a single, uniform measure to be sent to the president for enactment.
- Nurses' calls, e-mails, and faxes to their senators voicing the need for increased funding to address the nursing shortage helped secure passage of an amendment during the consideration of the fiscal year 2004 Labor, Health and Human Services, and Education appropriations measure that boosted funding for the Nurse Reinvestment Act by $50 million.

These are just a few examples of how people who took a few minutes to communicate with policymakers made a difference for patients for years to come.

Not only can one letter result in one law, but one letter, e-mail, or phone call can count more than once. This is what I refer to as the "cockroach theory"—a concept based on the idea that when you see one cockroach crawling across a kitchen counter, it represents 100–1,000 cockroaches crawling in the walls of the kitchen. Although this is not the most appealing analogy, the theory applies to communications with policymakers. They know that where there is one advocate, there are more. One letter, e-mail, phone call, or fax represents many constituents who support its contents.

Each policymaker's office has its own procedures for handling constituent communication and its own formula for the relative weight of a communication. For example, in some offices, 5–10 letters about an issue can constitute a critical mass or major trend and warrants extra attention and response. Thus, your communication represents more than just your opinion to your elected officials. Although it may not always seem or feel like it, your correspondence is counted, and the policymaker is informed that constituents are communicating and requesting action on a particular issue.

Communicate Effectively With Members of Congress

Policymakers expect to hear from their constituents. Systems, processes, and staff are devoted solely to being responsive to input and requests from the public. Although thousands of important proposals are introduced every year in the U.S. Congress and state legislatures, policymakers often say they will not lend their support until they "hear from home" about the need to cosponsor or vote for a particular measure. Therefore, letters, e-mails, phone calls, or faxes from people in their districts or states asking them to lend support (or oppose a proposal) can spur them to take action on issues of priority to nurses and patients.

Many ways to communicate with policymakers exist: letters, e-mails, phone calls, faxes, postcards, and face-to-face meetings (see Figure 36-4). Advocates often wonder which method is most effective and whether all are counted equally. Each Congressional office has its own calculus for different communications. Generally, each policymaker gets a weekly report from staff regarding how many letters, postcards,

---

Figure 36-4. Top Ten Tips for Writing a Letter, Fax, or E-mail

When writing to policymakers, be sure to use personal stationery or your personal e-mail account, as your employer might not share your views on the topic. For all forms of communication, be sure to include your full name, any degrees, return mailing address, e-mail address, and phone number. Keep a hard copy of what you send, as sometimes faxes, e-mails, or letters are lost and you may need to send a second copy to ensure a response. (For tips regarding placing phone calls to Congressional offices, visit www.ons.org/LAC/pdf/10TipsCalls.pdf.)

(1) **Always be polite.** When addressing correspondence to any government official, be sure to use the proper forms of address. Even if you are angry, frustrated, or disappointed, always be sure to use a polite tone and appropriate language. The most effective way to communicate with your members of Congress is the way you communicate with your patients—clearly, concisely, and with respect and honesty. For a sample letter, visit www.ons.org/LAC/pdf/hptk/appendix6.pdf and www.ons.org/LAC/pdf/hptk/appendix7.pdf.

(2) **Be clear as to who you are and why you are writing.** In the opening sentence, identify yourself as a registered voter, constituent, and an oncology nurse, and make your request up front. For example: *As an oncology nurse who lives, votes, and works in your district, I am writing to request your support for increased funding for the Nurse Reinvestment Act.* If you know the member or staff aide, say so at the beginning of your message. This may alert the aide reading your correspondence to give your message special attention.

(3) **Be concise and informed.** You do not need to be an expert on the issue, but you should be familiar with the basic facts and points (e.g., name of the legislation, the associated bill number, why it should be supported or opposed). Do not include extraneous details or too much scientific information. To the degree possible, try to keep your letter to a single page. If you are requesting that the policymaker cosponsor a particular measure or are writing to express disappointment at a particular vote the policymaker cast, check the list of cosponsors and the vote record first at thomas.loc.gov to ensure that you have your facts straight. The template letter/e-mail text provided by your professional organization assists with these details.

(Continued on next page)

Figure 36-4. Top Ten Tips for Writing a Letter, Fax, or E-mail *(Continued)*

(4) **Personalize your message.** Remember, you are an expert in nursing care and have many experiences to share. Tell your own story—or that of a patient—and explain the relevance to the issue at hand. Although form letters and postcards are "counted," they often do not elicit a response from a Congressional office. Policymakers and their staff more easily remember personal stories and illustrations of local impact than statistics and generic examples. Moreover, personal stories often are what spur policymakers to action—not statistics. The reality is that our policymakers often legislate by anecdote. Your own words are best and can influence the legislator's response or vote. If you are using a template letter, be sure to take a few moments to personalize it with your own experience and expertise. Also, if you can, include relevant information from your district or state and explain how the issue affects your community.

(5) **Be honest.** If you are including a personal story about a patient, be sure to protect your patients' privacy by not using full names. Be sure to get the facts straight in your personal story, as you never know when that story may be told again on the House or Senate floor by a member who has been moved and touched by the personal account. If you are including statistics or other scientific information, be sure to verify your sources and have them handy should the Congressional office follow up and want additional information.

(6) **Be modest in your request.** Although you may wish to address multiple issues, be sure not to "kitchen-sink" in your communication. It is best to focus on one or two issues that are of top priority to you. By concentrating on only a few issues, policymakers or staffers will be more receptive because you have not overwhelmed them with too many requests or concerns.

(7) **Be of assistance and serve as a resource.** Policymakers and their staffers are overworked and overwhelmed; offer your assistance and expertise to them. They will appreciate your input and help. If you have an article of interest or relevance, be sure to include it with your correspondence, or refer to it and indicate that you would be happy to provide it should they be interested.

(8) **Express appreciation.** Too many times we just "spank" and forget to "thank." Be sure to say thank you and acknowledge the policymakers' or staffers' attention to your concerns. If you receive a letter in response to an earlier correspondence informing you that the member shares your views or took the action you requested, write back to express your thanks for the response and support. If you learn through the newspaper, your organization's grassroots network, or other means that the policymaker recently cosponsored a bill you support or voted the way you hoped, send a letter articulating your pleasure in his or her action. At the close of your correspondence, be sure to thank the member for his or her attention to your concerns.

(9) **Ask for a response.** Because policymakers and their staffers work for you, you have every right to ask for a response and hold them accountable. Be sure to specify in your written or verbal communication that you want and expect a response. In fact, entire systems, processes, and staff exist in Congressional offices to respond to constituent input. It is important to note, however, that because of the volume of constituent input, there often is a delay of a few weeks or a month before you may receive a response.

(10) **Be sure to follow up.** If you do not receive a response in a timely fashion (in excess of a month for most offices, a little bit longer for Senators from large states such as California and Texas), be sure to follow up with the office by phone or with another letter with your original correspondence attached. If you receive an unsatisfactory response, you should write or call again to express appreciation for the response and be polite, yet firm, in communicating that the response was not what you anticipated or requested. Reiterate your points and address any concerns or points the policymaker has made on the issue in the correspondence. Keep in touch with the office so as to establish a relationship and make yourself available as a local resource on healthcare concerns.

(Continued on next page)

Figure 36-4. Top Ten Tips for Writing a Letter, Fax, or E-mail *(Continued)*

Specific Tips About "Snail Mail"
As a result of the anthrax attack in the fall of 2001, the way in which the U.S. Postal Service mail is handled by Congressional post offices has changed. Most of the incoming mail is irradiated to ensure that it is safe for handling by Congressional staff and members of Congress. Therefore, the content of such mail is oftentimes damaged; therefore, enclosing items such as photographs, originals of articles, or other enclosures is not recommended. It is best to save these items for hand delivery or drop off when you have a meeting in the office, either in Washington, DC, or in your community.

Specific Tips About E-mail
Each Congressional office maintains a different policy about how e-mail from constituents is handled. Most members of Congress have a public e-mail address to which e-mail can be sent. To access the e-mail addresses, you either can visit the individual member's Web page (via either www.house.gov or www.senate.gov) or locate them through the ONS Legislative Action Center (www.onslac.org).

Many Congressional offices provide a generic, automatic acknowledgment that your e-mail has been received but then will follow up with either a specific e-mail response to your issue or a letter via regular U.S. Postal Service. A handful of offices still do not respond individually to e-mail but count the input, as mentioned earlier. It is best to contact your members' offices to learn about their individual policies about constituent correspondence.

Note. From *Top Ten Tips for Writing a Letter, Fax, or E-mail to Your Member of Congress,* by the Oncology Nursing Society, 2003. Retrieved November 3, 2003, from http://www.ons.org/LAC/pdf/10TipsLetters.pdf. Copyright 2003 by the Oncology Nursing Society. Adapted with permission.

---

e-mails, phone calls, and faxes have been received recently on various issues, what positions constituents are advocating, and which issues are of concern.

- When sending an e-mail, fax, or letter by U.S. Postal Service, include your full home mailing address so the office can verify that you are a constituent and send you a response.
- When you call a member's office, leave your full name and mailing address with the staffer so your opinion can be logged, and be sure to specify that you want a written response.
- Personal notes (e.g., handwritten letters either mailed or faxed) are very effective because they illustrate that the authors took the time to send in personal missives on particular issues.
- When an issue is time sensitive, phone calls are the most effective because they allow citizens to weigh in and have their opinions be counted immediately.
- It is important to note that since the anthrax attack in 2001, new mail handling precautions were instituted on Capitol Hill. Thus, the effectiveness of mailing letters via the U.S. Postal Service is tenuous because prompt and intact delivery cannot be guaranteed. Therefore, e-mails and faxes ensure a more timely delivery.

Regardless of your mode of communication, be sure to keep a copy of your correspondence and/or make a note of the day you called and the name of the staffer with whom you spoke. In the event you do not receive a response, this record will help you follow up with the office and receive a response (see Figure 36-5).

Figure 36-5. Examples of Effective Health Policy Advocacy Activities

- Write letters, send e-mails and faxes, and place phone calls to policymakers' offices to voice opinions about issues and request that they take specific action (e.g., vote in favor of increased funding for the Nurse Reinvestment Act).

- Meet with policymakers and their staff either in Washington, DC, or at home in their district offices to discuss issues of concern and request specific actions and/or develop a working relationship with the member and staffers for future collaboration on issues of mutual interest and priority.

- Attend town hall meetings to voice concerns to policymakers or ask questions about what they are doing to address particular problems.

- Submit a letter to the editor or an op-ed piece to a local newspaper to educate policymakers and the public about specific issues or problems.

- Develop a coalition of like-minded organizations interested in advancing or defeating the same legislative proposal (e.g., an alliance of local organizations seeking to ban smoking in public places).

- Submit comments to the Centers for Medicare and Medicaid Services (CMS)—the federal agency responsible for administering the Medicare and Medicaid programs—on Medicare reimbursement issues affecting nurses and patients.

- Volunteer to be nominated by your professional organization to serve on an advisory panel or committee that works to review and develop policies (e.g., the National Cancer Advisory Board, the Secretary's Advisory Committee on Genetics, Society, and Health).

- Join both the national and local/state chapter of your professional organization to ensure that you are up-to-date and informed on the issues concerning your practice and patients.

- If your professional organization has a "key contacts" grassroots effort or other legislative or advocacy program, be sure to add your name, e-mail, and address to the list. Most of these initiatives provide members with action alerts, legislative newsletters, heads up about action on key items, advocacy training, opportunities to visit Washington, DC, and have meetings on Capitol Hill, and other tools and resources to increase advocacy activity and effectiveness. For example, ONS has ONStat (http://www.ons.org/lac/onstat.shtml)—the electronic grassroots advocacy network. To register, visit http://onsopcontent.ons.org/interactive/onstat/signup.aspx and click on ONStat Program.

- Testify before committees or panels about particular legislative or regulatory measures.

- Serve as a resource and provide input and counsel to policymakers and their staff as they review, develop, and analyze legislative or regulatory proposals.

When communicating with policymakers, do not worry about party affiliation (see Figure 36-6). At some point in every policymaker's life, he or she or his or her family members will need the care and assistance of a nurse. To that end, nursing touches everyone's lives, and this ubiquity is recognized and appreciated. When contacting or meeting with policymakers and their staff, identify yourself as a voter, a constituent, and a nurse; these are suitable qualifications for you to be treated with respect.

The two most important things are (a) to weigh in with your elected officials to ensure your voice is heard and (b) to exercise your right to vote. If you are not registered, the League of Women Voters' Web site allows men and women to register to vote online at www.lwv.org/voter/register.html.

Figure 36-6. Health Policy and Advocacy Resources

Agency for Healthcare Research and Quality—www.ahcpr.gov

American Academy of Nurse Practitioners Legislation and Practice—www.aanp.org/Practice +Policy+and+Legislation/Practice+and+Policy.asp

American College of Nurse Practitioners Public Policy Information—www.nurse.org/acnp/leg /index.shtml

American Nurses Association Government Affairs—www.nursingworld.org/gova/

Cable News Network (CNN) Politics—www.cnn.com/allpolitics

Cable Satellite Public Affairs Network (CSPAN)—www.c-span.org

(U.S.) Centers for Disease Control and Prevention—www.cdc.gov

Centers for Medicare and Medicaid Services—www.cms.hhs.gov

(U.S.) Congress—http://thomas.loc.gov

Congress.org—www.congress.org

Congressional Quarterly (one of the most read periodicals on Capitol Hill)—www.cq.com

(U.S.) Department of Health and Human Services—www.dhhs.gov

Federal Register—www.access.gpo.gov

(U.S.) General Accounting Office—www.gao.gov

(U.S.) Government Printing Office—www.access.gpo.gov

Health Resources and Services Administration—www.hrsa.gov

(U.S.) House of Representatives—www.house.gov

League of Women Voters—www.lwv.org/

National Association of Counties—www.naco.org

National Association of Pediatric Nurse Practitioners—http://napnap.org (click on advocacy)

National Cancer Institute—www.nci.nih.gov

National Conference of State Legislatures—www.ncsl.org

National Governors Association—www.nga.org

National Institutes of Health—www.nih.gov

National Journal (one of the most read periodicals on Capitol Hill)—www.nationaljournal.com

Oncology Nursing Society. *Addressing correspondence*—www.ons.org/LAC/pdf/hptk /appendix7.pdf

Oncology Nursing Society. *Advocacy action alerts* (updated regularly)—http://capwiz.com/ona/ home/

Oncology Nursing Society. *Become a member of the elite Oncology Nursing Society grassroots response network: ONStat*—www.ons.org/lac/onstat.shtml

Oncology Nursing Society. *Branches of the U.S. federal government*—www.ons.org/LAC/pdf/hptk/ appendix3.pdf

Oncology Nursing Society. *Federal budget and appropriations primer*—www.ons.org/LAC/pdf/hptk/ appendix4.pdf

Oncology Nursing Society. *Congressional offices: The real deal and who's who*—www.ons.org/lac/ hptk/ch13.shtml

Oncology Nursing Society. *Health policy tool kit*—www.ons.org/lac/pdf/HPTK/hptk03.pdf

Oncology Nursing Society. *How a bill becomes a law*—www.ons.org/LAC/hptk/ch6.shtml

Oncology Nursing Society. *How to work with congressional staff*—www.ons.org/lac/hptk/ch14. shtml

Oncology Nursing Society Legislative Action Center—www.onslac.org

Oncology Nursing Society Online Advocacy Course—http://onsopcontent.ons.org//meetings/ healthpolicy/home.html

Oncology Nursing Society. *Top ten advocacy myths debunked*—www.ons.org/LAC/pdf /Advocacy_Myths.pdf

Oncology Nursing Society. *Top ten tips for calling your members of Congress and their staff*— www.ons.org/LAC/pdf/CallsToCong.pdf

Oncology Nursing Society. *Top ten tips for meeting with your member of Congress and his or her staff*—www.ons.org/LAC/hptk/ch12.shtml

(Continued on next page)

Figure 36-6. Health Policy and Advocacy Resources *(Continued)*

Oncology Nursing Society. *Top ten tips for working successfully with other organizations*—www. ons.org/LAC/pdf/Working_Successfully.pdf

Oncology Nursing Society. *Top ten tips for writing a letter, fax, or e-mail to your member of Congress*—www.ons.org/lac/pdf/toptenwriting.pdf

Oncology Nursing Society. *Sample letters to elected officials*—www.ons.org/LAC/pdf/hptk /appendix6.pdf

Project Vote Smart—www.vote-smart.org/

Roll Call (one of the most read newspapers on Capitol Hill)—www.rollcall.com

Roster of National Nurse Practitioner and Nursing Organizations—www.nurse.org

(U.S.) Senate—www.senate.gov

U.S. Conference of Mayors—www.usmayors.org/uscm/home.asp

White House—www.whitehouse.gov

Become a Special Advisor and Help Shape Public Policy

A significant proportion of the staff on Capitol Hill is under the age of 30, and a vast majority of the health legislative assistants are women in their mid-20s who have a bachelor degree in political science, no formal training in science or health care, and whose main knowledge of the healthcare system is through their own annual well-woman examination. Despite this limited knowledge and expertise in health care, as a group, these staffers are intelligent, hard working, committed to the elected officials for whom they work, earnest in their interest in health policy, overworked, and underpaid. To that end, most eagerly welcome an opportunity to develop a collaborative relationship with constituents who have specific expertise and can serve as trusted resources for them and their member of Congress. This provides an excellent opportunity for nurses to become key counselors to Congressional staff and members on issues of concern to the nursing and healthcare communities.

To initiate such a relationship, call each of the Washington, DC, offices of your members of Congress, ask to speak with the health legislative assistant, introduce yourself and your area of expertise, and explain that you would like to be of assistance. After the conversations with the staffers, be sure to follow up with an e-mail or a faxed letter thanking them for their time, provide them with your contact information, and reiterate your interest in working with them on issues of mutual interest and priority. If you have a short article, newsletter, or other information that you think would be of interest to the staffer, feel free to include that in your follow-up correspondence.

Conclusion

Nurses represent and address the needs of patients every day by caring for them, bringing their concerns to their physicians, and working with their health insurance companies. The skill set and characteristics that nurses maintain—intelligence, compassion, clear communication, caring, concern, and specialized knowledge of nursing and healthcare delivery—convey perfectly to the policymaking environment. Nurses are a powerful and well-respected constituency, and their active involvement in health policy advocacy will help to ensure policymakers take action on key issues, such as increasing funding for the Nurse Reinvestment Act and other federal nursing workforce programs at the Health Resources and Services Administration within the U.S. Department of Health and Human Services. Active and effective health policy advocacy by nurses will help to preserve workplace safety standards; ensure laws, regulations, and programs are in place to help prevent and reduce medical errors and promote patient safety; secure increased funding for biomedical research, ensuring access to quality care for all patients in need; and sustain the long-term viability of the Medicare and Medicaid programs. However, the corollary is that if nurses fail to communicate with policymakers about key issues of concern, legislative and regulatory proposals will be crafted and enacted without the benefit of nurses' expertise and perspective and may not be in the best interest of patients or nurses.

Policymakers and their staff expect, welcome, and appreciate input from constituents, especially those with understanding and experience. Nursing organizations recognize that engaging nurses in health policy advocacy is essential to ensuring that their views and priorities are received and addressed by policymakers. Nurses can and should become involved in health policy advocacy. Using available resources, such as those on ONS's Legislative Action Center (www.onslac.org), nurses have the tools necessary to be effective health advocates at the national, state, and local levels. Being a citizen-lobbyist is easy, can be very effective and fun, and proves to be a natural extension to nursing.

CHAPTER 37

Managerial Rejuvenation

Brenda M. Nevidjon, RN, MSN

Nurse managers have the most demanding and complex role in the healthcare system. Not only are they expected to be clinically competent, perhaps even clinically expert, but they also must create an environment for high-quality, low-cost patient care and for high employee satisfaction and retention. They are the translators of organizational initiatives to the employees and of employee concerns to the executives. In times of nursing shortages, they frequently become part of the staffing for patient care. The business and human resource literature has long identified that the frontline manager's relationship with employees is key to employee satisfaction (Shortell & Kaluzny, 2000). It is thus not surprising that in the current nursing shortage, the nurse manager is being promoted as the chief retention officer.

Although attention on direct care nurse satisfaction is comprehensive, less attention has been given to the well-being of managers. Healthcare executives must develop supportive environments for their managers with specific opportunities for their development. The nurse manager also must design strategies of self-care that integrate the multiple demands of work and home. Managerial rejuvenation ensures that the nurse manager is fully engaged with work. This chapter reviews conditions for managerial burnout and provides suggestions on self-care and organizational strategies.

Managerial Burnout

The phenomenon and term "burnout" emerged in the 1970s and was identified with people working in the human services careers, nursing being one. Initially seen as pop psychology because it lacked the traditional top down theoretically derived approach, burnout has been extensively researched and has generated theoretical models that illustrate the relationship that people have with work. Maslach (2001) summarized the research on job burnout and defined it as a psychological syndrome characterized by overwhelming exhaustion, feelings of cynicism, and a sense of ineffectiveness or lack of accomplishment. Defined further, *exhaustion* is the feeling of being overextended, depleted emotionally and physically; *cynicism* and *depersonalization* are negative, disparaging responses to the job and can be seen as disconnection from the work; and *ineffectiveness* is the feeling of incompetence and lack of achievement.

Exhaustion is the most central characteristic of burnout. Typically, when people say they are "burned out" they are referring to their experience of exhaustion. The other two characteristics fully define the phenomenon. Research indicates that when one is exhausted, *cynicism* and *depersonalization* may be one way to cope (Maslach, 2001). For a nurse manager, that may be manifested as being less available to staff or approaching staff in a less personal and supportive way, not recognizing the uniqueness of each member of the staff. Another sign is the use of skeptical responses to organizational initiatives or indifference to organizational actions. Both of these characteristics can be related to work overload and conflict. Exhaustion and depersonalization may make it difficult to feel effective, but also a lack of key resources may contribute to *ineffectiveness*.

Research also has shown that women managers face greater sources of stress than their male colleagues (Fielden & Cooper, 2001). As they noted, historically, most research on occupational stress focused on white, professional men. Research that had been conducted with women produced conflicting results. Their analysis showed that some studies indicated that the multiple roles working women have increased stress. Other studies show that the number of roles does not influence a woman's mental health, but the quality of experiences across the roles does. However, there is an indication that women in management face greater sources of stress. Given that nursing continues to be a predominantly female profession, healthcare organizations likely have more women in nurse manager roles and should consider what organizational support can be provided.

Causes of Managerial Burnout

The simplest and most logical answer to what causes burnout is that there is an excessive workload (Al-Assaf & Taylor, 1992; Moore, 2000). However, workload alone does not explain burnout. Recent theoretical frameworks about burnout are integrating personal and situational factors rather than giving an either/or explanation (Moore). Although the idea of person-job fit is acknowledged at the point of hire and system entry, Maslach (2001) has expanded the concept of match/mismatch between the person and six domains of the job environment. Briefly, these domains are

- Workload: a mismatch can occur because of an excessive amount of work or the wrong work for the person's skill set.
- Control: person has insufficient control over needed resources, or responsibility exceeds authority.
- Reward: insufficient financial rewards or lack of social rewards (work is not appreciated).
- Community: isolation, impersonal contact, or unresolved conflicts produce continuous negative feelings.
- Fairness: inequity of workload or pay, evaluations and promotions handled inappropriately, and grievance procedures do not allow voice to both sides of the conflict.
- Values: conflict between personal values and what is asked in the job or conflict between the values of the organization and the actual practice.

Job-related stressors can include specific tasks, demands of the position, interpersonal relationships, and the physical environment. Research has shown antecedents to work exhaustion are more commonly situational, such as overload, role conflict and ambiguity, lack of autonomy, interpersonal conflict, and lack of rewards (Moore, 2000). Cooper, Manning, and Poteet (1988) reviewed organizational and personal factors that may contribute to stress. Organizational factors include those intrinsic to the job, the role in the organization, career development, and relationships in the organization. Crabtree (2003), with the Gallup organization, speculated that with an uncertain economy, employees, specifically baby boomers who are at the peak of their careers, work longer hours. Although research shows that regular vacations lower the risk of death for men and the rate of heart attacks in women, the pace of the work environment continues to escalate (Rives, 2003). Covey, Merrill, and Merrill (1994) noted that being busy has come to symbolize being important. Many workplaces have cultures of workaholism, and managers, in particular, feel the pressure to work long hours.

Factors external to the organization include family and community relationships and activities. These can be extensive, as many managers are active as volunteers and community leaders. Specific focus on women in the workplace outlines factors unique to women (Bolton, 2000; Hochschild, 1997; Kaltrieder, 1997). These authors described the multiple factors that affect women in the workplace by looking at the total environment in which women interact.

Being a nurse manager may coincide with several other critical life events. Most nurse managers are over 30 and may have many roles. For example, the manager may be starting or have a young family. In 1995, one in five women had a first child after 35 (American Society for Reproductive Medicine, 1995). As a mother, the manager not only has childrearing stresses, but also may be a volunteer for her children's activities. As a daughter, the manager may be helping aging parents make decisions about health care, finances, where they should live, and if they can live independently. This also may include providing physical care to parents or other relatives, as nurses often are called to do in their families. The manager may be in school to obtain an advanced degree or active in professional organizations, such as the American Nurses Association, the Oncology Nursing Society, or the American Association of Critical Care Nurses. The potential combinations of roles are many. Any of these roles can conflict with another, adding to the stress of the manager.

Signs and Symptoms of Burnout

As with cancer, prevention is the best approach to managing burnout. There are many strategies to develop a life that integrates the dimensions of self, family, work, community, and spirituality. However, when these strategies lose their effect or when organizational demands become excessive, a person can begin to show signs of stress and burnout. Early detection of the signs of burnout allows early intervention and better outcomes. Employees are a good barometer and know when a nurse manager may be in need of rejuvenation. The manager also needs to know when demands are becoming overwhelming. Figure 37-1 lists many of the signs of a person who is stressed and possibly experiencing the triad of exhaustion, cynicism, and ineffectiveness. Recognizing personal cues of stress is the first step in stopping a progression to burnout.

Figure 37-1. Signs and Symptoms of Stress

Personal
- Regularly waking up tired
- Experiencing irritability, insomnia, migraines, aches and pains, or a change in weight
- Easily frustrated
- Becoming cynical about self, others, work, or home
- Experiencing great conflict with partner, children, or others
- Increasing use of drugs or alcohol
- Finding no pleasure in favorite activities
- Inability to concentrate
- Accident-prone

Work Related
- Calling in sick or arriving late more frequently
- Behaving negative in most interactions
- Losing compassion for staff
- Dissatisfaction with job activities
- Increased complaints about job
- Decreased productivity
- Negative attitude toward the organization and its executives
- Dysfunctional work relationships
- Faulty decision making

Interventions

Work and personal factors contribute to an individual's overall well-being. Thus, for a manager who feels overworked, exhausted, or burned out, interventions are not singular. Employers who balance the financial goals of the organization with humanistic concerns for their employees often are recognized on lists of family friendly workplaces or best employers for working mothers. Magazines, books, tapes, workshops, and television shows abound that advise people how to achieve balance, manage time and multiple demands, remove personal clutter from their lives, and have a fulfilling life.

Organizational Strategies

The literature has documented for decades occupational stress and the importance of work environment changes (Cooper & Marshall, 1976; Phelan et al., 1991; Swanson, 2000). Employers have slowly recognized that interventions to make the workplace a healthier environment incorporate both changes in the psychosocial aspects of the workplace and the availability of specific services. The latter depends on the size of the organization and resources that can be directed at employee development and support. Employee assistance and counseling referral programs are typical employer supported resources. Employer sponsored child care, eldercare resources, on-site fitness programs, and concierge services (banking, dry cleaning, take-home meals) are examples of programs that are less frequently offered but can be found in progressive healthcare employers.

The nursing shortage has revealed many reasons why people have not been choosing nursing as a career and why nurses have left the profession. To recruit and retain staff, as addressed in previous chapters, employers have initiated a myriad of programs: sign-on bonuses, retention bonuses, flexible scheduling, specialized overtime options, recognition programs, and clinical ladders. Frontline managers communicate and oversee many of these programs while recognizing that they do not benefit from them. Organizations must not neglect to attend to the needs of all employees. With the attention on the nursing shortage, the negative work environment and psychosocial factors, such as abuse and disrespect of nurses, also have gained attention. These factors are not unique to direct care nurses; nurse managers, too, encounter disrespect and lack of acknowledgment and recognition, which are antecedents of stress. Organizations must have procedures for building collaborative relationships among all staff and be prepared to deal with abusive behavior in the workplace.

Actual workload for nurse managers increased substantially in the 1990s as care delivery redesign resulted in managers having a broader scope of supervision and additional responsibilities added to their job description. A broader scope is not in and of itself a problem when coupled with necessary support systems and personnel. For instance, in an inpatient environment, it may be advantageous to have a nurse manager of two or three acute care units or the continuum of inpatient and outpatient units to ensure a standard of practice and effective coordination of care. However, that manager needs assistant managers and secretarial support. Too often, those supports are reduced or eliminated. In redesign efforts or when budget reductions are taken, the executive team should assess the impact on manager workload.

Frequently, nurse managers are selected based on their successful performance as clinical practitioners. Just as frequently, organizations expect the nurse to become a manager by osmosis and do not develop an educational plan in which the nurse manager begins to acquire managerial skills. These skills range from strategic thinking to fiscal planning to counseling employees through a conflict. Learning must be ongoing and not framed only as an orientation for new managers. Examples of organizational support for ongoing learning include monthly business meetings in which a brief (10–15 minute) educational presentation is incorporated, annual or semiannual retreats in which more in-depth education can occur, individualized development plans, funding for attendance at professional development conferences, and mentor programs in which experienced managers or executives coach a new manager. Judkins and Ingram (2002) found that a self-paced learning module could be used to help managers develop hardiness, which protects against stress.

Senior executives must recognize that the nurse managers whom they expect to lead and implement organizational changes also are affected by those changes. Thus, with major initiatives, time may be needed to support the managers' understanding of the change and to deal with their feelings of loss and transition. Trust can be eroded during times of change, and a manager who has enjoyed close, trusting relationships with staff may find these replaced with distance and suspicion. In situations in which layoffs are occurring, the nurse manager may be concerned with personal job security. Organizational support to prevent manager burnout is a key workplace variable. In particular, supervisors have a direct effect on burnout and staff intentions to quit (Kalliath & Beck, 2001).

Supervisor support often is identified as a key intervention to modulate the effects of stressors, but the research is not conclusive (Kalliath & Beck, 2001; Kickul & Posig, 2001). Support can be emotional, defined as active listening and caring about the employee, or instrumental, defined as giving tangible assistance to help the employee complete a task (Kickul & Posig). In studying the relationship between the types of support and two specific stressors, role conflict and time pressure, Kickul and Posig found a reverse buffering effect of emotional support. They believed that this is because of the demands initiated by the supervisor, which cause stress. In applying their findings to the situation of a supervisor supporting a manager, one can see how a manager would benefit more by supervisory behavior that gives them assistance or tools to accomplish the very tasks that the supervisor is delegating. There is also a message in this research for executives initiating systemwide changes: ensure that the managers accountable for the change have the tools and expertise they need.

Self-Care Strategies

Taking care of self is essential, and managers can use many strategies to offset the stresses of their jobs. However, recognizing the 24 hours, 7 days a week nature of managerial work may be unnoticed by nurses considering a managerial career. The workload for managers frequently exceeds the typical hours in the workweek because there are increased responsibilities and decreased resources in most healthcare organizations. Also, nurses attracted to a managerial career may have unrealistic expectations of themselves and be vulnerable to the "super nurse" syndrome (David-hizar & Shearer, 1999). Similar to new graduates who have a desire for perfection, managers, too, may expect they can be all things to all people: staff, supervisor, physicians, patients, and colleagues. The very strategies that a nurse manager might use to help a new graduate deal with being overwhelmed by the desire for perfection can be effective in coping with personal stresses.

Because being a manager, particularly on the frontline, means a blurring of the boundary of work and home, recognizing signs of personal stress is key. Signs may be as diverse as increased hair loss, exhaustion regardless of the amount of sleep, coworkers asking if the manager is feeling well, or ceasing routines such as exercise. Parts of the job that were challenges become problems, or parts that were rewarding become tasks to be completed. At home, hobbies may become burdensome rather than pleasurable. The feeling of caring about others or activities or self may disappear. These are signs that rejuvenation is needed.

No one can avoid stress, but how one adapts or reacts to stress has long-lasting effects. In addition to participating in the organization's support strategies, the manager also must choose personal approaches to counter the demands of the job and to remain positively engaged in the workplace. These approaches include both work and personal behaviors (see Figure 37-2).

> ### Figure 37-2. Behavioral Strategies for Stress Management
>
> **Work Related**
> - Time management
> - Setting priorities
> - Organizing the work space
> - Managing mail/e-mail
> - Developing peer support
>
> **Personal**
> - Exercise and nutrition
> - Setting priorities
> - Relaxation
> - Saying "no"
> - Developing social support

Work Behaviors

Time management is often a beginning point of focus for managers who feel stressed. There are any number of books, seminars, daily planners, and personal coaches for developing time management skills. However, time management is not so much about managing time but managing what is important (Bennett & Lando, 1999). Covey et al. (1994) comprehensively described the various approaches to time management and noted that what they call the first three generations of time management has resulted in people being able to do more in less time. A common tool used to learn what activities are important is the time management matrix (see Figure 37-3). While over time managers have activities in all quadrants, quadrant IV is the least desirable quadrant because the activities here are not important or urgent. However, managers can find that much of their day and week can be consumed by not important, not urgent activities causing them to feel that they have not accomplished anything. A skill for the manager to develop is to evaluate what she is doing against this matrix and learn to put more energy into quadrant II.

Setting goals clarifies what is important. By reviewing the organizational goals, the manager can articulate what is important at the local level and ask with each situation, "Is this important to meeting my/our unit's/the organization's goals?" If the answer is "no," then the task is not one that should be given lengthy time. If the answer is "unsure," then the first step is to discuss with the supervisor its importance.

Setting priorities interfaces with time management. Paradoxically, high priority tasks often may be handled last. Several reasons may be the cause: the task seems unpleasant, it looks like the time needed is more than the manager has, interruptions delay it, or the priority of the task has not been consciously established. The latter, in particular, can lead to frustration and guilt if goals are not being achieved. Identifying goals and the necessary activities to accomplish them, whether on a daily, weekly, or annual basis, will assist priority setting. The activities are not only tasks, but include relationship development, too. The proverbial "to do" list is a tool to remind the manager of what is more important, and should crises occur, as they will, the list helps the manager to refocus her time and energy once the crisis has ended. By taking time to plan and understand what needs to come first, the manager benefits from seeing goals accomplished. Positive feelings and completed work are powerful offsets to the multiple demands that pull a manager in many directions.

Figure 37-3. Time Management Matrix

	Urgent	Not Urgent
Important	I	II
Not Important	III	IV

There is no one right way to **organize a work space**, but every manager needs to have a system that works. Defining that system and using it can reduce stress, but trying to use a process that is a burden can aggravate the stress level. People who function well using piles can become more stressed trying to create and maintain a file system. Common considerations in organizing the work space are to designate an area that is free of clutter, have readily available the tools needed every day so it is not necessary to hunt for them, and think ergonomically about the chair, lighting, and computer keyboard. Some managers find that creating a personalized work environment provides relief from stress. That may include stress reducers such as toys, scented candles, music, and framed sayings that remind them to take a break and relax or put work in perspective. Personalizing the work space also may include photos, children's art, or other symbols of family, friends, and fun. Although some organizations may have rules about decorating the work space, most managers have private offices that are not affected by such policies.

Similar strategies can be helpful in **managing mail and e-mail.** When e-mail first started being used more frequently as a main means of communication, many thought that the volume of paper they needed to handle would decrease. However, most managers find that they still receive a lot of paper, and handling the paper and electronic communication is time-consuming. The manager should develop the skill to discard some e-mails without opening them. Just as managers have received junk mail, they now receive junk e-mail. Certain types of issues are best dealt with in person and should not have a written reply. Scheduling a time for reading and responding to correspondence has several benefits: others learn that there is a specific time in which the manager will review messages, it blocks time for reading lengthier documents, and it limits the time the manager spends on correspondence. With e-mail, there are other considerations such as being selective about distributing one's e-mail address or blocking e-mail from certain sources, something that cannot be done with regular mail. Also, most organizations have antispamming policies, which reduce unwanted messages. Managers always need to remember that paper or electronic communication does not substitute for face-to-face communication (Shearer, Davidhizar, & Castro, 1999).

The saying, "birds of a feather, flock together" can be a useful image of how to **develop peer support**. Managers share common issues, and finding time to meet on a regular basis to share stories can be cathartic and energizing. A commitment to meeting for coffee, lunch, or after work unites managers to exchange ideas and solve problems.

Personal Behaviors

Volumes have been written about the importance of **exercise and nutrition** in managing stress. The literature outlines the health benefits of regular exercise, stress reduction being one benefit. Key is to pick something one likes. There are conflicting messages about what is and is not healthy about food, but managers need to remember that food is their source of energy. Days can be so busy that it may be tempting to skip meals and rely on coffee to keep going. Likewise, exercise can be viewed as one more task to fit into an already overloaded day. However, being creative and incorporating simple activities to the day can reduce stress. Scheduling meals with a colleague ensures taking time to eat something nourishing. Walking and climbing stairs as much as possible brings exercise into the day. When office-bound by projects, managers must consciously take breaks. Taking a short walk helps returning to the project with renewed energy.

Coupled with exercise, **relaxation** brings a positive physiologic balance to stress. Relaxation does not need to be time consuming, and there are many ways to learn and to practice relaxation. Rejuvenation can result from an activity as simple as deep breathing for a minute or two each hour or from a more complex activity as a guided relaxation response for 15 minutes on a regular basis. The key to making relaxation beneficial is to practice it, which can be done anywhere.

As in the workplace, **setting priorities** and having a **social support network** in one's personal life mitigate burnout. Much has been written about the second shift phenomenon that women experience (Hochschild & Machung, 1989). First shift is their job, and second shift is all the activities at home, from child rearing to house cleaning. Taking time to decide what is important and how critical it is will put things in perspective, although meshing work and personal priorities can result in conflict. For example, a high priority organizational meeting might conflict with a high priority family event. Having a well-developed social support network can be advantageous to a manager who is developing skill in negotiating and integrating work and personal priorities. That network includes family, friends, and social acquaintances, such as members of a church or volunteer group. Choosing friends wisely means finding ones who will be honest, supportive, and compassionate.

One of the most important personal behaviors for managers to develop is the ability to say "no." This is also one the most difficult behaviors to develop. "No" can be a difficult word to use because managers often have become managers because of their willingness to say "yes." However, learning to say "no" can have positive results—time and energy needed for other things. It takes practice to say "no," but with practice, the to do list will not grow, and feelings of being burdened will diminish. Saying "no" builds upon the effort that the manager has given to identifying goals, at work and at home, because they guide priority setting. If something is not a priority and does not contribute to a goal, then it can be declined, even if it looks interesting. Having fun is important, too, but not at the expense of feeling stressed.

A career in management can be rewarding as long as the manager recognizes that she or he is in a position characterized by conflicting demands and expectations at work and between work and their personal lives. Healthcare organizations must attend not only to their financial well-being but also to the humanistic needs of staff, most importantly the managers. Investment in the ongoing development and support of managers is key to organizational performance. Managers also must recognize that they have a responsibility to take care of themselves through any number of self-care strategies and engagement in organizational support. Managerial rejuvenation is not elective but rather required to ensure excellence in quality care and professional nursing practice. Rejuvenation is critical to having the strength and stamina to mentor and develop future healthcare leaders. The care of self ensures that the manager can care for others, including family, patients, and staff.

References

Al-Assaf, A.F., & Taylor, T.L. (1992). Managerial burnout. *The Health Care Manager, 11*(2), 32–38.

American Society for Reproductive Medicine. (1995). *Guidelines for practice: Age related infertility.* Birmingham, AL: Author.

Bennett, S., & Lando, A. (1999). Manager, manage thyself! *Seminars for Nurse Managers, 7*(2), 63–66.

Bolton, M. (2000). *The third shift: Managing hard choices in our careers, homes, and lives as women.* San Francisco: Jossey-Bass.

Cooper, C., Manning, C., & Poteet, G. (1988). Stress, mental health & job satisfaction among nurse managers. *Health Services Management Research, 1*(1), 51–58.

Cooper, C., & Marshall, J. (1976). Occupational sources of stress: A review of the literature relating to coronary heart disease and mental ill health. *Journal of Occupational Psychology, 49,* 11–28.

Covey, S., Merrill, A.R., & Merrill, R. (1994). *First things first: To live, to love, to learn, to leave a legacy.* New York: Simon and Schuster.

Crabtree, S. (2003). *Boomers need to pick up the pace.* Retrieved July 22, 2003, from http://www.gallup.com/poll/tb/healthcare/20030708.asp

Davidhizar, R., & Shearer, R. (1999). The "super nurse" syndrome. *Seminars for Nurse Managers, 7*(2), 59–62.

Fielden, S., & Cooper, C. (2001). Women managers and stress: A critical analysis. *Equal Opportunities International, 20*(1/2), 3–16.

Hochschild, A., & Machung, A. (1989). *The second shift.* New York: Penguin Books.

Hochschild, A. (1997). *The time bind: When work becomes home and home becomes work.* New York: Metropolitan Books.

Judkins, S., & Ingram, M. (2002). Decreasing stress among nurse managers: A long-term solution. *Journal of Continuing Education in Nursing, 33,* 259–264.

Kalliath, T., & Beck, A. (2001). Is the path to burnout and turnover paved by a lack of supervisory support? A structural equations test. *New Zealand Journal of Psychology, 30*(2), 72–79. Retrieved October 8, 2003, from http://web5.infotrac.galegroup.com/itw/infomark/737/132/42805522w5/purl=rc1_ITOF_0_A83447488&dyn=4!xrn_1_0_A83447488?sw_aep=duke_perkins

Kaltrieder, N. (1997). *Dilemmas of a double life: Women balancing careers and relationships.* Northvale, NJ: Jason Aronson.

Kickul, J., & Posig, M. (2001). Supervisory emotional support and burnout: An explanation of reverse buffering effects. *Journal of Managerial Issues, 13,* 328–347.

Maslach, C. (2001). Job burnout. *Annual Review of Psychology, 52*(1), 397–422.

Moore, J. (2000). Why is this happening? A causal attribution approach to work exhaustion consequences. *Academy of Management Review, 25*(2). Retrieved October 8, 2003, from

http://web5.infotrac.galegroup.com/itw/infomark/769/730/42805937w5/purl=rc1_ITOF_0_
A62197043&dyn=5!xrn_1_0_A62197043?sw_aep=duke_perkins

Phelan, J., Schwartz, J., Bromet, E., Dew, M., Parkinson, D., Schulberg, H., et al. (1991). Work stress, family stress and depression in professional and managerial employees. *Psychological Medicine, 21,* 999–1012.

Rives, K. (2003, June 22). Vacation starvation. *News and Observer.* Retrieved November 10, 2003, from http://archives.newsbank.com

Shearer, R., Davidhizar, R., & Castro, B. (1999). Dilemma for the nurse manager: Managing e-mail overload. *Seminars for Nurse Managers, 7*(2), 93–96.

Shortell, S., & Kaluzny, A. (2000). *Health care management: Organization design and behavior* (4th ed.). Albany, NY: Delmar Thomson Learning.

Swanson, N. (2000). Working women and stress. *Journal of American Medical Women's Association, 55*(2), 76–79.

APPENDICES

Appendix A. Glossary

ABN (advance beneficiary notice)—Implications for patient and provider. An ABN is a written notice (the standard government form CMS-R-131 [PDF, 100k]) that is received from physicians, providers, or suppliers before furnishing a service or item that notifies the patient that Medicare will probably deny payment for that specific service or item. Information provided includes the reason the physician, provider, or supplier expects Medicare to deny payment and that the patient will be held personally and fully responsible for payment if Medicare denies payment. An ABN is to be provided to patients in advance of services so that the patient may refuse services if he or she wishes.

AHRQ (Agency for Healthcare Research and Quality)—Group performs research on issues related to healthcare delivery systems, guidelines, and disease outcomes and disease management protocols.

APC (ambulatory payment classification)—All services paid under the new prospective payment system are classified into groups call APCs. Services in each APC are similar clinically and in terms or the resources they require. A payment rate is established for each APC. Depending on the services provided, hospitals may be paid for more than one APC for an encounter.

AWP (average wholesale price)—Average priced drugs are sold to institutions.

Case Mix—A method of grouping hospital patients according to a predefined set of characteristics. Used to determine percentage of patients by insurance carrier.

Chargemaster—A financial management form that provides information about the organization charges for the healthcare services it provides to patients.

CMS (Centers for Medicare and Medicaid Services)—Known as Health Care Financing Administration (HCFA) prior to 2001. CMS is the division of the Department of Health and Human Services responsible for developing and enforcing regulations.

CPT (current procedural terminology) Coding—A medical code set of physician and other services maintained and copyrighted by the American Medical Association (AMA) and adopted by the government as the standard for reporting physician and other services on standard transactions.

DRG (diagnosis-related group)—A classification system that groups patients according to diagnosis, type of treatment, age, and other relevant criteria. Under the prospective payment system, hospitals are paid a set fee for treating patients in a single DRG category, regardless of the actual cost of care for the individual.

E & M (evaluation and management) Coding—CPT codes used to report evaluation and management services provided in the physician's office or other ambulatory facility. A patient is considered an outpatient until inpatient admission to a healthcare facility occurs.

HCFA (Health Care Financing Administration)—Founded in 1977, renamed the Centers for Medicare and Medicaid Services in June 2001.

HCPC (health care procedure coding) System—A list of codes used to report services to Medicare. This terminology is used to describe supplies, materials injections, and procedures as well as certain services. Q codes are temporary codes that are assigned to injections and infusions.

HCUP (Healthcare Cost and Utilization Project)—HCUP consists of a set of databases that include information on inpatients from all payment sources. Researchers use these data to compare treatments, outcomes, and costs.

HMO (health maintenance organization)—Competitive medical plans, including Medicare + Choice, which has contracts with CMS on a prospective capitation payment basis for providing health care to Medicare beneficiaries.

ICD-9-CM (International Classification of Disease)—Clinical modification. A classification system used in the United States to report morbidity and mortality information.

(Continued on next page)

Appendix A. Glossary *(Continued)*

Indemnity Plan—Health insurance coverage provided in the form of cash payments to patients or providers.

Managed Care—Broad term used to describe several types of prepaid healthcare plans. Common types of managed care plans include HMOs, PPOs, and POSs.

Medicaid—Medicaid is an assistance program. Medicaid bills are paid from federal, state, and local tax funds. It serves low-income people of every age. Patients usually pay no part of costs for covered medical expenses. A small co-payment is sometimes required. Medicaid is a federal-state program. It varies from state to state. State and local governments within federal guidelines run it.

Medicare—Medicare is an insurance program. Medical bills are paid from trust funds, which those covered have paid into. It primarily serves people older than 65, whatever their income, and serves younger disabled people and dialysis patients. Patients pay part of costs through deductibles for hospital and other fees. Small monthly premiums are required for non-hospital coverage. Medicare is a federal program. It is basically the same everywhere in the United States and is run by CMS.

Medicare Part A—For inpatient hospital, hospice, and skilled nursing facility services and post-hospital care provided by a home health agency. Medicare Part A is designed to defray expenses incurred by hospitalization and related care.

Medicare Part B—Medicare supplementary medical insurance. An individual must enroll during the enrollment period and pay the required premiums. Part B covers
* Home health services not covered by Part A
* Physician services
* Hospital outpatient services
* Diagnostic services
* Vaccines and other outpatient services listed.

POS (point of service)—A type of managed care health plan in which subscribers are encouraged to select a provider from within a network. Subscribers may seek care outside the network but will be responsible for a larger share of cost than network providers.

PPO (preferred provider organization)—Managed care in which you use doctors, hospitals, and providers that belong to the network. You can use doctors, hospitals, and providers outside of the network for an additional cost.

PPS (prospective payment system)—A method of reimbursement in which Medicare payment is made based on a predetermined, fixed amount. The payment amount for a particular service is derived based on the classification system of that service (i.e., DRGs for inpatient hospital services).

Prospective Capitation—Reimbursement based on a preset amount, rather than actual charges billed.

UB-92—Standardized billing form required by Medicare for hospital inpatients and outpatients. This form also is used to bill third party payors by most hospitals.

Appendix B. Warning Letter Format

MEMO TO: Employee

FROM: Manager

DATE: June x, 2xxx

SUBJECT: Written warning for unacceptable conduct

State the purpose of the employee conference or memorandum. "The purpose of this memorandum is to discuss some issues with your recent job performance (or conduct)."

Summarize the facts. "On (date) you were given a warning for (state performance issue)." *Describe the expectations that were set for correcting the performance problem and then summarize the new problems or conduct.* "On (date) you . . . *(describe the subsequent conduct or work rule violation)*."

Cite the objective or work rule violation. "Our Staff Handbook on page xx *(or cite other sources for the work rule or performance expectation such as the Policies and Procedures Manual)* states . . . "

State or restate the expectations and describe the strategies for correcting the problem. "You are expected to…" *Refer the employee to any resources or training that may be appropriate. Incorporate acceptable suggestions or strategies for addressing the problem.* "We agreed that you will . . ."

Describe the action(s) being taken. "This is a written warning and will be placed in your personnel file. If you fail to immediately and continually meet the expectations, you will be subject to further disciplinary action, up to and including termination."

End with a statement of your confidence in the employee. "You are a valuable employee in our organization, and I fully expect that you can meet these expectations. I hope you will take the necessary actions to correct this situation."

Employee Signature: _____

(Signing this memo does not indicate that you agree with the contents but certifies that it has been discussed with you.)

(Make a note on the signature line if the employee refuses to sign.)

Appendix C. Written Warning Sample Letter

MEMO TO: Employee

FROM: Manager

DATE: June x, 2xxx

SUBJECT: Written warning for unacceptable conduct

The purpose of this memorandum is to discuss recent issues with your conduct on the job.

On June 20, 2xxx, we met, and you were given a warning for the verbal altercation you had with another staff member. At that time, I explained to you that such conflicts were not acceptable and cited our policy for avoiding fighting. On July 6, 2xxx, you had another incident with the same employee and you became loud and angry in my office on July 8, 2xxx, when we met to discuss the incident.

This disruptive conduct is unacceptable and will not be tolerated. You are expected to comply with our policies and to avoid further confrontations.

Employee, this is a written warning and will be placed in your personnel file. If you fail to immediately and continually meet these expectations for acceptable conduct, you will be subject to further disciplinary action, up to and including dismissal.

You are a valuable employee and we fully expect that you can meet these expectations. I hope you will take the necessary actions to correct this situation.

Employee Signature: _____

(Signing this letter does not indicate that you agree with the contents but certifies that it has been discussed with you.)

Appendix D. Sample Notice of Dismissal

MEMO TO: Employee

FROM: Manager

DATE: June 1, 2xxx

SUBJECT: Notice of dismissal

Over the past few months, you have received a verbal warning, a written warning, and a final written warning for poor work performance. At the time of the final warning, I indicated that I expected an immediate and sustained improvement in your performance or you would be subject to dismissal.

Over the last two weeks, the problem areas cited in the warning letter have continued and we have not seen any sustained improvement in your job performance. For example, _____. Due to continued unacceptable performance, your employment with Company is terminated effective today, June 1, 2xxx.

Your final paycheck, which will include hours worked through close of business today, also will include any unused vacation hours.

For benefits information, please contact Jane Doe, Benefits Specialist, at xxx-xxx-xxxx.

I have read and received a copy of this document.

_____   _____

Employee Signature   Date

Appendix E. Sample Corrective Action Form

Employee Name: _____   Job Title: _____
Department: _____   Location: _____
Date of Incident: _____   Today's Date: _____

Recommended Action: Prior Corrective Actions/Dates:
Step 1. Written counseling   _____
Step 2. Written counseling with plan for improvement   _____
Step 3. Suspension up to five days without pay   _____
Step 4. Termination   _____

This employee has shown unacceptable work performance in the following manner:
_____
_____
_____
_____

Future action if performance is not improved: _____
_____
_____

Recommended plan to improve performance: _____
_____
_____

Is follow-up required? _____ Yes _____ No. If so, when? _____

Employee's action plan to correct/improve: _____
_____
_____

I have reviewed offense(s) with employee: I have read and understand this report.
                                            My signature does not indicate agreement.

_____   _____
Signature of Supervisor   Signature of Employee

_____   _____
Administrator/Department Director Signature   Date

This report will be made a part of the employee's human resources file as of this date.

_____   _____
Human Resources   Date

Appendix F. Family and Medical Leave Act

Certification of Health Care Provider
(Family and Medical Leave Act of 1993)

U.S. Department of Labor
Employment Standards Administration
Wage and Hour Division

*(When completed, this form goes to the employee, **Not to the Department of Labor**.)*

OMB No.:
Expires:

1. Employee's Name

2. Patient's Name *(If different from employee)*

3. Page 4 describes what is meant by a **"serious health condition"** under the Family and Medical Leave Act. Does patient's condition[1] qualify under any of the categories described? If so, please check the applicable category.

   (1) _____ (2) _____ (3) _____ (4) _____ (5) _____ (6) _____ , or None of the above _____

4. Describe the **medical facts** which support your certification, including a brief statement as to how the medical fact the criteria of one of these categories:

5. a. State the approximate **date** the condition commenced, and the probable duration of the condition (and also the probable duration of the patient's present **incapacity**[2] if different):

   b. Will it be necessary for the employee to take work only **intermittently or to work on a less than full schedul** result of the condition (including for treatment described in Item 6 below)?

   If yes, give the probable duration:

   c. If the condition is a **chronic condition** (condition #4) or **pregnancy**, state whether the patient is presently incap and the likely duration and frequency of **episodes of incapacity**[2]:

[1] Here and elsewhere on this form, the information sought relates **only** to the condition for which the employee is taking FMLA leave.

[2] "Incapacity," for purposes of FMLA, is defined to mean inability to work, attend school or perform other regular daily activities due to the serious condition, treatment therefor, or recovery therefrom.

Page 1 of 4

Revised

(Continued on next page)

Appendix F. Family and Medical Leave Act *(Continued)*

Certification of Health Care Provider
(Family and Medical Leave Act of 1993)

U.S. Department of Labor
Employment Standards Administration
Wage and Hour Division

*(When completed, this form goes to the employee, **Not to the Department of Labor**.)*

OMB No.: 1215-0181
Expires: 07/31/07

1. Employee's Name

2. Patient's Name *(If different from employee)*

3. Page 4 describes what is meant by a **"serious health condition"** under the Family and Medical Leave Act. Does the patient's condition[1] qualify under any of the categories described? If so, please check the applicable category.

   (1) _____   (2) _____   (3) _____   (4) _____ (5) _____   (6) _____ , or None of the above _____

4. Describe the **medical facts** which support your certification, including a brief statement as to how the medical facts meet the criteria of one of these categories:

5. a. State the approximate **date** the condition commenced, and the probable duration of the condition (and also the probable duration of the patient's present **incapacity**[2] if different):

   b. Will it be necessary for the employee to take work only **intermittently or to work on a less than full schedule** as a result of the condition (including for treatment described in Item 6 below)?

   If yes, give the probable duration:

   c. If the condition is a **chronic condition** (condition #4) or **pregnancy**, state whether the patient is presently incapacitated[2] and the likely duration and frequency of **episodes of incapacity**[2]:

[1] Here and elsewhere on this form, the information sought relates **only** to the condition for which the employee is taking FMLA leave.

[2] "Incapacity," for purposes of FMLA, is defined to mean inability to work, attend school or perform other regular daily activities due to the serious health condition, treatment therefor, or recovery therefrom.

Page 1 of 4

Form WH-380
Revised December 1999

(Continued on next page)

Appendix F. Family and Medical Leave Act *(Continued)*

6. a. If additional **treatments** will be required for the condition, provide an estimate of the probable number of such treatments.

        If the patient will be absent from work or other daily activities because of **treatment** on an **intermittent** or **part-time** basis, also provide an estimate of the probable number of and interval between such treatments, actual or estimated dates of treatment if known, and period required for recovery if any:

  b. If any of these treatments will be provided by **another provider of health services** (e.g., physical therapist), please state the nature of the treatments:

  c. **If a regimen of continuing treatment** by the patient is required under your supervision, provide a general description of such regimen (*e.g.*, prescription drugs, physical therapy requiring special equipment):

7. a. If medical leave is required for the employee's **absence from work** because of the **employee's own condition** (including absences due to pregnancy or a chronic condition), is the employee **unable to perform work** of any kind?

  b. If able to perform some work, is the employee **unable to perform any one or more of the essential functions of the employee's job** (the employee or the employer should supply you with information about the essential job functions)? If yes, please list the essential functions the employee is unable to perform:

  c. If neither a. nor b. applies, is it necessary for the employee to be **absent from work for treatment**?

Page 2 of 4

(Continued on next page)

Appendix F. Family and Medical Leave Act *(Continued)*

8. a. If leave is required to **care for a family member** of the employee with a serious health condition, **does the patient require assistance** for basic medical or personal needs or safety, or for transportation?

    b. If no, would the employee's presence to provide **psychological comfort** be beneficial to the patient or assist in the patient's recovery?

    c. If the patient will need care only **intermittently** or on a part-time basis, please indicate the probable **duration** of this need:

_____   _____
Signature of Health Care Provider   Type of Practice

_____   _____
Address   Telephone Number

                                                      _____
                                                      Date

To be completed by the employee needing family leave to care for a family member:

State the care you will provide and an estimate of the period during which care will be provided, including a schedule if leave is to be taken intermittently or if it will be necessary for you to work less than a full schedule:

_____   _____
Employee Signature   Date

(Continued on next page)

Appendix F. Family and Medical Leave Act *(Continued)*

A **"Serious Health Condition"** means an illness, injury impairment, or physical or mental condition that involves one of the following:

1. Hospital Care

   Inpatient care (*i.e.*, an overnight stay) in a hospital, hospice, or residential medical care facility, including any period of incapacity[2] or subsequent treatment in connection with or consequent to such inpatient care.

2. Absence Plus Treatment

   (a) A period of incapacity[2] of **more than three consecutive calendar days** (including any subsequent treatment or period of incapacity[2] relating to the same condition), that also involves:

      (1) **Treatment**[3] **two or more times** by a health care provider, by a nurse or physician's assistant under direct supervision of a health care provider, or by a provider of health care services (*e.g.*, physical therapist) under orders of, or on referral by, a health care provider; or

      (2) **Treatment** by a health care provider on **at least one occasion** which results in a **regimen of continuing treatment**[4] under the supervision of the health care provider.

3. Pregnancy

   Any period of incapacity due to **pregnancy**, or for **prenatal care**.

4. Chronic Conditions Requiring Treatments

   A **chronic condition** which:

      (1) Requires **periodic visits** for treatment by a health care provider, or by a nurse or physician's assistant under direct supervision of a health care provider;

      (2) Continues over an **extended period of time** (including recurring episodes of a single underlying condition); and

      (3) May cause **episodic** rather than a continuing period of incapacity[2] (*e.g.*, asthma, diabetes, epilepsy, etc.).

5. Permanent/Long-term Conditions Requiring Supervision

   A period of **Incapacity**[2] which is **permanent or long-term** due to a condition for which treatment may not be effective. The employee or family member must be **under the continuing supervision of, but need not be receiving active treatment by, a health care provider**. Examples include Alzheimer's, a severe stroke, or the terminal stages of a disease.

6. Multiple Treatments (Non-Chronic Conditions)

   Any period of absence to receive **multiple treatments** (including any period of recovery therefrom) by a health care provider or by a provider of health care services under orders of, or on referral by, a health care provider, either for **restorative surgery** after an accident or other injury, **or** for a condition that **would likely result in a period of Incapacity**[2] **of more than three consecutive calendar days in the absence of medical intervention or treatment**, such as cancer (chemotherapy, radiation, etc.), severe arthritis (physical therapy), and kidney disease (dialysis).

This optional form may be used by employees to satisfy a mandatory requirement to furnish a medical certification (when requested) from a health care provider, including second or third opinions and recertification (29 CFR 825.306).

Note: Persons are not required to respond to this collection of information unless it displays a currently valid OMB control number.

---

[3] Treatment includes examinations to determine if a serious health condition exists and evaluations of the condition. Treatment does not include routine physical examinations, eye examinations, or dental examinations.

[4] A regimen of continuing treatment includes, for example, a course of prescription medication (*e.g.*, an antibiotic) or therapy requiring special equipment to resolve or alleviate the health condition. A regimen of treatment does not include the taking of over-the-counter medications such as aspirin, antihistamines, or salves; or bed-rest, drinking fluids, exercise, and other similar activities that can be initiated without a visit to a health care provider.

Public Burden Statement

We estimate that it will take an average of 20 minutes to complete this collection of information, including the time for reviewing instructions, searching existing data sources, gathering and maintaining the data needed, and completing and reviewing the collection of information. If you have any comments regarding this burden estimate or any other aspect of this collection of information, including suggestions for reducing this burden, send them to the Administrator, Wage and Hour Division, Department of Labor, Room S-3502, 200 Constitution Avenue, N.W., Washington, D.C. 20210.

DO NOT SEND THE COMPLETED FORM TO THIS OFFICE; IT GOES TO THE EMPLOYEE.

Page 4 of 4   *U.S. GPO: 2000-461-954/25505

(Continued on next page)

Appendix F. Family and Medical Leave Act *(Continued)*

Employer Response to Employee
Request for Family or Medical Leave
(Optional Use Form -- See 29 CFR § 825.301)

U.S. Department of Labor
Employment Standards Administration
Wage and Hour Division

(Family and Medical Leave Act of 1993)

OMB No. : 1215-0181
Expires : 08-31-07

Date:

To: _____
(Employee's Name)

From: _____
(Name of Appropriate Employer Representative)

Subject: **REQUEST FOR FAMILY/MEDICAL LEAVE**

On _____ , you notified us of your need to take family/medical leave due to:
(Date)

☐ The birth of a child, or the placement of a child with you for adoption or foster care; or

☐ A serious health condition that makes you unable to perform the essential functions for your job: or

☐ A serious health condition affecting your ☐ spouse, ☐ child, ☐ parent, for which you are needed to provide care.

You notified us that you need this leave beginning on _____ and that you expect
(Date)

leave to continue until on or about _____
(Date)

Except as explained below, you have a right under the FMLA for up to 12 weeks of unpaid leave in a 12-month period for the reasons listed above. Also, your health benefits must be maintained during any period of unpaid leave under the same conditions as if you continued to work, and you must be reinstated to the same or an equivalent job with the same pay, benefits, and terms and conditions of employment on your return from leave. If you do not return to work following FMLA leave for a reason other than: (1) the continuation, recurrence, or onset of a serious health condition which would entitle you to FMLA leave; or (2) other circumstances beyond your control, you may be required to reimburse us for our share of health insurance premiums paid on your behalf during your FMLA leave.

This is to inform you that: *(check appropriate boxes; explain where indicated)*

1. You are ☐ eligible ☐ not eligible for leave under the FMLA.

2. The requested leave ☐ will ☐ will not be counted against your annual FMLA leave entitlement.

3. You ☐ will ☐ will not be required to furnish medical certification of a serious health condition. If required, you must furnish certification by _____ *(insert date)* (must be at least 15 days after you are notified of this requirement), or we may delay the commencement of your leave until the certification is submitted.

4. You may elect to substitute accrued paid leave for unpaid FMLA leave. We ☐ will ☐ will not require that you substitute accrued paid leave for unpaid FMLA leave. If paid leave will be used, the following conditions will apply: *(Explain)*

Form WH-381
Rev. June 1997

(Continued on next page)

Appendix F. Family and Medical Leave Act *(Continued)*

5. (a) If you normally pay a portion of the premiums for your health insurance, these payments will continue dur the period of FMLA leave. Arrangements for payment have been discussed with you, and it is agreed that you will make premium payments as follows: *(Set forth dates, e.g., the 10th of each month, or pay periods, etc. that specifically cover the agreement with the employee.)*

   (b) You have a minimum 30-day *(or, indicate longer period, if applicable)* grace period in which to make premium payments. If payment is not made timely, your group health insurance may be cancelled, *provided* we notify you in writing at least 15 days before the date that your health coverage will lapse, or, at our option, we may pay your share of the premiums during FMLA leave, and recover these payments from you upon your return to work. We ☐ will ☐ will not pay your share of health insurance premiums while you are on leave.

   (c) We ☐ will ☐ will not do the same with other benefits *(e.g.,* life insurance, disability insurance, etc.) while you are on FMLA leave. If we do pay your premiums for other benefits, when you return from leave you ☐ will ☐ will not be expected to reimburse us for the payments made on your behalf.

6. You ☐ will ☐ will not be required to present a fitness-for-duty certificate prior to being restored to employment. If such certification is required but not received, your return to work may be delayed until certification is provided.

7. (a) You ☐ are ☐ are not a "key employee" as described in § 825.217 of the FMLA regulations. If you are a "key employee:" restoration to employment may be denied following FMLA leave on the grounds that such restoration will cause substantial and grievous economic injury to us as discussed in § 825.218.

   (b) We ☐ have ☐ have not determined that restoring you to employment at the conclusion of FMLA leave will cause substantial and grievous economic harm to *us. (Explain (a) and/or (b) below. See §825.219 of the FMLA regulations.)*

8. While on leave, you ☐ will ☐ will not be required to furnish us with periodic reports every _____ _____ *(indicate interval of periodic reports, as appropriate for the particular leave situation)* of your status and intent to return to work *(see § 825.309 of the FMLA regulations).* If the circumstances of your leave change and you are able to return to work earlier than the date indicated on the reverse side of this form, you ☐ will ☐ will not be required to notify us at least two work days prior to the date you intend to report to work.

9. You ☐ will ☐ will not be required to furnish recertification relating to a serious health condition. *(Explain below. if necessary, including the interval between certifications as prescribed in §825.308 of the FMLA regulations.)*

This optional use form may be used to satisfy mandatory employer requirements to provide employees taking FMLA leave with Written notice detailing spectfic expectations and obligations of the employee and explaining any consequences of a failure to meet these obligations. (29 CFR 825.301(b).)

Note: Persons are not required to respond to this collection of information unless it displays a currently valid OMB control number.

Public Burden Statement

We estimate that it will take an average of 5 minutes to complete this collection of information, including the time for reviewing instructions. searching existing data sources, gathering and maintaining the data needed, and completing and reviewing the collection of information. If you have any comments regarding this burden estimate or any other aspect of this collection of information, including suggestions for reducing this burden. send them to the Administrator, Wage and Hour Division, Department of Labor, Room S-3502. 200 Constitution Avenue, N.W., Washington. D.C. 20210.

DO NOT SEND THE COMPLETED FORM TO THE OFFICE SHOWN ABOVE.

Note. Figure courtesy of the U.S. Department of Labor. Used with permission.

INDEX

The letter f *indicates that relevant content appears in a figure; the letter* t, *in a table.*